My iPhone® for Seniors

FOURTH EDITION

Brad Miser

que®

800 East 96th Street,
Indianapolis, Indiana 46240 USA

My iPhone® for Seniors, Fourth Edition

Copyright © 2018 by Pearson Education, Inc.

ISBN-13: 978-0-7897-5869-9

ISBN-10: 0-7897-5869-5

Library of Congress Control Number: 2017957344

1   17

Trademarks

Warning and Disclaimer

Special Sales

For information about buying this title in bulk quantities, or for special sales opportunities (which may include electronic versions; custom cover designs; and content particular to your business, training goals, marketing focus, or branding interests), please contact our corporate sales department at corpsales@pearsoned.com or (800) 382-3419.

For government sales inquiries, please contact governmentsales@pearsoned.com.

For questions about sales outside the United States, please contact intlcs@pearson.com.

Editor-in-Chief
Greg Wiegand

Senior Acquisitions Editor
Laura Norman

Marketing
Stephane Nakib

Director, AARP Books
Jodi Lipson

Development Editor
Charlotte Kughen

Managing Editor
Sandra Schroeder

Project Editor
Mandie Frank

Copy Editor
Charlotte Kughen

Indexer
Ken Johnson

Proofreader
Debbie Williams

Editorial Assistant
Cindy Teeters

Designer
Chuti Prasertsith

Compositor
Tricia Bronkella

Contents at a Glance

To access the online chapters, go to informit.com/myiphoneseniors and click the Downloads tab below the book description. Click the link to download the chapter.

Table of Contents

3 Setting Up and Using an Apple ID, iCloud, and Other Online Accounts   105

10 Managing Calendars 457

11 Working with Siri 493

To access the online chapters, go to informit.com/myiphoneseniors and click the Downloads tab below the book description. Click the link to download the chapter.

About the Author

Brad Miser has written extensively about technology, with his favorite topics being the amazing "i" devices, especially the iPhone, that make it possible to take our lives with us while we are on the move. In addition to *My iPhone for Seniors*, Fourth Edition, Brad has written many other books, including *My iPhone*, Eleventh Edition. He has been an author, development editor, or technical editor for more than 60 other titles.

Brad is or has been a sales support specialist, the director of product and customer services, and the manager of education and support services for several software development companies. Previously, he was the lead proposal specialist for an aircraft engine manufacturer, a development editor for a computer book publisher, and a civilian aviation test officer/engineer for the U.S. Army. Brad holds a bachelor of science degree in mechanical engineering from California Polytechnic State University at San Luis Obispo and has received advanced education in maintainability engineering, business, and other topics.

Brad would love to hear about your experiences with this book (the good, the bad, and the ugly). You can write to him at bradmiser@icloud.com.

Dedication

To those who have given the last full measure of devotion so that the rest of us can be free.

Acknowledgments

To the following people on the *My iPhone for Seniors* project team, my sincere appreciation for your hard work on this book:

Laura Norman, my acquisitions editor, who envisioned the original concept for *My iPhone for Seniors* and works very difficult and long hours to ensure the success of each edition. Laura and I have worked on many books together, and I appreciate her professional and effective approach to these projects. Thanks for putting up with me yet one more time! Frankly, I have no idea how she does all the things she does and manages to be so great to work with given the incredible work and pressure books like this one involve!

Charlotte Kughen, my development and copy editor, who helped craft this book so that it provides useful information delivered in a comprehensible way. Thanks for your work on this book!

Mandie Frank, my project editor, who skillfully managed the hundreds of files and production process that it took to make this book. Imagine keeping dozens of plates spinning on top of poles and you get a glimpse into Mandie's daily life! (And no plates have been broken in the production of this book!)

Cindy Teeters, who handles the administrative tasks associated with my books. Cindy does her job extremely well and with a great attitude. Thank you!

Chuti Prasertsith for the cover of the book.

Que's production and sales team for printing the book and getting it into your hands.

We Want to Hear from You!

As the reader of this book, *you* are our most important critic and commentator. We value your opinion and want to know what we're doing right, what we could do better, what areas you'd like to see us publish in, and any other words of wisdom you're willing to pass our way.

We welcome your comments. You can email or write to let us know what you did or didn't like about this book—as well as what we can do to make our books better.

Please note that we cannot help you with technical problems related to the topic of this book.

When you write, please be sure to include this book's title and author as well as your name and email address. We will carefully review your comments and share them with the author and editors who worked on the book.

Email: feedback@quepublishing.com

Mail: Que Publishing
          ATTN: Reader Feedback
          800 East 96th Street
          Indianapolis, IN 46240 USA

Reader Services

Register your copy of *My iPhone for Seniors* at quepublishing.com for convenient access to downloads, updates, and corrections as they become available. To start the registration process, go to quepublishing.com/register and log in or create an account*. Enter the product ISBN, 9780789758699, and click Submit. Once the process is complete, you will find any available bonus content under Registered Products.

*Be sure to check the box that you would like to hear from us in order to receive exclusive discounts on future editions of this product.

Using This Book

This book has been designed to help you transform an iPhone into *your* iPhone by helping you learn to use it easily and quickly. As you can tell, the book relies heavily on pictures to show you how an iPhone works. It is also task-focused so that you can quickly learn the specific steps to follow to do lots of cool things with your iPhone.

Using an iPhone involves lots of touching its screen with your fingers. When you need to tap part of the screen, such as a button or keyboard, you see a callout with the step number pointing to where you need to tap. When you need to swipe your finger along the screen, such as to browse lists, you see the following icons:

The directions in which you should slide your finger on the screen are indicated with arrows. When the arrow points both ways, you can move your finger in either direction. When the arrows point in all four directions, you can move your finger in any direction on the screen.

To zoom in or zoom out on screens, you unpinch or pinch, respectively, your fingers on the screen. These motions are indicated by the following icons:

When you need to tap twice, such as to zoom out or in, you see the following icon:

If you use an iPhone 6s/6s Plus or later model, you can use pressure on the screen to activate certain functions. The following icons indicate when you should apply some pressure (called a Peek) or slightly more pressure (called a Pop):

Sometimes, you should touch your finger to the screen and leave it there without applying pressure to the screen. The following icon indicates when you should do this:

When you should rotate your iPhone, you see this icon:

As you can see on its cover, this book provides information about iPhone models that can run iOS 11. These models are: 5s, SE, 6, 6 Plus, 6s, 6s Plus, 7, 7 Plus, 8, 8 Plus, and X. Each of these models has specific features and capabilities that vary slightly from the others. Additionally, they have different screen sizes, with the SE being the smallest and the Plus models being the largest.

Because of the variations between the models, the figures you see in this book might be slightly different than the screens you see on your iPhone. For example, the iPhone 8 has settings that aren't on the 5s or SE. In most cases, you can follow the steps as they are written with any of these models even if there are minor differences between the figures and your screens.

When the model you are using doesn't support a feature being described, such as the Display Zoom that is on the iPhone 6 and later but not on earlier models, you can skip that information or read it to help you decide if you want to upgrade to a newer model.

The most "different" model of iPhone that runs iOS 11 is the iPhone X. To maximize screen space, the iPhone X does not have the Touch ID/Home button all the other models do. It also uses Face ID instead of Touch ID when user authentication is required, such as when you unlock the phone. Most of the tasks in this book are the same on the X as on other models. In some cases, there are minor variations for the X, which are explained in this book. In a few cases, tasks are substantially different on the X than on the other models. If you use an X, please download the online supplement *My iPhone X* by going to www.informit.com/myiphoneseniors to get the details for these tasks that are unique to the iPhone X.

The iPhone 7 Plus, 8 Plus, and X have additional photographic capabilities because these models have two cameras on their backsides instead of just one. If you have one of these models, check out the online supplement *My iPhone X* for the detailed step-by-step instructions to use their unique photo-taking features.

If you review this book's Table of Contents, you see that two chapters and the *My iPhone X* supplement are provided online. You can download these elements by performing the following steps:

1. Use a web browser to go to www.informit.com/myiphoneseniors.

2. Click the Downloads tab.

3. Click the content you want to download. The content opens in a web browser window.

4. Download the content to your computer or other device. You can then read that content using a PDF viewing application, such as Acrobat Reader.

Getting Started

Learning to use new technology can be intimidating. Don't worry; with this book as your guide, you'll be working with your iPhone like you've been using it all your life in no time at all.

There are several ways you can purchase an iPhone, such as from an Apple Store, from a provider's store (such as AT&T or Verizon), or from a website. You may be upgrading from a previous iPhone or other type of cell phone, in which case you are using the same phone number, or you might be starting with a completely new phone and phone number. However you received your phone, you need to turn it on, perform the basic setup (the iPhone leads you through this step-by-step), and activate the phone.

If you purchased your phone in a physical store, you probably received help with these tasks and you are ready to start learning how to use your iPhone. If you purchased your iPhone from an online store, it came with basic instructions that explain how you need to activate your phone; follow those instructions to get your iPhone ready for action.

For this book, I've assumed you have an iPhone in your hands, you have turned it on, followed the initial setup process it led you through, and activated it.

With your iPhone activated and initial setup complete, you are ready to learn how to use it. This book is designed for you to read and do at the same time. The tasks explained in this book contain step-by-step instructions that guide you; to get the most benefit from the information, perform the steps as you read them. This book helps you learn by doing!

As you can see, this book has quite a few chapters. However, there are only a few that you definitely should read as a group as you get started. You can read the rest of them as the topics are of interest to you. Most of the chapters are designed so that they can be read individually as you move into new areas of your iPhone.

After you've finished reading this front matter, I recommend you read and work through Chapter 1, "Getting Started with Your iPhone," Chapter 2, "Using Your iPhone's Core Features," and Chapter 3, "Setting Up and Using an Apple ID, iCloud, and Other Online Accounts" in their entirety. These chapters give you a good overview of your iPhone and help you set up the basics you use throughout the rest of the book.

From there, read the parts of Chapter 4, "Customizing How Your iPhone Works," and Chapter 5, "Customizing How Your iPhone Looks and Sounds," that are interest to you (for example, in Chapter 5, you find out how to change allpaper image that you see in the background of the Home and Lock . Tasks covering how to protect your iPhone with a passcode and ve your iPhone recognize your fingerprints to unlock it and to make rom the iTunes Store (tasks that are covered in Chapter 4) should be oriority list. Chapters 4 and 5 are good references whenever you hanges to how your iPhone is configured.

After you've finished these core chapters, you're ready to explore the rest of the book in any order you'd like. For example, when you want to learn how to use your iPhone's camera and work with the photos you take, see Chapter 13, "Taking Photos and Video with Your iPhone," and Chapter 14, "Viewing and Editing Photos and Video with the Photos App."

You'll soon wonder
how you ever got
along without one!

In this chapter, you get introduced to the amazing iPhone! Topics include the following:

→ Getting to know your iPhone's external features
→ Getting to know your iPhone's software

Getting Started with Your iPhone

Your iPhone is one of the most amazing handheld devices ever because of how well it is designed. It has only a few external features you need to understand. For most of the things you do, you just use your fingers on your iPhone's screen (which just seems natural), and the iPhone's consistent interface enables you to accomplish most tasks with similar steps.

Getting to Know Your iPhone's External Features

Take a quick look at the iPhone's physical attributes. It doesn't have many physical buttons or controls because you mostly use software to control it.

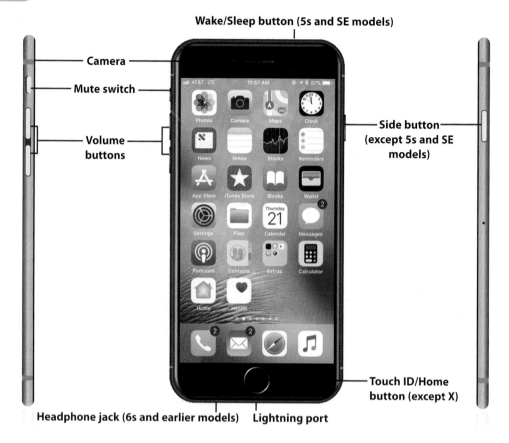

Wake/Sleep button (5s and SE models)

Camera

Mute switch

Volume buttons

Side button (except 5s and SE models)

Touch ID/Home button (except X)

Headphone jack (6s and earlier models)   Lightning port

- **Cameras**—One of the iPhone's camera lenses is located on its backside near the top-left corner (the iPhone 7 Plus, 8 Plus, and X have two lenses there); the other is on the front at the top near the center of the phone. When you take photos or video, you can choose the cameras on either side. All iPhone models have a flash located near the camera on the backside. The iPhone 6s and later models also have a flash on the front that comes from the screen; for the 5s and SE, there is no flash when you use the camera on the front.

- **Side button**—Press this button (called the Sleep/Wake button on the 5s and SE and located on the top of the phone instead of on the side of those models) to lock the iPhone's screen and put it to sleep. Press it again to wake the iPhone from Sleep mode. You also use this button to shut down the iPhone and to power it up. On the iPhone X, it has other uses, such as activating Siri when you hold it down for a couple of seconds.

- **Mute switch**—This switch determines whether the iPhone makes sounds, such as ringing when a call comes in or making the alert noise for notifications, such as for an event on a calendar. Slide it toward the front of the iPhone to hear sounds. Slide it toward the back of the iPhone to mute all sound. When muted, you see orange in the switch.

- **Volume**—Press the upper button to increase volume; press the lower button to decrease volume. These buttons are contextual; for example, when you are listening to music, they control the music's volume, but when you aren't, they control the ringer volume. When you are using the Camera app, pressing either button takes a photo.

- **Lightning port**—Use this port, located on the bottom side of the iPhone, to plug in the Lightning headphones (iPhone 7/7 Plus or later models) or connect it to a computer or power adapter using the included USB cable. There are also accessories that connect to this port. The Lightning port accepts Lightning plugs that are flat, thin, rectangular plugs. It doesn't matter which side is up when you plug something into this port.

  The iPhone 7/7Plus and later models come with an adapter that enables you to plug devices that have a 3.5 mm plug (such as prior versions of the EarPods) into the Lightning port.

- **Headphone jack (5s, SE, 6/6 Plus, and 6s/6s Plus)**—This standard 3.5 mm jack can be used for headphones (such as the older EarPods) and powered speakers.

- **Touch ID/Home button (all iOS 11 compatible models except the X)**—This serves two functions.

  The Touch ID sensor recognizes your fingerprint, so you can simply touch it to unlock your iPhone, sign in to the iTunes Store, use Apple Pay, and enter your password in Touch ID-enabled apps. On the iPhone 7/7s and later models, it technically isn't even a button, rather it is a sensor only (though it still works like a button because you press it).

  It also serves as the Home button. When the iPhone is asleep, press it to wake up the iPhone; press it again to unlock the iPhone (if you have Touch ID enabled, this also enters your passcode; if not, you have to manually enter the passcode to unlock the phone). When the iPhone is awake and unlocked, press this button to move to the all-important Home screens; press it twice quickly to open the App Switcher. Press and hold the Home button to activate Siri to speak to your iPhone. You can also configure it so you can use it to perform other actions, such as pressing it three times to open the Magnifier.

Camera

Mute switch

Volume buttons

Side button

Lightning port

One of the most significant hardware changes that Apple made for the iPhone X was to remove the Touch ID/Home button. This enables the iPhone X to have a larger screen than similarly sized iPhone models, such as the 7 or 8. Gestures and different button combinations replace some of the functions of the Touch ID/ Home button while Face ID replaces the Touch ID function of this button.

So Many iPhones, So Few Pages

The iPhone is now in its eleventh generation of software that runs on multiple generations of hardware. Each successive generation has added features and capabilities to the previous version. All iPhone hardware runs the iOS operating system. However, this book is based on the current version of this operating system, iOS 11. iOS 11 is compatible with the 5s, SE, 6, 6 Plus, 6s, 6s Plus, 7, 7 Plus, 8, 8 Plus, and X. If you don't have one of these models, this book helps you see why it is time to upgrade, but most of the information contained herein won't apply to your iPhone until you do.

There are also differences even among the models of iPhones that can run iOS 11. For example, the iPhone 7 Plus, 8 Plus, and X have dual cameras on the backside that provide additional photographic features, including telephoto and portrait photographs.

Most of the information in this book is based on iPhone 7, 7 Plus, 8, and 8 Plus. If you don't use one of these models, there might be slight differences between what you see on your screen and the steps and figures in this book (if you use an iPhone X, make sure to read the next sidebar). These differences aren't significant and shouldn't stop you from accomplishing the tasks as described in this book.

X Marks the Spot

Because of the differences in the iPhone X hardware and the rest of the models, it has an online companion supplement to this book called *My iPhone X*. You can download this supplement by using a web browser to visit www.informit.com/myiphone-seniors. While almost all of the tasks in this book can be followed as written with an iPhone X, the supplement provides detailed steps for those tasks that are unique to the X, such as configuring and using Face ID. Also, some of the photographic tasks that only the 7 Plus, 8 Plus, and X can do are covered in this supplement.

Getting to Know Your iPhone's Software

You might not suspect it based on the iPhone's simple and elegant exterior, but this powerhouse runs very sophisticated software that enables you to do all sorts of great things. The beauty of the iPhone's software is that it is both very powerful and also easy to use—once you get used to its user interface (UI for the more technical among you). The iPhone's UI is so well designed that after a few minutes, you might wish everything worked so well and was so easy to use.

Using Your Fingers to Control Your iPhone

Apple designed the iPhone to be touched. Most of the time, you control your iPhone by using your fingers on its screen to tap icons, select items, swipe on the screen, zoom, type text, and so on. If you want to get technical, this method of interacting with software is called the multi-touch interface.

Going Home

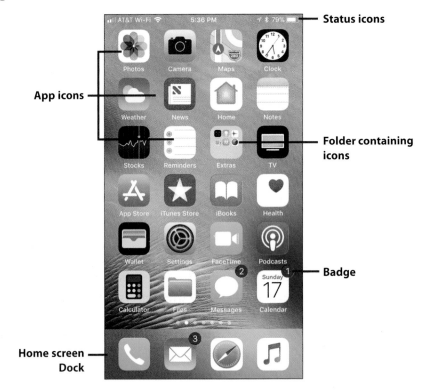

Almost all iPhone activities start at the Home screen, or Home screens, to be more accurate, because the Home screen consists of multiple pages. When your iPhone is unlocked and you are using an app, you get to the Home screen by pressing the Touch ID/Home button once (all models except iPhone X) or touching and swiping up from the bottom of the screen (iPhone X). You move to the Home screen automatically any time you restart your iPhone and unlock it. Along the bottom of the Home screen (or along the side on an iPhone Plus model when held horizontally) is the Dock, which is always visible on the Home screens. This gives you easy access to the icons it contains; up to four icons can be placed on this Dock. Above the Dock are apps that do all sorts of cool things. As you install apps, the number of icons on the Home screens increases. To manage these icons, you can organize the pages of the Home screens in any way you like, and you can place icons into folders to keep your Home screens tidy. At the top of the screen are status icons that provide you with important information, such as whether you are connected to a Wi-Fi network and the current charge of your iPhone's battery.

Touching the iPhone's Screen

The following figures highlight the major ways you control an iPhone:

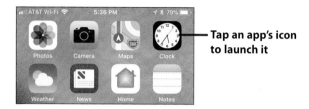

Tap an app's icon to launch it

- **Tap**— Briefly touch a finger to the iPhone's screen and then lift your finger again. When you tap, you don't need to apply pressure to the screen, simply touch your finger to it. For example, to open an app, you tap its icon.

- **Double-tap**—Tap twice. You double-tap to zoom in on something; for example, you can double-tap on a web page to view something at a larger size.

- **Swipe**—Touch the screen at any location and slide your finger (you don't need to apply pressure, just touching the screen is enough). You use the swipe motion in many places, such as to browse a list of options or to move among Home page screens. Whatever you are swiping on moves in the direction that you swipe.

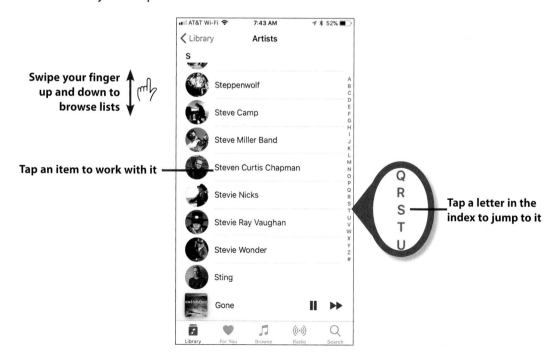

Swipe your finger up and down to browse lists

Tap an item to work with it

Tap a letter in the index to jump to it

- **Drag**—Touch and hold an object and move your finger across the screen without lifting it up; the faster you move your finger, the faster the resulting action happens. (Again, you don't need to apply pressure, just make contact.) For example, you can drag icons around the Home screens to rearrange them.

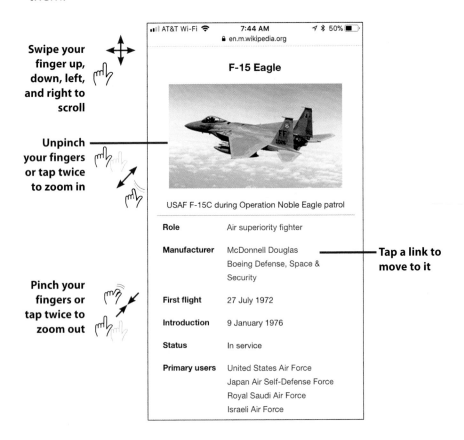

- **Pinch or unpinch**—Place two fingers on the screen and drag them together or move them apart; the faster and more you pinch or unpinch, the "more" the action happens (such as a zoom in). When you are viewing photos, you can unpinch to zoom in on them or pinch to zoom out again.

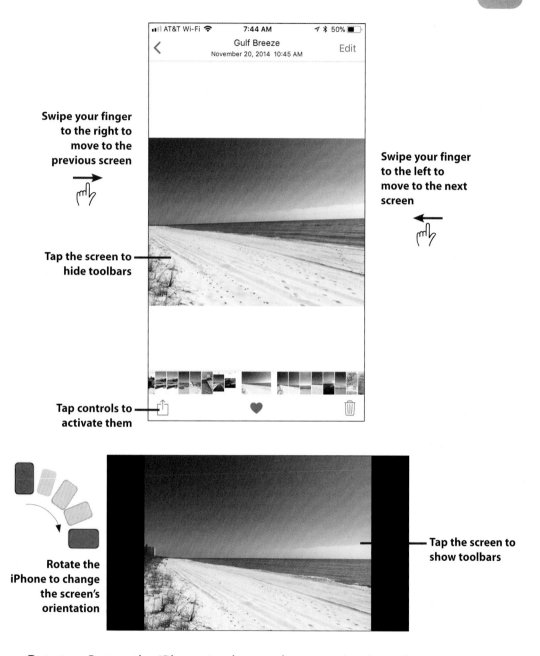

Swipe your finger to the right to move to the previous screen

Swipe your finger to the left to move to the next screen

Tap the screen to hide toolbars

Tap controls to activate them

Rotate the iPhone to change the screen's orientation

Tap the screen to show toolbars

• **Rotate**—Rotate the iPhone to change the screen's orientation.

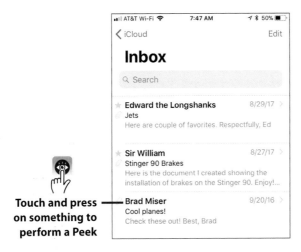

Touch and press
on something to
perform a Peek

Swipe up on a Peek to reveal menus with
actions you can select to perform them

A Peek is a quick way to
look at something without
actually opening it

When you swipe up on a Peek, you get
a menu; tap an action to perform it

- **Peek**—On an iPhone that supports 3D Touch (iPhone 6s and later models), you can take action on something by applying pressure to the screen when you touch it. When you are looking at a preview of something, such as an email, touch and put a small amount of pressure on the screen to perform a Peek. A Peek causes a window to open that shows a preview of the object. You can preview the object in the Peek window; if you swipe up on a Peek, you get a menu of commands related to the object. For example, when you perform a Peek on an email and then swipe up on the Peek, you can tap Reply to reply to the email.

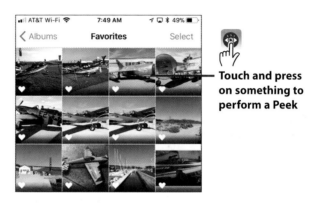

Touch and press
on something to
perform a Peek

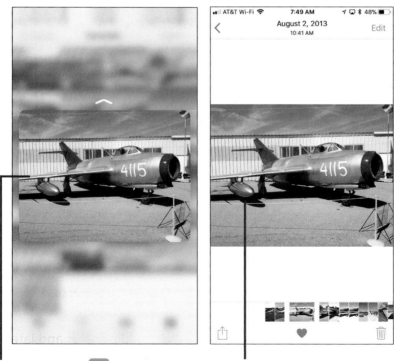

Press slightly harder on a
Peek to perform a Pop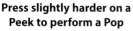

When you perform a Pop, the object
opens in the associated app

- **Pop**—When you are looking at a Peek, apply slightly more pressure on the screen to perform a Pop, which opens the object in its app. For example, you can perform a Peek on a photo's thumbnail to preview it. Apply a bit more pressure (a Pop) on the preview to "pop" it open in the Photos app (for example, to crop your finger out of the photo).

Working with iPhone Apps

When you tap an app's icon, it opens and fills the iPhone's screen

One of the best things about an iPhone is that it can run all sorts of applications, or in iPhone lingo, *apps*. It includes a number of preinstalled apps, such as Mail, Safari, and so on, but you can download and use thousands of other apps, many of which are free, through the App Store. You learn about many of the iPhone's preinstalled apps as you read through this book. And as you learned earlier, to launch an app, you simply tap its icon. The app opens and fills the iPhone's screen. You can then use the app to do whatever it does.

Pressing on an app's icon pops open the Quick Actions menu

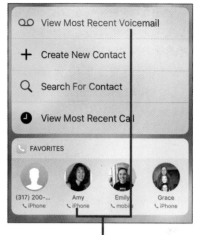

Tap a Quick Action to perform it

On an iPhone that supports 3D Touch (iPhone 6s and later models), you can press on an app's icon to open its Quick Actions menu; tap an action to take it. For example, when you open the Quick Actions menu for the Phone app, you can place calls to people you have designated as favorites.

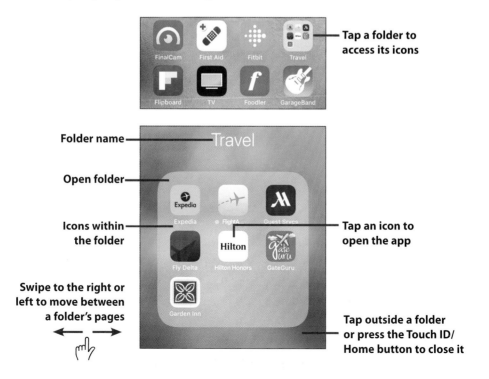

Tap a folder to access its icons

Folder name

Open folder

Icons within the folder

Tap an icon to open the app

Swipe to the right or left to move between a folder's pages

Tap outside a folder or press the Touch ID/ Home button to close it

In Chapter 5, "Customizing How Your iPhone Looks and Sounds," you learn how you can organize icons in folders to keep your Home screens tidy and make getting to icons faster and easier. To access an icon that is in a folder, tap the folder. It opens and takes over the screen. Under its name is a box showing the apps it contains. Like the Home screens, folders can have multiple pages. To move between a folder's pages, swipe to the left to move to the next screen or to the right to move to the previous one. Each time you "flip" a page, you see another set of icons. You can close a folder without opening an app by tapping outside its borders or by pressing the Touch ID/Home button (except the iPhone X).

To open an app within a folder, tap its icon.

When you are done using an app, press the Touch ID/Home button (all models except the iPhone X) or swipe up from the bottom of the screen (iPhone X). You return to the Home screen you were most recently using.

When you move out of an app by pressing the Touch ID/Home button or swiping up from the bottom of the screen (iPhone X only), the app moves into the background but doesn't stop running (you can control whether or not apps are allowed to work in the background using the Settings app, which you use throughout this book). So, if the app has a task to complete, such as uploading photos or playing audio, it continues to work behind the scenes. In some cases, most notably games, the app becomes suspended at the point you move it into the background by switching to a different app or moving to a Home screen. In addition to the benefit of completing tasks when you move into another app, the iPhone's capability to multitask means that you can run multiple apps at the same time. For example, you can run an Internet radio app to listen to music while you switch over to the Mail app to work on your email.

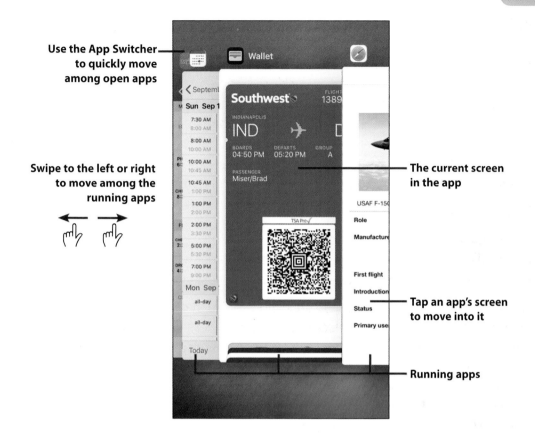

Use the App Switcher to quickly move among open apps

Swipe to the left or right to move among the running apps

The current screen in the app

Tap an app's screen to move into it

Running apps

You can control apps by using the App Switcher. To see this, quickly press the Touch ID/Home button twice (all models except the iPhone X) or swipe up from the bottom of the screen and pause near the middle of the screen (iPhone X). The App Switcher appears.

At the top of the App Switcher, you see icons for apps you are currently using or have used recently. Under each app's icon, you see a thumbnail of that app's screen. You can swipe to the left or right to move among the apps you see. You can tap an app's screen to move into it. That app takes over the screen, and you can work with it, picking up right where you left off the last time you used it.

When you open the App Switcher, the app you were using most recently comes to the center to make it easy to return to. This enables you to toggle between two apps easily. For example, suppose you need to enter a confirmation number from one app into another app. Open the app into which you want to enter the number. Then open the app containing the number you need to enter. Open the

App Switcher and tap the previous app to return to it quickly so that you can enter the number.

To close the App Switcher without moving into a different app, press the Touch ID/Home button once (all models except iPhone X) or tap outside the App Switcher (iPhone X). You move back into the app or Home screen you were most recently using.

Swipe up on an app's screen to force it to close

iPhone X App Switching

On the iPhone X, you can switch apps by swiping to the left or right along the bottom of the screen (without opening the App Switcher). Refer to the online supplement *My iPhone X* by going to www.informit.com/myiphoneseniors for more details about using an iPhone X.

In some cases, you might want to force an app to quit, such as when it's using up your battery too quickly or it has stopped responding to you. To do this, open the App Switcher. Swipe up on the app you want to stop. The app is forced to quit, its icon and screen disappear, and you remain in the App Switcher. You should be careful about this, though, because if the app has unsaved data, that data is lost when you force the app to quit. The app is not deleted from the iPhone—it is just shut down until you open it again (which you can do by returning to the Home screen and tapping the app's icon).

Tap to return to the app you were previously using

Sometimes, a link in one app takes you into a different app. When this happens, you see a left-facing arrow with the name of the app you were using in the upper-left corner of the screen. You can tap this to return to the app you came from. For example, you can tap a link in a Mail email message to open the associated web page in Safari. To return to the email you were reading in the Mail app, tap the Mail icon in the upper-left corner of the screen.

Swipe all the way to the right to access widgets

Widgets

Swipe up and down to see all the widgets

Music widget — MUSIC ——— Tap to show less

Tap an album to play it

Mail widget — MAIL ——— Tap to show more

Tap a VIP to read email from him

Apps can provide widgets, which make it easy to work with those apps from the Widget Center. To access these widgets, swipe all the way to the right from a Home screen or from the Lock screen (more on this later). You see widgets for various apps. Swipe up or down the screen to browse all the widgets available to you. Tap Show Less to collapse a widget or tap Show More to expand it. Tap something inside a widget to use that app. For example, tapping an album in the Music widget plays it. You learn more about how to use widgets in Chapter 2, "Using Your iPhone's Core Features" and how to configure the Widget Center in Chapter 4, "Customizing How Your iPhone Works."

Using the Home Screens

Previously in this chapter, you read that the Home screen is the jumping-off point for many of the things you do with your iPhone because that is where you access the icons you tap to launch things such as apps you've saved there.

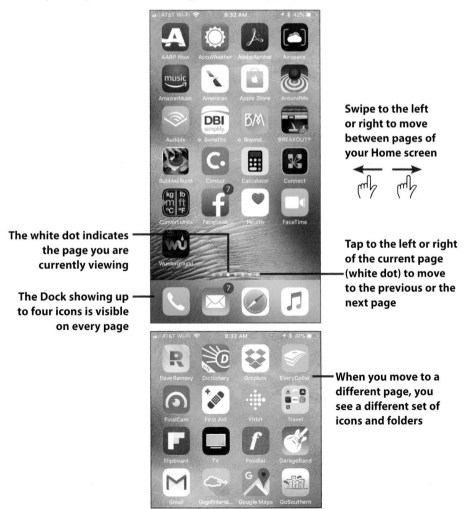

Swipe to the left or right to move between pages of your Home screen

The white dot indicates the page you are currently viewing

Tap to the left or right of the current page (white dot) to move to the previous or the next page

The Dock showing up to four icons is visible on every page

When you move to a different page, you see a different set of icons and folders

The Home screen has multiple pages. To change the page you are viewing, swipe to the left to move to later pages or to the right to move to earlier pages. The dots above the Dock represent the pages of the Home screen; the white dot represents the page being displayed. You can also change the page by tapping to the left of the white dot to move to the previous page or to the right of it to move to the next page.

Using the iPhone Plus' Split-Screen

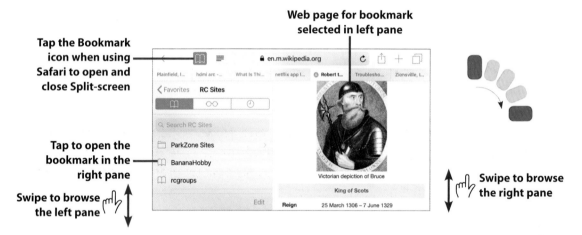

Web page for bookmark selected in left pane

Tap the Bookmark icon when using Safari to open and close Split-screen

Tap to open the bookmark in the right pane

Swipe to browse the left pane

Swipe to browse the right pane

When you hold an iPhone Plus in the horizontal orientation, you can take advantage of the Split-screen feature in many apps (not all apps support this). In Split-screen mode, the screen has two panes. The left pane is for navigation, whereas the right pane shows the content selected in the left pane. The two panes are independent, so you can swipe up and down on one side without affecting the other. In most apps that support this functionality, there is an icon you can use to open or close the split screen. This icon changes depending on the app you are using. For example, when you are using Safari to browse the Web, tap the Bookmark icon to open the left pane and tap it again to close the left pane (while the left pane is open, you can select bookmarks and see the associated web pages in the right pane). As another example, in the Mail app, you tap the Full Screen icon (two arrows pointing diagonally away from each other) to open or close the left pane.

Preinstalled apps that support this functionality include Settings, Mail, Safari, and Messages; you see examples showing how Split-screen works in those apps later in this book. You should hold your iPhone Plus horizontally when using your favorite apps to see if they support this feature.

Home screen pages ——

Dock

When you hold an iPhone Plus horizontally and move to the Home screen, the Dock moves to the right side of the screen and you see the Home screen's pages in the left part of the window. Though this looks a bit different, it works the same as when you hold an iPhone vertically.

Working with the Control Center

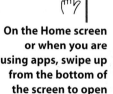

On the Home screen or when you are using apps, swipe up from the bottom of the screen to open the Control Center (except iPhone X)

On an iPhone X, swipe down from the upper-right corner of the screen to open the Control Center

On the Lock screen, swipe up from the bottom of the screen to open the Control Center

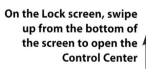

Press home to unlock

The Control Center provides quick access to a number of very useful controls. To access it, swipe up from the bottom of the Home screen (all models except the iPhone X) or swipe down from the upper-right corner of the screen (iPhone X). If your iPhone is asleep/locked, press the Side or Touch ID/Home button or lift the phone to wake it up and then swipe up from the bottom of the Home screen (all models except the iPhone X) or swipe down from the upper-right corner of the screen (iPhone X). When the Control Center opens, you have easy and quick access to a number of controls.

Control Center Tip

Some apps have their own Dock at the bottom of the screen. When you are using such an app, make sure you don't touch an icon on the Dock when you are trying to open the Control Center because you'll do whatever the icon is for instead. Just swipe up on an empty area of the app's Dock and the Control Center opens. On the iPhone X, this isn't an issue because your swipe down from the upper-right corner of the screen instead.

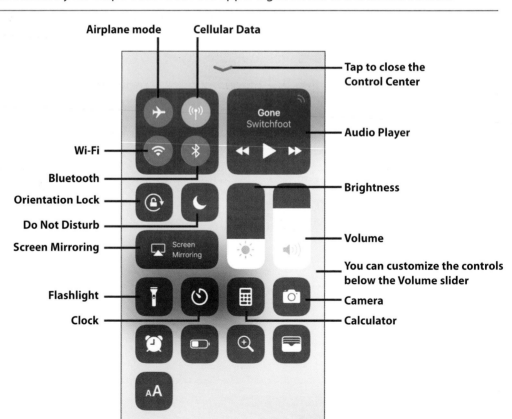

In the top-left quadrant of the Control Center are icons you can use to turn on or turn off important functions, which are Airplane mode, Cellular Data, Wi-Fi, Bluetooth, Orientation Lock, and Do Not Disturb mode. To activate a function, tap its icon, which changes color to show the function is active. To disable a function, tap the icon so that it becomes gray to show you it is inactive. For example, to lock the orientation of the iPhone's screen in its current position, tap the Orientation Lock icon so it becomes red. Your iPhone screen's orientation no longer changes when you rotate the phone. To make the orientation change when you rotate the phone again, tap the Orientation Lock icon to turn it off again. You learn about the Airplane and Do Not Disturb modes later in this chapter. Wi-Fi and Cellular Data are explained in Chapter 2. You learn about using Bluetooth in the online Chapter 15, "Working with Other Useful iPhone Apps and Features."

In the upper-right quadrant, you see the Audio Player. You can use this to control music, podcasts, and other types of audio that are playing in their respective apps (you learn about the Music app in the online Chapter 15).

Just below the Audio Player are the Brightness and Volume sliders. You swipe up or down on these to increase or decrease the screen's brightness and the volume of whatever you are hearing on your phone.

The controls above the first row of four icons are always on the Control Center; you can't change them in any way. However, below those are a section of controls you can change. By default, you see the Flashlight, Clock, Calculator, Camera, and others in this area. Like the icons toward the top of the screen, tap these icons to perform the associated action, such as using the iPhone's flash as a flashlight, or opening an app—the Clock app, for example. You can configure the controls that are in this area by adding, removing, and organizing them; you learn how to configure your Control Center in Chapter 4.

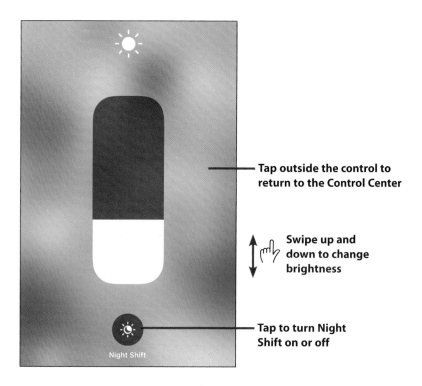

Tap outside the control to return to the Control Center

Swipe up and down to change brightness

Tap to turn Night Shift on or off

When you press on some of the controls, such as the Brightness slider, you see additional options. You should press the controls you use to see what options are available. For example, when you press the Brightness slider, you see a larger slider and have access to the Night Shift icon (you learn about Night Shift in Chapter 5).

When you're done using the Control Center, tap the downward-facing arrow at the top of the screen and the Control Center is hidden.

Examples of using the controls on the Control Center are throughout the rest of this book.

Working with the Notification Center

Your iPhone has a lot of activity going on, from new emails to reminders to calendar events. The iOS notification system keeps you informed of these happenings through a number of means. Visual notifications include banners and badges. Alert sounds can also let you know something has happened, and vibrations make you feel the new activity.

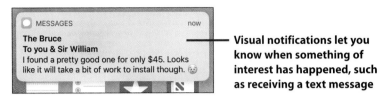

Visual notifications let you know when something of interest has happened, such as receiving a text message

Individual notifications (onscreen alerts, sounds, or vibrations) arrive with the events with which they are associated such as new emails, messages, and updated information from apps. For example, you can have banner notifications and a sound when you receive new text messages.

You learn how to work with the notifications your iPhone uses in Chapter 2. Because there is likely to be a lot of activity on your iPhone, you want to customize the notifications you receive so you are aware of important information but not distracted or annoyed by less important activity; configuring notifications is explained in Chapter 4.

Swipe down from the top of the screen to open the Notification Center when your iPhone is unlocked

Swipe up from the middle of the screen to open the Notification Center when your iPhone is locked

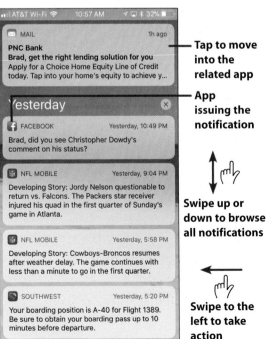

Tap to move into the related app

App issuing the notification

Swipe up or down to browse all notifications

Swipe to the left to take action

You can also access groups of notifications on the Notification Center, which you open by swiping down from the top of the screen when your iPhone is unlocked or swiping up from the middle of the screen when it is locked. The Notification Center opens and displays notifications grouped by day and the app from which they come. You can read the notifications by swiping up and down the screen. You can work with the notifications on the Notification Center just as you work with individual notifications (see Chapter 2). For example, on an iPhone with 3D Touch, press on a notification to pop it open to read more of it or to take action on it; press a little harder to open the associated app. On iPhones without 3D Touch, tap a notification to move into the associated app.

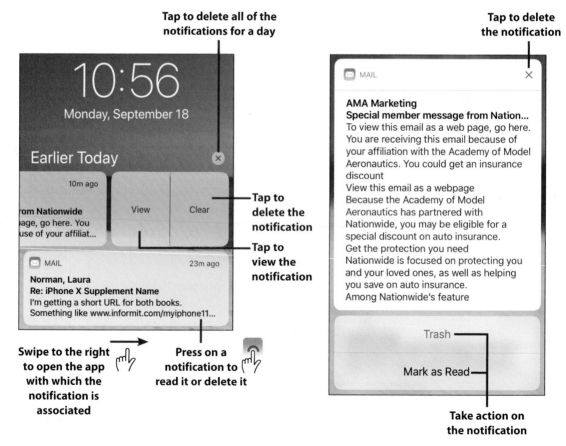

Tap to delete all of the notifications for a day

Tap to delete the notification

Tap to delete the notification

Tap to view the notification

Swipe to the right to open the app with which the notification is associated

Press on a notification to read it or delete it

Take action on the notification

When you swipe to the left on a notification, you can tap Clear to delete the notification or View to open it. If you swipe to the right on a notification, you open the app that generated it (if your iPhone is locked, you need to unlock it to move into the app). If you press on a notification, it opens in a window that enables you to read the notification, such as an email, and take action on it.

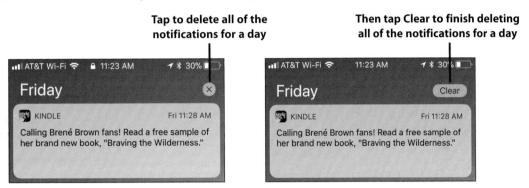

Tap to delete all of the notifications for a day

Then tap Clear to finish deleting all of the notifications for a day

You can remove all the notifications for a day by tapping its Delete (x) icon and then tapping Clear.

To close the Notification Center when your iPhone is unlocked, move back to the Home screen (press the Touch ID/Home button except on the iPhone X where you swipe up from the bottom of the screen). When the iPhone is locked, just press the Side button to put the phone to sleep to hide the Notification Center.

Using Siri Suggestions

Search your iPhone

Tap to close SIRI SUGGESTIONS

Tap to show fewer apps

Tap an app to open it

Tap to run a suggested search

Earlier, you learned how to access apps from the Home page and App Switcher. Your iPhone can make recommendations about apps that you might want to use based on those you have most recently used, your current activity, and even your location. You can see these suggestions by swiping down from about ¾ up the screen (if you swipe down from the top, you open the Notification Center instead). In the SIRI APP SUGGESTIONS panel, you see the apps being suggested. Tap an app to open it. You can show more apps by tapping Show More, or if the panel is already expanded, tap Show Less to show fewer apps.

At the top of the screen is the Search bar, which you can use to search your phone (this is covered in Chapter 2).

In the SIRI SEARCH SUGGESTIONS panel, you can tap a suggested search to run it (this is also covered in Chapter 2).

If you don't want to use any of the apps shown or perform a search, tap Cancel to return to the previous screen.

Using the Do Not Disturb Mode

All the notifications your iPhone uses to communicate with you are useful, but at times, they can be annoying or distracting. When you put your iPhone in Do Not Disturb mode, its visual, audible, and vibration notifications are disabled so that they won't bother you. For example, the phone won't ring if someone calls you unless you specify certain contacts whose calls you do want to receive while your phone is in this mode.

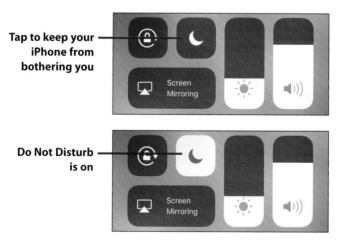

Do Not Disturb is on

To put your iPhone in Do Not Disturb mode, open the Control Center and tap the Do Not Disturb icon. It becomes purple and the Do Not Disturb: On status appears at the top of the Control Center. Your iPhone stops notifications. The Do Not Disturb status icon appears at the top of the Home screens so you know your iPhone is silent.

To make your notifications active again, tap the Do Not Disturb icon so it is gray; your iPhone resumes trying to get your attention when it is needed, and the Do Not Disturb status icon disappears from the top of the Home screens.

In Chapter 4, you learn how to set a schedule for Do Not Disturb so that your iPhone goes into this mode automatically at certain times, such as from 10 p.m. to 6 a.m. You can also configure certain exceptions, including whose calls come in even when your iPhone is in Do Not Disturb mode.

Using Airplane Mode

Although there's a debate about whether cellular devices such as iPhones pose any real danger to the operation of aircraft, there's no reason to run any risk by using your iPhone's cellular functions while you are on an airplane. (Besides, not following crew instructions on airplanes can lead you to less-than-desirable interactions with the flight crew.) When you place your iPhone in Airplane mode, its cellular transmitting and receiving functions are disabled, so it poses no threat to the operation of the aircraft. While it is in Airplane mode, you can't use the phone, the Web, Siri, or any other functions that require cellular communication between your iPhone and other devices or networks. You can continue to use Wi-Fi networks to access the Internet and Bluetooth to communicate with Bluetooth devices.

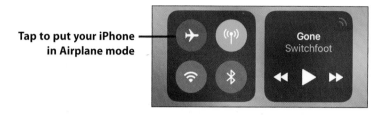

Tap to put your iPhone in Airplane mode

To put your iPhone in Airplane mode, open the Control Center and tap the Airplane mode icon. All connections to the cellular network stop, and your iPhone doesn't broadcast or receive any cellular signals. The Airplane mode icon becomes orange, and you see the Airplane mode status icon at the top of the screen.

This iPhone is in Airplane mode

In Airplane mode, you can use apps that don't require a cellular connection; for example, you can connect to a Wi-Fi network to work with email or browse the Web.

This iPhone is in Airplane mode

Tap to turn off Airplane mode

To turn off Airplane mode, open the Control Center and tap the Airplane mode icon; it becomes gray again and the Airplane mode status icon disappears. The iPhone resumes transmitting and receiving cellular signals, and all the functions that require a cellular connection start working again.

Meeting Siri

Siri is the iPhone's voice-recognition and control software. This feature, which now sounds more natural and less robotic than it did with previous versions of the iOS, enables you to accomplish many tasks by speaking. For example, you can create and send text messages, reply to emails, make phone calls, get directions, and much more. (Using Siri is explained in detail in Chapter 11, "Working with Siri.")

When you perform actions, Siri uses the related apps to accomplish what you've asked it to do. For example, when you create a meeting, Siri uses the Calendar app.

Siri is a great way to control your iPhone, especially when you are working in handsfree mode.

Your iPhone has to be connected to the Internet for Siri to work. That's because the words you speak are sent over the Internet, transcribed into text, and then sent back to your iPhone. If your iPhone isn't connected to the Internet, this can't happen and Siri reports that it can't connect to the network or simply that it can't do what you ask right now.

Using Siri is pretty simple because it follows a consistent pattern and prompts you for input and direction.

Siri is ready to do your bidding —

Activate Siri by pressing and holding down the Touch ID/Home button (all models except iPhone X) or pressing and holding the Side button (iPhone X) until you hear the Siri chime. If so configured (see Chapter 11), you can say "Hey Siri" to activate it, too. And, if those ways aren't enough, you can press and hold down the center part of the buttons on the right EarPod wire.

All of these actions put Siri in "listening" mode, and the "What can I help you with?" text appears on the screen (although when you use "Hey Siri" to activate it, the onscreen text is skipped and Siri gets right to work). This indicates Siri is ready for your command.

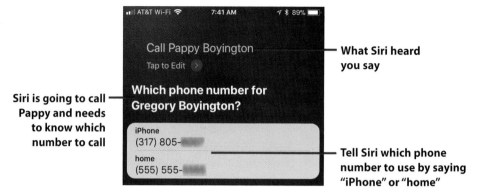

What Siri heard you say

Siri is going to call Pappy and needs to know which number to call

Tell Siri which phone number to use by saying "iPhone" or "home"

Speak your command or ask a question. When you stop speaking, Siri goes into processing mode. After Siri interprets what you've said, it provides two kinds of feedback to confirm what it heard: It displays what it heard on the screen and provides audible feedback to you. Siri then tries to do what it thinks you've asked and shows you what it is doing. If it needs more input from you, you're prompted to provide it and Siri moves into "listening" mode automatically.

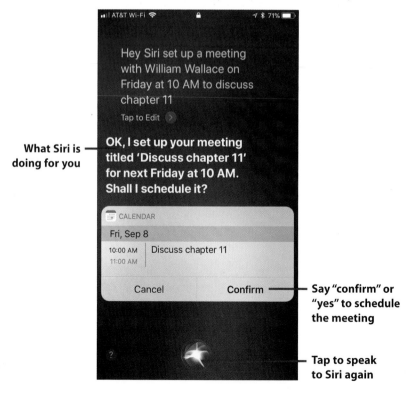

What Siri is doing for you

Say "confirm" or "yes" to schedule the meeting

Tap to speak to Siri again

If Siri requests that you confirm what it is doing or make a selection, do so. Siri completes the action and displays what it has done; it also audibly confirms the result.

Siri isn't quite like using the computer on the Starship Enterprise on *Star Trek*, but it's pretty darn close. Mostly, you can just speak to Siri as you would talk to someone else, and it is able to do what you want or asks you the information it needs to do what you want.

Understanding iPhone Status Icons

At the top of the screen is the Status bar with various icons that provide you with information, such as if you are in Airplane mode, whether you are connected to a Wi-Fi or cellular data network, the time, whether the iPhone's orientation is locked, the state of the iPhone's battery, and so on. Keep an eye on this area as you use your iPhone. The following table provides a guide to the most common of these icons.

Icon	Description	Where to Learn More
	Signal strength—Indicates how strong the cellular signal is.	Chapter 2
AT&T	Provider name—The provider of the current cellular network.	Chapter 2
LTE	Cellular data network—Indicates which cellular network your iPhone is using to connect to the Internet.	Chapter 2
	Wi-Fi—Indicates your phone is connected to a Wi-Fi network.	Chapter 2
Wi-Fi	Wi-Fi calling—Indicates your phone can make voice calls over a Wi-Fi network.	Chapter 2
	Do Not Disturb—Your iPhone's notifications and ringer are silenced.	Chapters 1, 4
	Bluetooth—Indicates if Bluetooth is turned on or off and if your phone is connected to a device.	Chapter 15
79%	Battery percentage—Percentage of charge remaining in the battery.	Chapter 16
	Battery status—Relative level of charge of the battery.	Chapter 16

Icon	Description	Where to Learn More
	Low Battery status—The battery has less than 20% power remaining.	Chapter 16
	Low Power mode—The iPhone is operating in Low Power mode.	Chapter 16
	Orientation Lock—Your iPhone's screen won't change when you rotate your iPhone.	Chapter 1
	Charging—The battery in the iPhone is being charged.	Chapter 16
	Location Services—An app is using the Location Services feature to track your iPhone's location.	Chapter 4
	Airplane mode—The cellular transmitting and receiving functions are disabled.	Chapter 1

Turning Your iPhone Off or On

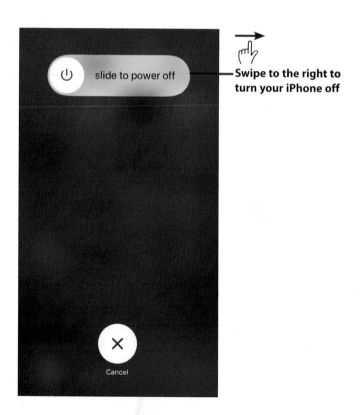

Swipe to the right to turn your iPhone off

You seldom need to turn your iPhone off, but when you do, press and hold the Side button until the slider appears at the top of the screen. (On an iPhone 5s or SE, use the Sleep/Wake button located on the topside of the phone to turn it off or on.) Swipe the slider to the right to shut down the iPhone. The iPhone shuts down.

To restart your iPhone, press and hold the Side button until the Apple logo appears on the screen, and then let go of the button.

After it starts up, assuming you have a passcode, you see the Enter Passcode screen. Enter your passcode to start using your phone; once your passcode is entered correctly, you move to the Home screen. (Even if you have Touch ID or Face ID enabled to unlock your phone, you must enter your passcode the first time you unlock it after a restart.)

If you don't have a passcode configured (you should have a passcode configured to protect your information), you move directly to the Home screen when the phone starts and it's ready for you to use. Keep in mind, if you do not have a passcode configured, your phone is vulnerable to anyone who gets hold of it. (See Chapter 5 for more information about configuring passcodes and Touch ID or the online supplement *My iPhone X* at informit.com/myiphoneseniors to learn how to work with Face ID.)

Sleeping/Locking and Waking/Unlocking Your iPhone

When your iPhone sleeps, it goes into a Low Power mode to extend battery life. Some processes keep working, such as playing music, whereas others stop until your iPhone wakes up. Almost all of the time, you'll put your iPhone to sleep rather than turning it off because it's much faster to wake up than to turn on. Because it uses so little power when it's asleep, there's not much reason to shut it down.

Also, when you put your iPhone to sleep, much of its functionality can't be used until it is unlocked; you can do a number of tasks, such as using widgets and viewing notifications, while the iPhone is awake, but locked. If you configure your iPhone to require a passcode to unlock, this also protects your information. Even when the iPhone is asleep, you can receive and work with notifications, such as when you receive emails or text messages. (See Chapter 4 to configure which notifications you see on the Lock screen and how you can interact with them.)

To put your iPhone to sleep and lock it, press the Side button (on an iPhone 5s or SE, use the Sleep/Wake button). The screen goes dark.

This iPhone is awake and locked

Swipe down from the top-right corner of the screen to open the Control Center (iPhone X)

Control audio that is playing

Swipe to the right to access widgets

Swipe to the left to take photos or video

Swipe up from the middle of the screen to open the Notification Center

Swipe up from the bottom of the screen to open the Control Center (all models except iPhone X)

When an iPhone is asleep/locked, you need to wake it up to use it. You can do this in several ways: touch or press the Touch ID/Home button, press the Side button (Sleep/Wake button on a 5s or SE) or simply raise the iPhone (on models that support the Raise to Wake feature). The Lock screen appears.

If you want to use app widgets (swipe to the right), access the Notification Center (swipe up from the middle of the screen), open the Control Center (swipe up from the bottom of the Home screen [all models except the iPhone X] or swipe down from the upper-right corner of the screen [iPhone X]), take photos or video (swipe to the left), or control audio playback (when audio is playing the controls appear on the Lock screen), you can do so directly on the Lock screen.

When you are ready to use apps or access your Home screens, you need to unlock your iPhone. How you unlock your iPhone depends on its state and the model you are using.

If you don't have a passcode (you should have a passcode to protect your information on the phone), you can press the Touch ID/Home button (all models except iPhone X) or swipe up from the bottom of the screen (iPhone X) to unlock it.

If you have configured a passcode (see Chapter 4), which you should have on your phone, there are two states your iPhone can be in; how you unlock it depends on its state.

Enter your passcode to start using your iPhone

If you restarted your iPhone, you need to enter its passcode, even if you have Touch ID or Face ID configured to unlock it.

If you have an iPhone with Touch ID configured to unlock it (see Chapter 4), press the Touch ID/Home button with a finger whose fingerprint has been stored for use; if you are using an iPhone 7 or later model (except the iPhone X), you don't need to press the Touch ID/Home button and can simply touch it instead. When your fingerprint is recognized, your iPhone unlocks and you can start using it.

If you have an iPhone X with Face ID configured to unlock it, you swipe up from the bottom of the screen and look at the screen. When the iPhone recognizes your face, the phone unlocks and you can use it.

If your iPhone doesn't have Touch ID or Face ID configured to unlock it, press the Touch ID/Home button (all models except iPhone X) or swipe up from the bottom of the screen (iPhone X) and enter your passcode to unlock your phone.

Be Recognized

To use the Touch ID, you need to train your iPhone to recognize the fingerprints you want to use. You were prompted to configure one fingerprint when you started your iPhone for the first time. You can change or add fingerprints for Touch ID at any time; see Chapter 4 for the details of configuring Touch ID.

iPhone X Face ID

Refer to the online supplement *My iPhone X* by going to www.informit.com/myiphoneseniors for the details of configuring and using Face ID on an iPhone X.

However you unlock the phone, when it unlocks, you move to the last screen you were using before it was locked.

If you don't use your iPhone for a while, it automatically goes to sleep and locks according to the preference you have set for it (this is covered in Chapter 5).

The Time Is Always Handy

If you use your iPhone as a watch the way I do, just wake it up. The current time and date appear; if you don't unlock it, the iPhone goes back to sleep after a few seconds.

Working with Touch ID or Face ID

You can use Touch ID and Face ID to quickly, easily, and securely provide a password or passcode in many different situations, such as unlocking your iPhone, downloading apps from the App Store, signing into an account in a banking or other app, and so on.

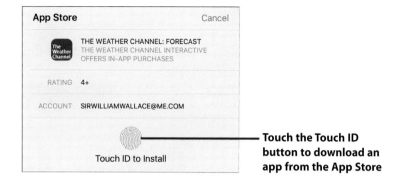

Touch the Touch ID button to download an app from the App Store

Once configured, using Touch ID is as simple as touching a recorded fingerprint to the Touch ID/Home button when you are prompted to do so. The resulting action is completed, such as downloading an app from the App Store. (As referenced in the prior note, you need to configure your iPhone to recognize your fingerprints to use Touch ID and to enable where it can be used; see Chapter 4 for details.)

Face ID works similarly except that instead of touching the Touch ID/Home button, you look at the screen. When the iPhone recognizes your face, the action is completed.

More iPhone X Face ID

Refer to the online supplement *My iPhone X* by going to www.informit.com/myiphoneseniors for the details of working with Face ID on an iPhone X.

If you don't have the settings configured to enable you to use Touch ID or Face ID or you use an app that doesn't support Touch ID or Face ID, you need to provide your password when prompted to do so. Whatever action you were performing is completed.

Setting Volume

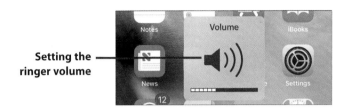

Setting the ringer volume

To change the iPhone's volume, press the up or down Volume button on the side of the iPhone. When you change the volume, your change affects the current activity. For example, if you are on a phone call, the call volume changes, or if you are listening to music, the music's volume changes. If you aren't on a screen that shows a Volume slider, an icon pops up to show you the relative volume you are setting and the type, such as setting the ringer's volume. When the volume is right, release the Volume button.

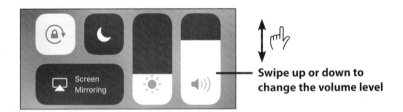

Swipe up or down to change the volume level

You can also use the Volume slider on the Control Center to change the volume level.

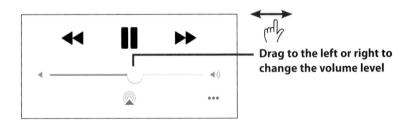

Drag to the left or right to change the volume level

When you are using an audio app, such as the Music app, you can also drag the volume slider in that app or on the Control Center to increase or decrease the volume. Drag the slider to the left to lower volume or to the right to increase it.

When you use the iPhone's EarPods, you can change the volume by pressing the upper part of the switch on the right EarPod's wire to increase volume or the lower part to decrease it.

To mute your phone's sounds, slide the Mute switch, located on the left side of the phone, toward the back of the phone. You see an on-screen indicator that the phone is muted and you see orange within the Mute switch on the side of the iPhone; notification and other sounds won't play. To restore normal sound, slide the switch toward the front of the phone.

Unintentional Muting

If your phone suddenly stops ringing when calls come in or doesn't play notification sounds that you think it should, always check the Mute switch to ensure it hasn't been activated accidentally or that you forgot that you had muted your iPhone. (There's no indication on the screen that the iPhone is currently muted, so you have to look at the switch to tell.)

Connect to the Internet via
Wi-Fi or a cellular network

Use the
Settings app
to configure
your iPhone

Notifications, such
as badges, keep
you informed

Use the iPhone's
great text tools in
many apps

Take advantage of an
Internet connection in
many different apps

Print email and other documents
from your phone

In this chapter, you learn to use some of your iPhone's core features. Topics include the following:

→ Getting started
→ Working with the Settings app
→ Connecting to the Internet using Wi-Fi networks
→ Connecting to the Internet using cellular data networks
→ Securing your iPhone
→ Working with text
→ Using widgets
→ Searching on your iPhone
→ Working with Siri Suggestions
→ Working with notifications
→ Printing from your iPhone

2

Using Your iPhone's Core Features

In Chapter 1, "Getting Started with Your iPhone," you learned how to interact with your iPhone, including navigating Home screens, using apps, locking and unlocking the phone, swiping to open and close things, and zooming in or out. In this chapter, you learn to use some of the iPhone's "core" features, meaning those that apply across multiple apps and functions of your phone.

Getting Started

Here are the core features and concepts you learn about in this chapter:

- **Settings app**—The iPhone's Settings app is where you do almost all of your phone's configuration, and you use it frequently throughout this book.

- **The Internet**—Your iPhone has many functions that rely on an Internet connection; most of the apps you use either require or can use a connection to the Internet to do what they do for you. For example, to send and receive email, your iPhone has to be connected to the Internet.

- **Wi-Fi**—Wi-Fi stands for Wireless Fidelity and encompasses a whole slew of technical specifications around connecting devices together without using cables or wires. Wi-Fi networks have a relatively short range and are used to create a Local Area Network (LAN). The most important thing to know is that you can use Wi-Fi networks to connect your iPhone to the Internet. This is great because Wi-Fi networks are available in many places you go. You probably have a Wi-Fi network available in your home to which you can connect your iPhone, too. (If you connect your computers to the Internet without a cable from your computer to a modem or network hub, you are using a Wi-Fi network.)

- **Cellular data networks**—In addition to your voice, your iPhone can transmit and receive data over the cellular network to which it is connected. This enables you to connect your iPhone to the Internet just about anywhere you are. You use the cellular network provided by your cell phone company. There are many different cell phone providers that support iPhones. In the United States, these include AT&T, Sprint, T-Mobile, and Verizon. You don't need to configure your iPhone to use the cellular data network, as it is set up from the start to do so.

- **Security**—Connecting your iPhone to the Internet enables you to do lots of useful, and sometimes amazing, things with it. But that connection does come with some risk because of the sensitive information you store on your iPhone and the tasks you perform with it. The good news is that you can protect your information with a few relatively simple precautions.

- **Text**—You enter text on your iPhone for many different purposes, including sending messages and emails and writing notes. You can type text using the iPhone's amazing onscreen keyboards. You can also dictate text wherever you might need to create it. The iPhone has many features to help you make the text you enter "just right." For example, text is automatically checked for correct spelling and the Predictive Text feature suggests text you might want to enter with just a tap.

- **Widgets**—Widgets are "mini" versions of apps installed on your iPhone that you can access easily and quickly from the Widget Center (you saw an introduction to this in Chapter 1).

- **Search**—Your iPhone has a lot of information on it. This includes apps, emails, music, and much more. The iPhone's Search tool enables you to find what you want to work with quickly and easily.

- **Siri Suggestions**—You frequently want to "go back" to something you were using recently, such as an app or a search. The Siri Suggestions tool presents these recent items to you so that you can return to them with a single tap. Siri can also learn from what you do and make suggestions about what you might find useful; for example, when you correct a text message that you've dictated, Siri can make suggestions about what you might have intended to say.

- **Notifications**—The iPhone's notification system keeps you informed about activity in which you may be interested, such as new emails, events, app updates, and so on. There are a number of types of these notifications that you experience. Visual notifications include banners and badges. Alert sounds can also let you know something has happened, and vibrations make you feel the new activity.

- **Print**—The paperless world has never become a reality—and probably never will. Fortunately, you can print emails, documents, and other content directly from your iPhone.

Working with the Settings App

Aptly named, the Settings app is where you configure the many settings that change how your iPhone looks, sounds, and works. In fact, virtually everything you do on your iPhone is affected by settings in this app. As you use and make an iPhone into *your* iPhone, you frequently visit the Settings app.

Using the Settings App on Any iPhone

You can work with the Settings app on any iPhone as follows:

(1) On the Home screen, tap Settings. The Settings app opens. The app is organized in sections starting at the top with your Apple ID information followed by Airplane Mode, Wi-Fi, Bluetooth, and Cellular.

(2) Swipe up or down the screen to get to the settings area you want to use.

(3) Tap the area you want to configure, such as Sounds & Haptics (iPhone 7 or later) or Sounds (earlier models).

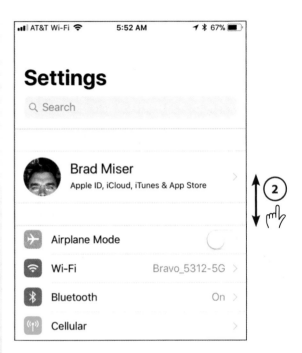

4. Use the resulting controls to configure that area. The changes you make take effect immediately.

5. When you're done, you can leave the Settings app where it is (it remains there when you come back to it) or tap the Back icon, which is always located in the upper-left corner of the screen (its name changes based on where you are in the app), until you get back to the main Settings screen to go into other Settings areas.

Searching for Settings

You can quickly find settings you need by searching for them:

1. Move into the Settings app. (If you aren't on the main Settings screen, tap the Back icon until you get there.)

2. Tap in the Search bar; if you don't see the Search bar, swipe down from the top of the Settings screen until it appears.

3. Type the setting for which you want to search. As you type, potential matches are shown on the list of results. Matches can include a settings area, such as Sounds & Haptics, or specific settings, such as the ringtone and vibrations used when you receive a call.

4. Tap the setting you want to use.

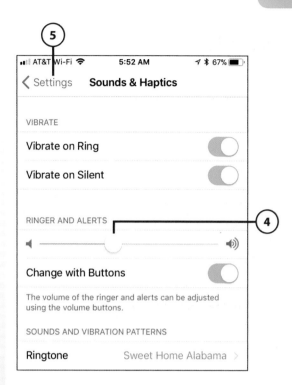

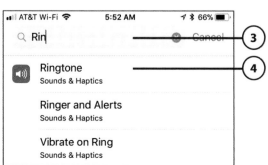

(5) Configure the setting you selected in the previous step.

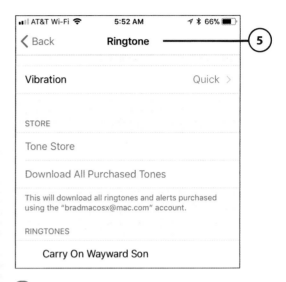

Using the Settings App on an iPhone Plus

When you hold an iPhone Plus in the
horizontal orientation and use the
Settings app, you can take advantage
of the Split-screen feature as follows:

(1) Hold the iPhone Plus so it is
horizontal.

(2) Tap the Settings app to open it.
In the left pane, you see the areas
of the Settings app that you can
configure. In the right pane, you
see tools you can use to configure the selected setting. The two
panes are independent, making
navigation easier than with other
iPhones.

(3) Swipe up or down on the left
pane until you see the function, feature, or app you want to
configure.

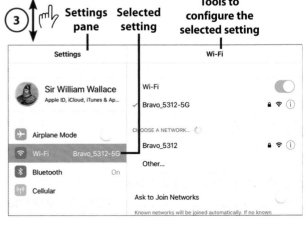

(4) Tap the function, feature, or app you want to configure, such as Sounds. Its controls appear in the right pane.

(5) Swipe up or down on the right pane until you see the specific setting you want to change.

(6) Tap the setting you want to configure, such as Ringtone. Its controls appear in the right pane.

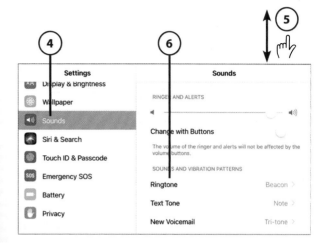

(7) Use the tools in the right pane to configure the setting you selected in step 6. These work just as described in the previous task and throughout this chapter except that you move within the right pane instead of changing the entire screen.

(8) To move back through the screens in the right pane, use the Back icon, which is labeled with the name of the screen you came from.

(9) Tap another area in the left pane to configure it. As you can see, the split screen makes it very easy to quickly switch between areas in the Settings app.

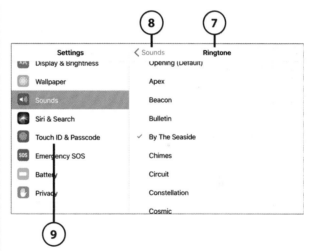

Connecting to the Internet Using Wi-Fi Networks

Your iPhone is designed to seamlessly connect to the Internet so apps that use the Internet to work, such as Safari to browse the Web, are always ready when you need them. Wi-Fi networks provide fast Internet connections and you usually have an unlimited amount of data to work with, so you don't have to worry about paying more based on how you are using your iPhone. Because of their speed and unlimited data (usually), Wi-Fi networks are the best way for your iPhone to connect to the Internet.

Wi-Fi networks are available just about everywhere you go, including homes, offices, hotels, restaurants, and other locations. Fortunately, it's very easy to connect your iPhone to the Wi-Fi networks you encounter. (If there isn't a Wi-Fi network available, your iPhone uses its cellular data network to connect to the Internet, which is covered later in this chapter.)

Almost all Wi-Fi networks broadcast their information so that you can easily see them with your iPhone; these are called open networks because anyone who is in range can attempt to join one because they appear on Wi-Fi devices automatically. The Wi-Fi networks you can see on your iPhone in public places (such as airports and hotels) are all open. Likewise, any Wi-Fi networks in your or other people's homes are very likely to be open as well. To connect your iPhone to an open network, you tap its name and then enter its password.

Your iPhone remembers Wi-Fi networks you've connected to previously and joins one of them automatically when available; these are called known networks. For example, if you have a Wi-Fi network at home and another in a coffee shop you frequent, when you change locations, your iPhone automatically changes Wi-Fi networks.

If your iPhone can't connect to a known network, it automatically searches for other Wi-Fi networks to join. If one or more are available, a prompt appears showing the networks available to your iPhone. You can select and join one of these networks by tapping its name on the list of networks and entering its password (if one is required, you need to obtain it from the source of the network, such as a hotel or restaurant).

If no Wi-Fi networks are available or you choose not to connect to one, your iPhone automatically switches to its cellular data connection (covered in "Connecting to the Internet Using Cellular Data Networks" later in this chapter).

Connecting to Open Wi-Fi Networks

To connect your iPhone to a Wi-Fi network, perform the following steps:

(1) On the Home screen, tap Settings. Next to Wi-Fi, you see the status of your Wi-Fi connection. It is Off if Wi-Fi is turned off, Not Connected if Wi-Fi is turned on and your phone isn't currently connected to Wi-Fi, or the name of the Wi-Fi network to which your iPhone is connected.

(2) Tap Wi-Fi.

(3) If Wi-Fi isn't enabled already, tap the Wi-Fi switch to turn it on (green) and your iPhone searches for available networks. A list of available networks is displayed in the CHOOSE A NETWORK section (it can take a moment for all the networks available in the area to be shown). Along with each network's name, icons indicating whether it requires a password (the padlock icon) to join and the current signal strength (the radio waves icon) are displayed.

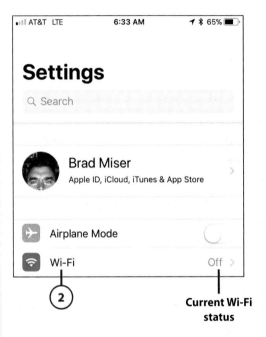

Current Wi-Fi status

Quick Access to the Wi-Fi Switch

You can quickly turn Wi-Fi on or off by swiping up from the bottom of the Home screen (all models except the iPhone X) or swiping down from the upper-right corner of the screen (iPhone X) to open the Control Center. If the Wi-Fi icon (it looks like the signal strength indicator on the Wi-Fi Setting screen) is blue, Wi-Fi is on. Tap that icon to turn Wi-Fi off (the icon becomes gray). Tap it again to turn Wi-Fi on and reconnect to a known network. See Chapter 1 for more information about working with the Control Center.

4 Tap the network you want to join. Of course, when a network requires a password, you must know that password to be able to join it. Another consideration should be signal strength; the more waves in the network's signal strength icon, the stronger the connection.

5 At the prompt, enter the password for the network you selected. If you aren't prompted for a password, skip to step 7. (You're likely to find networks that don't require a password in public places; see the next section for information on these types of networks.)

6 Tap Join. If you provided the correct password, your iPhone connects to the network and gets the information it needs to connect to the Internet. If not, you're prompted to enter the password again. After you successfully connect to the network, you return to the Wi-Fi screen.

7 Review the network information. The network to which you are connected appears just below the Wi-Fi switch and is marked with a check mark. You also see the signal strength for that network.

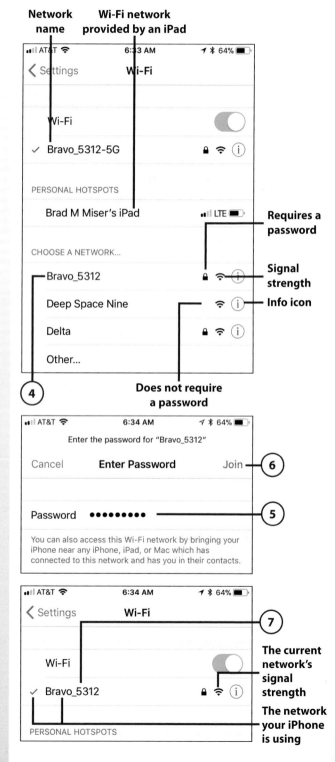

Network name

Wi-Fi network provided by an iPad

Requires a password

Signal strength

Info icon

Does not require a password

The current network's signal strength

The network your iPhone is using

8 Try to move to a web page, such as www.bradmiser.com, to test your Wi-Fi connection. (See Chapter 12, "Surfing the Web," for details.) If the web page opens, you are ready to use the Internet on your phone. You can also tell that your iPhone is connected to a Wi-Fi network by the "waves" icon that appears just to the right of your cell phone provider's name (such as AT&T). If you are taken to a login web page for a Wi-Fi provider rather than the page you were trying to access, see the next task. If you see a message saying the Internet is not available, there is a problem with the network you joined. Go back to step 4 to select a different network.

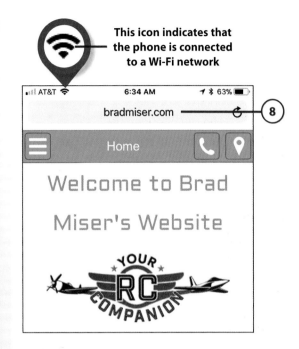

This icon indicates that the phone is connected to a Wi-Fi network

>>>Go Further
CONNECTING TO WI-FI NETWORKS

As you connect to Wi-Fi networks, consider the following:

- **Typing passwords**—As you type a password, each character is hidden by a dot in the Password field except for the last character you entered, which is displayed on the screen for a moment. Keep an eye on characters as you enter them because you can fix a mistake as soon as you make it rather than finding out after you've entered the entire password and having to start over.

- **Changing networks**—You can use these same steps to change the Wi-Fi network you are using at any time. For example, if you have to pay to use one network while a different one is free, simply choose the free network in step 4.

- **Be known**—After your iPhone connects to a Wi-Fi network successfully, it becomes a known network. This means that your iPhone remembers its information so you don't have to enter it again. Your iPhone automatically connects to known networks when it needs to access the Internet. So unless you tell your iPhone to forget a network (explained later in this chapter), you need to enter its password only the first time you connect to it.

- **Security recommendation**—If you are connected to a network that doesn't use what Apple considers sufficient security, you see the words "Security Recommendation" under the network's name. If you tap the Info (i) icon for that network, you see its Info screen. At the top of that screen, you see the type of security the network is using and a recommendation about the type of security it should use. If the Wi-Fi network comes from a router or modem you own or rent, contact your Internet service provider, such as a cable company, to learn how the security provided by that router or modem can be reconfigured to be more secure. If the network is in a public place or business, you just have to use it as is (unless you can contact the administrator of that network to see if better security is available).

- **Personal hotspots**— iPhones and iPads can share their cellular Internet connection (how to do this is covered in a later Go Further sidebar) with other devices by providing a Wi-Fi network to which you can connect your iPhone. The icons for these networks are a bit different, being two connected loops that indicate the network is from a hotspot. You can select and use these networks just like the other types of networks being described in this chapter. The speed of your access is determined mostly by the speed of the device's cellular data connection. Also, the data you use while connected to the hotspot's network counts against the data plan for the device to which you are connected.

Connecting to Public Wi-Fi Networks

Many Wi-Fi networks in public places, such as hotels or airports, require that you pay a fee or provide other information to access the Internet through that network; even if access is free, you usually have to accept terms and conditions for the network to be able to use it.

When you connect to one of these public networks, you're prompted to provide whatever information is required. This can involve different details for different networks, but the general steps are the same. You're prompted to provide whatever information required. Then, follow the instructions that appear.

Following are the general steps to connect to many types of public Wi-Fi networks:

(1) Move to the Settings screen.

(2) Tap Wi-Fi.

(3) Tap the network you want to join. You move to that network's Log In screen. Follow the onscreen prompts to complete the process. This often involves selecting a connection option and providing payment or identification information, as this example of connecting to a hotel's Wi-Fi network shows.

(4) Choose the connection option you want to use.

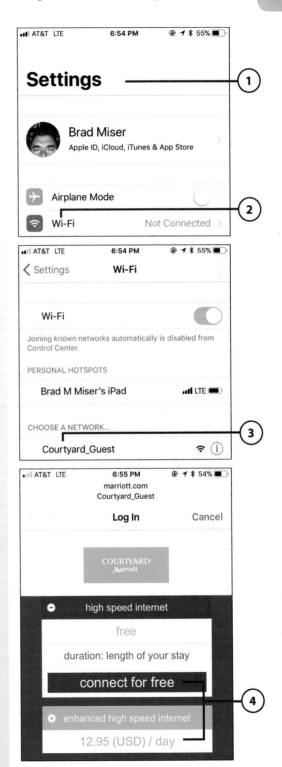

5 Provide the information required to join the network, such as a last name and room number. If a fee is required, you have to provide payment information. In many cases, you at least have to indicate that you accept the terms and conditions for using the network, which you typically do by checking a check box.

6 Tap the icon to join the network. This icon can have different labels depending on the type of access, such as Connect, Authenticate, Done, Free Access, Login, and so on. If you haven't already accepted terms and conditions, doing so is usually inherent in joining the network.

7 Tap Done (if required).

8 Try to move to a web page, such as www.wikipedia.org, to test your Wi-Fi connection (not shown in a figure). (See Chapter 12 for details.) If the web page opens, you are ready to use the Internet on your phone. If you are taken to a login web page for the Wi-Fi network's provider, you need to provide the required information to be able to use the Internet. For example, when access is free, as it is at most airports, you usually just have to indicate you accept the terms of use for that network.

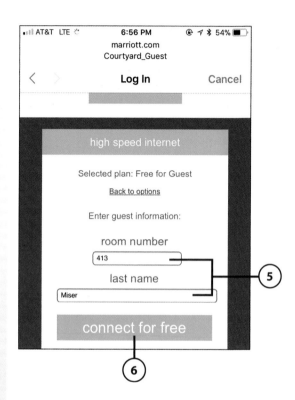

Terms and Conditions?

In order to join a Wi-Fi network, you must accept its terms and conditions. You can click a link to actually read those terms and conditions. They are typically quite long and complicated, almost always being written in complex legal language. Usually, they boil down to you agreeing that you won't do anything harmful to others, participate in illegal activities, hold the network provider liable for anything that happens to you because of your use of the network, and so on. Terms and conditions are a "take it or leave it" proposition. If you don't accept them, you won't be able to use the network.

No Prompt?

Not all public networks prompt you to log in as these steps explain. Sometimes, you use the network's website to log in instead. After you join the network (step 3), your iPhone is connected to the network without any prompts. When you try to move to a web page as explained in step 8, you're prompted to log in to or create an account with the network's provider on the web page that appears.

Disabling Automatic Prompting

When your iPhone can't find a known network—meaning one that you've used before—it presents a prompt showing you the currently available networks. You can use this prompt to select and join one of these networks. This can be useful because you don't have to use the Settings app to find a network to which you are going to connect; instead, you can just tap a network at the prompt to join it.

However, this automatic prompting for networks can be as annoying as it is helpful. It is helpful in that your iPhone prompts you when it comes into range of a network it doesn't know, which can make it easier to know when a network is available to you. It can be annoying when you are moving around a lot because what you are doing can be frequently interrupted by the prompt, even if you don't want to connect to one of the available networks. For example, when you walk through an airport, the prompt can appear multiple times as you move between networks.

To disable automatic network prompting, perform the following steps:

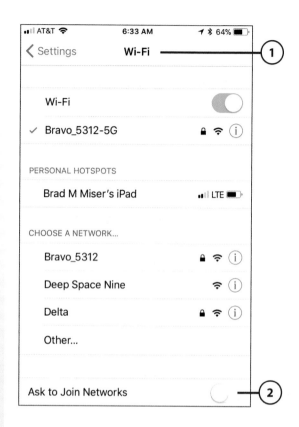

(1) Open the Settings app and move to the Wi-Fi screen.

(2) Set the Ask to Join Networks switch to off (white). To connect to unknown networks, you need to use the Settings app as described in the previous tasks because your iPhone no longer automatically prompts you to join unknown networks. (Remember that it still joins known networks, meaning those you have used before, automatically.)

Forgetting Wi-Fi Networks

As you learned earlier, your iPhone remembers networks you have joined and connects to them automatically as needed; these are known networks. Although this is mostly a good thing, there are times when you no longer want to use a particular network any more. For example, when in an airport, you might decide to connect to a network for which you have to pay for faster Internet access, or you might prefer to access the Internet using cellular service. Each time you move through that airport, your iPhone connects to that network again automatically, which might not be what you want it to do.

To have your iPhone forget a network so it doesn't automatically connect to it in the future, do the following:

(1) Tap Wi-Fi in the Settings app to view the Wi-Fi screen.

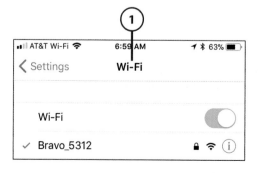

2 Tap the Info (i) icon for the network that you want your iPhone to forget. (You can forget a network only if you are or have previously been connected to it.)

3 Tap Forget This Network.

Forget Versus Auto-Join

When you forget a network, your iPhone stops connecting to it automatically and erases the network's password so you have to enter it again if you want to re-join that network. If you just want to stop automatically joining the network but keep its password on your iPhone, set the Auto-Join switch to off (white) instead of performing step 3. Your iPhone stops automatically connecting to that network, but you can re-join it at any time by tapping it on the CHOOSE A NETWORK list (you don't have to re-enter the password as you do if you forget a network).

4 Tap Forget in the resulting prompt. Your iPhone stops using and forgets the network. You return to the Wi-Fi screen. If another known network is available, your iPhone connects to it automatically. If a network you've forgotten is still in range of your iPhone, it continues to appear in the CHOOSE A NETWORK section, but your iPhone no longer automatically connects to it. You can re-join a forgotten network at any time, just as you did the first time you connected to it.

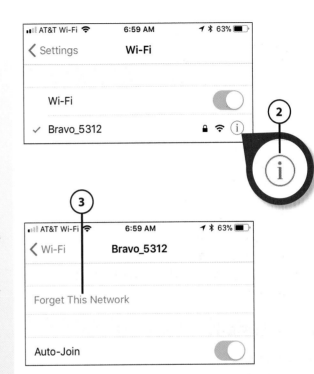

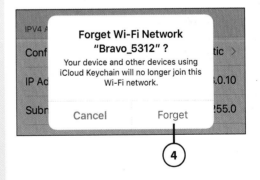

Cell Phone Provider Wi-Fi Networks

Many cell phone providers also provide other services, particularly public Wi-Fi networks. In some cases, you can access that provider's Internet service through a Wi-Fi network that it provides; often, you can do this at no additional charge. So, you can take advantage of the speed a Wi-Fi connection provides without paying more for it. You connect to these networks just like any other by selecting them on the network list. What happens next depends on the specific network. In some cases, you need to enter your mobile phone number and then respond to a text message to that phone number. Check your provider's website to find out whether it offers this service and where and how you can access it.

Connecting to the Internet Using Cellular Data Networks

When you don't have a Wi-Fi network available or you don't want to use one that is available (such as if it has a fee or is slow), your iPhone can connect to the Internet through a cellular data network.

The provider for your iPhone also provides a cellular data connection your iPhone uses to connect to the Internet automatically when you aren't using a Wi-Fi network (such as when you are in a location that doesn't have one). (Your iPhone tries to connect to an available Wi-Fi network before connecting to a cellular data connection, because Wi-Fi is typically less expensive and faster to use.) These cellular networks cover large geographic areas and the connection to them is automatic; your iPhone chooses and connects to the best cellular network currently available. Access to these networks is part of your monthly account fee; you choose from among various amounts of data per month for different monthly fees.

Most providers have multiple cellular data networks, such as a low-speed network that is available widely and one or more higher-speed networks that have a more limited coverage area. Your iPhone chooses the best connection available automatically.

The cellular data networks you can use are determined based on your provider, your data plan, the model of iPhone you are using, and your location within your provider's networks or the roaming networks available, when you are outside of your provider's coverage area. The iPhone automatically uses the fastest connection available to it at any given time (assuming you haven't disabled that option, as explained later).

In the United States, the major iPhone providers are AT&T, Verizon, T-Mobile, and Sprint. There are also other smaller providers, such as Virgin Mobile. All these companies offer high-speed Long Term Evolution (LTE) cellular networks (these are also referred to as true 4G networks) along with the slower 4G and 3G networks. In other locations, the names and speeds of the networks available might be different.

The following information is focused on LTE networks because I happen to live in the United States and use AT&T as my cell phone provider. If you use another provider, you are able to access your provider's networks similarly, though your details might be different. For example, the icon on the Home screen reflects the name of your provider's network, which might or might not be LTE.

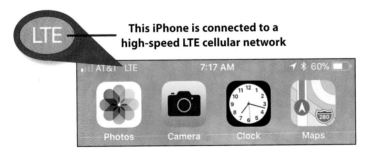

This iPhone is connected to a high-speed LTE cellular network

LTE high-speed wireless networks provide very fast Internet access from many locations. (Note: LTE networks might not be available everywhere, but you can usually access them near populated areas.) To connect to the LTE network, you don't need to do anything. If you aren't connected to a Wi-Fi network, you haven't turned off LTE, and your iPhone isn't in Airplane mode, the iPhone automatically connects to an LTE network when available. When you are connected to the LTE network, you see the LTE indicator at the top of the iPhone's screen. If you can't access the LTE network, such as when you aren't in its coverage area, the iPhone automatically connects to the next fastest network available, such as 4G. If that isn't available, it connects to the next fastest and so on until it finds a network to which it can connect if there is one available. If it can't connect to any network, you see No Service instead of a network's name; this indicates that you currently can't connect to any network, and so you aren't able to access the Internet.

One thing you do need to keep in mind when using a cellular network is that your account might include a limited amount of data per month. When your data use exceeds this limit, you might be charged overage fees, which can be very expensive. Most providers send you warning texts or emails as your data use approaches your plan's limit, at which point you need to be careful about what you do while using the cellular data network to avoid an overage fee. Some tasks, such as watching YouTube videos or downloading large movie files, can chew up a lot of data very quickly and should be saved for when you are on a Wi-Fi network to avoid exceeding your plan's monthly data allowance. Other tasks, such as using email, typically don't use very much.

Unlimited Data

If you don't already have an account with unlimited data, check with your provider periodically to see if an unlimited data plan is available for a reasonable price. As competition has increased among cell providers, unlimited data plans have become more common and less expensive in many areas. If other cell providers are available to you, check to see if they offer unlimited data plans; if so, you can consider changing providers or using a competitor's plan to lower the cost of your plan. Having an unlimited data plan is good because you don't need to worry about overage charges from using more data than your plan allows.

An App for That

Various apps are available in the App Store that you can install on your iPhone that monitor how much data you are using. These apps are a good way to know where your data use is relative to your plan's monthly allowance so that you can avoid an overage situation. To get information on finding, downloading, and installing apps, see the section "Using the App Store App to Find and Install iPhone Apps" in Chapter 4, "Customizing How Your iPhone Works." (To find an app for this purpose, search for "data monitoring app.")

When you move outside your primary network's geographic coverage area, you are in roaming territory, which means a different provider might provide cellular phone or data access, or both. The iPhone automatically selects a roaming provider, if there is only one available, or allows you to choose one, if there is more than one available.

When you are outside of your primary provider's coverage area, roaming charges can be associated with calls or data use. These charges are often very expensive. The roaming charges associated with phone calls are easier to manage, because it's more obvious when you make or receive a phone call in a roaming area. However, data roaming charges are much more insidious, especially if Push functionality (where emails and other updates are pushed to your iPhone from the server automatically) is active. And when you use some applications, such as Maps to navigate, you don't really know how much data is involved. Because data roaming charges are harder to notice, the iPhone is configured by default to prevent data roaming. When data roaming is disabled, the iPhone is unable to access the Internet when you are outside of your cellular network, unless you connect to a Wi-Fi network. (You can still use the cellular roaming network for telephone calls.)

You can configure some aspects of how your cellular network is used, as the following task demonstrates. You can also allow individual apps to use, or prevent them from using, your cellular data network. This is especially important when your data plan has a monthly limit.

In some cases, the first time you launch an app, you're prompted to allow or prevent it from using cellular data. At any time, you can use the Cellular Data options in the Settings app to enable or disable an app's access to your cellular data network.

The options you have for configuring how your iPhone uses its cellular data connection depend on the provider your iPhone is connected to and the model of iPhone you use. For example, if you live in the United States and use Sprint as your cellular provider, the Cellular screens in the Settings app look a bit different than the figures in this section (which are based on AT&T's service). Regardless of the specific options you see on your phone, the basic purpose is the same, which is to configure how your iPhone uses its high-speed network and to enable and disable roaming.

Configuring Cellular Data Use

The following steps show configuring cellular data use on an iPhone using AT&T in the United States; you can use similar steps to configure these options on an iPhone from a different provider:

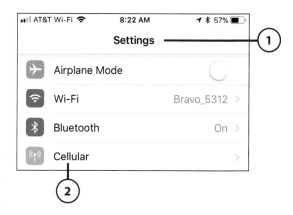

(1) Open the Settings app.

(2) Tap Cellular.

(3) To use a cellular Internet connection, set the Cellular Data switch to on (green) and move to step 4; if you don't want to use a cellular Internet connection, set this switch to off (white) and skip the rest of these steps. To use the Internet when the Cellular Data switch is off, you have to connect to a Wi-Fi network that provides Internet access.

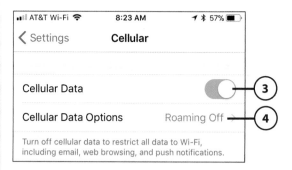

(4) Tap Cellular Data Options.

(5) To configure the high-speed network, tap Enable *high-speed network*, where *high-speed network* is the name of the high-speed network your provider has. With some providers, this is a switch that enables or disables the high-speed network; set the switch to be on or off and skip to step 8 (if you set the switch to off, the iPhone can't use the higher-speed network, but can still use slower networks).

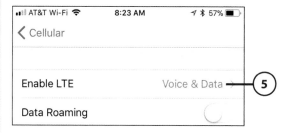

6 To disable the high-speed network, tap Off; to use it for both voice and data, tap Voice & Data; or to use it only for data, tap Data Only. (When you enable the high-speed network for voice, the quality of the sound of your calls may be better.)

7 Tap the Back icon.

8 If you want to allow data roaming, set the Data Roaming switch to the on (green) position. With some providers, Roaming is an option instead of a switch; tap Roaming and use the resulting switches to enable or disable roaming for voice or data and then tap the back icon.

9 Tap Cellular.

10 Use the controls in the *PROVIDER*, where *PROVIDER* is the name of your provider (AT&T in this example), to configure how the cellular service interacts with other services, such as to enable Wi-Fi calling, calls on other devices, and so on. These settings are explained in Chapter 7, "Communicating with the Phone and FaceTime Apps."

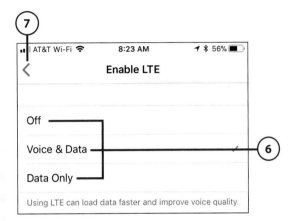

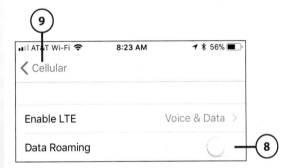

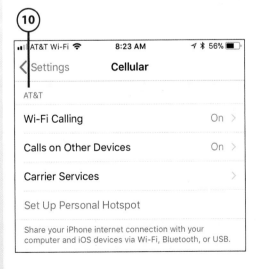

11 Swipe up the screen until you see the CELLULAR DATA section. This section enables you to allow or prevent individual apps from accessing a cellular data network. To limit the amount of data you use, it's a good idea to review this list and allow only those apps that you rely on to use the cellular data network. (Of course, if you are fortunate enough to have an unlimited cellular data plan, you can leave cellular data for all the apps enabled.) This list can be quite long if you have a lot of apps stored on your iPhone.

12 Set an app's switch to on (green) if you want it to be able to use a cellular data network to access the Internet.

13 Set an app's switch to off (white) if you want it to be able to access the Internet only when you are connected to a Wi-Fi network.

14 Set the Wi-Fi Assist switch to on (green) if you want your iPhone to automatically switch to its cellular connection when the Wi-Fi connection is weak. If you have a limited cellular data plan, you might want to set this switch to off (white) to minimize cellular data use.

15 If you want to access files on your iCloud drive when you aren't using a Wi-Fi network, set the iCloud Drive switch to on (green). If you set this switch to off, files are synced only when you are connected to a Wi-Fi network.

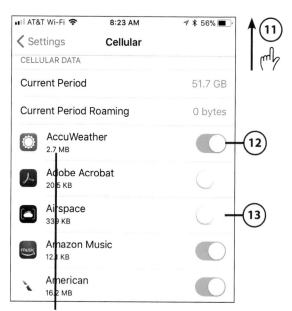

Amount of data the app has used since last reset

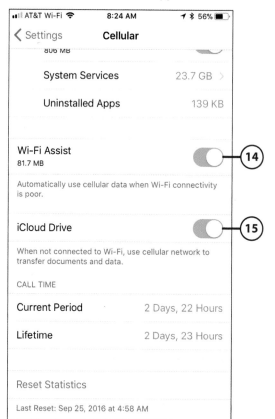

>>>*Go Further*

MORE ON CELLULAR DATA

Using a cellular network to connect to the Internet means you seldom have to be without a connection unless you choose to be. Here are some things to keep in mind as you keep connected:

- **Unlimited data but limited speed**—Under an unlimited data plan, some providers limit the speed at which your cellular data service operates if you pass a threshold amount of data used that month. You can continue to use all the data you want, but the performance of the connection might be slower. Check your plan's details to see what the threshold is and what speed reduction is applied. You probably won't hit that threshold unless you watch a lot of video on your phone, but it's good to be aware of such limitations on your account.

- **GSM versus CDMA**—There are two fundamental types of cellular networks, which are GSM (Global System for Mobile Communications) or CDMA (Code-Division Multiple Access). The cellular provider you use determines which type of network your iPhone uses; the two types are not compatible. GSM is used by most of the world whereas some very large carriers in the United States (such as Verizon and Sprint) use CDMA. There are differences between the two, which is why you might see different cellular options than shown in the figures here (which show the options for AT&T, which uses GSM). If your iPhone uses CDMA, you see the International CDMA switch on the Roaming screen. If your phone has poor performance when you are roaming in different countries, set this switch to off (white).

- **Cellular data usage**—In the Cellular Data section, you see how much data you've used for the current period and how much you've used while roaming. This can help you see where your use is compared to your monthly plan allowance (if you have a monthly plan allowance of course) so you know whether you are getting close to exceeding that allowance (thus incurring overage charges). This isn't proactive at all, as you have to remember to check the information. If you are concerned about data use, you're better off getting an app with more active monitoring, as discussed earlier in this chapter in the "An App for That" note.

If you tap System Services at the bottom of the list of apps on the Cellular screen, you see the data usage for core system functions, such as Time & Location, Messaging Services, and Siri. This can be useful information to see how much data these services use, especially when you are in a roaming situation. You can limit the data use by some of these services by not accessing the related function; for example, you can turn off Siri to prevent it from using cellular data.

- **Higher-speed networks use more power**—Using a higher-speed network, such as an LTE network, also uses somewhat more battery power than using a slower network. If getting the absolute maximum time on a charge is important, you might want to disable the high-speed network.

- **Apps' cellular data use**—Just under each app's name in the CELLULAR DATA section, you see how much data the app has used since the counter was reset. This number can help you determine how much data a particular app uses. For example, if an app's use is shown in megabytes (MB), it's used a lot more data than an app whose use is shown in kilobytes (KB).

- **Cellular data use reset**—You can reset all of the statistics on the Cellular screen by swiping up until you reach the bottom of the screen and tapping Reset Statistics. Tap Reset Statistics again to complete the reset.

- **Personal hotspot**—The iPhone can be a personal hotspot, which is when it provides an Internet connection to computers or other devices through its cellular data connection. This is useful when you are in a location where you can't connect a computer or other device to a Wi-Fi or cellular network with Internet access (or don't want to spend the money to do so) but can access the Internet with the iPhone's cellular data connection.

  There are a lot of caveats to this service, including whether your provider offers it, additional costs, and so on. Check with your provider to see if the personal hotspot feature is supported and if there are additional fees to use it. If it is provided and the fees are acceptable, this is a good way to provide Internet access to other devices when a Wi-Fi or cellular connection either isn't available or is too expensive for those devices.

  First, add the personal hotspot service to your cellular account. Second, move to the Cellular screen in the Settings app, and then tap Set Up Personal Hotspot (if you don't see this option, your provider doesn't offer personal hotspot service). Follow the onscreen prompts to complete the configuration of the personal hotspot; the details depend on the specific provider you are using. After your iPhone is configured as a hotspot, it can share its Internet connection with other devices. To allow access to the Internet through your phone's hotspot, provide the name of its network and password (which are both automatically generated when you enable the hotspot) to the people you want to allow to use your hotspot.

Securing Your iPhone

Even though you won't often be connecting a cable to it, an iPhone is a connected device, meaning that it sends information to and receives information from other devices, either directly or via the Internet, during many different activities. Some are obvious, such as sending text messages or browsing the Web, whereas others might not be so easy to spot, such as when an app is determining your iPhone's location. Whenever data is exchanged between your iPhone and other devices, there is always a chance your information will get intercepted by someone you didn't intend or that someone will access your iPhone without you knowing about it.

The good news is that with some simple precautions, the chances of someone obtaining your information or infiltrating your iPhone are quite small (much less than the chance of someone obtaining your credit card number when you use it in public places, for example). Following are some good ways to protect the information you are using on your iPhone:

- Always have a passcode on your iPhone so it can't be unlocked without entering the passcode. Configuring a passcode is explained in Chapter 4.

- Use Touch ID (all models except iPhone X) or Face ID (iPhone X) to make entering your passcode and passwords much easier and more secure. Configuring Touch ID is also explained in Chapter 4. To learn how to use Face ID on an iPhone X, download *My iPhone X* from www.informit.com/myiphoneseniors.

- Never let someone you don't know or trust use your iPhone, even if he needs it "just for a second to look something up." If you get a request like that, look up the information for the person and show him rather than letting him touch your iPhone.

- Learn how to use the Find My iPhone feature in case you lose or someone steals your iPhone. This is explained in the online Chapter 16, "Maintaining and Protecting Your iPhone and Solving Problems," which you'll find on this book's website (see the back cover for the information you need to access it).

- Never respond to an email that you aren't expecting that directs you to click a link to verify your account. If you haven't requested some kind of change, such as signing up for a new service, virtually all such requests are scams, seeking to get your account information, such as username and password, or your identification, such as full name and Social Security number. And many of these scam attempts look like email from actual organizations. For example, I receive many of these emails that claim, and sometimes even look like, they are from Apple. However, Apple doesn't request updates to account information using a link in an email unless you have made some kind of change, such as registering a new email address for iMessages. Legitimate organizations never include links in an email to update account information when you haven't requested or made any changes.

  To reinforce this concept, there are two types of requests for verification you might receive via email. The legitimate type is sent to you after you sign up for a new service, such as creating a new account on a website, to confirm that the email address you provided is correct and that you are really you. If you make changes to an existing account, you might also receive confirmation request emails. You should respond to these requests to finish the configuration of your account.

  If you receive a request for account verification, but you haven't done anything with the organization from which you received the request, don't respond to it. For example, if you receive a request that appears to be from Apple, PayPal, or other organizations, but you haven't made any changes to your account, the email request is bogus and is an attempt to scam you. Likewise, if you have never done anything with the organization apparently sending the email, it is also definitely an attempt to scam you.

  If you have any doubt, contact the organization sending the request before responding to the email.

- If you need to change or update account information, you can go directly to the related website using an address that you type in or have saved as a bookmark using the Safari app. This protects you because it ensures you can move directly to the legitimate website rather than clicking a link that might take you to a fraudulent website.

- Be aware that when you use a Wi-Fi network in a public place, such as a coffee shop, hotel, or airport, there is a chance that the information you send over that network might be intercepted by others. The risk of this is usually quite small, but you need to be aware that there is always some level of risk. To have the lowest risk, don't use apps that involve sensitive information, such as an online banking app, when you are using a Wi-Fi network in a public place.

- If you don't know how to do it, have someone who really knows what they are doing set up a wireless network in your home. Wireless networks need to be configured properly, so they are secure. Your home's Wi-Fi network should require a password to join.

- For the least risk, only use your home's Wi-Fi network (that has been configured properly) or your cellular data connection (you can turn Wi-Fi off when you aren't home) for sensitive transactions, such as accessing bank accounts or other financial information.

- Never accept a request to share information from someone you don't know. In the online Chapter 15, "Working with Other Useful iPhone Apps and Features," you learn about AirDrop, which enables you to easily share photos and lots of other things with other people using iOS devices. If you receive an AirDrop request from someone you don't recognize, always decline it. In fact, if you have any doubt, decline such requests. It's much easier for someone legitimate to confirm with you and resend a request than it is for you to recover from damage that can be done if you inadvertently accept a request from someone you don't know.

- Only download apps through Apple's App Store through the App Store app on your iPhone. Fortunately, the way the iPhone is set up, you have to do something very unusual to install apps outside of the App Store. As long as you download apps only as described in this book, you are free of apps that can harm your information because Apple has strict controls over the apps that make it into the App Store. (Downloading apps is explained in Chapter 4, "Customizing How Your iPhone Works.")

Reality Check

Internet security is a complex topic, and it can be troublesome to think about. It's best to keep in mind the relative level of risk when you use your iPhone compared to other risks in the physical world that most of us don't think twice about. For example, every time you hand your credit card to someone, there is a chance that that person will record the number and use it without your knowledge or permission. Even when you swipe a credit card in a reader, such as at a gas station, that information is communicated across multiple networks and can be intercepted. (For example, there have been numerous compromises of credit card information at a number of well-known retailers.) If you take basic precautions like those described here, the risks to you when you are using your iPhone are similar to the other risks we all face in everyday life.

My recommendation is to take the basic precautions, and then don't worry about it overly much. It is a good idea to have identity theft insurance in case your information is compromised, which can happen whether you use an iPhone or don't use one. Try to find an insurance company that assigns someone to do the work of recovering for you should your identity be stolen because that can be very time-consuming and difficult.

Working with Text

You can do lots of things with an iPhone that require you to provide text input. There are a couple of ways you can do this, the most obvious of which is by typing. The iPhone's keyboard is quite amazing. Whenever you need it, whether it's for emailing, messaging, entering a website URL, performing a search, or any other typing function, it pops up automatically.

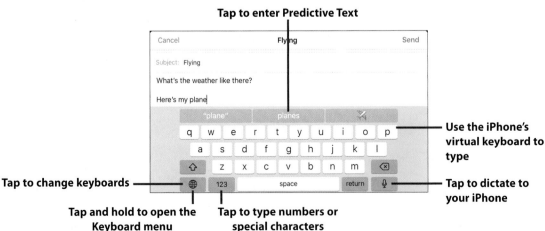

Tap to enter Predictive Text

Use the iPhone's virtual keyboard to type

Tap to dictate to your iPhone

Tap to change keyboards

Tap and hold to open the Keyboard menu

Tap to type numbers or special characters

To type, just tap the keys. As you tap each key, you hear audio feedback (you can disable this sound if you want to) and the key you tapped pops up in a magnified view on the screen. The keyboard includes all the standard keys, plus a few for special uses. To change from letters to numbers and special characters, just tap the 123 key. Tap the #+= key to see more special characters. Tap the 123 key to move back to the numbers and special characters or the ABC key to return to letters. The keyboard also has contextual keys that appear when you need them. For example, when you enter a website address, the .com key appears so you can enter these four characters with a single tap.

Working with Predictive Text

You can also use Predictive Text, which is the feature that tries to predict text you want to enter based on the context of what you are currently typing and what you have typed before. Predictive Text appears in the bar between the text and the keyboard and presents you with three options. If one of those is what you want to enter, tap it and it is added to the text at the current location of the cursor. If you don't see an option you want to enter, keep typing and the options change as the text you are typing changes. You can tap an option at any time to enter it. The nice thing about Predictive Text is that it gets better at predicting your text needs over time. In other words, the more you use it, the better it gets at predicting what you want to type. You can also enable or disable Predictive Text, as you see shortly.

Predictive Text Need Not Apply

When you are entering text where Predictive Text doesn't apply, such as when you are typing email addresses, the Predictive Text bar is hidden and can't be enabled. This makes sense because there's no way text in things such as email addresses can be predicted. When you move back into an area where it does apply, Predictive Text becomes active again.

Working with Keyboards

The great thing about a virtual keyboard like the iPhone has is that it can change to reflect the language or symbols you want to type. As you learn in Chapter 4, you can install multiple keyboards, such as one for your primary language and more for your secondary languages. You can also install third-party keyboards to take advantage of their features (this is also covered in Chapter 4).

By default, two keyboards are available for you to use. One is for the primary language configured for your iPhone (for example, mine is U.S. English). The other is the Emoji keyboard (more on this shortly). How you change the keyboard you are using depends on whether you have installed additional keyboards and the orientation of the iPhone.

If you haven't installed additional keyboards, you can change keyboards by tapping the Emoji key, which has a smiley face on it.

If you have installed other keyboards, you change keyboards by tapping the Globe key.

Each time you tap this key (Globe if available, Emoji if there isn't a Globe), the keyboard changes to be the next keyboard installed; along with the available keys changing, you briefly see the name of the current keyboard in the space key. When you have cycled through all the keyboards, you return to the one where you started.

The Keys, They Are A-Changin'

The keys on the keyboard can change depending on the orientation of the iPhone. For example, when you have more than one keyboard installed and hold the iPhone vertically, the Emoji key disappears and you see only the Globe key. Not to worry though, you can still get to the Emoji keyboard by tapping the Globe key until the Emoji keyboard appears, or by opening the Keyboard menu and tapping Emoji. When you have installed additional keyboards and hold the iPhone horizontally, you see both the Globe and Emoji keys. Tap the Emoji key to switch to that keyboard or the Globe key to cycle through all the keyboards.

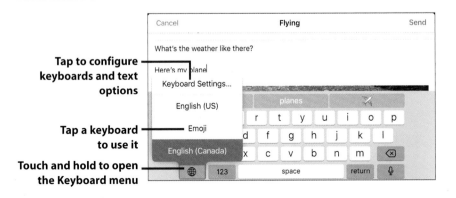

Tap to configure keyboards and text options

Tap a keyboard to use it

Touch and hold to open the Keyboard menu

You can also select the specific keyboard you want to use and access keyboard and text options by touching and holding on the Globe key (or the Emoji key, if you don't see the Globe key). The Keyboard menu appears. Tap a keyboard to switch to it. Tap Keyboard Settings to jump to the Keyboards screen in the Settings app where you can configure keyboards and enable or disable text options (these settings are covered in Chapter 4).

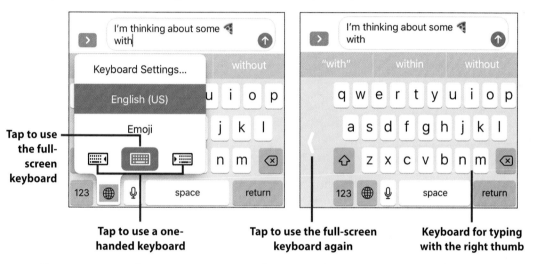

Tap to use the full-screen keyboard

Tap to use a one-handed keyboard

Tap to use the full-screen keyboard again

Keyboard for typing with the right thumb

Because you often type on your iPhone while you are moving around, it has a one-handed keyboard. This keyboard "squishes" all the keys to the left or right side of the screen to suit typing with a thumb. To use a one-handed keyboard, tap and hold the Globe or Emoji key to open the keyboard menu (this only works when the iPhone is held vertically). Tap the left or right keyboard; the keyboard compresses toward the side you selected and you can more easily tap its keys with one thumb. To return to the full-screen keyboard, tap the right- or left-facing arrow that appears in the "empty" space on the side of the screen not being used for the keyboard or open the Keyboard menu and tap the full-screen keyboard.

Using Emojis

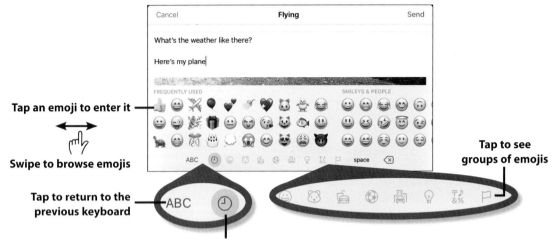

Tap an emoji to enter it

Swipe to browse emojis

Tap to return to the previous keyboard

Tap to see emojis you've used frequently

Tap to see groups of emojis

Emojis are icons you insert into your text to liven things up, communicate your feelings, or just to have some fun (if you don't have this keyboard installed, see Chapter 4). You can open the Emoji keyboard by tapping its key (the smiley face) or by selecting it on the Keyboard menu. You see a palette containing many emojis, organized into groups. You can change the groups of emojis you are browsing by tapping the icons at the bottom of the screen. Swipe to the left or right on the emojis to browse the emojis in the current group. Tap an emoji to enter it at the cursor's location in your message, email, or other type of document. To use an emoji you've used often, tap the Clock icon to see emojis you've used frequently; you'll probably find that you use this set of emojis regularly so this can save a lot of time. To return to the mundane world of letters and symbols, tap the ABC key.

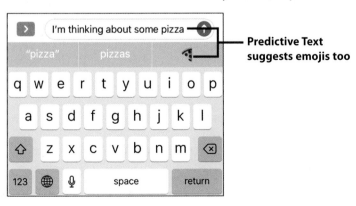

Predictive Text suggests emojis too

The Predictive Text feature also suggests emojis when you type certain words; just tap the emoji to replace the word with it.

Emoji Options

If you tap and hold on some emojis, you see options. For example, if you tap and hold on the thumbs-up emoji, you see a menu with the emoji in different flesh tones. Slide your finger over the menu and tap the version you want to use. The version you select becomes the new default for that emoji. You can go back to a previous version by opening the menu and selecting it.

Emojis Galore

Emojis are very widely used in text messages because you can communicate a lot with a single icon. The Messages app enables you to access many kinds of emojis through the apps you can install within the Messages app itself; these are often called stickers, but they work the same way as emojis. See Chapter 9, "Sending, Receiving, and Managing Texts and iMessages," to learn how to add and use sticker apps within the Messages app.

What's Your Typing Orientation?

Like many other tasks, you can rotate the iPhone to change the screen's orientation while you type. When the iPhone is in the horizontal orientation, the keyboard is wider, making it easier to tap individual keys, and you have access to more keys. When the iPhone is in vertical orientation, the keyboard is narrower, but you can see more of the typing area. So, try both to see which mode is most effective for you.

Correcting Spelling as You Type

If you type a word that the iPhone doesn't recognize, that word is flagged as a possible mistake and suggestions are made to help you correct it. How this happens depends on whether or not Predictive Text is enabled.

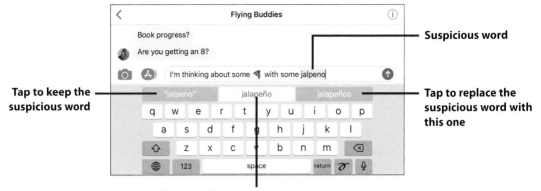

Tap to keep the suspicious word

Tap to replace the suspicious word with this one

Suspicious word

If you tap the space key, the suspicious word is replaced with this one

If Predictive Text is enabled, potential replacements for suspicious words appear in the Predictive Text bar. When you tap the space key, the suspicious word is replaced with the word in the center of the Predictive Text bar. Tap the word on the far left to keep what you've typed (because it isn't a mistake) or tap the word on the right end of the bar to enter it instead of what you've typed.

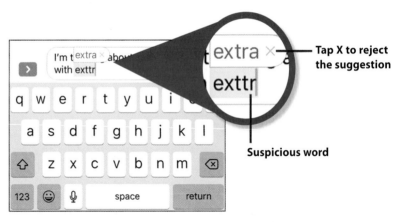

Tap X to reject the suggestion

Suspicious word

If Predictive Text isn't enabled, a suspicious word is highlighted and a suggestion about what it thinks is the correct word appears in a pop-up box. To accept the suggestion, tap the space key; the suspicious word is replaced with the suggested word. To reject the suggestion, tap the Close (x) icon in the pop-up box to close it and keep what you typed. You can also use this feature for shorthand typing. For example, to type "I've" you can simply type "Ive" and iPhone suggests "I've," which you can accept by tapping the space key.

Typing Tricks

Many keys, especially symbols and punctuation, have additional characters. To see a character's options, touch it and hold down. If it has options, a menu pops up after a second or so. To enter one of the optional characters, drag over the menu until the one you want to enter is highlighted, and then lift your finger off the screen. The optional character you selected is entered. For example, if you tap and hold on the period, you can select .com, .edu, and so on, which is very helpful when you are typing a website or email address.

Your Own Text Replacements

You can create your own text shortcuts so you can type something like "eadd" and it is automatically replaced with your email address. See Chapter 4 for the details.

By default, the iPhone attempts to correct the capitalization of what you type. It also automatically selects the Shift key when you start a new sentence, start a new paragraph, or in other places where its best guess is that you need a capital letter. If you don't want to enter a capital character, simply tap the Shift key before you type. You can enable the Caps Lock key by tapping the Shift key twice. When the key is highlighted (the upward-facing arrow is black), everything you type is in uppercase letters.

Editing Text

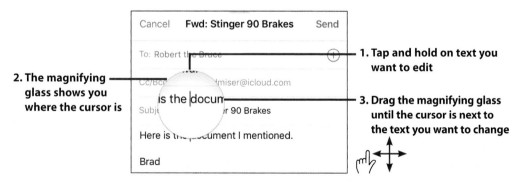

2. The magnifying glass shows you where the cursor is

1. Tap and hold on text you want to edit

3. Drag the magnifying glass until the cursor is next to the text you want to change

To edit text you've typed, touch and hold on the area containing the text you want to edit. A magnifying glass icon appears on the screen, and within it you see a magnified view of the location of the cursor. Drag the magnifying glass to position the cursor where you want to start making changes, and then lift your finger from the screen. The cursor remains in that location, and you can use the keyboard to make changes to the text or to add text at that location, or you can make a selection on the menu that appears.

Using 3D Touch with Text

When you are using an iPhone that supports 3D Touch (6s and later models), you can apply slight pressure when you touch the screen to have the closest word selected automatically; it is highlighted in blue to show you that it is selected. To place the cursor without selecting words that are near your finger, just touch the screen without applying any pressure.

Options, Options

Using the Keyboards screen in the Settings app, you can enable or disable text-related functions, such as Auto-Capitalization. See Chapter 4 for details.

Selecting, Copying, Cutting, or Pasting Text

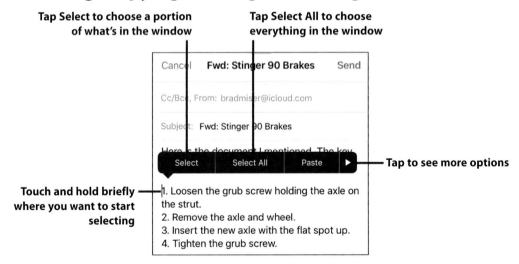

Tap Select to choose a portion of what's in the window

Tap Select All to choose everything in the window

Cancel   **Fwd: Stinger 90 Brakes**   Send

Cc/Bcc, From: bradmiser@icloud.com

Subject: Fwd: Stinger 90 Brakes

Here is the document I mentioned. The key

| Select | Select All | Paste | ▶ |

Tap to see more options

Touch and hold briefly where you want to start selecting

1. Loosen the grub screw holding the axle on the strut.
2. Remove the axle and wheel.
3. Insert the new axle with the flat spot up.
4. Tighten the grub screw.

You can also select text or images to copy and paste the selected content into a new location or to replace that content. Touch and hold down briefly where you want to start the selection until the magnifying glass icon appears; then lift your finger off the screen. The Select menu appears. Tap Select to select part of the content on the screen, or tap Select All to select everything in the current window.

More Commands

Some menus that appear when you are making selections and performing actions have a right-facing arrow at the right end. Tap this to see a new menu that contains additional commands. These commands are contextual, meaning that you see different commands depending on what you are doing at that specific time. You can tap the left-facing arrow to move back to a previous menu.

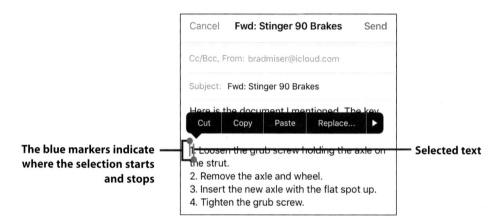

The blue markers indicate where the selection starts and stops

Selected text

You see markers indicating where the selection starts and stops. (The iPhone attempts to select something logical, such as the word or sentence.) New commands appear on the menu; these provide actions for the text currently selected.

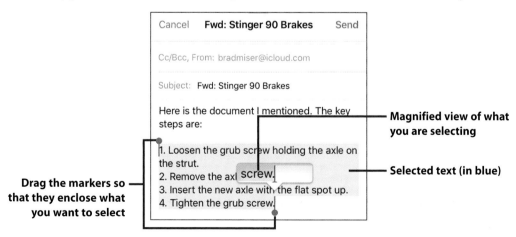

Magnified view of what you are selecting

Selected text (in blue)

Drag the markers so that they enclose what you want to select

Drag the two markers so that the content you want to select is between them; the selected portion is highlighted in blue. As you drag, you see a magnified view of where the selection marker is, which helps you place it more accurately. When the selection markers are located correctly, lift your finger from the screen. (If you tapped the Select All command, you don't need to do this because the content you want is already selected.)

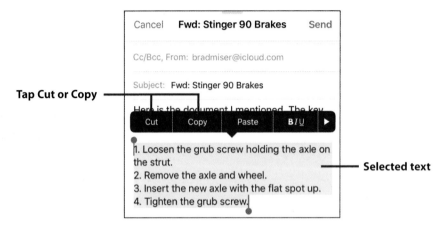

Tap Cut to remove the content from the current window, or tap Copy to just copy it.

Have I Got a Suggestion for You!

As you select different items, explore the menu to see commands that might be useful to you. These commands are contextual so they change based on what you have selected. For example, when you have a word or phrase selected, one of the suggestions might be Look Up, which opens Siri Suggestions for the word or phrase you selected. The results can include dictionary or Wikipedia entries, suggested apps, and so on. Tap Done to return to the text with which you were working. As you use your iPhone, check out the options on this menu because you'll find some very useful tricks tucked away there.

Format It!

If you tap BIU on the menu, you can tap Bold, Italics, or Underline to apply those formatting options to the selected text. You also can tap multiple format options to apply them at the same time. You might need to tap the right-facing arrow at the end of the menu to see these commands, depending on how many commands are on the menu.

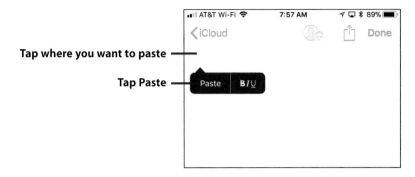

Tap where you want to paste

Tap Paste

Move to where you want to paste the content you selected; for example, use the App Switcher to change to a different app. Tap where you want the content to be pasted. (For a more precise location, tap and hold and then use the magnifying glass icon to move to a specific location.) Lift your finger off the screen and the menu appears. Then tap Paste.

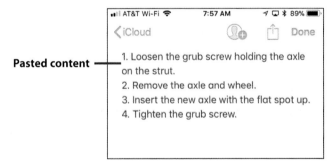

Pasted content

The content you copied or cut appears where you placed the cursor.

Correcting Spelling After You've Typed

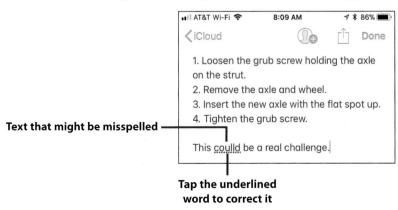

Text that might be misspelled

Tap the underlined word to correct it

The iPhone also has a spell-checking feature that comes into play after you have entered text (as opposed to the Predictive Text and autocorrect/suggests features that change text as you type it). When you've entered text the iPhone doesn't recognize, it is underlined in red.

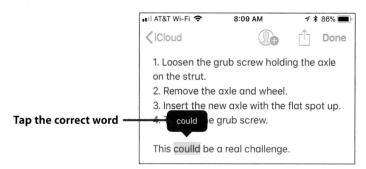

Tap the correct word

Tap the underlined word. It is shaded in red to show you what is being checked, and a menu appears with one or more replacements that might be the correct spelling. If one of the options is the one you want, tap it. The incorrect word is replaced with the one you tapped.

Contextual Menus and You

In some apps, tapping a word causes a menu with other kinds of actions to appear; you can tap an action to make it happen. For example, in the iBooks app, when you tap a word, the resulting menu enables you to look up the word in a dictionary. Other apps support different kinds of actions, so it's a good idea to try tapping words in apps that involve text to see which commands are available.

Undo

The iPhone has a somewhat hidden undo command. To undo what you've just done, such as typing text, gently shake your phone back and forth a couple of times. An Undo Typing prompt appears on the screen. Tap Undo to undo the last thing you did or tap Cancel if you activated the undo command accidentally.

Dictating Text

You can also enter text by dictating it. This is a fast and easy way to type, and you'll be amazed at how accurate the iPhone is at translating your speech into typed words. Dictation is available almost anywhere you need to enter text. (Exceptions are passcodes and passwords, such as for your Apple ID.)

Tap to put the cursor where you want dictated text to start

Tap the Microphone key to start dictation

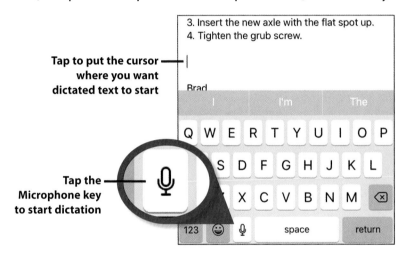

To start dictating, tap the Microphone key. The iPhone goes into Dictation mode. A gray bar appears at the bottom of the window. As the iPhone "hears" you, the line oscillates.

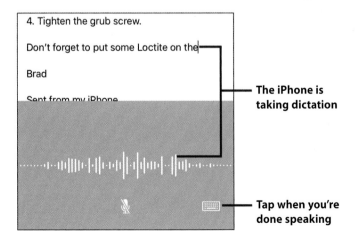

The iPhone is taking dictation

Tap when you're done speaking

Start speaking the text you want the iPhone to type. As you speak, the text is entered starting from the location of the cursor. Speak punctuation when you want to enter it. For example, when you reach the end of a sentence, say "period," or to enter a colon say "colon." To start a new paragraph, say "new paragraph."

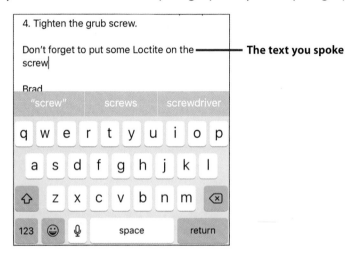

When you've finished dictating, tap the keyboard icon. The keyboard reappears and you see the text you spoke. This feature is amazingly accurate and can be a much faster and more convenient way to enter text than typing it.

You can edit the text you dictated just like text you typed using the keyboard.

Drawing in Text

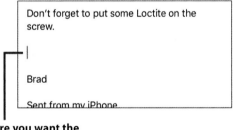

Tap where you want the drawing to be inserted

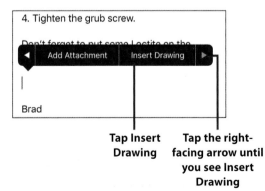

Tap Insert Drawing   **Tap the right-facing arrow until you see Insert Drawing**

You can use the iOS drawing tool to create and insert drawings that include shapes, text, colors, and other elements into places where you create text, such as emails. Tap in the window where you want the drawing to be. On the menu, tap the right-facing arrow until you see Insert Drawing and then tap that command.

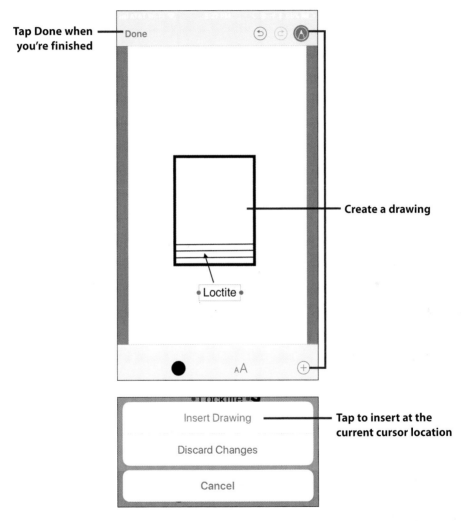

Tap Done when you're finished

Create a drawing

Tap to insert at the current cursor location

Use the drawing tool to create the drawing. Tap Add (+) to add shapes, lines, or text. Tap text to edit it. Tap Signature to sign your name. You can tap objects to select them to move or change them. You can use the format tools (color and font) to format objects. When you're done, tap Done. Then tap Insert Drawing to place the drawing where the cursor was located.

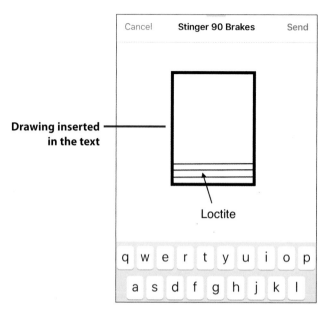

Drawing inserted in the text

When you move back to the text, you see the drawing you created. You can then complete what you were doing, such as finishing and sending an email message.

Using Widgets

Widgets are "mini" versions of apps installed on your iPhone that you can access easily and quickly from the Widget Center.

 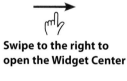

Swipe to the right to open the Widget Center

You can open the Widget Center in a number of ways:

- Wake your iPhone and swipe to the right on the Lock screen.
- Move to a Home page and swipe to the right.
- Swipe down the screen to open the Notification Center and then swipe to the right.

Tap Show Less to collapse a widget

Tap to call or FaceTime a favorite

Swipe up and down to browse your widgets

See your next event

Tap to move into the widget's app

Widget name

At the top of the Widget Center, you see the Search tool (more on this later). If you open the Widget Center from the Lock screen, you see the current time and date under the Search tool; if you open it from a Home or app's screen, you don't see the date or time. Beneath that, you see widgets for apps installed on your iPhone. Swipe up and down the screen to browse your widgets.

Configuring the Widget Center

You can choose the widgets that appear in the Widget Center and the order in which those widgets are shown on the screen. See "Configuring the Widget Center" in Chapter 4 for the step-by-step instructions to configure your Widget Center.

Each widget provides information or functions based on its app. For example, you can use the FAVORITES widget to place phone calls using the Phone app or to make FaceTime calls to your contacts you've designated as Favorites (you learn how to do this in Chapter 7). You can see your daily calendar in the CALENDAR widget, get news in the NEWS widget, or listen to music in the MUSIC widget.

You can expand a widget to show all of its information or tools by tapping the Show More command or collapse it to a more minimal state by tapping the Show Less command.

You can interact with widgets in several ways. Some widgets provide information that you can view within the widget, such as CALENDAR, STOCKS, or UP NEXT. Some apps provide options you can tap to perform specific actions; these include FAVORITES and MUSIC. When you tap something within a widget, the associated app opens and either performs the task you indicated or shows more information about what you selected.

Some apps even have multiple widgets. For example, the Calendar app has the UP NEXT widget that shows you the next events on your calendar and the CALENDAR widget that shows the events on the current date.

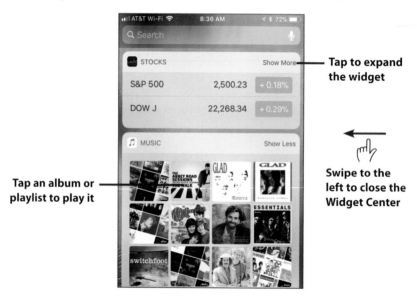

Tap to expand the widget

Tap an album or playlist to play it

Swipe to the left to close the Widget Center

If you don't move into an app from a widget, you can close the Widget Center by swiping to the left. You move back to the screen you came from, such as a Home screen. If you do move into an app from a widget, you work with that app just as if you moved into it from a Home screen.

Searching on Your iPhone

You can use the Search tool to search your iPhone to find many different types of information, including locations, emails, messages, apps, and so on.

Swipe down from the center part of the screen to search your iPhone

There are a couple of ways you can start a search:

- Swipe to the right to open the Widget Center. The Search bar is at the top of the screen.

- On a Home screen, swipe down from the center of the screen. The Search bar appears at the top of the screen.

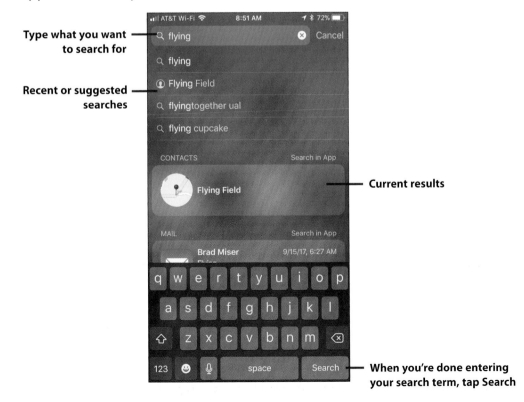

Type what you want to search for

Recent or suggested searches

Current results

When you're done entering your search term, tap Search

To perform a search, tap in the Search bar and type the search term using the onscreen keyboard. As you type, recent or suggested searches appear just below the Search bar; tap a search to perform it. Under the search list, you see the current items that match your search. If you don't tap one of the recent or suggested searches, when you finish typing the search term, tap Search to see the full list of results.

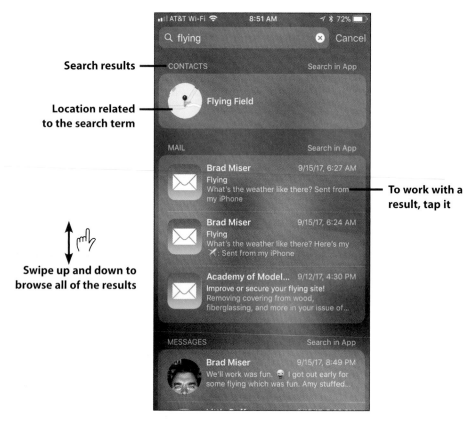

Search results —

Location related to the search term —

Swipe up and down to browse all of the results

To work with a result, tap it

The results are organized into sections, such as CONTACTS, MAIL, MESSAGES, APPLICATIONS, MAPS, MUSIC, and so on. Swipe up and down the screen to browse all of the results. To work with an item you find, such as to view a location you found, tap it; you move to a screen showing more information or into the associated app and see the search result that you tapped.

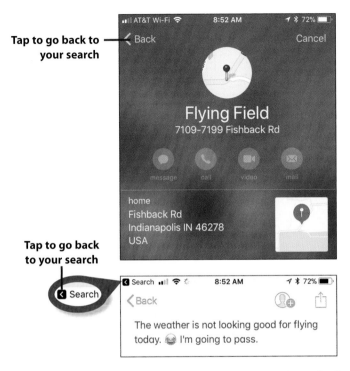

Tap to go back to your search

Tap to go back to your search

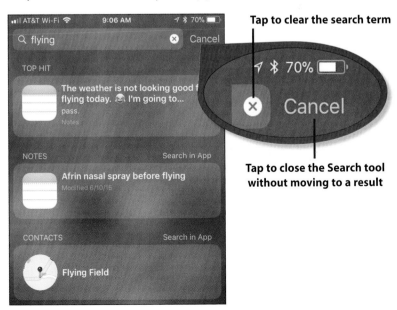

The results remain in the Search tool as you work with them. To move back to the search results, tap the Back icon in the upper-left corner of the screen or tap Search (which you see depends on the result you tapped on).

Tap to clear the search term

Tap to close the Search tool without moving to a result

The results of the most recent search are still listed. To clear the search term, tap Clear (x). To close the Spotlight tool without going to one of the results, tap Cancel.

Tell Me More

If one of the categories you find in a search has a lot of entries, you see the Show More command. Tap this to show more of the results for that category. Tap Show Less to collapse the category again. When you can search within an app, you see the Search in App text on the right side of the screen aligned with the results section; tap this to open the app and perform the search within that app.

Working with Siri Suggestions

Siri Suggestions can make it easy to get back to apps, searches, or other items you've used recently. Using Siri Suggestions can also lead you to useful things you weren't necessarily looking for. These suggestions show up in many different areas on your iPhone and you can access them directly at any time.

Swipe down from the center part of the screen to see Siri Suggestions

Tap to open an app

Tap to run a search

To access Siri Suggestions, swipe down from the center of a Home screen. Just under the Search bar, you see the SIRI APP SUGGESTIONS panel. This panel shows you apps you've used recently or apps that might be useful to you based on your location. For example, the Starbucks app may be suggested when you are near a Starbucks location. Tap an app to open it.

There's a Widget for That

You can also use the SIRI APP SUGGESTIONS widget in the Widget Center to quickly access recently used or suggested apps. This widget works just like the SIRI APP SUGGESTIONS panel because it's basically the same thing.

Siri Suggestions can also appear in other apps. Siri monitors your activity and "learns" from what you do in order to improve the suggestions it makes. These suggestions can appear in many different places, such as when you are entering email addresses in a new email, dealing with new contact information, performing searches, editing a text message, and so on. When you see a list of Siri Suggestions, you can tap the suggestion you want to use. For example, if it is an email address, that address is entered for you. If it is a search, the search is performed.

You can enable or disable the apps and services that Siri can access to make these suggestions; the information to do this is provided in Chapter 11, "Working with Siri." For example, if you don't want Siri to be able to make suggestions based on a specific app, you can disable the Search & Siri Suggestions setting for that app.

Working with Notifications

As you learned in Chapter 1, the iPhone's notification system keeps you informed of activity in which you may be interested, such as new emails, events, app updates, and so on. There are a number of types of these notifications that you will experience. Visual notifications include banners and badges. Alert sounds can also let you know something has happened, and vibrations make you feel the new activity.

You can determine which types of notifications are used for specific activity on your iPhone. This might be one of the most important areas to configure because you want to make sure you are aware of activity that is important to you, but too many notifications can be disruptive and annoying. So, you want to strike a good balance between being aware and being annoyed.

Notification Center

In Chapter 1, you learned how to use the Notification Center to work with groups of notifications. This can be a more efficient way to deal with notifications since you can access "batches" of them instead of dealing with each one individually. You might want to configure individual notifications for the activity that is most important to you and access the rest via the Notification Center.

Working with Visual Notifications

There are three types of visual notifications: badges, persistent banners, and temporary banners.

Badges appear on an app's or a folder's icon to let you know something has changed, such as when you have received new email.

Badges are purely informational, meaning you can't take any action on these directly as you can with the other visual notifications. They inform you about an event so that you can take action, such as to download and install an update to your iPhone's iOS software or read new text messages.

Badges on Folders

In Chapter 5, you learn how to organize apps in folders. When apps in folders have badges enabled, the badge you see on a folder is a total count of the badges on the apps within that folder. The only way to know which apps that are in the folders have badges is to open the folder so you can see the individual app icons and badges.

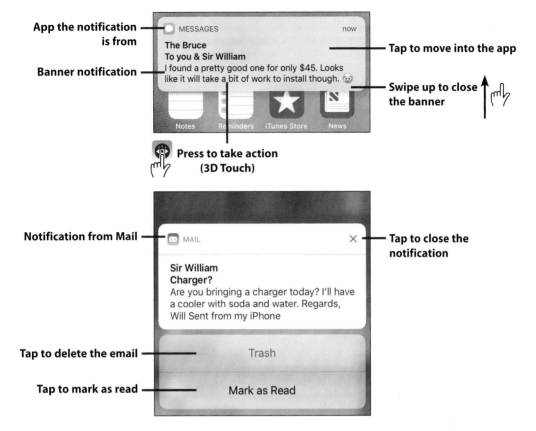

App the notification is from

Banner notification

Tap to move into the app

Swipe up to close the banner

Press to take action (3D Touch)

Notification from Mail

Tap to close the notification

Tap to delete the email

Tap to mark as read

Banner notifications provide information for you, and you can take action related to the event that generated the notification. For example, you can respond to a text message directly from its notification.

There are two types of banner notifications. Persistent banner notifications remain on the screen until you take action on them, which can be closing them, responding to them, etc. Temporary banner notifications appear on the screen for a few seconds and if you don't take action on them, they rotate off the screen to get out of your way.

When your iPhone is unlocked, banner notifications appear at the top of the screen. They provide a summary of the app and the activity that has taken place, such as a new email or text message. When a banner appears, you can view its information; if it is a temporary banner, it rotates off the screen after displaying for a few seconds; if it is a persistent banner, you need to do something to cause it to disappear. You can tap it to move into the app to take some action, such as to read an email. You can swipe up from the bottom of the banner to close it. For some apps, such as Mail, you can press on the notification to open a menu of commands.

No 3D Touch?

If your iPhone doesn't support 3D Touch (it's not an iPhone 6s or later model), you can swipe down on a notification to take action on it, such as to reply to a text message.

Banner notification on the Lock screen

Press to take action (3D Touch)

Tap to close the notification

New message

Reply to the message

Banner notifications can also appear on the Lock screen, which is really convenient because you can read and take action on them directly from that screen. If your phone is asleep, the notifications appear briefly on the screen and then it goes dark again; you can press the Side button or the Touch/ID Home button or raise your phone to see your notifications without unlocking the iPhone. You can swipe up or down the screen to browse the notifications.

To respond to a notification or take other action on it, press it to open it (3D Touch iPhones) or swipe to the right on it (non-3D Touch iPhones) and then take action, such as replying to a message. In some cases, you might need to unlock your phone to complete an action associated with a notification. In those cases, you're prompted to use Touch ID, Face ID, or your passcode to proceed.

If don't want the banner notifications to appear, you can disable them.

Configuring Your Notifications

It's a good idea to configure the notifications your iPhone uses so that you are aware of important activity, such as new work emails, without being distracted by constant notifications for things that don't require your immediate attention (such as a post to Facebook). To learn how to configure your notifications, see "Configuring Notifications" in Chapter 4.

Working with Other Types of Notifications

Sounds are audible indicators that something has happened. For example, you can be alerted to a new email message by a specific sound. You can choose global sound notifications, such as a general ringtone, and specific ones, such as a special ringtone when someone in your contacts calls you.

Vibrations are a physical indicator that something has happened. Like sounds, you can configure general vibrations, and you can also configure an app's vibration pattern for its notifications.

You learn how to configure sounds and vibrations in Chapter 5.

Printing from Your iPhone

You can print directly from your iPhone to AirPrint-compatible printers.

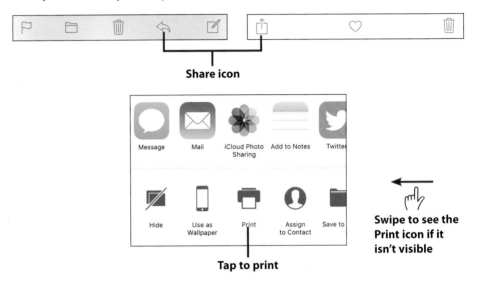

Share icon

Swipe to see the Print icon if it isn't visible

Tap to print

First, set up and configure your AirPrint printer (see the instructions that came with the printer you use).

It Depends

When you tap the Share icon, you might see a menu containing commands instead of the grid of icons shown in the figure. The way it appears is dependent upon the app you are using. If you see a menu, tap Print to move to the Printer Options screen.

AirPrint?

AirPrint is an Apple technology that enables an iOS device to wirelessly print to an AirPrint-compatible printer without installing any printer drivers on the iOS device. To be able to print directly to a printer via Wi-Fi, the printer must support AirPrint (a large number of them do). When an iOS device, such as your iPhone, is on the same Wi-Fi network as an AirPrint printer, it automatically detects that printer and is able to print to it immediately.

When you are in the app from which you want to print, tap the Share icon. Tap Print on the resulting menu. You might need to swipe to the right to expose the

Print command. (If you don't see the Share icon or the Print command, the app you are using doesn't support printing.)

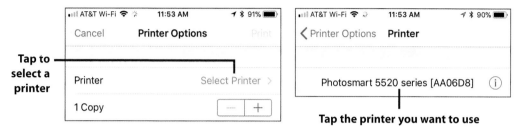

Tap to select a printer

Tap the printer you want to use

The first time you print, you need to select the printer you want to use. On the Printer Options screen, tap Select Printer. Then tap the printer you want to use. You move back to the Printer Options screen and see the printer you selected.

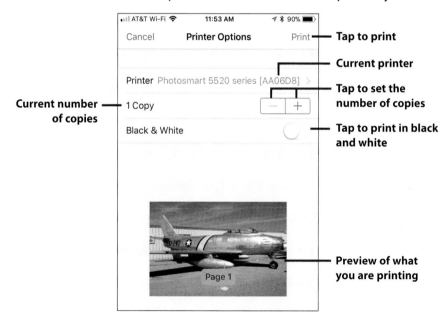

Tap to print

Current printer

Tap to set the number of copies

Current number of copies

Tap to print in black and white

Preview of what you are printing

Tap the – or + to set the number of copies; the current number of copies is shown to the left of the controls. You can use other controls that appear to configure the print job, such as the Black & White switch to print in black and white on a color printer; the controls you see depend on the capabilities of the printer you selected. Tap Print to print the document.

The next time you print, if you want to use the same printer, you can skip the printer selection process because the iPhone remembers the last printer you used. To change the printer, tap Printer and tap the printer you want to use.

Go here to configure and manage your Apple ID, iCloud, and other online accounts

Store files on the cloud

Use iCloud, Google, and other accounts to store the data your apps use on the cloud

In this chapter, you learn how to configure an Apple ID on your iPhone and to set up various types of accounts, such as iCloud and Google, so that apps on your iPhone can access data stored on the Internet cloud. Topics include the following:

→ Getting started
→ Configuring an Apple ID
→ Configuring and using iCloud
→ Setting up other types of online accounts on your iPhone
→ Setting how and when your accounts are updated

Setting Up and Using an Apple ID, iCloud, and Other Online Accounts

Connecting your iPhone to the Internet enables you to share and sync a wide variety of content using popular online accounts such as iCloud and Google. Using iCloud, you can put your email, contacts, calendars, photos, and more on the Internet so that multiple devices—most importantly your iPhone—can connect to and use that information. (There's a lot more you can do with iCloud, too, as you learn throughout this book.) There are other online accounts you might also want to use, such as Google for email, calendars, and contacts as well as email accounts provided by your Internet Service Provider, such as a cable company.

To use iCloud and access other services provided by Apple, such as the App Store, iTunes Store, and iMessage, you need to have an Apple ID configured on your iPhone. The Apple ID connects the services Apple provides to you on all of your devices.

You need to configure these accounts on your iPhone to be able to use them; this chapter includes sections for several different online accounts you might want to use. Of course, you need to refer only to the sections related to the accounts you actually use.

This chapter also explains how to configure how and when your information is updated and demonstrates tasks you might find valuable as you manage the various accounts on your iPhone.

Getting Started

You can configure your iPhone to use various types of online accounts that offer different types of services and information. Here are some of the key terms for this chapter:

- **Apple ID**—An Apple ID enables you to access many Apple services, especially iCloud, and make purchases from the App Store, iTunes Store, and Apple's online store. An Apple ID also enables you to use iMessage to send and receive messages via the Messages app. An Apple ID is the "connector" between all your devices; it enables you to start tasks on one device, such as writing an email on your iPhone, and finish them on another, such as an iPad. Similarly, if you subscribe to Apple's Music Library, your Apple ID provides access to that music on each of your devices (iPhones, iPads, or computers).

- **iCloud**—This is Apple's online service that offers lots of great features that you can use for free; if you store a lot of information online, you might need to add storage to your account for an additional fee. It includes email, online photo storage and sharing, backup, calendars, Find My iPhone, and much more. This chapter explains how to set up iCloud on your iPhone; you find examples of how to use iCloud services in this chapter and throughout the rest of this book.

- **Family Sharing**—This Apple service allows you to share content with a group of people. (They don't actually have to be related to you.) For example, you can share music you download from the iTunes Store—when you set people up in your "family" group. This service is free.

- **Google account**—A Google account is similar to an iCloud account except it is provided by Google instead of Apple. It also offers lots of features, such as email, calendars, and contacts. You can use iCloud and a Google account on your iPhone at the same time.

- **Push, Fetch, or Manual**—Information has to get from your online account onto your iPhone. For example, when someone sends an email to you, it actually goes to an email server, which then sends the message to devices that are configured with your email account. You can choose how and when new data is provided to your phone. The three ways data gets moved onto your iPhone (Push, Fetch, Manual) are explained in "Setting How and When Your Accounts Are Updated" later in this chapter.

Configuring an Apple ID

An Apple ID is required to access Apple's online services, including iCloud, the App Store, iTunes, and the online store. You can access all of these services with one Apple ID.

An Apple ID has two elements. One is the email address associated with your account; this can be one provided by Apple or you can choose to use an address from a different service (such as Google Gmail). The other element is a password.

In addition to your email address and password, your contact information (such as physical address and phone number) and payment information (if you make purchases through your account, such as apps or storage upgrades) is also part of your Apple ID.

If you have used Apple technology or services before, you probably already have an Apple ID. If you don't already have one, obtaining an Apple ID is simple and free.

If you have any of the following accounts, you already have an Apple ID:

- **iTunes Store**—If you've ever shopped at the iTunes Store, you created an Apple ID.

- **Apple Online Store**—As with the iTunes Store, if you made purchases from Apple's online store, you created an account with an Apple ID.

- **Find My iPhone**—If you obtained a free Find My iPhone account, you also created an Apple ID.

Another way you might have already obtained an Apple ID is during the initial iPhone startup process when you were prompted to sign in to or create an Apple ID.

If you don't have an Apple ID, read the next section to obtain one. If you already have an Apple ID, move to "Signing into Your Apple ID" to learn how to sign into it on your iPhone. If you both have an Apple ID and have already signed into it on your iPhone, skip to the section "Changing the Personal Information Associated with Your Apple ID" to learn how to configure it.

Obtaining an Apple ID

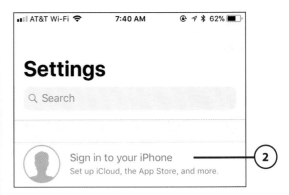

If you don't have an Apple ID, you can use your iPhone to create one by performing the following steps:

(1) On the Home screen, tap Settings.

(2) Tap Sign in to your iPhone.

(3) Tap Don't have an Apple ID or forgot it?.

(4) Tap Create Apple ID.

(5) Provide the information required on the following screens; tap Next to move to the next screen after you've entered the required information. You start by entering your birthday, providing your name, and so on. You are guided through each step in the process.

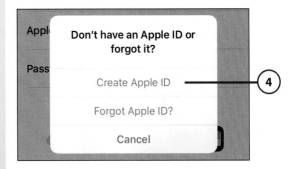

During the process, you're prompted to use an existing email address or to create a free iCloud email account. You can choose either option. The email address you use becomes your Apple ID that you use to sign in to iCloud. If you create a new iCloud email account, you can use that account from any email app on any device, just like other email accounts you have.

You also create a password, enter a phone number and verification method, verify the phone number you entered, and agree to license terms. When your account has been created, you sign into iCloud, which you do by entering your iPhone's passcode.

You might then be prompted to merge information already stored on your iPhone, such as Safari bookmarks, onto iCloud. Tap Merge to copy the information that currently is stored on your iPhone to the cloud or Don't Merge to keep it out of the cloud.

When you've worked through merging your information, you're prompted to sign in to the iTunes and App Stores to make sure your new account can work with those services, too. You can choose to review your account information now or skip it and configure it at another time.

When the process is complete, you're signed into your new Apple ID; skip ahead to "Changing the Personal Information Associated with Your Apple ID" to learn how to change its settings.

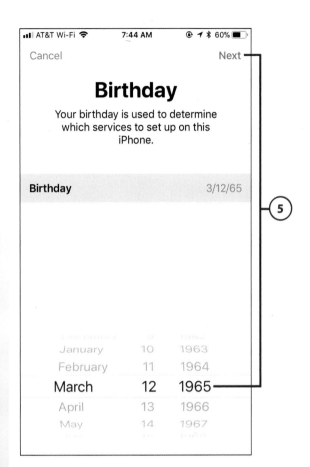

Signing In to Your Apple ID

You can sign in to an existing Apple ID on your iPhone by doing the following:

1. On the Home screen, tap Settings.

2. Tap Sign in to your iPhone.

3. Enter your Apple ID (email address).

4. Enter your password.

5. Tap Sign In. If you are using the same Apple ID on other devices, you're prompted to enter the verification code sent to those devices. See the sidebar "Two-Factor Authentication" for more information.

6. Enter your verification code; if you weren't prompted to enter a code, skip this step.

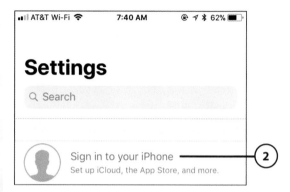

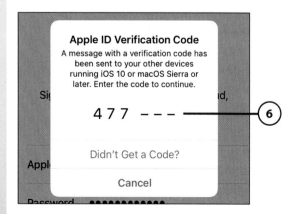

(7) Enter your iPhone's passcode. You might be prompted to merge existing information on the iPhone onto your iCloud storage.

(8) Tap Merge to copy information from your iPhone onto the cloud or Don't Merge if you don't want that information copied to the cloud. You might be prompted to perform this merge step more than once depending on the kind of information already stored on your iPhone. If you don't have any information that can be merged, you skip this step entirely.

When you've finished these steps, you are signed in to your Apple ID and can configure it further using the information in the next section.

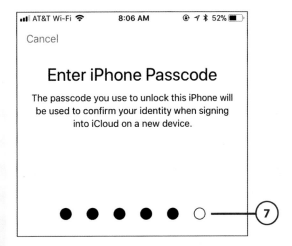

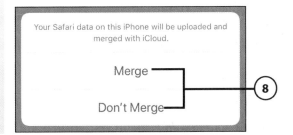

Two-Factor Authentication

Apple uses two-factor authentication for its services. This requires that you have two pieces of information to be able to access your Apple accounts. One is your Apple ID login information (email and password). The other is a verification code that is sent to other devices on which the Apple ID is already configured (called trusted devices). This makes using Apple services more secure because even if someone was able to get your Apple ID and password (which is unlikely), he would still need the verification code to be able to sign in to your account (meaning he would also have to be able to access another device on which your Apple ID is already configured, which is very, very unlikely). In general, you should use two-factor authentication when it is available (it requires you have at least two devices that can use your Apple ID, such as an iPhone and a Mac).

You can configure two-factor authentication for your Apple ID in the Password & Security settings, which are described in the next section.

Changing the Personal Information Associated with Your Apple ID

When you create or sign in to your Apple ID, the personal information associated with your account is used on your iPhone. You can change this information on your phone, for example, if you want to change your contact information or how you pay for purchases from Apple. Following are the steps you can use to change the personal information associated with your Apple ID:

(1) On the Home screen, tap Settings.

(2) Tap your Apple ID, which appears immediately under the Search bar at the top of the Settings screen. The Apple ID screen has four sections. The top section shows your Apple ID and photo (if you have one) and provides access to your account's primary settings, which are contact information, security, and payment information.

(3) To set or change the photo associated with your Apple ID, tap the image shown just above your name.

4 Tap Take Photo to take a new photo for your Apple ID or Choose Photo to use an existing photo; then use the resulting tools to configure the photo for your Apple ID (detailed information about working with the iPhone's photo tools is provided in Chapter 13, "Taking Photos and Video with Your iPhone," and Chapter 14, "Viewing and Editing Photos and Video with the Photos App"). When you're done configuring the photo, you return to the Apple ID screen and see the new photo at the top of the screen.

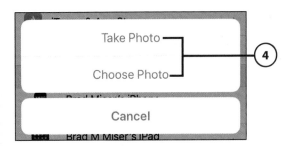

5 To change your contact information, tap Name, Phone Numbers, Email.

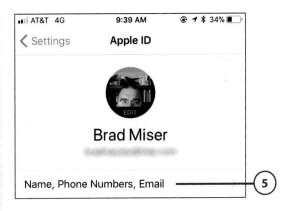

6 To change the name associated with your account, tap the name shown and edit it on the resulting screen; when you're done, tap Back to move to the previous screen (this step is not shown in the figures).

7 To change the email addresses with which you can be contacted in various apps, such as FaceTime, tap Edit.

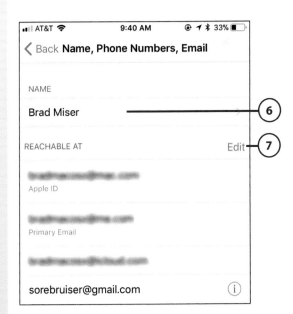

Address Info

If an email address has the Info icon (i) next to it, you can tap that icon to verify the address or see information about it (such as a message for your primary Apple ID address stating that you can't remove it).

8 To remove an address, tap its Unlock icon.

9 Tap Delete. That address is removed from the list and can't be used for associated apps.

10 To add more email addresses or phone numbers, tap Add Email or Phone Number.

11 Tap Add an Email Address to associate a new email or tap Add a Phone Number to add a phone number. Follow the resulting steps to complete the process. For example, enter the new email and then respond to the verification email sent to the address.

Done Is Done

When you make some changes, such as adding a new email address, you exit Edit mode automatically. You have to tap Edit again to make more changes. If a change you make doesn't automatically move you out of Edit mode, tap Done when you are finished making changes.

12 If you need to change the birthday for your account, tap it and make the change on the resulting screen.

13 To receive emails from Apple for various types of information, set the associated switch to On (green) or to prevent such messages from being sent, set the switch to Off (white).

14 When you're done making changes to your personal information, tap Back.

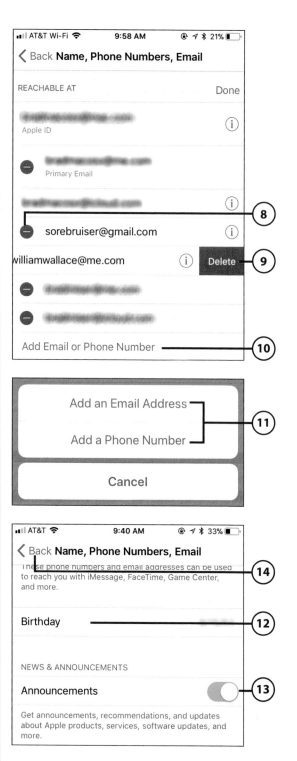

Confirmations Galore

Many changes you make to your Apple ID, such as adding a new email address or changing security settings, result in you receiving confirmation emails and notifications from Apple on all of the devices tied to your account. These are helpful because they confirm the actions you are taking. If you ever receive such a notification but you haven't changed your account, carefully review it. In many cases, especially email notifications, these unexpected notifications are attempts to get your information for nefarious purposes. Don't respond to emails you don't expect even if they appear to be from Apple (if you make a change to your account information and then receive an email, that is expected). Instead, log in directly to your account on your iPhone or other device to make sure it hasn't been changed by someone else.

Changing Your Apple ID's Password and Security Settings

To access the security settings for your Apple ID, perform the following steps:

(1) Move to the Apple ID screen.

(2) Tap Password & Security.

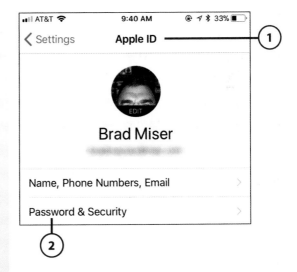

(3) To change your password, tap Change Password and follow the onscreen instructions to make the change. You need to enter your iPhone's passcode and then you'll be able to change the password.

(4) If two-factor authentication isn't currently enabled, tap Turn on Two-Factor Authentication and then tap Continue to complete the process; if it is already enabled, you see the On status (as shown in the figure).

(5) To change the phone number used for account verification, tap Edit and use the resulting tools to delete or change existing numbers or add new ones.

(6) If you need a verification code for another device with which you are trying to access your Apple ID information, tap Get Verification Code. The code appears on the screen and you can enter that code on the other device to verify it; tap OK to close the code dialog.

(7) When you're done making changes, tap Apple ID.

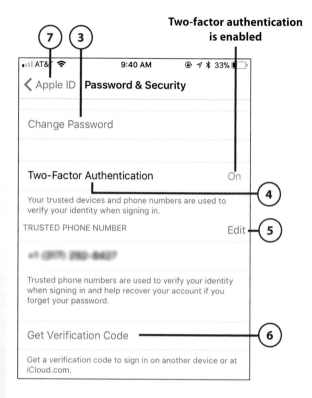

Two-factor authentication is enabled

(7) (3)

●ıll AT&T 🤖   9:40 AM   @ ✈ ✳ 33% 🔋

< Apple ID   **Password & Security**

Change Password

Two-Factor Authentication   On   (4)

Your trusted devices and phone numbers are used to verify your identity when signing in.

TRUSTED PHONE NUMBER   Edit   (5)

Trusted phone numbers are used to verify your identity when signing in and help recover your account if you forget your password.

Get Verification Code   (6)

Get a verification code to sign in on another device or at iCloud.com.

Changing Your Apple ID's Payment and Shipping Information

To change the payment and shipping information for your Apple ID, perform the following steps:

(1) Move to the Apple ID screen.

(2) Tap Payment & Shipping.

(3) To change your payment information, tap the current payment method (which is what will be used for all purchases made under your account, such as from the App Store).

(4) Use the fields on the resulting screen to provide or change your name, credit or debit card information, and the address associated with the payment method.

(5) Tap Save when you have updated the information.

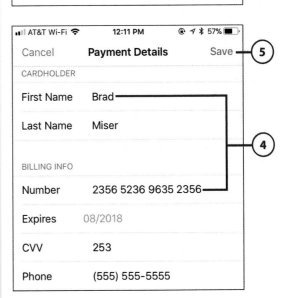

6 To change your shipping address, tap the current address.

7 Use the fields on the resulting screen to provide or change the address to which items you purchase from Apple should be delivered.

8 Tap Done when you have updated the information.

9 Tap Apple ID to return to the Apple ID screen.

Configuring Services that Use Your Apple ID

In the center part of the Apple ID screen, you see tools you can use to configure iCloud (covered in "Configuring and Using iCloud" later in this chapter) and the iTunes and App Stores (covered in "Customizing How Your iPhone Works with Apps" in Chapter 4, "Customizing How Your iPhone Works"). Family Sharing enables you to configure a group of people with whom you share content related to your Apple ID (such as music you purchase from the iTunes Store and apps you download from the App Store). You can use the Family Sharing option to configure your Family Sharing group and determine the access this group has to your account.

Changing the Devices Using Your Apple ID

You will likely have more than one device that uses your Apple ID. For example, you might have an iPad on which you want to be able to access the same information as you can on your iPhone. You can get information about the devices currently using your Apple ID like so:

1. Move to the Apple ID screen.

2. Tap the device about which you want to get information.

3. Review the information about the device. (If the device is also an iPhone, you can enable or disable some iCloud functions from this screen.)

4. If you don't recognize the device, tap Remove from Account and follow the onscreen prompts to disconnect the device from your Apple ID. You should also immediately change your Apple ID password.

5. To return to the Apple ID screen, tap Apple ID.

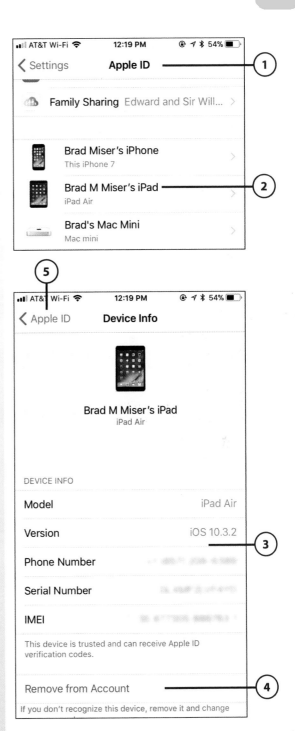

Signing Off

If don't want to continue accessing your Apple ID on your iPhone or you want to sign into a different Apple ID, tap Sign Out at the bottom of the Apple ID screen. If Find My iPhone is enabled, you need to enter your password and tap Turn Off to continue the process. You might be prompted to keep some information on your iPhone; if you choose to keep that information, it remains on your iPhone but is no longer synchronized to the information stored on the cloud. After you have completed the process, you can sign in to the same or a different Apple ID using the information in "Signing In to Your Apple ID" earlier in this chapter.

Configuring and Using iCloud

iCloud is a service provided by Apple that provides you with your own storage space on the Internet. You can store content from your computer or devices in your storage space on the cloud, and because it is on the Internet, all your devices are able to access that information at the same time. This means you can easily share your information on your iPhone, a computer, and iPad, so that the same information and content is available to you no matter which device you are using at any one time.

Although your iPhone can work with many types of online/Internet accounts, iCloud is integrated into the iPhone like no other (not surprising because the iPhone and iCloud are both Apple technology). An iCloud account is part of an Apple ID; if you have an Apple ID, you also have an iCloud account.

An iCloud account is useful in a number of ways, including the following:

- **Photos**—You can store your photos in iCloud to back them up and to make them easy to share.

- **Email**—An iCloud account includes an @icloud.com email address if you chose to create one when you created an Apple ID. You can configure any device to use your iCloud email account, including an iPhone, an iPad, and a computer.

- **Contacts**—You can store your contact information in iCloud.

- **Calendars**—Putting your calendars in iCloud makes it much easier to manage your time.

- **Reminders**—Through iCloud, you can be reminded of things you need to do or anything else you want to make sure you don't forget.

- **Notes**—With the Notes app, you can create text notes, draw sketches, and capture photos for many purposes; iCloud enables you to use these notes on any iCloud-enabled device.

- **Messages**—This puts all of your text messages on the cloud so you can access the same messages from any device.

- **Safari**—iCloud can store your bookmarks, letting you easily access the same websites from all your devices. And you can easily access websites currently open on other devices, such as a Mac, on your iPhone.

- **News**—iCloud can store information from the News app online, making reading news on multiple devices easier.

- **Health**—This causes the information stored using the Health app to be available to multiple devices. For example, you might track information on your Apple Watch and want to be able to analyze it on your iPhone.

- **Wallet**—The Wallet app stores coupons, tickets, boarding passes, and other documents so you can access them quickly and easily. With iCloud, you can ensure that these documents are available on any iCloud-enabled device.

- **Game Center**—This capability stores information from the Game Center app on the cloud.

- **Siri**—It can be helpful to manage Siri information on multiple devices; this setting puts that information on the cloud.

- **Keychain**—The Keychain securely stores sensitive data, such as passwords, so that you can easily use that data without having to remember it.

- **Find My iPhone**—This service enables you to locate and secure your iPhone and other devices.

- **iCloud Backup**—You can back up your iPhone to the cloud so that you can recover your data and your phone's configuration should something ever happen to it.

- **iCloud Drive**—iCloud enables you to store your documents and other files on the cloud so that you can seamlessly work with them using different devices.

- **App Data**—When iCloud Drive is enabled, you can allow or prevent apps from storing data there.

You can also manage your iCloud storage space, share your location, and configure some aspects of iCloud mail.

You learn about iCloud's many useful features throughout this book (such as using iCloud with your photos, which is covered in Chapter 14). The tasks in this chapter show you how to set up and configure the iCloud features you want to use.

One at a Time Please

You can have more than one iCloud account. However, you can be signed in to only one iCloud account on your iPhone at a time.

I'm In

To configure your iCloud account, sign in to your Apple ID as described in "Signing In to Your Apple ID" earlier in this chapter.

Configuring iCloud to Store Photos

Storing your photos on the cloud provides many benefits, not the least of which is that the photos you take with your iPhone are automatically saved on the cloud so that you can access them from computers and other iOS devices (such as iPads), and your photos remain available even if something happens to your iPhone, such as losing it. Using iCloud also makes it easy for you to share your photos with others. To configure your photos to be stored in iCloud, do the following:

① Open the Apple ID screen.

② Tap iCloud.

③ On the iCloud screen, tap Photos.

4 To store your entire photo library on the cloud, set the iCloud Photo Library switch to on (green). This stores all of your photos and video in iCloud, which both protects them by backing them up and makes them accessible on other iOS devices (iPads, iPod touches, iPhones) and computers (Macs and Windows PCs).

5 If you enable the iCloud Photo Library feature, tap Optimize iPhone Storage to keep lower-resolution versions of photos and videos on your iPhone (this means the file sizes are smaller so that you can store more of them on your phone), or tap Download and Keep Originals if you want to keep the full-resolution photos on your iPhone. In most cases, you should choose the Optimize option so that you don't use as much of your iPhone's storage space for photos.

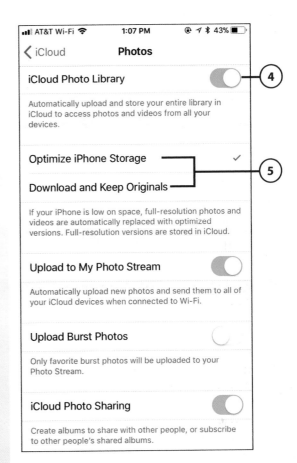

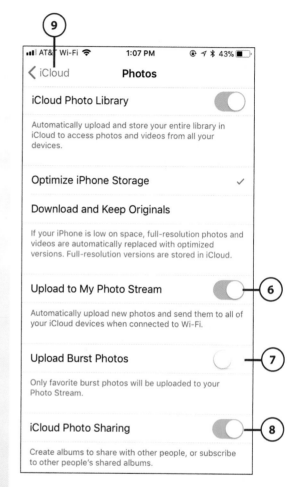

6 Ensure the Upload to My Photo Stream switch is on (green) (if you aren't using the iCloud Photo Library, this switch is called My Photo Stream); if you set it to off (white) instead, skip to step 8. Any photos you take with the iPhone's camera are copied onto iCloud, and from there they're copied to your other devices on which the Photo Stream is enabled. Note that Photo Stream affects only photos that you take with the iPhone from the time you enable it, whereas the iCloud Photo Library feature uploads all of your photos—those you took in the past and will take in the future.

7 If you want all of your burst photos (photos taken in sequence, such as for action shots) to be uploaded to iCloud, set the Upload Burst Photos switch to on (green). In most cases, you should leave this off (white) because you typically don't want to keep all the photos in a burst. When you review and select photos to keep (this is explained in Chapter 14), the ones you keep are uploaded.

8 To be able to share your photos and to access photos other people share with you, set the iCloud Photo Sharing switch to on (green).

9 Tap iCloud.

Enabling iCloud to Store Information on the Cloud

One of the best things about iCloud is that it stores email, contacts, calendars, reminders, bookmarks, notes, and other data on the cloud so that all your iCloud-enabled devices can access the same information. You can choose the types of data stored on the cloud by performing the following steps:

(1) Move to the iCloud screen. Just below the Storage information are the iCloud data options. Some of these have a right-facing arrow that you tap to configure options, and others have a two-position switch. The types of data that have switches are Mail, Contacts, Calendars, Reminders, Notes, Messages, Safari, News, Health, Wallet, Game Center, and Siri. When a switch is green, it means that switch is turned on and the related data is stored to your iCloud account and kept in sync with the information on the iPhone.

(2) To store data on the cloud, set its switch to On (green). You might be prompted to merge that information with that already stored on the cloud. For example, if you have contacts information on your iPhone already and want to merge that with the contacts already on the cloud, tap Merge. If you don't want the contacts copied to the cloud, tap Don't Merge.

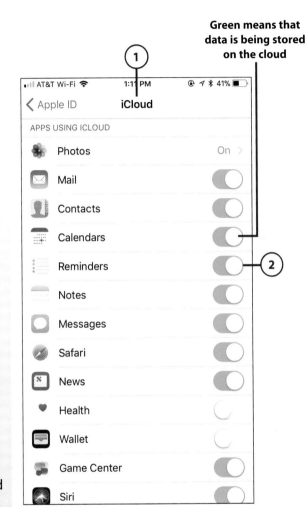

Green means that data is being stored on the cloud

(3) If you don't want a specific type of data to be stored on the cloud and synced to your iPhone, tap its switch to turn that data off (the switch becomes white instead of green).

When you turn off a switch because you don't want that information stored on the cloud any more, you might be prompted to keep the associated information on your iPhone or delete it.

If you choose Keep on My iPhone, the information remains on your iPhone but is no longer connected to the cloud; this means any changes you make exist only on the iPhone. If you choose Delete from My iPhone, the information is erased from your iPhone. Whether you choose to keep or delete the information, any information of that type that was previously stored on the cloud remains available there; the delete action affects only the information stored on the iPhone.

After you've configured each data switch on the iCloud screen, you're ready to configure the rest of the data options, which are explained in the following tasks.

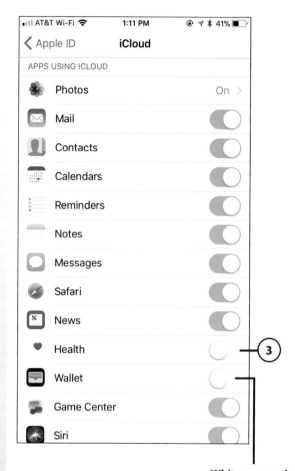

White means the data is not being stored on the cloud

Configuring Your iCloud Keychain

A keychain can be used to store user-names, passwords, and credit cards so you can access this information with-out retyping it every time you need it. Enabling keychain syncing through iCloud makes this information avail-able on multiple devices. For example, if you've configured a website's pass-word on your keychain on a Mac, that password is available in the Safari app on your iPhone if the keychain is synced via iCloud. Follow these steps to enable keychain syncing through iCloud:

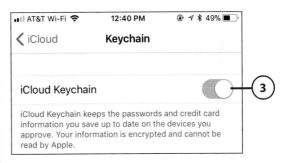

(**1**) On the iCloud screen, tap Keychain.

(**2**) If prompted to do so, enter your Apple ID password and tap OK (not shown in the figures).

(**3**) Set the iCloud Keychain switch to on (green).

Your Experience May Vary

How iCloud Keychain syncing is configured can vary based on the current status of your keychain. These steps assume your keychain is already configured on another device, such as a Mac, and your iPhone is connecting to that keychain. If you don't have any keychain syncing configured, you might see additional steps when you perform step 3. In that case, just follow the onscreen prompts to com-plete the process.

>>>Go Further

PROCEED WITH CAUTION

If you store a lot of sensitive information in your keychain on a Mac, such as usernames and passwords to websites, credit cards, and such, be careful about enabling keychain syncing. When you enable this iCloud feature, all this data becomes available on your iPhone and can be used by anyone who can use your phone. Assuming you have a passcode to the phone, you are protected from someone using your phone without you knowing it, but if you let someone use your phone, they can also use your sensitive information. You might choose to leave keychain syncing off and just keep a minimum amount of sensitive information on your phone.

>>>Go Further

CONFIGURING FIND MY iPHONE

Find My iPhone enables you to locate and secure your iPhone if you lose it (you learn how to do this in the online Chapter 16, "Maintaining and Protecting Your iPhone and Solving Problems"). This feature is enabled by default when you sign in to your iCloud account. You should usually leave it enabled so that you have a better chance of locating your iPhone should you lose it—or in case you need to delete its data should you decide you won't be getting the iPhone back. There are a couple of configuration tasks you can do for Find My iPhone:

- To disable Find My iPhone, open the iCloud settings screen and tap Find My iPhone. Set the Find My iPhone switch to off (white) and enter your Apple ID password at the prompt. You can no longer access your iPhone via the Find My iPhone feature.

- To send the last known location of the iPhone to Apple when power is critically low, open the Find My iPhone settings screen and set the Send Last Location switch to on (green). When your iPhone is nearly out of power, its location is sent to Apple. You can contact Apple to try to determine where your iPhone was when the battery was almost out of power.

Configuring Your iCloud Backup

Like other digital devices, it is important to back up your iPhone's data so that you can recover should something bad happen to your iPhone. You can back up your iPhone's data and settings to iCloud, which is really useful because that means you can recover the backed-up data using a different device, such as a replacement iPhone. Configure your iCloud backup with the following steps:

1. On the iCloud settings screen, tap iCloud Backup.

2. Set the iCloud Backup switch to on (green). Your iPhone's data and settings are backed up to the cloud automatically when your iPhone is connected to a Wi-Fi network.

3. Tap iCloud.

Back Me Up on This

You can manually back up your iPhone's data and settings at any time by tapping Back Up Now on the Backup screen. This can be useful to ensure recent data or settings changes are captured in your backup. For example, if you know you are going to be without a Wi-Fi connection to the Internet for a while, back up your phone to ensure that your current data is saved in the backup.

Configuring iCloud Drive

iCloud Drive, which is enabled by default, stores files (such as Keynote presentations) on the cloud so that you can work with those documents on any device. For example, you can create a Keynote presentation on a Mac and then access it on your iPhone to present it. To configure your iCloud Drive, perform the following steps:

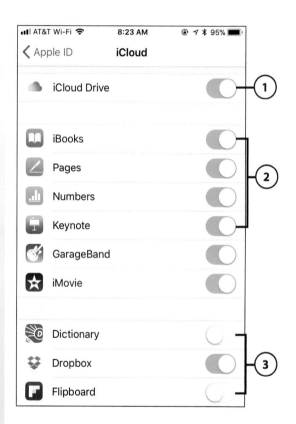

(1) On the iCloud settings screen, set the iCloud Drive switch to on (green).

(2) Set the switch to on (green) for those apps that you do want to use the iCloud Drive to store data.

(3) Set the switch to off (white) for any apps that you don't want to use your iCloud Drive.

Managing Your iCloud Storage

Your iCloud account includes storage space that you can use for your data including photos, documents, and so on. By default, your account includes 5 GB of free storage space. For many people, that is enough, but if you take a lot of photos and video and use the iCloud Photo Library feature, you might find that you need more space. It is easy (and relatively inexpensive) to upgrade the amount of room you have on your iCloud Drive. You can use the STORAGE section on the iCloud settings screen to manage your storage space as follows:

(1) Move to the top of the iCloud settings screen. Here you see a gauge that displays the amount of space you have and how that space is currently being used. The gray portion of the bar indicates how much free space you have; if this portion of the bar is very small, you might want to consider upgrading your storage space.

(2) Tap Manage Storage. At the top of the iCloud Storage screen, you see the same storage information as on the prior screen. Under that, you see the tools you can use to manage your storage.

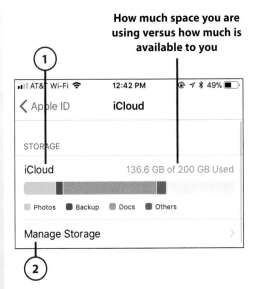

How much space you are using versus how much is available to you

(**3**) To change the amount of storage space available to you, tap Change and follow the onscreen prompts to upgrade (or downgrade) your storage.

(**4**) If you use the Family Sharing feature, tap Share With Family to enable the people in your sharing group to store content on your iCloud drive (not shown on figures).

(**5**) When the Share With Family feature is enabled, you can tap Family Usage to see how much space each member of the group is using (you can disable this feature through the Family Sharing option on the Apple ID screen).

(**6**) Swipe up the screen to review all of the apps that are currently using iCloud storage space.

(**7**) Tap an app to get details about how it is using iCloud space.

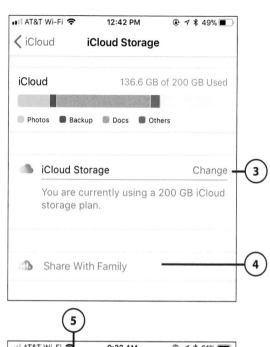

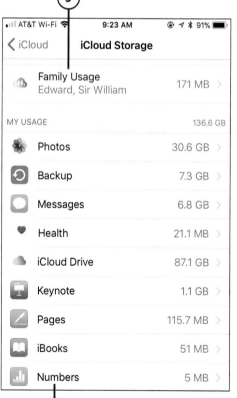

8 If the app works with documents, you see the list of documents and how much space each is using (if it doesn't use documents, you only see a total).

Delete or Disable?

When you delete documents or data from your iCloud storage, it is removed from the cloud. This also means it is removed from every device using that data on the cloud. If you want the app to stop storing data on the cloud, but keep the data on the devices currently using it, prevent it from using iCloud storage as described in "Configuring iCloud Drive" instead.

9 To remove documents and data from iCloud, tap Delete Documents & Data, Disable & Delete, or Delete Data. After you confirm the deletion, the app's data is deleted from your iPhone.

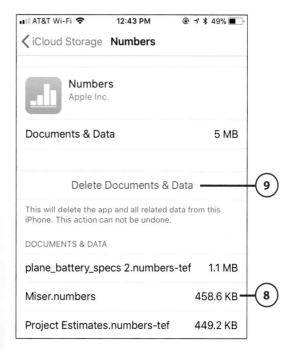

>>>Go Further

YET EVEN MORE iCLOUD CONFIGURATION OPTIONS

Most of the time, you can use your iCloud account just fine if you only configure it as described in the previous tasks. However, there are some other configuration options located at the bottom of the iCloud settings screen that you might want to use at some point:

- **Look Me Up**. Some iCloud-aware apps can look you up via your Apple ID; people who do this see your first and last names. You can tap Look Me Up to see which apps and people have accessed this information.

- **Share Your Location**. With this feature, you can share your location with others. You can enable the feature by setting its switch to on (green) and choosing which of your iCloud devices is used to determine your location. You can share your location in Messages, and you can enable people you've included in your Family Sharing group to view your location.

- **Mail**. Use this option to configure certain aspects of your iCloud email. These options are explained in Chapter 8, "Sending, Receiving, and Managing Email."

>>>Go Further

EMAIL ALIASES

One of the great features of iCloud is using email aliases. You can create alias addresses for specific purposes, such as avoiding spam or just to use an email address you prefer. Email sent to one of your aliases comes into your normal inbox. When you send email from an alias, it appears to be from the alias address, even though any aliases are still related to the same email account. You can create email aliases for your iCloud account using your iCloud website, available at www.icloud.com. Log in to your iCloud account, and then open the Mail app. Open the Mail Preferences dialog by clicking the gear icon and choosing Preferences. Then, click the Accounts tab, where you can create and manage up to three aliases.

Setting Up Other Types of Online Accounts on Your iPhone

Many types of online accounts provide different services, including email, calendars, contacts, social networking, and so on. To use these accounts, you need to configure them on your iPhone. The process you use for most types of accounts is similar to the steps you used to set up your iCloud account. In this section, you learn how to configure a Google account and an account that you might have through your Internet provider, such as a cable company.

Configuring a Google Account

A Google account provides email, contacts, calendar, and note syncing that are similar to iCloud. To set up a Google account on your iPhone, do the following:

1. On the Home screen, tap Settings.
2. Tap Accounts & Passwords.
3. Tap Add Account.

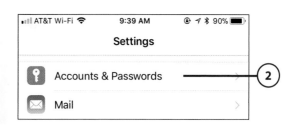

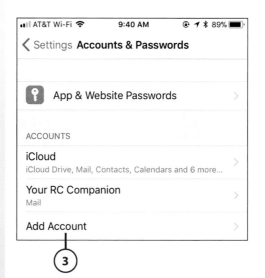

(4) Tap Google.

(5) Enter your Google email address.

(6) Tap Next.

(7) Enter your Google account password.

(8) Tap Next.

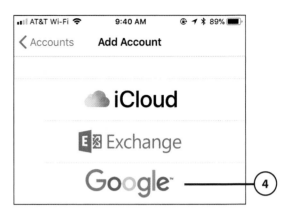

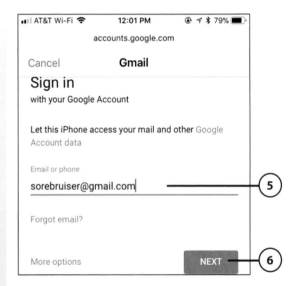

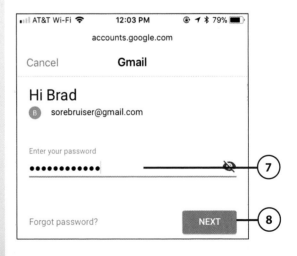

9 Enable the features of the account you want to access on the iPhone—which are Mail, Contacts, Calendars, and Notes— by setting the switch to on (green) for the types of data you do want to use or to off (white) for the types of data you don't want to use.

10 Tap Save. The account is saved, and the data you enabled becomes available on your iPhone.

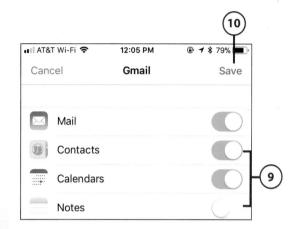

Advanced Google

Similar to iCloud, a Google account has some settings you aren't likely to use, but it's good to know how to get to them in case you need them. To access these settings, move to the Accounts & Passwords screen and tap your Google account. On the Gmail account's screen, you can change the types of data you are syncing by setting the switches to on or off. Tap Account, and then tap Advanced to see additional settings. Working with these is similar to working with iCloud. For example, you can determine where draft email messages are stored, such as on the Gmail server or on your iPhone.

You can't change the password for a Google account in the Settings app on your iPhone. You have to change the password elsewhere, such as by accessing your Google account via the Google website. After your Google password has been changed, you're prompted to enter the new password the first time your iPhone attempts to access your account.

Setting Up an Online Account that Isn't Built In

You can access many types of online accounts on your iPhone. These include accounts that are "built in," which include AOL, Exchange, Google, iCloud, Outlook.com, and Yahoo! Setting up an AOL, Exchange, Outlook.com, or Yahoo! account is similar to configuring a Google or iCloud account on your iPhone. Just select the account type you want to use and provide the information for which you are prompted.

There are other types of accounts you might want to use that aren't "built in." An email account included with an Internet access account, such as one from a cable Internet provider, is one example. Support for these accounts isn't built in to the iOS; however, you can usually set up such accounts on your iPhone fairly easily.

When you obtain an account, such as email accounts that are part of your Internet service, you should receive all the information you need to configure those accounts on your iPhone. If you don't have this information, visit the provider's website and look for information on configuring the account in an email application. You need to have this information to configure the account on the iPhone.

With the configuration information for the account you want to use on your iPhone in hand, you're ready to set it up:

(1) On the Home screen, tap Settings.

(2) Tap Accounts & Passwords.

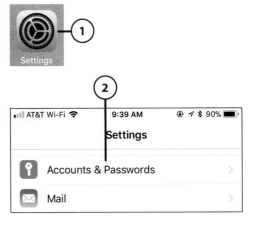

3 Tap Add Account.

4 Tap Other.

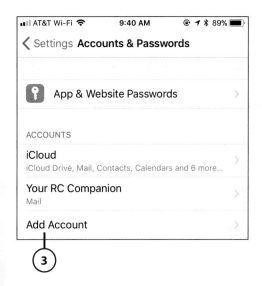

(5) Tap the type of account you want to add. For example, to set up an email account, tap Add Mail Account.

(6) Enter the information by filling in the fields you see; various types of information are required for different kinds of accounts. You just need to enter the information you received from the account's provider.

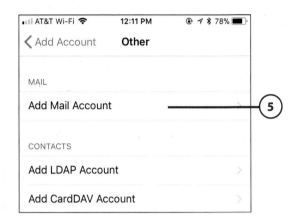

(7) Tap Next. If the iPhone can set up the account automatically, its information is verified and it's ready for you to use (if the account supports multiple types of information, you can enable or disable the types with which you want to work on your iPhone). If the iPhone can't set up the account automatically, you're prompted to enter additional information to complete the account configuration. When you're done, the account appears on the list of accounts and is ready for you to use.

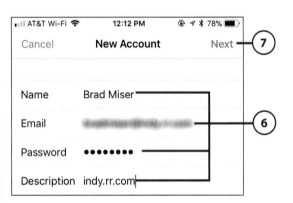

(8) Configure the switches for the data sync options you see. For example, to use the account for email, set the Mail switch to on (green).

(9) Tap Save. The account you configured is available in the related app, such as Mail if you set up an email account.

Multiple Accounts

There is no limit (that I have found so far) on the number of online accounts (even of the same type, such as Gmail) that you can access on your iPhone. (You can only have one iCloud account configured on your iPhone at the same time.)

Configuring Social Media Accounts on Your iPhone

Social media apps are useful for doing things such as keeping in touch with others, sharing your opinions and reading the opinions of others, and exchanging photos. Examples of these types of social media include Facebook, Instagram, and Twitter. Your iPhone is ideally suited to these because you can easily download and configure these apps to work on your phone.

Unlike Google, iCloud, and other accounts that are configured through the Settings app, you configure your social media accounts directly in their apps.

To use a social media app, you perform the following three steps:

1. Download and install the app you want to use.

2. Configure the app to access your social media account.

3. Configure other settings for the social media app.

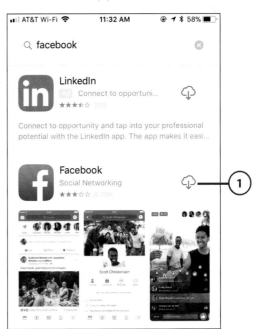

The steps to find and download apps are provided in Chapter 4. Examples of the second and third steps follow.

Facebook is one of the most popular social media channels you can use to keep informed about other people and inform them about you. Use these steps to download and configure Facebook on your iPhone:

1 Use the App Store app to download and install the Facebook app on your iPhone (see Chapter 4 for the details of working with the App Store app).

(**2**) Tap the Facebook icon on a Home screen to open the app.

(**3**) If you have previously signed into Facebook on the phone, tap the account shown. You're prompted to enter your password; when you do, you sign in and can jump to step 10. If you haven't signed into an account before, you won't have this option and instead immediately go to the login page as described in step 5.

(**4**) To sign into a different Facebook account than the one shown, tap Log Into Another Account.

Don't Have a Facebook Account?

If you don't already have a Facebook account, you can create one by tapping Sign Up for Facebook on the opening screen in the app or on the Log In screen. Follow the onscreen instructions to create a new Facebook account and log into it.

(**5**) Tap in the Email or phone number field.

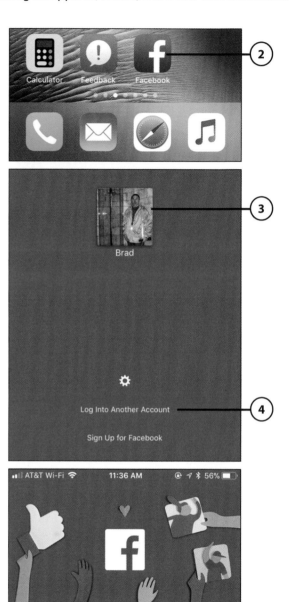

6 Enter the email address, phone number, or Facebook account name associated with your account.

7 Enter your password. (If you don't know your password, tap Forgot Password? and follow the onscreen instructions to reset it.)

8 Tap Log In.

9 If you want to receive notifications from Facebook, such as when someone posts on your Timeline, tap Allow; if you don't want these notifications, tap Don't Allow. (You can always change these notification settings as described in Chapter 4.)

10 Use the Facebook app to post comments, add photos, and so on. You can use the app with its default settings. Perform steps 11 and 12 when you want to make changes to how the app works.

11 Further configure the app by tapping Facebook on the Settings screen.

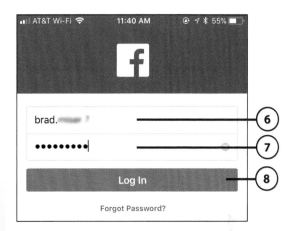

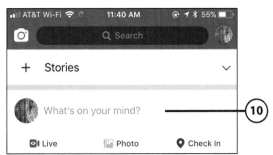

12 Use the app's settings to configure how it works for you. For example, you can configure notifications, determine if it uses cellular data, and so on.

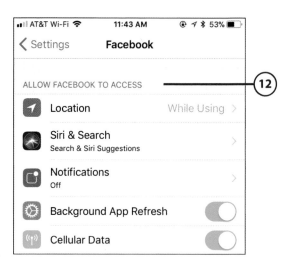

More About Social Media

If you'd like to learn more about various social media, check out *My Social Media for Seniors*, Second Edition by Michael Miller (Que Publishing, 2017).

Setting How and When Your Accounts Are Updated

The great thing about online accounts is that their information can be updated any time your iPhone can connect to the Internet. This means you have access to the latest information, such as new emails, changes to your calendars, and so on. There are three basic ways information gets updated:

- **Push**—When information is updated via Push, the server pushes (thus the name) updated information onto your iPhone whenever that information changes. For example, when you receive a new email, that email is immediately sent (or pushed) to your iPhone. Push provides you with the most current information all the time but uses a lot more battery than the other options.

- **Fetch**—When information is updated via Fetch, your iPhone connects to the account and retrieves the updated information according to a schedule, such as every 15 minutes. Fetch doesn't keep your information quite as current as Push does, but it uses much less battery than Push does.

- **Manual**—You can cause an app's information to be updated manually. This happens whenever you open or move into an app or by a manual refresh. For example, you can get new email by moving onto the Inboxes screen in the Mail app and swiping down from the top of the screen.

You can configure the update method that is used globally, and you can set the method for specific accounts. Some account types, such as iCloud, support all three options whereas others might support only Fetch and Manual. The global option for updating is used unless you override it for individual accounts. For example, you might want your work account to be updated via Push so your information there is always current, whereas configuring Fetch on a personal account might be frequent enough.

Configuring How New Data Is Retrieved for Your Accounts

To configure how your information is updated, perform the following steps:

1. Move to the Accounts & Passwords screen of the Settings app.

2. Tap Fetch New Data.

3. To enable data to be pushed to your iPhone, slide the Push switch to on (green). To disable push to extend battery life, set it to off (white). This setting is global, meaning that if you disable Push here, it is disabled for all accounts even though you can still configure Push to be used for individual accounts. For example, if your iCloud account is set to use Push but Push is globally disabled, the iCloud account's setting is ignored and data is fetched instead.

4. To change how an account's information is updated, tap it. The account's screen displays. The options on this screen depend on the kind of account it is. You always have Fetch and Manual; Push is displayed only for accounts that support it.

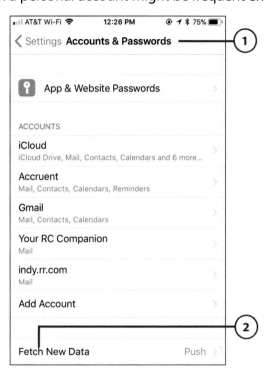

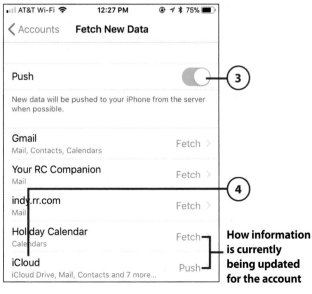

How information is currently being updated for the account

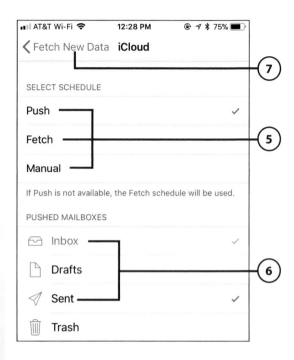

(5) Tap the option you want to use for the account: Push, Fetch, or Manual.

If you choose Manual, information is retrieved only when you manually start the process by opening the related app (such as Mail to get your email) or by using the refresh gesture, regardless of the global setting.

If you choose Fetch, information is updated according to the schedule you set in step 9.

(6) If you choose the Push option in step 5 and are working with an email account, choose the mailboxes whose information you want to be pushed by tapping them so they have a check mark; to prevent a mailbox's information from being pushed, tap it so that it doesn't have a check mark. (The Inbox is selected by default and can't be unselected.)

(7) Tap Fetch New Data.

(8) Repeat steps 5–7 until you have set the update option for each account. (The current option is shown to the right of the account's name.)

(9) Tap the amount of time when you want the iPhone to fetch data when Push is turned off globally or for those accounts for which you have selected Fetch or that don't support Push; tap Manually if you want to manually check for information for Fetch accounts or when Push is off. Information for your accounts is updated according to your settings.

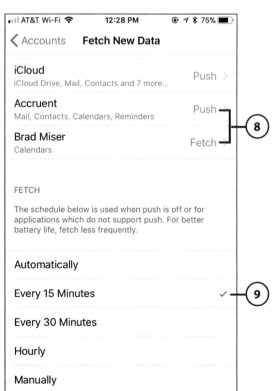

>>>Go Further

TIPS FOR MANAGING YOUR ACCOUNTS

As you add and use accounts on your iPhone, keep the following points in mind:

- You can temporarily disable any data for any account by moving to the Accounts & Passwords screen and tapping that account. Set the switches for the data you don't want to use to off (white). You might be prompted to keep or delete that information; if you choose to keep it, the data remains on your iPhone but is disconnected from the account and is no longer updated. If you delete it, you can always recover it again by simply turning that data back on. For example, suppose you are going on vacation and don't want to deal with work email, meeting notifications, and so on. Move to your work account and disable all its data. That data disappears from the related apps; for example, the account's mailboxes no longer appear in the Mail app. When you want to start using the account again, simply re-enable its data.

- If you want to completely remove an account from your iPhone, move to its configuration screen, swipe up the screen, and tap Delete Account. Tap Delete in the confirmation dialog box and the account is removed from your iPhone. (You can always sign in to the account to start using it again.)

- You can have different notifications for certain aspects of an account, such as email. See Chapter 2, "Using Your iPhone's Core Features," for information about using notifications and Chapter 4 for the steps to configure the notifications for your online accounts. For example, you might want to hear a different sound when you receive work emails versus those sent to your personal account.

- You can change how information is updated at any time, too. If your iPhone is running low on battery, disable Push and set Fetch to Manually so you can control when the updates happen. When your battery is charged again, you can re-enable Push or set a Fetch schedule.

Tap to personalize
your iPhone to
make it your own

Install apps so you
can do all kinds of
useful and fun things
with your iPhone

Configure notifications from apps
so they provide the right amount of
information at the right times

In this chapter, you learn how to make an iPhone into *your* iPhone. Topics include the following:

→ Getting started
→ Configuring notifications
→ Scheduling Do Not Disturb
→ Configuring the Control Center
→ Configuring the Widget Center
→ Setting keyboard, language, and format options
→ Setting Privacy and Location Services preferences
→ Configuring passcode, Touch ID, and content restrictions
→ Setting accessibility options
→ Customizing how your iPhone works with apps

Customizing How Your iPhone Works

You can configure the iPhone to make it work how you want it to. Taking the time to tailor your iPhone to your personal preferences and how you want to use it makes the iPhone easier and more fun to use.

Getting Started

As you've seen in previous chapters, the Settings app enables you to configure various aspects of your iPhone, such as connecting your iPhone to a Wi-Fi network and configuring iCloud. The Settings app provides many other configuration tools that you can use to tailor how your iPhone works to suit your preferences. Perhaps the most important of these is the security of your iPhone that you can configure by setting a passcode and fingerprint recognition using Touch ID (all models except iPhone X) or facial recognition using Face ID (iPhone X). You can also configure the keyboards available, language and region format options, accessibility options, and how content on your phone can be accessed. Throughout this chapter, you see how to use the Settings app to customize the iPhone in all of these areas.

Although the Settings app enables you to customize how your iPhone works in many ways, installing apps on your iPhone enables it to do so much more than it can "out of the box." You'll want to explore and download apps to completely customize how you use your iPhone; the possibilities of what your phone can do with apps are limitless!

Configuring Notifications

In Chapter 2, "Using Your iPhone's Core Features," you learned how to work with the various types of notifications your iPhone presents to keep you informed of important (and at times, not-so-important) information. Notifications can become distracting or overwhelming because the apps on your phone can provide notifications about all manner of things—incoming mail, messages, news updates, and so on. If an app manages a lot of activity, it can generate multiple notifications over a short period of time.

You can configure how apps can provide notifications and, if you allow notifications, which type. You can also configure other aspects of notifications, such as whether an app's notifications appear in the Notification Center or if they appear on the Lock screen. Apps can support different notification options; some apps, such as Mail, support notification configuration by account (for example, you can set a different alert sound for new mail in each account). You can follow the same general steps to configure notifications for each app; you should explore the options for the apps you use most often to ensure they work the best for you.

The steps in the following task show you how to configure Mail's notifications, which is a good example because it supports a lot of notification features; the notification settings for other apps might have fewer features or might be organized slightly differently. But configuring the notifications for any app follows a similar pattern as exemplified by the steps for Mail's notification settings.

To configure notifications from the Mail app, perform the following steps:

1. Tap Settings on the Home screen.

2. Tap Notifications.

3. Tap Show Previews. As you may recall from Chapter 2, alerts from an app can contain a preview of the information related to the alert, such as part of an email message.

4. To have alerts always show the preview, tap Always; tap When Unlocked to show previews only when your iPhone is unlocked; or tap Never to hide previews. This is a global setting for all apps. However, you can override this for individual apps. (How to do this is shown in later steps.)

5. Tap Notifications. In the Notification Style section, you see all the apps installed on your phone. Along with the app name and icon, you see the current status of its notifications.

6. Swipe up or down the screen to locate the app whose notifications you want to configure. (The apps are listed in alphabetical order.)

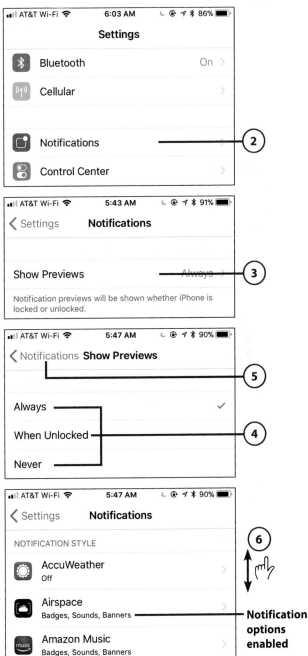

⑦ Tap the app whose notifications you want to configure.

⑧ If you want the app to provide notifications, set the Allow Notifications switch to on (green) and move to step 9. If you don't want notifications from the app, set the Allow Notifications switch to off (white) and skip to step 25.

⑨ Tap the account for which you want to configure notifications; if the app doesn't support accounts, skip this step.

⑩ Tap Sounds.

⑪ Use the resulting Sounds screen to choose the alert sound and vibration for new email messages to the account (see "Choosing the Sounds and Vibratory Feedback Your iPhone Uses" in Chapter 5, "Customizing How Your iPhone Looks and Sounds," for the details about configuring sounds and vibrations).

⑫ Tap the Back icon located in the upper-left corner of the screen (how it is labeled depends on what you are working with; for example, it shows the account name when you are working with a Mail account).

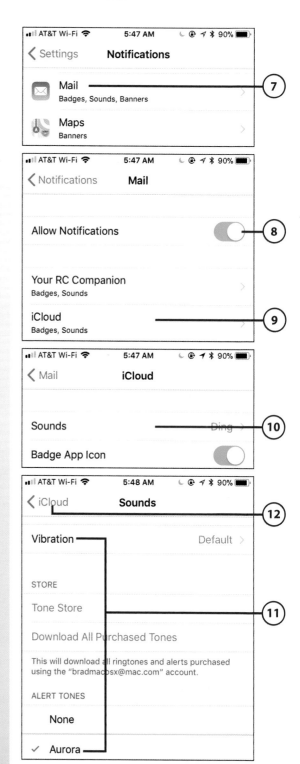

(13) To display the app's badge (which shows the number of new items in that app or account), set the Badge App Icon switch to on (green). (If you set this to off (white) for an account, new items sent to that account won't be included in the count of new items shown on the badge.)

(14) If you want the app's or account's notifications to appear on the Lock screen, slide the Show on Lock Screen switch to on (green). If you receive sensitive information to the account, you might want to leave this off so that this information isn't displayed on the Lock screen, which anyone who has access to your iPhone can view.

(15) To show notifications from the app/ account in the Notification Center, set the Show in History switch to on (green); if you set this to off (white), notifications from the app/account are not shown in the Notification Center.

(16) If you want to receive banner notifications for the account, set the Show as Banners switch to on (green); if you don't want banner notifications, leave this set to off (white) and skip to step 18.

(17) Tap Temporary if you want banners to appear on the screen for a few seconds and then disappear or Persistent if you want them to remain on the screen until you take action on them (such as reading the associated email). You know which type is currently selected because its name is marked with an oval around it.

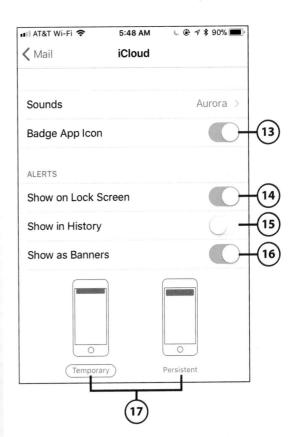

18 Tap Show Previews.

19 Tap Always (Default) if you always want previews to appear in notifications; When Unlocked if you want them to appear only when your iPhone is unlocked; or Never if you don't want previews to be displayed at any time. This setting overrides the global setting you configured earlier for the app whose notifications you are configuring.

20 Tap the Back icon, which is located in the upper-left corner of the window.

21 Tap the Back icon, which is located in the upper-left corner of the window.

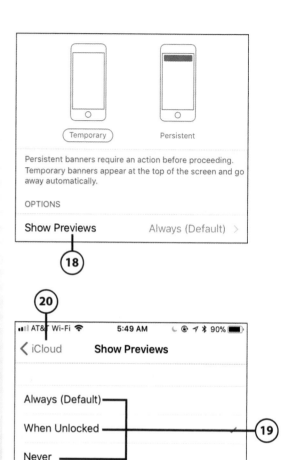

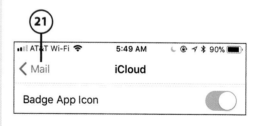

22 Configure notifications for the other accounts used in the app.

23 Configure notifications for VIP email and threads.

24 Tap Notifications.

25 Repeat steps 6 through 24 for each app shown on the Notifications screen. Certain apps might not have all the options shown in these steps, but the process to configure their notifications is similar.

26 Swipe up until you reach the bottom of the screen.

27 Configure any special notifications you see. What you see here depends on the country or region your phone is associated with. For example, where I live in the United States, the GOVERNMENT ALERTS section includes two notifications. AMBER Alerts are issued when a child is missing and presumed abducted, whereas Emergency Alerts are issued for things such as national crises, local weather, and so on. You can use the switches to enable (green) or prevent (white) these types of alerts, but you can't configure them.

More Options

Some apps provide notifications for the types of activity they manage. For example, the Calendar app enables you to configure notifications for upcoming events, invitations, and so on. Open the Notification Settings screen for the apps you use frequently to explore the notification options they offer.

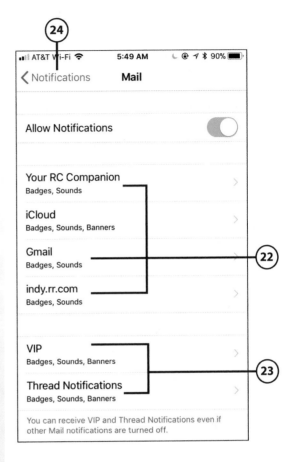

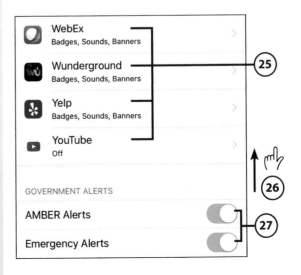

>>>Go Further

NOTIFY THIS

Here are some other hopefully useful notification tidbits for your consideration:

- **VIPs**—Mail supports VIPs, which are people from whom email messages are treated specially, such as having a dedicated mailbox in the Mail app. You can apply specific notification settings to VIP messages using the VIP notification option. These override the notification settings for the email account to which messages from VIPs are sent.

- **Threads**—Mail can keep related messages together as threads. Like VIP messages, you can override Mail's notifications for messages that are part of threads using the Thread Notifications option.

- **Special sounds and vibrations for contacts**—You can override some app's sounds and vibration notification settings for individuals in your Contacts app. For example, you can configure a specific ringtone, new text tone, and vibrations for calls or texts from a contact. You do this using the contact information screen as explained in Chapter 6, "Managing Contacts."

- **Installed app not shown**—You must have opened an app at least once for it to appear on the Notifications screen.

- **Initial notification prompt**—The first time you open many apps, you are prompted to allow that app to send you notifications. If you allow this, the app is able to send notifications about its activity. If you deny this, the app isn't able to send notifications. You can always configure the app's notifications using the steps in this task regardless of your initial decision.

- **Lots of apps**—If you have a lot of apps or activity on your iPhone, notifications can become disruptive. It can take a little time to set each app's notifications, but making sure you receive only the notifications that are important to you prevents your iPhone from bothering you unnecessarily.

- **Limiting notifications**—Visual and auditory notifications can be distracting and annoying. You should configure these so they happen only when something you really care about occurs, such as when you receive a new email from a VIP or a text message arrives. For less important activity, configure the app's notifications so that they appear in the Notification Center, but have no banner, audible, or vibratory options enabled. For those apps whose activity is not important at all, disable all notifications.

Scheduling Do Not Disturb

As you learned in Chapter 1 "Getting Started with Your iPhone," the Do Not Disturb feature enables you to temporarily silence notifications; you can also configure quiet times during which notifications are automatically silenced by performing the following steps:

(1) Open the Settings app and tap Do Not Disturb.

(2) To activate Do Not Disturb manually, set the Manual switch to on (green). (This does the same thing as activating it from the Control Center as explained in Chapter 1.)

(3) To configure Do Not Disturb to activate automatically on a schedule, set the Scheduled switch to on (green).

(4) Tap the From and To box.

⑤ Tap From.

⑥ Swipe on the time selection wheels to select the hour and minute (AM or PM) when you want the Do Not Disturb period to start.

⑦ Tap To.

⑧ Swipe on the time selection wheels to set the hour and minute (AM or PM) when you want the Do Not Disturb period to end.

⑨ Tap Back.

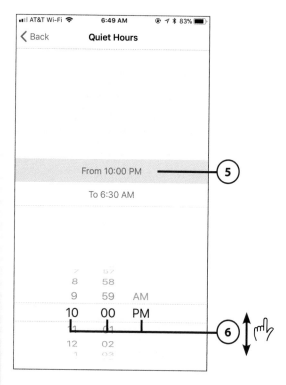

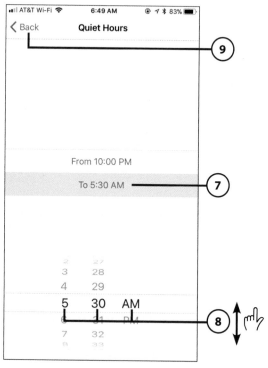

10 If you want notifications to be silenced during the Do Not Disturb period only when your phone is locked, tap While iPhone is locked. Tap Always if you want notifications to be silenced regardless of the Lock status. The While iPhone is locked setting presumes that if your iPhone is unlocked, you won't mind taking calls or having notifications even if it is within the Do Not Disturb period because you are probably using the phone.

11 Tap Allow Calls From.

12 Tap the option for the group of people whose calls should be allowed during the Do Not Disturb period. The options are Everyone, which allows all calls to come in; No One, which sends all calls directly to voicemail; Favorites, which allows calls from people on your Favorites lists to come through but calls from all others go to voicemail; or one of your contact groups, which allows calls from anyone in the selected group to come through while all others go to voicemail.

13 Tap Back.

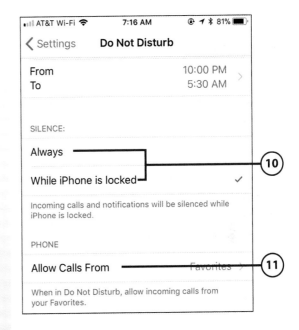

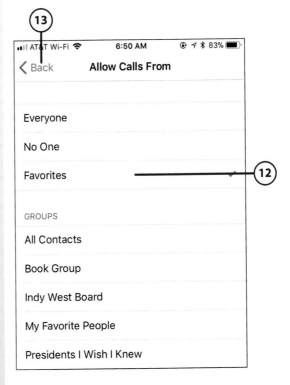

14 Set the Repeated Calls switch to on (green) if you want a second call from the same person within three minutes to be allowed through. This feature is based on the assumption that if a call is really important, the person calling you will try again immediately.

15 Tap Activate in the DO NOT DISTURB WHILE DRIVING section.

16 To have Do Not Disturb activate automatically when you are driving, tap Automatically to have this based on your iPhone's motion (once the iPhone's accelerometer detects that the phone has reached a particular speed) or When Connected to Car Bluetooth to have Do Not Disturb active whenever your iPhone is connected to your car's Bluetooth system; to prevent this type of automatic activation, tap Manually.

17 Tap Do Not Disturb.

18 Tap Auto-Reply To.

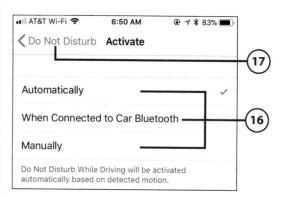

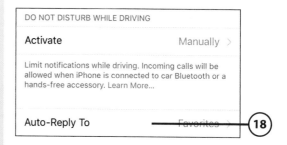

19 Configure when you want automatic replies to be sent when Do Not Disturb is on (regardless of how it was activated) by tapping No One to prevent automatic replies; Recents to send replies to people on your recent lists (such as calls you have recently received); Favorites to send replies to your favorites; or All Contacts to automatically reply to anyone on your Contacts lists.

20 Tap Back.

21 Tap Auto-Reply.

22 Type the message you want to be automatically sent.

23 Tap Do Not Disturb. During the Do Not Disturb period or based on the DO NOT DISTURB WHILE DRIVING setting, your iPhone is silent, except for any exceptions you configured. Automatic replies are sent according to your configuration. When the scheduled Do Not Disturb period ends, your iPhone resumes its normal notification activity.

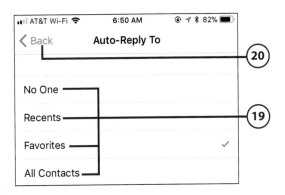

Configuring the Control Center

As you learned in Chapters 1 and 2, the Control Center provides quick access to a number of your iPhone's features and tools. The top part of the Control Center screen always contains the same controls, but you can configure the controls toward the bottom of the Control Center by performing the following steps:

(1) Open the Settings app and tap Control Center.

(2) To be able to access the Control Center while you are using apps, set the Access Within Apps switch to on (green). If you set this to off, you need to move back to a Home or the Lock screen to use the Control Center.

(3) Tap Customize Controls. The Customize screen has two sections: INCLUDE shows the tools installed in your Control Center, whereas MORE CONTROLS shows tools that are available for you to add to the Control Center.

(4) To remove a tool from the Control Center, tap its Unlock (–) icon.

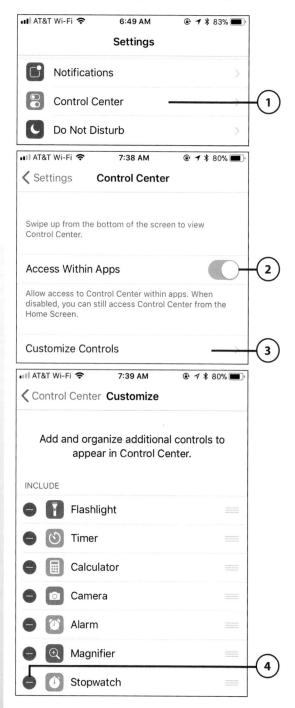

5 Tap Remove. The tool is moved from the INCLUDE list to the MORE CONTROLS list. This means it no longer appears on the Control Center, but remains available should you want to add it again.

6 To add a control to the Control Center, tap its Add (+) icon. The control moves to the bottom of the INCLUDE list.

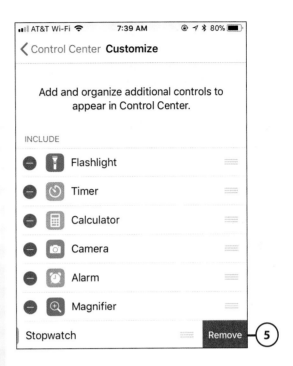

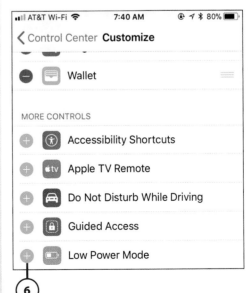

7) Move a control higher on the Control Center by dragging its Order (three lines) icon up the INCLUDE list or move it lower by dragging its Order icon down the list. The top four controls on the list appear first in the customizable part of the Control Center; the next four are below those, and so on.

8) Repeat steps 4 through 7 until you have all the controls you want on the Control Center in the order you want them. The next time you open the Control Center, it reflects the changes you made.

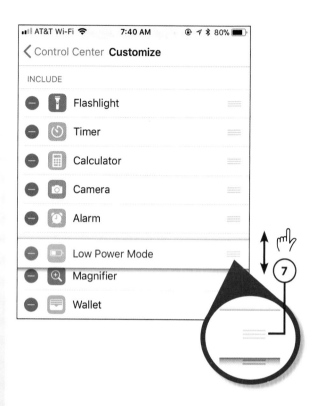

Your Control Center Options Are Limited

There are more controls on the Control Center than you see on the Customize screen. You can't change some of the Control Center's options. For example, you always see the Airplane Mode, Cellular Data, Wi-Fi, and Bluetooth icons on the Control Center. The area you can customize is below the Screen Mirroring, Brightness, and Volume controls.

Configuring the Widget Center

As described in Chapters 1 and 2, the Widget Center provides quick access to widgets that enable you to take action or to view information. You can determine which widgets are shown in the Widget Center and the order in which those widgets appear on the screen; for example, you might want your most frequently used widgets to be at the top of the screen.

To configure the Widget Center, perform the following steps:

(1) Open the Widget Center by moving to a Home screen and swiping all the way to the right.

(2) Swipe all the way up the screen.

(3) Tap Edit. You see the Add Widgets screen. This screen has two sections. At the top are the currently installed widgets; installed widgets have the Unlock icon next to their icons. Toward the bottom of the screen, you see the MORE WIDGETS section that shows you available widgets that aren't currently in your Widget Center.

(4) To remove a widget from the Widget Center, tap its Unlock (–) icon.

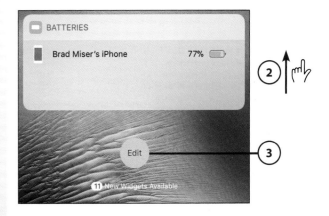

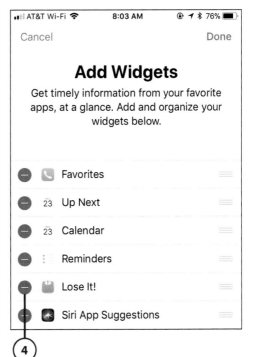

5 Tap Remove. The widget is removed from your Widget Center and moved onto the MORE WIDGETS list.

6 Swipe up the screen until you see the MORE WIDGETS section. Widgets that are new since the last time you viewed this list are marked with a blue circle.

7 To add a widget to the Widget Center, tap its Add (+) icon. The widget jumps up the screen to become the last widget on the list of widgets in the Widget Center.

8 To change where a widget appears in the Widget Center, drag its Order icon up or down the screen. When it is in the position you want, take your finger off the screen and the widget is placed there.

9 Repeat steps 4 through 8 until the Widget Center contains the widgets you want to access, in the order in which you want them to be shown.

10 When you're done making changes to the Widget Center, tap Done. You return to the Widget Center and see the results of the changes you've made.

New Widgets

When new widgets become available, you see a message under Edit on the Widget Center screen. Tap this to move into Edit mode, so you can see the new widgets and add them to the Widget Center if you want to use them.

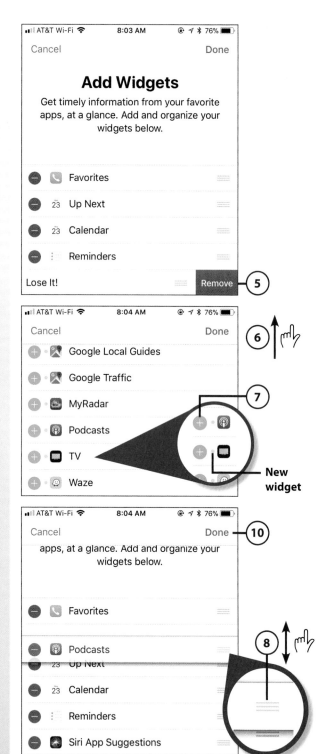

New widget

Setting Keyboard, Language, and Format Options

You'll be working with text in many apps on your iPhone. You can customize a number of keyboard- and format-related options so text appears and behaves the way you want it to.

Setting Keyboard Preferences

You use the iPhone's keyboard to input text in many apps, including Mail, Messages, and so on. A number of settings determine how the keyboard works.

1. On the Settings screen, tap General.

2. Swipe up the screen.

3. Tap Keyboard.

4. Tap Keyboards. This enables you to activate more keyboards so that you can choose a specific language's keyboard when you are entering text. At the top of the screen, you see the keyboards that are available to you.

5. Tap Add New Keyboard.

Fun in Text

The Emoji keyboard allows you to include a huge variety of smiley faces, symbols, and other icons whenever you type. The Emoji keyboard is active by default; however, if you don't see it on the list of active keyboards, you can use these steps to activate it.

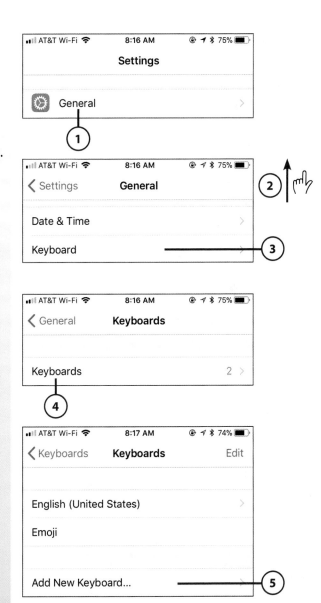

6. Swipe up and down the screen to browse the available keyboards.

7. Tap the keyboard you want to add.

8. Tap the keyboard you added in step 7.

9. Tap the keyboard layout you want to use. (Not all keyboards support options; if the one you are configuring doesn't, skip this step.)

10. Tap Keyboards.

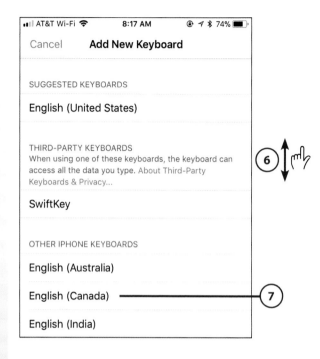

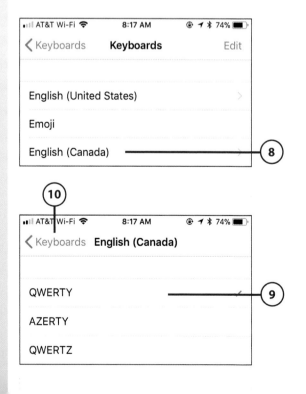

11 Repeat steps 5–10 to add and configure additional keyboards.

12 Tap Keyboards.

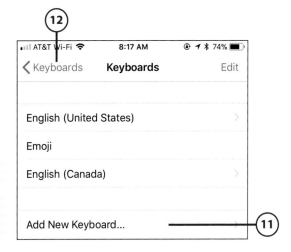

>>>Go Further

THIRD-PARTY KEYBOARDS

You can install and use keyboards from third parties (meaning not Apple) on your iPhone. To do this, open the App Store app and search for "keyboards for iPhone" or you can search for a specific keyboard by name if you know of one you want to try. (See "Using the App Store App to Find and Install iPhone Apps," later in this chapter for help using the App Store app.) After you have downloaded the keyboard you want to use, use steps 1–5 to move back to the Keyboards Settings screen. When you open the Add New Keyboard screen, you see a section called THIRD-PARTY KEYBOARDS in which you see the additional keyboards you have installed. Tap a keyboard in this section to activate it as you do with the default keyboards. When you move back to the Keyboards screen, you see the keyboard you just activated. Tap it to configure its additional options. Then you can use the new keyboard just like the others you have activated. Make sure you check out the documentation for any keyboards you download so you take advantage of all of their features.

(13) Tap One Handed Keyboard.

(14) To be able to use the one-handed keyboard (which squishes all the keys toward one side of the screen), tap Left to place it on the left side or Right to put it on the right side of the screen; tap Off if you don't want to use the one-handed keyboard.

(15) Tap Back.

(16) To prevent your iPhone from automatically capitalizing as you type, set Auto-Capitalization to off (white).

(17) To disable the automatic spell checking/correction, set Auto-Correction to off (white).

(18) To disable the iPhone's Spell Checker, set the Check Spelling switch to off (white).

(19) To disable the Caps Lock function, set the Enable Caps Lock to off (white).

(20) To disable the iPhone's Predictive Text feature (see Chapter 2), set the Predictive switch to off (white).

Language Options

The keyboard options you see depend on the language being used. For example, if settings apply only to a specific language, you see them in that language's section.

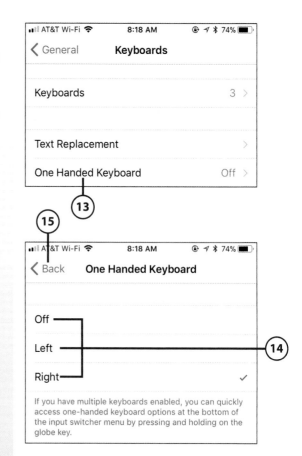

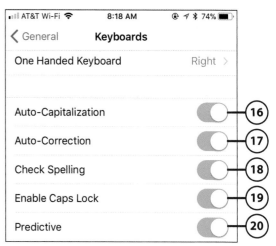

(21) To prevent the iPhone from automatically trying to correct your punctuation, set the Smart Punctuation switch to off (white).

(22) To prevent the character you type from being shown in a magnified pop-up as you type it, set the Character Preview switch to off (white).

(23) To disable the shortcut that types a period followed by a space when you tap the space key twice, set the "." Shortcut switch to off (white). You must tap a period and the space key to type these characters when you end a sentence.

(24) To disable the iPhone's dictation feature, set the Enable Dictation switch to off (white). The microphone key won't appear on the keyboard and you won't be able to dictate text.

(25) If dictation is enabled, tap Dictation Languages.

(26) If you don't want to be able to use dictation with a language, tap it so that it doesn't have a check mark. If you do want to be able to dictate in a listed language, ensure it has a check mark (if it doesn't, tap it).

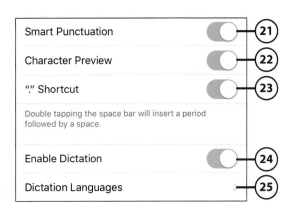

Changing Keyboards

To delete a keyboard, move to the Keyboards Settings screen and swipe to the left on the keyboard you want to remove. Tap Delete. The keyboard is removed from the list of activated keyboards and is no longer available to you when you type. (You can always activate it again later.) To change the order in which keyboards appear, move to the Keyboards screen, tap Edit, and drag the keyboards up and down the screen. When you've finished, tap Done. (An explanation of how to switch between keyboards when you type is provided in Chapter 2.)

Creating and Working with Text Replacements

Text replacements are useful because you can use just a few letters to type a series of words. You type the replacement, and it is replaced by the phrase with which it is associated. To configure your text replacements, do the following:

1. Move to the Keyboards screen as described in steps 1–3 in the previous task.

2. Tap Text Replacement.

3. Review the current replacements.

4. To add a replacement, tap Add (+).

5. Type the phrase for which you want to create a replacement.

6. Type the shortcut you want to be replaced by the phrase you created in step 5.

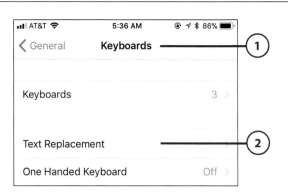

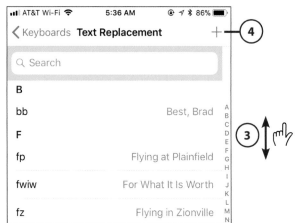

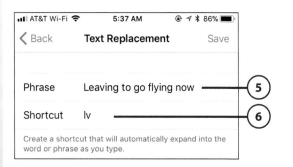

(**7**) Tap Save. If the replacement doesn't contain any disallowed characters, it is created and you move back to the Text Replacement screen where you see your new text replacement. If there is an error, you see an explanation of the error; you must correct it before you can create the replacement. When you type the shortcut, it is replaced by the phrase associated with it.

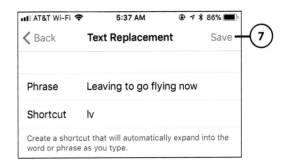

(**8**) Repeat steps 4–7 to create other text replacements.

(**9**) When you've created all the replacements you want, tap Keyboards.

Shortcuts to Replacements

To change a replacement, tap it. Use the resulting screen to change the phrase or shortcut, and tap Save to update the replacement. To remove a replacement, swipe to the left on it and tap Delete. To search for a replacement, tap in the Search bar at the top of the screen and type the replacements you want to see; you can also use the index along the right side of the screen to find replacements. You can also tap Edit on the Shortcuts screen to change your replacements. And, yes, you can create a phrase without a shortcut, but I don't really see much use for that!

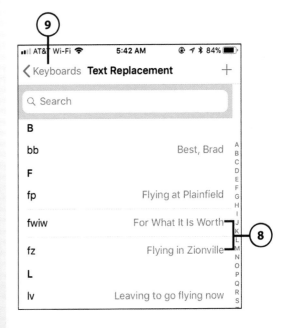

Setting Language and Region Preferences

There are a number of formatting preferences you can set that determine how information is formatted in various apps. For example, you can choose how addresses are formatted by default by choosing the region whose format you want to follow.

① On the Settings screen, tap General.

② Swipe up the screen.

③ Tap Language & Region.

④ Tap iPhone Language.

⑤ Swipe up and down the screen to view the languages with which your iPhone can work or tap in the Search bar and type a language you want to use to find it. The current language is marked with a check mark.

⑥ Tap the language you want to use.

⑦ Tap Done.

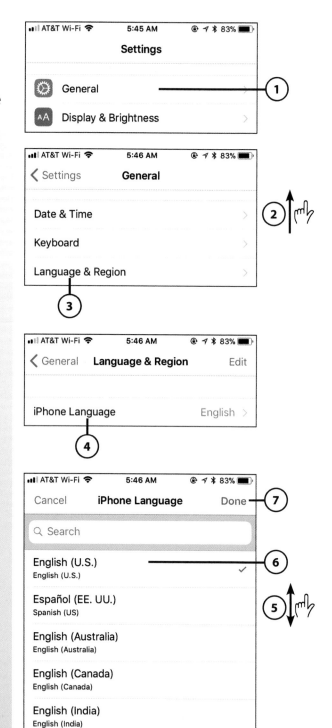

8 Tap to confirm the change in language you indicated. Your iPhone screen goes dark while the iPhone switches to the new language. When it comes back, you return to the Language & Region screen, and the language you selected starts being used.

9 Tap Add Language.

10 Using steps 5–7, find and tap a secondary language. This language is used when your primary language can't be, such as on websites that don't support your primary language.

11 Tap Done.

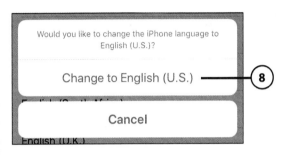

Would you like to change the iPhone language to English (U.S.)?

Change to English (U.S.) —— **8**

Cancel

English (U.K.)

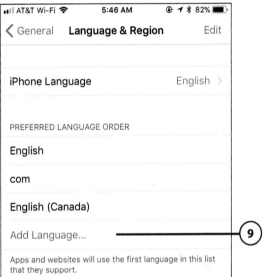

AT&T Wi-Fi ❤   5:46 AM   @ ✈ ✳ 82% ■

‹ General   **Language & Region**   Edit

iPhone Language   English ›

PREFERRED LANGUAGE ORDER

English

com

English (Canada)

Add Language... ———————————— **9**

Apps and websites will use the first language in this list that they support.

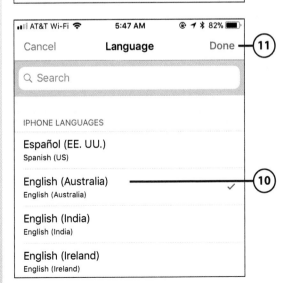

AT&T Wi-Fi ❤   5:47 AM   @ ✈ ✳ 82% ■

Cancel   **Language**   Done —— **11**

Q Search

IPHONE LANGUAGES

Español (EE. UU.)
Spanish (US)

English (Australia) ———————————— **10**
English (Australia)   ✓

English (India)
English (India)

English (Ireland)
English (Ireland)

12 Tap the language you want to be primary to confirm it. The language you selected is configured and you move back to the Language & Region screen. The new language is shown on the list in the center of the screen.

Order, Order!

To change the order of preference for the languages you have configured, tap Edit, drag the languages up or down the screen to set their order, and tap Done to save your changes.

13 To add more languages, tap Add Language and follow steps 10–12 to add more languages.

14 Tap Region.

15 Swipe up and down the regions available to you. The current region is marked with a check mark.

16 Tap the region whose formatting you want to use; if there are options within a region, you move to an additional screen and can tap the specific option you want to use.

17 Tap Done.

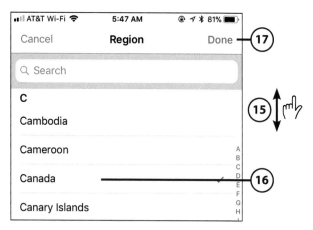

18 If you've changed the region, tap the language you want to use as the primary iPhone language. Your iPhone starts using the formatting associated with the region you selected.

19 Tap Calendar.

20 Tap the calendar you want your iPhone to use.

21 Tap Back.

22 Tap Temperature Unit.

23 Tap the unit in which you want temperatures to be displayed.

24 Tap Back.

25 Swipe up until you see the bottom of the screen where there are examples of the format options you have selected, such as the time and date format.

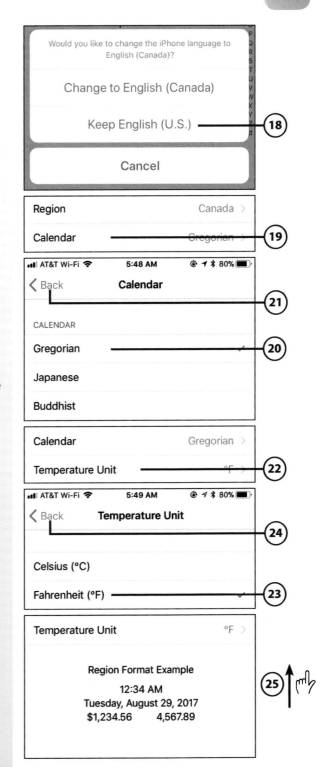

Setting Privacy and Location Services Preferences

Using its GPS or network connection, your iPhone's Location Services feature can determine where the phone is. This is useful in many situations, such as in the Maps app when you want to generate directions. Lots of other apps use this capability, too, such as apps that provide you location-specific information (the Uber app uses it to determine your location when you request a ride, for example). You can configure certain aspects of how these services work. And, if you don't want specific apps to be able to access your iPhone's current location, you can disable this feature for those apps. Of course, if you do, apps that rely on this capability don't work properly (they prompt you to allow access to this service as you try to use them).

You can also determine which apps can access certain kinds of information, such as the apps that are able to access your contact information in the Contacts app.

To configure privacy settings, do the following:

(1) Move to the Settings screen and tap Privacy.

(2) Tap Location Services.

3 To disable Location Services for all apps, set the Location Services switch to off (white); to leave it enabled, skip to step 5.

4 Tap Turn Off at the prompt. No apps are able to identify your location; skip the rest of these steps because they don't apply when Location Services is disabled.

5 Tap Share My Location. You can share your location with others in several areas, such as the Messages app.

6 To prevent your location from being shared, set the Share My Location switch to off (white) and skip to step 10. If you leave this switch on (green), move to the next step.

7 Tap From.

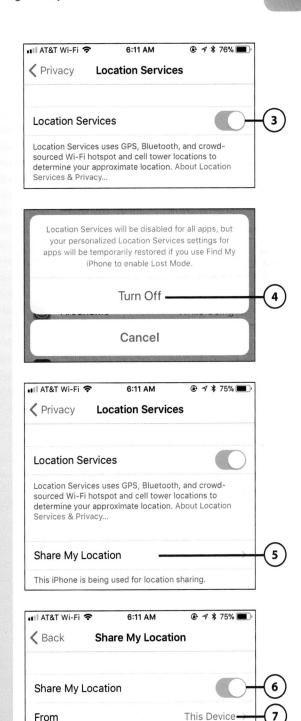

8 Tap the device that should be used to identify your location (this only applies if you have multiple devices configured with your Apple ID).

9 Tap Back.

10 Tap Back.

11 Swipe up and down the list of apps on the Location Services screen. These are all the apps that have requested access to your iPhone's location. Along the right side of the screen, you see the current status of Location Sharing for the app. Always means that the app can always access your location. While Using means the app can only access your location information while you are using it. Never means that using location information for the app has been disabled (some apps don't work properly when set to this status). Apps marked with a purple arrow have recently accessed your location; those that have done so within the past 24 hours are marked with a gray arrow. An outline purple arrow indicates that the app is using a geofence, which is a perimeter around a location that defines an area that is used to trigger some event, such as a reminder.

12 Tap an app to configure its access to Location Services.

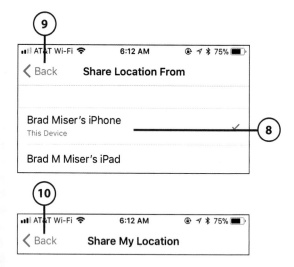

9

| ₌₁₁ AT&T Wi-Fi 🗢 | 6:12 AM | @ ⌁ ⚹ 75% ▪️ |

‹ Back   **Share Location From**

Brad Miser's iPhone
This Device   ✓   **8**

Brad M Miser's iPad

10

| ₌₁₁ AT&T Wi-Fi 🗢 | 6:12 AM | @ ⌁ ⚹ 75% ▪️ |

‹ Back   **Share My Location**

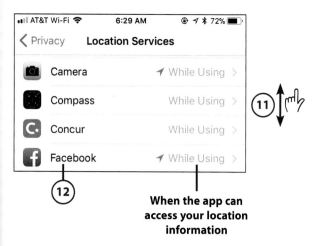

| ₌₁₁ AT&T Wi-Fi 🗢 | 6:29 AM | @ ⌁ ⚹ 72% ▪️ |

‹ Privacy   **Location Services**

📷 Camera   ⌁ While Using ›

▦ Compass   While Using ›

C. Concur   While Using ›

f Facebook   ⌁ While Using ›

11

12

When the app can
access your location
information

Share with Family?

The iPhone's Family Sharing feature enables you to designate up to five other people as a family (they don't actually have to be related to you in any way). When you do this, you can allow members of this group to share content you have downloaded, such as music or movies, from the iTunes Store. You can also share your location information with them. When Family Sharing is enabled, you see the members of the family group on the Share My Location screen. You can tap each person and tap Share My Location to share your location with that person. The people in your family with whom you share your location can see it in the Find Friends app.

13 Tap the status in which you want to place the app's access to your location. Some apps only have the Always or Never options, whereas others also have the While Using the App option.

14 Tap Back.

15 Repeat steps 12–14 for each app whose access to your location you want to configure.

16 Tap System Services.

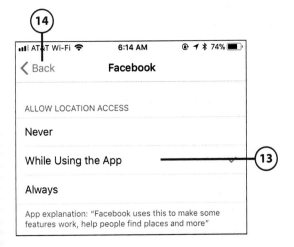

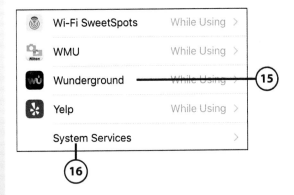

17 Enable or disable Location Services for the System Services you see. As with apps, if you disable Location Services for a system function, it might not work properly.

18 Tap Back.

19 Tap Privacy. Next, allow or prevent apps or other services from accessing data stored on your iPhone.

20 Tap an app or service on the list; this example shows Bluetooth Sharing. A list of apps that have requested to use the app's data or a service (in this example, Bluetooth) is displayed. If the requesting app or service is able to use the app's data, its switch is on (green).

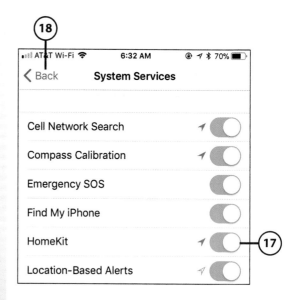

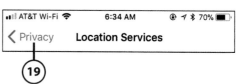

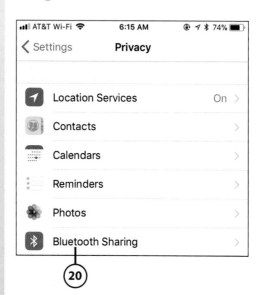

(21) Prevent a requesting app or service from accessing the app's data by setting its switch to off (white). That app is no longer able to use the data it requested (which can inhibit some of its functionality).

(22) Tap Privacy.

(23) Repeat steps 20–22 for each app or service on the list. Most of time, you can just leave the permissions with the default setting (unless you want to block a specific app from using a certain kind of data).

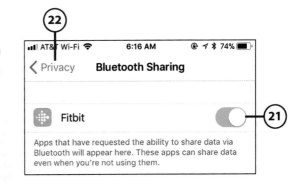

>>>Go Further
MORE ON SYSTEM SERVICES

One of the System Services is Significant Locations. This service tracks places you visit. This information is used to improve the performance of some apps. If you want to prevent this, tap Significant Locations, enter your passcode or touch the Touch ID/Home button, and then set the Significant Locations switch to off (white).

You can use the switches in the PRODUCT IMPROVEMENT section to enable or disable various types of information from being collected, such as what is popular near you.

Use the Status Bar Icon switch to enable or disable the Location Services arrow at the top of the screen when a system service is accessing location information. (This arrow always appears when apps use location information.)

>>>Go Further
MORE ON PRIVACY

At the bottom of the Privacy screen, you see Analytics. Under this section, you can determine if information about performance of apps and your device is communicated back to Apple. You can also determine if information about the performance of apps is shared with app developers.

You also see the Advertising option. If you tap this, you can limit the tracking of ads you view by setting the Limit Ad Tracking switch to on (green). Typically, this tracking is used by advertisers to present ads that are related to ads you have viewed (the point being to make the ads more effective). You can reset the identifier used to identify you by tapping Reset Advertising Identifier and then tapping Reset Identifier. You can tap View Ad Information to see your status with respect to advertising in Apple apps.

Configuring Passcode, Touch ID, and Content Restrictions

Your iPhone contains data you probably don't want others to access. You can (and should) require a passcode so your iPhone can't be unlocked without the proper passcode being entered. This gives you a measure of protection should you lose control of your phone. If you have an iPhone 5s or later, you can record your fingerprints so that you can unlock your phone (by automatically entering the passcode) and enter your Apple ID password by touching the Touch ID/Home button. The capability can also be used in other apps and services that require confirmation, such as Apple Pay, banking apps, and others.

You can also restrict the access to specific content and apps on your phone. Suppose you let other people borrow your iPhone but don't want them to use certain apps or to see data you'd rather keep to yourself. You can enable a restriction to prevent someone from accessing these areas without entering the restriction code. You can also restrict the use of apps, movies, music, and other content based on the age rating that the app or other content has.

Configuring Your Passcode and Touch ID

To configure the passcode you have to enter to unlock your iPhone, perform the following steps (note these steps show an iPhone that supports Touch ID; if your model doesn't have this, the steps are slightly different as you will only be configuring a passcode):

iPhone X and Face ID

The iPhone X uses Face ID instead of Touch ID. For help configuring and working with Face ID, download the online supplement *My iPhone X* by going to www.informit.com/myiphoneseniors.

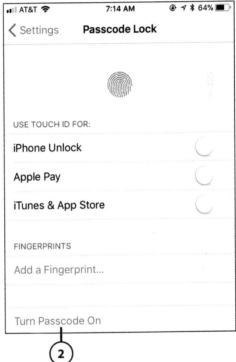

1 On the Settings screen, tap Touch ID & Passcode.

2 Tap Turn Passcode On.

Already Have a Passcode?

When you first turned your iPhone on, you were prompted to create a passcode and to record a fingerprint for Touch ID. If your iPhone already has a passcode set, when you perform step 1, you're prompted to enter your current passcode. When you enter it correctly, you move to the Passcode Lock screen, and you can make changes to the current passcode, add new fingerprints, and so on. In that case, you can skip directly to step 5. If you want to change your current passcode, tap Change Passcode and follow steps 3 and 4 to change it. Then continue with step 5.

3 Enter a six-digit passcode.

4 Re-enter the passcode. If the two passcodes match, the passcode is set.

5 If you have an Apple ID config-ured, enter your Apple ID pass-word; if you don't have an Apple ID configured, skip to step 7.

6 Tap Continue.

7 Tap Require Passcode; when you use Touch ID to unlock your iPhone, you don't have an option for when the passcode is required, so if you are going to or already use Touch ID, skip to step 10.

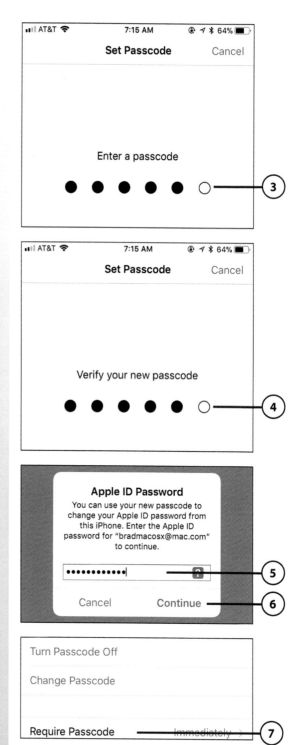

(8) Tap the amount of time the iPhone is locked before the passcode takes effect. The shorter this time is, the more secure your iPhone is, but also the more frequently you'll have to enter the passcode if your iPhone locks frequently.

(9) Tap Back.

(10) If you have an iPhone 5s or later, tap Add a Fingerprint and continue to step 11; if you have a model that doesn't support Touch ID, skip to step 25.

(11) Touch the finger you want to record to the Touch ID/Home button, but don't press it. An image of a fingerprint appears.

(12) Leave your finger on the Touch ID/Home button until you feel the phone vibrate, which indicates part of your fingerprint has been recorded and you see some segments turn red. The parts of your fingerprint that are recorded are indicated by the red segments; gray segments are not recorded yet. This step captures the center part of your finger.

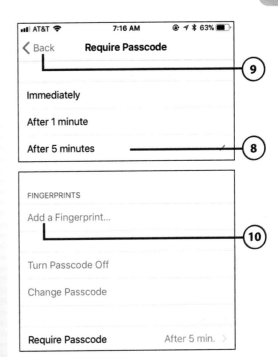

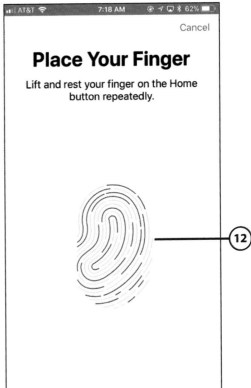

13 Lift your finger off the Touch ID/ Home button and touch the button again, adjusting your finger on the button to record other parts that currently show gray lines instead of red ones. Other segments of your fingerprint are recorded.

14 Repeat step 13 until all the segments are red. You are prompted to change your grip so you can record more of your fingerprint.

15 Tap Continue.

16 Repeat step 13, again placing other areas of your finger to fill in more gray lines with red. This step captures the fingerprints more toward the edges of your fingers. When the entire fingerprint is covered in red lines, you see the Complete screen.

17 Tap Continue. The fingerprint is recorded and you move back to the Touch ID & Passcode screen. You see the fingerprint that has been recorded.

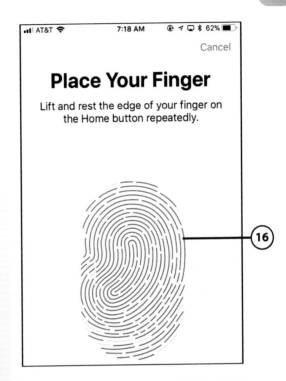

18 Tap the fingerprint you recorded.

19 Give the fingerprint a name.

20 Tap Passcode Lock.

21 Repeat steps 10–20 to record up to five fingerprints. These can be yours or someone else's if you want to allow another person to access your iPhone.

22 To be able to use Touch ID to unlock your iPhone, ensure the iPhone Unlock switch is set to on (green).

23 To use your fingerprint to make Apple Pay payments, set the Apple Pay switch to on (green). (Refer to the online Chapter 15, "Working with Other Useful iPhone Apps and Features," for more information about Apple Pay.)

24 If it isn't enabled already and you want to also be able to enter your Apple ID password by touching your finger to the Touch ID/Home button, set the iTunes & App Store switch to on (green). You need to enter your Apple ID password and tap Continue to complete this configuration.

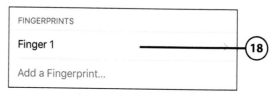

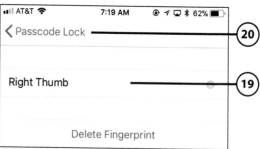

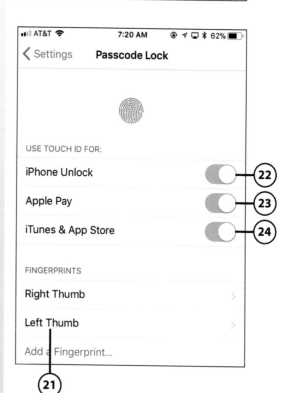

25 Swipe up the screen until you see the Voice Dial switch.

26 To prevent Voice Dial from working, set the Voice Dial switch to off (white). (Voice Dial enables you to make calls by speaking even if you don't use Siri.)

27 Use the switches in the ALLOW ACCESS WHEN LOCKED section to enable or disable the related functions when your iPhone is locked. The options include Today View (the Today section of the Notification Center), Recent Notifications, Control Center, Siri, Reply with Message, Home Control, Wallet, and Return Missed Calls. If you set a switch to off (white), you won't be able to access the corresponding function when your iPhone is locked.

28 If you want the iPhone to automatically erase all your data after an incorrect passcode has been entered 10 times, set the Erase Data switch to on (green). If someone was trying to guess your passcode so they could unlock your iPhone, all its data would be erased when the tenth try failed.

29 Tap Enable.

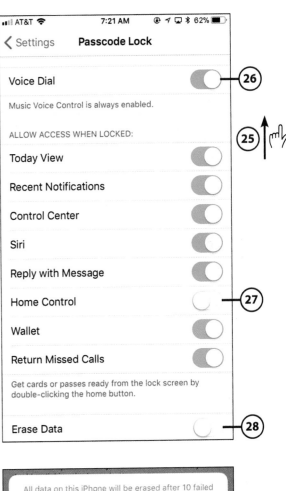

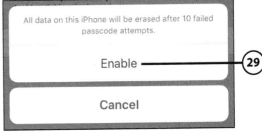

>>>Go Further

BE SECURE

Here are some additional tidbits to help you with your iPhone's security:

- **Touch ID and Apps**—The first time you launch an app that supports Touch ID, you're prompted to enable Touch ID in that app. If you allow this, you can log into the associated account by touching the Touch ID button, just like you unlock your phone or use Apple Pay.

- **Automatic Erase**—When you have enabled the Erase Data function and you enter an incorrect passcode when unlocking your iPhone, you see a counter showing the number of unsuccessful attempts. When this reaches 10, all the data on your iPhone is erased on the next unsuccessful attempt.

- **Making Changes**—Any time you want to make changes to your passcode and fingerprint (iPhone 5s or later) settings, move back to the Passcode Lock screen by tapping Touch ID & Passcode and entering your passcode. To disable the passcode (not recommended), tap Turn Passcode Off, tap Turn Off, and enter the passcode. To change your passcode, tap Change Passcode. You then enter your current passcode and enter your new passcode twice. You return to the Passcode Lock screen, and the new passcode takes effect. You can change the other settings similar to how you set them initially as described in these steps. For example, you can add new fingerprints. To remove a fingerprint, move to the Fingerprints screen, swipe to the left on the fingerprint you want to remove, and tap Delete.

- **Automatic Locking**—For security purposes, you should configure your iPhone so that it locks automatically after a specific amount of idle time passes. To do this, you use the Auto-Lock setting on the Display & Brightness settings screen as explained in Chapter 5.

- **Complex Passcode**—By default, your passcode is a simple six-digit number. If you want to have a more complex (and more secure) passcode, on the Create or Change Passcode screen, tap Passcode Options. You are prompted to create a new, complex passcode. You can choose Custom Alphanumeric Code, Custom Numeric Code, or 4-Digit Numeric Code (this is a less secure option and I don't recommend it). Choose the option you want and then follow the onscreen prompts to create it. The Alphanumeric Code option is the most secure, especially if you use a code that is eight characters or longer that includes both letters and numbers. The steps to set a complex passcode are similar; the difference is that you use the keyboard and numeric keypad to configure the passcode instead of just the numeric keypad.

Setting Restrictions for Content and Apps

To restrict access to content or apps, perform the following steps:

1. On the Settings screen, tap General.

2. Swipe up the screen until you see Restrictions.

3. Tap Restrictions.

4. Tap Enable Restrictions.

5. Create a Restrictions Passcode. You have to enter this passcode to change the content restrictions or to be able to access restricted content.

6. Re-enter your Restrictions Passcode. You return to the Restrictions screen, and the Allow switches are enabled.

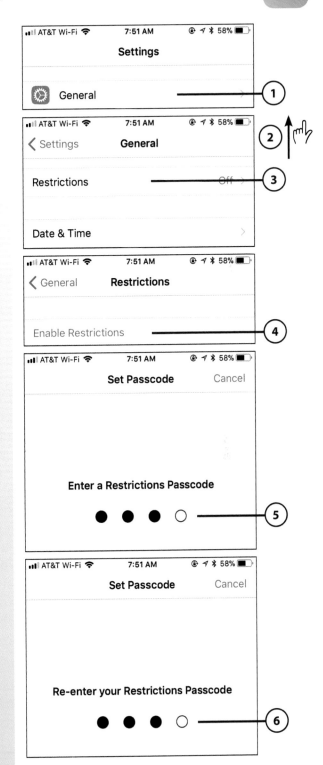

(7) In the ALLOW section, set the switch next to each function you want to disable to off (white). For example, to prevent FaceTime calls, set the FaceTime switch to off (white); the FaceTime icon is removed from the Home screen and can't be used. With the other controls, you can prevent access to Safari, the Camera, Siri & Dictation, AirDrop, CarPlay, the iTunes Store, and so on.

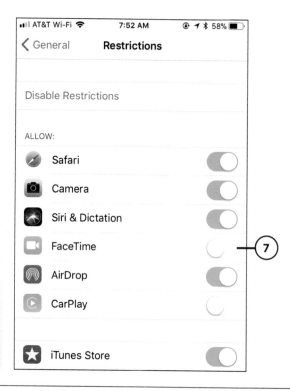

Dueling Passcodes

Your iPhone can have two passcodes: the Lock passcode and the Restrictions passcode. Each controls access to its respective functions. Limiting access to content and apps likely means you will be letting someone else use your phone. The person who will be using your iPhone might need to be able to unlock it unless you want to have to unlock it for them. If you want to allow them to unlock the phone but want to restrict access to your Apple Pay information or Apple ID, create a fingerprint for that person, but disable Touch ID for Apple Pay and iTunes & App Stores (see the previous task for details). This enables the person to unlock and use your iPhone; you can control what they can do by setting a Restrictions passcode and configuring permissions as described in these steps. (You don't want to give the person the passcode to the phone as that defeats the purpose of configuring restrictions.)

In-App Purchases

Some apps, especially games, allow you to make purchases while you are using the app. For example, you can buy additional levels for a game. To prevent in-app purchases, set the In-App Purchases switch to off (white). This is especially important if you let your phone be used by children or others who might inadvertently make purchases you don't want made.

8 Swipe up to see the ALLOWED CONTENT section.

9 Tap Ratings For.

10 Tap the country whose rating system you want to use for content on your iPhone.

Whose Ratings?

The country you select in step 10 determines the options you see in the remaining steps because the restrictions available depend on the location you select. These steps show the United States rating systems; if you select a different country, you see rating options for that country instead.

11 Tap Restrictions.

12 Tap Music, Podcasts & News.

13 To prevent content tagged as explicit from being played, set the EXPLICIT switch to off (white). Explicit content will not be available in the associated apps, such as Music or News.

14 Tap Back.

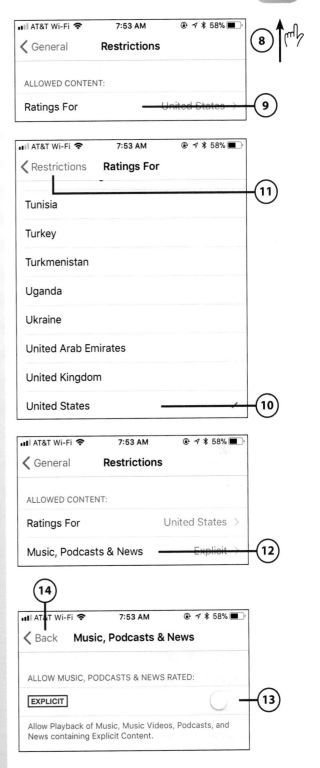

15 Tap Movies.

16 Tap the highest rating of movies
that you want to be playable (for
example, tap PG-13 to prevent
R and NC-17 movies from playing); tap Allow All Movies to allow
any movie to be played; or tap
Don't Allow Movies to prevent
any movie content from playing. Prevented movie ratings are
highlighted in red.

17 To prevent movies from being
streamed to the iPhone, set the
Show Movies in the Cloud switch
to off (white).

18 Tap Restrictions.

19 Tap TV Shows and use the resulting screen to set the highest
rating of TV shows that you want
to be playable (for example, tap
TV-14 to prevent TV-MA shows
from playing); tap Allow All TV
Shows to allow any show to be
played; or tap Don't Allow TV
Shows to prevent any TV content
from playing. Prevented ratings
are highlighted in red. Use the
Show TV Shows in the Cloud
switch to allow or prevent TV
content from streaming on the
iPhone. Tap Restrictions to return
to the Restrictions screen.

20 Use the Books option to enable
or disable access to sexually
explicit books.

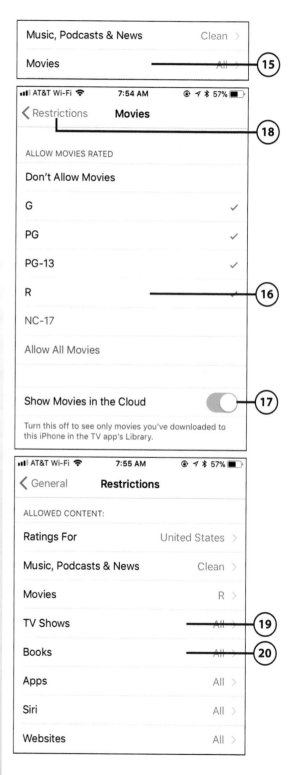

21 Tap Apps and set the highest rating of app that you want to be available (for example, tap 12+ to prevent 17+ applications from working); tap Allow All Apps to allow any application to be used; or tap Don't Allow Apps to prevent all applications. Tap Restrictions to return to the Restrictions screen.

22 Use the Siri option to restrict explicit language or content during web searches.

23 Use the Websites option to control the websites that can be accessed. The options are to limit sites with adult content or to allow only specific websites to be visited. When you select the Specific Websites Only option, you can create a list of sites and only those sites can be visited.

24 Swipe up the screen until you see the PRIVACY section.

25 Use the settings in the PRIVACY section to determine whether apps can access information stored in each area and whether they should be locked in their current states. For example, you can prevent apps from accessing your calendars or photos. Configuring these is similar to the Privacy settings you read about earlier in this chapter.

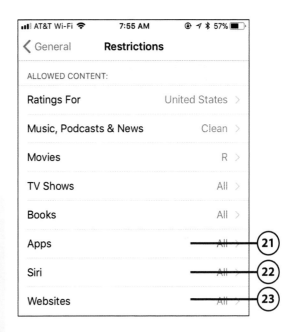

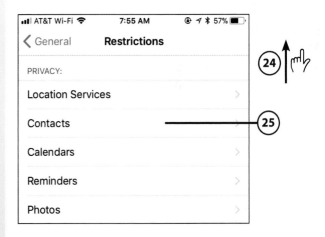

(26) Swipe up the screen until you see the ALLOW CHANGES section.

(27) Tap areas that you want to restrict, such as Cellular Data or Volume Limit, and then tap Don't Allow Changes to prevent changes to that area.

(28) To prevent multiplayer games in the Game Center, set the Multiplayer Games switch to off (white). Users will no longer be able to play games against other people.

(29) To prevent new friends from being added in the Game Center, set the Adding Friends switch to off (white). Players will be restricted to the friends already allowed.

(30) To prevent the screen from being recorded during game play associated with the Game Center, set the Screen Recording switch to off (white).

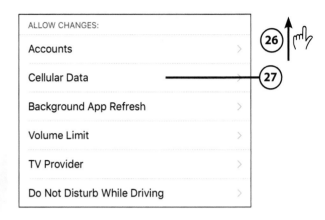

Removing Restrictions

To remove all restrictions, move to the Restrictions screen (your Restrictions passcode is required) and tap Disable Restrictions. Enter your Restrictions passcode, and all restrictions are removed.

Setting Accessibility Options

The iPhone has many features designed to help people who have hearing impairments, visual impairments, or other physical challenges to be able to use it effectively.

You can enable and configure the Accessibility features on the Accessibility Settings screen.

(**1**) On the Settings screen, tap General.

(**2**) Swipe up the screen until you see Accessibility.

(**3**) Tap Accessibility. The Accessibility screen is organized into different sections for different kinds of limitations. The first section is VISION, which includes options to assist people who are visually impaired.

(**4**) Use the controls in the VISION section to change how the iPhone's screens appear. Some of the options include the following:

- **VoiceOver**—The iPhone guides you through screens by speaking their contents. To configure this, tap VoiceOver and set the VoiceOver switch to on (green) to turn it on. The rest of the settings configure how VoiceOver works. For example, you can set the rate at which the voice speaks, what kind of feedback you get, and many more options.

- **Zoom**—This magnifies the entire screen. Tap Zoom and then turn Zoom on. Use the other settings to change how the zoom works, such as whether it follows where you are focused on the screen or remains fixed.

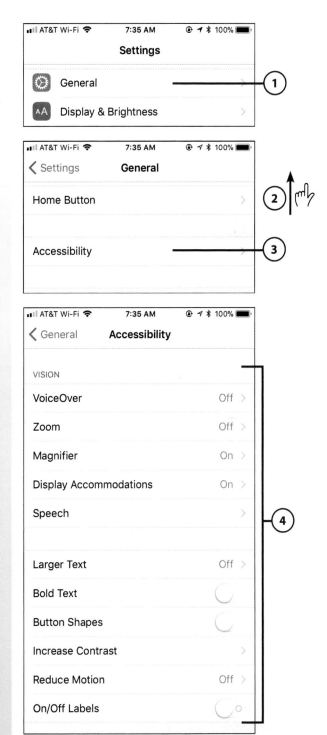

- **Magnifier**—This feature enables you to use your iPhone's camera like a magnifying glass. When you enable this, you can triple-press the Touch ID/Home button to activate it. You can also add its control to the Control Center using the steps provided earlier in the chapter.

- **Display Accommodations**—These options change how your iPhone uses color. You can use the Invert Colors function to reverse the color on the screen so that what is light becomes dark and vice versa. The Color Filters tool enables you to customize how colors appear on the screen. The Auto-Brightness switch controls whether the iPhone's screen automatically dims or not. The Reduce White Point switch, when enabled, reduces the intensity of bright colors.

- **Speech**—Under the Speech option, Speak Selection causes a Speak button to appear when you select text, and Speak Screen provides the option to have the screen's content spoken. You can also determine whether you hear feedback while you type, and you can configure the voices used, the rate of speech, and pronunciations.

- **Larger and Bold Text**—These increase the text size and add bold; these are in addition to the Text Size and Bold settings that you learn about in Chapter 5.

- **Other options**—You can also change button shapes, change contrast, reduce motion, and turn labels on or off.

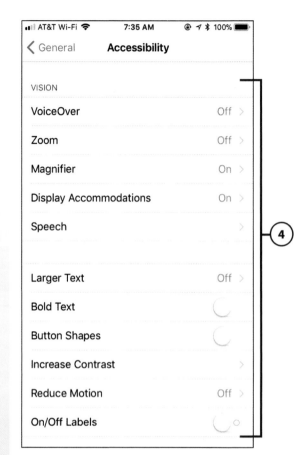

5 Swipe up to see the INTERACTION section.

6 Use the controls in this section to adjust how you can interact with the iPhone. The controls here include the following:

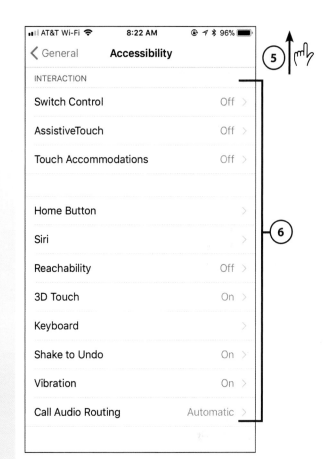

- **Switch Control**—The controls on this screen enable you to configure an iPhone to work with an adaptive device so that you can control the iPhone with that device.

- **AssistiveTouch**—These controls make an iPhone easier to manipulate; if you enable this, a white button appears on the screen at all times. You can tap this to access the Home screen, Notification Center, and other areas. You can also create new gestures to control other functions on the iPhone.

- **Touch Accommodations**— You can use the Touch Accommodations options to make it easier for you to use the touch screen. For example, you can change the amount of time you must touch the screen before it is recognized as a touch.

- **Home Button**—Use this switch to set the rate at which you press the Touch ID/Home button to register as a double- or triple-press.

- **Siri**—You can determine if the Type to Siri function is active and when voice feedback is provided to you when you are working with Siri.

- **Reachability**—When you enable this switch, you can jump to the top of the screen by tapping the Touch ID/Home button twice.

- **3D Touch**—This setting, which is available only on iPhone models that support 3D Touch, enables you to turn the 3D Touch feature off or on. If 3D Touch is on, you can determine how much pressure you need to apply to the screen to activate it.

- **Keyboard**—Using these options, you can show or hide lowercase letters and change how the keys react to your touches.

- **Shake to Undo**—This setting enables you to turn off the shake motion to undo your most recent action.

- **Vibration**—This setting enables you to enable or disable vibrations. It overrides the vibration settings in other areas, such as notifications.

- **Call Audio Routing**—Use this to configure where audio is heard during a phone call or FaceTime session, such as headset or speaker. If you select Automatic, the iPhone chooses the routing based on how it is configured. You can select Bluetooth Headset or Speaker to always use one of those options first instead. You can also have the phone automatically answer calls.

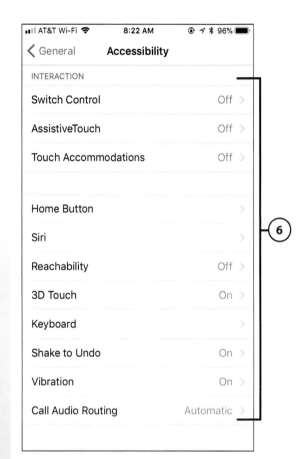

7 Swipe up the Accessibility screen to see the HEARING section.

8 Use the controls in this section to configure sounds and to configure the iPhone to work with hearing-impaired people. The controls in this section include the following:

- **MFi Hearing Aids**—When you activate this setting, you can pair an iPhone to work with MFi hearing aids. (You pair other types of hearing aids using Bluetooth.)

- **TTY**—These controls enable you to use your iPhone with a TTY device.

- **LED Flash for Alerts**—When you set this switch to on (green), the flash flashes whenever an alert plays on the phone.

- **Mono Audio**—This causes the sound output to be in mono instead of stereo.

- **Phone Noise Cancellation**—This switch turns noise cancellation on and off. Noise cancellation reduces ambient noise when you are using the Phone app.

- **Balance**—Use this slider to change the balance of stereo sound between left and right.

- **Hearing Aid Compatibility**—If you enable this switch, the sound quality is improved for some types of hearing aids. When you use hearing aids with your iPhone, try setting this switch to on (green) to see if you can hear more clearly.

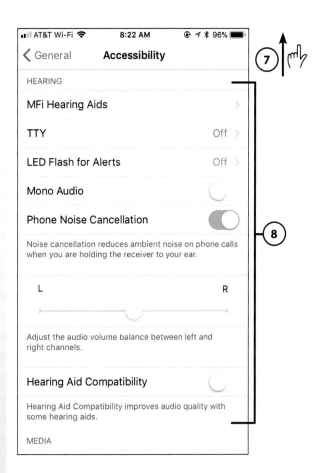

(9) Swipe up to see the MEDIA section.

(10) Use the controls in this section to add features to video playback, including the following:

- **Subtitles & Captioning—** Use these controls to enable subtitles and captions for video and choose the style of those elements on the screen.

- **Audio Descriptions—**This causes an audio description of media to be played when available.

(11) Use the Guided Access setting if you want to limit the iPhone to using a single app and to further configure the features, such as Passcode Settings and Time Limits.

(12) Use the Accessibility Shortcut control to determine what happens when you press the Touch ID/Home button three times.

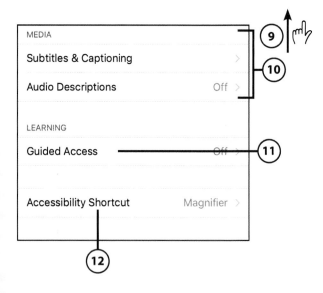

Customizing How Your iPhone Works with Apps

Installing apps on your iPhone enables you to add more functionality than you can probably imagine. As the old Apple ad use to proclaim, "There's an app for that." And in all likelihood, there probably is an app for a lot of what you would like to use your iPhone for. The App Store app enables you to find, download, and install apps onto your iPhone.

Before you jump into the App Store, take a few moments to ensure your iPhone is configured for maximum ease and efficiency of dealing with new apps.

Configuring Your iPhone to Download and Maintain Apps

To download apps from the App Store, you need an Apple ID (if you need help getting or configuring an Apple ID, see Chapter 3, "Setting Up and Using an Apple ID, iCloud, and Other Online Accounts"). With your Apple ID configured on your phone in the iCloud area, make sure it is also ready to go for the App Store and ensure you can use Touch ID when you download apps (instead of typing your password).

1. Open the Settings app.

2. Tap iTunes & App Store.

3. Ensure the Apple ID you want to use to download apps is shown at the top of the screen; if it isn't tap the Apple ID shown, tap Sign Out, and then sign into your Apple ID.

4. Ensure the Apps switch is on (green); this causes any apps you download to your iPhone to also automatically be downloaded to other devices (with which the apps are compatible, of course) that use the same Apple ID.

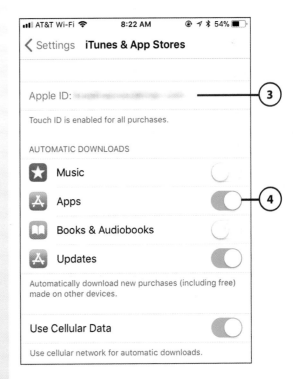

5 Ensure the Updates switch is on (green); this causes any updates to apps you have installed on your iPhone to be downloaded and installed automatically. I recommend you use this option so you can be sure you are always running the most current versions of your apps.

6 If you don't have an unlimited cellular data plan, you might want to set Use Cellular Data to off (white) so apps and other content are downloaded only when you are on a Wi-Fi network. If this is enabled (green), apps and content can be downloaded to your iPhone when you are using a cellular network, which can consume significant amounts of your data plan. (Some apps or content are so large, they can only be downloaded when you are using a Wi-Fi connection.)

7 Use the information in the task "Configuring Your Passcode and Touch ID" to ensure the iTunes & App Store switch is enabled (green) so that you can use Touch ID to download apps instead of typing your password. (If it isn't enabled, tap the switch, enter your Apple ID password, and tap OK to enable it.)

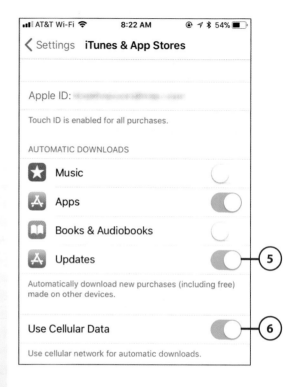

Using the App Store App to Find and Install iPhone Apps

The App Store app enables you to quickly and easily browse and search for apps, view information about them, and then download and install them on your iPhone with just a few taps.

When you use the App Store app, you can find apps to download using any of the following options:

- **Today**—This tab takes you to apps featured in the App Store on the day you go into the store. They are grouped in various ways, such as APP OF THE DAY, based on what is trending, and so on. When you tap any of the items on the Today screen, you move into the group or app on which you tapped.

- **Games**—Easily the most popular category of apps, Games enables you to find those critical games you need to prove your skills and pass the time. When you move into the Games area, the games are also grouped in various ways, such as Top Paid, Top Free, Top Categories, etc.

- **Apps**—This category leads you to apps that aren't games. On this screen, in addition to the Top Paid and Top Free lists, you see apps organized by category. Tap a category to explore the apps it contains.

- **Updates**—Through this option, you can update your apps (if you don't have automatic updates set as described earlier) or if you have automatic updates enabled, you see the list of updates made to the apps on your iPhone along with those that are pending.

- **Search**—This tool enables you to search for apps. You can search by name, developer, and other keywords.

Finding and downloading any kind of app follows this same pattern:

1. **Find the app you are interested in.** You can use the options described in the previous list to find apps by browsing for them, or you can use the search option to find a specific app quickly and easily.

2. **Evaluate the app.** The information screen for apps provides lots of information that you can use to decide whether you want to download an app (or not). The information available includes a text description, screenshots, ratings and reviews from users, and so on.

3. **Download and install the app.**

The following tasks provide detailed examples for each of these steps.

Searching for Apps

If you know something about an app, such as its name, its developer, its purpose, or just about anything else, you can quickly search the App Store to find the app. Here's how to search for an app:

1. Move to the Home screen and tap App Store.

2. Tap Search.

3. Tap in the Search box.

4. Type a search term. This can be the type of app you are looking for based on its purpose (such as *travel apps*) or the name of someone associated with the app, its title, its developer, or even a topic. As you type, the app suggests searches that are related to what you are typing.

5. Tap the search you want to perform or tap the Search key on the keyboard to search for the term you entered in step 4. The apps that meet your search term appear.

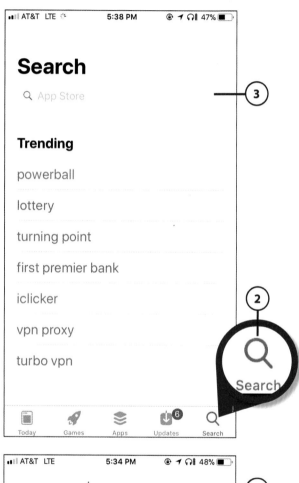

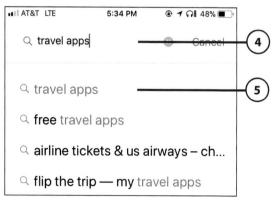

(6) Swipe up and down on the screen to review the apps in the search results.

(7) If none of the apps are what you are looking for, tap Clear (x) in the Search box and repeat steps 4–6.

(8) When you find an app of interest to you, tap it. You move to the app's information screen.

(9) Use the app's information on the information screen to evaluate the app and decide if you want to download it. You can read about the app, see screenshots, and read other peoples' reviews to help you decide. If you want to download the app, see "Downloading Apps" later in this chapter for the details.

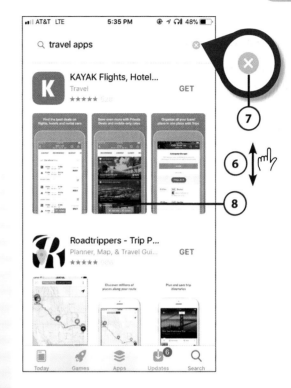

Follow the Trends?

Before you enter a search term on the Search screen, you see the Trending Searches, which are the searches that are being performed most frequently. You can tap one of these to use it to search for apps.

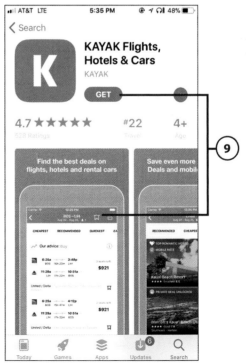

Browsing for Apps

If you don't know of a specific app you want, you can browse the App Store. To browse, you can tap any graphics or links you see in the App Store app. One of the most useful ways to browse for apps is by using categories:

(1) Open the App Store app.

(2) Tap Apps (browsing for games or using the Today option works very similarly).

(3) Swipe up the screen until you see the Top Categories section.

(4) Tap See All to browse all available categories.

(5) Tap a category in which you are interested.

(6) Swipe up and down to browse the groupings of apps, such as Apps We Love, Top Paid, and so on.

(7) Tap See All for a grouping to browse the apps it contains.

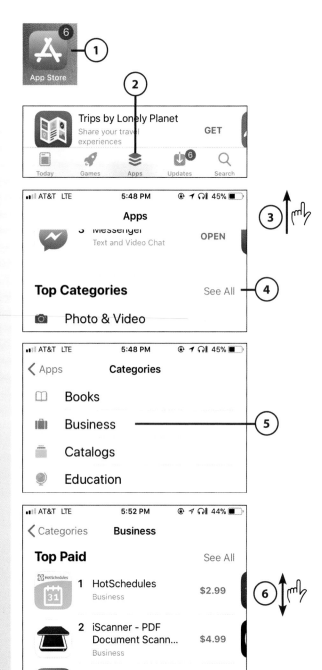

8 Swipe up and down to browse the apps in the group you selected in step 7.

9 Tap an app in which you are interested. You move to that app's information screen.

10 Use the information on the information screen to decide whether you want to download the app. You can read about the app, see screenshots, and read other peoples' reviews to help you decide. If you want to download the app, see "Downloading Apps" later in this chapter for the details. Or, you can continue browsing by tapping the Back icon in the top-left corner of the screen to return to the category list.

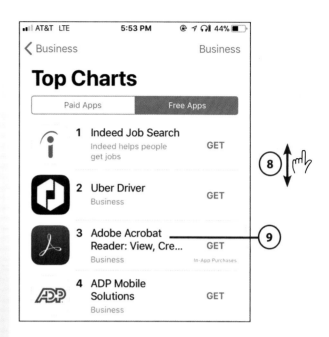

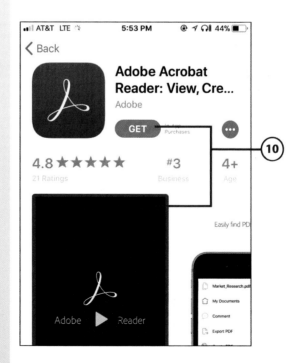

>>>Go Further

MORE ON FINDING APPS

Following are a few pointers to help you use the App Store:

- When you see a + inside an app's price or Get button, that means the app is a universal app, which means it runs equally as well on iPhones, iPads, and iPod touches.

- Some apps include video previews. When you see the Play icon on an image, it is a video preview. Tap the Play icon to watch it. Tap Done in the upper-left corner of the screen to move back to the screenshots.

- After you have used an app, you can add your own review by moving back to its Reviews tab and tapping Write a Review. You move to the Write a Review screen where you have to enter your iTunes Store account information before you can write and submit a review.

- You can read user reviews of the apps in the App Store. You should take these with a grain of salt. Some people have an issue with the developer or the type of app; are reviewing an older version of the app; or are commenting on issues unrelated to the app itself; and these issues can cause them to provide unfairly low ratings. The most useful individual user reviews are very specific, as in "I wanted the app to do x, but it only does y." It can be more helpful to look at the number of reviews and the average user rating than reading the individual reviews.

Downloading Apps

Downloading and installing apps is about as easy as things get, as you can see:

(1) In the App Store, view the app you want to download.

(2) Tap GET (for free apps) or the price (for apps that have a license fee). The icon then becomes INSTALL, if it is a free app, or BUY if it has a license fee.

(3) Tap Install or Buy. Depending on your iTunes & App Store settings, you might be prompted to sign in with your Apple ID and password to start the download. If you aren't prompted to confirm the download, you can skip the next step because the app starts downloading immediately.

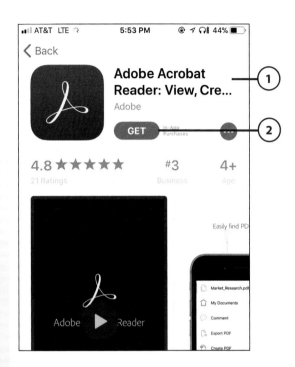

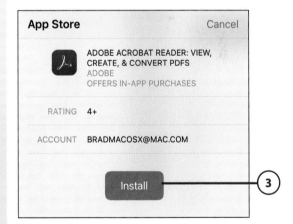

4 If you are prompted to confirm the download, and you are using an iPhone 5s or later and have enabled Touch ID for store downloads, touch the Touch ID/Home button at the prompt; if you are using another model, or you don't use Touch ID for store downloads, type your Apple ID password, and then tap Sign In.

Face ID

If you have an iPhone X, you can configure Face ID so that you can confirm an app download by looking at your phone. See the online supplement *My iPhone X* by going to www.informit.com/myiphoneseniors for the details.

You see the progress of the process.

App being downloaded

When the process is complete, the status information is replaced by the OPEN button. You can tap OPEN to start working with the app right away.

Or, you can move to the Home screen on which it is installed and tap its icon to launch the app at any time. (New apps are installed in the first available space on your Home screens. You can move them wherever you want them to be using the information provided in Chapter 5.)

App is ready to use

>>>Go Further
MORE ON APPS

As you use the App Store app to install apps on your iPhone, keep the following hints handy:

- Like other software, apps are updated regularly to fix problems, add features, or make other changes. If you set the iTunes & App Store Updates setting to on (green) as described earlier in this chapter, updates to your apps happen automatically in the background. Your apps are always current so you don't have to update them manually. (More information on updating apps is in the online Chapter 16, "Maintaining and Protecting Your iPhone and Solving Problems.")

- If you see the Download icon next to an app rather than Get or Buy, that means you have previously downloaded (and paid for if it isn't free) the app but it is not currently installed on your iPhone. Tap the icon to download and install it.

- To let someone else know about an app, tap the Share icon and then tap how you want to let him know; the options include AirDrop, Message, Mail, Twitter, and Facebook. To buy an app for someone, tap Gift.

- Apps can work in the background to keep their information current, such as Weather and Stocks. To configure this, open the Settings app, tap General, and tap Background App Refresh. Tap Background App Refresh and tap Off to disable this, Wi-Fi to enable it only when your iPhone is connected to a Wi-Fi network, or Wi-Fi & Cellular Data to allow it any time your iPhone is connected to the Internet. Tap the Back icon, located in the upper-left corner of the screen, to see the list of apps installed on your iPhone. To enable an app to work in the background, set its switch to on (green). To disable background activity for an app, set its switch to off (white).

- After you install an app, move to the Settings screen and look for the app's icon. If it is there, the app has additional settings you can use to configure the way it works. Tap the app's icon in the Settings app and use its Settings screen to configure it.

Tap to configure your
iPhone's screen and sounds

Customize the layout of
the icons on your Home
screens by placing icons
where you want them

Choose the image you
want as wallpaper

Place icons in folders
to keep your Home
screens organized

In this chapter, you learn how to make an iPhone look and sound the way you want it to. Topics include the following:

→ Getting started
→ Customizing your Home screens
→ Setting the screen's brightness, lock/wake, text, view, and wallpaper options
→ Choosing the sounds and vibratory feedback your iPhone uses

Customizing How Your iPhone Looks and Sounds

There are lots of ways that you can customize an iPhone to make it *your* iPhone so that it looks and sounds the way you want it to. You can design your Home screens; set the screen's brightness, text size, and wallpaper; and choose the sounds your iPhone makes.

Getting Started

In Chapter 4, "Customizing How Your iPhone Works," you learned how to change many aspects of how your iPhone works. This chapter focuses on how you can change the way you interact with your iPhone and how it interacts with you. Following are key areas you can configure to personalize your iPhone's personality:

- **Home screens**—The iPhone's Home screens are the starting point for most everything you do because these screens contain the icons that you tap to access the apps that you want to use. You see and use the Home screens constantly, so it's a good idea to customize them to your preferences. You can place icons on specific screens, and you can use folders to make your Home screens work better for you.

- **Screen brightness, Auto-Lock, Raise to Wake, text, view, and wallpaper options**—There are a number of ways you can change how your iPhone's screen looks and works. For example, you can set its brightness level and text size. You can also change the view you have; one option causes the screen to be zoomed in so icons and text are larger and easier to see.

- **Sounds**—Sound is one important way your iPhone uses to communicate with you. The most obvious of these sounds is the ringtone that plays when you receive a call. However, there are many other sounds you can choose to help you know when something is happening. You can also choose to disable sounds so that your iPhone isn't so noisy. You can also have your iPhone vibrate in conjunction with, or instead of, making sounds.

Notifications

Notifications are the primary way your iPhone communicates with you and there are many options you can configure to change your iPhone's visual, auditory, and vibratory notifications. How to use notifications is explained in Chapter 2, "Using Your iPhone's Core Features," while in Chapter 4, you learn how to configure the types of notifications your iPhone uses to communicate with you.

Customizing Your Home Screens

The iPhone's Home screens are the starting point for anything you do because these screens contain the icons and folders of icons that you tap to access the apps that you want to use. You see and use the Home screens constantly, so it's a good idea to customize them to your preferences.

In the background of the Lock screen and every Home screen is the wallpaper image. In the section called "Setting the Wallpaper on the Home and Lock Screens," you learn how to configure your iPhone's wallpaper in both locations.

As you know, you can access apps on your Home screens by tapping them. The Home screens come configured with icons in default locations. You can change the location of these icons to be more convenient for you. As you install more apps on your iPhone, it's a good idea to organize your Home screens so that you can quickly get to the apps you use most frequently. You can move icons around the same screen, move icons between the pages of the Home screen, and organize icons within folders. You can even change the icons that appear on the Home screen Dock. You can also delete icons you no longer need.

Moving Icons Around Your Home Screens

You can move icons around on a Home screen, and you can move icons among screens to change where they are located.

1. Move to a Home screen by pressing the Touch ID/Home button (except iPhone X) or swiping up from the bottom of the screen (iPhone X).

2. Swipe to the left or right across the Home screen until the page containing an icon you want to move appears.

3. Touch (don't tap because if you do, the app opens instead) and hold on any icon. After a moment, the icons begin jiggling, which indicates that you can move icons on the Home screens. You also see the Delete symbol (x) in the upper-left corner of some icons, which indicates that you can delete both the icon and app (more on this later in this section).

Touch But Don't Press (3D Touch Models)

If you are working with an iPhone 6s/6s Plus or later model that supports 3D Touch, don't press on icons when you want to move them; just touch your finger lightly to the screen. If you apply pressure, you might open the Quick Action menu instead. When you just touch an icon and leave your finger on the screen without any pressure, the icons become fuzzy briefly, and then start jiggling to indicate you can move them.

4 Touch and hold an icon you want to move; it becomes darker to show that you have selected it.

5 Drag the icon to a new location on the current screen; as you move the icon around the page, other icons separate and are reorganized to enable you to place the icon in its new location.

6 When the icon is in the location you want, lift your finger. The icon is set in that place. (You don't have to be precise; the icon automatically snaps into the closest position when you lift your finger off the screen.)

7 Tap and hold on an icon you want to move to a different page.

8 Drag the icon to the left edge of the screen to move it to a previous page or to the right edge of the screen to move it to a later page. As you reach the edge of the screen, you move to the previous or next page.

9 Drag the icon to its new location on the Home screen and lift your finger off the icon. Lift your finger off the screen. The icon is set in its new place.

10 Continue moving icons until you've placed them in the locations you want; then press the Touch ID/Home button once. The icons are locked in their current positions, they stop jiggling, and the Delete symbols disappear.

iPhone X

Because it doesn't have a Touch ID/Home button, arranging icons and folders on the Home screens on an iPhone X requires slightly different steps. Refer to the online supplement *My iPhone X* by going to www.informit.com/myiphoneseniors for the steps that are specific to the iPhone X.

Creating Folders to Organize Apps on Your Home Screens

You can place icons into folders to keep them organized and to make more icons available on the same page. To create a folder, do the following:

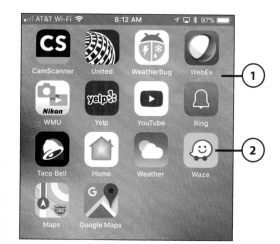

1. Move to the Home screen containing icons you want to place in a folder.

2. Touch and hold an icon until the icons start jiggling; the Delete symbols appear.

3. Drag one icon on top of another one that you want to be in the new folder together.

4. When the first icon is on top of the second and a folder appears, lift your finger. The two icons are placed into the new folder, which is named based on the type of icons you place within it. The folder opens and you see its default name.

5. Edit the name by tapping in the name field.

6. Delete the current name by tapping the Delete icon.

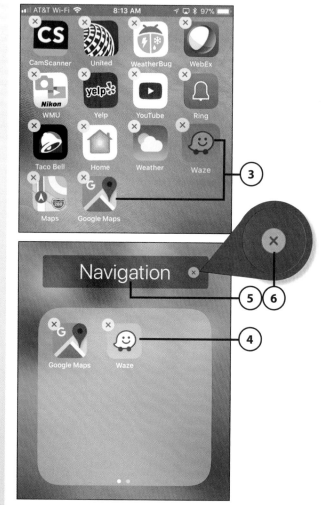

7 Change the default name for the folder or type a completely new name if you deleted the previous one.

8 Tap Done.

9 Tap outside the folder to close it.

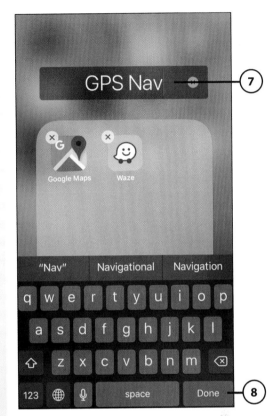

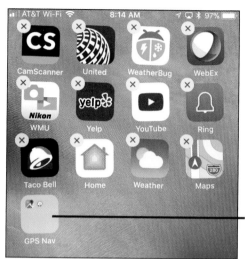

10 If you're done organizing the Home screen, press the Touch ID/Home button. The icons stop jiggling.

The new folder

Locating Folders

You can move a folder to a new location in the same way you can move any icon. Touch and hold (don't tap or it opens instead) the folder's icon until the icons start jiggling. Drag the folder icon to where you want it to be.

Placing Icons in Existing Folders

You can add icons to an existing folder like so:

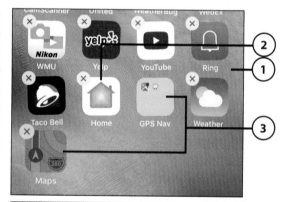

1 Move to the Home screen containing an icon you want to place in a folder.

2 Touch and hold an icon until the icons start jiggling and the Delete symbols appear.

3 Drag the icon you want to place into a folder on top of the folder's icon so that the folder opens. (The icon doesn't have to be on the same Home screen page; you can drag an icon from one page and drop it on a folder on a different page.)

4 When the folder opens, lift your finger from the screen. The icon is placed within the folder.

Adding Apps to Folders Quickly

If you don't want to change the icon's location when you place it in the folder, lift your finger as soon as the folder's icon is highlighted; this places the icon in the folder but doesn't cause the folder to open. This is faster than waiting for the folder to open, but doesn't allow you to position the icon within the folder.

(5) Drag the new icon to its location within the folder.

(6) Tap outside the folder. The folder closes.

(7) When you're done adding icons to folders, press the Touch ID/ Home button.

Removing Icons from Folders

To remove an icon from a folder, tap the folder from which you want to remove the icon to open it. Touch and hold the icon you want to remove until it starts jiggling. Drag the icon you want to remove from inside the folder to outside the folder. When you cross the border of the folder, the folder closes and you can place the icon on a Home screen.

Folders and Badges

When you place an icon that has a badge notification (the red circle with a number in it that indicates the number of new items in an app) in a folder, the badge transfers to the folder so that you see it on the folder's icon. When you place more than one app with a badge notification in the same folder, the badge on the folder becomes the total number of new items for all the apps in the folder. You need to open a folder to see the badges for the individual apps it contains.

**The folder now contains
the app you placed in it**

Configuring the Home Screen Dock

The Dock on the bottom of the Home screen appears on every page. You can place any icons on the Dock that you want, including folder icons.

1. Move to the Home screen containing an icon you want to place on the Dock.

2. Touch and hold an icon until the icons start jiggling and the Delete symbols appear.

3. Drag an icon that is currently on the Dock from the Dock onto the Home screen to create an empty space on the Dock.

4. Drag an icon or folder from the Home screen onto the Dock.

5. Drag the icons on the Dock around so they are in the order you want them to be.

6. Press the Touch ID/ Home button to set the icons in their current places.

New icon on the Dock

Deleting Icons

You can delete icons from a Home screen to remove them from your iPhone. When you delete an app's icon, its data is also deleted and you won't be able to use the app anymore (of course, you can download it again if you change your mind).

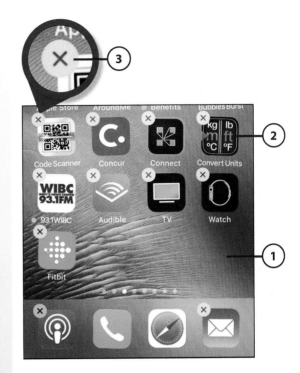

(**1**) Move to the Home screen containing an icon you want to delete.

(**2**) Touch and hold an icon until the icons start jiggling and the Delete symbols appear (you can delete icons that are inside folders, too).

(**3**) Tap the icon's Delete symbol.

(**4**) Tap Delete. The app and any associated data on your iPhone are deleted.

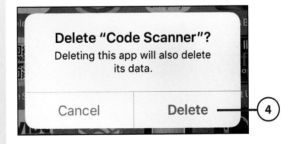

Delete "Code Scanner"?
Deleting this app will also delete its data.

Cancel   Delete

>>>Go Further
MORE ON ORGANIZING HOME SCREENS

Organizing your Home screens can make the use of your iPhone more efficient. Here are a few more things to keep in mind:

- You can place many icons in the same folder. When you add more than nine, any additional icons are placed on new pages within the folder. As you keep adding icons, pages keep being added to the folder to accommodate the icons you add to it. You can swipe to the left or right within a folder to move among its pages, just as you can to move among your Home screens. You can also drag icons between pages in a folder, just like on a Home screen.

- To change an existing folder's name, move to a screen showing the folder whose name you want to change. Touch and hold an icon until the icons jiggle. Tap the folder so that it opens, and then tap the current name. Edit the name, tap Done, and tap outside the folder to close it. Press the Touch ID/Home button to complete the process.

- To delete a folder, remove all the icons from it. The folder is deleted as soon as you remove the last icon from within it.

- You can delete icons for apps you've added to your iPhone or some of the default apps, such as the Stocks app. You can't delete some of the default apps, which is why their icons don't have Delete symbols like apps that you install do. If you don't use some of these default apps that you can't delete, move them to pages of your Home screen that you don't use very often so they don't get in your way, or create a folder for unused icons and store them there, out of your way.

- To return your Home screens to how they were when you first started using your iPhone, open the Settings app, tap General, Reset, Reset Home Screen Layout, and Reset Home Screen. The Home screens return to their default configurations. Icons you've added are moved onto the later pages.

Setting the Screen's Brightness, Lock/Wake, Text, View, and Wallpaper Options

There are a number of settings you can configure to suit your viewing preferences and how your iPhone locks/wakes:

- **Brightness**—Because you continually look at your iPhone's screen, it should be the right brightness level for your eyes. However, the screen is also a large user of battery power, so the dimmer an iPhone's screen is, the longer its battery lasts. You should find a good balance between viewing comfort and battery life.

- **Night Shift**—This feature changes the color profile of the screen after dark. It is supposed to make the light produced by the iPhone more suitable to darker conditions. You can set the color temperature to your preferences and can set a schedule if you want Night Shift to be activated automatically.

- **Auto-Lock**—The Auto-Lock setting causes your iPhone to lock and go to sleep after a specific amount of inactivity. This is good for security as it is less likely someone can pick up and use your phone if you let it sit for a while. It also extends battery life because it puts the iPhone to sleep when you aren't using it.

- **Raise to Wake**—This setting, available on iPhone 6s/6s Plus and later models, enables you to wake up the iPhone by lifting it up. This is useful because you don't even need to press a button, just lift the phone and you see the Lock screen, giving you quick access to the current time, the Audio Player, notifications, and widgets. However, some people find this feature more annoying than helpful, so if the phone waking when you lift it up bothers you, disable this setting on your phone.

- **Text Size/Bold**—As you use your iPhone, you'll be constantly working with text so it's also important to configure the text size to meet your preferences. You can use the Bold setting to bold text to make it easier to read.

- **View**—The iPhone 6 and later models offer two views. The Standard view maximizes screen space and the Zoomed view makes things on the screen larger, making them easier to see, but less content fits on the screen. You can choose the view that works best for you.

- **Wallpaper**—Wallpaper is the image you see "behind" the icons on your Home screens. Because you see this image so often, you might as well have an image that you want to see or that you believe makes using the Home screens easier and faster. You can use the iPhone's default wallpaper images, or you can use any photo available on your iPhone. You can also set the wallpaper you see on the iPhone's Lock screen (you can use the same image as on the Home screens or a different one). Although it doesn't affect productivity or usability of the iPhone very much, choosing your own wallpaper to see in the background of the Home and Lock screens makes your iPhone more personal to you and is just plain fun.

Setting the Screen Brightness and Night Shift Using the Settings App

To set the screen brightness and Night Shift, perform the following steps:

1. In the Settings app, tap Display & Brightness.

2. Drag the slider to the right to raise the base brightness or to the left to lower it. A brighter screen uses more power but is easier to see.

3. Tap Night Shift.

4. To have Night Shift activate automatically, set the Scheduled switch to on (green); if you don't want it to activate automatically, skip to step 11.

5. Tap the From/To setting.

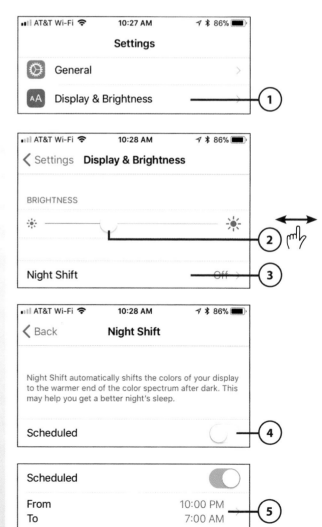

6 To have Night Shift on between sunset and sunrise, tap Sunset to Sunrise and skip to step 10.

7 To set a custom schedule for Night Shift, tap Custom Schedule.

8 Tap Turn On At and swipe up or down on the hour, minute, and AM/PM wheels to set the time when you want Night Shift to activate.

9 Tap Turn Off At and use the time wheels to set when you want Night Shift to turn off.

10 Tap Night Shift.

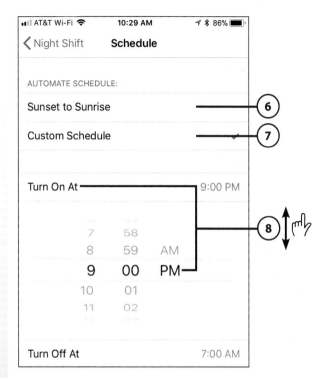

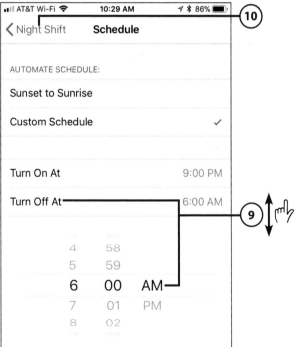

(11) To manually turn Night Shift on at any time, set the Manually Enable Until Tomorrow switch to on (green). Night Shift activates and remains on until sunrise when it shuts off automatically. (You can manually turn off Night Shift by setting the Manually Enable Until Tomorrow switch to off [white].)

(12) Drag the COLOR TEMPERATURE slider to the right to make the Night Shift effect more pro- nounced or to the left to make it less warm. If Night Shift isn't active when you drag the slider, it goes into effect as you move the slider so you can see the effect the temperature you select has.

(13) Tap Back.

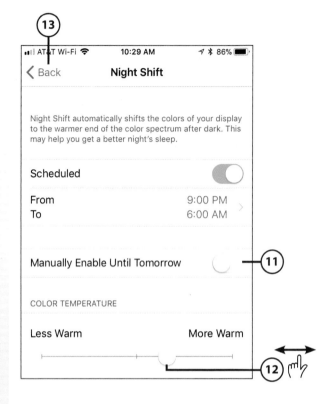

Setting the Screen Brightness and Night Shift Using the Control Center

You can use the Control Center to quickly adjust brightness and Night Shift as follows:

(1) Swipe up from the bottom of the Home screen (all models except the iPhone X) or swipe down from the upper-right corner of the screen (iPhone X, not shown in the figure) to open the Control Center.

2 Swipe up or down on the Brightness slider to increase or decrease the brightness, respectively.

3 To turn Night Shift on or off, press and hold on the Brightness slider.

4 Use the Brightness slider to change the screen's brightness (this does the same thing as using the slider on the Control Center, but since it is larger here, it is a bit easier to use).

5 Tap the Night Shift icon to turn Night Shift on. When on, the Night Shift icon is orange.

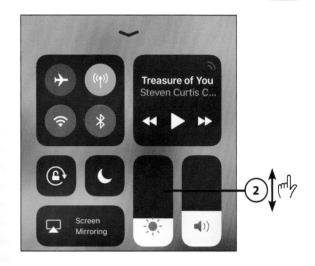

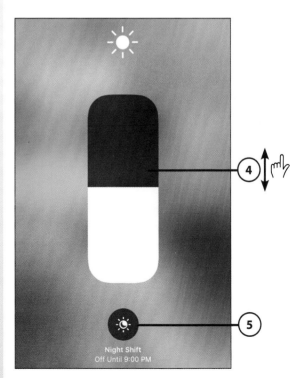

6. Tap the Night Shift icon to turn Night Shift off. When off, the Night Shift icon is white.

7. Tap outside the tools to return to the Control Center.

8. Tap the downward-facing arrow at the top of the Control Center to close it.

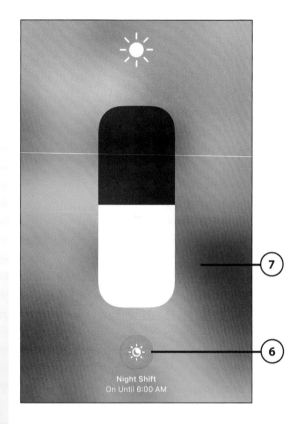

Setting Auto-Lock and Raise to Wake

To set Auto-lock and Raise to Wake, perform the following steps:

(**1**) In the Settings app, tap Display & Brightness to open the Display & Brightness settings screen.

(**2**) Tap Auto-Lock.

(**3**) Tap the amount of idle time you want to pass before the iPhone automatically locks and goes to sleep. You can choose from 30 seconds or 1 to 5 minutes; choose Never if you want to only manually lock your iPhone. I recommend that you keep Auto-Lock set to a relatively small value to conserve your iPhone's battery and to make it more secure. Of course, the shorter you set this time to be, the more frequently you have to unlock your iPhone.

(**4**) Tap Back.

(**5**) If you want to be able to wake your phone by lifting it, set the Raise to Wake switch to on (green); to disable this feature, set the switch to off (white).

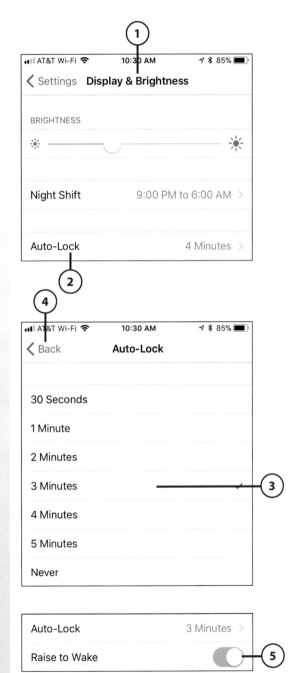

Setting Text Size and Bold

To change the text size or make all text bold, perform the following steps:

1. In the Settings app, tap Display & Brightness to open the Display & Brightness settings screen.

2. Tap Text Size. This control changes the size of text in all the apps that support the iPhone's Dynamic Type feature.

3. Drag the slider to the right to increase the size of text or to the left to decrease it. As you move the slider, the text at the top of the screen resizes so you can see the effect of the change you are making.

4. When you are happy with the size of the text, tap Back.

5. If you want to make all of the text on your iPhone bold, set the Bold Text switch to on (green) and move to step 6. If you don't want to bold the text, skip the next step.

6. Tap Continue. Your iPhone restarts. All the text is in bold, making it easier to read.

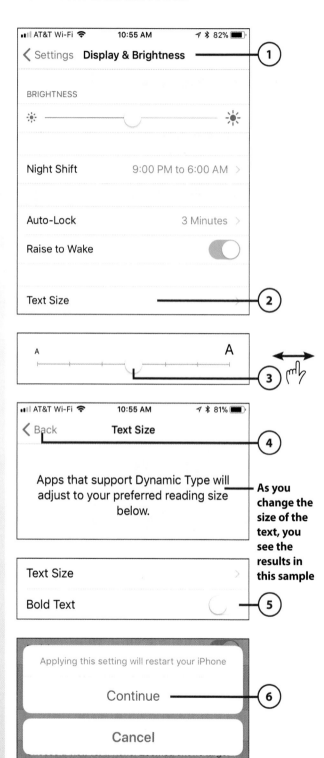

As you change the size of the text, you see the results in this sample

Setting Text Size Using the Control Center

To change the text size with the Control Center, perform the following steps:

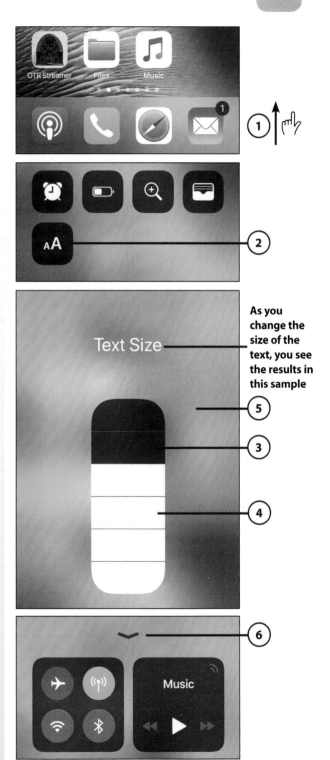

As you change the size of the text, you see the results in this sample

(1) Swipe up from the bottom of the Home screen (all models except the iPhone X) or swipe down from the upper-right corner of the screen (iPhone X, not shown in the figure) to open the Control Center.

(2) Tap the Text Size icon. (If you don't see this icon, you need to add it to the Control Center. See Chapter 4, "Customizing How Your iPhone Works," for details.)

(3) Tap above the shaded area to increase the text size.

(4) Tap below the shaded area to decrease the text size.

(5) Tap outside the tool to return to the Control Center.

(6) Tap the downward-facing arrow at the top of the Control Center to close it.

Choosing a View

To configure the view you use, perform the following steps:

1. In the Settings app, tap Display & Brightness to open the Display & Brightness settings screen.

2. Tap View; if you don't see this option, your iPhone doesn't support it and you can skip the rest of these steps.

3. Tap Standard.

4. Look at the sample screen.

5. Swipe to the left or right to see examples of what other screens look like in the Standard view.

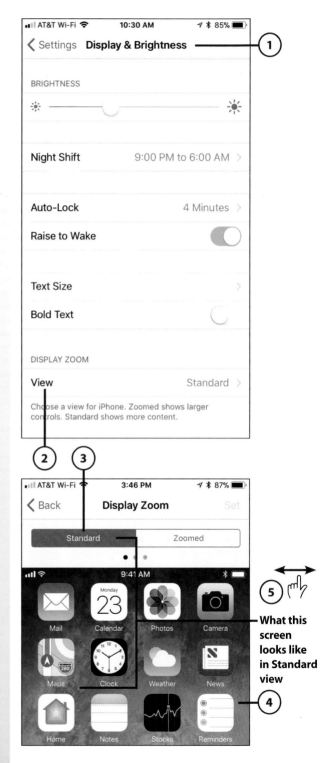

What this screen looks like in Standard view

(6) Look at the next sample screen.

(7) Swipe to the left or right to see examples of what other screens look like in the Standard view.

(8) Tap Zoomed. The sample screens change to reflect the Zoomed view.

(9) Swipe to the left and right to preview the other sample screens in the Zoomed view.

(10) If you want to keep the current view, tap Cancel and skip the rest of these steps.

(11) To change the view, tap the view you want.

(12) Tap Set (if Set is grayed out, the view you selected is already set and you can skip the rest of these steps).

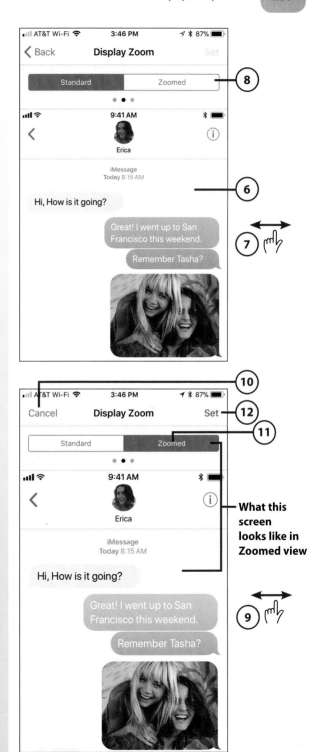

What this screen looks like in Zoomed view

13 Tap Use Zoomed (this is Use Standard if you are switching to the Standard view). Your iPhone restarts and uses the new view.

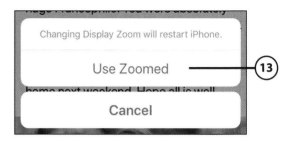

A Home screen in Zoomed view

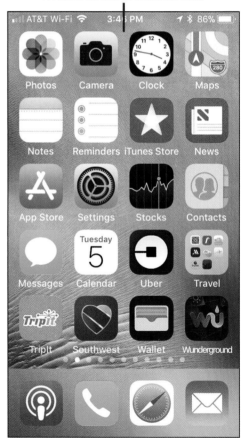

Setting the Wallpaper on the Home and Lock Screens

To configure your wallpaper, perform the following steps:

(1) In the Settings app, tap Wallpaper. You see the current wallpaper set for the Lock and Home screens.

(2) Tap Choose a New Wallpaper. The Choose screen has two sections. The top section enables you to choose one of the default wallpaper images (Dynamic, Stills, or Live), whereas the lower section shows you the photos available on your iPhone. If you don't have any photos stored on your iPhone, you can only choose from the default images. To choose a default image, continue with step 3; to use one of your photos as wallpaper, skip to step 8.

(3) Tap Dynamic if you want to use dynamic wallpaper, Stills if you want to use a static image, or Live if you want to use a Live Photo. These steps show selecting a Live Photo, but using a dynamic or still image is similar.

Current wallpaper on your Lock screen

Current wallpaper on your Home screens

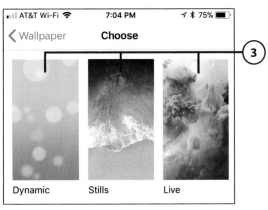

④ Swipe up and down the screen to browse the images available to you.

⑤ Tap the image you want to use as wallpaper.

⑥ Tap Perspective to use the Perspective view of the wallpaper, tap Still if you want a static version of the image, or tap Live Photo to use a Live Photo. (See the sidebar "More on View Options" for an explanation of these terms.)

⑦ Tap Set and move to step 15.

Wallpaper Options Explained

Dynamic wallpaper has motion (kind of like a screen saver on a computer). Stills are static images. Live Photos show motion when you touch and hold on them. Live Photos are available only on iPhone 6s/6s Plus or later models. On other models, you see only the Dynamic and Stills options.

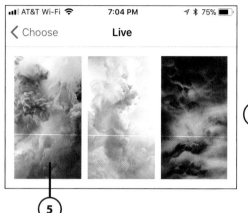

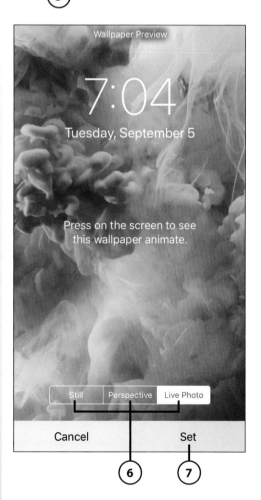

8 To use a photo as wallpaper, swipe up the screen to browse the sources of photos available to you; these include All Photos, Favorites, Selfies, albums, and so on.

Working with Photos

To learn how to work with the photos on your iPhone, see Chapter 14, "Viewing and Editing Photos and Video with the Photos App."

9 Tap the source containing the photo you want to use.

10 Swipe up and down the selected source to browse its photos.

11 Tap the photo you want to use. The photo appears on the Move and Scale screen, which you can use to resize and move the image around.

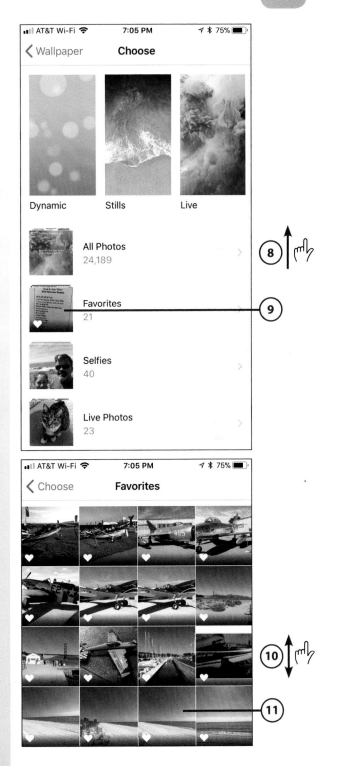

More on View Options

The Perspective view can be a bit difficult to describe because it is subtle. This view magnifies the wallpaper image when you tilt your iPhone. It is sometimes noticeable and sometimes not, depending on the image you are using for wallpaper. The best thing to do is to enable it to see if you notice any difference or disable it if you prefer not to use it for the specific images you use as wallpaper. You can enable or disable it at any time for your wallpaper on the Lock and Home screens. To change the view without changing the wallpaper, move to the Wallpaper screen and tap the wallpaper (tap the Lock or Home screen) you want to change. Tap Perspective to use the Perspective view or Still if you want the image to be static. To save the view, tap Set or to leave it as it is, tap Cancel.

When you choose a Live Photo as wallpaper, you can touch and hold on the screen to see the image's motion. Note that when you apply a Live Photo to the Home screen wallpaper, it becomes a static image for which you can choose the Still or Perspective view.

12 Use your fingers to unpinch to zoom in or pinch to zoom out, and hold down and drag the photo around the screen until it appears how you want the wallpaper to look.

13 Tap Perspective to use the Perspective view of the wallpaper (see the sidebar "More on View Options"), tap Still to use a static version of the image, or tap Live Photo to use a Live Photo (available only when you are working with a Live Photo on iPhone 6s or iPhone 6s Plus or later models).

14 Tap Set.

15 Tap Set Lock Screen or Set Home Screen to apply the wallpaper to only one of those screens; tap Set Both to apply the same wallpaper in both locations. The next time you move to the screen you selected, you see the wallpaper you chose.

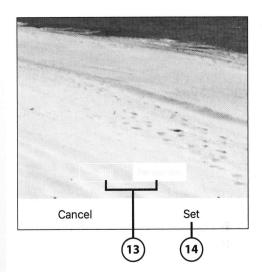

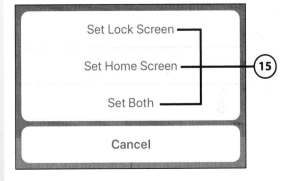

(16) If you set the wallpaper in only one location, tap Choose (not shown on a figure) to move back to the Choose screen and repeat steps 3–15 to set the wallpaper for the other location.

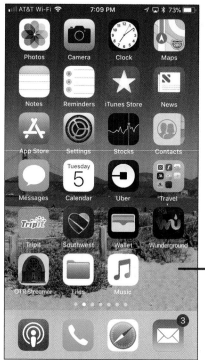

New wallpaper on the Home screen

New wallpaper on the Lock screen

Choosing the Sounds and Vibratory Feedback Your iPhone Uses

Sound and vibrations are two ways your iPhone uses to communicate with you. You can configure the sounds and vibrations the phone uses in two ways. One is by choosing the general sounds and vibrations your iPhone makes, which is covered in this section. You can also configure the sounds and vibrations that apps use for notifications about certain events; this is covered in Chapter 4.

If you have an iPhone 7 or later model, it offers haptic feedback, which means the phone vibrates slightly when something happens, such as when you make a choice on a selection wheel. You can determine whether you want to feel this feedback or not. If you don't have one of these models, you won't see references to haptics on your Sounds screens.

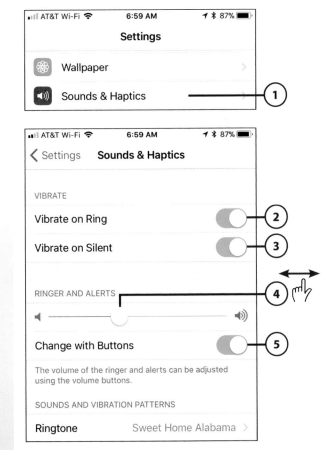

To configure your iPhone's general sounds, do the following:

1. On the Settings screen, tap Sounds & Haptics (iPhone 7 and later) or Sounds (earlier models).

2. Set the Vibrate on Ring switch to on (green) if you want your iPhone to also vibrate when it rings.

3. Set the Vibrate on Silent switch to on (green) if you want your iPhone to vibrate when you have it muted.

4. Set the volume of the ringer and alert tones by dragging the slider to the left or right.

5. Set the Change with Buttons switch to on (green) if you want to also be able to change the ringer volume using the Volume buttons on the side of the phone.

⑥ Tap Ringtone. On the resulting screen, you can set the sound and vibration your iPhone uses when a call comes in.

Individual Ringtones and Vibrations

The ringtone and vibration you set in steps 6–14 are the default or general settings. These are used for all callers except for people in your Contacts app for whom you've set specific ringtones or vibrations. In that case, the contact's specific ringtone and vibration are used instead of the defaults. See Chapter 6, "Managing Contacts," to learn how to configure specific ringtones and vibrations for contacts.

⑦ Swipe up and down the screen to see all the ringtones available to you. There are two sections of sounds on this screen: RINGTONES and ALERT TONES. These work in the same way; alert tones tend to be shorter sounds. At the top of the RINGTONES section, you see any custom ringtones you have configured on your phone; a dark line separates those from the default ringtones that are below the custom ones.

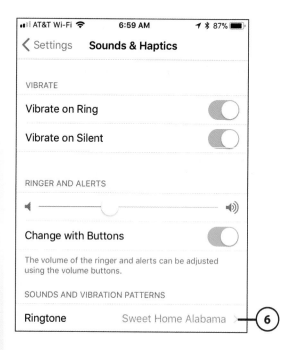

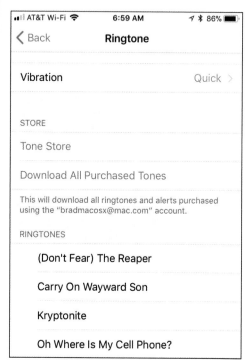

8 Tap a sound, and it plays; tap it again to stop it.

9 Repeat steps 7 and 8 until you have selected the sound you want to have as your general ringtone.

10 If necessary, swipe down the screen so you see the Vibration section at the top.

11 Tap Vibration. A list of Standard and Custom vibrations is displayed.

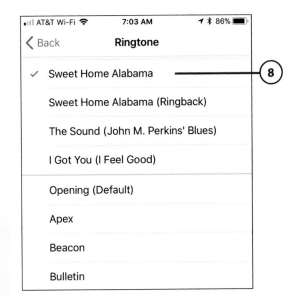

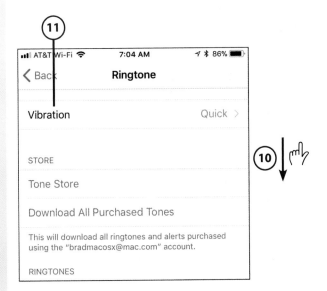

12 Swipe up and down the screen to see all the vibrations available. The STANDARD section contains the default vibrations, and in the CUSTOM section you can tap Create New Vibration to create your own vibration patterns, as discussed in the "Sounding Off" sidebar at the end of this section.

13 Tap a vibration. It "plays" so you can feel it; tap it again to stop it.

14 Repeat steps 12 and 13 until you've selected the general vibration you want to use; you can tap None at the bottom of the Vibration screen (not shown on the figure) below the CUSTOM section if you don't want to have a general vibration.

15 Tap Ringtone.

16 Tap Back. The ringtone you selected is shown on the Sounds and Haptics (or Sounds) screen next to the Ringtone label.

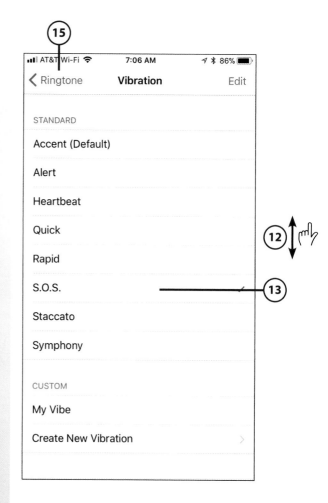

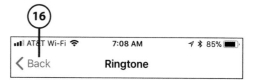

(17) Tap Text Tone.

(18) Use steps 7–14 with the Text
Tone screen to set the sound and
vibration used when you receive
a new text. The process works the
same as for ringtones, though
the screens look a bit different.
For example, the ALERT TONES
section is at the top of the screen
because you are more likely to
want a short sound for new texts.

(19) When you're done setting the
text tone, tap Back.

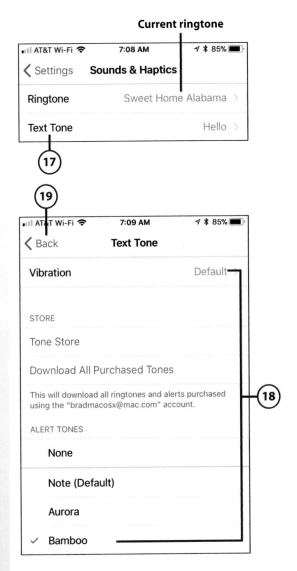

20 Using the same process as you did for ringtones and text tones, set the sound and vibrations for the rest of the events on the list.

21 If you don't like the audible feedback when you tap keys on the iPhone's virtual keyboard, slide the Keyboard Clicks switch to off (white) to disable that sound. The keyboard is silent as you type on it.

22 If you don't want your iPhone to make a sound when you lock it, slide the Lock Sound switch to off (white). Your iPhone no longer makes this sound when you press the Side button to put it to sleep and lock it.

23 Set the System Haptics switch to off (white) if you prefer not to experience vibratory feedback for events. (System Haptics are available on iPhone 7 or later models.)

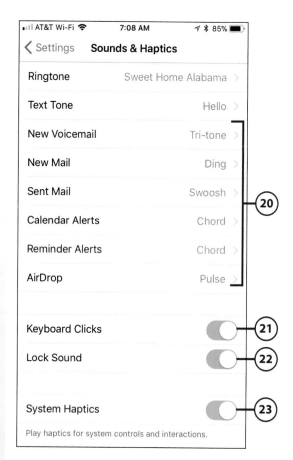

>>>Go Further
SOUNDING OFF

Following are two more sound- and vibration-related pointers:

- You can tap the Store icon on the Ringtone, Text Tone, and other screens to move to the iTunes Store, where you can purchase and download ringtones and other sounds to your iPhone.

- You can create custom vibration patterns. On the Vibration screen, tap Create New Vibration. Tap the vibration pattern you want to create; when you're done tapping, tap Stop. Tap Record to start over if you don't like the one you created. When you're done, tap Save. Name the pattern and tap Save. The patterns you create are available in the CUSTOM section on the Vibration screen, so you can use them just like the iPhone's default vibration patterns. To remove a custom pattern, swipe to the left on it and tap Delete.

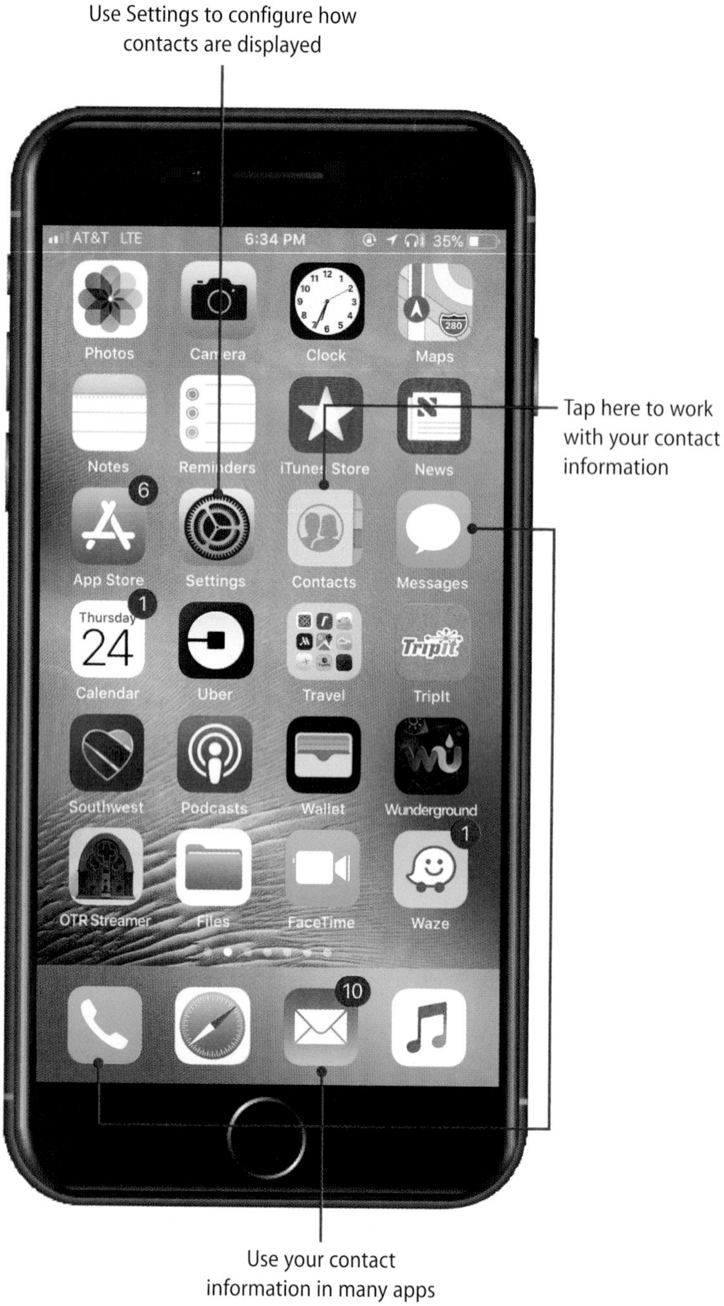
Use Settings to configure how contacts are displayed
Tap here to work with your contact information
Use your contact information in many apps
AT&T LTE
6:34 PM
35%
Photos
Camera
Clock
Maps
Notes
Reminders
iTunes Store
News
App Store
Settings
Contacts
Messages
Thursday
24
Calendar
Uber
Travel
TripIt
Southwest
Podcasts
Wallet
Wunderground
OTR Streamer
Files
FaceTime
Waze

In this chapter, you learn how to ensure that your iPhone has the contact information you need when you need it. Topics include the following:

→ Getting started
→ Setting your Contacts preferences
→ Creating contacts on your iPhone
→ Working with contacts on your iPhone
→ Managing your contacts on your iPhone

Managing Contacts

You'll be using your iPhone to make calls, get directions, send emails, and do many other tasks that require contact information, including names, phone numbers, email addresses, and physical addresses. It would be time-consuming and a nuisance to have to remember and retype this information each time you use it. Fortunately, you don't have to do either because the Contacts app puts all your contact information at your fingertips (literally).

Getting Started

The Contacts app makes using your contact information extremely easy. This information is readily available on your phone in all the apps, such as Mail, Messages, and Phone, in which you need it. And, you don't need to remember or type the information because you can enter it by choosing someone's name, a business's name, or other information that you know about the contact. You can also access your contact information directly in the Contacts app and take action on it (such as placing a call).

To use contact information, it must be stored in the Contacts app. This can be accomplished in several ways. When you configure an online account on your iPhone—such as iCloud or Google—to include contact information, the contact information stored in that account is immediately available on your phone without you having to do anything else. (See Chapter 3, "Setting Up and Using an Apple ID, iCloud, and Other Online Accounts," for the steps to enable contact information in online accounts.) You can manually add new contact information to the Contacts app by capturing that information when you perform tasks (such as reading email). You can also enter new contact information directly in the Contacts app.

The Contacts app also makes it easy to keep your contact information current by doing such things as adding more information, updating existing contacts, or removing contacts you no longer need.

Setting Your Contacts Preferences

Use the Accounts & Passwords settings to configure the online accounts in which you store contact information. (Refer to Chapter 3 for help setting up online accounts.)

Using the Contacts settings, you can determine whether contact information can be used in Siri and other apps, how contacts are sorted and displayed, if or how names are shortened on various screens, your contact information, and which account should be the default for contact information. You can probably work with your contacts just fine without making any changes to these Contacts settings, but if you want to make adjustments, open the Settings app and tap Contacts.

Use the information in the following table to configure your contact settings.

Settings App Explained

To get detailed information on using the Settings app, see "Working with the Settings App" in Chapter 2, "Using Your iPhone's Core Features."

Contacts Settings

Setting	Description
Accounts & Passwords	Use the Accounts & Passwords settings to configure the online accounts you use to store contact information (see Chapter 3).
Siri & Search	Set the Search & Siri Suggestions switch to off (white) if you don't want to use contact information in searches or to allow Siri to access your contact information. Set Find Contacts in Other Apps to off (white) if you don't want contact information in the various apps to be suggested to you, such as to automatically complete addresses when you create emails, or try to identify callers when a number calling you is unknown. You typically should leave both of these on (green) unless you find the automatic contact suggestions annoying or not helpful.
Sort Order	Tap First, Last to have contacts sorted by first name and then last name or tap Last, First to have contacts sorted by last name and then first name.
Display Order	To show contacts in the format *first name, last name,* tap First, Last. To show contacts in the format *last name, first name,* tap Last, First.
Short Name	You can choose whether short names are used and, if they are, what form they take. Short names are useful because more contact information can be displayed in a smaller area, and they look "friendlier." To use short names, move the Short Name switch to the on position (green). Tap the format of the short name you want to use. You can choose from a combination of initial and name or just first or last name. If you want nicknames for contacts used for the short name when available, set the Prefer Nicknames switch to on (green).
My Info	Use this setting to find and tap your contact information in the Contacts app, which it can insert for you in various places and which Siri can use to call you by name; your current contact information is indicated by the label "me" next to the alphabetical index.
Default Account	Tap the account in which you want new contacts to be created by default (which is then marked with a check mark). If you have only one account configured for contacts, you don't have this option.

Where Contacts Are Stored Matters

You should store your contacts in an online account (for example, iCloud or Google), because the information is accessible on many devices and it is also backed up. If you don't have an online account, contact information is stored only on your iPhone. This is not good because, if something happens to your phone, you can lose all of your contacts.

Creating Contacts on Your iPhone

You can create new contacts on an iPhone in a number of ways. You can start with some information, such as the email address on a message you receive, and create a contact from it, or you can create a contact by manually filling in the contact information. In this section, you learn how to create a new contact starting with information in an email message and how to create a new contact manually.

Creating New Contacts from Email

When you receive an email, you can easily create a contact to capture the email address. (To learn how to work with the Mail app, see Chapter 8, "Sending, Receiving, and Managing Email.")

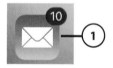

(1) On the Home screen, tap Mail.

(2) Use the Mail app to read an email message.

(3) Tap the email address for which you want to create a new contact; if the address isn't in blue as shown, tap Details before tapping the address. The contact's Info screen appears. You see as much information as could be gleaned from the email address, which is typically the sender's name and email address.

4 Tap Create New Contact. The New Contact screen appears. The name, email address, and any other information that can be identified are added to the new contact. The email address is labeled with iPhone's best guess, such as other or home.

5 Use the New Contact screen to enter more contact information or update the information that was added (such as the label applied to the email address) and save the new contact by tapping Done. This works just like when you create a new contact manually, except that you already have some information—most likely, a name and an email address. For details on adding and changing more information for the contact, see the next task, "Creating Contacts Manually."

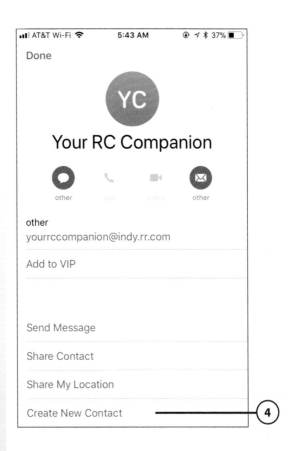

More Information for New Contacts

In some cases, such as when an email comes from an email server that includes full contact information, you see a bar at the top of the email message above the From and To section. This bar shows the sender's name and phone number. Under this, you see Ignore and Add to Contacts. Tap Ignore to ignore this additional contact information. Tap Add to Contacts to create a new contact with all of the information available; this does the same thing as steps 3 through 5 except the resulting new contact contains more information with the name and email address; for example, phone numbers.

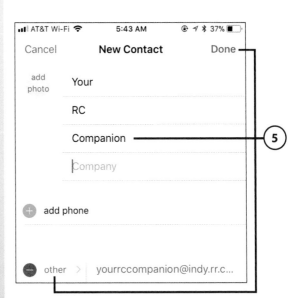

>>>*Go Further*

MORE ON CREATING CONTACTS FROM APPS

It's useful to be able to create contact information by starting with some information in an app. Keep these points in mind:

- Mail is only one of the apps from which you can create contacts. You can start a contact in just about any app you use to communicate, such as Messages, or get information, such as Maps. The steps to start a contact in these apps are similar to those for Mail. Tap the Info (i) icon for the person or address for which you want to create a contact, and then tap Create New Contact. The Contacts app fills in as much of the information as it can, and you can complete the rest yourself.

- You can also add more contact information to an existing contact from an app you are currently using. You can do this by viewing the contact information (such as a phone number) and tapping Add to Existing Contact (instead of Create New Contact). You then search for and select the contact to which you want to add the additional information. After it's saved, the additional information is associated with the contact you selected. For example, suppose you have created a contact for a company but all you have is its phone number. You can quickly add the address to the contact by using the Maps app to look it up and then add the address to the company's existing contact information by tapping the location, tapping Add to Existing Contact, and selecting the company in your contacts.

Creating Contacts Manually

Most of the time, you'll want to get some basic information for a new contact from an app, as the previous task demonstrated, or through an online account, such as contacts stored in your iCloud account. If these aren't available, you can also start a contact from scratch and manually add all the information you need to it. Also, you use the same steps to add information to or change information for an existing contact that you do to create a new one, so even if you don't start from scratch often, you do need to know how to do so.

The Contacts app leads you through creating each type of information you might want to capture. You can choose to enter some or all of the default information on the New Contact screen, or add additional fields as needed.

The following steps show creating a new contact containing the most common contact information you are likely to need:

1. On the Home screen, tap Contacts. (If you don't see the Contacts app on a Home screen, tap the Extras folder to open it and you should see the app's icon. You might want to move the Contacts icon from this folder to a more convenient location on your Home screen; see Chapter 5, "Customizing How Your iPhone Looks and Sounds," for the steps to do this.) The Contacts screen displays.

   If you see the Groups screen instead, tap Done located in the upper-right corner of the screen to move to the Contacts screen. (Groups are covered later.)

2. Tap Add (+). The New Contact screen appears with the default fields.

3. To associate a photo with the contact, tap add photo. You can choose a photo already on your phone or take a new photo. These steps show using an existing photo. See the "Taking Photos" note for the steps to take a new photo.

4. Tap Choose Photo.

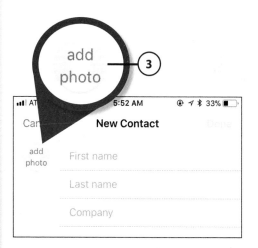

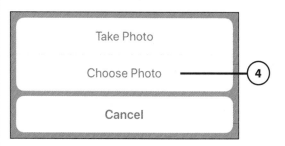

5 Use the Photos app to move to, select, move, and size the photo you want to associate with the contact (see Chapter 14, "Viewing and Editing Photos and Video with the Photos App," for help with the Photos app).

6 Tap Choose. You return to the New Contact screen where the photo you selected is displayed.

7 Tap in the First name field and enter the contact's first name; if you are creating a contact for an organization only, leave both name fields empty. (The Display Order preference determines whether the First name or Last name field appears at the top of the screen.)

8 Tap in the Last name field and enter the contact's last name.

9 Enter the organization, such as a company, with which you want to associate the contact, if any.

10 Tap add phone to add a phone number. A new phone field appears along with the numeric keypad.

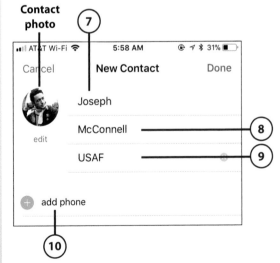

Taking Photos

To take a new photo for a contact, tap Take Photo in step 4 instead of Choose Photo. The Camera app's screen appears. Use the iPhone's camera to capture the photo you want to associate with the new contact (taking photos is covered in Chapter 13, "Taking Photos and Video with Your iPhone"). Use the Move and Scale screen to adjust the photo so it is what you want to use; then tap Use Photo. The photo is pasted into the image icon on the New Contact screen.

(11) Use the numeric keypad to enter the contact's phone number. Include any prefixes you need to dial it, such as area code and country code. The Contacts app formats the number for you as you enter it.

(12) Tap the label for the phone number, such as home, to change it to another label. The Label screen appears.

(13) Swipe up and down the Label screen to see all the options available.

(14) Tap the label you want to apply to the number, such as iPhone. That label is applied and you move back to the New Contact screen.

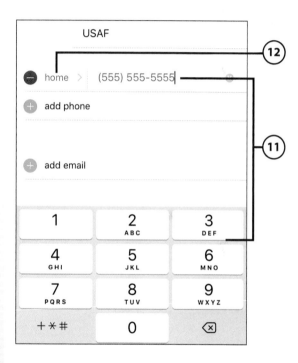

(15) Repeat steps 10–14 to add more phone numbers to the contact.

(16) Swipe up the screen until you see add email.

(17) Tap add email. The keyboard appears.

A Rose by Any Other Name Isn't the Same

The labels you apply to contact information, such as phone numbers, become important when a contact has more than one type of that information. For example, a person might have several phone numbers, such as for home, an iPhone, and work. Applying a label to each of these numbers helps you know which number is for which location. This is especially useful when you use Siri as you can tell Siri which number to use to place a call, such as "Call Sir William Wallace home" to call the number labeled as home on William's contact card.

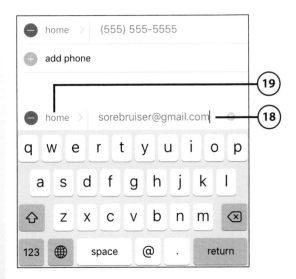

(18) Type the contact's email address.

(19) Tap the label for the email address to change it.

(20) Tap the label you want to apply to the email address. You move back to the New Contact screen.

21 Repeat steps 17–20 to add more email addresses.

22 If necessary, swipe up the screen until you see Ringtone.

23 Tap Ringtone. The list of ringtones and alert tones available on your iPhone appears.

24 Set the Emergency Bypass switch to on (green) if you want sounds and vibrations for phone calls or new messages associated with the contact you are creating to play even when Do Not Disturb is on. (For more about Do Not Disturb, see Chapter 1, "Getting Started with Your iPhone" and for information about working with notifications, see Chapter 2, "Using Your iPhone's Core Features.")

25 Swipe up and down the list to see all of the tones available.

26 Tap the ringtone you want to play when the contact calls you. When you tap a ringtone, it plays so you can experiment to find the one that best relates to the contact. Setting a specific ringtone helps you identify a caller without looking at your phone. (For more on working with sounds and vibrations, see Chapter 5.)

27 Tap Vibration and use the resulting screen if you want to set a specific vibration for the contact (this is also covered in Chapter 5).

28 Tap Done. You return to the New Contact screen.

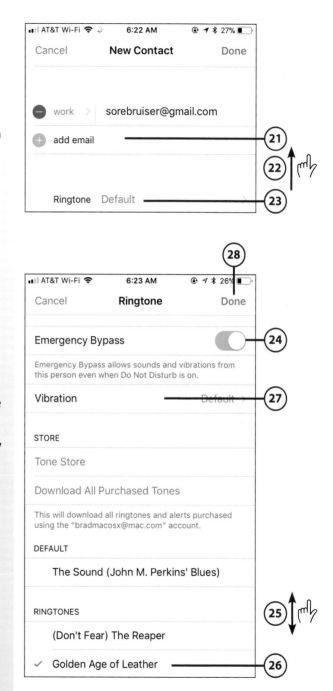

29 Using the pattern you have learned in the previous steps, move to the next item you want to set and tap it.

30 Use the resulting screens to enter the information you want to configure for the contact. After you've done a couple of the fields, it is easy to do the rest because the same pattern is used throughout.

31 When you've added all the information you want to capture, tap Done. The New Contact screen closes and the new contact is created and ready for you to use in Contacts and other apps. It is also moved onto other devices with which your contact information is synced. See the "Creating Contacts Expanded" Go Further sidebar for additional information on syncing and maintaining contacts.

Joseph's contact information is now readily available in many apps

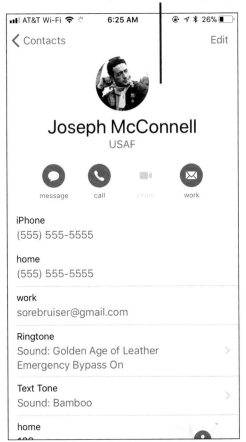

>>>Go Further
CREATING CONTACTS EXPANDED

Contacts are useful in many ways, so you should make sure you have all the contact information you need. Here are a few points to ponder:

- You can (and should) sync contacts on multiple devices (computers and other iOS devices) by using iCloud, Gmail, or other similar online accounts to store your contact information on the cloud from where all your devices can access it. Refer to Chapter 3 for the details of setting up online accounts.

- Syncing your contacts works in both directions. Any new contacts you create or any changes you make to existing contact information on your iPhone move back to your other devices through the sync process.

- To remove a field in which you've entered information, tap Edit, tap the red circle with a dash in it next to the field, and then tap Delete. If you haven't entered information into a field, just ignore it because empty fields don't appear on a contact's screen.

- The address format on the screens in the Contacts app is determined by the country you associate with the address. If the current country isn't the one you want, tap it and select the country in which the address is located before you enter any information. The fields appropriate for that country's addresses appear on the screen.

- If you want to add a type of information that doesn't appear on the New Contact screen, swipe up the screen and tap add field to see a list of fields you can add. Tap a field to add it; for example, tap Nickname to add a nickname for the contact. Then, enter the information for that new field.

- When you add more fields to contact information, those fields appear in the appropriate context on the Info screen. For example, if you add a nickname, it is placed at the top of the screen with the other "name" information. If you add an address, it appears with the other address information.

- As you learn in Chapter 7, "Communicating with the Phone and FaceTime Apps," you can configure the Phone app to announce the name of callers when you receive calls. This can be even more useful than setting a specific ringtone for your important contacts.

Working with Contacts on Your iPhone

There are many ways to use contact information. The first step is always finding the contact information you need, typically by using the Contacts app. Whether you access it directly or through another app (such as Mail), it works the same way. Then, you select the information you want to use or the action you want to perform.

Using the Contacts App

You can access your contact information directly in the Contacts app. For example, you can search or browse for a contact and then view the detailed information for the contact in which you are interested.

(1) On the Home screen, tap Contacts. (If you don't see the Contacts app on the Home screen, tap the Extras folder to open it and you see the Contacts app. You might want to move the Contacts icon from this folder to a more convenient location on your Home screen; see Chapter 5 for the steps to do this.) The Contacts screen displays with the contacts listed in the view and sort format determined by the Contacts settings. (If the Groups screen appears, tap Done, which is located in the upper-right corner of the screen. You move back to the Contacts screen.)

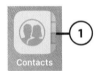

You can find a contact to view by browsing (step 2), using the index (step 3), or searching (step 4). You can use combinations of these, too, such as first using the index to get to the right area and then browsing to find the contact in which you are interested.

(2) Swipe up or down to scroll the screen to browse for contact information; swipe up or down on the alphabetical index to browse rapidly.

(3) Tap the index to jump to contact information organized by the first letter of the format you selected in the Contact Preferences (last name or first name).

(4) Use the Search tool to search for a specific contact; tap in the tool, type the name (you can type last, first, company, and nickname), and then tap the contact you want to view on the results list.

(5) Tap a contact to view that contact's information.

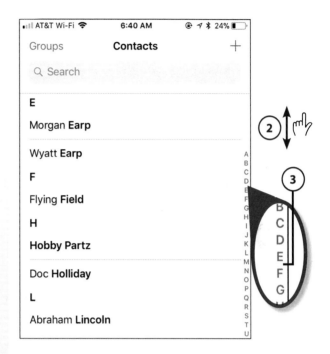

6 Swipe up and down the screen to view all the contact's information.

7 Tap the data or icons on the screen to perform actions, including the following:

- **Phone numbers**—Tap a phone number to call it. You can also tap one of the phone icons just under the contact's image to call that number. For example, to call the number labeled as mobile, tap the mobile icon.

- **Email addresses**—Tap an email address or the icon with the address's label (such as other for the email address labeled as other) on it to create a new message to that address.

- **URLs**—Tap a URL to open Safari and move to the associated website.

- **Addresses**—Tap an address to show it in the Maps app.

- **FaceTime**—Tap video or FaceTime to start a FaceTime call with the contact. (If an icon, such as video, is disabled, you don't have that type of information stored for the contact.)

- **Text**—Tap the message icon or tap Send Message and choose the phone number or email address to which you want to send a text message.

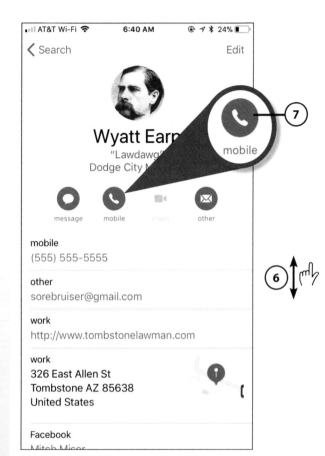

- **Share Contact**—Tap Share Contact. The Share menu appears. To share the contact via email, tap Mail; to share it via a text, tap Message; or to share it using AirDrop, tap AirDrop. You can also share via Twitter or Facebook. Then, use the associated app to complete the task.

- **Favorites**—Tap Add to Favorites and choose the phone number or email address you want to designate as a favorite. You can use this in the associated app to do something faster. For example, if it's the Phone app, you can tap the Favorites tab to see your favorite contacts and quickly dial one by tapping it. You can also quickly access favorites from the FAVORITES widget by swiping to the right when you are on the Lock screen. You can add multiple items (such as cell and work phone numbers) as favorites for one contact.

8 To return to the prior screen without performing an action, tap the Back icon located in the upper-left corner of the screen.

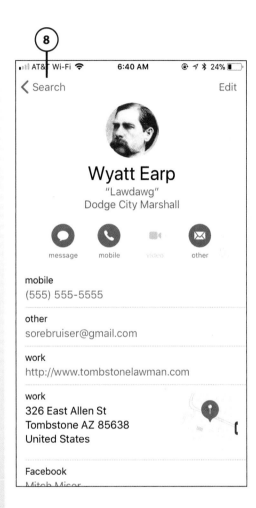

>>>Go Further

MAKE CONTACT

When working with your contacts, keep the following points in mind:

- **Last known contact**—The Contacts app remembers where you last were and takes you back there whenever you move into the Contacts app. For example, if you view a contact's details and then switch to a different app to send a message, and then back to Contacts, you are returned to the screen you were last viewing. To move back to the main Contacts screen, tap the Back icon (it is labeled with the previous screen's name, such as Search or Contacts) in the upper-left corner of the screen.

- **Groups**—In a contact app on a computer, such as Contacts on a Mac, contacts can be organized into groups, which in turn can be stored in an online account, such as iCloud. When you sync, the groups of contacts move onto the iPhone. You can limit the contacts you browse or search by group; to do this, tap Groups, which is located in the upper-left corner of the Contacts screen.

  The Groups screen displays the accounts (such as iCloud or Google) with which you are syncing contact information; under each account are the groups of contacts stored in that account. If a group has a check mark next to it, its contacts are displayed on the Contacts screen. To hide a group's contacts, tap it so that the check mark disappears. To hide or show all of a group's contacts, tap All *account*, where *account* is the name of the account in which those contacts are stored. To make browsing contacts easier, tap Hide All Contacts to hide all the groups and contacts; then, tap each group whose contacts you want to show on the Contacts screen.

  Tap Done, which is located in the upper-right corner of the Groups screen, to move back to the Contacts screen.

- **Speaking of contacts**—You can use Siri to speak commands to work with contacts, too. You can get information about contacts by asking for it, such as "What is William Wallace's work phone number?" If you want to see all of a contact's information, you can say "Show me William Wallace." When Siri displays contact information, you can tap it to take action, such as tapping a phone number to call it. (See Chapter 11, "Working with Siri," for more on using Siri.)

It's Not All Good

Managing Contact Groups

When you create a new contact, it is associated with the account you designated as the default in the Contacts settings and is stored at the account level (not in any of your groups). You can't create groups in the Contacts app, nor can you change the group with which contacts are associated. You have to use a contacts app on a computer to manage groups and then sync your iPhone (which happens automatically when you use an online account, such as iCloud) to see the changes you make to your contact groups.

Accessing Contacts from Other Apps

You can also access contact information while you are using a different app. For example, you can use a contact's email address when you create an email message. When you perform such actions, you use the Contacts app to find and select the information you want to use. The following example shows using contact information to send an email message, and using your contact information in other apps (such as Phone or Messages) is similar.

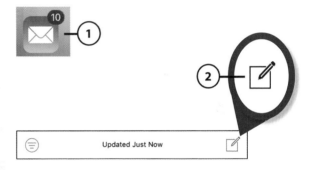

(1) Open the app from which you want to access contact information (this example uses Mail).

(2) Tap the Compose icon.

(3) Tap Add (+) in the To field.

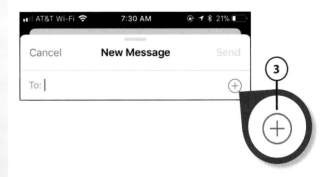

4 Search, browse, or use the index to find the contact whose information you want to use. If you browse or use the index, you see the contacts on the screen and can skip to step 5. If you searched for the contact, you see the results of your search under the Search bar. The text that matches your search is shown in bold. For example, if you search for Wal, you see people named Wallace, Walker, Walken, etc., and "Wal" is shown in bold in each result.

5 Tap the contact whose information you want to use. (If a contact doesn't have relevant information; for example, if no email address is configured when you are using the Mail app, that contact is grayed out and can't be selected.)

If the contact has only one type of the relevant information (such as a single email address, if you started in the Mail app), you immediately move back to the app and the appropriate information is entered, and you can skip to step 7.

6 If the contact has multiple entries of the type you are trying to use, tap the information you want to use—in this case, the email address. The information is copied into the app and entered in the appropriate location.

7 Complete the task you are doing, such as sending an email message.

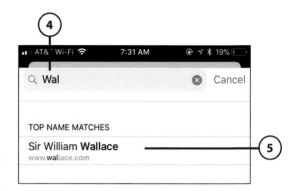

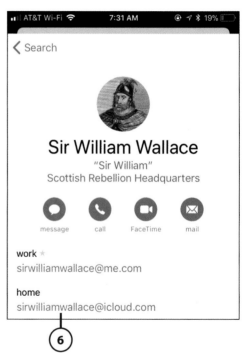

Managing Contacts on Your iPhone

When you sync contacts with an iCloud, Google, or other account, the changes go both ways. For example, when you change a contact on the iPhone, the synced contact manager application, such as Outlook, makes the changes for those contacts on your computer. Likewise, when you change contact information in a contact manager on your computer, those changes move to the iPhone. If you add a new contact in a contact manager, it moves to the iPhone, and vice versa. You can also change contacts manually in the Contacts app on your iPhone.

Updating Contact Information

You can change any information for an existing contact, such as adding new email addresses, deleting outdated information, and changing existing information.

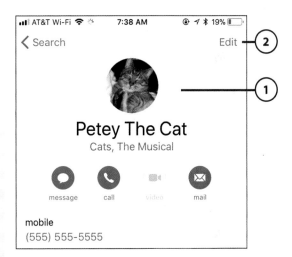

1. Use the Contacts app to find and view the contact whose information you want to change.

2. Tap Edit. The contact screen moves into Edit mode, and you see Unlock icons.

3. Tap current information to change it; you can change a field's label by tapping it, or you can change the data for the field by tapping the information you want to change. Use the resulting tools, such as the phone number entry keypad, to make changes to the information. These tools work just like when you create a new contact (refer to "Creating Contacts Manually," earlier in this chapter).

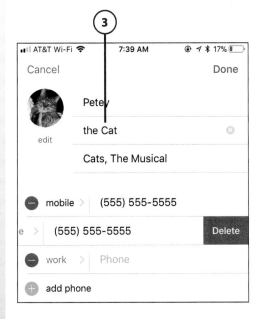

(4) To add more fields, tap the Add (+) icon in the related section, such as add phone in the phone number section; then, select a label for the new field and complete its information. This also works just like adding a new field to a contact you created manually.

(5) Tap a field's Unlock (–) icon to remove that field from the contact.

(6) Tap Delete. The information is removed from the contact.

(7) To change the contact's photo, tap the current photo, or the word *edit* under the current photo, and use the resulting menu and tools to select a new photo, take a new photo, delete the existing photo, or edit the existing one.

(8) When you finish making changes, tap Done. Your changes are saved, and you move out of Edit mode.

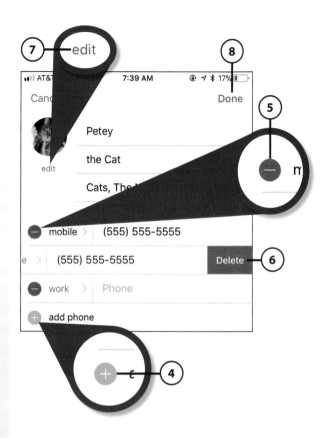

No Tones or Vibes?

If you leave the default tones or vibration patterns set for a contact, you won't see those fields when you view the contact. However, when you edit a contact, all the fields you need to add these to a contact become available.

Adding Information to an Existing Contact While Using Your iPhone

As you use your iPhone, you'll encounter information related to a contact that isn't currently part of that contact's information. For example, a contact might send you an email from a different email address than the one you have stored for her. When this happens, you can easily add the new information to the existing contact. Just tap the information to view it (such as an email address), and then tap Add to Existing Contact. Next, select the existing contact to which you want to add the new information. The new information is added to the contact. Depending on your iPhone model, tap Update or Done (or Cancel, if you decide not to keep the new information) to return to the app you're working in.

Deleting Contacts

To get rid of contacts, you can delete them from the Contacts app.

1. Find and view the contact you want to delete.

2. Tap Edit.

3. Swipe up to get to the bottom of the Info screen.

4. Tap Delete Contact.

5. Tap Delete Contact to confirm the deletion. The app deletes the contact, and you return to the Contacts screen.

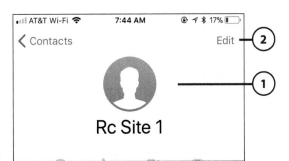

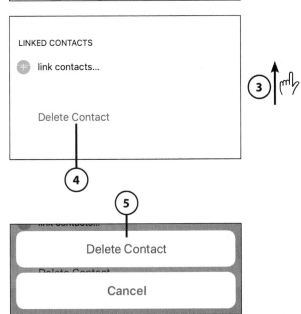

When it's Gone, it's Gone

Be aware that deleting the contact information from your iPhone also deletes it from the associated account through which it is stored. It is also deleted from other devices that access your contact information. In other words, when you delete a contact using the Contacts app on your iPhone, it is deleted from everywhere you use it.

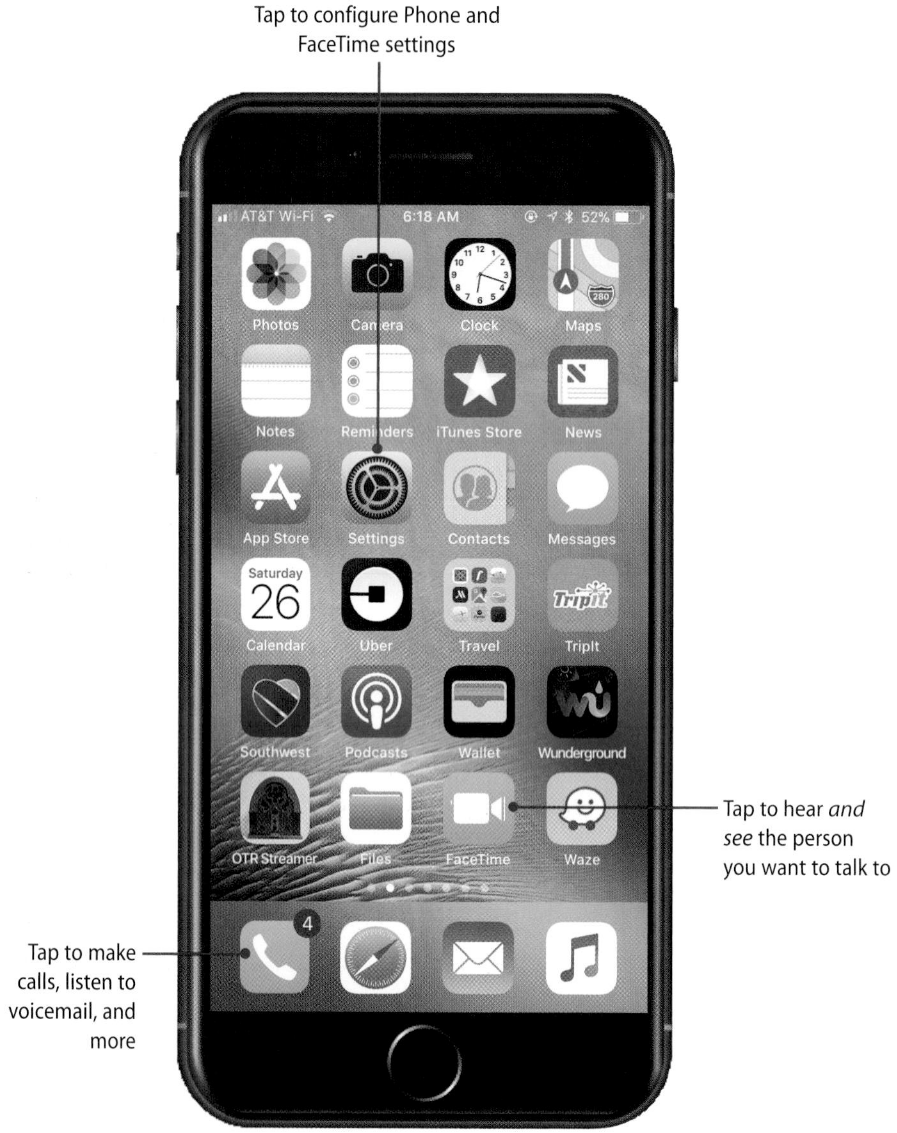
Tap to configure Phone and FaceTime settings
Tap to hear *and see* the person you want to talk to
Tap to make calls, listen to voicemail, and more
AT&T Wi-Fi
6:18 AM
52%
Photos
Camera
Clock
Maps
Notes
Reminders
iTunes Store
News
App Store
Settings
Contacts
Messages
Saturday
26
Calendar
Uber
Travel
TripIt
Southwest
Podcasts
Wallet
Wunderground
OTR Streamer
Files
FaceTime
Waze
4

In this chapter, you explore all the cell phone and FaceTime functionality that your iPhone has to offer. Topics include the following:

→ Getting started
→ Configuring phone settings
→ Making voice calls
→ Managing in-process voice calls
→ Receiving voice calls
→ Managing voice calls
→ Using visual voicemail
→ Communicating with FaceTime

Communicating with the Phone and FaceTime Apps

Although it's also a lot of other great things, such as a music player, web browser, email tool, and such, there's a reason the word *phone* is in iPhone. It's a feature-rich cell phone that includes some amazing features, two of which are visual voicemail and FaceTime. Other useful features include a speakerphone, conference calling, and easy-to-use onscreen controls. Plus your iPhone's phone functions are integrated with its other features. For example, when using the Maps application, you might find a location, such as a business, that you're interested in contacting. You can call that location just by tapping the number you want to call directly on the Maps screen.

Getting Started

Some of the key concepts you'll learn about in this chapter include:

- **Phone app**—The iPhone can run many different kinds of apps that do all sorts of useful things. The iPhone's cell phone functionality is provided by the Phone app. You use this app whenever you want to make calls, answer calls, or listen to voicemail.

- **Visual Voicemail**—The Phone app shows you information about your voice-mails, such as the person who left each message, a time and date stamp, and the length of the message. The Phone app provides a lot more control over your messages, too; for example, you can easily fast forward to specific parts of a message that you want to hear. (This is particularly helpful for capturing information, such as phone numbers.) And if that wasn't enough, you can also read transcripts of voicemails so you don't have to listen to them at all.

- **FaceTime**—This app enables you to have videoconferences with other people (using iPhones or Mac computers) so that you can both see and hear them. Using FaceTime is intuitive so you won't find it any more difficult than making a phone call.

- **FaceTime Audio**—You can make FaceTime calls using only audio; this is simi-lar to making a phone call. One difference is that when you are using a Wi-Fi network to place a FaceTime audio call, there are no extra costs for the call, no matter if you are calling someone next-door or halfway around the world.

Configuring Phone Settings

Of course, we all know that your ringtone is the most important phone set-ting, and you'll want to make sure your iPhone's ringtones are just right. Use the iPhone's Sounds settings to configure custom or standard ringtones and other phone-related sounds, including the new voicemail sound. You can also config-ure the way your phone vibrates when you receive a call. These are explained in Chapter 5, "Customizing How Your iPhone Looks and Sounds."

You can also have different ringtones and vibrations for specific people so you can know who is calling just by the sound and feel when a call comes in (config-uring contacts is explained in Chapter 6, "Managing Contacts").

And you'll want to configure notifications for the Phone app. These include alerts, the app's badge, sounds, and vibrations. Configuring notifications is explained in Chapter 4, "Customizing How Your iPhone Works."

It is likely that you can use the Phone app with its default settings just fine. However, you might want to take advantage of some of its features by configuring the settings described in the following table. To access these settings, open the Settings app and tap Phone.

Provider Differences

The settings for the Phone app depend on the cell phone provider you use. The table lists most, but certainly not all, of the options you might have available. Depending on the provider you use, you may see more, fewer, or different settings than shown in the table. It's a good idea to open your Phone settings to see the options available to you.

Phone Settings

Section	Setting	Description
N/A	My Number	Shows your phone number for reference purposes.
CALLS	Announce Calls	When you enable this setting, the name of the caller (when available) is announced when the phone rings. Tap Always to always have the name announced, Headphones & Car to have the caller announced only when you are using headphones or your car's audio system, Headphones Only to have announcements only when you are using headphones, or Never if you don't want these announcements.
CALLS	Call Blocking & Identification	Tap this to see a list of people who you are currently blocking. You can tap someone on the list to see more information or swipe to the left and tap Unblock to unblock someone. Tap Block Contact to block someone in your Contacts app.

Section	Setting	Description
CALLS	Wi-Fi Calling	When enabled, you can place and receive calls via a Wi-Fi network. This is particularly useful when you are in a location with poor cellular reception, but you have access to a Wi-Fi network. When you set the Wi-Fi Calling on This iPhone switch to on (green), you're prompted to confirm your information. When you do, the service starts and you see the Update Emergency Address option; this is used to record your address so if you can place emergency calls via Wi-Fi, your location can be determined.
CALLS	Calls on Other Devices	When enabled, and your iPhone is on the same network as other iOS devices (such as iPads) or Macs configured with your information, you can take incoming calls and place calls from those devices. This can be useful when you aren't near your phone or simply want to use a different device to have a phone conversation. It can also be annoying because when a call comes in, all the devices using this feature start "ringing." When the Allow Calls on Other Devices switch is on (green), you can choose the specific devices calls are allowed on by setting their switches to on (green).
CALLS	Respond with Text	When calls come in, you have the option to respond with text. For example, you might want to say "Can't talk now, will call later." There are three default text responses or you can use this setting to create your own custom text responses.
CALLS	Call Forwarding	Enables you to forward incoming calls to a different phone number. Set the Call Forwarding switch to on (green) and enter the number to which you want calls forwarded. Set the switch to off (white) to stop your calls from being forwarded.
CALLS	Call Waiting	Enables or disables the call waiting feature.

Section	Setting	Description
CALLS	Show My Caller ID	Shows or hides your caller ID information when you place a call.
N/A	Change Voicemail Password	Use this option to change your voicemail password.
N/A	Dial Assist	Enable the Dial Assist feature if you want the correct country code to be added to numbers in your country when dialing those numbers from outside your country or if you want the correct area codes to be added when you dial a local number. For example, if you live in the United States and don't want the correct prefixes added to U.S. phone numbers when you dial them from outside the United States, turn off Dial Assist (white). You then have to add any prefixes manually when dialing a U.S. number from outside the United States.
N/A	SIM PIN	Your iPhone uses a Subscriber Identity Module (SIM) card to store certain data about your phone; the SIM PIN setting enables you to associate a personal ID number (PIN) with the SIM card in an iPhone. To use your account with a different phone, you can remove the SIM card from your iPhone and install it in other phones that support these cards. If you set a PIN, that PIN is required to use the card in a different phone.
N/A	*Provider* Services, where *Provider* is the name of your provider	This area provides information about your account, such as the numbers you can dial for checking bill balances, paying bills, and other account management. You can also access your account by tapping the link at the bottom of the screen.

Making Voice Calls

There are a number of ways to make calls with your iPhone; after a call is in progress, you can manage it in the same way no matter how you started it.

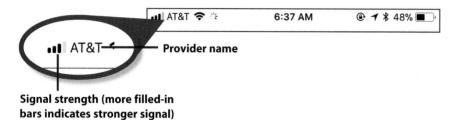

Signal strength (more filled-in
bars indicates stronger signal)

You can tell you are able to make a call or receive calls using your cellular network when you see your provider's information at the top of the screen along with the strength of the signal your phone is receiving. As long as you see at least one bar shaded in, you should be able to place and receive calls via the cellular network. More shaded bars are better because they mean you have a stronger signal, meaning the call quality will be better.

Wi-Fi calling is available

If the Wi-Fi calling feature is enabled and your phone is connected to a Wi-Fi network, you see the Wi-Fi calling icon for your provider at the top of the screen.

With a reasonably strong cellular signal or connection to a Wi-Fi network with Wi-Fi calling enabled, you are ready to make calls.

Which Network?

When you leave the coverage area for your provider and move into an area that is covered by another provider that supports roaming, your iPhone automatically connects to the other provider's network. When you are roaming, you see a different provider near the signal strength indicator at the top of the screen. For example, if AT&T is your provider and you travel to Toronto, Canada, the provider might become Rogers instead of AT&T, which indicates you are roaming. (In most cases, your provider sends a text message to you explaining the change in networks, including information about roaming charges.) Although the change to a roaming network is automatic, you need to be very aware of roaming charges, which can be significant depending on where you use your iPhone and what your default network is. Before you travel outside of your default network's coverage, check with your provider to determine the roaming rates that apply to where you are going. Also, see if there is a discounted roaming plan for that location. If you don't do this before you leave, you might get a nasty surprise when the bill arrives because roaming charges can be substantial.

Dialing with the Keypad

The most obvious way to make a call is to dial the number.

1. On the Home screen, tap Phone. The Phone app opens.

② If you don't see the keypad on the screen, tap Keypad.

③ Tap numbers on the keypad to dial the number you want to call. If you dial a number associated with one or more contacts, you see the contact's name and the type of number you've dialed just under the number. (If you make a mistake in the number you are dialing, tap the Delete icon located to the right of the Call icon to delete the most recent digit you entered.)

④ Tap the Call icon. The app dials the number, and the Call screen appears.

⑤ Use the Call screen to manage the call (not shown in the figure); see "Managing In-Process Voice Calls" later in this chapter for the details.

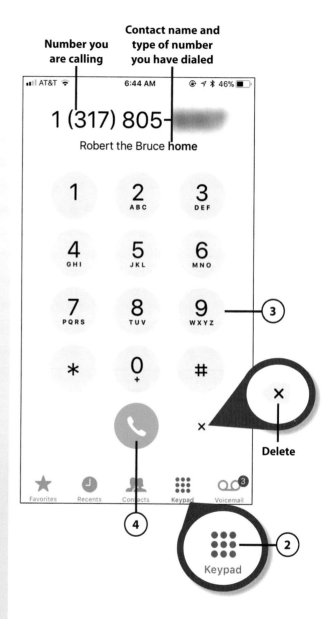

Number you are calling

Contact name and type of number you have dialed

Delete

Keypad

Dialing with Contacts

As you saw in Chapter 6, the Contacts app is a complete contact manager so you can store various kinds of phone numbers for people and organizations. To make a call using a contact, follow these steps.

(1) On the Home screen, tap Phone.

(2) Tap Contacts.

(3) Browse the list, search it, or use the index to find the contact you want to call. (Refer to Chapter 6 for information about using the Contacts app.)

(4) Tap the contact you want to call.

(5) Tap the number you want to dial; or tap the Call icon that is labeled with the type of number under the contact's name (if the person has more than one phone number, you are then prompted to tap the number you want to call). The app dials the number, and the Call screen appears.

(6) Use the Call screen to manage the call (not shown in the figure); see "Managing In-Process Voice Calls" later in this chapter for the details.

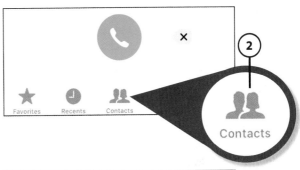

Call Icon

At the top of a contact's screen, you see the Call icon (the receiver). If a contact has only one number, this icon is labeled with the label applied to that number, such as iPhone or mobile; tap the icon to call that number. If the person has more than one number, the icon is labeled with call; when you tap the call icon, you see all of the person's numbers and can tap the number you want to dial.

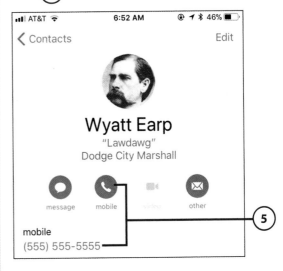

Dialing with Favorites

You can save contacts as favorites to make calling or videoconferencing them even simpler. (You learn how to save favorites in various locations later in this chapter. You learn how to make a contact into a favorite in Chapter 6.)

1. On the Home screen, tap Phone.

2. Tap the Favorites icon.

3. Browse the list until you see the favorite you want to call. Under the contact's name, you see the type of favorite, such as a phone number (identified by the label in the Contacts app, for example, iPhone or mobile) or FaceTime.

4. Tap the favorite you want to call; to place a voice call, tap a phone number (if you tap a FaceTime contact, a FaceTime call is placed instead). The app dials the number, and the Call screen appears.

5. Use the Call screen to manage the call (not shown in the figure); see "Managing In-Process Voice Calls" later in this chapter for the details.

Nobody's Perfect

If your iPhone can't complete the call for some reason, such as not having a strong enough signal, the Call Failed screen appears. Tap Call Back to try again and maybe try moving to another location that might have a stronger signal or tap Done to give up. When you tap Done, you return to the screen from which you came.

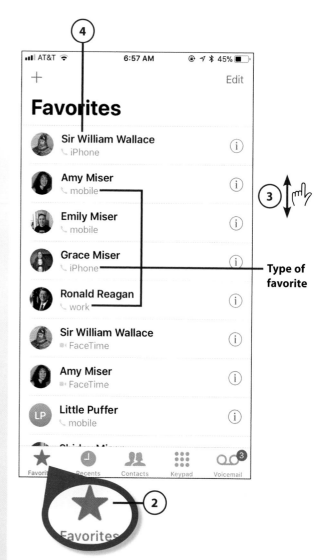

Type of favorite

Dialing with Recents

As you make, receive, or miss calls, your iPhone keeps tracks of all the numbers on the Recents list. You can use the Recents list to make calls.

(1) On the Home screen, tap Phone.

(2) Tap Recents.

(3) Tap All to see all calls.

(4) Tap Missed to see only calls you missed.

(5) If necessary, browse the list of calls.

(6) To call the number associated with a recent call, tap the title of the call, such as a person's name, or the number if no contact is associated with it. The app dials the number, and the Call screen appears. Skip to step 10.

(7) To get more information about a recent call, for example, to see exactly what time yesterday they called, tap its Info (i) icon. The Info screen appears.

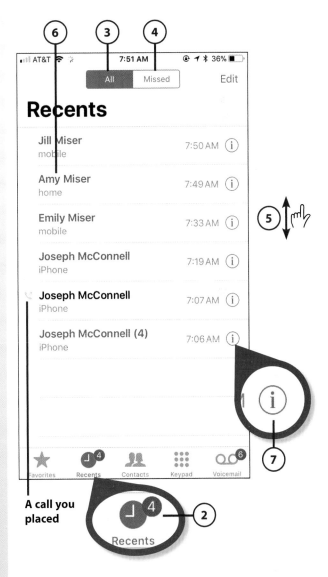

A call you placed

Info on the Recents Screen

If you have a contact on your iPhone associated with a phone number, you see the person's name and the label for the number (such as mobile). If you don't have a contact for a number, you see the number itself. If a contact or number has more than one call associated with it, you see the number of recent calls in parentheses next to the name or number. If you initiated a call, you see the phone icon next to the contact's name and label.

8 Read the information about the call or calls. For example, if the call is related to someone in your Contacts list, you see detailed information for that contact. If there are multiple recent calls, you see information for each call, such as its status (Missed Call, Canceled Call, or Outgoing Call, for example) and time.

9 Tap a number on the Info screen. The app dials the number, and the Call screen appears.

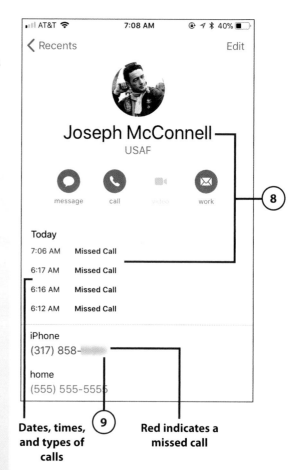

Going Back
To return to the Recents screen without making a call, tap Recents.

10 Use the Call screen to manage the call (not shown in the figure); see "Managing In-Process Voice Calls" later in this chapter for the details.

Dates, times, and types of calls

Red indicates a missed call

Dialing from the FAVORITES Widget

Using the FAVORITES widget, you can quickly call a favorite. Use the following steps.

Managing Widgets
If you don't see the FAVORITES widget, you need to add it. See Chapter 4 for the steps to manage your widgets.

1 From the Home or Lock screen, swipe to the right to open your widgets.

(2) Swipe up or down until you see the FAVORITES widget.

(3) Tap Show More to see the full list of favorites. The list expands.

(4) Tap the person you want to call.

(5) Use the Call screen to manage the call (not shown in the figure); see the next section for the details.

You've Got the Touch

If your iPhone supports 3D Touch (iPhone 6s/6s Plus and later), you can also place calls to favorites by pressing on the Phone app. The FAVORITES pane appears; tap a favorite to place a call. You can also access the most recent voicemail or see the most recent call.

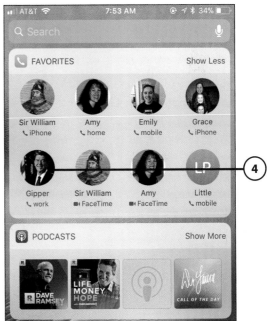

Managing In-Process Voice Calls

When you place a call, there are several ways to manage it. The most obvious is to place your iPhone next to your ear and use your iPhone like any other phone you've ever used. As you place your iPhone next to your ear, the controls on its screen become disabled so you don't accidentally tap onscreen icons with the side of your face or your ear. When you take your iPhone away from your ear, the Call screen appears again and the Phone app's controls become active again.

When you are on a call, press the Volume buttons on the left side of the iPhone to increase (top button) or decrease (bottom button) its volume. Some of the other things you can do while on a call might not be so obvious, as you learn in the next few tasks.

Following are some of the icons on the Call screen that you can use to manage an active call:

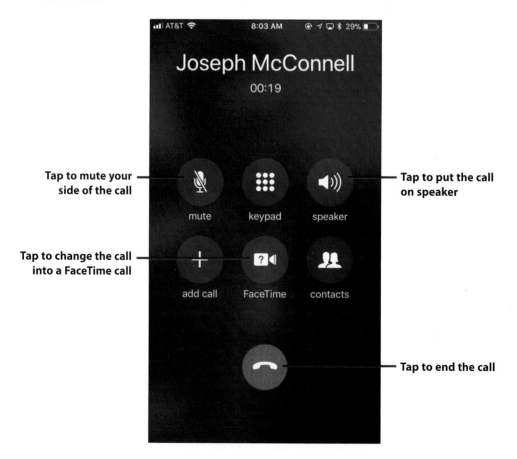

Tap to mute your side of the call — mute

keypad

Tap to put the call on speaker — speaker

Tap to change the call into a FaceTime call — add call

FaceTime

contacts

Tap to end the call

- Mute your side of the call by tapping mute. You can hear the person on the other side of the call, but he can't hear anything on your side.

- Tap speaker to use the iPhone's speakers to hear the call. You can speak with the phone held away from your face, too.

- Tap FaceTime to convert the voice call into a FaceTime call (read more on FaceTime later in this chapter).

- When you're done with the call, tap the Receiver icon to end it.

Contact Photos on the Call Screen

If someone in your contacts calls you, or you call her, the photo associated with the contact appears on the screen. Depending on how the image was captured, it either appears as a small icon at the top of the screen next to the contact's name or fills the entire screen as the background wallpaper.

Entering Numbers During a Call

You often need to enter numbers during a call, such as to log in to a voicemail system, access an account, or enter a meeting code for an online meeting.

1. Place a call using any of the methods you've learned so far.

2. Tap keypad.

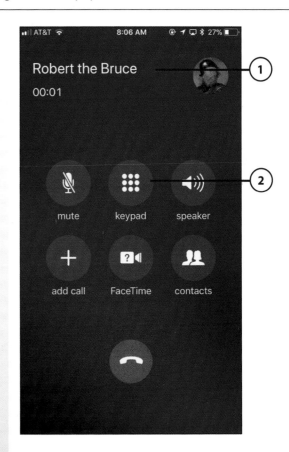

3 Tap the numbers you want to enter.

4 When you're done, tap Hide. You return to the Call screen.

Making Conference Calls

Your iPhone makes it easy to talk to multiple people at the same time. You can have two separate calls going on at any point in time. You can even create conference calls by merging them together. Not all cell providers support two on-going calls or conference calling, though. If yours doesn't, you won't be able to perform the steps in this section.

1 Place a call using any of the methods you've learned so far.

2 Tap add call.

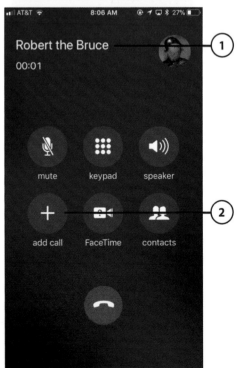

(3) Tap the icon you want to use to place the next call. Tap Favorites to call a favorite, tap Recents to use the Recents list, tap Contacts to place the call using the Contacts app, or tap Keypad to dial the number. These work just as they do when you start a new call.

(4) Place the call using the option you selected in step 3. Doing so places the first call on hold and moves you back to the Call screen while the Phone app makes the second call. The first call's information appears at the top of the screen, including the word hold so you know the first call is on HOLD. The app displays the second call just below that, and it is currently the active call.

Similar but Different

If you tap contacts instead of add call, you move directly into the Contacts screen. This might save you one screen tap if the person you want to add to the call is in your Contacts app.

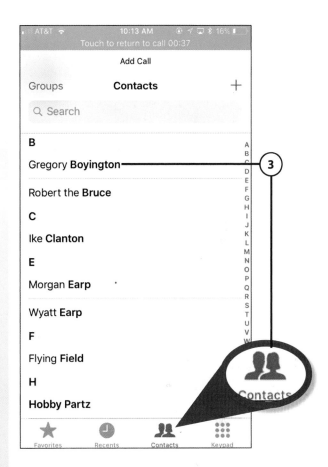

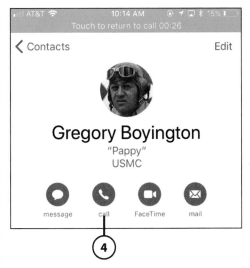

5. Talk to the second person you called; the first remains on hold.

6. To switch to the first call, tap it on the list or tap swap. This places the second call on hold and moves it to the top of the call list, while the first call becomes active again.

7. Tap merge calls to join the calls so all parties can hear you and each other. The iPhone combines the two calls, and you see a single entry at the top of the screen to reflect this.

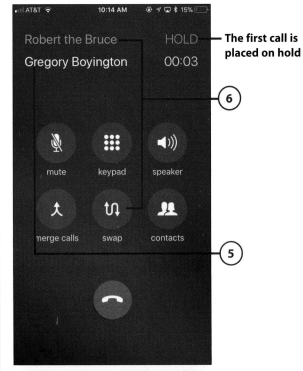

The first call is placed on hold

Merging Calls

As you merge calls, your iPhone attempts to display the names of the callers at the top of the Call screen. As the text increases, your iPhone scrolls it so you can read it. Eventually, the iPhone replaces the names with the word Conference.

Number of Callers

Your provider and the specific technology of the network you use can limit the number of callers you place in a conference call. When you reach the limit, the add call icon is disabled.

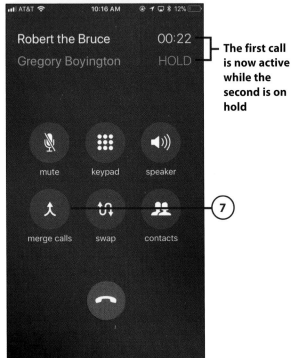

The first call is now active while the second is on hold

(8) To add another call, repeat steps 2–7. Each time you merge calls, the second line becomes free so you can add more calls.

(9) To manage a conference call, tap the Info (i) icon at the top of the screen.

(10) To speak with one of the callers privately, tap Private (if the Private icons are disabled, you can't do this with the current calls). Doing so places the conference call on hold and returns you to the Call screen showing information about the active call. You can merge the calls again by tapping merge calls.

(11) Tap End to remove a caller from the call. The app disconnects that caller from the conference call. When you have only one person left on the call, you return to the Call screen and see information about the active call.

(12) Tap Back to move back to the Call screen. You move to the Call screen and can continue working with the call, such as adding more people to it.

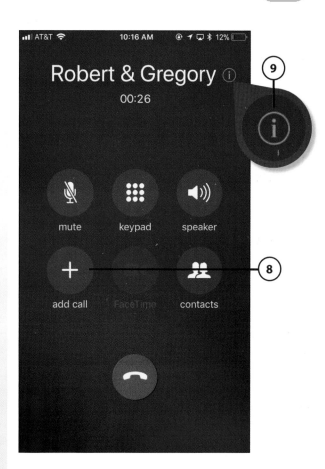

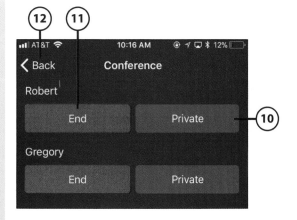

13 To end the call for all callers, tap the Receiver icon.

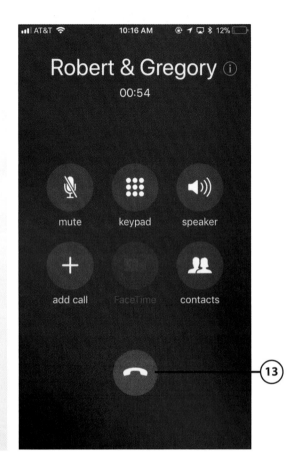

It's Not All Good

Watch Your Minutes

When you have multiple calls combined into one, depending on your provider, the minutes for each call can continue to count individually. So if you've joined three people into one call, each minute of the call might count as three minutes against your calling plan. Before you use this feature, check with your provider to determine what policies govern conference calling for your account.

Using Another App During a Voice Call

A call is active, and you can use other apps while still talking

Tap to return to the call

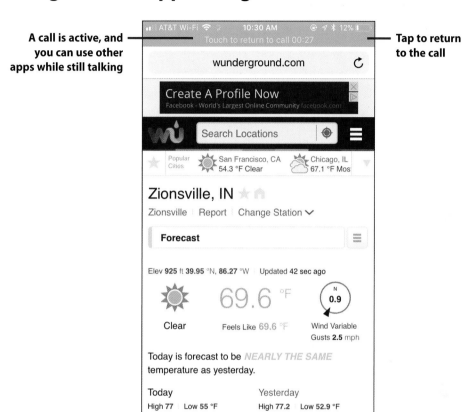

If your provider's technology supports it, you can use your iPhone for other tasks while you are on a call. When you are on a call, press the Touch ID/Home button (all models except iPhone X) or swipe up from the bottom of the screen (iPhone X) to move to a Home screen and then tap a different app (placing the call in speaker mode before you switch to a different app or using headphones are best for this). Or, you can press the Touch ID/Home button twice (all models except iPhone X) or swipe up from the bottom of the screen and pause toward the middle of the screen (iPhone X) to open the App Switcher to move into a different app. The call remains active and you see the active call information in a green bar at the top of the screen. You can perform other tasks, such as looking up information, sending emails, and visiting websites. You can continue to talk to the other person just like when the Call screen is showing. To return to the call, tap the green bar.

Receiving Voice Calls

Receiving calls on your iPhone enables you to access the same great tools you can use when you make calls, plus a few more for good measure.

Answering Calls

Person calling you ⸺ Joseph McConnell / iPhone

Tap to decline and be reminded of the call later ⸺ Remind Me

Tap to decline and respond with a message ⸺ Message

Tap to decline and send the call to voicemail ⸺ Decline

Tap to answer ⸺ Accept

When your iPhone rings, it's time to answer the call—or not. If you configured the ringer to ring, you hear your default ringtone or the one associated with the caller's contact information when a call comes in. If vibrate is turned on, your iPhone vibrates whether the ringer is on or not. If you enabled the announce feature, the name of the caller is announced (if available). And if those ways aren't enough, a message appears on your iPhone's screen to show you information about the incoming call. If the number is in your Contacts app, you see the contact with which the number is associated, the label for the number, and the contact's image if there is one. If the number isn't in your contacts, you see the number only.

Wallpaper

If the photo associated with a contact was taken with your iPhone or came from a high-resolution image, you see the contact's image at full screen when the call comes in, instead of the small icon at the top of the screen.

Calls on Other Devices

By default, when you receive a call on your iPhone, it also comes to any iOS 8 or later devices or Macs running Yosemite or later that are on the same Wi-Fi network, and you can take the call on those devices. To disable this, set the Calls on Other Devices setting to off as described earlier in this chapter.

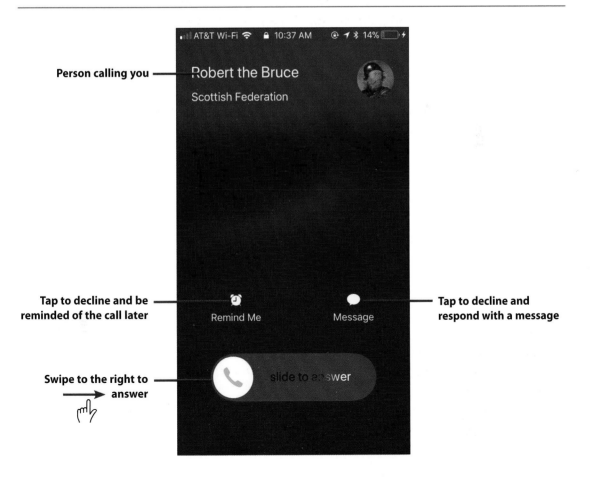

Person calling you — Robert the Bruce / Scottish Federation

Tap to decline and be reminded of the call later — Remind Me

Tap to decline and respond with a message — Message

Swipe to the right to answer — slide to answer

If your iPhone is locked when a call comes in, swipe the slider to the right to answer it or use the Remind Me and Message icons, which work just like they do when a call comes in when the iPhone isn't locked.

When you receive a call, you have the following options:

- **Answer**—Tap Accept (if the iPhone is unlocked) or swipe the slider to the right (if the iPhone is locked) to take the call (you don't have to unlock the phone to answer a call). You move to the Call screen and can work with the call just like calls you place. For example, you can add a call, merge calls, place the call on hold, or end the call.

- **Decline**—If you tap Decline (when the iPhone is unlocked), the Phone app immediately routes the call to voicemail. You can also decline a call by quickly pressing the Side button twice.

- **Silence the ringer**—To silence the ringer without sending the call directly to voicemail, press the Side button once or press either volume button once. The call continues to come in, and you can answer it even though you shut off the ringer.

- **Respond with a message**—Tap Message to send the call to voicemail and send a message back in response. You can tap one of the default messages, or you can tap Custom to create a unique message (the table at the beginning of the chapter explains where to find the setting to create custom messages). Of course, the device the caller is using to make the call must be capable of receiving messages for this to be useful.

- **Decline the call but be reminded later**—Tap Remind Me and the call is sent to voicemail. Tap When I leave, When I get home, When I get to work, or In 1 hour to set the timeframe in which you want to be reminded. A reminder is created in the Reminders app to call back the person who called you, and it is set to alert you at the time you select.

Silencio!

To mute your iPhone's ringer, slide the Mute switch located above the Volume switch toward the back so the orange line appears. The Mute icon (a bell with a slash through it) appears on the screen to let you know you turned off the ringer. To turn it on again, slide the switch forward. The bell icon appears on the screen to show you the ringer is active again. To set the ringer's volume, use the Volume controls (assuming that setting is enabled) when you aren't on a call and aren't listening to an app, such as the Music app.

Answering Calls During a Call

As mentioned earlier, your iPhone can manage multiple calls at the same time. If you are on a call and another call comes in, you have a number of ways to respond.

- **Decline incoming call**—Tap Send to Voicemail to send the incoming call directly to voicemail.

- **Place the first call on hold and answer the incoming call**—Tap Hold & Accept to place the current call on hold and answer the incoming one. After you do this, you can manage the two calls just as when you call two numbers from your iPhone. For example, you can place the second call on hold and move back to the first one, merge the calls, and add more calls.

- **End the first call and answer the incoming call**—Tap End & Accept to terminate the active call and answer the incoming call.

- **Respond with message or get reminded later**—These options work just as they do when you are dealing with any incoming phone call.

Auto-Mute

If you are listening to music or video when a call comes in, the app providing the audio, such as the Music app, automatically pauses. When the call ends, that app picks up right where it left off.

Managing Voice Calls

You've already learned most of what you need to know to use your iPhone's cell phone functions. In the following sections, you learn the rest.

Clearing Recent Calls

Previously in this chapter, you learned about the Recents tool that tracks call activity on your iPhone. As you read, this list shows both completed and missed calls; you can view all calls by tapping the All tab or only missed calls by tapping Missed. On either tab, missed calls are always in red, and you see the number of missed calls since you last looked at the list in the badge on the Recents tab. You also learned how you can get more detail about a call, whether it was missed or made.

Over time, you'll build a large Recents list, which you can easily clear.

1 Tap Phone.

2 Tap Recents.

3 Tap Edit.

4 Tap Clear to clear the entire list; to delete a specific recent call, skip to step 6.

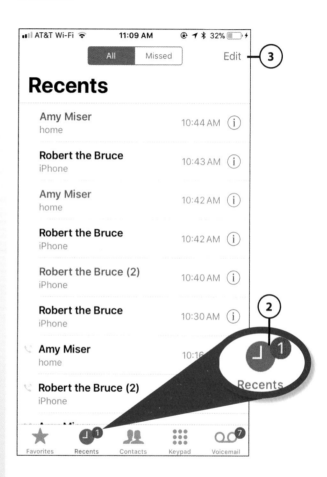

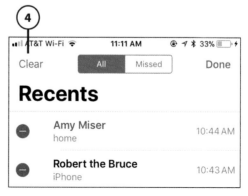

(5) Tap Clear All Recents. The Recents list is reset and you can skip to the rest of these steps.

Delete Faster

On the Recents screen, you can delete an individual recent item by swiping to the left on it (starting to the left of the i icon) and tapping Delete.

(6) Tap a recent item's Unlock (–) icon.

(7) Tap Delete. The recent item is deleted.

(8) When you are done managing your recent calls, tap Done.

Clear All Recents — **5**

Cancel

Favorites   Recents   Contacts   Keypad   Voicemail

(6)

AT&T Wi-Fi 🛜   11:11 AM   @ ✈ ✳ 33% 🔋 ⚡

Clear   [All]   Missed   Done — **8**

Recents

⊖   Amy Miser   10:44 AM
      home

Robert the Bruce   10:43 AM   **Delete** — **7**
Phone

⊖   Amy Miser   10:42 AM
      home

Adding Calling Information to Favorites

Earlier you learned how simple it is to place calls to someone on your Favorites list. There are a number of ways to add people to this list, including adding someone on your Recents list.

(1) Move to the Recents list.

(2) Tap the Info (i) icon for the person you want to add to your favorites list. The Info screen appears. If the number is associated with a contact, you see that contact's information.

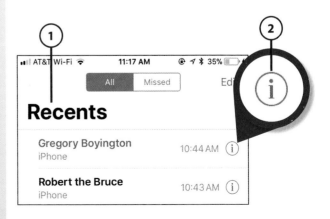

(1)   **(2)**

AT&T Wi-Fi 🛜   11:17 AM   @ ✈ ✳ 35% 🔋

                        [All]   Missed   Ed ⓘ

Recents

Gregory Boyington   10:44 AM ⓘ
iPhone

Robert the Bruce   10:43 AM ⓘ
iPhone

③ Swipe up to move to the bottom of the screen.

④ Tap Add to Favorites. If the person has multiple types of contact information, such as phone numbers, email addresses, and so on, you see each type of information available.

⑤ Tap the type of information you want to add as a favorite, such as Call to make a phone number a favorite.

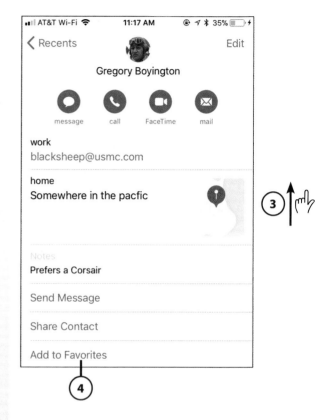

6. Tap the number or email address you want to add as a favorite.

7. Repeat steps 5 and 6 if you want to add the contact's other numbers or addresses to the favorites list. (If all the numbers and email addresses are assigned as favorites, Add to Favorites doesn't appear on the contact's screen.)

Make Contact First

To make someone a favorite, he needs to be a contact in the Contacts app. Refer to Chapter 6 to learn how to make someone who has called you into a contact.

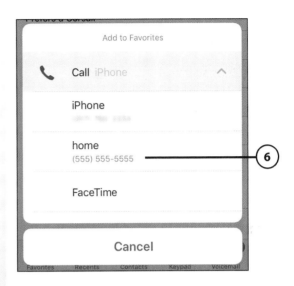

Using the iPhone's Headset for Calls

Your iPhone includes an EarPods headset with a microphone on one of its cords. The mic includes a button in the center of the switch on the right side of the EarPod's cable that you can use to do the following:

- **Answer**—Press the mic button once to answer a call.

- **End a call**—Press the mic button while you are on a call to end it.

- **Decline a call**—Press and hold the mic button for about two seconds. Two beeps sound when you release the button to let you know that your iPhone sent the call to voicemail.

- **Put a current call on hold and switch to an incoming call**—Press the mic button once and then press again.

- **End a current call on hold and switch to an incoming call**—Press the mic button once and hold for about two seconds. Release the button and you hear two beeps to let you know you ended the first call. The incoming call is ready for you.

- **Activate Siri**—Press and hold the mic button until you hear the Siri chime. This is useful when you want to make a call to someone without looking at or touching your phone.

Oh, That Ringing in My Ears

When you have EarPods plugged into your iPhone and you receive a call, the ringtone plays on both the iPhone's speaker (unless the ringer is muted, of course) and through the EarPods.

Using Visual Voicemail

Visual voicemail just might be the best of your iPhone's many great features. No more wading through long, uninteresting voicemails to get to one in which you are interested. You simply jump to the message you want to hear. If that isn't enough for you, you can also jump to any point within a voicemail to hear just that part, such as to repeat a phone number that you want to write down. Even better, the iPhone creates a transcript of voicemails, so you can read them instead of listening to them.

The Phone app can access your voicemails directly so don't need to log in to hear them.

Recording a New Greeting

The first time you access voicemail, you are prompted to record a voicemail greeting. Follow the onscreen instructions to do so.

You can also record a new greeting at any time.

1 Move to the Phone screen and tap Voicemail. If badge notifications are enabled for the Phone app, you see the number of voicemails you haven't listened to yet in the badge on the Voicemail icon.

2 Tap Greeting.

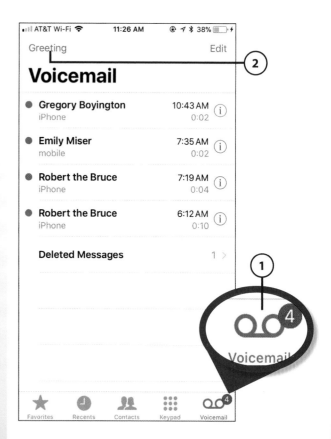

3. To use a default greeting that provides only the iPhone's phone number, tap Default and skip to step 10.

4. Tap Custom to record a personalized greeting. If you have previously used a custom greeting, it is loaded into the editor. You can replace it by continuing with these steps.

5. Tap Record. Recording begins.

6. Speak your greeting. As you record your message, the red area of the timeline indicates (relatively) how long your message is.

7. When you're done recording, tap Stop.

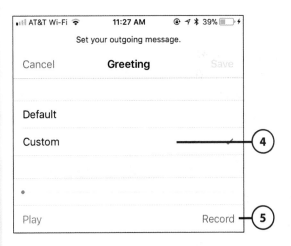

For the Very First Time

Some providers require that you dial into your voicemail number the first time you use it. If you tap Voicemail and the phone starts to dial instead of you seeing Visual Voicemail as shown in these figures, this is your situation. You call the provider's voicemail system, and you're prompted to set up your voicemail. When you've completed that process, you can use these steps to record your greeting.

Your message being recorded

8 Tap Play to hear your greeting.

9 If you aren't satisfied, drag the Playhead to the beginning and repeat steps 5–8 to record a new message.

10 When you are happy with your greeting, tap Save. The Phone app saves the default or custom greeting as the active greeting and returns you to the Voicemail screen.

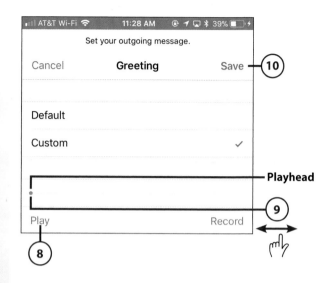

Adding to a Custom Message

To add onto or replace part of an existing greeting, drag the playhead to where you want to start recording and tap Record. Tap Stop when you're done.

No Visual Voicemail?

If your voicemail password isn't stored on your iPhone when you tap Voicemail, your phone dials into your voicemail instead of moving to the Voicemail screen. If that happens, something has gone wrong with your password and you need to reset it. Follow your provider's instructions to reset the password. When you have the new password, open the Phone Settings screen, tap Change Voicemail Password, enter the reset password, create a new password, and re-enter your new password. (You need to tap Done after each time you enter a password.)

Change Greeting

To switch between the default and the current custom greeting, move to the Greeting screen, tap the greeting you want to use (which is marked with a check mark), and tap Save. When you choose Custom, you use the custom greeting you most recently saved.

Listening to, Reading, and Managing Voicemails

Unless you turned off the voicemail sound, you hear the sound you selected each time a caller leaves a voicemail for you. The number in the badge on the Phone icon and on the Voicemail icon on the Phone screen increases by 1 (unless you've disabled the badge). (Note that the badge number on the Phone icon includes both voicemails left for you and missed calls, whereas the badge number on the Voicemail icon indicates only the number of voicemails left for you.) (A new voicemail is one to which you haven't listened, not anything to do with when it was left for you.) If you've configured visual notifications for new voicemails (see Chapter 4), you see those on the screen as well.

If you receive a voicemail while your iPhone is locked, you see a message on the screen alerting you that your iPhone received a voicemail (unless you have disabled these notifications from appearing on the Lock screen). (It also indicates a missed call, which is always the case when a call ends up in voicemail.) Press (3D Touch iPhones) or swipe to the right (non-3D Touch models) on the notification to jump to the Voicemail screen so that you can work with your messages.

And in yet another scenario, if you are using your iPhone when a message is left, you see a notification (unless you have turned off notifications for the Phone app) that enables you to deal with the new message.

Missing Password

If something happens to the password stored on your iPhone for your voicemail, such as if you restore the iPhone, you are prompted to enter your password before you can access your voicemail. Do so at the prompt and tap OK. The iPhone signs you in to voicemail, and you won't have to enter your password again (unless something happens to it again of course).

Contacts or Numbers?

Like phone calls, if a contact is associated with a number from which you've received a voicemail, you see the contact's name associated with the voicemail message. If no contact exists for the number, you see the number only.

Finding and Listening to Voicemails

Working with voicemails is simple and quick.

(1) Move into the Phone app and tap Voicemail (if you pressed or swiped on a new message notification, you jump directly to the Voicemail screen).

(2) Swipe up and down the screen to browse the list of voicemails. Voicemails you haven't listened to are marked with a blue circle.

(3) To listen to or read a voicemail, tap it. You see the timeline bar and controls and the message plays.

(4) Read the message if you don't want to listen to it.

(5) Tap the Pause icon to pause a message.

(6) Tap Speaker to hear the message on your iPhone's speaker.

Voicemail you haven't listened to

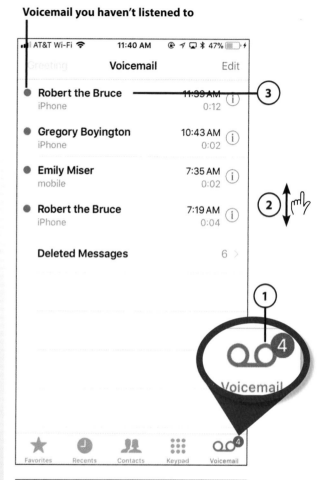

7 To move to a specific point in a message, drag the Playhead to the point at which you want to listen.

Moving Ahead or Behind

You can also drag the Playhead while a message is playing to rewind or fast-forward it. This is also helpful when you want to listen to specific information without hearing the whole message again.

8 Tap Call Back to call back the person who left the message.

9 Tap Delete to delete the message.

10 Tap the Share icon to share the message, and then tap how you want to share it, such as Message or Mail. For example, when you tap Mail, you send the voice-mail to someone else using the Mail app, so he can listen to the message.

11 Tap the Info (i) icon to get more information about a message. The Info screen appears. If the person who left the message is on your contacts list, you see her contact information. The number associ-ated with the message is high-lighted in blue.

12 Swipe up or down the screen to review the caller's information.

13 Tap Voicemail.

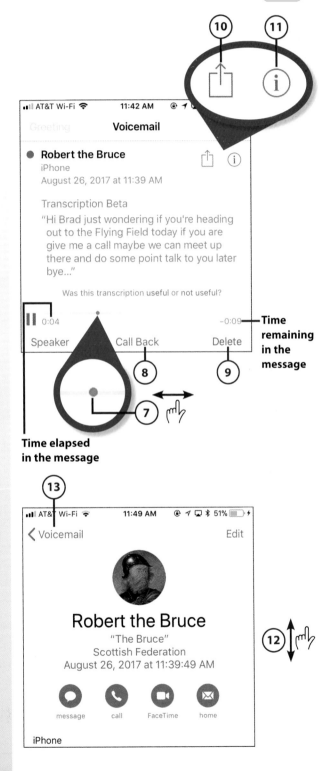

(14) To listen to a message you have listened to before (one that doesn't have a blue dot), tap the message and then tap the Play icon. It begins to play. You can also read its transcript (if available).

Deleting Messages

To delete a voicemail message that isn't the active message, tap it so it becomes the active message and then tap Delete. Or swipe to the left on the message you want to delete and tap Delete. Or swipe quickly all the way to the left on the message to delete it.

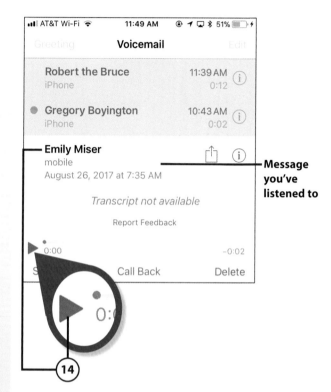

Message you've listened to

Listening to and Managing Deleted Voicemails

When you delete messages, they are moved to the Deleted Message folder. You can work with deleted messages as follows:

(1) Move to the Voicemail screen.

(2) If necessary, swipe up the screen until you see the Deleted Messages option.

(3) Tap Deleted Messages.

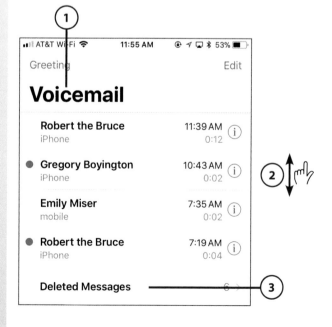

What's Missed?

In case you're wondering, your iPhone considers any call you didn't answer to be a missed call. So if someone calls and leaves a message, that call is included in the counts of both missed calls and new voicemails. If the caller leaves a message, you see a notification informing you that you have a new voicemail and showing who it is from (if available). If you don't answer and the caller doesn't leave a message, it's counted only as a missed call and you see a notification showing a missed call along with the caller's identification (if available).

4 Swipe up or down the screen to browse all the deleted messages.

5 Tap a message to listen to it or to read its transcript.

6 Tap the Play icon to hear the message. You can use the other playback tools just like you can with undeleted messages.

7 Tap Undelete to restore the deleted message. The iPhone restores the message to the Voicemail screen.

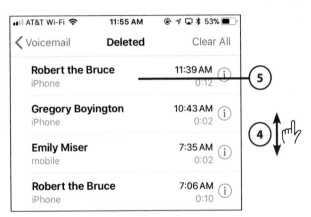

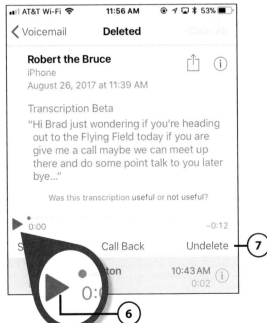

8. Tap Clear All to remove all deleted messages permanently. (If this is disabled, close the open message by tapping it.)

9. Tap Clear All at the prompt. The deleted messages are erased and you return to the Deleted screen.

10. Tap Voicemail to return to the Voicemail screen.

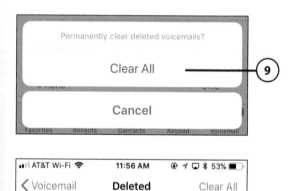

Lost/Forgot Your Password?

If you have to restore your iPhone or it loses your voicemail password for some other reason and you can't remember it, you need to have the password reset to access your voicemail on the iPhone. For most cell phone providers, this involves calling the customer support number and accessing an automated system that sends a new password to you via a text message. For AT&T, which is one of the iPhone providers in the United States, call 611 on your iPhone and follow the prompts to reset your password (which you receive via a text). No matter which provider you use, it's a good idea to know how to reset your voicemail password because it is likely you will need to do so at some point.

Communicating with FaceTime

FaceTime enables you to see, as well as hear, people with whom you want to communicate. This feature exemplifies what's great about the iPhone; it takes complex technology and makes it simple. FaceTime works great, but there are two conditions that have to be true for you and the people you want some

FaceTime with. To be able to see each other, both sides have to use a device that has the required cameras (this includes iPhone 4s and newer, iPod touches third generation and newer, iPad 2s and newer, and Macs running Snow Leopard and newer), and have FaceTime enabled (via the settings on an iOS device that are explained below or via the FaceTime application on a Mac). And each device has to be able to communicate over a network; an iPhone or cellular iPad can use a cellular data network (if that setting is enabled) or a Wi-Fi network while Macs have to be connected to the Internet through a Wi-Fi or other type of network. When these conditions are true, making and receiving FaceTime calls are simple tasks.

In addition to making video FaceTime calls, you can also make audio-only FaceTime calls. These work similarly to making a voice call except the minutes don't count against your voice plan when you use a Wi-Fi network (if you are making the call over the cellular network, the data does count against your data plan, so be careful about this).

Assuming you are in a place where you don't have to pay for the data you use, such as when you use a Wi-Fi network, you don't have to pay for a FaceTime call (video or audio-only) either.

Configuring FaceTime Settings

FaceTime is a great way to use your iPhone to hear and see someone else. There are a few FaceTime settings you need to configure for FaceTime to work. You can connect with other FaceTime users via your phone number or an email address.

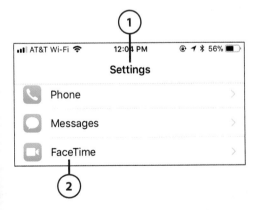

1. Move to the Settings screen.

2. Tap FaceTime.

3 If the FaceTime switch is off (white), tap the FaceTime switch to turn it on (green). If the FaceTime switch is on and you see an Apple ID, you are already signed into an account; in this case, you see the current FaceTime settings and can follow along starting with step 7 to change these settings. You can sign out of the current account by tapping it, and then tapping Sign Out; proceed to step 4 to sign in with a different account.

4 To use your Apple ID for FaceTime calls, tap Use your Apple ID for FaceTime (if you haven't signed into an Apple ID account, see Chapter 3, "Setting Up and Using an Apple ID, iCloud, and Other Online Accounts" to do so and then come back here to enable FaceTime). If you don't sign in to an Apple ID, you can still use FaceTime, but it is always via your cellular connection, which isn't ideal because then FaceTime counts under your voice minutes on your calling plan or as data on your data plan.

5 Configure the email addresses you want people to be able to use to contact you for FaceTime sessions by tapping them to enable each address (enabled addresses are marked with a check mark) or to disable addresses (these don't have a check mark). (If you don't have any email addresses configured on your iPhone, you are prompted to enter email addresses.)

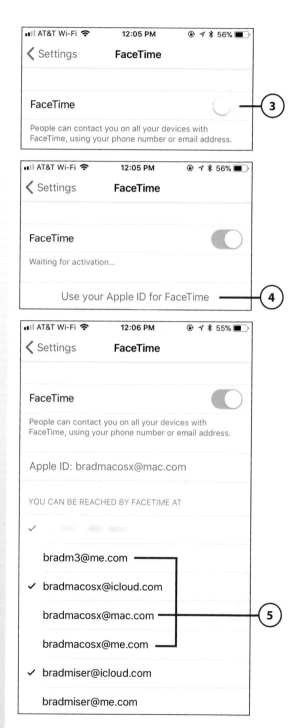

(6) Tap the phone number or email address by which you will be identified to the other caller during a FaceTime call.

(7) If you want to allow Live Photos to be captured while you are in a FaceTime session, set the FaceTime Live Photos switch to on (green); if you disable this, photos you take during FaceTime calls are static images instead. (To learn more about Live Photos, see Chapter 13, "Taking Photos and Video with Your iPhone.")

Blocking FaceTime

If you tap Blocked at the bottom of the FaceTime Settings screen, you see the names, phone numbers, and email addresses that are currently blocked from making calls, sending messages, or making FaceTime requests to your iPhone. To block someone else, tap Add New and then tap the contact you want to block.

Making FaceTime Calls

FaceTime is a great way to communicate with someone because you can hear and see him (or just hear him if you choose an audio-only FaceTime call). Because iPhones have cameras facing each way, it's also easy to show something to the person you are talking with. You make FaceTime calls starting from the FaceTime, Contacts, or Phone apps and from the FAVORITES widget. No matter which way you start a FaceTime session, you manage it in the same way.

Careful

If your iPhone is connected to a Wi-Fi network, you can make all the FaceTime calls you want (assuming you have unlimited data on that network). However, if you are using the cellular data network, be aware that FaceTime calls may use data under your data plan. If you have a limited plan, it's a good idea to use FaceTime primarily when you are connected to a Wi-Fi network. (Refer to Chapter 2, "Using Your iPhone's Core Features," for information on connecting to Wi-Fi networks.)

To start a FaceTime call from the Contacts app, do the following:

1. Use the Contacts app to open the contact with whom you want to chat (refer to Chapter 6 for information about using the Contacts app).

2. To place an audio-only FaceTime call, tap the FaceTime audio icon. (The rest of these steps show a FaceTime video call, but a FaceTime audio-only is very similar to voice calls described earlier in this chapter.)

3. Tap the contact's FaceTime icon. The iPhone attempts to make a FaceTime connection. You hear the FaceTime "chirping" and see status information on the screen while the call is attempted. When the connection is complete, you hear a different tone and see the other person in the large window and a preview of what she is seeing (whatever your iPhone's front-side camera is pointing at—most likely your face) in the small window. If the person you are trying to FaceTime with isn't available for FaceTime for some reason (perhaps she doesn't have a FaceTime-capable device or is not connected to the Internet), you see a message saying that the person you are calling is unavailable for FaceTime, and the call terminates.

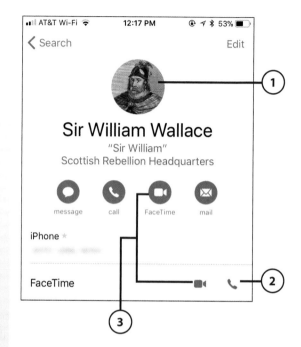

Playing Favorites

If you've set a FaceTime contact as a favorite, you can open the Phone app, tap Favorites, and tap the FaceTime favorite to start the FaceTime session.

(4) After the call is accepted, manage the call as described in the "Managing FaceTime Calls" task later in this chapter.

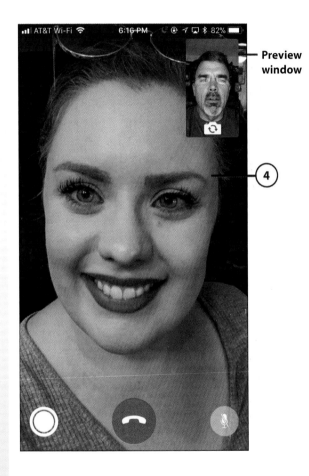

Preview window

>>>Go Further

MORE INFORMATION ABOUT FACETIME CALLS

As you make FaceTime calls, following are some other bits of information for your consideration:

- **Failing FaceTime**—If a FaceTime request fails, you can't really tell the reason why. It can be a technical issue, such as none of the contact information you have is FaceTime-enabled or the person is not signed into a device. Or, the person you are calling might have declined the request. If you repeatedly have trouble connecting with someone, contact him to make sure he has a FaceTime-capable device and that you are using the correct FaceTime contact information.

- **Leave a Message**—On the FaceTime Unavailable screen, you can tap Leave a Message to send a text or iMessage message to the person with whom you are trying to FaceTime.

- **Transform a call**—You can transform a voice call into a FaceTime session by tapping FaceTime on the Call screen. When you transform a call into a FaceTime session, the minutes no longer count against the minutes in your calling plan because all communication happens over the Wi-Fi network or your cellular data plan if you enabled that option and aren't connected to a Wi-Fi network. (The voice call you started from automatically terminates when you make the switch.)

- **FaceTime app**—To use the FaceTime app to start a call, tap the FaceTime icon on the Home screen. Tap the Video tab to make a video call or the Audio tab to make an audio-only call. Tap Add (+) to use your contacts to start the call. You can also enter a name, email address, or phone number in the bar at the top of the screen (if you haven't made or received any FaceTime calls before, you won't see the tabs until you make your first call). Tap a person on the Recents list to place a FaceTime call to that person. Once you've connected, you manage the FaceTime session as described in the rest of this chapter.

- **FaceTime with Siri**—You can also place a FaceTime call using Siri by activating Siri and saying "FaceTime *name*" where *name* is the name of the person with whom you want to FaceTime. If there are multiple options for that contact, you must tell Siri which you want to use. After you've made a selection, Siri starts the FaceTime call.

- **FaceTime with the FAVORITES widget**—You can open the FAVORITES widget and tap the FaceTime icon for the person with whom you want to have a FaceTime conversation.

Receiving FaceTime Calls

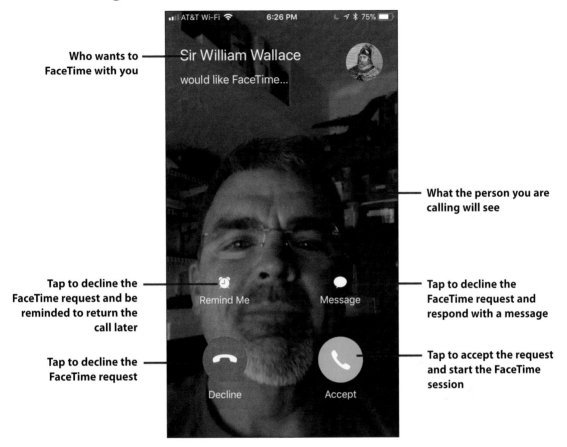

Who wants to FaceTime with you — Sir William Wallace would like FaceTime...

What the person you are calling will see

Tap to decline the FaceTime request and be reminded to return the call later — Remind Me

Tap to decline the FaceTime request and respond with a message — Message

Tap to decline the FaceTime request — Decline

Tap to accept the request and start the FaceTime session — Accept

When someone tries to FaceTime with you, you see the incoming FaceTime request screen message showing who is trying to connect with you and the image you are currently broadcasting. Tap Accept to accept the request and start the FaceTime session. Manage the FaceTime call as described in the "Managing FaceTime Calls" task.

Tap Remind Me to decline the FaceTime request and create a reminder or Message to decline the request and send a message. These options work just as they do for a voice call (you have the same custom message options). You can also press the Side button to decline the request.

When a FaceTime request comes in while your iPhone is locked, you swipe to the right on the slider to accept the call or use the Remind Me or Message options if you don't want to take the call (this is the same as when you receive a voice call via the Phone app).

If you decline the FaceTime request, the person trying to call you receives a message that you're not available (and a message if you choose that option). She can't tell whether there is a technical issue or if you simply declined to accept the request.

Tracking FaceTime Calls

FaceTime calls are tracked just as voice calls are. Open the FaceTime app and tap Video to see recent video FaceTime calls or Audio to see recent audio FaceTime calls. On the recents list, FaceTime calls are marked with the video camera icon. FaceTime audio-only calls are marked with a telephone receiver icon. FaceTime calls that didn't go through are in red and are treated as missed calls. You can do the same tasks with recent FaceTime calls that you can with recent voice calls.

Managing FaceTime Calls

Drag to change the location of the preview window

Tap to change the camera you are using

Tap to take a photo

Tap to mute your side of the call

During a FaceTime call (regardless of who placed the call initially), you can do the following:

- Drag the preview window, which shows the image that the other person is seeing, around the screen to change its location. It "snaps" into place in the closest corner when you lift your finger up.

- Move your iPhone and change the angle you are holding it to change the images you are broadcasting to the other person. Use the preview window to see what the other person is seeing.

- Tap Mute to mute your side of the conversation. Your audio is muted and you see the Mute icon in the preview window. Video continues to be broadcast so the other person can still see you.

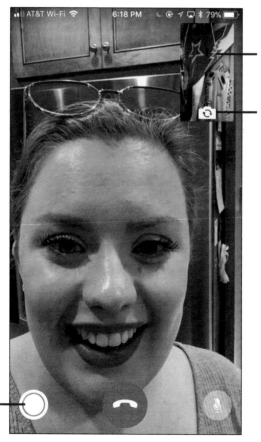

The other person is seeing what the backside camera is showing

Tap to change the camera you are using

Tap to take a photo

- To use the camera on the backside of the iPhone, tap the Change Camera icon. The other person now sees whatever you have the camera on the back of the iPhone pointed at. If the other person changes her camera, you see what her backside camera is pointing at.

- Tap the Shutter icon to take a Live Photo (if that setting is enabled) or a static photo of the image you are seeing in the FaceTime window.

Tap the screen to make the controls reappear

- After a few moments, the controls disappear. Tap the screen to make them reappear.

Preview shows the landscape orientation

FaceTime works in landscape orientation too

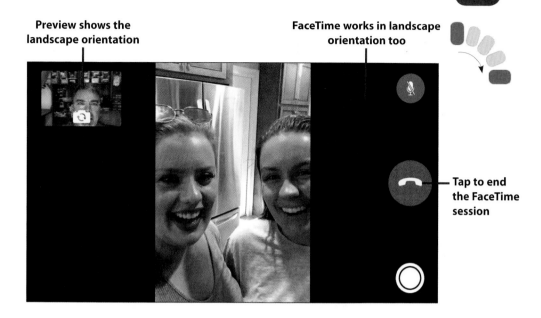

Tap to end the FaceTime session

- Rotate your iPhone to change the orientation to horizontal. This affects what the other person sees (as reflected in your preview), but you continue to see the other person in her iPhone's current orientation.

- Tap the Receiver icon to end the FaceTime session.

FaceTime Break

Just like when you are in a voice call, you can move into and use other apps (if your provider's technology supports this functionality). You see the green FaceTime in progress bar at the top of the screen. The audio part of the session continues, but the other person sees a still image with a Camera icon and the word "Paused." As soon as you move back into the FaceTime session, the video resumes. Likewise, if the other person moves out of the FaceTime app, you see the Paused icon.

Tap to configure
email settings

Tap to use email

In this chapter, you explore all the email
functionality that your iPhone has to offer.
Topics include the following:

→ Getting started
→ Configuring email accounts
→ Setting Mail app preferences
→ Working with email
→ Managing email

Sending, Receiving, and
Managing Email

For most of us, email is an important way we communicate with others,
both in our public and personal lives. Fortunately, your iPhone has great
email tools so you can work with email no matter where you are.

Getting Started

To use email on your iPhone, you use the Mail app to access your email
accounts over the Internet. The Mail app has lots of great features that
help you really take advantage of all that email offers; you learn how to
use these features throughout this chapter.

You configure your email accounts in the Mail app to be able to access
them; configuring email accounts is described in the next section.

You need to be connected to the Internet through a Wi-Fi or cellular
data connection to send or receive email—although you can read
downloaded messages, reply to messages, and compose messages

when you aren't connected. In Chapter 2, "Using Your iPhone's Core Features," you find out how to connect your iPhone to the Internet.

As you use email, it's helpful to understand that email isn't sent between devices, for example from an email application on a computer to Mail on an iPhone. Rather, all email flows through an email server. When you send an email, it moves from your iPhone to an email server. From there, it moves from the server onto each device configured with the email account to which you sent it, such as an iPhone or a computer. The process is the same when someone sends email to you. The email travels from the device sending it to the email server that handles email for your email account. From there, it is available on every device configured with your email address. This means you can have the same email messages on more than one device at a time. You can determine how often email is moved from the server onto your iPhone.

Configuring Email Accounts

Before you can start using an iPhone for email, you have to configure the email accounts you want to access with it. The iPhone supports many kinds of email accounts, including iCloud, Gmail, an account from your Internet service provider (such as a cable company), and so on. Setting up the most common types of email accounts is covered in Chapter 3, "Setting Up and Using an Apple ID, iCloud, and Other Online Accounts," so if you haven't done that already, go back to that chapter and get your accounts set up. Then come back here to start using those accounts for email.

You can have multiple email accounts configured on your iPhone at the same time—for example, an iCloud account and a Google account. If you have only one email account on your iPhone, some of the screens you see on your iPhone might look a bit different than those in this chapter. The information contained in this chapter still applies; some of the steps might be slightly different for you as noted in those steps.

Setting Mail App Preferences

There are a number of settings that affect how the Mail app works. The good news is that you can use the Mail app with its default settings just fine. However, you might want to tweak how it works for you by making changes using the Settings app; you can use the information in the table that follows to understand the options available to you.

To access the settings in the table, first tap the Settings icon on the Home screen, tap the option listed in the Settings Area column, and then move to the location to make changes to the setting (for example, to change the amount of text shown in email previews, open the Settings app; tap Mail; move to the MESSAGE LIST section; and then tap Preview). For each setting, you see a description of what it does along with options (if applicable).

Settings App Explained

To get detailed information on using the Settings app, see "Working with the Settings App" in Chapter 2.

Mail and Related Settings

Settings Area	Location	Setting	Description
Accounts & Passwords	ACCOUNTS	Email accounts	You can configure the accounts used in the Mail app to determine which account can receive or send email on your iPhone (see Chapter 3 for details).
Accounts & Passwords	N/A	Fetch New Data	Determines when new email is downloaded to your iPhone (see Chapter 3 for an explanation of the options).
Mail	ALLOW MAIL TO ACCESS	Siri & Search	When enabled (green), Search, Siri, and other elements of the iOS can use information in the Mail app. For example, when you search for a person, the Search tool can search your email for relevant information. If you don't want your email information to be used, set the switch to off (white).

Settings Area	Location	Setting	Description
Mail	ALLOW MAIL TO ACCESS	Notifications	Configure the type of notifications the Mail app uses. See "Configuring Notifications" in Chapter 4, "Customizing How Your iPhone Works," for a detailed explanation.
Mail	ALLOW MAIL TO ACCESS	Cellular Data	When enabled (green), Mail can send and receive email when your iPhone is connected to the Internet using the cellular data network. Email typically doesn't use a lot of data, but if you receive many emails with very large attachments and have a limited data plan, you might want to set this switch to off (white).
Mail	MESSAGE LIST	Preview	Determines the number of lines you want to display for each email when you view the Inbox and in other locations, such as alerts. This preview enables you to get the gist of an email without opening it. More lines give you more of the message but take up more space on the screen.
Mail	MESSAGE LIST	Show To/Cc Label	Slide the switch to on (green) to always see a To or Cc label next to the subject line on messages in your inboxes. This helps you know when you are included in the To line or as a Cc, which usually indicates whether you need to do something with the message or if it is just for your information.

Settings Area	Location	Setting	Description
Mail	MESSAGE LIST	Swipe Options	Changes what happens when you swipe to the left or right on email when you are viewing an Inbox. You can set the Swipe Left motion to be None, Mark as Read, Flag, or Move Message. When you do a partial swipe to the left, you see the More icon, which leads to a menu of actions, and the option you configure for the Left Swipe setting. When you do a full swipe to the left, a message is deleted. You can set the Swipe Right motion to be None, Mark as Read, Flag, Move Message, or Archive. When you swipe all the way to the right on a message, the action you configure for the Swipe Right is performed. When you do a partial swipe, you see an icon that you can tap to perform the action. Note that you can't have the same option configured for both directions.
Mail	MESSAGE LIST	Flag Style	Determines how messages you flag are marked; you can choose a colored circle or a Flag icon. Flagging messages marks messages that you want to know are important or that need your attention.
Mail	MESSAGES	Ask Before Deleting	When this switch is on (green), you're prompted to confirm when you delete or archive messages. When this switch is off (white), deleting or archiving messages happens without the confirmation prompt.

Settings Area	Location	Setting	Description
Mail	MESSAGES	Load Remote Images	When this switch is on (green), images in HTML email messages are displayed automatically. When this switch is off (white), you have to manually load images in a message. (If you receive a lot of spam, you should turn this off so that you won't see images in which you might not be interested.)
Mail	THREADING	Organize By Thread	When this switch is on (green), messages in a conversation are grouped together as a "thread" on one screen. This makes it easier to read all the messages in a thread. When this switch is off (white), messages are listed individually. (You learn more about working with threads in the "Working with Email" task later in this chapter.)
Mail	THREADING	Collapse Read Messages	When enabled and you read messages in a thread, the thread collapses so you see the thread rather than the individual messages in the thread.
Mail	THREADING	Most Recent Message on Top	With this switch set to on (green), the most recent message in a thread appears at the top of the thread and the messages move backward in time as you move down the list of messages. When disabled (white), the first message in the thread displays at the top with the next oldest message appearing next, and so on until the last message, which is the most recent message in the thread.

Settings Area	Location	Setting	Description
Mail	THREADING	Complete Threads	With this switch enabled (green), all the messages in a thread are displayed when you view the thread, even if you've moved messages to a different folder (other than the Inbox).
Mail	COMPOSING	Always Bcc Myself	When this switch is on (green), you receive a blind copy of each email you send; this means that you receive the message, but you are hidden on the list of recipients. When this switch is off (white), you don't receive a blind copy.
Mail	COMPOSING	Mark Addresses	This feature highlights addresses in red that are not from domains that you specify. You enter the domains (everything after the @ in email addresses, such as icloud.com) from which you do not want addresses to be marked (highlighted in red) when you create email. You can add multiple domains to the list by separating them with commas. All addresses from domains not listed will be marked in red. To disable this feature, delete all the domains from the list.
Mail	COMPOSING	Increase Quote Level	When this option is enabled (green), the text of an email you are replying to or forwarding (quoted content) is automatically indented. Generally, you should leave this enabled so it is easier for the recipients to tell when you have added text to an email, versus what is from the previous email messages' quoted content.

Settings Area	Location	Setting	Description
Mail	COMPOSING	Signature	Signatures are text that is automatically added to the bottom of new email messages that you create. For example, you might want your name and email address added to every email you create. You can configure the same signature for all your email accounts or have a different signature for each account. If you don't want to use a signature, delete any signatures that are currently configured. (Note that the default signature is "Sent from my iPhone.")
Mail	COMPOSING	Default Account	Determines which email account is the default one used when you send an email (this setting isn't shown if you have only one email account). You can override the default email account for an email you are sending by choosing one of your other email addresses in the From field.
Display & Brightness	N/A	Text Size	Changes the size of text in all apps that support Dynamic Type (Mail does). Drag the slider to the right to make text larger or to the left to make it smaller.
Display & Brightness	N/A	Bold Text	Changes text to be bold when the Bold Text switch is set to on (green).
Control Center	N/A	Text Size	Changes the size of text; you can add the Text Size tool to your Control Center to make it quicker and easier to use. See "Configuring the Control Center" in Chapter 4 for the steps to configure your Control Center.

More on Marking Addresses

When you configure at least one address on the Mark Addresses screen, all addresses from domains except those listed on the Mark Addresses screen are in red text on the New Message screen. This is useful to prevent accidental email going to places where you don't want it to go. For example, you might want to leave domains associated with a club off this list so that whenever you send email to addresses associated with your club, the addresses appear in red to remind you to pay closer attention to the messages you are sending.

Email Notifications and Sounds

If you want to be alerted whenever new email is received and when email you create is sent, be sure to configure notifications for the Mail app. These include whether unread messages are shown in the Notification Center, the type of alerts, whether the badge appears on the Mail icon, whether the preview is shown, the alert sound, and whether new messages are shown on the Lock screen. For a detailed explanation of configuring notifications, refer to Chapter 4.

Working with Email

The Mail app offers lots of great features and is ideally suited for working with email on your iPhone. This app offers a consolidated Inbox, so you can view email from all your accounts at the same time. Also, the app organizes your email into threads (assuming you didn't disable this feature), which makes following a conversation convenient.

You've got email

When you move to a Home screen, you see the number of new email messages you have in the badge on the Mail app's icon (assuming you haven't disabled this); tap the icon to move to the app. Even if you don't have any new email, the Mail icon still leads you to the Mail app. Other ways Mail notifies you of new messages include by displaying visual notifications and the new mail sound. (You determine which of these options is used for each email account by configuring its notifications as explained in the "Email Notifications and Sounds" note earlier in this chapter.)

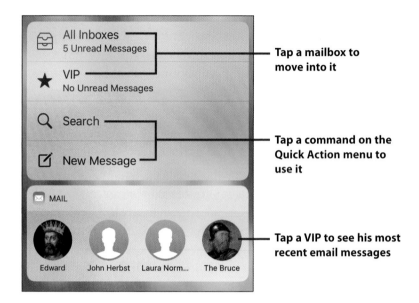

Tap a mailbox to move into it

Tap a command on the Quick Action menu to use it

Tap a VIP to see his most recent email messages

If you are using an iPhone that supports 3D Touch (6s/6s Plus or later models), you can press on the Mail icon to open the Quick Actions menu and choose an action you want to perform. For example, you can start a new email message by tapping New Message or move directly to your VIP email by tapping VIP. You can move to the most recent messages from one of your VIPs by tapping him in the MAIL widget.

VIP

You can designate people with whom you correspond as a Very Important Person (VIP). Mail has options specifically for your VIPs, such as a dedicated inbox, the MAIL widget, and so on. You learn more about working with VIPs later in this chapter.

About Assumptions

The steps and figures in this section assume you have more than one email account configured and are actively receiving email from those accounts on your iPhone. If you have only one email account active, your Mailboxes screen contains that account's folders instead of mailboxes from multiple accounts and the Accounts sections that appear in these figures and steps. Similarly, if you disable the Organize by Thread setting, you won't see messages in threads as these figures show. Instead, you work with each message individually.

The Mail app enables you to receive and read email for all the email accounts configured on your iPhone. The Mailboxes screen is the top-level screen in the app and is organized into two sections.

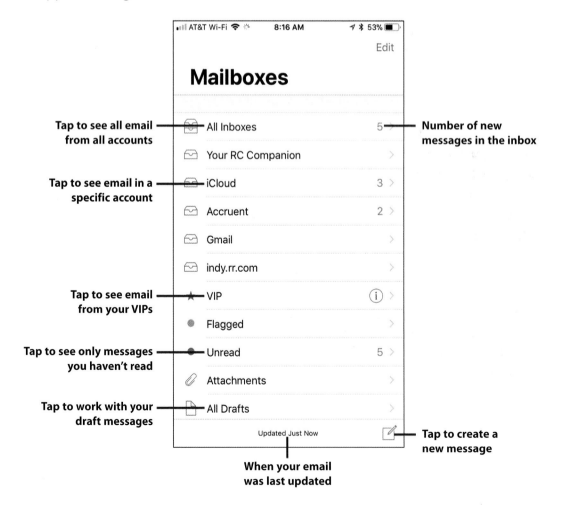

The Inboxes section shows the Inbox for each account along with folders for email from people designated as VIPs, your unread messages, and your draft messages (those you've started but haven't sent yet). Next to each Inbox or folder is the number of new emails in that Inbox or folder. (A new message is simply one you haven't viewed yet.) At the top of the section is All Inboxes, which shows the total number of new messages to all accounts; when you tap this, the integrated Inbox containing email from all your accounts is displayed.

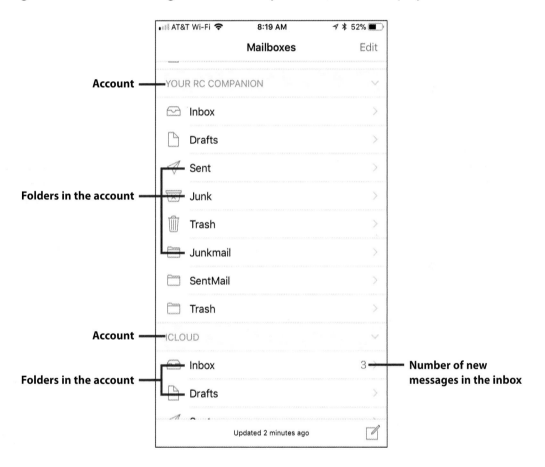

The Accounts section, which is underneath the Inboxes section on the screen, shows the set of inboxes and folders within each email account. The difference between these sections is that the Inbox options take you to just the Inbox for one or all of your accounts or specific folders (such as the VIP folder), whereas the Account options take you to all the folders under each account. You can tap any folder or inbox under an account to view the emails stored in that folder or inbox.

Receiving and Reading Email

To read email you have received, perform the following steps:

(1) On the Home screen, tap Mail. When you open Mail (assuming you didn't use the App Switcher to quit the app when you left it), you move back to the screen you were last on; for example, if you were reading an email you return to it. If the Mailboxes screen isn't showing, tap the Back icon in the upper-left corner of the screen until you reach the Mailboxes screen.

(2) To read messages, tap the Inbox that contains messages you want to read, or tap All Inboxes to see the messages from all your email accounts. Various icons indicate the status of each message, if it has attachments, if it is from a VIP, or if it is part of a thread. A message is part of a thread when it has double right-facing arrows along the right side of the screen—individual messages have only one arrow.

(3) Swipe up or down the screen to browse the messages. You can read the preview of each message to get an idea of its contents.

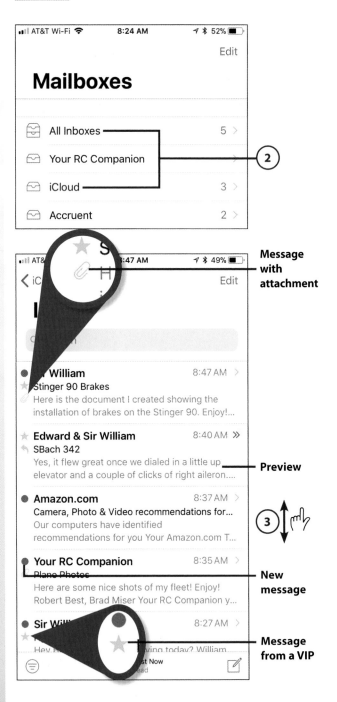

(4) If a message you are interested in is in a thread, tap its arrows. (If it isn't part of a thread, skip to step 6.) The thread expands (the double arrows point down instead of to the right) and you can see the messages it contains. The first message in the thread appears in a gray bar. The responses to the message appear under it in a lighter shade of gray; the responses don't have a subject because they are all related to the subject of the thread.

Thread

Pulling on Threads

A thread is a group of emails that are related to the same subject. For example, if someone sends an email to you saying how wonderful the *My iPhone* book is, and you reply with a message saying how much you agree, those two messages would be grouped into one thread. Other messages with the same subject are also placed in the thread.

Collapsing Threads

To collapse an expanded thread, tap the downward-facing arrows. You see only the most recent message in the thread again.

5 Swipe up or down the screen to browse the messages in the thread.

6 To read a message (whether in a thread or not), tap it. As soon as you open a message, it's marked as read and the new mail counter reduces by one. You see the message screen with the address information at the top, including whom the message is from and whom it was sent to. Under that the message's subject along with time and date it was sent are displayed. Below that is the body of the message. If the message has an attachment or is a reply to another message, the attachment or quoted text appears toward the bottom of the screen.

7 Swipe up and down the screen to read the entire message.

Standard Motions Apply

You can use the standard finger motions on email messages, such as unpinching or tapping to zoom, swiping directions to scroll, and so on. You can also rotate the phone to change the orientation of messages from vertical to horizontal; this makes it easier to type.

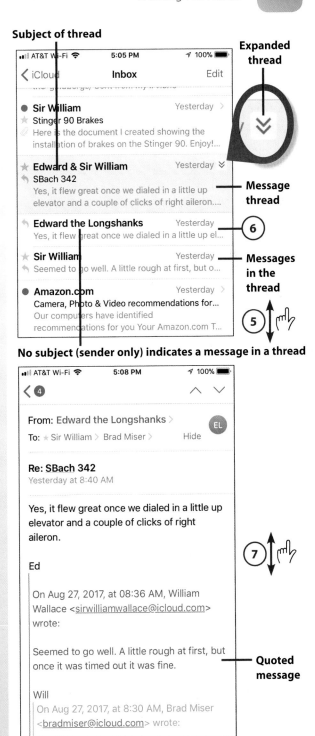

Subject of thread

Expanded thread

Message thread

Messages in the thread

No subject (sender only) indicates a message in a thread

Quoted message

8 If the message contains an attachment, swipe up the screen to get to the end of the message. Some types of attachments, most notably photos, appear directly in the message and you don't have to download them to the device. If an attachment hasn't been downloaded yet, it starts to download automatically (unless it is a large file). If the attachment hasn't been downloaded auto-matically, which is indicated by "Tap to Download" in the attach-ment icon, tap it to download it into the message. When an attachment finishes download-ing, its icon changes to represent the type of file it is. If the icon remains generic, it might be of a type the iPhone can't display, and you would need to open it on a computer or other device.

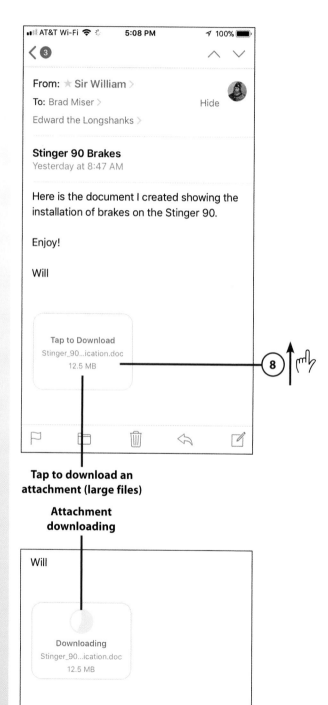

Tap to download an attachment (large files)

Attachment downloading

9. Tap the attachment to view it.

10. Scroll the document by swiping up, down, left, or right on the screen.

11. Unpinch or double-tap to zoom in.

12. Pinch or double-tap to zoom out.

13. Tap the Share icon to see the available actions for the attachment.

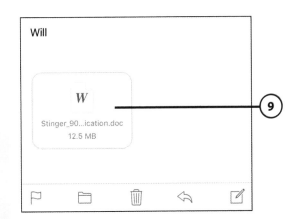

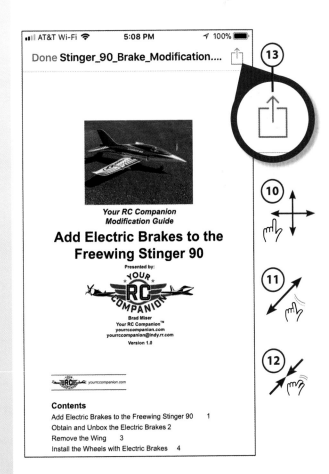

14 Swipe to the left or right to see all the available options.

15 Tap the action you want to take, such as opening the attachment in a different app, printing it, sharing it via email, and so on. Tap Cancel to return to the attachment if you don't want to do any of these. If you open the attachment in an app, work with the attachment in that app. To return to the email, tap Mail in the top-left corner of the screen to return to the Mail app (not shown in the figures).

16 Tap Done (depending on the type of attachment you were viewing, you might tap the Back icon instead).

17 To view information for an email address, such as who sent the message, tap it. The Info screen appears. On this screen, you see as much information for the person as is available. If it is someone in the Contacts app, you see all of the information stored there, and you can place a call, send a message, etc. If it is not someone in the Contacts app, you see the person's email address along with actions you might want to perform, such as creating a contact for him or adding new information to an existing contact. (See Chapter 6, "Managing Contacts," for information about working with contacts.)

18 Tap Done to return to the message.

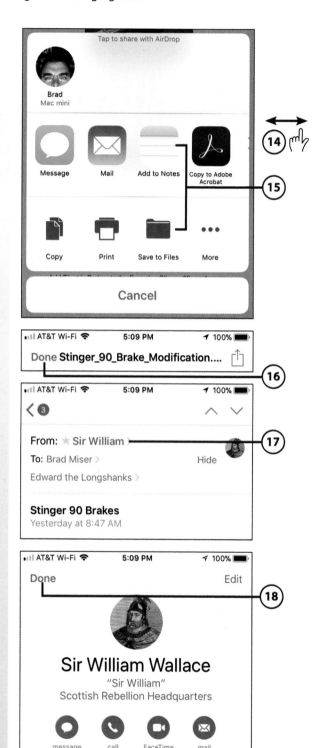

19 To read the next message in the current Inbox, tap the down arrow. (If the arrow is disabled, you are viewing the most recent email in the inbox.)

20 To move to a previous message in the current Inbox, tap the up arrow. (If the arrow is disabled, you are viewing the oldest message in the inbox.)

21 To move back to see the inbox again, tap the Back icon, which shows the number of unread messages in the inbox from which you came (all your inboxes if you were viewing them all).

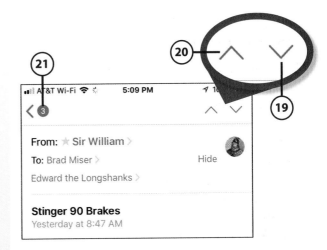

Reading Threads

If you want to read all the messages in a thread instead of individual messages it contains, tap the thread (instead of tapping its arrows to expand it). The thread opens, and you see the title of the thread at the top of the screen in a gray bar. You can browse up and down the thread's screen to read all of the messages it contains. When you are done with the thread, tap the Back icon located in the upper-left corner of the screen.

Two Other Ways to Open New Email

You canview a preview of email messages in notifications you receive and press or swipe on the notification to get to the full message. You can also use Siri to get and read new email. If those aren't enough ways, you can also use the MAIL widget to quickly get to email from your VIPs.

Receiving and Reading Email on an iPhone Plus

The larger screens on the iPhone Plus models (6, 7, and 8) provide some additional functionality that is unique to those models. You can access this by holding the Plus horizontally when you use the Mail app.

(1) Open the Mail app and hold the iPhone so it is oriented hori-zontally. The mail window splits into two panes. On the left is the Navigation pane, where you can move to and select items you want to view. When you select something in the left pane, it appears in the Content pane on the right, which shows the email message you were most recently reading.

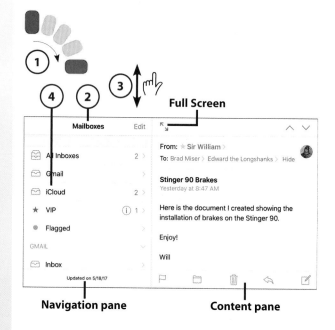

(2) In the left pane, navigate to the Mailboxes screen by tapping the Back icon until it disappears.

(3) Swipe up or down the Navigation pane to browse the mailboxes and accounts available to you. Notice that the two panes are independent. When you browse the left pane, the right pane doesn't change.

(4) Tap the mailbox or account whose contents you want to view.

5 Swipe up and down the messages to browse all of them in the mailbox you selected.

6 Tap the message or thread that you want to read. If you tap a thread, the messages it contains appear in the left pane; browse the messages in the thread by swiping up and down the screen and then tap the message in the thread that you want to read. The message currently selected is highlighted in gray.

7 Read the message.

8 Use the other tools to work with it; these work just like they do on other models and when you hold the iPhone vertically. For example, tap the up arrow to move to the previous message in the current Inbox.

9 To read the message in full screen, tap the Full Screen icon. The Content pane uses the entire screen.

10 Work with the message.

11 When you're done, tap the Back icon, which shows the number of unread messages in the selected inbox from which you came (all your inboxes if you were viewing them all). The screen splits into two panes again.

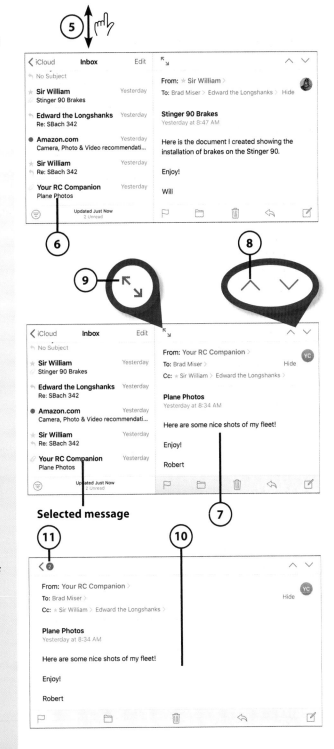

Selected message

12 Select and read other messages.

13 When you're done, tap the Back icon, which is labeled with the name of the inbox or folder whose contents you are browsing.

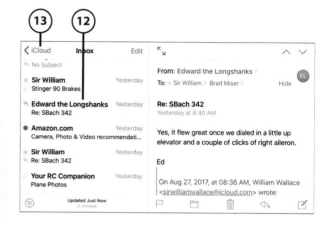

Using 3D Touch for Email

You can use the 3D Touch feature (iPhone 6s/6s Plus or later models) for email as follows:

1 Browse a list of email messages.

2 Press and hold on an email in which you are interested. A Peek of that email appears.

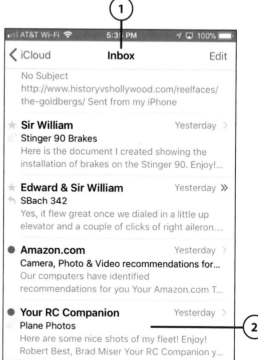

3 Review the preview of the email that appears in the Peek.

4 To open the email so you can read all of it, press down slightly harder until it pops open and use the steps in the earlier task to read it (skip the rest of these steps).

5 To see actions you can perform on the email, swipe up on the Peek.

6 Tap the action you want to perform, such as Reply All, to reply to the email.

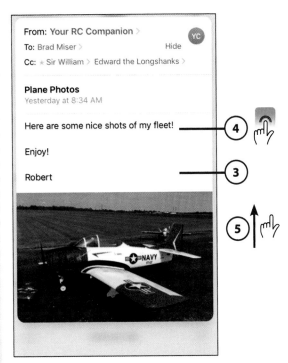

From: Your RC Companion >
To: Brad Miser >   Hide
Cc: ⋆ Sir William > Edward the Longshanks >

Plane Photos
Yesterday at 8:34 AM

Here are some nice shots of my fleet! —— **4**

Enjoy!

Robert —— **3**

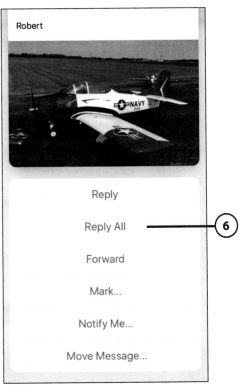

Robert

Reply

Reply All —— **6**

Forward

Mark...

Notify Me...

Move Message...

>>>Go Further

MORE ON RECEIVING AND READING EMAIL

Check out these additional pointers for working with email you receive:

- If more messages are available than are downloaded, tap Load More Messages. The additional messages download to the inbox you are viewing.

- You can change the amount of detail you see at the top of the message screen by tapping Details to show all of the detail, such as the entire list of recipients, or Hide to collapse that information.

- A thread is started based on its subject and sender. As replies are made, the messages continue to be categorized by subject because Re: is appended to it. It even remains in the thread if the initial subject continues to be in the message but other words are added.

- If a message includes a photo, Mail displays the photo in the body of the email message if it can (if the image is large, you might have to download it to see it). You can zoom in or out and scroll to view it just as you can for photos in other apps.

- If you tap a PDF attachment in a message and the iBooks app is installed on your iPhone, you're prompted to select Quick Look or Open in iBooks. If you select Open in iBooks, the document opens in the iBooks app where you can read it using the powerful features it offers for reading ebooks and other documents.

- Some emails, especially HTML messages, are large and don't immediately download in their entirety. When you open a message that hasn't been fully downloaded, you see a message stating that this is the case. Tap the link to download the rest of the message.

- If you have other apps with which an attachment is compatible, you can open the attachment in that app. For example, if you have Pages installed on your iPhone and are viewing a Word document attachment, you can tap the Share icon and tap Open in Pages to open the document in the Pages app. You can get the same options by touching and holding on the attachment's icon in the body of a message until the Share menu appears.

Sending Email

You can send email from any of your accounts. Follow these steps for a basic walk-through of composing and sending a new email message:

(1) Tap the Compose icon at the bottom of any Mail screen. (If you are using an iPhone that supports 3D Touch, you can press down on the Mail app's icon and choose New Message to create a new email from a Home page.) A new email message containing your signature is created. (For an explanation of where to configure a signature, see the table at the beginning of the chapter.)

(2) Tap the To field and type the first recipient's email address. As you type, Mail attempts to find matching addresses in your Contacts list, or in emails you've sent or received, and displays the matches it finds. These can include individuals or groups with which you've emailed. To select one of those addresses, tap it. Mail enters the rest of the address for you. Or, just keep entering information until the address is complete.

(3) Address the email using your Contacts app by tapping Add (+).

(4) Use the Contacts app to find and select the contact to whom you want to address the message. (Refer to Chapter 6 for the details about working with contacts.) When you tap a contact who has only one email address, that address is pasted into the To field and you return to the New Message window. When you tap a contact with more than one email address, you move to that contact's screen, which shows all available addresses; tap the address to which you want to send the message.

(5) Repeat steps 2–4 to add other recipients to the message.

(6) Tap the Cc/Bcc, From line. The Cc and Bcc lines expand.

(7) Follow the same procedures from steps 2–4 to add recipients to the Cc field.

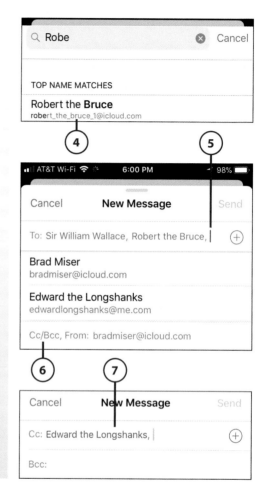

Have Multiple Email Accounts?

If you have more than one email account, it's important to know from which account you are sending a new message. If you tap the Compose icon while you are on the Mailboxes screen or the Inboxes screen, the From address is the one for the account you set as your default; otherwise, the From address is the email account associated with the Inbox you are in.

Removing Addresses

To remove an address, tap it so it is highlighted in a darker shade of blue; then tap Delete (x) on the iPhone's keyboard.

8 Follow the same procedures from steps 2–4 to add recipients to the Bcc field.

9 If the account from which you want to send the message is shown, skip to step 11; to change the account from which the email is sent, tap the From field. The account wheel appears at the bottom of the screen.

10 Swipe up or down the wheel until the From address you want to use is in the center of the bottom box and is the most prominent.

11 Tap in the Subject line. The account selection wheel closes.

12 Type the subject of the message.

13 If you want to be notified when someone replies to the message you are creating, tap the bell; if not, skip to step 16.

14 Tap Notify Me. When anyone replies to the message, you are notified.

15 If you don't see the body of the message, swipe up the screen and it appears.

16 Tap in the body of the message, and type the message above your signature. Mail uses the iOS's text tools, attempts to correct spelling, provides Predictive Text, and makes suggestions to complete words. (Refer to Chapter 2 for the details of working with text.)

17 To make the keyboard larger, rotate the iPhone so that it is horizontal.

18 When you finish the message, tap Send. The progress of the send process is shown at the bottom of the screen; when the message has been sent, you hear the Sent Mail sound you configured, which confirms that the message has been sent. If you enabled the reply notification for the message, you are notified when anyone replies to it.

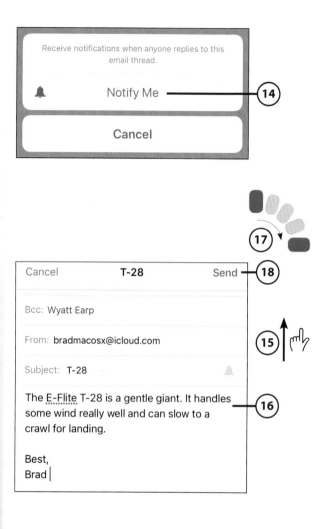

Receive notifications when anyone replies to this email thread.

🔔 Notify Me ——— **14**

Cancel

Cancel   T-28   Send —— **18**

Bcc: Wyatt Earp

From: bradmacosx@icloud.com   **15**

Subject: T-28

The E-Flite T-28 is a gentle giant. It handles some wind really well and can slow to a crawl for landing.   **16**

Best,
Brad |

Start Writing Now, Finish Writing and Send Later

If you want to save a message you are creating without sending it, tap Cancel. A prompt appears; select Save Draft to save the message; if you don't want the message, tap Delete Draft instead. When you want to work on a draft message again, touch and hold down the Compose icon. After a moment, you see your most recent draft messages; tap the draft message you want to work on. You can make changes to the message and then send it or save it as a draft again. (You can also move into the Drafts folder to select and work with draft messages; moving to this folder is covered later in this chapter.)

Using Mail's Suggested Recipients

As you create messages, Mail suggests recipients based on the new message's current recipients. For example, if you regularly send emails to a group of people, when you add two or more people from that group, Mail suggests others you might want to include. As you add others to the message, Mail continues suggesting recipients based on the current recipient list. You can use these suggestions to quickly add more recipients to a new message.

1 Create a new message.

2 Add at least two recipients. Just below the To line, Mail suggests additional recipients for the new message based on other messages you have created.

3 Tap the additional recipients you want to add to the new message. (Mail sometimes suggests multiple recipients as a group if you have emailed that group before.) As you select these recipients, Mail keeps making suggestions and new people appear in the gray bars.

4 When you're done adding To recipients, tap in the next field you want to complete and continue creating the new message.

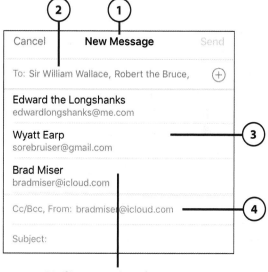

Mail's suggestions for more recipients for the new message

Replying to Email

Email is all about communication, and Mail makes it simple to reply to messages.

1. Open the message you want to reply to.

2. Tap the Arrow icon.

3. Tap Reply to reply to only the sender or, if there was more than one recipient, tap Reply All to reply to everyone who received the original message. The Re: screen appears showing a new message. Mail pastes the contents of the original message at the bottom of the body of the new message below your signature. The original content is in blue and is marked with a vertical line along the left side of the screen.

4. Use the message tools to add or change the To, Cc, or Bcc recipients.

5. Write your response.

6. Tap Send. Mail sends your reply.

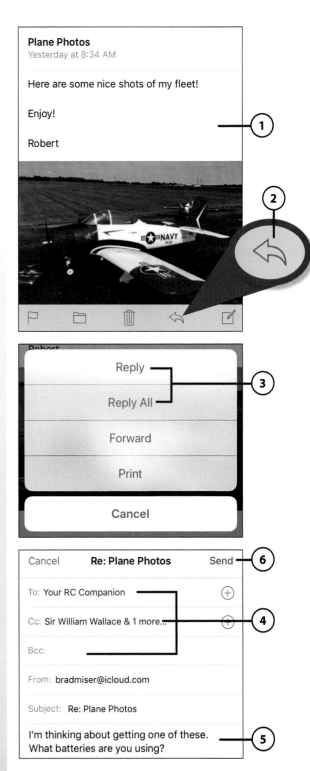

Plane Photos
Yesterday at 8:34 AM

Here are some nice shots of my fleet!

Enjoy!

Robert

Reply
Reply All
Forward
Print
Cancel

Cancel   **Re: Plane Photos**   Send

To: Your RC Companion

Cc: Sir William Wallace & 1 more...

Bcc:

From: bradmiser@icloud.com

Subject: Re: Plane Photos

I'm thinking about getting one of these. What batteries are you using?

Including a Photo or Video in a Message

To add a photo or video to a message you create (new, reply, or forward), tap twice in the body. Swipe to the left on the resulting toolbar (if you don't see it immediately) until you see the Insert Photo or Video command, and then tap it. Use the Photos app (see Chapter 14, "Viewing and Editing Photos and Video with the Photos App," for information about this app) to move to and select the photo or video you want to attach. Tap Choose. The photo or video you selected is added to the message.

Sending Email from All the Right Places

You can send email from a number of places on your iPhone. For example, you can share a photo with someone by viewing the photo, tapping the Share icon, and then tapping Mail. Or you can tap a contact's email address to send an email from your contacts list. In all cases, the iPhone uses Mail to create a new message that includes the appropriate content, such as a photo or link; you use Mail's tools to complete and send the email.

Print Email from Your iPhone

If you need to print a message, tap the Arrow icon at the bottom of the screen and tap Print. To learn about printing from your iPhone, refer to Chapter 2.

Forwarding Emails

When you receive an email you think others should see, you can forward it to them.

1. Read the message you want to forward.

2. If you want to include only part of the current content in the message you forward, tap where you want the forwarded content to start. This is useful (and considerate!) when only a part of the message applies to the people to whom you are forwarding it. If you want to forward the entire message, skip to step 4.

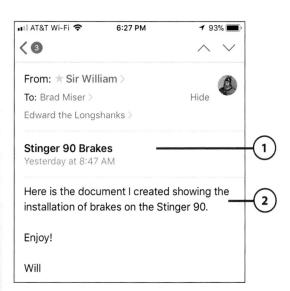

3 Use the text selection tools to select the content you want to include in your forwarded message.

4 Tap the Arrow icon.

5 Tap Forward.

6 If the message includes attachments, tap Include at the prompt if you also want to forward the attachments, or tap Don't Include if you don't want them included. The Forward screen appears. Mail pastes the contents of the message that you selected, or the entire content if you didn't select anything, at the bottom of the message below your signature. If you included attachments, they are added to the new message as well.

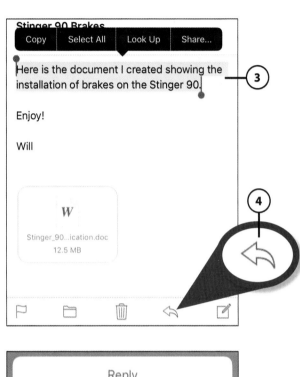

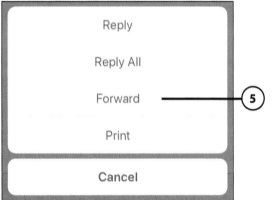

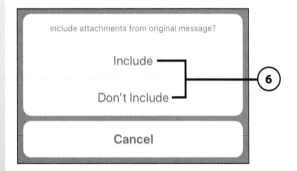

7 Address the forwarded message using the same tools you use when you create a new message.

8 Type your commentary about the message above your signature.

9 Tap Send. Mail forwards the message.

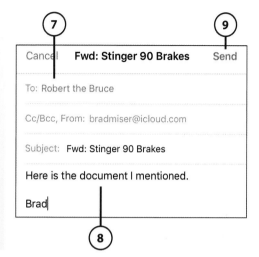

Large Messages

Some emails, especially HTML messages, are so large that they don't immediately download in their entirety. When you forward a message whose content or attachments haven't fully downloaded, Mail prompts you to download the "missing" content before forwarding. If you choose not to download the content or attachments, Mail forwards only the downloaded part of the message.

Managing Email

Following are some ways you can manage your email. For example, you can check for new messages, see the status of messages, delete messages, and organize messages using the folders associated with your email accounts.

Checking for New Email

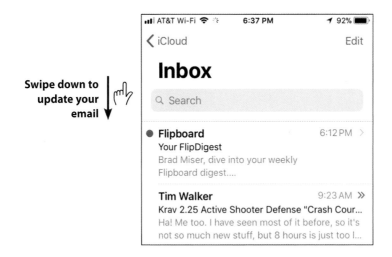

Swipe down to update your email

To manually retrieve messages, swipe down from the top of any Inbox or the Mailboxes screen. The screen "stretches" down and when you lift your finger, the Mail app checks for and downloads new messages.

How many unread messages you have in the current Inbox

When your email was last updated

Mail also retrieves messages whenever you move into the app or into any Inbox or all your Inboxes. Of course, it also retrieves messages according to the selected Fetch New Data option. It downloads new messages immediately when they arrive in your account if Push is enabled or automatically at defined intervals if you've set Fetch to get new email periodically. (Refer to Chapter 3 for an explanation of these options and how to set them.)

The bottom of the Mailboxes or an Inbox screen always shows when email was most recently downloaded to your iPhone; on the bottom of Inbox screens, you also see the number of new email messages (if there are any unread messages).

Understanding the Status of Email

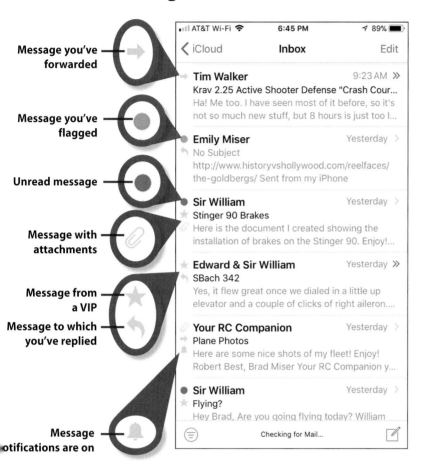

Message you've forwarded

Message you've flagged

Unread message

Message with attachments

Message from a VIP

Message to which you've replied

Message notifications are on

When you view an Inbox or a message thread, you see icons next to each message to indicate its status (except for messages that you've read but not done anything else with and that aren't from a VIP, which aren't marked with any icon).

Managing Email from the Message Screen

Tap to delete a message

To delete a message while reading it, tap the Trash Can. If you enabled the warning preference, confirm the deletion and the message is deleted. If you disabled the confirmation prompt, the message is deleted immediately.

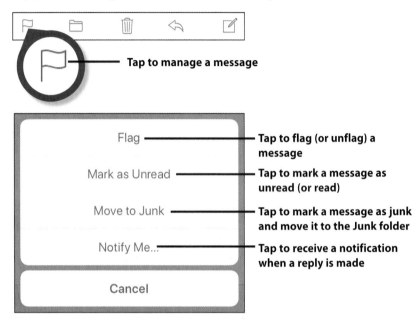

Tap to manage a message

Flag — Tap to flag (or unflag) a message

Mark as Unread — Tap to mark a message as unread (or read)

Move to Junk — Tap to mark a message as junk and move it to the Junk folder

Notify Me... — Tap to receive a notification when a reply is made

Cancel

To take other action on a message you are reading, tap the Flag icon. On the menu that opens, you can choose a number of commands. The action you select is performed on the message you are viewing.

Dumpster Diving

As long as an account's trash hasn't been emptied, you can work with a message you've deleted by moving to the account's screen and opening its Trash folder. Over time, a lot of deleted messages can accumulate in the Trash folder. To get rid of these messages, open the Trash folder under the account. Tap Delete All and tap Delete All again at the prompt. The deleted messages are removed from the folder and are gone forever. This frees up space on the cloud as well as on your iPhone.

Where Has My Email Gone?

When you send an email to the Archive folder, it isn't deleted. To access messages you've archived, tap the Back icon in the upper-left corner of the screen until you get to the Mailboxes screen. Tap the Archive folder under the account to which email you've archived was sent.

Managing Email from an Inbox

Previously in this chapter, you saw the settings options for swipe actions for email. You can use those to configure how right and left swipes affect your email from an Inbox screen, such as flagging a message with a left swipe. (Depending on the choices you set for the swipe preferences, the results you see when you swipe might be different than shown here. However, the swipe right or swipe left actions still reveal commands you can use unless you chose None in the settings, in which case nothing happens when you swipe on a message.)

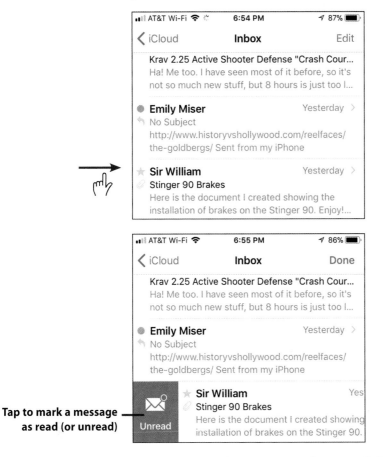

Tap to mark a message as read (or unread)

Swipe to the right on a message to change its read status. If the message has been read, you can reset its status to unread, or, if it hasn't been read, you can mark it as read.

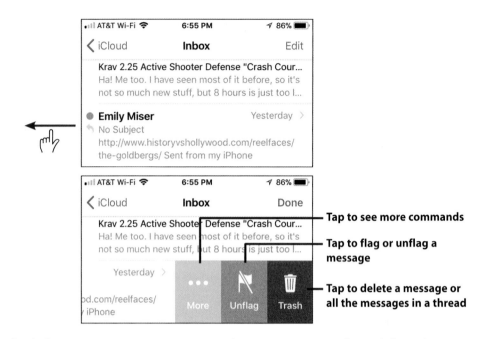

Tap to see more commands

Tap to flag or unflag a message

Tap to delete a message or all the messages in a thread

Swipe to the left on a message to see several options. Tap Trash to delete the message or messages if you swiped on a thread (the number of messages that will be deleted is shown in parentheses). Tap Flag to flag the message or Unflag to remove the flag. Tap More to open a menu of additional commands.

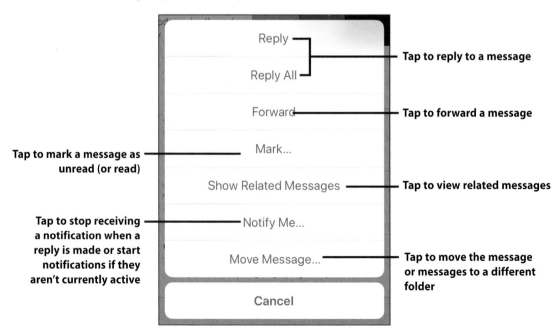

Tap to reply to a message

Tap to forward a message

Tap to mark a message as unread (or read)

Tap to view related messages

Tap to stop receiving a notification when a reply is made or start notifications if they aren't currently active

Tap to move the message or messages to a different folder

When you tap More, you see other commands for actions you can take on the message, such as replying to it or moving it to a different folder.

No-Stop Swiping to Delete

If you quickly swipe all the way to the left on a message on an Inbox screen, the message is deleted in one fell swipe.

Managing Multiple Emails at the Same Time

You can also manage email by selecting multiple messages on an Inbox screen, which is more efficient because you can take action on multiple messages at the same time.

1. Move to an Inbox screen showing messages you want to manage.

2. Tap Edit. A selection circle appears next to each message, and actions appear at the bottom of the screen.

3 Select the message(s) you want to manage by tapping their selection circles. As you select each message, its selection circle turns blue and is marked with a check mark. At the top of the screen, you see how many messages you have selected.

When you use an iPhone Plus in the horizontal orientation, you see the selection screen on the left and a preview of what you have selected in the right pane. Even though it looks a bit different, it works in the same way.

4 To delete the selected messages, tap Trash. Mail deletes the selected messages and exits Edit mode. (If you enabled the warning prompt, you have to confirm the deletion.)

5 To change the status of the selected messages, tap Mark.

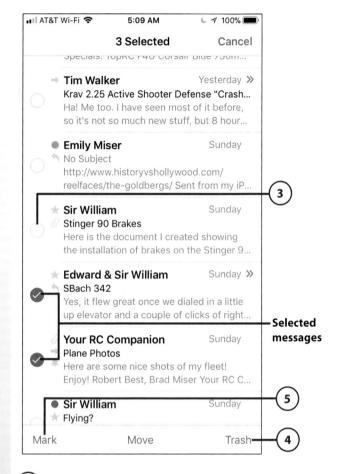

Selected messages

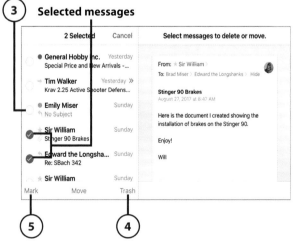

3 Selected messages

6 Tap the action you want to take on the selected messages. You return to the Inbox screen and exit Edit mode.

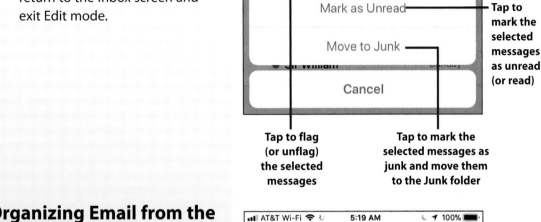

Tap to flag (or unflag) the selected messages

Tap to mark the selected messages as junk and move them to the Junk folder

Tap to mark the selected messages as unread (or read)

Organizing Email from the Message Screen

You can have various folders to organize email, and you can move messages among these folders. For example, you can recover a message from the Trash by moving it from the Trash folder back to the Inbox.

1 Open a message you want to move to a different folder.

2 Tap the Mailboxes icon. You're prompted to move the messages into the folder you most recently moved messages into or to choose a different folder.

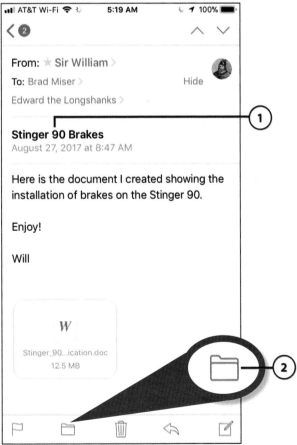

3 To move the messages into a folder you have previously used, tap Move to "*foldername*" where *foldername* is the name of that folder and skip the rest of these steps.

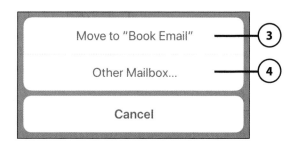

4 To move the message into a folder that wasn't the one you used most recently, tap Other Mailbox. The Mailboxes screen appears. At the top of this screen is the message you are moving. Under that are the mailboxes available under the current account.

Move to Other Accounts

If you want to move selected messages to a folder under a different account, tap Accounts in the upper-left corner of the screen. Tap the account to which you want to move the message (not all accounts will be available; if an account is grayed out, you can't move a message to it). Then tap the mailbox into which you want to move the message.

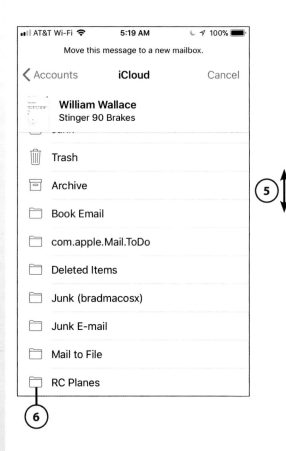

5 Swipe up and down the screen to browse the mailboxes available in the current account.

6 Tap the mailbox into which you want to move the message. The message moves to that mailbox, and you move to the next message in the list you were viewing.

When you use an iPhone Plus in the horizontal orientation, you see the list of folders you are navigating in the left pane and a preview of the messages you have selected in the right pane.

Makin' Mailboxes

You can create a new mailbox to organize your email. Move to the Mailboxes screen and tap Edit. Then, tap New Mailbox located at the bottom of the screen. Type the name of the new mailbox. Tap the Mailbox Location and then choose where you want the new mailbox located (for example, you can place the new mailbox inside an existing one). Tap Save. You can then store messages in the new mailbox.

Organizing Email from the Inbox

Like deleting messages, organizing email from the Inbox can be made more efficient because you can move multiple messages at the same time.

1. Move to an Inbox screen showing messages you want to move to a folder.

2. Tap Edit. A selection circle appears next to each message. Actions appear at the bottom of the screen.

3. Select the messages you want to move by tapping their selection circles. As you select each message, its selection circle turns blue and is marked with a check mark.

4. Tap Move. You're prompted to move the messages into the folder you most recently moved messages into or to choose a different folder.

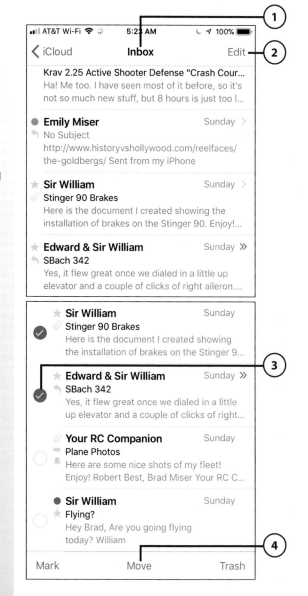

5 To move the messages into a folder you have previously used, tap Move to *"foldername"* where *foldername* is the name of that folder and skip the rest of these steps.

6 To move the message into a folder that wasn't the one you used most recently, tap Other Mailbox. The Mailboxes screen appears. At the top of this screen is the message you are moving. Under that are the mailboxes available under the current account.

7 Swipe up and down the screen to browse the mailboxes available in the current account.

On an iPhone Plus held horizontally, you see the list of folders in the left pane and a preview of the selected messages in the right pane.

8 Tap the mailbox to which you want to move the selected messages. They are moved into that folder, and you return to the previous screen, which is no longer in Edit mode.

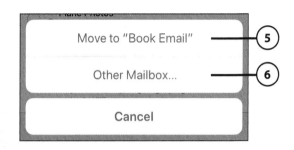

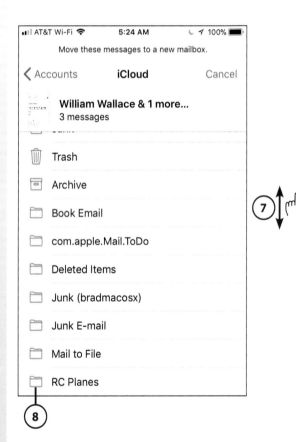

Threading Your Way Through Email

When you select a thread, you select all the messages in that thread. Whatever action you select is taken on all the thread's messages at the same time.

Viewing Messages in a Mailbox

You can open a mailbox within an account to work with the messages it contains. For example, you might want to open the Trash mailbox to recover a deleted message.

(1) Move to the Mailboxes screen.

(2) If necessary, swipe up the screen to see the email accounts you are using. Each account has its own section showing the mailboxes stored on that account.

(3) If you don't see an account's mailboxes, expand the account by tapping the right-facing arrow at the edge of the screen.

(4) Tap the folder or mailbox containing the messages you want to view. You see the messages it contains. In some cases, this can take a few moments for the messages to be downloaded if that folder or mailbox hasn't been accessed recently.

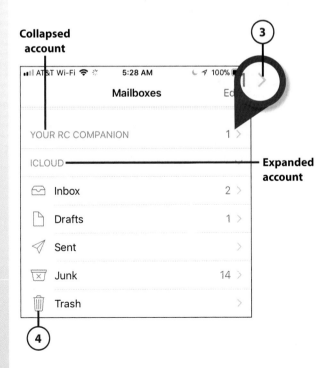

(5) Tap a message or thread to view it. (If you want to move messages, such as to recover messages that are in the Trash, see "Organizing Email from the Inbox.")

Changing Mailboxes

You can change the mailboxes that appear on the Mailboxes screen. Move to the Mailboxes screen and tap Edit. To cause a mailbox to be visible, tap it so that it has a check mark in its circle. To hide a mailbox, tap its check mark so that it shows an empty circle. For example, you can display the Attachments mailbox to make messages with attachments easier to get to. Drag the Order icon for mailboxes up or down the screen to change the order in which mailboxes appear. Tap Add Mailbox to add a mailbox not shown on the list. Tap Done to save your changes.

Saving Images Attached to Email

Email is a great way to share photos. When you receive a message that includes photos, you can save them on your iPhone.

(1) Move to the message screen of an email that contains one or more photos or images.

(2) Swipe up the message to see all the images it contains.

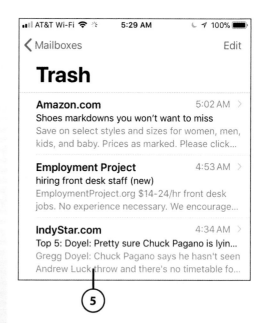

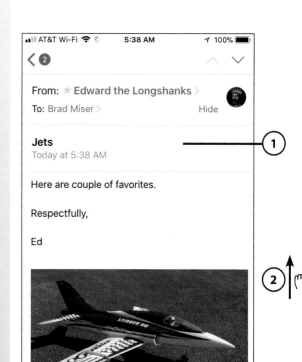

(3) Touch and hold on an image (if you are using an iPhone that supports 3D Touch, don't press down when you touch or you Peek at the image instead).

(4) Swipe to the left until you see the Save Image icons.

(5) Tap Save Image to save just the image you touched or tap Save X Images, where X is the number of images attached to the message, to save all the attachments. (If there is only one image, the command is just Save Image.) The images are saved in the Photos app on your iPhone. (See Chapter 14 for help working with the Photos app.)

Filtering Email

You can quickly filter the email messages in an inbox as follows:

(1) Open the inbox you want to filter.

(2) Tap the Filter icon. The contents of the inbox are filtered by the current criteria, which is indicated by the terms under "Filtered by." The Filter icon is highlighted in blue to show the inbox is filtered.

3 Tap the current filter criteria.

4 Set the criteria by which you want to filter the messages in the inbox; the current criteria are indicated by check marks or green switches. For example, tap To: Me to only show messages on which you are included in the To block.

5 Tap Done. You return to the inbox and only messages that meet your filter criteria are shown.

6 Tap the Filter icon to turn off the filters and display all the messages again.

Searching Your Email

As you accumulate email, you might want to find specific messages. For example, suppose you want to retrieve an email message that was related to a specific topic, but you can't remember where you stored it. Mail's Search tool can help you find messages like this quite easily.

1 Move to the screen you want to search, such as an account's Inbox or a folder's screen. (This is optional as you can choose an area to search later in the process.)

2 If necessary, swipe down to move to the top of the screen to display the Search tool.

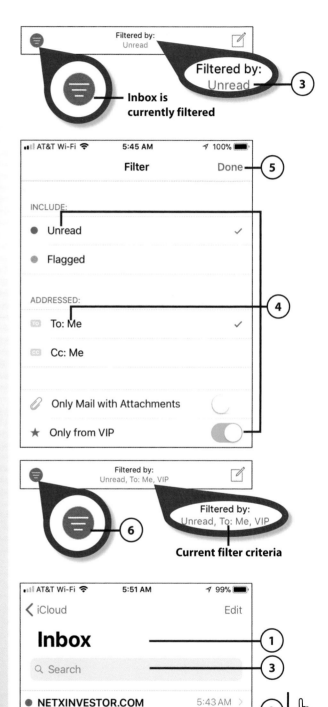

Filtered by:
Unread

Filtered by:
Unread — **3**

Inbox is
currently filtered

AT&T Wi-Fi 5:45 AM 100%

Filter Done — **5**

INCLUDE:
● Unread ✓
● Flagged

ADDRESSED: **4**
TO To: Me ✓
CC Cc: Me

⌀ Only Mail with Attachments
★ Only from VIP

Filtered by:
Unread, To: Me, VIP

Filtered by:
Unread, To: Me, VIP

6

Current filter criteria

AT&T Wi-Fi 5:51 AM 99%
‹ iCloud Edit

Inbox — **1**

🔍 Search — **3**

● NETXINVESTOR.COM 5:43 AM ›
JPMORGAN FUNDS Important Information
Shareholder Communications Account: **2**

3 Tap in the Search tool.

4 Enter the text for which you want to search. As you type, Mail makes suggestions about what you might be searching for. These appear in different sections based on the type of search Mail thinks you are doing, such as People, Subjects, and more.

5 To use one of Mail's suggestions to search, such as a subject, tap it; or continue typing your search term and when you are done, tap Search. Mail searches for messages based on your search criterion and you see the results.

6 To search for the term in the sub-ject field, tap Subject, or to search in the body, tap Message.

7 Tap Search.

Mail's search suggestions

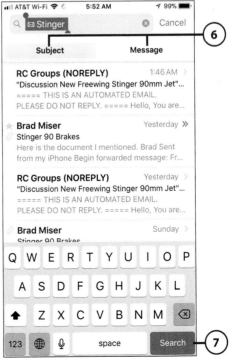

(8) To search in all your mailboxes, tap All Mailboxes, or to search in only the current mailbox, tap Current Mailbox.

(9) Work with the messages you found, such as tapping a message to read it. Tap the Back icon in the upper-left corner of the screen to return to the search results.

(10) To clear a search and exit Search mode, tap Cancel.

(11) To clear a search but remain in Search mode, tap Clear (x).

When you use an iPhone Plus horizontally, searching is even better, because you can select a found message in the search results in the left pane and read it in the right pane.

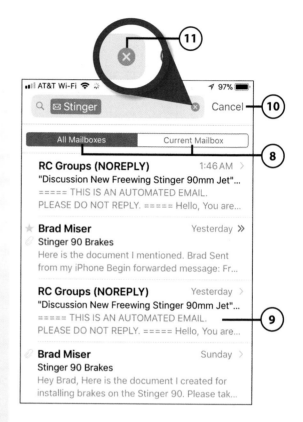

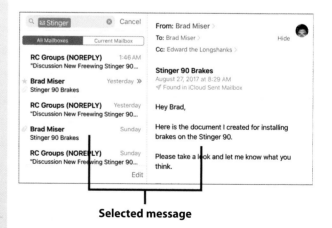

Selected message

Working with VIPs

The VIP feature enables you to indicate specific people as your VIPs. When a VIP sends you email, it is marked with a Star icon and goes into the special VIP mailbox so you can access these important messages easily. You can also create specific notifications for your VIPs, such as a unique sound when you receive email from a VIP (see Chapter 4).

Designating VIPs

To designate someone as a VIP, perform the following steps:

1. View information about the person you want to be a VIP by tapping his name in the From or Cc fields as described earlier in the chapter.

2. On the Info screen, tap Add to VIP. The person is designated as a VIP and any email from that person receives the VIP treatment.

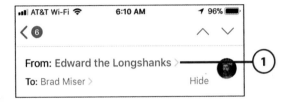

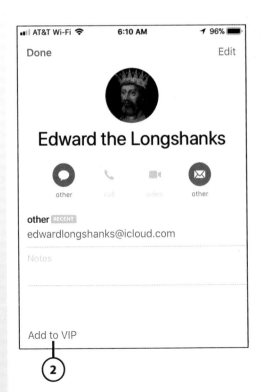

Accessing VIP Email

To work with VIP email, do the
following:

① Move to the Mailboxes screen.

② Tap VIP.

③ Work with the VIP messages you
see.

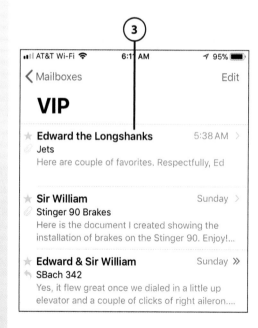

>>>*Go Further*

MORE ON VIPS

Here are a few more tidbits on VIPs:

- Messages from VIPs are marked with the Star icon no matter in which mailbox you see the messages. If you haven't read a VIP message, the star is blue. If you have read it, the star is gray.

- To see the list of your current VIPs, move to the Mailboxes screen and tap the Info (i) icon for the VIP mailbox. You see everyone currently designated as a VIP. Tap Add VIP to add more people to the list. Tap VIP Alerts to create special notifications for VIPs.

- To return a VIP to normal status, view his information and tap Remove from VIP.

Managing Junk Email

Junk email, also known as spam, is an unfortunate reality of email. No matter what precautions you take, you are going to receive some spam emails. Of course, it is good practice to be careful about where you provide your email address to limit the amount of spam you receive.

Consider using a "sacrificial" email account when you shop, post messages, and in the other places where you're likely to get spammed. If you do get spammed, you can stop using the sacrificial account and create another one to take its place. Or you can delete the sacrificial account from your iPhone and continue to use it on your computer where you likely have better spam tools in place. If you have an iCloud account, you can set up and use email aliases for this purpose.

The Mail app on the iPhone includes a very basic junk management tool. However, if you use an account or an email application on a computer that features a junk mail/spam tool, it acts on mail sent to your iPhone, too. For example, if you configure spam tools for a Gmail account, those tools act on email before it reaches your iPhone. Similarly, if you use the Mail app on a Mac, its rules and junk filter work on email as you receive it; the results of this are also reflected on your iPhone. To change how you deal with junk email on your iPhone, change the junk email settings for your account online (such as for Gmail) or by changing how an email app on a computer deals with junk mail. The results of these changes are reflected in the Mail app on your iPhone.

Many email accounts, including iCloud and Google, have Junk folders; these folders are available in the Mail app on your iPhone. You can open the Junk folder under an account to see the messages that are placed there.

Marking Junk Email

You can perform basic junk email management on your iPhone by doing the following:

1 When you view a message that is junk, tap the Flag button.

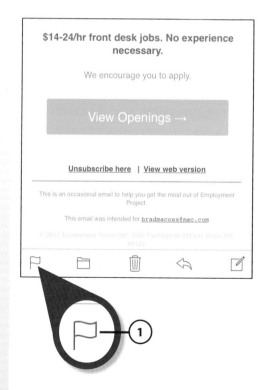

(2) Tap Move to Junk. The message
is moved from the inbox to the
Junk folder for the account to
which it was sent. Future messages from the same sender go into
the Junk folder automatically.

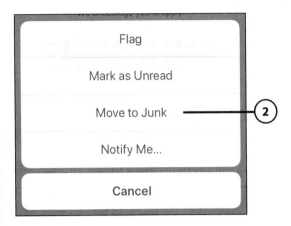

Junk It

You can also move a message to the
Junk folder by swiping slowly to the left
on it, tapping More, and then tapping
Move to Junk. If you swipe quickly all
the way to the left side of the screen,
you'll delete the message instead.

Junk It or Trash It?

The primary difference between moving a message to the Junk folder or
deleting it is that when you mark a
message as junk, future messages from
the same sender are moved to the Junk
folder automatically. When you delete a
message, it doesn't change how future
messages from the same sender are
handled.

Tap to configure
Messages

Send messages from
other apps too, such
as to share photos

Tap to send and
receive text messages,
photos, video, and
more

In this chapter, you'll explore the texting and messaging functionality your iPhone has to offer. Topics include the following:

→ Getting started
→ Preparing the Messages app for messaging
→ Sending messages
→ Receiving, reading, and replying to messages
→ Working with messages

Sending, Receiving, and Managing Texts and iMessages

You can use the Messages app to send messages (also known as texts), receive messages, and converse with others; you can also send and receive images, videos, audio, and links. You can maintain any number of conversations with other people at the same time, and your iPhone lets you know whenever you receive a new message via audible and visible notifications that you can configure. In addition to text conversations with other people, many organizations use text messaging to send important updates, such as airlines communicating flight status changes. You might find messaging to be one of the most used functions of your iPhone.

Getting Started

Texting, also called messaging, is an especially great way to communicate with others when you have something quick you want to say, such as an update on your arrival time. It's much easier to send a quick text, "I'll be there in 10 minutes," than it is to make a phone call or send an email. Texting/messaging is designed for relatively short messages. It is also a great way to share photos and videos quickly and easily. And if you communicate with younger people, you might find they tend to respond quite well since texting is a primary form of communication for them.

There are two types of messages that you can send with and receive on your iPhone using the Messages app.

The Messages app can send and receive text messages via your cell network based on telephone numbers. Using this option, you can send text messages to and receive messages from anyone who has a cell phone capable of text messaging.

You can also use the iMessage function within the Messages app to send and receive messages via an email account, to and from other iOS devices (using iOS 5 or newer), or Macs (running OS X Lion or newer). This is especially useful when your cell phone account has a limit on the number of texts you can send via your cell account; when you use iMessage for texting, there is no limit on the amount of data you can send when you are connected to the Internet using a Wi-Fi network and so you incur no additional costs for your messages. This is also really useful because you can send messages to, and receive messages from, iPod touch, iPad, Apple Watch, and Mac users. The limitations to iMessage are that it only works on those supported devices, and the people with whom you are messaging have to set up iMessage on their device (which isn't difficult).

You don't need to be overly concerned about which type is which because the Messages app makes it clear which type a message is by color and text. It uses iMessage when available and automatically uses cellular texting when it isn't possible to use iMessage.

You can configure iMessage on multiple devices, such as an iPhone and an iPad. This means you have the same text messages on each device. So, you can start a conversation on your iPhone, and then continue it on an iPad at a later time.

Preparing the Messages App for Messaging

Like most of the apps described in this book, there are settings for the Messages app you can configure to choose how the app works for you. For example, you can configure iMessage so you can communicate via email addresses, configure how standard text messages are managed, and so on. You can also choose to block messages from specific people.

Setting Your Text and iMessage Preferences

Perform the following steps to set up Messages on your iPhone:

(1) Move to the Settings app and tap Messages.

(2) Set the iMessage switch to on (green).

(3) Set the Show Contact Photos switch to on (green) if you want images associated with your contacts to appear in messages.

(4) Slide the Send Read Receipts switch to on (green) to notify others when you read their messages. Be aware that receipts apply only to iMessages (not texts sent over a cellular network).

(5) Slide the Send as SMS switch to on (green) to send texts via your cellular network when iMessage is unavailable. If your cellular account has a limit on the number of texts you can send, you might want to leave this set to off (white) so you use only iMessage when you are texting. If your account has unlimited texting, you should set this to on (green).

(6) Tap Send & Receive.

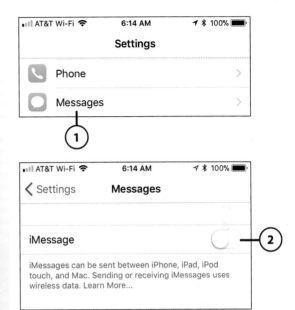

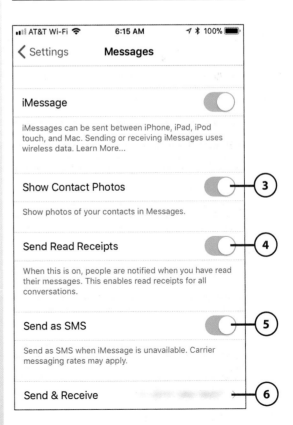

(7) Tap Use your Apple ID for iMessage. You sign into your Apple ID. At the top of the iMessage screen, you see your Apple ID. You also see the phone number of your iPhone and the email addresses associated with your Apple ID that can be used in the Messages app.

(8) To prevent an email address from being available to others to send you messages, in the YOU CAN BE REACHED BY IMESSAGE AT section, tap it so it doesn't have a check mark.

(9) To enable an address so it can be used for messages, tap it so it does have a check mark.

(10) Tap the phone number or email address you want to use by default when you start a new text conversation in the START NEW CONVERSATIONS FROM section. Because there are no data or media limitations with iMessages, you usually want to choose an email address as the default way to start a conversation.

(11) Tap Messages.

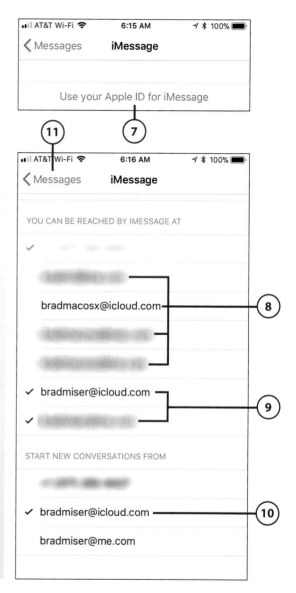

Apple ID?

These steps assume you are already signed into an Apple ID on your iPhone (see Chapter 3, "Setting Up and Using an Apple ID, iCloud, and Other Online Accounts" for help with an Apple ID). If you haven't, when you perform step 7, you're prompted to provide an Apple ID and password to sign into that Apple ID. If you are already signed into an Apple ID for Messages and see your Apple ID at the top of the iMessage screen, you can skip step 7. If you want to change the Apple ID currently being used for iMessage, tap Send & Receive, tap the Apple ID shown at the top of the iMessage screen, and then tap Sign Out. You can then sign in to a different Apple ID for Messages.

12 Tap Text Message Forwarding; if you don't see this option, your cell phone carrier doesn't support it and you can skip to step 14.

13 Set the switch to on (green) for devices on which you want to be able to receive and send text messages using your iPhone's cell phone function (this doesn't affect messages sent via iMessages because they go to all the devices on which your Apple ID is being used for iMessages automatically).

Code Required?

In some cases, when you perform step 13, you are prompted to enter a code for that device. This code appears on the device you are enabling; for example, if you turned the switch for a Mac on, the code appears on that Mac. You need to enter that code at the prompt on your iPhone and tap Allow to finish the process.

14 Tap Back.

15 Swipe up the screen to see the SMS/MMS section.

16 Set the MMS Messaging switch to off (white) if you don't want to allow photos and videos to be included in messages sent via your phone's cellular network. You might want to disable this option if your provider charges more for these types of messages—or if you simply don't want to deal with anything but text in your messages.

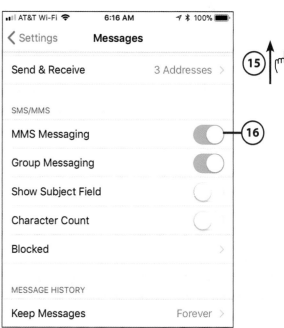

(17) Set the Group Messaging switch to on (green) to keep messages you send to a group of people organized by the group. When enabled, replies you receive to messages you send to groups (meaning more than one person on a single message) are shown on a group message screen where each reply from anyone in the group is included on the same screen. If this is off (white), when someone replies to a message sent to a group, the message is separated out as if the original message was just to that person. (The steps in this chapter assume Group Messaging is on.)

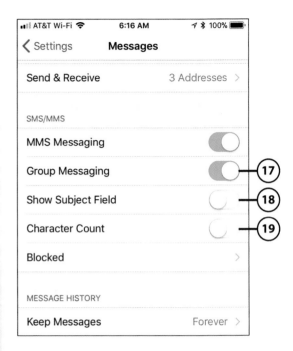

(18) Set the Show Subject Field switch to on (green) to add a subject field to your messages. This divides text messages into two sections; the upper section is for a subject, and you type your message in the lower section. This is not commonly used in text messages, and the steps in this chapter assume this setting is off.

(19) Set the Character Count switch to on (green) to display the number of characters you've written compared to the number allowed (such as 59/160). When it is off, you don't see a character count for messages you send. Technically, text messages you send via the cellular network are limited to 160 characters, so showing the character count helps you see where you are relative to this limit (iMessages don't have a limit). I don't use this setting so you won't see it in the figures in this chapter, but if character count is important to you, you should enable this.

20 Use the Blocked option to block people from texting you (see the next task).

21 Tap Keep Messages.

22 Tap the length of time for which you want to keep messages.

23 If you tapped something other than Forever, tap Delete. The messages on your iPhone older than the length of time you selected in step 22 are deleted.

24 Tap Messages.

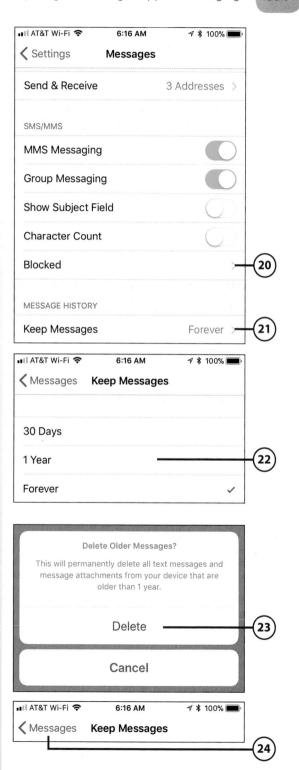

(25) If you want messages from people or organizations not in the Contacts app to be put on a separate list, set the Filter Unknown Senders switch to on (green). When this switch is on, you see a separate tab for messages from people you might not know; notifications for those messages are also disabled. This can be useful if you receive a lot of messages from people you don't know and don't want to be annoyed by notifications about those messages. (This feature is explained in the section "Working with Messages from People You Might Not Know" later in this chapter.)

(26) Tap Expire.

(27) Choose the time after which you want audio messages to expire and be deleted from your iPhone. The options you see depend on your cell phone provider. For example, if you tap After 2 Minutes, audio messages are automatically deleted two minutes after you listen to them. This is good because audio messages require a lot of storage space, and deleting them keeps that space available for other things. Other choices might be After 1 Year or Never (if you don't want audio messages to ever be deleted).

(28) Tap Messages.

(29) To be able to listen to audio messages by lifting the phone to your ear, set the Raise to Listen switch to on (green). If you set this to off (white), you need to manually start audio messages.

(30) To have the images in your messages sent at a lower quality level, set the Low Quality Image Mode switch to on (green). This can be a useful setting if you or the other recipients of your messages have limited data plans because lower quality images require less data to transmit and receive. If you tend to use all or most of your data allowance each month and send a lot of images, you might want to enable this setting and see if that reduces your data use.

Expire	After 2 Minutes >
Raise to Listen	⬤○ —(29)

Raise to Listen allows you to quickly listen and reply to incoming audio messages by raising the phone to your ear.

| Low Quality Image Mode | ○ —(30) |

When this is on, images sent will be lower quality.

Audio Messages

There are two types of audio messages you can send via the Messages app. Instant audio messages are included as part of the message itself. Audio, such as voice memos, can also be attached to messages. The Expire settings only affect instant audio messages. Audio that is attached to messages is not deleted automatically.

Blocking People from Messaging or Texting You

If you want to block someone before they send messages to you, configure that person's contact information so you can easily block his messages. Refer to Chapter 6, "Managing Contacts," for the steps to create contacts. (You can also block someone after you have received messages you don't want, which doesn't require that there be a contact first; those steps are provided later in this chapter.) Use the following steps to block a contact from sending messages to you:

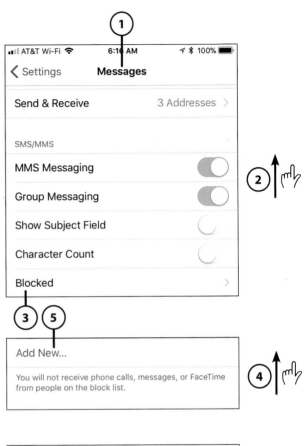

(1) Move to the Messages screen in the Settings app.

(2) Swipe up the Messages screen.

(3) Tap Blocked.

(4) If necessary, swipe up the screen.

(5) Tap Add New.

(6) Use the Contacts app to find and tap the contact you want to block. (Note that contacts without email addresses or phone numbers that don't have the potential to send messages to you are grayed out and cannot be selected.) You return to the Blocked screen and see the contact on your Blocked list. Any messages, phone calls, and FaceTime requests from the contact, as long as they come from an email address or phone number included in his contact information, won't be sent to your iPhone.

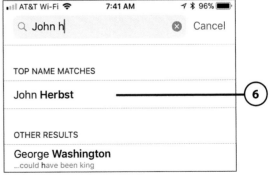

>>>Go Further

MORE ON MESSAGES CONFIGURATION

Following are a few more Messages configuration tidbits for your consideration:

- You can use only one Apple ID for iMessages at a time. To change the account you are using, move to the iMessage screen by tapping Send & Receive on the Messages Settings screen. Then tap the Apple ID shown. Tap Sign Out. You can then sign in to a different Apple ID.

- SMS stands for Short Message Service, which is what text messages use. MMS stands for Multimedia Messaging Service, which adds the ability to include multimedia elements (photos, video, sound, and so on) in text messages. All text devices and accounts support SMS, but they don't all support MMS.

- In the Notifications settings, you can configure the notifications the Messages app uses to communicate with you. You can configure the alert styles (none, temporary banners, or persistent banners), badges on the Messages icon to show you the number of new messages, sounds and vibrations when you receive messages, and so on. Messages also supports repeated alerts, which by default is to send you two notifications for each message you receive but don't read. Configuring notifications is explained in detail in Chapter 4, "Customizing How Your iPhone Works."

- To unblock someone so you can receive messages from them again, move to the Messages screen in the Settings app, tap Blocked, swipe to the left across the contact you want to unblock, and tap Unblock.

- You can also block someone without having a contact for them. To do this, move to the details screen for the conversation containing the person you want to block (you learn how to work with conversations later in this chapter). Tap the person, email address, or number you want to block. On the resulting screen, tap Block this Caller. Tap Block Contact at the prompt. That person is blocked from sending you messages.

Sending Messages

You can use the Messages app to send messages to people using a cell phone number (as long as the device receiving it can receive text messages) or an email address that has been registered for iMessage. If the recipient has both a cell number and iMessage-enabled email address, the Messages app assumes you want to use iMessage for the message.

When you send a message to more than one person and at least one of those people can use only the cellular network, all the messages are sent via the cellular network and not as an iMessage.

More on Mixed Recipients

If one of a message's recipients has an email address that isn't iMessage-enabled (and doesn't have a phone number), the Messages app attempts to send the message to that recipient as an email message. The recipient receives the email message in an email app on his phone or computer instead of through the Messages app.

Whether messages are sent via a cellular network or iMessage isn't terribly important, but there are some differences. If your cellular account has a limit on the number of texts you can send, you should use iMessage when you can because those messages won't count against your limit. Also, when you use iMessage, you don't have to worry about a limit on the number of characters in a message. When you send a message via a cellular network, your messages might be limited to 160 characters.

When you send messages to or receive messages from a person or a group of people, you see those messages in a conversation. Every message sent among the same people is added to that conversation. When you send a message to a person or group you haven't messaged before, a new conversation is created. If you send a message to a person or group you have messaged before, the message is added to the existing conversation.

Messages on an iPhone running iOS 10 or later can include lots of different elements, including effects, Digital Touches, content from apps, and more. When you include these items in your messages sent to other people using devices running iOS 10 or later, they'll be received as you intended. If they are using devices that aren't running iOS 10 or later or Macs running macOS Sierra or later, messages with these enhancements might or might not be what you intended. For example, if the recipient is using an older version of the iOS, a Digital Touch message comes in as a static image. If the recipient is using a device not running the iOS at all, such as an Android device, it can be hard to predict what will happen to messages if you enhance them. So, keep the recipients of your messages in mind and adjust the content you send to them accordingly.

Creating a New Message and Conversation

You can send messages by entering a number or email address manually or by selecting a contact from your contacts list.

1 On the Home screen, tap Messages.

2 Tap the Compose icon (if you don't see this icon, tap the Back icon in the upper-left corner of the screen until you do). If you haven't used the Messages app before, you skip this step and move directly to the New Message screen in the next step.

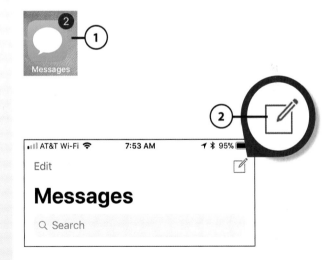

3 Type the recipient's name, email address, or phone number. As you type, the app attempts to match what you type with a saved contact or to someone you have previously messaged and shows you a list of suggested recipients. You see phone numbers or email addresses for each recipient on the list. Phone numbers or addresses in blue indicate the recipient is registered for iMessages and your message is sent via that means. Messages to phone numbers in green are sent as text messages over the cellular network. If a number or email address is gray, you haven't sent any messages to it yet; you can tap it to attempt to send a message. You also see groups you have previously messaged.

4 Tap the phone number, email address, or group to which you want to send the message. The recipients' names are inserted into the To field. Or, if the information you want to use doesn't appear, just type the complete phone number (as you would dial it to make a call to that number) or email address.

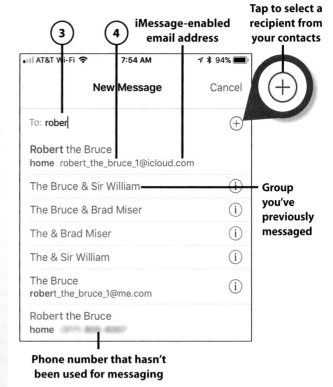

Tap to select a recipient from your contacts

iMessage-enabled email address

Group you've previously messaged

Phone number that hasn't been used for messaging

Straight to the Source
You can tap Add (+) in the To field to use the Contacts app to select a contact to whom you want to address the message (see Chapter 6 for the details of using the Contacts app).

Go to the Group
You can tap the Info (i) icon next to a group on the suggested recipients list to see the people that are part of that group.

5 If you want to send the message to more than one recipient, tap in the space between the current recipient and the Add (+) icon and use steps 3 and 4 to enter the other recipients' information, either by selecting contacts using the Add (+) icon, or by entering phone numbers or email addresses. As you add recipients, they appear in the To field. (If you addressed the message to a number or email address that matches a number in your contacts, the contact's name replaces the number in the To field. If not, the number or email address remains as you entered it.)

6 Tap in the Message bar, which is labeled iMessage if you entered iMessage addresses or Text Message if you entered a phone number. The cursor moves into the Message bar and you are ready to type your message.

7 Type the message you want to send in the Message bar.

8 Tap the Send icon, which is blue if you are sending the message via iMessage or green if you are sending it via the cellular network. The Send status bar appears as the message is sent; when the process is complete, you hear the message sent sound and the status bar disappears.

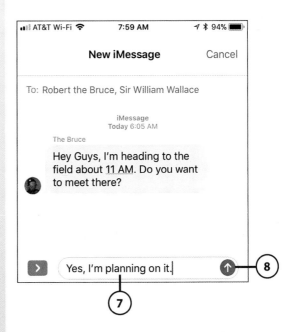

Change Your Mind?

To remove a contact or phone number from the To box, tap it once so it becomes highlighted in blue and then tap Delete on the keyboard.

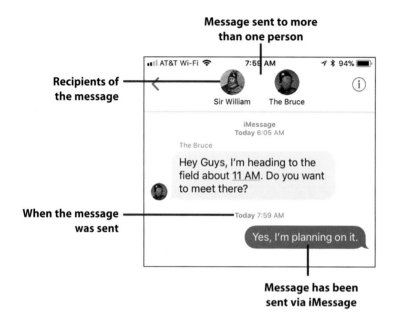

Message sent to more than one person

Recipients of the message

When the message was sent

Message has been sent via iMessage

If the message is addressed to iMessage recipients, your message appears in a blue bubble in a section labeled iMessage. If the person to whom you sent the message enabled his read receipt setting, you see when he reads your message.

Recipient of the message

Message has been sent via a cellular network

If you sent the message via the cellular network instead of iMessage, you see your message in a green bubble in a section labeled Text Message.

When you send a message, you see a new conversation screen if the message was not sent to someone or a group of people with whom you were previously messaging. If you have previously sent messages to the same recipient or recipients, you move back to the existing conversation screen and your new message is added to that conversation instead.

In a group conversation, you see icons and the names of each person who received the message; if there are more than two or three people, the icons "stack" on top of each other. (If you sent a message via a cellular text, you only see the person's name or number.)

>>>Go Further

TEXT ON

Following are some additional points to help you take your texting to the next level (where is the next level, anyway?):

- **iMessage or cell**—If the recipient has an iOS device or Mac that has been enabled for iMessage, text messages are sent via iMessage when possible even if you choose the recipient's phone number.

- **Group messaging**—If you've enabled the Group Messaging setting, when you include more than one recipient, any messages sent in reply are grouped in one conversation. If this setting isn't enabled, each reply to your message appears in a separate conversation.

- **Larger keyboard**—Like other areas where you type, you can rotate the iPhone to be horizontal where the keyboard is larger as is each key. This can make texting easier, faster, and more accurate.

- **Recents**—When you enter To information for a new message, included on the list of potential recipients are people being suggested to you by your iPhone. When a suggested recipient has an Info (i) icon, tap that icon, tap Ignore Contact, and then tap Ignore at the prompt to prevent that person from being suggested in the future.

Sending Messages in an Existing Conversation

As you learned earlier, when you send a message to or receive a message from one or more people, a conversation is created. You can add new messages to a conversation as follows:

(1) On the Home screen, tap Messages. You see a list of conversations on the Messages screen. If you were previously in a conversation, you see the messages in that conversation and the people involved at the top of the screen instead. Tap the Back icon, which is the left-facing arrow in the top-left corner of the screen to return to the conversation list on the Messages screen.

On the list, the conversation containing the most recent message you've sent or received is at the top; conversations get "older" as you move down the screen.

(2) Swipe up or down the screen or tap in the Search bar and type names, numbers, or email addresses to find the conversation to which you want to add a message.

(3) Tap the conversation to which you want to add a message. At the top of the screen, you see the people involved in the conversation. Under that, you see the current messages in the conversation.

④ Tap in the Message bar.

⑤ Type your message.

⑥ Tap the Send icon. Your new message is added to the conversation and sent to everyone participating in the conversation.

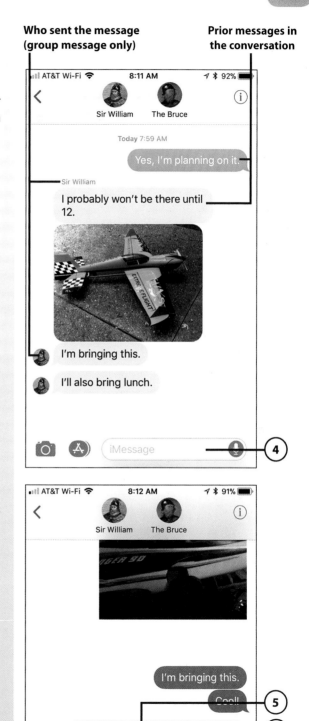

Who sent the message (group message only)

Prior messages in the conversation

Applying Effects to Messages You Send

The Messages app enables you to apply effects to your messages. Bubble Effects apply to the message you send, whereas Screen effects fill the screen when your message is read. There are quite a few effects you can use, and they are easy to apply using the following steps:

1. Create a new message or add a message to an existing conversation.

2. Touch and hold on the Send icon. The Send with effect screen appears.

No iOS 10 or later?

Recipients must be using devices running iOS 10 or later or Macs running macOS Sierra for these effects to play as you see them when you send them. You can send messages with effects to people not using iOS 10 or later devices or Macs running macOS Sierra; the messages are delivered, but the effects are not.

3. Tap Bubble to apply a Bubble Effect; to apply a Screen Effect instead, skip to step 7.

4. Tap an effect. It is applied to the current message so you see how it will look.

5. Tap other effects to see what they do.

Ah, Forget It

If you decide you don't want to add an effect, tap Delete (x) at the bottom of the screen and you return to your unadorned message, which you can then send without any bells or whistles.

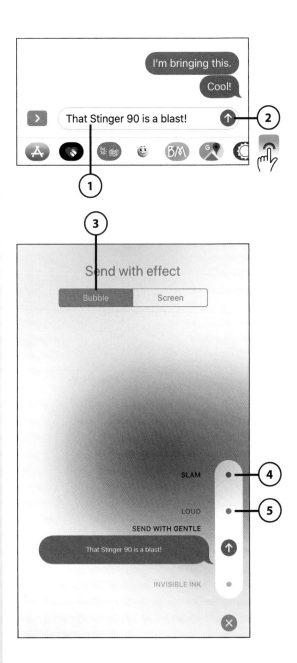

6 To send the message with the current Bubble Effect, tap the Send icon and skip the rest of these steps. Your message is sent and the recipient sees the effect on the message's bubble when he opens the message.

7 Tap Screen to apply a Screen Effect.

8 Swipe to the left or right. Each time you swipe, a new Screen Effect is applied and you see it on the screen.

9 When you find the effect you want to use, tap the Send icon. Your message is sent and each recipient sees the effect in the background of the Messages screen when she opens the message. You also see the effect applied to the message on your iPhone.

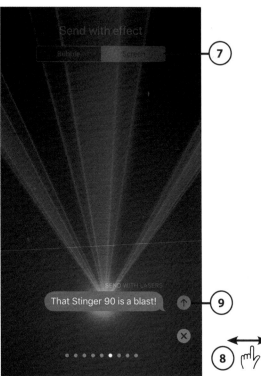

Including Photos or Video You've Recently Taken in Messages You Send

It's easy to use Messages to quickly send photos or video you've taken recently to other people as you see in the following steps:

(1) Move into the conversation with the person or people to whom you want to send a photo, or start a new conversation.

(2) Tap the Camera icon. In the photo pane, you see the photos and video you've taken recently.

Send a Video? No Problemo.

The steps in this task and the following two tasks show including photos in messages you send. You can send videos using very similar steps.

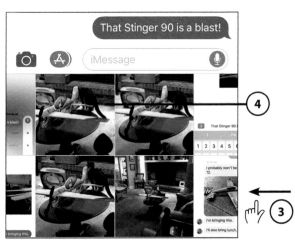

(3) Swipe to the left on the photo panel to browse the recent photos and videos.

(4) Tap the first photo or video you want to send. It is marked with a check mark and is added to the message you are sending.

(5) Swipe to the left or right to review more recent photos and videos.

(6) Tap the next photo or video you want to send. It is also marked with a check mark and added to the message.

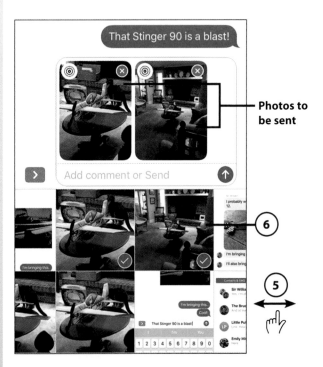

Photos to be sent

7 Repeat steps 5 and 6 until you've added all the photos and videos you want to send.

Limitations, Limitations

Not all cell carriers support MMS messages (the type that can contain images and video), and the size of messages can be limited. Check with your carrier for more information about what is supported and whether there are additional charges for using MMS messages. If you're using iMessage, you don't have this potential limit and are always able to include images and video in your texts. Also be sure your recipient can receive MMS messages before you send one.

8 Tap in the Message bar.

9 Type the comments you want to send with the photos or videos.

10 Tap the Send icon. The photos, videos, and comments are added to the conversation.

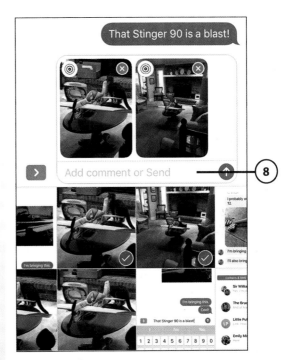

This message includes Live Photos

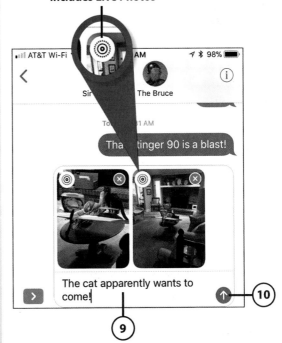

Including Photos or Video Stored on Your iPhone in Messages You Send

You can add any image, photo, or video stored on your iPhone in a conversation by performing the following steps:

1. Move into the conversation with the person or people to whom you want to send a photo or video, or start a new conversation.

2. Tap the Camera icon.

3. Swipe to the right until you see the Photos icon.

4. Tap Photos.

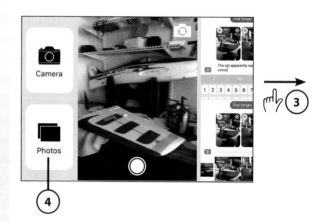

5. Swipe up or down the screen to find the source containing the photos or videos you want to send. (For more information about using the Photos app to find and select photos, see Chapter 14, "Viewing and Editing Photos and Video with the Photos App.")

6. Tap the source containing the photos or videos you want to send.

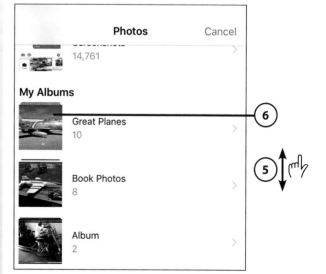

7 Swipe up or down the screen until you see the photo or video you want to send.

8 Tap the photo or video you want to send.

9 Tap Choose. You move back to the conversation and see the image or video in the Message bar.

10 Tap in the Message bar.

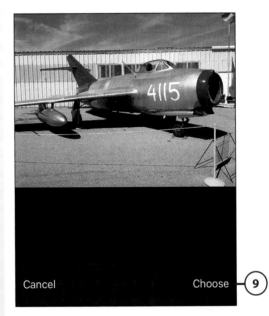

(11) Type the message you want to send with the photo or video.

(12) Tap the Send icon.

Taking Photos or Video and Sending Them in Messages

You can capture new photos and video using the iPhone's cameras and immediately send them to others via Messages as follows:

(1) Move into the conversation with the person or people to whom you want to send a photo or video, or start a new conversation.

(2) Tap the Camera icon.

(3) To use the full Camera app to take the photo or video, go on to step 4; to take a photo using the small camera window you see on the screen, position the image that you want to take and tap the Shutter icon. The photo is taken and added to the message; skip to step 10.

(4) Tap the Camera icon. (If you don't see the Camera icon, swipe to the right on the bottom of the screen until you see it.)

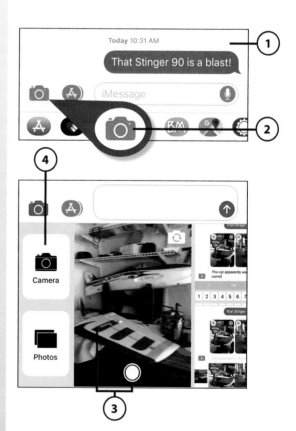

5 Use the Camera app to take the photo or video you want to send. (For more information about taking photos or videos, see Chapter 13, "Taking Photos and Video with Your iPhone.")

6 Use the tools you see to modify the photo or video, such as to add markups or edit it (see Chapter 14 for details).

(7) Use the tools you selected in the previous step to make changes to the photo or video. This example shows adding a markup to a photo.

(8) Tap Save.

(9) Tap Done.

(10) Tap in the Message bar.

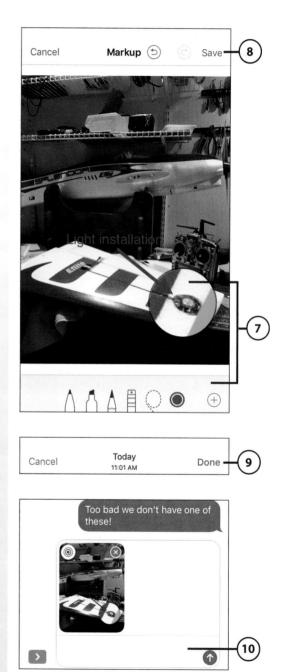

(11) Type the message you want to send with the photo.

(12) Tap the Send icon. The photo and message are added to the conversation.

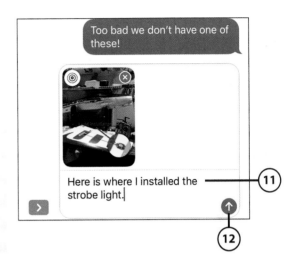

This Isn't Houston, but There Is a Problem

If a message you try to send is undeliverable or has some other problem, it is marked with an error icon, which is an exclamation point inside a red circle. The most common cause of this issue is a poor Internet connection. Tap the error icon and tap Try Again to attempt to resend the message. If it doesn't work again, you might need to wait until you have a better connection.

Sharing with Messages

You can share all sorts of information via Messages from many apps, such as Safari, Contacts, Maps, and so on. From the app containing the information you want to share, tap the Share icon. Then tap Messages. The information with which you are working is automatically added to a new message. Use the Messages app to complete and send the message.

Using Digital Touches in Messages You Send

You can enhance your messages with Digital Touches, which are dynamic images you draw with your fingers, or you can use the default images.

(1) Move into the conversation with the person or people to whom you want to send a Digital Touch.

(2) If you see the Digital Touch icon, skip to step 3; if not, tap the app icon.

(3) Tap the Digital Touch icon. The Digital Touch panel opens.

(4) Tap the upward-facing arrow to open the Digital Touch screen in full screen mode.

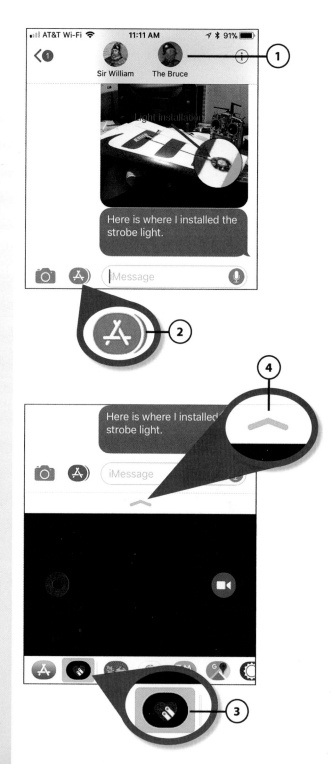

5 To send one of the default Digital Touches, move to step 8; to create your own Digital Touch, tap the color you want to use. The current color's icon has a dot in the center to show it's selected.

6 Use your finger to draw or write on the screen. You can change the color at any time; for example, you can use different colors in a drawing or for each letter in a word. Drawing on the Digital Touch screen is much like using colored pencils on paper.

7 Tap the Send icon to send it. The full screen mode digital pane collapses and you see a preview of your Digital Touch as it sends.

Use the Small Screen

You can create Digital Touches directly in the small Digital Touch panel that appears when you tap the Digital Touch icon. Putting it in full screen mode gives you more room to work but takes slightly longer. To create a touch directly in the panel, use the Digital Touch drawing tools directly in the small window and then tap the Send icon to send it.

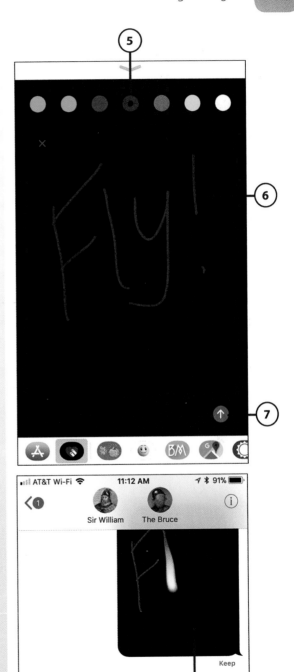

A preview of your digital touch plays so you see what the recipients will see

8 Tap the Info (i) icon. You see a list of all the gestures you can use to add a Digital Touch to a conversation. (This step is optional. If you know the gesture to create the Digital Touch you want to send, skip to step 11.)

9 Review the default Digital Touches.

10 Tap the Close (x) icon to close the list.

iOS 10 Required

Like effects, the recipient must be using a device running iOS 10 or later or a Mac running macOS Sierra to receive Digital Touches as you see them when you send them. If you send a Digital Touch message to devices not running iOS 10 or later, they appear as a static image in the message.

Start Over

To get rid of the contents of the Digital Touch screen, tap Delete (x).

11 Use the finger gesture to add the default Digital Touch you want to the conversation. You see a preview in the Digital Touch pane, and the Digital Touch is immediately sent to the recipients and added to the conversation.

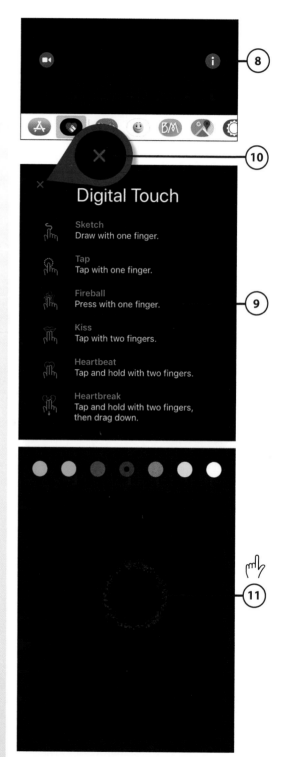

>>>Go Further

YOU'VE GOT THE TOUCH

Here are a few more touch-related tidbits:

- You can collapse the full screen Digital Touch pane by tapping the downward-facing arrow in the top-right corner of the screen.

- By default, Digital Touch messages you send or receive expire after two minutes. If you want to keep a Digital Touch message, tap Keep, which appears at the bottom of the message as soon as you send it. The Digital Touch message remains until you delete it manually or it is deleted with the other messages based on the Messages app's settings.

- You can't stop a default Digital Touch once you make its gesture. As soon as you make the gesture, it is sent.

- You can take a video or photo and create a Digital Touch on top of it by tapping the Video Camera icon in the Digital Touch pane. The camera view opens and you can take a photo or video. You can draw on or apply a Digital Touch before or during a video capture. You can send the photo or video by tapping the Send icon.

Adding Apps to Messages

You can use apps to add content to your messages. You can use the default apps installed in Messages (examples are provided later in this chapter) and you can add more apps as follows:

(1) Open Messages and move into a conversation.

(2) Tap the Apps icon. The App Drawer opens and you see the installed apps at the bottom of the screen. The app you used most recently is selected automatically.

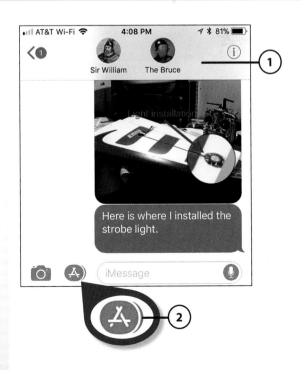

3 Tap the App Store app (if you don't see this app, swipe to the left or right on the App Drawer until you see it).

4 Tap Visit Store. You move into the App Store and see apps that work within Messages.

5 Browse or search within the App Store to find apps you want to add to Messages, such as stickers you can insert into your messages. This works very similarly to using the App Store app, which is covered in Chapter 4. Note that if you just browse you only see Messages-compatible apps, but if you search you see both "regular" apps and Messages apps.

6 Tap the Get icon for a free app or the price icon for an app with a license fee. You might have to touch the Touch ID button, use Face ID, or enter your Apple ID password to complete the process. Just like other apps, it is downloaded to your iPhone, but it's installed in the Messages App Drawer instead of on a Home screen.

After the app is downloaded, it appears in the App Drawer, and you can use it.

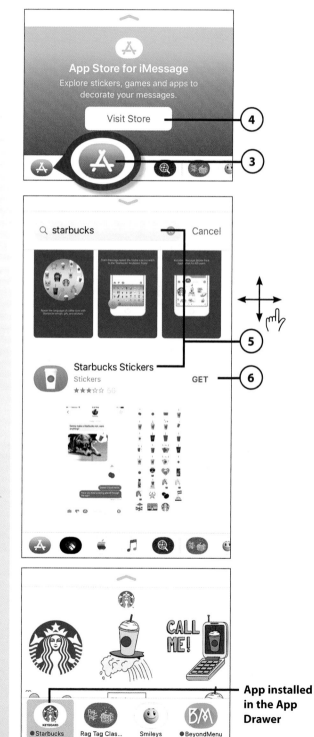

App installed in the App Drawer

Managing Apps in Messages

You can configure the apps in the App Drawer by performing the following steps:

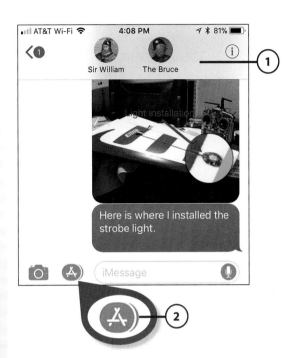

(1) Open Messages and move into a conversation.

(2) Tap the Apps icon. The App Drawer opens.

(3) Swipe to the left on the App Drawer until you see the More icon. As you swipe on the App Drawer, it enlarges so you can more clearly see the app icons.

(4) Tap More. You see apps currently installed on the App Drawer. There are two sections. FAVORITES are apps you've tagged as your favorites; these appear on the left end of the App Drawer and so are easier to access. In the MORE APPS section, you see the other apps in the App Drawer. You can use the apps in either section.

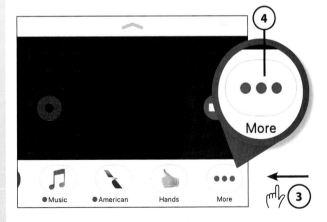

(5) Tap Edit.

(6) If you don't want to see an app in the App Drawer, set its switch to off (white). It no longer appears in the App Drawer, but remains available so you can re-enable it again.

Get Rid of It

If you want to remove an app from the App Drawer, perform steps 1 through 4. Swipe to the left on the app you want to remove. Tap Delete. The app is removed from the App Drawer.

(7) To move an app into the FAVORITES section, tap Add (+). It jumps up to the FAVORITES section.

(8) To move an app from FAVORITES to MORE APPS, tap its Unlock (–) icon.

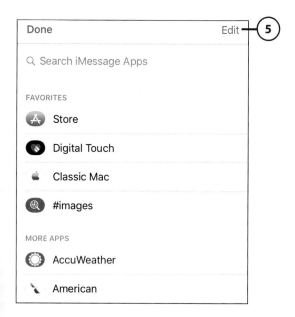

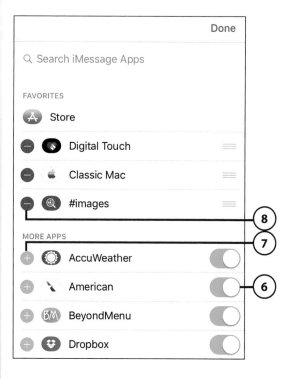

9 Tap Remove from Favorites. The app moves to the lower section, but remains in the App Drawer.

10 To change the order of the apps in the FAVORITES section, drag apps up or down the list by their Order (three lines) icon.

11 When you're done managing apps, tap Done.

12 Tap Done.

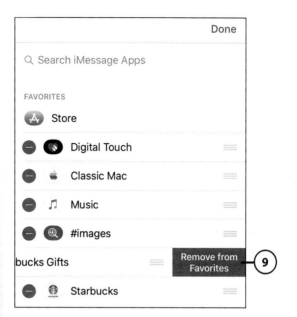

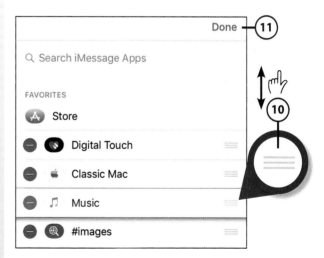

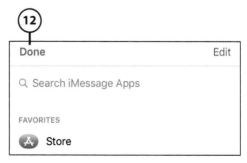

Adding Content from Apps to Messages You Send

You can use the apps on the Messages' App Drawer to add content to the messages you send. As you saw in the previous task, there are many different types of apps available and each works according to the type of content you can use. Some are quite simple, such as providing icons or images (sometimes called stickers) you can easily add to messages. Others are a bit more complicated; for example, you can use the #images app to search for and add images to your messages. Using any of these apps to add content to your messages follows a similar pattern, so once you see how to use one of them, you can use any of them fairly easily.

This example shows you how to use the #images app to add static images and animated gifs to your messages:

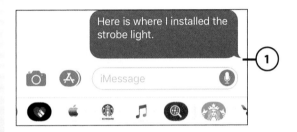

1. Move into a conversation or start a new one.

2. If you don't see the app you want to use, swipe to the left or right until you do. (If you don't see the App Drawer, tap the Apps icon to open it first.)

3. Tap the app you want to use.

4. Tap the up-facing arrow to expand the app to full screen; this step is optional because you can use the app in the collapsed view in the same way.

(5) Type a search term. Search terms that match what you type are listed.

(6) Tap the search you want to perform. (If you don't see a search you want to use, complete your search phrase and tap the Search key on the keyboard.)

(7) Swipe up and down the screen to browse all the images that match your search.

(8) Tap the image you want to add to the conversation.

(9) Tap in the Message bar. In many cases, you'll skip adding a message (steps 9 and 10) and just send the content by skipping to step 11.

(10) Type a comment you want to send with the content you added.

Delete It

To delete the content without sending it, tap Delete (x) that appears on the content you've added to the conversation.

(11) Tap the Send icon to send the app content you've added.

Tap to delete content

Including Instant Audio in Messages You Send

You can send audio messages that you record via a message by performing the following steps:

(1) Move to the conversation to which you want to add an audio message, or start a new conversation.

(2) Touch and hold on the Microphone in the Message bar (not the one on the keyboard). Recording starts.

(3) Speak your message; keep your finger touching the Microphone while you speak.

(4) When you're done recording, take your finger off the screen.

(5) Tap the Play icon to replay your message.

(6) If you don't want to send the message, delete it by tapping Delete (x).

(7) Tap the Send icon to send the message. The audio message is added to the conversation and the recipients are able to listen to it.

Your message is being recorded

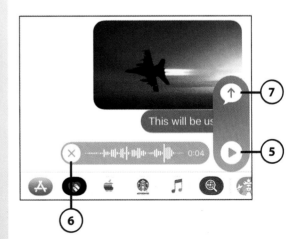

Adding Your Location to Messages You Send

Location information can be available for the participants in a conversation so you can see where others are, and they can see where you are. You can add your location information to a conversation as follows:

(1) Move to the conversation to which you want to add your location information.

(2) Tap the Info (i) icon.

(3) To share your current location as a snapshot, tap Send My Current Location. Your current location is captured and sent to the recipients of the message.

(4) To dynamically share your location so that it updates as you move around, tap Share My Location.

(5) Tap how long you want your location information to be shared.

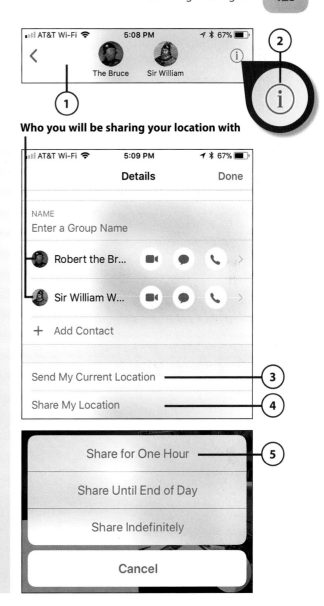

Who you will be sharing your location with

Current Locations

When a current location is added to a conversation, it is static, meaning it is only the location at that point in time. It appears as a map thumbnail in the conversation. Recipients can tap it to zoom in on the location, and then tap Directions to Here to generate directions from their location to the one sent as the current location.

Which Device?

If you have multiple devices that can provide your location, you can configure which device is used to determine your location by opening the Settings app, tapping Privacy, tapping Location Services, tapping Share My Location, tapping From, and then tapping the device that should be used for your position.

(6) To stop sharing your location, tap Stop Sharing My Location. If you selected to share it for one hour or until the end of the day, location sharing stops automatically at the time you selected.

(7) Tap Done to return to the conversation.

Using Quick Actions to Send Messages

You can use the Quick Actions feature on iPhones that support 3D Touch with the Messages app as follows:

(1) Press on the Messages icon. The Quick Actions menu appears.

(2) Tap the person to whom you want to send a message or tap New Message to send a message to someone not shown on the list. If you choose a person, you move into an existing conversation with that person or a new conversation is started. If you choose New Message, you move to the New Message screen.

(3) Complete and send the message.

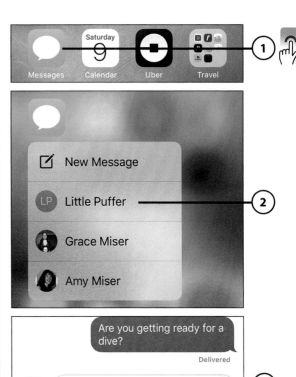

Receiving, Reading, and Replying to Messages

Text messaging is about communication, so when you send messages you expect to receive responses. People can also send new messages to you. As you learned earlier, the Messages app keeps messages grouped as a conversation consisting of messages you send and replies you receive to the same person or group of people.

Receiving Messages

Swipe to the right on the notification to move into the Messages app to read the entire message

Message alert notification on the Lock screen

Press the notification to read all of it and respond (3D Touch only)

Tap to open the message in the Messages app

Message alert notification on the Home screen

Press the notification to read all of it and respond (3D Touch only)

When you aren't currently using the Messages screen in the Messages app and receive a new message (as a new conversation or as a new message in an ongoing conversation), you see, hear, and feel the notifications you have configured for the Messages app. (Refer to Chapter 4 to configure your Messages notifications.)

If you are on the Messages screen in the Messages app when a new message comes in, you hear and feel the new message notification sound and/or vibration, but a notification does not appear. On the conversation list, any conversations containing a new message are marked with a blue circle showing the number of new messages in that conversation.

If a new message is from someone with whom you have previously sent or received a message, and you haven't deleted all the messages to or from those recipients (no matter how long it has been since a message was added to that conversation), the new message is appended to an ongoing conversation. That conversation then moves to the top of the list of conversations in the Messages app. If there isn't an existing message to or from the people involved in a new message, a new conversation is started and the message appears at the top of that list.

Speaking of Texting

Using Siri to hear and speak text messages is extremely useful. Check out Chapter 11, "Working with Siri," for examples showing how you can take advantage of this great feature. One of the most useful Messages commands is to activate Siri and say "Get new messages." Siri reads any new messages you have received.

Reading Messages

You can get to new messages you receive by doing any of the following:

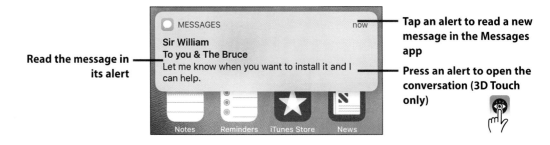

Read the message in its alert

Tap an alert to read a new message in the Messages app

Press an alert to open the conversation (3D Touch only)

- Read a message in its alert. Tap a banner alert notification from Messages to move into the message's conversation in the Messages app.

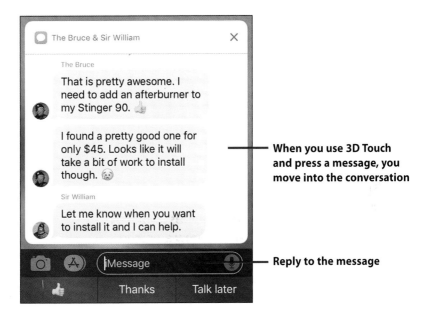

When you use 3D Touch and press a message, you move into the conversation

Reply to the message

- If you are using an iPhone that supports 3D Touch, you can press on an alert to open the conversation to which the message was added. You can read all the messages it contains and reply to those messages.

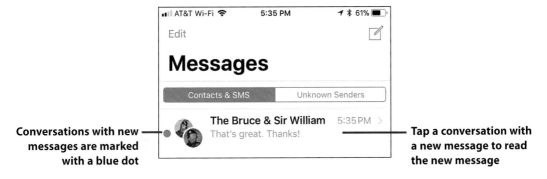

Conversations with new messages are marked with a blue dot

Tap a conversation with a new message to read the new message

- Open the Messages app and tap a conversation containing a new message; these conversations appear at the top of the Messages list and are marked with a blue circle. The conversation opens and you see the new message.

- Swipe to the right on a message notification when it appears on the Lock screen. You move into the conversation to which the message was sent (you might need to unlock your phone first).

- If you receive a new message in a conversation that you are currently viewing, you immediately see the new message.

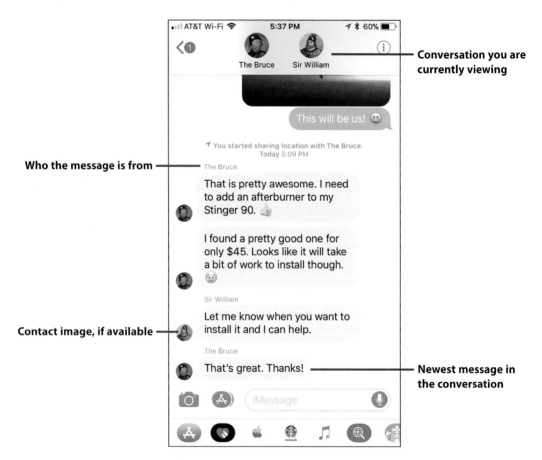

However you get to a message, you see the new message in either an existing conversation or a new conversation. The newest messages appear at the bottom of the screen. You can swipe up and down the screen to see all of the messages in the conversation. As you move up the screen, you move back in time.

Messages sent to you are on the left side of the screen and appear in gray bubbles. Just above the bubble is the name of the person sending the message; if you have an image for the contact, that image appears next to the bubble. The color of your bubbles indicates how the message was sent: blue indicates an iMessage while green indicates a cellular message.

Viewing Images or Video You Receive in Messages

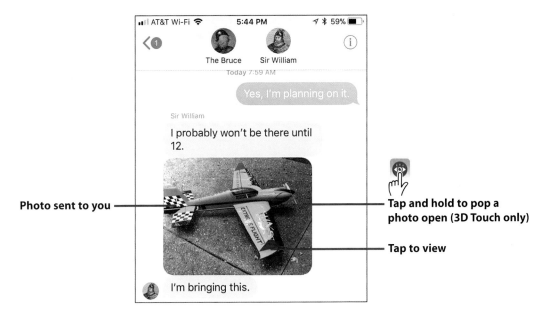

Photo sent to you

Tap and hold to pop a photo open (3D Touch only)

Tap to view

When you receive a photo or video as an attachment, it appears in a thumbnail along with the accompanying message.

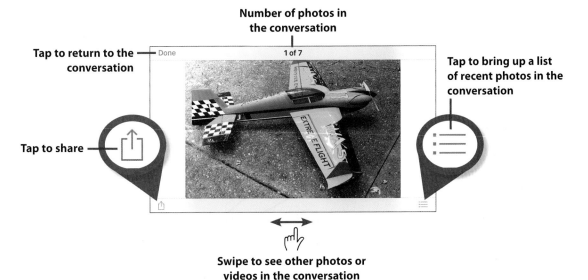

Number of photos in the conversation

Tap to return to the conversation

Tap to bring up a list of recent photos in the conversation

Tap to share

Swipe to see other photos or videos in the conversation

To view a photo or video attachment, tap it. You see the photo or video at a larger size. You can rotate the phone, zoom, and swipe around the photo just like viewing photos in the Photos app (see Chapter 14 for details). You can watch a video in the same way, too.

Tap the Share icon to share the photo with others via a message, email, tweet, Facebook, and so on. (When you hold an iPhone Plus horizontally, all the icons are at the top of the screen.)

If there is more than one photo or video in the conversation, you see the number of them at the top of the screen. Swipe to the left or right to move through the available photos.

Tap the List icon to see a list of the recent photos in the conversation (this only appears if there is more than one photo in the conversation).

Tap a photo on the list to view it. Tap Close to return to the photo you were viewing.

To move back to the conversation, tap Done.

When you use an iPhone that supports 3D Touch and you press on a photo, it opens in a Peek. If you continue pressing on the photo, it opens in the view window just like when you tap on it in the conversation.

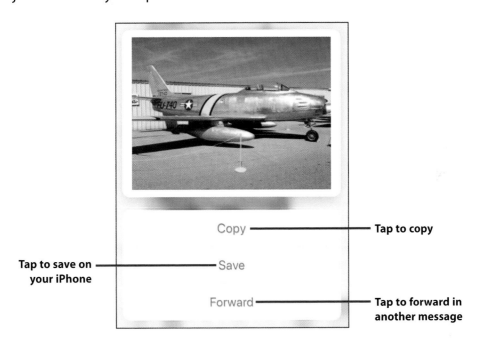

Copy ——————————— **Tap to copy**

Tap to save on ——————————— Save
your iPhone

Forward ——————————— **Tap to forward in**
another message

When you are peeking at a photo, swipe up on it to reveal options. You can copy the photo so you can paste it elsewhere, save the photo in the Photos app, or forward it to others.

No 3D Touch?

If your iPhone doesn't support 3D Touch, you can save a photo by touching the photo (don't apply pressure) and using the Save Image command on the resulting menu. You can also copy or forward it from this menu.

Listening to Audio You Receive in Messages

Audio message

Tap to listen via the speakerphone

Tap to play

When you receive an audio message, you can tap the Play icon to play it, or, if you enabled the Raise to Listen option, lift the phone to your ear and the message plays automatically. Tap the Speaker icon to hear the message via the iPhone's speakerphone.

Tap to pause

While the message is playing, you see its status along with the Pause icon, which you can tap to pause the audio message. After the message finishes, you see a message saying that it expires in 2 minutes or 1 year, depending on your settings. That message is quickly replaced by Keep.

Keep

Tap to save the audio message

Tap Keep to save the message on your phone. (Keep disappears indicating the audio is saved.)

Kept Audio Messages

When one or more of the recipients of an audio message that you sent keeps it, a status message is added to the conversation on your phone, so you know who keeps audio messages you have sent. And, others know when you keep their messages, too.

Replying to Messages from the Messages App

To reply to a message, read the message and do the following:

① Read, watch, or listen to the most recent message.

② Use the photos, Digital Touch, or App tools to reply with content of that type as you learned about earlier in this chapter.

③ Tap in the Message bar if you want to reply with text.

④ Type your reply or use the Dictation feature to speak your reply (this is translated to text; it's not recording and embedding an audio message).

⑤ Tap the Send icon.

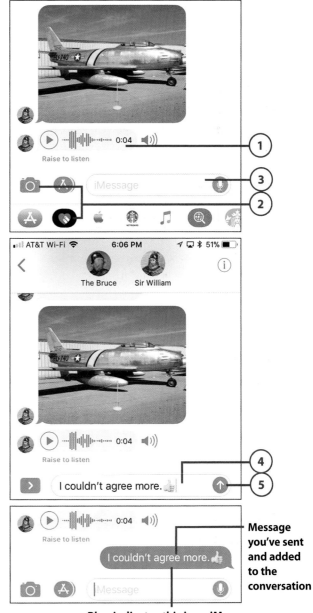

Message you've sent and added to the conversation

Blue indicates this is an iMessage

Mix and Match

The Messages app can switch between types of messages. For example, if you have an iMessage conversation going but can't access the iMessage service for some reason, the app can send messages as a cellular text. It can switch the other way, too. The app tries to send iMessages first if it can but chooses whichever method it needs to get the messages through. (If you disabled the Send as SMS option, messages are only sent via iMessage.)

More Tricks of the Messaging Trade

My Acquisitions Editor Extraordinaire pointed out that people can't receive messages when their phones aren't connected to the Internet (via Wi-Fi or cell). You don't see a warning in this case; you can only tell the message wasn't delivered because the Delivered status doesn't appear under the message. The message is delivered as soon as the other person's phone is connected to the Internet again, and its status is updated accordingly on your phone. Also, when an iMessage can't be delivered, you can tap and hold on it; then tap Send as Text Message. The app tries to send the message via SMS instead of iMessage.

Replying to Messages from a Banner Alert

If you have banner alerts configured for your messages, you can reply directly from the alert from either the Home or Lock screens:

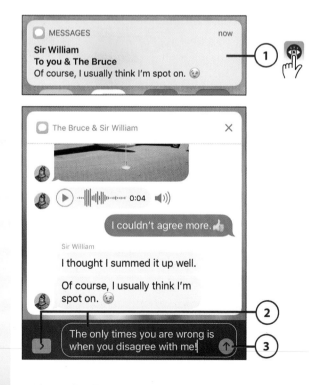

1. Press on the notification (3D Touch) or swipe to the right (non-3D Touch). The conversation opens.

2. Type your reply or tap the right-facing arrow to add other types of content to your response.

3. Tap the Send icon. Your message is added to the conversation.

Having a Messages Conversation

Messaging is all about the back-and-forth communication with one or more people. You've already learned the skills you need, so put them all together. You can start a new conversation by sending a message to one or more people with whom you don't have an ongoing conversation; or you can add to a conversation already underway.

(1) Send a new message to a person or add a new message to an existing conversation. You see when your message has been delivered. If you sent the message to an individual person via iMessages and he has enabled his Read Receipt setting, you see when he has read your message and you see a bubble as he is composing a response. (If you are conversing with more than one person, the person doesn't have her Read Receipt setting enabled, or the conversation is happening via the cellular network, you don't see either of these.)

As the recipient composes a response, you see a bubble on the screen where the new message will appear when it is received (again, only if it is an iMessage with a single individual). Of course, you don't have to remain on the conversation's screen waiting for a response. You can move to a different conversation or a different app. When the response comes in, you are notified per your notification settings.

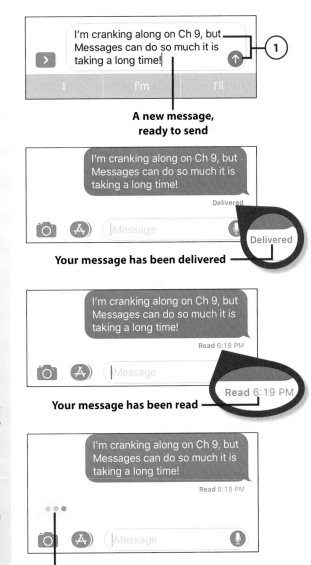

A new message, ready to send

Your message has been delivered

Your message has been read

The recipient is composing a response

2 Read the response.

3 Send your next message.

4 Repeat these steps as long as you want. Conversations remain in the Messages app until you remove them. Messages within conversations remain forever (unless you delete them, for one year, or for 30 days depending on your Keep Messages setting as shown earlier in this chapter).

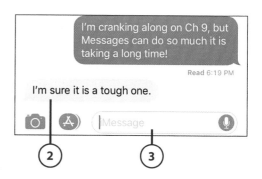

Seen But Not Read

Don't take the Read status too literally. All it means is that the conversation to which your message was added has been viewed. Of course, the Messages app can't know whether the recipient actually read the message.

The iMessage Will Be With You...Always

Messages that are sent with iMessage move with you from device to device, so they appear on every device configured to use your iMessage account. Because of this, you can start a conversation on your iPhone while you are on the move and pick it up on your iPad or Mac later.

Working with Messages

As you send and receive messages, the interaction you have with each person or group becomes a separate conversation. A conversation consists of all the messages that have gone back and forth. You manage your conversations from the Messages screen.

Multiple Conversations with the Same People

The Messages app manages conversations based on the phone number or email address associated with the messages in that conversation rather than the people (contacts) involved in the conversation. So, you might have multiple conversations with the same person if that person used a different means, such as a phone number and an email address, to send messages to you.

Managing Messages Conversations

Use the Messages screen to manage your messages.

1 On the Home screen, tap Messages.

The Messages screen showing conversations you have going appears, or you move into the conversation you were most recently using (tap the left-facing arrow at the top of the screen to move back to the conversation list). Conversations containing new messages appear at the top of the list. The name of the conversation is the name of the person or people associated with it, or it might be labeled as Group if the app can't display the names. If a contact can't be associated with the person, you see the phone number or email address you are conversing with instead of a name.

If you have the badge enabled, you see the number of new messages on the Messages icon

Information Messages

Many organizations use messages to keep you informed. Examples are airlines that send flight status information, retailers that use messages to keep you informed about shipping, and so on. These messages are identified by a set of numbers that don't look like a phone number. You can't send a response to most of these messages; they are one-way only. In some cases, you can issue commands related to the texts from that organization, such as "Stop" to stop further texts from being sent.

(**2**) Swipe up and down the list to see all the conversations.

(**3**) Tap a conversation you want to read or reply to. The conversation screen appears; the name of the screen is the people with whom you are conversing, either by name if they are a contact or email address or phone number if they aren't.

Conversation with new messages

Day or time of most recent message

Who is involved in the conversation

4 Read the new messages or view other new content in the conversation. Your messages are on the right side of the screen in green (cell network) or blue (iMessage), whereas the other people's messages are on the left in gray. Messages are organized so the newest message is at the bottom of the screen.

5 Swipe up and down the conversation screen to see all the messages it contains.

6 To add a new message to the conversation, tap in the Message bar, type your message or use an app to add content, and tap the Send icon.

7 Swipe down to scroll up the screen and move back in time in the conversation.

8 To see details about the conversation, tap the Info (i) icon. The Details screen appears. At the top of the screen, you see location information for the people with whom you are texting if it is available.

See the Time of Every Message

To see the time or date associated with every message in the conversation being displayed, swipe to the left and hold your finger down on the screen. The messages shift to the left and the time of each message appears along the right side of the screen. The date associated with each message appears right before the first message on that date.

(9) If you are working with a group message and want to give it a name, tap Enter a Group Name. If you are working with a conversation involving one other person or don't want to name the group, skip to step 11.

What's in a Name?

When you name a group (conversation), that name is applied to the conversation for all the participants.

(10) Enter the name of the group, and tap Done.

(11) To place a voice call or audio-only FaceTime call to one of the participants in the conversation, tap the Phone icon. If the person has a phone number configured, you're prompted to choose Voice Call or FaceTime Audio. When you make a choice, that call is placed. If the person only has an email address, an audio-only FaceTime call is placed over the Internet. You move into the Phone or FaceTime app and use that app to complete the call. (See Chapter 7, "Communicating with the Phone and FaceTime Apps," for the details about those apps.) Move to the Home screen and tap Messages or use the App Switcher to return to the Messages app.

(12) Send a private message to one of the participants by tapping the Messages icon.

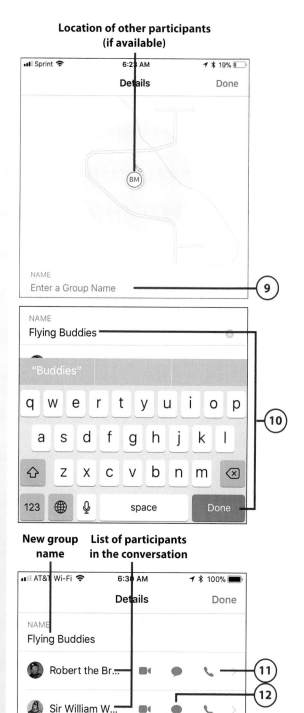

Location of other participants (if available)

NAME
Enter a Group Name — (9)

New group name   List of participants in the conversation

13. Place a FaceTime video call by tapping the Video Camera icon. You move into the FaceTime app to complete the call. When you're done, move to the Home screen and tap Messages or use the App Switcher to return to the Messages app.

14. To view a participant's contact information or send an email, tap the person whose information you want to view.

15. Work with the contact information as described in Chapter 6.

16. Tap the Back icon to return to the Details screen and click Done to return to the conversation screen.

Receiving and Reading Messages on an iPhone Plus

The larger screen on the iPhone Plus provides some additional functionality that is unique to it. You can access this by holding the iPhone Plus horizontally when you use the Messages app.

1. Open the Messages app and hold the iPhone so it is oriented horizontally. The window splits into two panes. On the left is the Navigation pane, where you can move to and select conversations you want to view. When you select a conversation in the left pane, its messages appear in the Content pane on the right.

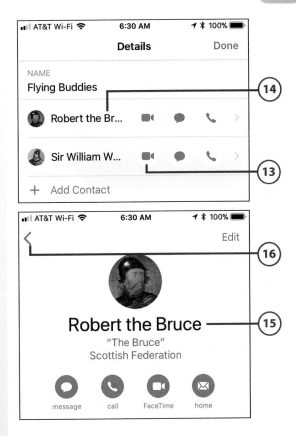

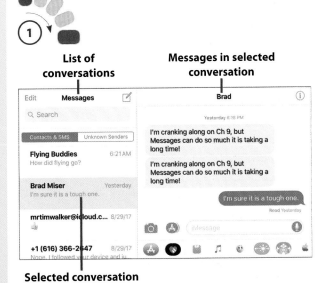

List of conversations

Messages in selected conversation

Selected conversation

(2) Swipe up or down the Navigation pane to browse the conversations available to you. Notice that the two panes are independent. When you browse the left pane, the right pane doesn't change.

(3) Tap the conversation containing messages you want to read. The messages in that conversation appear in the Content pane on the right.

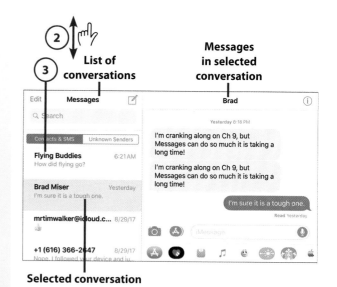

List of conversations

Messages in selected conversation

Selected conversation

(4) Swipe up and down the Content pane to read the messages in the conversation.

(5) Work with the messages in the conversation just like when the iPhone is held vertically.

(6) To add a message to the conversation, tap in the Message bar, type your message, and tap Send. Of course, you can embed audio, attach photos or video, add content from apps, or send your location just as you can when using Messages when you hold the iPhone vertically.

(7) Work with the conversation's details by tapping the Info (i) icon.

(8) Change conversations by tapping the conversation you want to view.

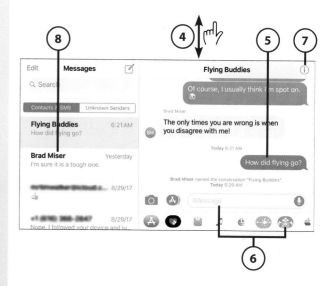

Using 3D Touch for Messages

You can use the 3D Touch feature (iPhone 6s and later models) with the Messages app as follows:

(1) Browse your messages.

(2) Tap and hold on a conversation in which you are interested. A Peek of that conversation appears.

(3) Review the preview of the messages that appear in the Peek.

(4) Open the conversation so you can read all of its messages by pressing down slightly harder until it pops open. Use the steps in the earlier task to read it (skip the rest of these steps).

(5) See actions you can perform on the message by swiping up on the Peek.

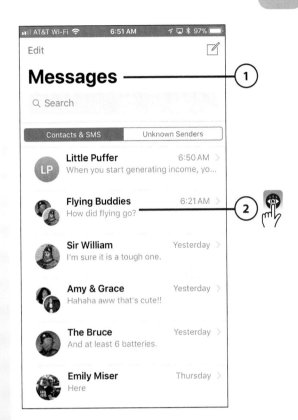

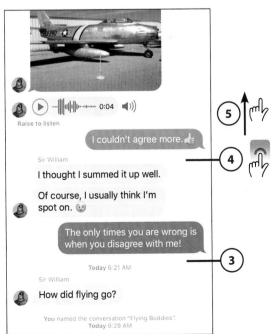

(6) Tap the reply you want to make, which is based on the context of the previous message, such as responding to the question "How did it go?," to reply to the message with that message. If you tap Custom, you can create a custom reply to the message as you can when you view the conversation.

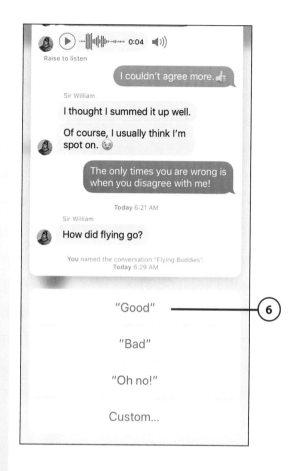

Browsing Attachments to Conversations

As photos, videos, and documents are added to a conversation, they are collected so you can browse and view them at any time:

(1) Move to the conversation in which you want to browse attachments.

(2) Tap the Info (i) icon.

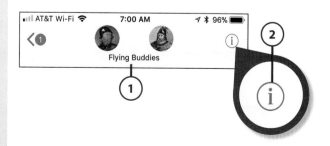

3. Swipe up until you see the Images and Attachments tabs.

4. Tap Images to see images attached to the conversation or Attachments to work with other types of attachments (such as PDF documents).

5. Swipe up and down on the attachments until you see one you want to view.

6. Tap the attachment you want to view.

7. View the attachment, such as looking at a photo.

8. Tap Done to return to the Details screen.

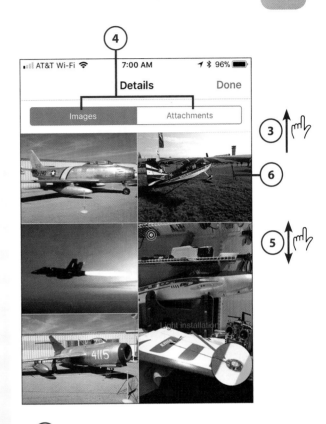

Keep Quiet!

You can disable notifications for a specific conversation by tapping its Info (i) icon to move to the Details screen. Set the Hide Alerts switch to on (green). You no longer are notified when new messages arrive in that conversation. Set the switch to off (white) to have notifications resume.

I'm Outta Here!

If you don't want to participate in a conversation any more, open the Details screen and tap Leave this Conversation.

Working with Messages from People You Might Not Know

As you use Messages, it is likely you'll receive messages from people who aren't in your contacts or who you haven't sent messages to before. Some of these will be legitimate contacts with whom you have messaged previously while some will just be because the person sending the message made a mistake, such as not typing the phone number correctly; others will be made for nefarious purposes. The Messages app can filter messages from unknown people for you and put them on the Unknown Senders tab so you can easily identify messages that are from people who you might not know.

To use this functionality, the Filter Unknown Senders switch on the Messages Settings screen must be turned on (green). (The details of configuring Messages settings are provided in "Setting Your Text and iMessage Preferences" earlier in this chapter.) When this switch is on, you see two tabs in the Messages app. The Contacts & SMS tab lists conversations with people who are contacts or with whom you have communicated previously. The Unknown Senders tab lists conversations from people who aren't contacts or with whom you haven't communicated previously. (If the Filter Unknown Senders switch is off, you don't see these tabs.)

If you enable the Filter Unknown Senders feature, you can work with "suspicious" messages as follows:

1. Open the Messages app.

2. Tap the Unknown Senders tab.

3. Tap a message to read it so you can determine if it is a legitimate message for you.

4. Review the identification of the sender as best Messages can determine it, such as an email address.

5. Read the message.

6. If the message is from someone you don't recognize and don't want to receive future messages from, tap Report Junk. The sender's message is deleted from the Messages app and the associated email address or phone number is blocked so you won't receive any more messages from the sender.

7. If you want to take other action on the sender, tap the Info (i) icon.

8. Tap the contact information for the sender.

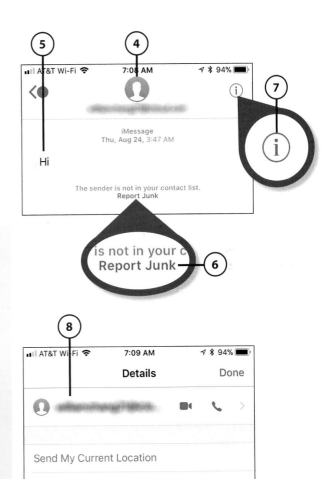

9 If you recognize the person, want to communicate with her, but don't have a contact configured for her, tap Create New Contact to create a new contact for the person. (For information about creating or updating contacts, see Chapter 6.)

10 If you recognize the person, want to communicate with her, and have a contact configured for her, tap Add to Existing Contact to update a current contact with new information.

11 If you don't want to receive future messages from the sender, tap Block this Caller.

12 Tap Block Contact.

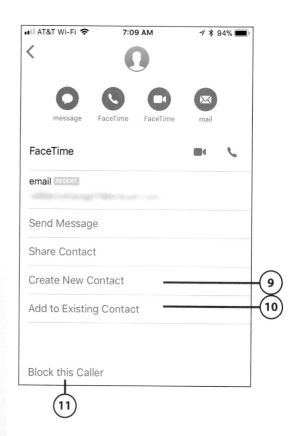

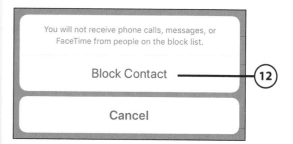

Junk or Block?

When you report a message as junk, the contact is blocked from communicating with you, but their information is not stored on your iPhone. When you block the contact instead, messages don't reach you, but the contact information is stored on the list of people you have blocked. You can unblock people from this list if you want to resume communicating with them. You can't resume communicating with someone whose messages you have marked as junk.

Responding to a Message with Icons

You can quickly respond to messages with an icon as follows:

1. View a conversation.

2. If you are using an iPhone with 3D Touch, press and hold on a message you want to respond to; if you are using a non-3D Touch phone, just touch and hold on a message. You can respond to any message, even if it's one you sent.

3. Tap the icon you want to add to the message; for example, tap the thumbs-up icon to indicate you like a message. The icon you select is added to the message.

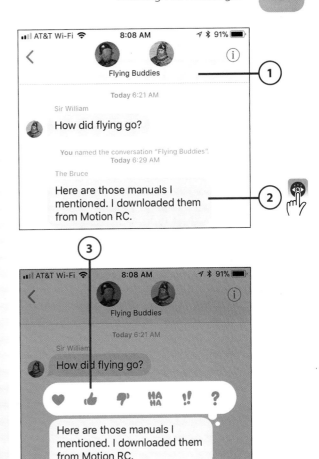

Deleting Messages and Conversations

Old text conversations never die, nor do they fade away (if you have your Keep Messages setting set to Forever, that is). All the messages you receive from a person or that involve the same group of people stay in the conversation. Over time, you can build up a lot of messages in one conversation, and you can end up with lots of conversations. (If you set the Keep Messages setting to be 30 Days or 1 Year, messages older than the time you set are deleted automatically.)

Long Conversation?

When a conversation gets very long, the Messages app won't display all its messages. It keeps the more current messages visible on the conversation screen. To see earlier messages, swipe down on the screen to move to the top and tap Load Earlier Messages.

When a conversation gets too long, if you just want to remove specific messages from a conversation, or, if you want to get rid of messages to free up storage space, take these steps:

(1) Move to a conversation containing an abundance of messages.

(2) If you are using an iPhone with 3D Touch, press and hold on a message you want to delete; if you are using a non-3D Touch phone, just touch and hold on a message to be deleted.

(3) Tap More. The message on which you tapped is marked with a check mark to show it is selected.

Be a Copycat

Tap Copy to copy a message so you can paste it in other messages or in other apps.

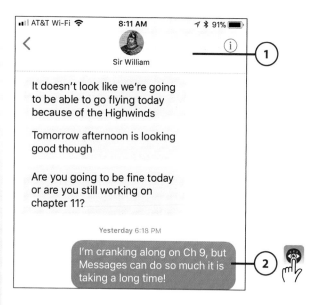

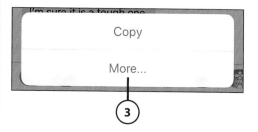

④ Tap other messages you want to delete. They are marked with a check mark to show you have selected them.

Delete Them All!

To delete all the messages in the conversation, instead of performing step 4, tap Delete All, which appears in the upper-left corner of the screen. Tap Delete Conversation in the confirmation box. The conversation and all its messages are deleted.

⑤ Tap the Trash Can.

⑥ Tap Delete *X* Messages, where *X* is the number of messages you have selected. The messages are deleted and you return to the conversation.

Pass It On

If you want to send one or more messages to someone else, perform steps 1–4. Tap the Forward icon that appears in the lower-right corner of the screen. A new message is created and the messages you selected are pasted into it. Select or enter the recipients to whom you want to send the messages, and tap Send.

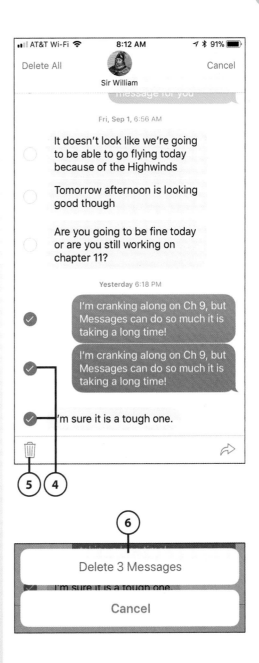

Deleting Conversations

If a conversation's time has come, you can delete it.

(1) Move to the Messages screen.

(2) Swipe to the left on the conversation you want to delete.

(3) Tap Delete. The conversation and all the messages it contains are deleted.

Gone, but Not Forgotten?

When you delete an iMessage conversation, it is removed from your iPhone. However, the actual conversation remains on the cloud and on other devices on which your iMessages account is configured. If you send a message to the same person or people who were on the conversation you deleted, it is restored to your iPhone.

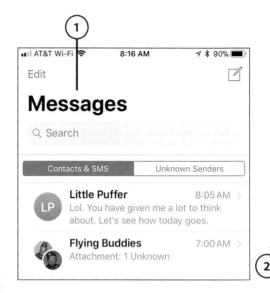

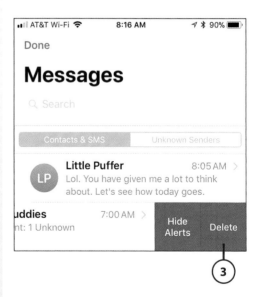

>>>Go Further

TEXTING LINGO

People frequently use shorthand when they text. Here is some of the more common shorthand you might see. This list is extremely short, but there are many websites dedicated to providing this type of information if you are interested. One that boasts of being the largest list of text message acronyms is www.netlingo.com/acronyms.php.

- **FWIW**—For What It's Worth
- **LOL**—Laughing Out Loud
- **ROTFL**—Rolling On the Floor Laughing
- **CU**—See You (later)
- **PO**—Peace Out
- **IMHO**—In My Humble Opinion
- **TY**—Thank You
- **RU**—Are You
- **BRB**—Be Right Back
- **CM**—Call Me
- **DND**—Do Not Disturb

- **EOM**—End of Message
- **FSR**—For Some Reason
- **G2G**—Got to Go
- **IDK**—I Don't Know
- **IKR**—I Know, Right?
- **ILU**—I Love You
- **NM or NVM**—Never Mind
- **OMG**—Oh My God
- **OTP**—On the Phone
- **P911**—Parent Alert
- **PLZ**—Please

Tap here to configure your
date and time preferences

Go here to figure
out where and when
you're supposed to be

In this chapter, you explore all the calendar functionality your iPhone has to offer. Topics include the following:

→ Getting started
→ Setting calendar, date, and time preferences
→ Working with calendars

10

Managing Calendars

When it comes to time management, your iPhone is definitely your friend. Using the iPhone's Calendar app, you can view calendars that are available on all your devices. You can also make changes to your calendars on your iPhone, and they appear on the calendars on your other devices so you have consistent information no matter which device you happen to be using at any time. You can also include other people in your events and manage events others invite you to attend.

Getting Started

The Calendar app does what it sounds like: It allows you to manage one or more calendars. This app has lots of features designed to help you work with multiple calendars and accounts, manage events that other people are invited to, and more. You don't have to use all these features, and you might just want to use its basic functionality, such as to record doctor appointments, dinner reservations, and similar events for which it is important to know the time and date (and be reminded when those times and dates are approaching).

Setting Calendar, Date, and Time Preferences

There are a number of time, date, and calendar settings that affect how you use your iPhone to manage your calendars and time. In most cases, you can leave these settings in their default configurations and start using the Calendar app right away (beginning with "Working with Calendars" later in this chapter).

Settings App Explained

To get detailed information on using the Settings app, see "Working with the Settings app" in Chapter 2, "Using Your iPhone's Core Features."

To be able to share your calendars among multiple devices, use an online account, such as iCloud or Google, to manage your calendar information. Before working with the calendar app, ensure you have at least one online account configured to manage calendar information on your iPhone. See Chapter 3, "Setting Up and Using an Apple ID, iCloud, and Other Online Accounts," for information about configuring online accounts.

To change the calendar settings, open the Settings app and tap Calendar. Use the settings described in the following list to make changes to how the app works.

- **Siri & Search**—Set the Search & Siri Suggestions switch to on (green) to allow information in your calendars to be searched and used by Siri. Set the Find Events in Other Apps switch to on (green) if you want information that appears to be calendar related (such as someone mentioning a time and place to meet for lunch in an email) to be highlighted so you can easily add it to your calendars. These are both enabled by default.

- **Time Zone Override**—When disabled, the time for events is based on your current time zone. When enabled, the time zone for events on the calendars is overridden with the time zone for a city you select. This is useful if you always want event times to be based on a specific time zone. (See the Go Further sidebar at the end of this list for a more in-depth explanation of this setting.)

- **Alternate Calendars**—You can choose among different types of calendars, such as Chinese or Hebrew.

- **Week Numbers**—When this switch is on (green), week numbers appear on your calendars in the Month view.

- **Show Invitee Declines**—When enabled (the switch is green) and someone declines a meeting, they are shown on the Invitee list as having declined. When disabled (the switch is white), invitees who decline an event are removed from the list.

- **Sync**—Determines how far back events are synced onto your calendars. You can choose 2 weeks, 1 month (the default), 3 months, 6 months, or all events.

- **Default Alert Times**—Determines the default alert times for birthdays, events, and all-day events. When you set the Time to Leave switch to on (green), the Calendar app can use your travel time to configure an event's alert. You can change the alert time for any event on your calendar; these settings just determine the initial alert time.

- **Start Week On**—Determines the first day of the week.

- **Default Calendar**—Determines which calendar is used for new events by default (you can override this setting for any events you create).

- **Location Suggestions**—When this switch is on (green), the Calendar app makes suggestions about the location of events when you create them.

>>>*Go Further*

MORE ON TIME ZONE OVERRIDE

The Time Zone Override feature can be a bit confusing. If Time Zone Override is on, the iPhone displays event times according to the time zone you select on the Time Zone Override screen. When Time Zone Override is off, the time zone used for calendars is the iPhone's current time zone, which is set automatically based on your location or your manual setting. This means that when you change time zones (automatically or manually), the times for calendar events shift accordingly. For example, if an event starts at 3:00 p.m. when you are in the Eastern time zone, its start time becomes 12:00 p.m. if you move into the Pacific time zone.

When Time Zone Override is on, the dates and times for events become fixed based on the time zone you select for Time Zone Override. If you change the time zone the iPhone is in, no change to the dates and times for events is shown on the calendar because they remain set according to the time zone you selected for the Time Zone Override. Therefore, an event's actual start time might not be accurately reflected for the iPhone's current time zone because it is based on the fixed Time Zone Override city instead of the time zone where you are currently located.

To configure how your iPhone displays and manages the date and time, open the Settings app, tap General, tap Date & Time, and change the settings described in the following list:

- **24-Hour Time**—Turning this switch on (green) causes the iPhone to display 24-hour instead of 12-hour time.

- **Set Automatically**—When this switch is on (green), your iPhone sets the current time and date automatically based on the cellular network it is using. When it is off (white), controls appear that you use to manually set the time zone, time, and date.

Notifications

The Calendar app can communicate with you in various ways, such as displaying banners when something happens that you might want to know about; for example, you can be alerted with a banner when you receive an invitation to an event. The information you need to configure notifications is explained in Chapter 4, "Customizing How Your iPhone Works."

Working with Calendars

The Calendar app helps you manage your calendars; notice I wrote calendars rather than calendar. That's because you can have multiple calendars in the app at the same time. For example, you might have a calendar for your personal events and another for club activities. Or, you might want a calendar dedicated to your travel plans, and then share that calendar with people who care about your location.

In most cases, you start by adding existing calendar information from an iCloud, Google, or similar account. From there, you can use the Calendar app to view your calendars, add or change events, and much more. Any changes you make in the Calendar app are automatically made in all the locations that use calendars from the same account.

Viewing Calendars and Events

You use the Calendar app to view and work with your calendars, and you can choose how you view them, such as by month, week, or day.

The badge indicates how many invitations to events you have received

To get into your calendars, move to the Home screen and tap the Calendar app (which shows the current day and date in its icon and a badge if you have at least one new invitation). The most recent screen you were viewing appears.

There are three modes you use in the app. The mode in which you'll spend most of your time is the one that displays your calendars in various views, such as showing a month, week, day, or event. Another mode is the Calendars tool that enables you to choose and edit the calendar information that is displayed. The third mode is your Inbox, which you use to work with event invitations you receive.

Configuring Calendars

To configure the calendar information you see in the app, perform the following steps:

(1) If you have only one calendar, skip to step 2. Otherwise, tap Calendars to see all of your calendars. If you don't see this at the bottom of the screen, you are already on the Calendars screen (look for "Calendars" at the top of the screen) or you are on the Inbox, in which case, tap Done.

The Calendars screen displays the calendars available, organized by the accounts from which they come, such as ICLOUD or GMAIL (the names you see are the descriptions of the accounts you created on your iPhone). By default, all your calendars are displayed, which is indicated by the circles with check marks next to the calendars' names. Any calendars that have an empty circle next to their names are not displayed when you view your calendars.

(**2**) Tap a calendar with a check mark to hide it. The check mark disappears and the calendar is hidden. (The calendar is still available in the app, you just won't see it when you are viewing your calendars.)

(**3**) To show a calendar again, tap its name. It is marked with a check mark and appears when you are viewing calendars.

(**4**) Tap the Info (i) icon to see or change a calendar's settings. Not all types of calendars support this function, and those that do can offer different settings. The following steps show an iCloud calendar; if you are working with a calendar of a different type, such as a Google calendar, you might not have all of the same options as those shown here. In any case, the steps to make changes are similar across all available types of calendars.

(**5**) Change the name of the calendar by tapping it and then making changes on the keyboard; when you're done making changes, swipe down the screen to close the keyboard.

(**6**) To share the calendar with someone, tap Add Person, enter the email address of the person with whom you are sharing it, and tap Add. (Sharing calendars is explained in more detail later in this chapter.)

7 If the calendar is shared and you don't want to be notified when shared events are changed, added, or deleted, set the Show Changes switch to off (white). When this switch is enabled (green) and a change is made to a shared calendar, you receive notifications about the changes that were made. If the calendar is not shared, you won't see this switch.

8 Swipe up the screen.

9 Tap the color you want events on the calendar to appear in.

10 If you want alerts to be enabled (active) for the calendar, set the Event Alerts switch to on (green).

11 To make the calendar public so that others can subscribe to a read-only version of it, set the Public Calendar switch to on (green), tap Share Link, and then use the resulting Share tools to invite others to subscribe to the calendar (more on this later in this chapter).

12 To remove the calendar entirely (instead of hiding it from view), tap Delete Calendar and then tap Delete Calendar at the prompt. The calendar and all its events are deleted. (It's usually better just to hide a calendar as described in step 2 so you don't lose its information.)

13 Assuming that you didn't delete the calendar, tap Done to save the changes you made.

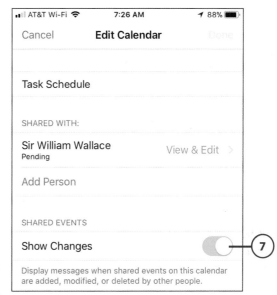

(14) Edit other calendars as needed.

(15) Tap Done. The app moves into viewing mode, and the calendars you enabled are displayed.

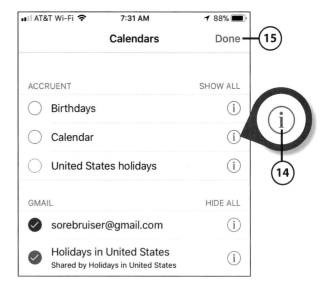

ALL OR NOTHING

You can make all your calendars visible by tapping Show All at the bottom of the screen; tap Hide All to do the opposite. After all the calendars are shown or hidden, you can tap individual calendars to show or hide them. You can show or hide all the calendars from the same account by tapping the SHOW/HIDE ALL command at the top of each account's calendar list.

Navigating Calendars

The Calendar app uses a hierarchy of detail to display your calendars. The highest level is the year view that shows the months in each year. The next level is the month view, which shows the days of the month (days with events are marked with a dot). This is followed by the week/day view that shows the days of the week and summary information for the events on each day. The most detailed view is the event view that shows all the information for a single event.

Viewing Calendars

You can view your calendars from the year level all the way down to the day/week view. It's easy to move among the levels to get to the time period you want to see. Here's how:

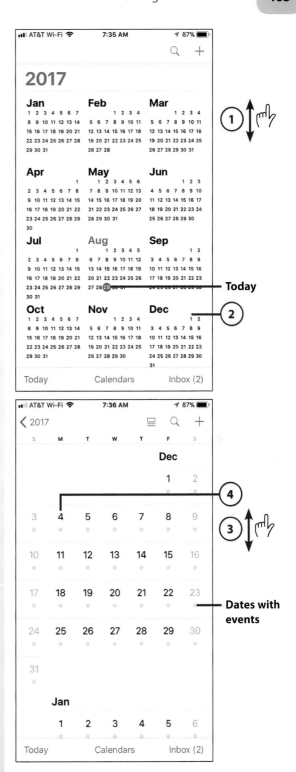

Today

Dates with events

(1) Starting at the year view, swipe up or down until you see the year in which you are interested. (If you aren't in the year view, keep tapping the Back icon located in the upper-left corner of the screen until that icon disappears.)

(2) Tap the month in which you are interested. The days in that month display, and days with events are marked with a dot.

(3) Swipe up and down the screen to view different months in the year you selected.

(4) To see the detail for a date, tap it. There are two ways to view the daily details: the Calendar view or the List view. Steps 5 through 8 show the Calendar view, whereas steps 9 through 11 show the List view. Each of these views has benefits, and, as you can see, it is easy to switch between them.

5 To see the Calendar view, ensure the List icon is not selected (isn't highlighted). At the top of the screen are the days of the week you are viewing. The date in focus is highlighted with a red circle when that day is today and a black circle for any other day. Below this area is the detail for the selected day showing the events on that day.

6 Swipe to the left or right on the dates or date being displayed to change the date for which detailed information is being shown.

7 Swipe up or down on the date detail to browse all its events.

8 Tap an event to view its detail and skip to step 12.

Today Is the Day

To quickly move to the current day, tap Today, which is located at the bottom-left corner of the screen.

9 See the events in List view by tapping the List icon so it is highlighted.

10 Swipe up and down to see the events for each day.

11 Tap an event to view its details.

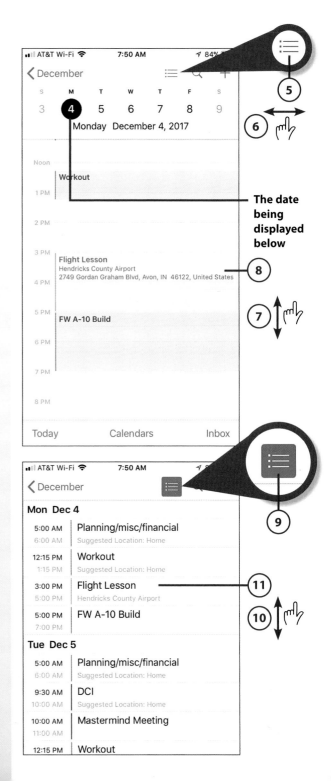

The date being displayed below

12 Swipe up and down the screen to see all of the event's information.

13 View information about the event, such as its location, repetition, and relationship to other events on the calendar.

14 Tap the Calendar or Alert fields to change these settings; tap the Invitees area to get information about people you've invited to the event.

15 Tap attachments to view them.

16 Tap any links to move to information related to the event.

17 Read notes associated with the event.

18 Tap a location to get directions to it.

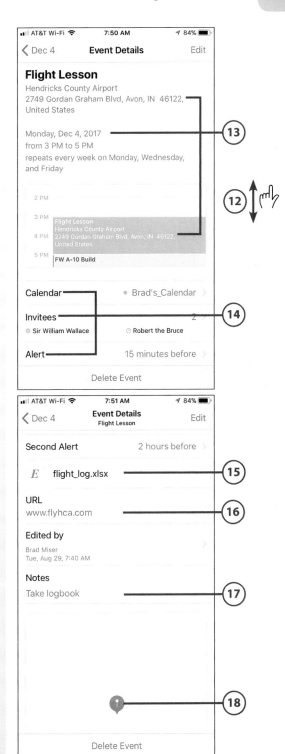

(19) Use the Maps app to get directions (see the online Chapter 15, "Working with Other Useful iPhone Apps and Features," for more information).

(20) Tap Calendar to return to the Calendar app.

(21) Tap the date to move back to the week/day view.

(22) Tap the Back icon (labeled with the month you are viewing) to move back to the month view.

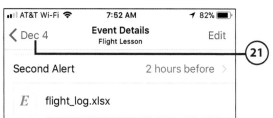

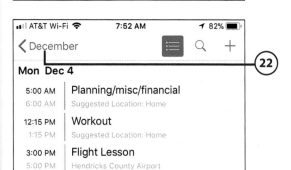

(23) To view your calendars in the multiday view, rotate your iPhone so it is horizontal. You can do this while in the week/day view or the month view.

(24) Swipe left or right to change the dates being displayed.

(25) Swipe up or down to change the time of day being displayed.

(26) Tap an event to see its details.

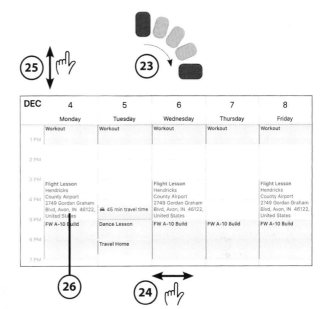

Current Time or Event

When you are viewing today in the Calendar view, the red line stretching horizontally across the screen indicates the current time, which is shown at the left end of that line. When you are viewing today in the List view, the current event is indicated by the text "Now" in red along the right edge of the screen.

Using 3D Touch for Events (iPhone 6s/6s Plus and Later)

You can use the 3D Touch feature on an iPhone 6s/6s Plus or later models with the Calendar app as follows:

(1) Browse events, such as when you use the List view.

(2) Tap and hold on an event in which you are interested. A Peek of that event appears.

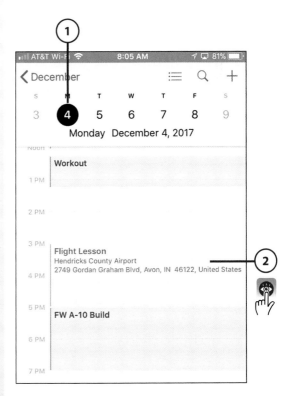

(3) Review the preview of the event that appears in the Peek.

(4) To open the event so you can see all of its detail, press down slightly harder until it pops open and use the steps in the earlier task to work with it (skip the rest of these steps).

(5) To see actions you can perform on the event, swipe up on the Peek.

(6) Tap the action you want to perform, such as Delete Event, to delete the event from your calendar.

Flight Lesson
Hendricks County Airport
2749 Gordan Graham Blvd, Avon, IN 46122,
United States

Monday, Dec 4, 2017
from 3 PM to 5 PM
repeats every week on Monday, Wednesday, and Friday

2 PM

3 PM   Flight Lesson
       Hendricks County Airport
4 PM   2749 Gordan Graham Blvd, Avon, IN 46122,
       United States

5 PM   FW A-10 Build

What's Next?

To quickly see the next event on your calendar, move to a Home screen or the Lock screen and swipe to the right to open the Widget Center. Find the UP NEXT widget, which shows you the next event on your calendar; you might want to move this to the top of the Widget Center if you use it regularly. (For more on configuring your widgets, see Chapter 4.)

2 PM

3 PM   Flight Lesson
       Hendricks County Airport
4 PM   2749 Gordan Graham Blvd, Avon, IN 46122,
       United States

5 PM   FW A-10 Build

Calendar   ● Brad's_Calendar >

Invitees   2 >
● Sir William Wallace   ○ Robert the Bruce

Alert   15 minutes before >

Delete Event ─────────── (6)

What's Next... Even Faster?

You can find out what's next even faster by activating Siri and saying, "What's next?" Siri shows you your next event and speaks the time and name of the event. Siri also can help with many other calendar-related tasks. (See Chapter 11, "Working with Siri," for the details.)

Adding Events to a Calendar

There are a number of ways you can add events to your calendar. You can create an event in an app on a computer, website, or other device and sync that event onto the iPhone through an online account. You can also manually create events in the Calendar app on the iPhone. You can also add an event by accepting an invitation (covered later in this chapter).

Your events can include a lot of information, or they can be fairly basic. You can choose to create the basic information on your iPhone while you are on the move and complete it later from a computer or other device, or you can fill in all the details directly in the Calendar app.

(1) Tap Add (+), which appears in the upper-right corner of any of the views when your phone is vertical (except when you are viewing an event's details). The initial date information is taken from the date currently being displayed, so you can save a little time if you view the date of the event before tapping Add (+).

(2) Tap in the Title field and type the title of the event.

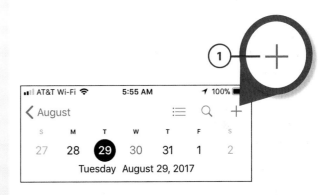

(3) Tap the Location bar and type the location of the event; if you allow the app to use Location Services, you're prompted to find and select a location; if not, just type the location and skip to step 6.

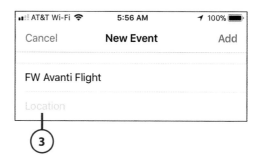

(4) Type the location in the Search bar. Sites that meet your search are shown below. The results screen has several sections including Recents, which shows locations you've used recently, and Locations, which are sites that the app finds that match your search criteria.

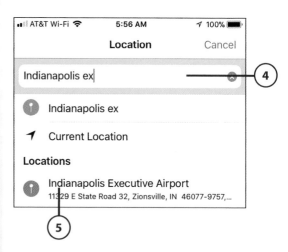

(5) Tap the location for the event; tap Current Location if the event takes place where you are. You return to the new event screen and see the location you entered.

(6) To set the event to last all day, set the All-day switch to the on position (green); when you select the All-day option, you provide only the start and end dates (you don't enter times as described in the next several steps). To set a specific start and end time, leave this setting in the off position (white); you set both the dates and times as described in the following steps.

(7) To set a timeframe for the event, tap Starts. The date and time tool appears.

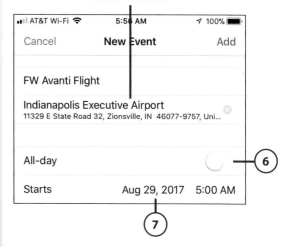

Location Prompt

The first time you create an event, you might be prompted to allow the Calendar app to access your location information. When you allow the app to use Location Services, you can search for and select event locations. The app can use this information to include an estimate of travel time for the event and to display events on a map when you view their detail.

8 Swipe up or down on the date wheel until the date on which the event starts appears in the center.

9 Swipe up or down on the hour wheel until the event's starting hour is shown.

10 Scroll and select the starting minute in the same way.

11 Swipe up or down on the hour wheel to select AM or PM.

12 If you want to associate the event with a specific time zone, tap Time Zone; if not, skip to step 14.

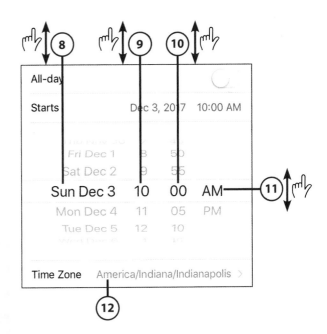

Your Results Might Vary

The fields and options available when you create a new event are based on the calendar with which the event is associated. For example, an iCloud calendar might have different options than a Google calendar does. If you aren't creating an event on your default calendar, it's a good idea to associate the event with a calendar before you fill in its details (to do that, perform step 30 before you do step 2).

(13) Search for and select the time zone with which the event should be associated.

(14) Tap Ends.

(15) Use the date and time wheels to set the ending date and time (if applicable) for the event; these work the same way as for the start date and time.

Different Ending Time Zone?

The Calendar app assumes the time zone associated with the ending date and time is the same as for the starting date and time. If you want to set a different ending time zone, tap Time Zone below the Ends section and choose a different time zone as described in steps 12 and 13.

(16) Tap Ends. The date and time tool closes.

(17) To make the event repeat, tap Repeat and follow steps 18–23. (For a nonrepeating event, keep the default, which is Never, and skip to step 24.)

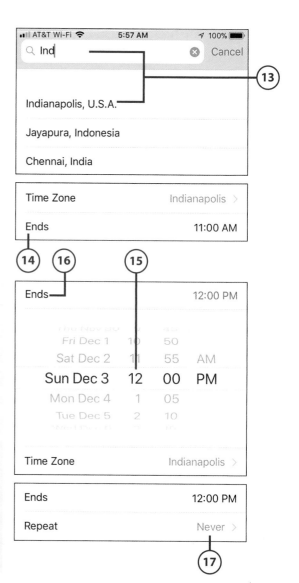

No Changes?

When you change a selection on most of the screens you see, you automatically return to the previous screen; for example, when you select a time zone, you immediately return to the New Event screen. If you don't make a change, you can return to the previous screen by tapping New Event in the upper-left corner of the screen. If you start to perform a search for something, such as time zone, but decide not to finish it, tap Cancel and then tap New Event.

18. Tap the frequency at which you want the event repeated, such as Every Day, Every Week, etc.; if you want to use a repeat cycle not shown, tap Custom and create the frequency with which you want the event to repeat.

19. Tap End Repeat to set a time at which the event stops repeating.

20. Tap Never to have the event repeat ad infinitum, and then skip to step 23.

21. Tap On Date to set an end to the repetition.

22. Use the date tool to set the date for the last repeated event.

23. Tap New Event.

Custom Repeat

To configure a custom repeat cycle for an event in step 18, such as the first Monday of every month, tap Custom on the Repeat screen. Then use the Frequency (Monthly for the example) and Every (for example, On the first Monday) settings to configure the repeat cycle. Tap Repeat to return to the Repeat screen and then tap New Event to get back to the event you are creating.

24. To configure travel time for the event, tap Travel Time; if you don't want to configure this, skip to step 30.

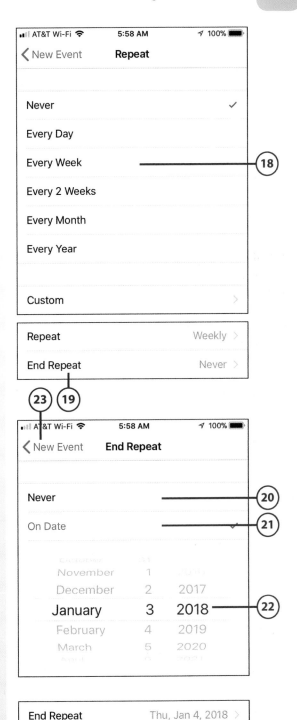

25 Set the Travel Time switch to on (green).

26 To manually set a travel time for the event, tap it and skip to step 29.

27 Tap Starting Location to build a travel time based on a starting location.

No Change Needed

If you don't make a change to one of the settings, such as on the Repeat screen, tap the Back icon (labeled New Event) in the upper-left corner of the screen to get back to the New Event screen.

28 To use your current location as the starting point, tap Current Location. Alternatively, use the search tool to find a starting location, and then tap it to select that location. This works just like setting a location for the event. The travel time is calculated based on the starting and ending locations entered for the new event. You can configure alerts based on this travel time, as described in later steps.

29 Tap New Event.

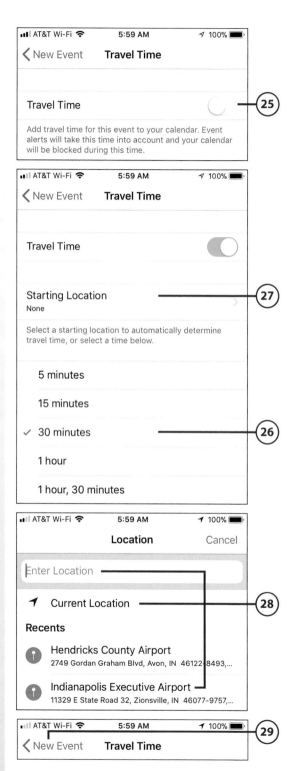

30 To change the calendar with which the event is associated, tap Calendar (to leave the current calendar selected, skip to step 32).

31 Tap the calendar with which the event should be associated.

32 To invite others to the event, tap Invitees; if you don't want to invite someone else, skip to step 37.

33 Enter the email addresses for each person you want to invite; as you type, the app tries to identify people who match what you are typing. You can tap a person to add him to the event or keep entering the email address until it is complete. You can also use the Add (+) icon to choose people in your Contacts app (see Chapter 6, "Managing Contacts," for help using that app).

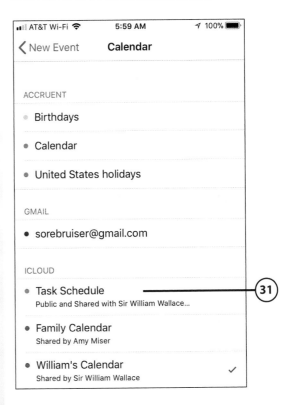

34 Repeat step 33 until you've added everyone you want to invite.

35 Tap Done. You move to the Invitees screen and see those whom you invited.

Automatic Sharing

When you add an event to a calendar that is shared with others, the people with whom the calendar is shared see the event automatically in their Calendar apps.

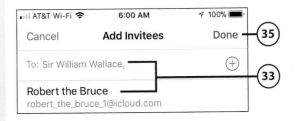

36 Tap New Event.

37 To set an alert for the event that is different than the default, tap Alert; if you want to use the default alert, skip to step 39.

38 Tap when you want to see an alert for the event. You can choose a time relative to the time you need to start traveling or relative to the event's start time.

39 To set a second alert that is different than the default, tap Second Alert; to use the default, skip to step 41.

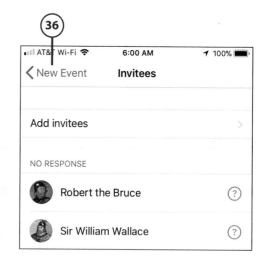

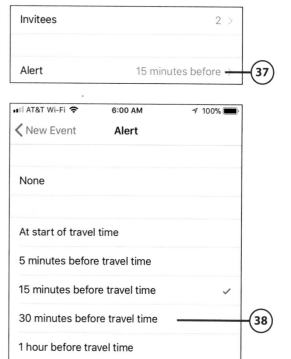

40 Tap when you want to see a second alert for the event. If you have included travel time in the event, the At or before start of travel time options are useful because they alert you relative to when your journey should begin.

41 To indicate your availability during this event, tap Show As.

42 Tap the availability status you want to indicate during the event. If someone can access your availability through their calendar application, this is the status they see if they try to book an event with you at the same time.

43 Tap in the URL field to enter a URL associated with the event.

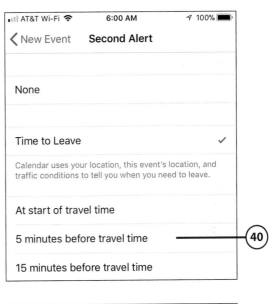

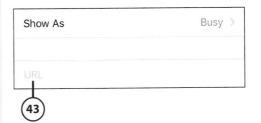

(44) Type the URL.

(45) Tap Done.

(46) Tap in the Notes field.

(47) Type the information you want to associate with the event.

(48) Tap Add. The event is added to the calendar you selected, and invitations are sent to its invitees. Alerts trigger according to the event's settings.

New event on the calendar

A Better Way to Create Events

Adding a lot of detail to an event in the Calendar app can be challenging. One effective and easy way to create events is to start with Siri. You can activate Siri and say something like "Create meeting with William Wallace in my office on November 15 at 10 a.m." Siri creates the event with as much detail as you provided (and might prompt you to provide additional information, such as which email address to use to send invitations). When you get to a computer or iPad, edit the event to add more information, such as website links. When your calendar is updated on the iPhone, via syncing, the additional detail for the event appears in the Calendar app, too. (See Chapter 11 for detailed information about using Siri.)

Using Quick Actions with the Calendar App (iPhone 6s/6s Plus and Later)

You can use the Quick Actions feature on an iPhone 6s/6s Plus or later models with the Calendar app as follows:

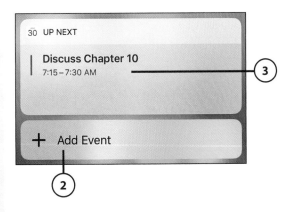

1. Press on the Calendar icon. The Quick Actions menu appears. At the top, you see the next event on your calendar.

2. To add a new event, choose Add Event and use the steps in the previous task to create the event.

3. Tap an event to view the event's details. You move to the event and can see all of its information.

Searching Calendars

You can search for events to locate specific ones quickly and easily. Here's how:

1. Tap the magnifying glass.

2. Type your search term. The events shown below the Search bar are those that contain your search term.

3. Swipe up or down the list to review the results.

4. Tap an event to see its detail.

5. Swipe up or down the event's screen to review its information.

6. Tap Back to return to the results.

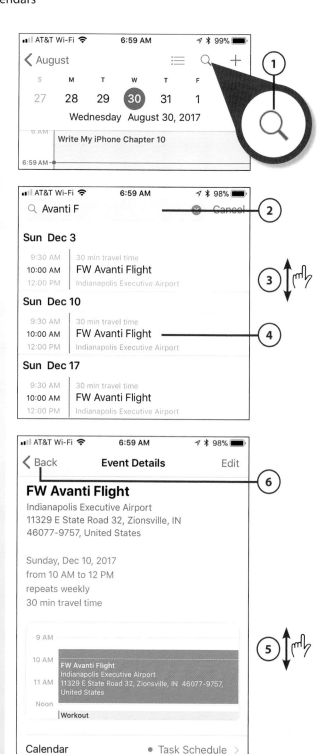

(7) Continue reviewing the results until you get the information for which you were searching.

(8) Tap Cancel to exit the search mode or the Clear (x) icon to clear the search but remain in search mode.

Working with Invitations

When someone invites you to an event, you receive an invitation notification in the Calendar app. You can accept these invitations, at which point the event is added to your calendar. You can tentatively accept, in which case the event is added to your calendar with a tentative status, or you can decline the event if you don't want it added to your calendar.

(1) Tap the Calendar app icon when you see the badge on the app's icon indicating how many invitations you've received but not dealt with. (You may also receive notifications about new invitations according to your notification settings.)

(2) Tap Inbox (the number in parentheses is the number of invitations you have received).

(3) If you have multiple invitations, swipe up and down the screen to browse them.

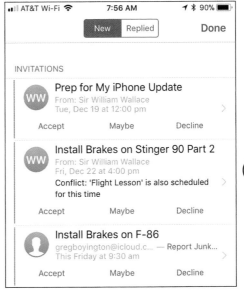

4 If you see enough information about the event to be able to make a decision about it, tap Accept, Maybe, or Decline. The event is added to your calendar if you tap Accept or Maybe. If you tap Decline, it is not added to a calendar.

5 Tap an invitation to see its detail.

6 Swipe up and down the Event Details screen to see all its information.

7 To see how the proposed event relates to other events on the same date, look at the section of the calendar during which the event is being proposed. You see any events that might conflict with the one to which you have been invited.

8 To choose the calendar on which the event should be shown, tap Calendar, and on the resulting screen, tap the calendar on which you want to store the event. Tap the Back icon located in the upper-left corner of the screen to return to the Event Details screen.

Invitation Notifications

You can use Notification settings to configure how the Calendar app informs you about invitations you receive. Refer to Chapter 4 for details. You can move to an invitation directly from its notification; for example, when a banner alert for an invitation appears on the screen, press it (3D Touch iPhones) or swipe it (non-3D Touch iPhones) to move to the invitation's details.

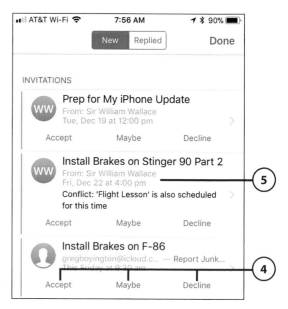

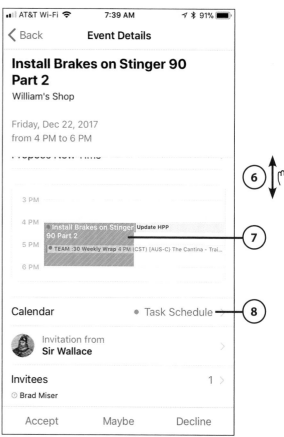

9 To view details about whom the invitation is from, tap the Invitation from bar. You move to the person's contact information (from Contacts if her information is stored there or as much as can be gleaned from the invitation if it isn't). Tap the Back icon located in the upper-left corner of those screens to return to the Event Details screen.

10 Tap Invitees to see the status for each invitee to the event. You see a list of each person to whom the invitation was sent along with his or her current status. Tap Back to return to the Event Details screen.

11 If you want to change the event's alert, tap Alert and use the resulting Alert screen to choose an alert.

12 Review any attachments or notes for the meeting.

13 Use the Travel Time option to configure your travel time to the event. This works just like when you create an event (see "Adding Events to a Calendar" earlier in this chapter).

14 To set your availability during the event, tap Show As and then tap your status during the event; in most cases, you tap Busy so others who want to schedule time with you will see that you aren't available.

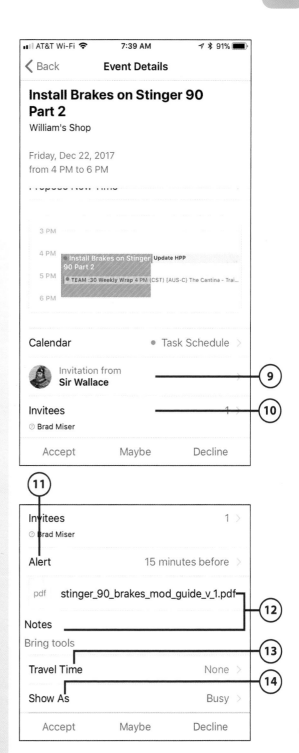

What You See Depends

Like when you create an event, the fields and options you see for an event to which you've been invited depend on the type of calendar the event is being sent from (for example, Google events may have different options than iCloud events do). Although the details for each type of calendar are slightly different, these steps help you deal with any invitations you receive.

(15) Indicate what you want to do with the event by tapping Accept, Maybe, or Decline. If you tap Accept or Maybe, the event is added to the calendar with the status you indicated. If you tap Decline, the event is not placed on a calendar, and the recipient receives a notice that you have declined.

After you make a decision, you move back to the Inbox. Any events you have accepted, indicated maybe, or declined disappear from the list of events on the New tab. Events that you have accepted from another device, such as from a computer, are shown with an OK icon, which you can tap to remove the invitation from the list.

(16) Use steps 5 through 15 to take action on other invitations you have received or tap OK to clear events you've dealt with on other devices.

(17) To review the invitations to which you've responded, tap Replied.

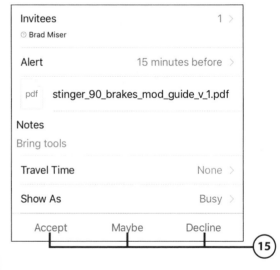

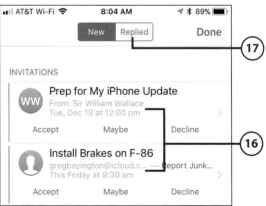

18 Swipe up and down the screen to review all the invitations to which you have responded. The highlighted box indicates your status for each event, such as Accept for those you have accepted or Decline for those you declined (these are also marked with a strikeout through their titles).

19 Tap an event to see its details.

20 To change your current status, tap one of the other status states. For example, to decline a meeting you previously accepted, tap Decline. The status changes immediately.

21 When you are done reviewing invitations, tap Done to close the Inbox. You move back to the calendar. If you accepted or indicated maybe for any events, they are added to your calendars.

Event you accepted

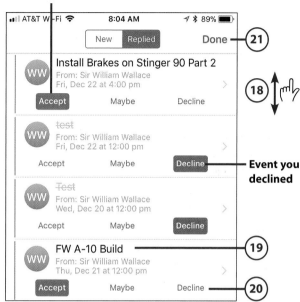

Event you declined

Sharing Calendars

You can share your calendars with other people to enable them to both see and change your calendar, according to the permissions you provide. If you set the View & Edit permission, the person is able to both see and change the calendar. If you set someone's permission to View Only, she can see, but not change, the calendar.

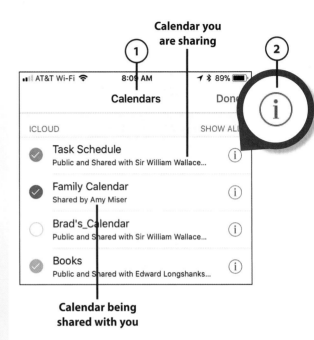

Calendar you are sharing

Calendar being shared with you

1. Move to the Calendars screen. Calendars you are sharing are indicated by the Shared with *name* text just under the calendar name, where *name* is the name of the person with whom you are sharing the calendar.

2. To see who is currently sharing a calendar, or to share a calendar, tap the Info (i) icon for the calendar to be shared. If the calendar is currently being shared, the SHARED WITH section appears on the Edit Calendar screen. This section contains the names of and permissions granted to the people who are sharing the calendar. The status of each person's acceptance is shown under his name (Accepted, Pending, or Declined).

3. Tap Add Person to share a calendar with someone else (whether it is currently shared or not).

4. Type a person's name or email address, tap a name or email address that the app suggests based on what you are typing, or use the Contacts app to choose the people with whom you want to share the calendar (you can add multiple people at the same time).

5. Tap Add. You return to the Edit Calendar screen, and see the person you added on the SHARED WITH list. The person you invited receives an invitation to join the calendar you are sharing. If he accepts, the shared calendar becomes available in the calendar app he uses. As people make decisions about the calendar you are sharing, the status below each invitee's name changes to reflect the current status. You also see notifications when an invitee responds if you allow the app to provide notifications to you.

6. If you don't want a person to be able to change the calendar, tap View & Edit.

7. Slide the Allow Editing switch to off (white); the person will be able to view but not change the calendar.

8. Tap Edit Calendar.

9. When you're done sharing the calendar, tap Done.

10. When you are finished configuring calendar sharing, tap Done.

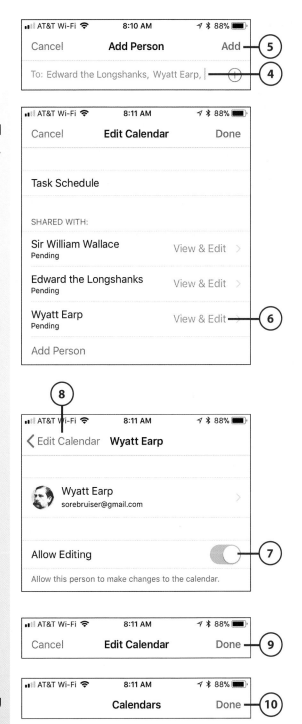

Managing Calendars, Events, and Invitations

Following are some more points about the Calendar app you might find helpful:

- You can also use the List view when you are viewing the calendar in month view. Tap the List icon (just to the left of the magnifying glass). The list opens at the bottom of the screen and shows the events on the day currently selected (the date is in a black circle unless the day selected is today, in which case the circle is red).

- You can see today's events at any time by opening the Widgets Center (move to a Home screen and swipe to the right). In the UP NEXT box, you see information about the next event on your calendar. You can view the current day's calendar in the CALENDAR widget; tap an event in the widget to see its detail. (See Chapter 2 for more information about working with the Notification Center and widgets.)

- When an event's alarm goes off, an onscreen notification appears (according to the notification settings for the Calendar app) and the calendar event sound you've selected plays. You can press (3D Touch) or tap (non-3D Touch) the event to view its details. If it is a persistent banner, you have to take action on it (such as viewing it) to clear it from the screen. If it is a temporary banner you can ignore it and it moves off the screen after a few moments. You can also swipe up from the bottom of a notification to manually close it.

- If an event gets canceled after you accept it or indicated maybe, you receive a notification in your Inbox that displays a strikethrough through the event's title. Tap Delete to remove the event from your calendar.

- When you receive an invitation, the event is tentatively added to your calendar until you make a decision about it. The status changes as you accept, tentatively accept (Maybe), or decline invitations.

- Siri is useful for working with calendars, especially for creating events. See Chapter 11 for detailed information about using Siri.

- You can publish a calendar by making it public. When you do this, anyone who can access the shared calendar on the Web can view, but not change, the published calendar. To make a calendar public, move to its Edit Calendar screen and slide the Public Calendar switch to on (green). Tap Share Link. Then tap Mail to send the link via email, tap Message to send it via the

Messages app, or tap Copy to copy the link so you can paste elsewhere. Tap AirDrop, Twitter, or Facebook to share the link in those ways. The link can be clicked to view your calendar or, if the person uses a compatible application, to subscribe to it so it appears in her calendar application.

>>>Go Further

OTHER USEFUL APPS FOR MANAGING YOUR TIME

Your iPhone includes a couple more apps that can help you manage your time. The Clock app enables you to easily see the current time in multiple locations, set alarms, set a consistent time for sleep every day, use a stopwatch, and count down time with a timer. The Reminders app enables you to create reminders for events, tasks you need to perform, or just about anything else. You can learn a bit more about these apps in the online Chapter 15.

Go here to set up Siri

Speak to Siri to send
and hear messages,
create and manage
events, make calls,
and much more

Dictate text input
instead of typing

In this chapter, you learn about all the great things you can do with your iPhone by speaking to it. Topics include the following:

→ Getting started
→ Setting up Siri
→ Understanding Siri's personality
→ Learning how to use Siri by example
→ Using dictation to speak text instead of typing

Working with Siri

Siri is Apple's name for the iPhone's and iPad's voice recognition feature. This technology enables your iPhone to "listen" to words you speak so that you can issue commands just by saying them, such as "Send text message to Sam," and the iPhone accomplishes the tasks you speak. This technology also enables the iPhone to take dictation; for example, you can speak words that you want to send in a text or email instead of typing them on the keyboard.

Getting Started

Siri gives you the ability to talk to your iPhone to control it, get information, and to dictate text. Siri also works with lots of iPhone apps—this feature enables you to accomplish many tasks by speaking instead of using your fingers on the iPhone's screen. For example, you can hear, create, and send text messages; reply to emails; make phone and FaceTime calls; create and manage events and reminders; and much more. Using dictation, you can speak text into any supported app instead of typing.

In fact, Siri does so many things, it's impossible to list them all in a short chapter like this one; you should give Siri a try for the tasks you perform and to get the information you need, and, in many cases, Siri can handle what you want to do.

Think of Siri as your personal, digital assistant to help you do what you want to do more quickly and easily (especially when you are working in handsfree mode).

You don't have to train Siri very much to work with your voice; you can speak to it normally, and Siri does a great job understanding what you say. Also, you don't have to use any specific kind of phrases when you have Siri do your bidding. Simply talk to Siri like you talk to people (well, you probably won't be ordering other people around like you do Siri, but you get the idea).

Your iPhone has to be connected to the Internet for Siri and dictation to work. That's because the words you speak are sent over the Internet, transcribed into text, and then sent back to your iPhone. If your iPhone isn't connected to the Internet, this can't happen, and if you try to use it, Siri reports that it can't complete its tasks.

Because your iPhone is likely to be connected to the Internet most of the time (via Wi-Fi or a cellular network when you have cellular data enabled), this really isn't much of a limitation—but it is one you need to be aware of.

Just start speaking to your phone and be prepared to be amazed by how well it listens! You'll find many examples in this chapter to get you going with specific tasks; from there, you can explore to learn what else Siri can do for you.

Setting Up Siri

There are several settings that affect how Siri works. In most cases, you can leave these settings in their default positions (including those you selected the first time you turned your iPhone on) and start using Siri right away (beginning with "Understanding Siri's Personality" later in this chapter).

If you decide you want to make changes to Siri's settings, you can use the information in the table that follows to understand the options available to you.

To access Siri's settings, tap Settings on the Home screen and then tap Siri & Search. For each of these settings, you see a description of what it does along with options (if applicable). (Siri must be enabled by setting the Siri switch to on [green] and then tapping Enable Siri before the rest of the settings become visible.)

The Settings App Explained

To get detailed information on using the Settings app, see "Working with the Settings App" in Chapter 2, "Using Your iPhone's Core Features."

Siri Settings

Setting	Description
Listen for "Hey Siri"	When this switch is on (green), you can activate Siri by saying, "Hey Siri" (along with the other options). The first time you turned your iPhone on, you were prompted to speak the five phrases Siri uses to recognize when you want its attention. When this switch is off (white), you can only activate Siri with the other options. When you enable it again, you might have to go through the recognition process again.
Press Home for Siri	This switch enables (green) or prevents (white) you from activating Siri by pressing and holding on the Touch ID/Home button. This setting doesn't apply to the iPhone X since it doesn't have a Touch ID/Home button.
Allow Siri When Locked	When this switch is on (green), you can activate and use Siri without unlocking your iPhone. This can be convenient, but it also makes your phone vulnerable to misuse because someone else may be able to activate Siri (for example, to send a text message) without using a passcode or providing a recognized thumbprint. For some tasks, Siri requires the phone to be unlocked to complete them, but some can be done while the phone is still locked.
Language	Set the language you want Siri to use to speak to you.
Siri Voice	Choose the accent and gender of the voice that Siri uses to speak to you (the options you see depend on the language you have selected).

Setting	Description
Voice Feedback	Choose when Siri provides verbal feedback as it works for you. When Always On is selected, Siri provides verbal feedback at all times. If you want to control Siri's voice feedback with the ring (Mute) switch, choose Control with Ring Switch. If you want voice feedback only when you are operating in handsfree mode, such as when you are using the iPhone's EarPods or a Bluetooth headset, tap Hands-free Only. Regardless of this setting, you always see Siri's feedback on the screen.
My Information	Choose your contact information in the Contacts app, which Siri uses to address you by name, take you to your home address, etc.
Suggestions in Search	When enabled (green), this switch allows Siri to make suggestions to you when you search. If you prefer not to have Siri make suggestions, set the switch to off (white).
Suggestions in Look Up	When enabled (green), this switch allows Siri to make suggestions when you use iOS's Look Up feature, that looks up information about a word or phrase you have selected on the screen. If you set this switch to off (white), Siri won't make suggestions when you use Look Up.
Apps	Toward the bottom of the Siri & Search screen, you see the list of apps installed on your iPhone. For each app, you can enable or disable Siri & Search Suggestions. When you enable this switch for an app, Siri can work within that app to make suggestions or learn from how you use the app. When you disable this switch, Siri is not able to work within the app for suggestions and search.

There are a couple of other settings that affect how you can speak to your iPhone:

- **Enable Dictation**—To access this setting, open the Settings app, tap General, and then tap Keyboard (you have to swipe up the screen to see it). At the bottom of the screen, you see the Enable Dictation switch. When this switch is on (green), you can tap the Microphone key on the keyboard to dictate text. When this switch is off (white), the Microphone key is hidden and you can't dictate text.

- **Cellular Data**—When enabled, this setting, located on the Cellular setting screen, allows your iPhone to access its cellular data network to connect to the Internet. This must be turned on for Siri to work when you aren't connected to the Internet via a Wi-Fi network.

---

iPhone X

The iPhone X doesn't have a Touch ID/Home button, so the Press Home for Siri setting doesn't apply. Download the online supplement *My iPhone X* from www.informit.com/myiphoneseniors to learn about the minor differences when using Siri on an iPhone X.

Understanding Siri's Personality

Siri works in two basic modes: when you ask it to do something or when it makes suggestions to you.

Telling Siri What to Do

When you ask Siri to do something, Siri's personality is pretty simple because it follows a consistent pattern when you use it, and it always prompts you for input and direction when needed.

If Siri is already active, tap the Listen icon at the bottom of the screen. Otherwise, activate Siri using one of the following methods:

- On all models except the iPhone X, pressing and holding the Touch ID/Home button until the Siri screen appears, you hear the Siri tone, and you feel the phone vibrate.

- On the iPhone X, pressing and holding the Side button for a couple of seconds until the Siri screen appears, you hear the Siri tone, and you feel the phone vibrate.

- Pressing and holding the center part of the buttons on the EarPods until the Siri screen appears and you hear the Siri tone.

- Saying "Hey Siri" (if you've enabled this setting).

Siri is ready for a task

Siri is listening to
you speak

This puts Siri in "listening" mode and the "What can I help you with?" text appears along with a line at the bottom of the screen that shows when Siri is hearing you. This screen indicates Siri is ready for your command; if you used the "Hey Siri" option to activate it, you don't see this text because Siri goes directly into listening mode. If you don't speak within a second or two, Siri starts prompting you for a request and presents examples of what you can do.

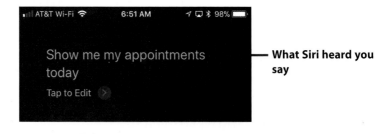

What Siri heard you
say

Speak your command or ask a question. As you speak, the line at the bottom of the screen oscillates to show you that Siri is hearing your input, and Siri displays what it is hearing you say at the top of the screen. When you stop speaking, Siri goes into processing mode.

After Siri interprets what you've said, it provides two kinds of feedback to confirm what it heard: It displays what it heard on the screen and provides audible feedback to you (unless it's disabled through the settings you learned about earlier). Siri then tries to do what it thinks you've asked and shows you the outcome.

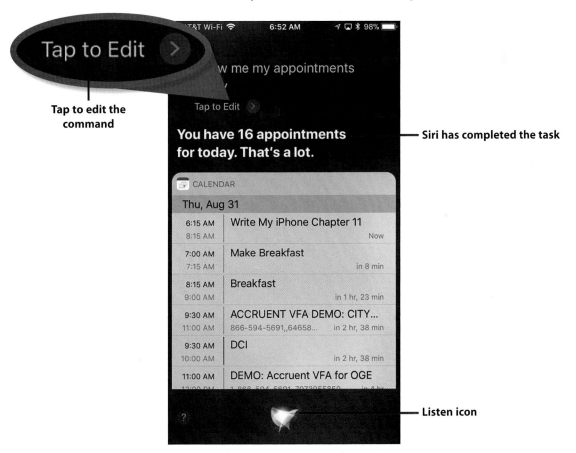

Tap to edit the command

Siri has completed the task

Listen icon

If it needs more input from you, you're prompted to provide it, and Siri moves into "listening" mode automatically. If Siri asks you to confirm what it is doing or to make a selection, do so. Siri completes the action and displays what it has done; it also audibly confirms the result (again unless audible feedback is disabled as described earlier). If you want Siri to do more for you, tap the Listen icon at the bottom of the screen and speak your command. If you want to work with the object Siri created for you in its associated app, tap the object Siri presents.

In some cases, you can edit the information you spoke to Siri to change it. For example, suppose you are sending a text message to Sir William Wallace but Siri didn't get the name quite right; you can tap Tap to Edit on the Siri screen and then change the name; this can sometimes be easier and faster than redoing the task from the beginning. You can also change the content of actions, such as what you are texting via Siri; if it isn't what you intended, you can tap the message to edit it before you send it.

Also, how Siri interacts with you can depend on how it was activated. For example, if you started the interaction using the verbal "Hey Siri" option, Siri assumes you want to interact verbally and might respond with other options than you would see or hear when you activate Siri manually. When you ask Siri to show you your appointments for the day in this mode, you see the summary, but then Siri asks if you want to hear the details; if you say yes, Siri reads each event to you. When you activate Siri by using the Touch ID/Home button with the same request, Siri stops after showing you the summary.

When you're done with Siri, press the Touch ID/Home button (all models except the iPhone X) to move back to the Home screen or to the app you were using. When you've finished with Siri on an iPhone X, swipe up from the bottom of the screen to move back to your previous location.

Siri uses this pattern for all the tasks it does, but often Siri needs to get more information from you, such as when there are multiple contacts that match the command you've given. Siri prompts you for what it needs to complete the work. Generally, the more specific you make your initial command, the fewer steps you have to work through to complete it. For example, if you say "Meet Will at the park," Siri might require several prompts to get you to tell it who Will is and what time you want to meet him at the park. If you say "Meet William Wallace at the park on 10/17 at 10 a.m.," Siri can likely complete the task in one step.

The best way to learn how and when Siri can help you is to try it—a lot. You find a number of examples in the rest of this chapter to get started.

Following are some other Siri tidbits:

- If Siri doesn't automatically quit "listening" mode after you've finished speaking, tap the oscillating line. This stops "listening" mode and Siri starts processing your request. You need to do this more often when you are in a noisy environment because Siri might not be able to accurately discern the sound of you speaking versus the ambient background noise.

- If you are having trouble with Siri understanding commands, speak a bit more slowly and make sure you firmly enunciate and end your words. If you tend to have a very short pause between words, Siri might run them all together, making them into something that doesn't make sense or that you didn't intend.

- However, you can't pause too long between words or sentences because Siri interprets pauses of a certain length to mean that you are done speaking, and it goes into processing mode. Practicing with Siri helps you develop a good balance between speed and clarity.

- If Siri doesn't understand what you want, or if you ask it a general question, it often performs a web search for you. Siri takes what it thinks you are looking for and does a search. You then see the results page for the search Siri performed, and you might have to manually open and read the results by tapping the listing you want to see. It opens in the Safari app. In some cases, Siri reads the results to you.

- When Siri presents information to you on the screen, you can often tap that information to move into the app with which it is associated. For example, when you tap an event that Siri has created, you move into the Calendar app, where you can add more detail using that app's tools, such as inviting people to an event, changing the calendar it's associated with, and so on.

- When Siri needs direction from you, it presents your options on the screen, including Yes, Cancel, Confirm, or lists of names. You can speak these items or tap them to select them.

- Siri is very useful for some tasks, such as creating reminders, responding to text messages, getting directions, and so on, but not so useful for others, such as inputting search criteria, because it can take longer to use Siri than to type your input.

- Siri is not so good at editing text you speak. You have to manually edit what Siri hears you say by tapping Tap to Edit and then using the keyboard to change what Siri heard or by selecting an option that Siri recommends. When you've finished making changes, tap Done. If you changed a command, Siri replaces the prior command with the edited version. If you changed content, Siri updates the content. After you've made changes, you can continue with the task.

- Siri might ask you to help it pronounce some terms, such as names. When this happens, Siri asks you to teach it to pronounce the phrase. If you agree, Siri presents a list of possible pronunciations, which you can preview. Tap the Select icon for the option you want Siri to use.

- To use Siri effectively, you should experiment with it by trying to say different commands or similar commands in different ways. For example, when sending email, you can include more information in your initial command to reduce the number of steps because Siri doesn't have to ask you for more information. Saying "Send an email to Wyatt Earp home about flying" requires fewer steps than saying "Send email" because you've given Siri more of the information it needs to complete the task, and so it won't have to prompt you for who you want to send it to, which address you want to use, or what the subject of the email is.

- When Siri can't complete a task that it thinks it should be able to do, it usually responds with the "I can't connect to the network right now," or "Sorry, I don't know what you mean." This indicates that your iPhone isn't connected to the Internet, the Siri server is not responding, or Siri just isn't able to complete the command for some other reason. If your iPhone is connected to the Internet, try the command again or try rephrasing the command.

- When Siri can't complete a task that it knows it can't do, it responds by telling you so. Occasionally, you can get Siri to complete the task by rephrasing it, but typically you have to use an app directly to get it done.

- If you have a passcode set to protect your iPhone's data (which you should), Siri might not be able to complete some tasks because the phone is locked. If that happens, Siri prompts you to unlock your phone, (which you can do by touching the Touch ID/Home button, using Face ID, or entering your passcode) and continue with what you were doing.

- Siri is really good at retrieving all sorts of information for you. This can include schedules, weather, directions, unit conversions, and so on. When you need something, try Siri first, as trying it is really the best way to learn how Siri can work for you.

- Siri sees all and knows all (well, not really, but it sometimes seems that way). If you want to be enlightened, try asking Siri questions, such as these:

  What is the best phone?
  Will you marry me?
  What is the meaning of life?
  Tell me a joke.

  Some of the answers are pretty funny, and you don't always get the same ones so Siri can keep amusing you. I've heard it even has responses if you curse at it, though I haven't tried that particular option.

Working with Siri Suggestions

When you enable the Suggestions in Search, Suggestions in Look Up settings, and the Search & Siri Suggestions setting for individual apps, Siri becomes pro-active and provides information or suggestions for you based on what you are doing and what you have done in the past. Over time, Siri "learns" more about you and tailors these suggestions to better match what you typically do. For example, when you create a text message and start to input a name, Siri can suggest potential recipients based on prior texts you've sent. Similarly, when you perform a search, Siri can tailor the search based on your history.

Because Siri works proactively in this mode, you don't do anything to cause Siri to take action. It works in the background for you and presents information or options at the appropriate times.

Learning How to Use Siri by Example

As mentioned earlier in this chapter, the best way to learn about Siri is to use it. Following are a number of tasks for which Siri is really helpful. Try these to get some experience with Siri and then explore on your own to make Siri work at its best for you.

Using Siri to Make Voice Calls

You can use Siri to make calls by speaking. This is especially useful when you are using your iPhone in handsfree mode.

(1) Activate Siri (such as by pressing and holding the Touch ID/Home button [on all models except the iPhone X] or the Side button [iPhone X]).

Speeding Up Siri

You can combine these steps by saying "Hey Siri, call Pappy Boyington iPhone." This is an example where providing Siri with more information when you speak gets the task done more quickly.

(2) Say "Call *name*," where *name* is the person you want to call. Siri identifies the contact you named. If the contact has only one number, Siri places the call and you move into the Phone app. If the person has multiple numbers, Siri lists the numbers available and asks you which number to use.

(3) Speak the label for the number you want to call, or tap it. Siri dials the number for you and you move to the Phone app as if you had dialed the number yourself.

Siri has found multiple numbers for Gregory "Pappy" Boyington

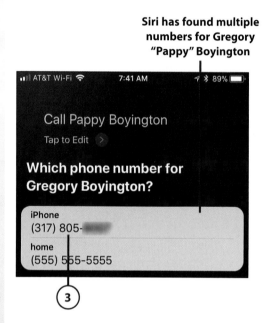

Siri Is Pretty Sharp

Siri can work with all kinds of variations on what you say. For example, if a contact has a nickname configured for him, you can use the nickname or the first name. If you want to call Gregory "Pappy" Boyington, you can say "Call Pappy Boyington" or "Call Gregory Boyington." If you say "Call Pappy" and there is only one contact with that nickname, Siri calls that contact. If more than one contact has "Pappy" as part of their contact information, Siri presents a list of contacts and prompts you to select one.

Placing FaceTime Calls

You can also use Siri to make FaceTime calls by saying "FaceTime *name*."

Composing New Email with Siri

To create email with Siri, do the following:

1. Say "Hey Siri, send email to *name*," where *name* is the person you want to email. Siri creates a new email addressed to the name you spoke. (If the recipient has more than one email address, Siri prompts you to choose the address you want to use.) Next, Siri asks you for the subject of the email.

2. Speak the subject of the email. Siri inserts the subject, and then prompts you for the body of the message.

More Than One Recipient?

To send an email to more than one recipient, say "and" between each name as in, "Send email to William Wallace and Edward Longshanks." Siri adds each address before and after the "and."

③ Speak the body of the email. As you speak, you can include punctuation; for example, to end a sentence, say the word "period" or to end a question, say the words "question mark." When Siri completes the email, it displays the message on the screen and prompts you to send it.

④ Review the message.

⑤ Change the message by tapping Tap to Edit.

6 Use the keyboard to change the body of the email.

7 Tap Done. Siri updates the content based on your changes and presents the edited content to you; it again prompts you to send the message.

8 Say "send" to send the email or "cancel" to delete it. If you say "send," Siri sends the message, confirms it will be sent, and plays the sent mail sound when it is.

What Am I Editing?

When you tap Tap to Edit, you edit the last thing you spoke to Siri. If this was a command, you edit the command. If it was content, such as a text message, you edit the content. You can edit only the most recent thing you spoke.

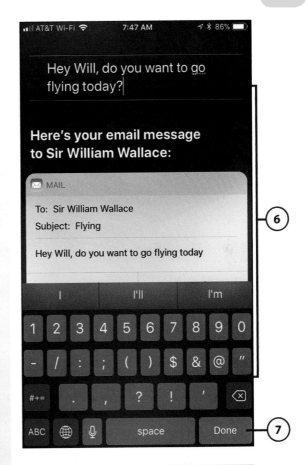

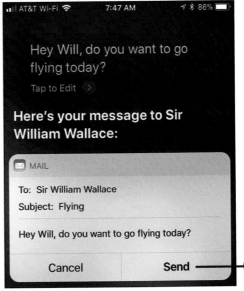

Replying to Emails with Siri

You can also use Siri to speak replies to emails you've read. Here's how:

(1) Open the message to which you want to reply.

(2) Say "Hey Siri, reply to this email." Siri prompts you for what you want your reply to say.

(3) Complete and send the reply; this works just like when you create a new message.

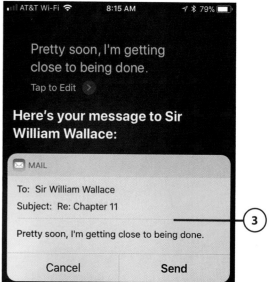

>>>*Go Further*
DOING MORE IN EMAIL WITH SIRI

Following are some other ways to use Siri for email:

- If you tell Siri to "Read email," Siri tells you how many emails are in your Inboxes and starts reading the time and date of the most recent email message followed by the subject and sender of the message. Siri then does the same for the next email until it has read a number of them. When it gets to the last message it reads, it prompts you to ask if you want to hear the entire list. On the screen, Siri lists the emails; you can tap an email message to read it yourself.

- Siri can read the content of email messages to you when you speak commands that tell it which email you want it to read, such as "Read most recent email," or "Read last email from William Wallace." Siri reads the entire message to you.

- To edit an email Siri created, say "Change." Siri prompts you to change the subject, change the message, cancel it, or send it. If you choose one of the change options, you can replace the subject or the body of the message. To change just some of the subject or body or to change the recipients, tap the message and edit it in the Mail app.

- You can start a new and completely blank email by saying "New email." Siri prompts you for the recipients, subject, and body.

- You can address a new email and add the subject with one statement, such as "Send email to William Wallace about flying."

- You can retrieve your email at any time by activating Siri and saying "Check email." Siri checks for new email and then announces how many emails you have received since the oldest message in your Inboxes was received. If you don't have any new email messages, Siri announces how many emails you have previously received and that remain in your Inbox.

- If you just want to know about new email messages, say "Check new email" instead. Siri reports back on new email you have received, but doesn't provide any information on email messages you've previously read.

- You can determine if you have emails from a specific person by asking something like, "Any email from William Wallace?" Siri's reply includes the number of emails in your Inboxes from William and displays them on the screen. Tap an email to read it.

- You can forward an email you are reading by saying "Forward this email" and then following Siri's lead to complete the process.

Having Messages Read to You

The Messages app is among the best to use with Siri because you can speak the most common tasks you normally do with messages. Especially useful is Siri's ability to read new messages to you. When you receive new text messages, do the following to have Siri read them to you:

(1) When you receive a text notification, activate Siri.

(2) Speak the command "Read text messages." (You can combine steps 1 and 2 by saying, "Hey Siri, read text messages.") Siri reads all the new text messages you've received, announcing the sender before reading each message. You have the option to reply (covered in the next task) or have Siri read the message again.

Siri reads each new message in turn until it has read all of them and then announces, "That's it" to let you know it has read all of them.

Siri only reads new text messages to you when you aren't on the Messages screen. If you've already read all your messages and you aren't in the Messages app, when you speak the command "Read text messages," Siri tells you that you have no new messages.

(2)

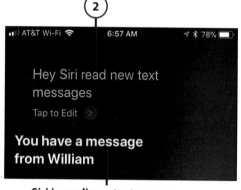

Siri is reading a text message

Reading Old Messages

To read an old message, move back to the conversation containing the message you want to hear. Activate Siri and say the command "Read text message." Siri reads the most recent text message to you.

Replying to Messages with Siri

You can also use Siri to speak replies to messages you've received. Here's how:

1. Listen to a message.

2. At the prompt asking if you want to reply, say "Yes." Siri prepares a reply to the message.

3. Speak your reply. Siri displays your reply.

4. If needed, change the message before you send it by tapping Tap to Edit.

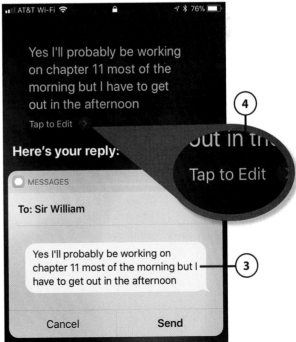

5 Use the keyboard to edit the message, or if you want to use Siri suggestions, skip to step 7.

6 Tap Done and skip to step 9.

7 Review Siri's suggestions for the message.

8 Tap a suggested message to use it.

9 At the prompt, say "Send" to send the message, "Cancel" to delete it, or "Change" to replace it. If you tell Siri that you want to send the message, Siri sends it and then confirms that it was sent.

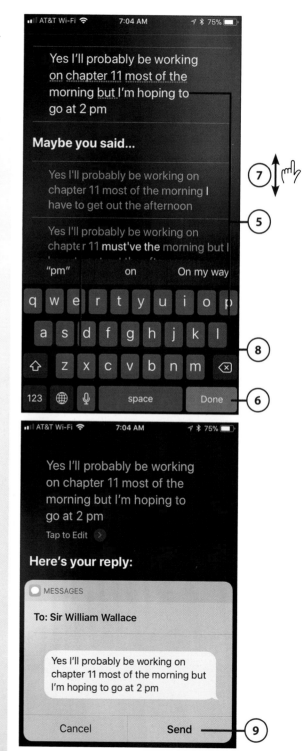

Sending New Messages with Siri

To send a new message to someone, do the following:

(1) Say "Hey Siri, send text message to *name*," where *name* is the person you want to text. Siri confirms your command and prepares to hear your text message.

(2) Speak your message. Siri listens and then prepares your message.

(3) If you want to send the message, say "Send." Siri sends the message.

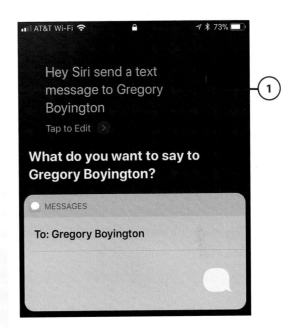

>>>Go Further

DOING MORE MESSAGING WITH SIRI

Following are some other ways to use Siri with messaging:

* If you say "Change" after you have created a new message, Siri prompts you to replace the message with a different one. If you say "Review" after creating a new message, Siri reads your message back to you. If you say "Cancel," Siri stops the process and deletes the message.

* You can use the Tap to Edit feature for any text message you are sending to manually edit it using the keyboard or to replace your message with one that Siri suggests.

* To send a text message to more than one recipient, say "and" between each name, as in, "Send text to William Wallace and Edward Longshanks."

* You can speak punctuation, such as "period" or "question mark" to add it to your message.

* You can tap icons that Siri presents on the screen, such as Send or Cancel, to take those actions on the message you are working on.

* Messages you receive or send via Siri appear in the Messages app just like messages you receive or send by tapping and typing.

* You can dictate into a text message you start in the Messages app (you learn about dictating later in this chapter).

Using Siri to Create Events

Siri is useful for capturing meetings and other events you want to add to your calendars. To create an event by speaking, use the following steps:

1. Activate Siri.

2. Speak the event you want to create. There are a number of variations in what you can say. Examples include "Set up a meeting with William Wallace on Friday at 10 a.m." or "Doctor appt on Thursday at 1 p.m." and so on. If you have any conflicts with the event you are setting up, Siri lets you know about them and asks you if you want to schedule the new event anyway.

3. Say "Confirm" if you don't have any conflicts or "Yes" if you do and you still want to have the appointment confirmed; you can also tap Confirm. Siri adds the event to your calendar. Say "Cancel" to cancel the event.

4. To add more information to an event Siri has created for you, tap it on the confirmation screen after you have confirmed it (not shown on the figure). You move into the Calendar app and can edit the event just like events you create within that app (see Chapter 10, "Managing Calendars" for information about the Calendar app).

Invitees

If you include the name of someone for whom you have an email address, Siri automatically sends invitations. If you include a name that matches more than one contact, Siri prompts you to choose the contact you want to invite. If the name doesn't match a contact, Siri enters the name but doesn't send an invitation.

Using Siri to Create Reminders

Creating reminders can be another useful thing you do with Siri, assuming you find reminders useful, of course. Here's how:

(1) Activate Siri.

(2) Speak the reminder you want to create. Here are some examples

Remind me to buy the A-10 at Motion RC.

Remind me to finish Chapter 10 at 10 AM on Saturday.

Remind me to buy milk when I leave work.

Siri provides a confirmation of what you asked. If you didn't mention a time or date when you want to be reminded, Siri prompts you to provide the details of when you want to be reminded.

(3) Speak the date and time when you want to be reminded. If you included a date and time in your original reminder request, you skip this step. Unlike some of the other tasks, Siri creates the reminder without confirming it with you.

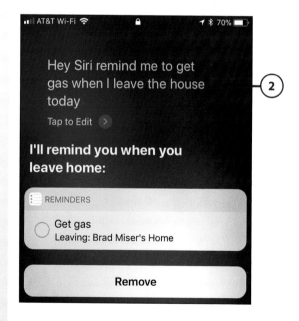

(4) If you don't want to keep the reminder, activate Siri and say "Remove" or tap Remove.

(5) To add detail to the reminder, tap it. You move into the Reminders app and can add more information to the reminder as you can when you create one manually.

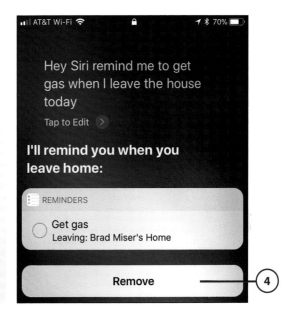

>>>Go Further

GOING FURTHER WITH SIRI TO MANAGE TIME

Following are some other ways to use Siri with the Calendar, Reminders, and Clock apps:

- You can change events with Siri, too. For example, if you have a meeting at 3 p.m., you can move it by saying something like "Move my 3 p.m. meeting to Friday at 6 p.m."

- You can get information about your events with Siri by saying things such as:

  Show me today's appointments.
  Do I have meetings on November 3?
  What time is my first appointment tomorrow?
  What are my appointments tomorrow?

  Siri tells you about the events and shows you what they are on the screen. You can tap any event to view it in the Calendar app.

- You can speak to your iPhone to set alarms. Tell Siri what you want and when you want the alarm to be set. For example, you can say something like "New alarm *alarmname* 6 a.m. tomorrow," where *alarmname* is the label of the alarm. Siri sets an alarm to go off at that time and gives it the label you speak. It displays the alarm on the screen along with a Status icon so you can turn it off if you change your mind. You don't have to label alarms, and you can just say something like "Set alarm 6 a.m. tomorrow." However, a label can be useful to issue other commands. For example, if an alarm has a name, you can turn it off by saying "Turn off *alarmname*." Any alarms you create with Siri can be managed just like alarms you create directly in the Clock app.

- To set a countdown timer, tell Siri to "Set timer for *x* minutes," where *x* is a number of minutes (you can do the same to set a timer for seconds or hours, too). Siri starts a countdown for you and presents it on the screen. You can continue to use the iPhone however you want. When the timer ends, you see and hear an alert. You can also reset the time, pause it, and so on by speaking.

- You can get information about time by asking questions, such as "What time is it?" or "What is the date?" You can add location information to the time information, too, as in "What time is it in London, England?"

- Tapping any confirmation Siri displays takes you back into the related app. For example, if you tap a clock that results when you ask what time it is, you can tap that clock to move into the Clock app. If you ask about your schedule today, you can tap any of the events Siri presents to move into the Calendar app to work with them.

- When you use Siri to create events and reminders, they are created on your default calendar (events) or reminder list (reminders).

Using Siri to Get Information

Siri is a great way to get information about lots of different topics in many different areas. You can ask Siri for information about a subject, places in your area, unit conversion (such as inches to centimeters), and so on. Just try speaking what you want to learn to best get the information you need. Here's an example looking for Chinese restaurants in my area:

(1) Activate Siri.

(2) Say something like, "Show me Chinese restaurants in my area." (Or a faster way is to combine steps 1 and 2 by saying "Hey Siri, show me Chinese restaurants in my area.") Siri presents a list of results that match your query and even provides a summary of reviews at the top of the screen. (You must have Location Services enabled for this to work. Refer to Chapter 4, "Customizing How Your iPhone Works," for information about configuring Location Services.)

Siri prompts you to take action on what it found. For example, if you asked for restaurants, Siri tells you about the closest one and then asks if you want to try it. If you say yes, Siri offers to call it for you or gives you directions. You can tap other items on the list to get more information or directions.

If you like Chinese food (or just about anything else), Siri can help you find it

(2)

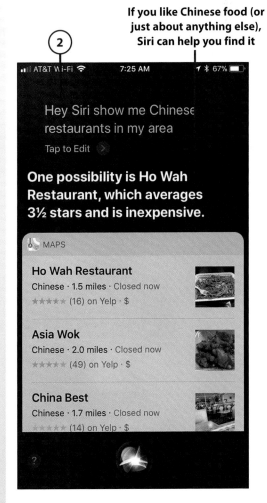

Siri is also useful for getting information about topics. Siri responds by conducting a web search and showing you the result. For example, suppose you want to learn about the F-15 fighter plane. Activate Siri and say, "Tell me about the F-15 Eagle." Siri responds with information about your topic. You can have Siri read the information by activating Siri and saying "Read." Siri reads the results (this doesn't always work; it works best when the results are presented via Wikipedia or something similar).

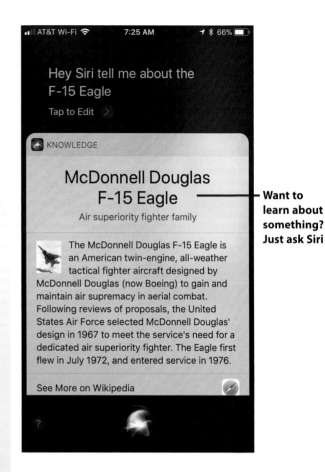

Want to learn about something? Just ask Siri

Using Siri to Play Music

You can also play music by telling Siri which music you want to hear.

(1) Activate Siri.

(2) Tell Siri the music you want to hear. There are a number of variations in what you can say. Here are some examples:

Play album Time of My Life.
Play song "Gone" by Switchfoot.
Play playlist Jon McLaughlin.

Siri provides a confirmation of what you asked and begins playing the music.

(3) Tap Open Music to move into the Music app to control the music with your fingers.

>>>Go Further

MORE SPOKEN COMMANDS FOR MUSIC

There are a number of commands you can speak to find, play, and control music (and other audio). "Play *artist*" plays music by the artist you speak. "Play *album*" plays the album you name. In both cases, if the name includes the word "the," you need to include "the" when you speak the command. "Shuffle" plays a random song. "Play more like this" uses the Genius to find songs similar to the one playing and plays them. "Previous track" or "next track" does exactly what they sound like they do. To hear the name of the artist for the song currently playing, say "Who sings this song?" You can shuffle music in an album or playlist by saying "Shuffle playlist *playlistname*." You can stop the music, pause it, or play it by speaking those commands.

Using Siri to Get Directions

With Siri, it's easy to get directions—you don't even have to stop at a gas station to ask.

1. Activate Siri.

2. Speak something like "Give me directions to the airport." If you want directions starting from someplace other than your current location, include that in the request, such as "Get directions from the Eagle Creek Airpark to the Indianapolis International Airport."

3. If Siri needs you to confirm one or more of the locations, tap the correct one.

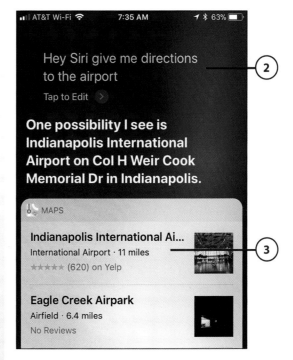

4   Tap Directions. Siri uses the Maps app to generate directions.

5   Tap Go to start turn-by-turn directions.

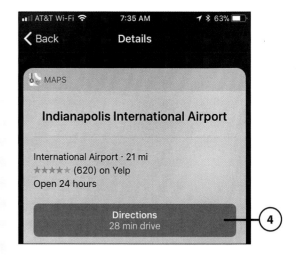

Using Siri to Open Apps

As you accumulate apps on your iPhone, it can take several taps and swipes to get to a specific app, such as one that is stored in a folder that isn't on the page of the Home screen you are viewing. With Siri, you can open any app on your phone with a simple command.

(1) Say "Hey Siri, open *appname*," where *appname* is the name of the app you want to open.

(2) If your phone needs to be unlocked to open the app, Siri prompts you to unlock it (such as by touching the Touch ID/Home button or using Face ID). Siri then opens the app for you, and you move to the last screen in that app you were using.

It's Not All Good

When Siri Misunderstands

Voice commands to Siri work very well, but they aren't perfect. Make sure you confirm your commands by listening to the feedback Siri provides when it repeats them or reviewing the feedback Siri provides on the screen. Sometimes, a spoken command can have unexpected results, which can include making a phone call to someone in the Contacts app. If you don't catch such a mistake before the call is started, you might be surprised to hear someone answering your call instead of hearing music you intended to play. You can put Siri in listening mode by tapping the Listen icon, and then saying "no" or "stop" to stop Siri should a verbal command go awry.

Using Siri to Translate

Siri can translate words and phrases from the language you are using into other languages. In the initial release of this feature, Siri supports the translation of English into French, German, Italian, Mandarin, and Spanish. Over time, Apple will add more capability to this, so you should try this translating function to see how it can work for you. Here's an example of translating an English phrase into Italian:

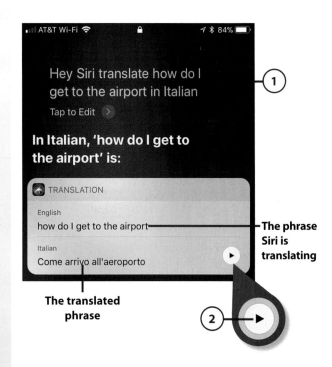

The phrase Siri is translating

The translated phrase

1. Say "Hey Siri, translate How do I get to the airport in Italian." Siri does the translation for you and speaks the translated phrase.

2. Tap the Play icon to have Siri speak the translation again.

No Can Do

If Siri is unable to complete the translation you requested, it speaks what it can do. For example, it speaks a list of currently supported languages.

Using Dictation to Speak Text Instead of Typing

You can use the iPhone's dictation capability to speak text into any app, such as Mail, Messages, and so on. In fact, any time you see the Microphone key on the keyboard, dictation is available to you.

Here's how this works:

(1) In the app you are using, put the cursor where you want the text you dictate to start. For example, if you are creating an email, tap in the body.

(2) Tap the Microphone key on the virtual keyboard. The dictation pane opens at the bottom of the screen. The oscillating line indicates Siri is listening to you and you can begin speaking.

(3) Speak the text you want to add. In addition to text, you can speak punctuation, such as saying "comma" when you want to insert a comma or "new paragraph" when you want to create a new paragraph. While you are speaking, you see the line that oscillates as you speak and the text you are speaking at the location of the cursor.

(4) Tap the Keyboard icon when you finish your dictation. The Dictation pane closes, and the keyboard reappears. The text you spoke is part of the message. From there, you can edit it just like text you've typed.

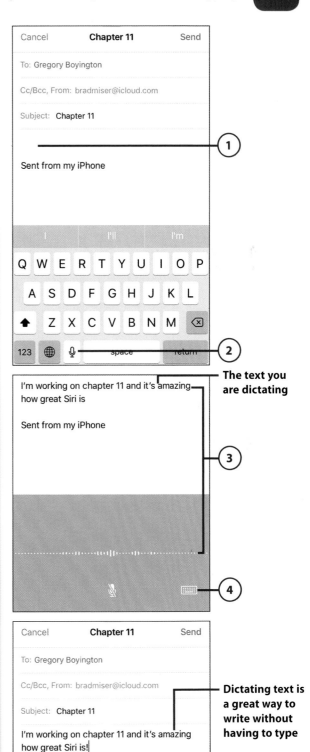

The text you are dictating

Dictating text is a great way to write without having to type

Tap to configure Safari

Tap to have the World Wide Web
in the palm of your hand

In this chapter, you explore the amazing web browsing functionality your iPhone has to offer. Topics include the following:

12

Surfing the Web

The Web has become an integral part of most of our lives. It is often the first step to search for information, make plans (such as travel arrangements), conduct financial transactions, shop, and so much more. Safari on the iPhone puts the entire Web in the palm of your hand. Safari is a full-featured web browser; anything you can do on a website in a browser on a computer can be done with Safari on your iPhone.

Getting Started

The World Wide Web, more commonly called the Web, is a great resource for finding information, planning travel, keeping up with the news, and just about anything else you want to do. Following are some of the more common terms you encounter as you use the Web:

• **Web page**—This is a collection of information (text and graphics) that is available on the Web. A web page is what you look at when you use the Web.

- **Website**—This is a collection of web pages that "go together." For example, most companies and other organizations have websites that contain information they use to help their customers or members, provide services, market and sell their products and services, and so on. A website organizes the web pages it contains and provides the structure you use to move among them.

- **Web browser**—This is the software you use to view web pages. There are many different web browsers available. Examples include Safari—which comes preinstalled on your iPhone—as well as Google Chrome, Internet Explorer, and Firefox. They all allow you to view and interact with web pages, and each has its own set of features. Some are available on just about every device there is, such as Safari and Google Chrome, while some are limited to certain devices, such as Internet Explorer that only runs on Windows computers.

- **Safari**—This is the default web browser on your iPhone; it is also the default web browser on Mac computers. You can download and install it on Windows computers, too.

- **URL**—A Uniform Resource Locator (URL) is a web page's or website's "address" on the Web. URLs allow you to direct your web browser to specific locations on the Web. Most URLs you deal with consist of text, such as www.apple.com or www.aarp.org. Some URLs are more complicated because they take you to specific web pages instead of a website. An example of this is www.aarp.org/health, which takes you to the Health web page on the AARP website. You seldom have to type URLs because you usually access web pages by tapping on links or using a bookmark, but it's good to know what they are and how to use them.

- **Link**—A link is a photo or other graphic, text, or other object that has a URL attached to it. When you tap a link, you move to the URL and open the web page associated with it. Most text links are formatted with a color so you can distinguish them from regular text. Links can also be attached to images, such as photos or other kinds of graphics.

- **Bookmark**—This is a saved location on the Web. When you visit a web page or website, you can save its URL as a bookmark so you can return to it with just a few taps instead of typing its URL. Safari allows you to save and organize your bookmarks on your iPhone.

- **Search engine or search page**—The Web contains information on every topic under the sun. You can use a search engine/page to search for information in which you are interested. There are a number of search engines available, with Google being the most popular. You access a search engine through a web browser. Safari uses Google by default, but you can choose Bing, DuckDuckGo, or Yahoo! as your default search engine if you prefer one of those instead.

Setting Safari Preferences

Like most apps, Safari offers settings you can use to adjust the way it works. You can likely use Safari with its default settings just fine; when the time comes that you want to tweak how Safari works for you, use the following table as a reference for the available settings. To access these settings, tap the Settings icon on the Home screen, and then tap Safari.

Safari Settings

Settings Area	Location	Setting	Description
ALLOW SAFARI TO ACCESS	Siri & Search	Siri & Search Suggestions	Set this switch to on (green) to allow information from Safari to be used in searches, when you perform lookups, and in other places. It also allows Siri to learn from how you use Safari to make better suggestions over time. If you don't want Safari information to be used in this way, set the switch to off (white).
SEARCH	Search Engine	Search Engine	Enables you to choose your default search tool; the options are Google (default), Yahoo, Bing, or DuckDuckGo.
SEARCH	N/A	Search Engine Suggestions	When this switch is on (green), Safari asks your default search engine for suggestions related to what you type in the Address/Search bar. This makes search easier because you can type your search term in the bar instead of first moving to the search web page.

Settings Area	Location	Setting	Description
SEARCH	N/A	Safari Suggestions	When this switch is on (green), Safari makes suggestions related to what you type in the Address/Search bar. This makes search easier because you can type a term in which you are interested in the bar instead of first moving to the search web page.
SEARCH	Quick Website Search	Quick Website Search	When this switch is on (green), you can perform a search at a specific website by typing its name before your search term. For example, you can type "wiki william wallace" in the Address/Search bar and the first section of the results will be entries in the Wikipedia related to William Wallace; this saves you the steps of moving to the search engine results, and then tapping the articles you want to read because you can do this directly from the Search screen instead.
SEARCH	N/A	Preload Top Hit	When this switch is on (green), the sites you move to or find more frequently are loaded while you search, making accessing them faster.
GENERAL	Autofill	N/A	These settings enable you to automatically log in to websites and to quickly complete forms on the Web by automatically filling in key information for you. Set the Use Contact Info switch to on (green), tap My Info, and tap your contact information in the Contacts app. When you use the Auto-Fill function, this is the information that is entered for you.

Settings Area	Location	Setting	Description
GENERAL	Autofill	N/A	You can determine what data is saved on your iPhone by setting the following switches on (green) or off (white): Names and Passwords or Credit Cards. If you want to be able to automatically sign into websites, the Names and Passwords switch must be on. The Credit Cards switch enables you to store credit cards on your iPhone so you can more easily enter their information to make purchases.
GENERAL	Autofill	Autofill	Tap Saved Credit Cards to view or change existing credit card information or to add new credit cards to Safari.
GENERAL	N/A	Frequently Visited Sites	When this switch is on (green) and you move into the Address/Search bar, Safari shows a section of sites that you visit frequently, making them easier to return to.
GENERAL	Favorites	Favorites	Use this option to choose the folder of bookmarks for sites that you use most frequently. The bookmarks in the folder you select appear at the top of the screen when you move into the Address/Search bar, making them fast and easy to use.
GENERAL	Open Links	Open Links	This tells Safari the option you want to see when you touch and hold a link on a current web page to open a new web page. The In New Tab option causes Safari to open and immediately take you to a new tab displaying the web page with which a link is associated. The In Background option causes Safari to open pages in the background for links you tap so you can view them later.

Settings Area	Location	Setting	Description
GENERAL	N/A	Block Pop-ups	Some websites won't work properly with pop-ups blocked, so you can use this setting to temporarily enable pop-ups by sliding the switch to off (white). When the Block Pop-ups switch is on (green), pop-ups are blocked.
PRIVACY & SECURITY	N/A	Prevent Cross-Site Tracking	When enabled (green), this feature attempts to limit tracking of your browsing history by websites that you visit. Its purpose is to limit the exposure of your private information by websites that try to track you as you visit other sites to collect information about you.
PRIVACY & SECURITY	N/A	Block All Cookies	When enabled (green), Safari doesn't allow cookies to be stored; cookies are bits of information that websites store about you to use to tailor your experience at that website. If you block all cookies, some sites might not work correctly. Safari only accepts cookies for websites you visit, so, in general, you should leave this feature disabled (white) so websites you visit work correctly.
PRIVACY & SECURITY	N/A	Ask Websites Not To Track Me	Some websites track your activity in order to tailor the site based on your browsing history. When enabled (green), Safari includes a request not to track you to each website you visit. If the website honors that request, you won't be tracked. However, it's up to each website to implement this.
PRIVACY & SECURITY	N/A	Fraudulent Website Warning	If you don't want Safari to warn you when you visit websites that appear to be fraudulent, set the Fraudulent Website Warning switch to off (white). You should leave this switch enabled (green).

Settings Area	Location	Setting	Description
PRIVACY & SECURITY	N/A	Camera & Microphone Access	When this switch is on (green) Safari can access the iPhone's microphone and camera to enable you to present video and transmit and receive audio communication via a website.
PRIVACY & SECURITY	N/A	Check for Apple Pay	When you visit websites that support Apple Pay with this switch enabled (green), you can use your Apple Pay account to make payments for goods or services. (Refer to the online Chapter 15, "Working with Other Useful iPhone Apps and Features," for information about Apple Pay.)
PRIVACY & SECURITY	N/A	Clear History and Website Data	When you tap this command and confirm it by tapping Clear History and Data at the prompt, Safari removes the websites you have visited from your history list. The list starts over, so the next site you visit is added to your history list again—unless you have enabled private browsing. It also removes all cookies and other website data that have been stored on your iPhone.
READING LIST	N/A	Automatically Save Offline	The Reading List enables you to store web pages on your iPhone for offline reading. If you want to allow pages to be saved to your iPhone automatically, slide this switch to the on (green) position.
Advanced	Website Data	Website Data	Website Data displays the amount of data associated with websites you have visited; swipe up on the screen and tap Remove All Website Data to clear this data.
Advanced	N/A	JavaScript	Set this switch to off (white) to disable JavaScript functionality (however, some sites won't work properly without JavaScript).

Settings Area	Location	Setting	Description
Advanced	N/A	Web Inspector	This switch controls a feature that is used by website developers to see how their sites work on an iPhone.

Where, Oh Where Are My Passwords?

When you enable Safari to save your names and passwords, they are stored under the App & Website Passwords settings, which you can access by tapping Accounts & Passwords on the main Settings screen. When you tap App & Website Passwords, you see a list of the usernames and passwords stored on your iPhone sorted by the URL of the website with which they are associated. You can tap a URL to see the username and password for that site and a list of all websites using that information. To remove a URL and its associated username and password from the list, swipe to the left on it and tap Delete. The next time you move to that site, you will need to manually enter your username and password again.

Visiting Websites

If you've used a web browser on a computer before, using Safari on an iPhone is a familiar experience. If you've not used a web browser before, don't worry because using Safari on an iPhone is simple and intuitive.

Syncing Bookmarks

Using iCloud, you can synchronize your Internet Explorer favorites or Safari bookmarks on a Windows PC—or Safari bookmarks on a Mac—to your iPhone so you have the same set of bookmarks available on your phone that you do on your computer and other devices, and vice versa (refer to Chapter 3, "Setting Up and Using an Apple ID, iCloud, and Other Online Accounts"). You should enable iCloud's Safari switch before you start browsing on your iPhone, so you avoid typing URLs or re-creating bookmarks. When you enable Safari syncing via iCloud, you can also view tabs open in Safari on other devices, such as a Mac or an iPad.

Using Bookmarks to Move to Websites

Using bookmarks you've synced via iCloud or created on your iPhone (you learn how later in this chapter) makes it easy to get to websites.

1. On the Home screen, tap Safari.
2. Tap the Bookmarks icon.
3. Tap the Bookmarks tab (the open book) if it isn't selected already. (If you don't see this tab, tap the Back icon, which is labeled with the name of the folder from which you moved to the current screen, in the upper-left corner of the screen until you do.)
4. Swipe up or down the list of bookmarks to browse the bookmarks and other folders of bookmarks available to you.
5. To move to a bookmark, skip to step 10; to open a folder of bookmarks, tap it.

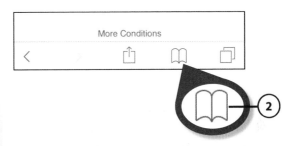

Back to the Bookmarks

The most recent Bookmarks screen is retained when you move away from Bookmarks and then come back. Each time you open your Bookmarks, you see the same screen you did when you left it.

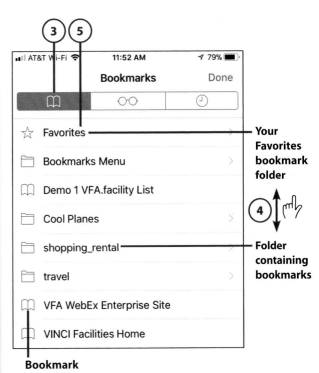

Your Favorites bookmark folder

Folder containing bookmarks

Bookmark

6 Swipe up or down the folder's screen to browse the folders and bookmarks it contains.

7 Tap a folder to see the bookmarks it contains.

Change Your Mind?
If you decide not to visit a bookmark, tap Done. You return to the website you were previously viewing.

8 To return to a previous screen, tap the Back icon in the upper-left corner of the screen, which is labeled with the name of the folder you previously visited (the parent folder); this disappears when you are at the top-level Bookmarks screen.

9 Repeat steps 5–8 until you see a bookmark you want to visit.

10 Tap the bookmark you want to visit. Safari moves to that website.

11 Use the information in the section "Viewing Websites" later in this chapter to get information on viewing the web page.

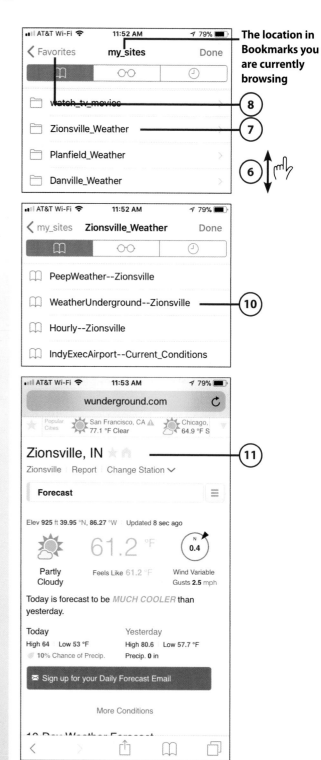

The location in Bookmarks you are currently browsing

Playing Favorites

You might see two Favorites folders on the Bookmarks screen. The folder marked with a star is the folder you designated, using the Safari settings described previously in this chapter, as the place to store Favorites on your iPhone. If you use Safari on a computer, you can also configure bookmarks and folders of bookmarks on its Bookmarks bar. When these bookmarks are synced from your computer to the iPhone, they might be stored in a folder of bookmarks also called Favorites and shown with the standard folder icon. If you set this synced folder in your iPhone's Safari settings to also be its Favorites folder, you won't have to deal with this potentially confusing situation of having two Favorites folders.

iPhone Web Pages

Some websites have been specially formatted for mobile devices. These typically have less complex information on each page, so they load faster. When you move to a site like this, you might be redirected to the mobile version automatically, or you might be prompted to choose which version of the site you want to visit. On the mobile version, there is typically a link that takes you to the "regular" version, too. (It's sometimes called the Desktop, Full, or Classic version.) Sometimes the version formatted for handheld devices offers less information or fewer tools than the regular version. Because Safari is a full-featured browser, you can use either version.

Using Your Favorites to Move to Websites

Using the Safari settings described earlier, you can designate a folder of bookmarks as your Favorites. You can get to the folders and bookmarks in your Favorites folder more quickly and easily than navigating to it as described in the previous section. Here's how to use your Favorites:

1. On the Home screen, tap Safari. (If you are in Safari and have the Bookmarks screen open, tap Done to close it.)

(2) Tap in the Address/Search bar (if you don't see the Address/Search bar, tap at the top of the screen to show it). Just below the Address/Search bar are your Favorites (bookmarks and folders of bookmarks). The keyboard opens at the bottom of the screen.

(3) Swipe up and down on your Favorites. The keyboard closes to give you more room to browse.

(4) To move to a bookmark, tap it and skip to step 8.

(5) Tap a folder to move into it.

More Commands

At the top of the Favorites screen, you might see two more commands. Tap Add to Favorites to add a bookmark to the current site to your Favorites folder. Tap Request Desktop Site if you are currently viewing the mobile version of a site and want to see the "full" version; you move to that version after you tap the command.

(6) Continue browsing your Favorites until you find the bookmark you want to use. Like using the Bookmarks screen, you can tap a folder to move into it, tap a bookmark to move to its website, or tap the Back icon to move to a previous screen.

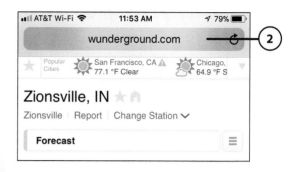

Folder of bookmarks

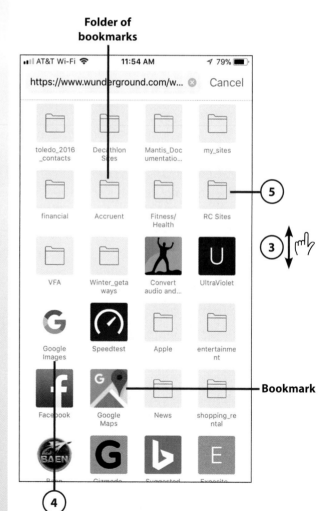

Bookmark

(7) Tap the bookmark for the site you want to visit.

(8) Use the information in the section "Viewing Websites" later in this chapter to view the web page.

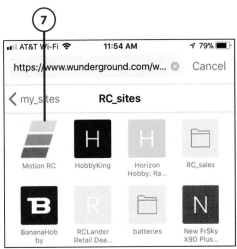

Typing URLs to Move to Websites

A Uniform Resource Locator (URL) is the Internet address of a web page. URLs can be relatively simple, such as www.apple.com, or they can be quite long and convoluted. The good news is that by using bookmarks, you can save a URL in Safari so you can get back to it using its bookmark (as you learned in the previous two tasks) and thus avoid typing URLs more than once. To use a URL to move to a website, do the following:

(1) On the Home screen, tap Safari. (If you are in Safari and have the Bookmarks screen open, tap Done to close it.)

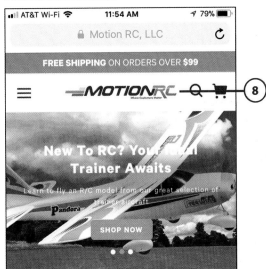

(2) Tap in the Address/Search bar
(if you don't see the Address/
Search bar, tap at the top of the
screen). The URL of the current
page becomes highlighted, or if
you haven't visited a page, the
Address/Search bar is empty. Just
below the Address/Search bar,
your Favorites are displayed. The
keyboard appears at the bottom
of the screen.

(3) If an address appears in the
Address/Search bar, tap the Clear
(x) icon to remove it.

(4) Type the URL you want to visit. If
it starts with www. (which almost
all URLs do), you don't have to
type "www." As you type, Safari
attempts to match what you are
typing to a site you have visited
previously and completes the URL
for you if it can. Just below the
Address/Search bar, Safari presents a list of sites that might be
what you are looking for, organized into groups, such as Top Hits
or Suggested Websites.

(5) If one of the sites shown is the
one you want to visit, tap it. You
move to that web page; skip to
step 8.

(6) If Safari doesn't find a match,
continue typing until you enter
the entire URL.

(7) Tap Go. You move to the web
page.

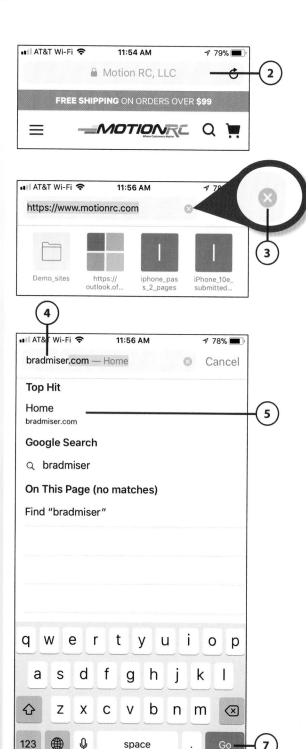

8 Use the information in the section "Viewing Websites" to view the web page.

Shortcut for Typing URLs

URLs include a top-level domain code that represents the type of site (theoretically anyway) that URL leads to. Common examples are .com (commercial sites) and .edu (educational sites). If you don't enter a code, Safari assumes .com since that is the most common one. To quickly enter a URL's code, tap and hold the period key to see a menu from which you can select other options, such as .net or .edu. Select the code you want on the keyboard, and it is entered in the Address/Search bar.

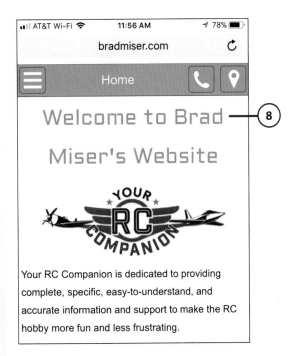

Using Your Browsing History to Move to Websites

As you move about the Web, Safari tracks the sites you visit and builds a history list (unless you enabled the Do Not Track option, in which case this doesn't happen and you can't use History to return to previous sites). You can use your browsing history list to return to sites you've visited.

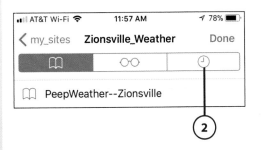

1 Tap the Bookmarks icon.

2 Tap the History tab.

③ Swipe up and down the page to browse all the sites you've visited. The more recent sites appear at the top of the screen; the further you move down the screen, the further back in time you go. Earlier sites are collected in folders for various times, such as This Morning or Monday Afternoon.

④ Tap the site you want to visit. The site opens and you can use the information in the section "Viewing Websites" to view the web page.

Erasing the Past

To clear your browsing history, tap Clear at the bottom of the History screen. At the prompt, tap the timeframe that you want to clear; the options are The last hour, Today, Today and yesterday, or All time. Your browsing history for the period of time you selected is erased. (Don't you wish it was this easy to erase the past in real life?)

Viewing Websites

Even though your iPhone is a small device, you'll be amazed at how well it displays web pages designed for larger screens.

1. Use Safari to move to a web page as described in the previous tasks.

2. To browse around a web page, swipe your finger right or left, or up or down.

3. Zoom in manually by unpinching your fingers.

4. Zoom in automatically by tapping twice on the screen.

Where Did the URL Go?

When you first move to a URL, you see that URL in the Address/Search bar. After you work with a site, the Address/Search bar and the toolbar are hidden and the URL is replaced with the high-level domain name for the site (such as sitename.com, sitename.edu, and so on). To see the Address/Search bar and toolbar again, tap the top or bottom of the screen. To see the full URL again, tap in the Address/Search bar.

5. Zoom out manually by pinching your fingers.

6. Zoom out on a column or a figure by tapping it twice.

7. Tap a link to move to the location to which it points. Links can come in many forms, including text (most text that is a link is in color and underlined) or graphics. The web page to which the link points opens and replaces the page currently being displayed.

8 To view the web page in land-scape orientation, rotate the iPhone so that it is horizontal.

9 Scroll, zoom in, and zoom out on the page to read it, as described in steps 2–7.

10 Tap Refresh to refresh a page, which causes its content to be updated. (Note: While a page is loading, this is the Stop [x] icon; tap it to stop the rest of the page from loading.)

11 To move to a previous page you've visited, tap the Back icon (left-facing arrow). (If the arrow is grayed out, it means you are at the beginning of the set of pages you have visited.)

12 To move to a subsequent page, tap the Forward icon (right-facing arrow). (If the arrow is grayed out, it means you are at the end of the set of pages you have visited.)

13 As you move around, the Address/Search bar at the top of the page and the toolbar at the bottom of the page are hidden automatically; to show them again, tap the top or bottom of the screen (on the iPhone 6/6s Plus or later models, tap the top of the screen when the phone is horizontal).

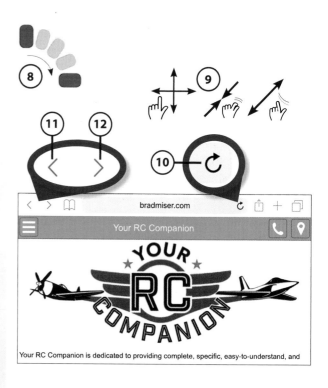

Do More with Links

To see options for a link, touch and hold your finger down for a second or so. (If you are using an iPhone that supports 3D Touch, this can be a bit tricky. If you apply pressure, a Peek appears instead of the menu. To see the menu, place your finger on the screen and hold it there, but don't put any pressure on the screen.) A menu appears. Tap Open to open the page to replace the current page at which the link points (this is the same as tapping a link once). Tap Open in Background to open the page in a new Safari window that opens in the background, or tap Open in New Tab to open the new page in the new tab. (The command that appears depends on the Open Links Safari setting that you learned about earlier in this chapter.) Tap Add to Reading List to add the page to your Reading List. If the link is an image, tap Save Image to save the image on your phone. Tap Copy to copy the link's URL so that you can paste it elsewhere, such as in an email message. Tap Share to open the Share menu that enables you to share the web page via email, a message, and so on. Tap Cancel to return to the current page and take no action.

Different Phones, Different Look

The type of iPhone you are using to browse the Web affects how pages look and where controls are located. For example, when you use an iPhone 5s, you see black at the top and bottom of the screen whereas you see white there on an iPhone 7. Also, when you rotate an iPhone 5s, the tools are at the top and bottom of the screen, but on an iPhone 7, the controls are all at the top of the screen. Regardless of where the controls appear on the screen, they work in the same way.

Working with Multiple Websites at the Same Time

When you move to a web page by using a bookmark, typing a URL, or tapping a link on the current web page, the new web page replaces the current one. However, you can also open and work with multiple web pages at the same time so that a new web page doesn't replace the current one.

When you work with multiple web pages, each open page appears in its own tab. You can use the tab view to easily move to and manage your open web pages.

You can also close open tabs, and you can even open web pages that are open on other devices on which your iCloud account has been configured and Safari syncing enabled.

There are two ways to open a new web page in a new tab. One is to touch and hold on a link on the current web page; you can use the resulting Open command to open the new page. There are two options for this approach; the one you use is determined by the Open Links preference set as described earlier in this chapter. The In Background option causes the new page to open and move to the background. This is most useful when you want to read the new page at a later time, such as when you are done with the current one. The In New Tab option causes the new page to open and move to the front so you see it instantly while moving the current page and its tab to the background.

The second way to open a new web page in a new tab is by using the Tab Manager.

These options are described in the following tasks.

Tapping Without Holding

When you tap, but don't hold down, a link on a web page, the web page to which the link points opens and replaces the current web page—no new tab is created. When you touch and hold down on a link, the behavior is determined by the setting you chose in the preferences as covered in a task earlier in this chapter ("Setting Safari Preferences"). To make things a bit more complicated, if your phone supports 3D Touch (iPhone 6s/6s Plus and later), don't apply pressure to the screen when you tap; if you do, a Peek appears instead (you learn about this in "Using 3D Touch with Safari").

Opening New Pages in the Background

If you enabled the In Background option for the Open Links preference, you can open new web pages by doing the following:

(1) Touch and hold (but don't press) on the link you want to open in the background.

(2) Tap Open in Background. The page to which the link points opens. The only result you see is the page associated with the link you touched "jumping" down to the Tab Manager icon in the lower-right corner of the screen.

(3) Continue opening pages in the background; see "Using Tab View to Manage Open Web Pages" to learn how to use the tab view to move to pages that are open in the background.

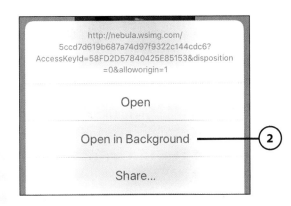

Opening New Pages in a New Tab

If you enabled the In New Tab option for the Open Links preference, you can open new pages by doing the following:

(1) Touch and hold on the link you want to open in the background.

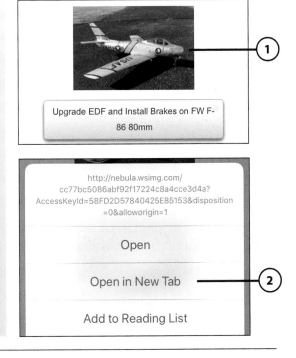

(2) Tap Open in New Tab. The tab view appears briefly, and a new tab opens and displays the page to which the link points. The web page from which you started moves into the background.

(3) Continue opening pages; see "Using Tab View to Manage Open Web Pages" to learn how to use the tab view to manage your open pages.

Just Open It

If you tap the Open command on the menu in step 2 of the previous tasks, the new web page replaces the one you were viewing on the current tab. This is the same as tapping a link on the page rather than touching and holding (but not pressing) on it.

Using Tab View to Manage Open Web Pages

As you open new pages, whether in the background or not, new tabs are opened. Safari's tab view enables you to view and work with your open pages/tabs. Here's how:

1. Tap the Tab View icon. Each open page appears on its own tab.

2. Swipe up or down on the open tabs to browse them.

3. Tap a tab/page to move into it. The page opens and fills the Safari window.

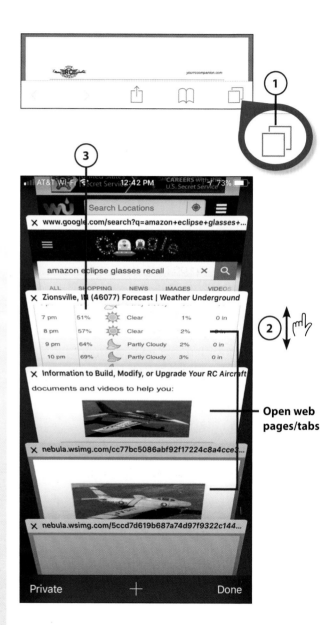

Open web pages/tabs

4 Work with the web page.

5 Tap the Tab View icon.

Tabs Are Independent

Each tab is independent. So, when you are working with a tab and use the Back/Forward icons to move among its pages, you are just moving among the pages open under that tab. Pages open in other tabs are not affected.

---

6 Tap a Close (x) icon to close a tab; alternatively swipe to the left on the tab you want to close.

7 To open a new tab, tap the Add (+) icon to create a new tab that shows your Favorites screen; navigate to a new page in that tab using the methods described in other tasks (tapping bookmarks or typing a URL).

8 Tap Done to close the tab view. The tab view closes, and the page you were most recently viewing is shown.

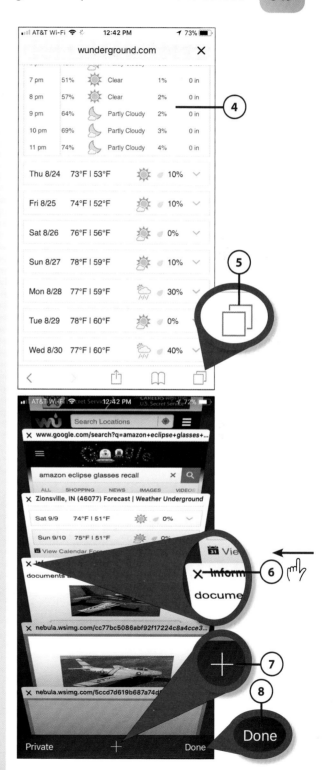

Opening Web Pages That Are Open on Other Devices

When you enable iCloud Safari syncing, iCloud tracks the websites you have open on all the devices on which you have Safari syncing enabled, including your iPhone, iPads, and Macs. This is really handy when you have pages open on another device and want to view them on your iPhone. (Web pages open on your iPhone are available on your other devices, too.) To view a page you have open on another device, do the following:

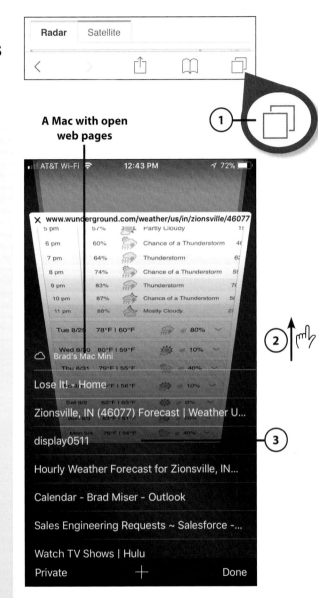

A Mac with open web pages

(1) Open the tab view.

(2) Swipe up the screen until you see the pages open on other devices. There is a section for each device; sections are labeled with the device's name. In each device's section, you see the pages open in Safari on those devices.

(3) Tap the page you want to view. The page opens on the iPhone and becomes a new tab.

Keep Private Things Private

If you aren't browsing in Private mode and tap the Private icon at the bottom of the tab view, Safari moves into Private mode and stops tracking the sites you visit. Tap the Private icon again to return to the previous state. If you are browsing in Private mode, tapping the Private icon shows or hides the tabs in the tab view.

Searching the Web

In the first section of this chapter, you learned that you can set Safari to search the Web using Google, Yahoo!, Bing, or DuckDuckGo. No matter which search engine you chose, you search the Web in the same way.

(1) Tap in the Address/Search bar (if you don't see this bar, tap at the top of the screen). The keyboard appears along with your Favorites.

(2) If there is any text in the Address/Search bar, tap the Clear (x) icon.

(3) Type your search word(s). As you type, Safari attempts to find a search that matches what you typed. The list of suggestions is organized in sections, which depend on what you are searching for and the search options you configured through Safari settings. One section, labeled with the search engine you are using (such as Google Search), contains the search results from that source. Other sections can include Bookmarks and History, or Apps (from the App Store). At the bottom of the list is the On This Page section, which shows the terms that match your search on the page you are browsing.

(4) To perform the search using one of the suggestions provided, tap the suggestion you want to use. The search is performed and you can skip to step 6.

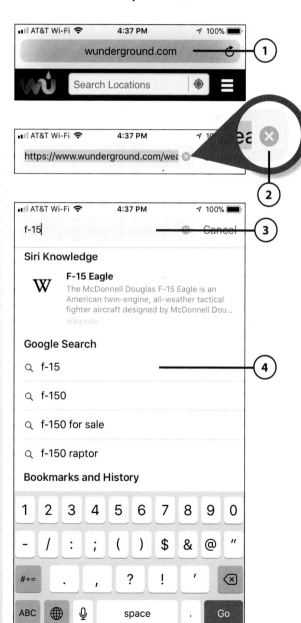

5 If none of the suggestions are what you want, keep typing until you have entered the entire search term, and then tap Go. The search engine you use performs the search and displays the results on the search results page.

Quick Website Search

If you enabled the Quick Website Search feature, you can include the site you want to search in the Address/Search bar, such as "Wiki F-15." When you do this, the results from the site you entered appear at the top of the list and you can access them directly by tapping the information that appears (as opposed to having to move to the search engine site first as in these steps).

6 Use the search results page to view the results of your search. These pages work just like other web pages. You can zoom, scroll, and tap links to explore results.

Searching on a Web Page

To search for words or phrases on a web page you are viewing, perform these steps, except in step 4, tap the word or phrase for which you want to search in the On This Page section (you might have to swipe up the screen to see this section). You return to the page you are browsing and each occurrence of your search term on the page is highlighted.

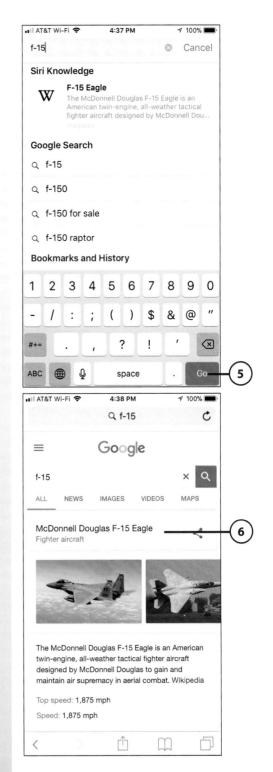

Saving and Organizing Bookmarks

In addition to moving bookmarks from a computer or iCloud onto your iPhone, you can save new bookmarks directly in your iPhone (they are synced onto other devices, too). You can also organize bookmarks on your iPhone to make them easier and faster to access.

Creating Bookmarks

When you want to make it easy to return to a website, create a bookmark with the following steps:

1. Move to a web page for which you want to save a bookmark.

2. Tap the Share icon.

3. Tap Add Bookmark. The Add Bookmark screen appears, showing the title of the web page you are viewing, which will also be the name of the bookmark initially; its URL; and the Location field, which shows where the bookmark will be stored when you create it.

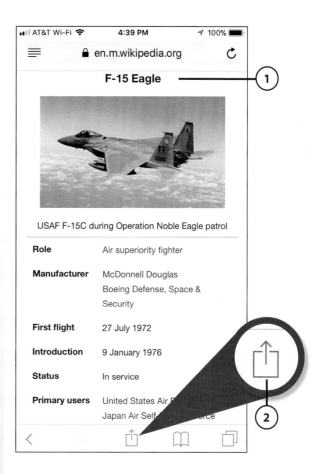

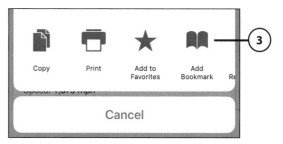

④ Edit the bookmark's name as needed, or tap the Clear (x) icon to erase the current name, and then type the new name of the bookmark. The titles of some web pages can be quite long, so it's a good idea to shorten them so the bookmark's name is easier to read on the iPhone's screen.

⑤ Tap the current folder shown under Location. The Location section expands and you see all of the folders of bookmarks on your phone. The folder that is currently selected is marked with a check mark.

⑥ Swipe up and down the screen to find the folder in which you want to place the new bookmark. You can choose any folder on the screen; folders are indented when they are contained within other folders.

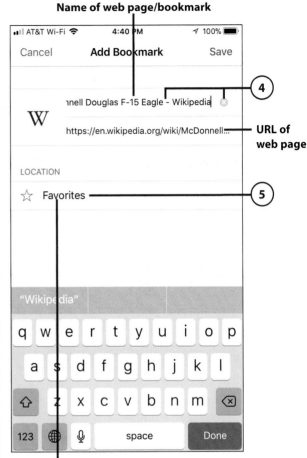

Name of web page/bookmark

URL of web page

Current bookmark location

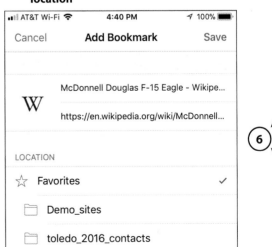

7 Tap the folder in which to store the new bookmark. You return to the Add Bookmark screen, which shows the location you selected.

8 Tap Save. The bookmark is created and saved in the location you specified. You can use the bookmark to return to the website at any time.

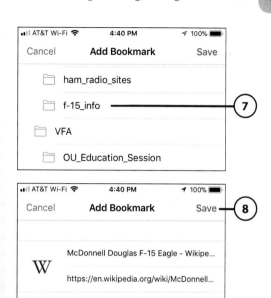

Organizing Bookmarks

You've seen how bookmarks can be contained in folders, which is a good thing because you're likely to have a lot of them. You can change the names and locations of your existing bookmarks and folders as follows:

1 Move to the Bookmarks screen showing the bookmarks and folders you want to change. (You can't move among the Bookmarks screens while you are in Edit mode so you need to start at the location where the items you want to change are located.)

2 Tap Edit. Unlock icons appear next to the folders and bookmarks you can change (some folders can't be changed and you won't see controls for those folders). The Order icons also appear on the right side of the screen, again only for folders or bookmarks you can change.

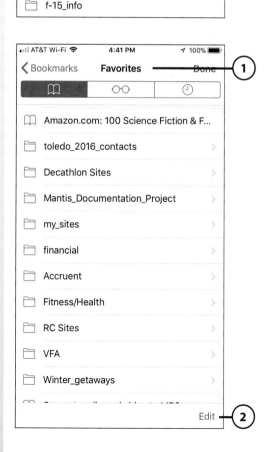

3 Drag the Order icon next to the bookmark or folder you want to move up or down the screen to change the order in which it appears on the screen. When you drag a folder or bookmark between other items, they slide apart to make room for the folder or bookmark you are dragging. The order of the items in the list is the order in which they appear on the Bookmarks screen.

4 Tap a folder to change its name or location.

5 Change the name in the name bar.

6 To change the location of the folder, tap the Location bar, which shows the folder's current location.

Can't Move?

If you have only one bookmark you've added, you can't move them around as described here because Safari won't let you "disturb" the default bookmarks and folders (such as Favorites). You can only delete default bookmarks.

7 Swipe up and down the list of folders until you see the folder in which you want to place the folder you are working with.

8 Tap the folder into which you want to move the folder you are editing.

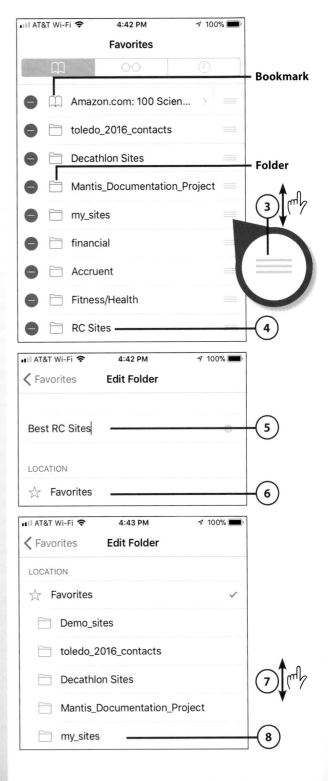

9 Tap the Back icon, which is labeled with the location from which you came. You move back to the prior Bookmarks screen, which reflects any changes you made.

10 Tap a bookmark you want to change.

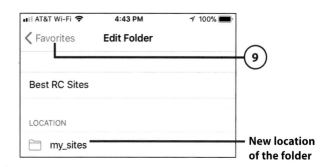

New location of the folder

Editing a Bookmark

If the bookmark you want to change isn't on the Bookmarks screen you are currently viewing, tap Done to exit Edit mode. Then open the folder containing the bookmark you want to change and tap Edit. You are able to change the bookmark.

11 Change the bookmark's name in the name bar.

12 If you want to change a bookmark's URL, tap the URL bar and make changes to the current URL. For example, you might want to change it to have the bookmark point to a site's home page rather than the page you are viewing.

13 To change the location of the folder or bookmark, tap the Location bar and follow steps 7 and 8.

14 Tap Done. You move back to the previous screen, and any changes you made—such as changing the name or location of a bookmark—are reflected.

15 Tap New Folder to create a new folder.

16 Enter the name of the folder.

17 Follow steps 6–8 to choose the location in which you want to save the new folder.

18 Tap Done. The new folder is created in the location you selected. You can place folders and bookmarks into it by using the Location bar to navigate to it.

19 Tap Done. Your changes are saved, and you exit Edit mode.

Browsing Both Ways

As you browse, make sure you try both the horizontal and vertical orientations. Safari sometimes offers different features in the two orientations on different models. For example, when you open the Bookmarks screen and rotate an iPhone 6 Plus, 6s Plus, or 7 Plus, the screen is divided into two panes. On the left is the Bookmarks pane you are viewing and the right pane shows the web page you were browsing. If you tap a bookmark, the web page in the right pane becomes the page at which the bookmark points.

Deleting Bookmarks or Folders of Bookmarks

You can get rid of bookmarks or folders of bookmarks you don't want any more by deleting them:

1. Move to the screen containing the folder or bookmark you want to delete.

2. Swipe to the left on the folder or bookmark you want to delete.

3. Tap Delete. The folder or bookmark is deleted. Note that when you delete a folder, all the bookmarks it contains are deleted, too.

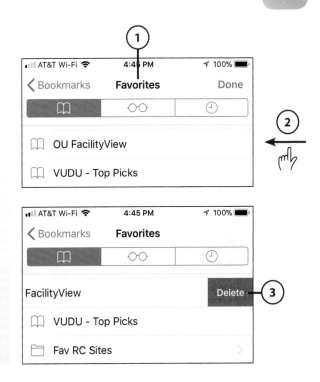

Using 3D Touch with Safari

Like other default iPhone apps, Safari supports 3D Touch (iPhone 6s and later models), which you can use in a couple of ways.

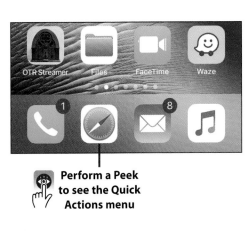

Perform a Peek to see the Quick Actions menu

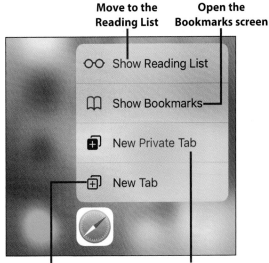

Move to the Reading List   Open the Bookmarks screen

Open a new tab and allow the sites to be tracked   Open a new tab in which the sites won't be tracked

When you press and hold on the Safari app's icon, you see the Quick Actions menu. You can select from among its options to quickly perform actions in Safari. For example, choose New Tab to open a new tab in which you can navigate to a web page, or choose Show Bookmarks to jump to the Bookmarks page.

Perform a Peek on links you are browsing

When you see this, you can swipe up the screen to see options

Perform a Pop to open the web page

Tap an action to perform it

When you are browsing links, such as when you have performed a search, or your bookmarks, press on a link or a bookmark in which you are interested to perform a Peek on it. In the Peek window, you see the web page for the link or web page on which you peeked. If you continue to press on the Peek, it pops open so you can view the web page in Safari. When you perform a Peek on some screens, such as the links resulting from a search, you see an upward-facing arrow at the top of the screen; this indicates you can swipe up the screen to reveal a menu of commands. Tap a command to perform it. For example, tap Open in New Tab to open the web page in a new tab in Safari.

Sharing Web Pages

Safari makes it easy to share web pages that you think will be valuable to others. There are many ways to share, including AirDrop, Message, Mail, Twitter, and Facebook. A couple of examples will prepare you to use any of them.

Emailing a Link to a Web Page

You can quickly email links to web pages you visit.

1. Use Safari to navigate to a web page whose link you want to email to someone.

2. Tap the Share icon.

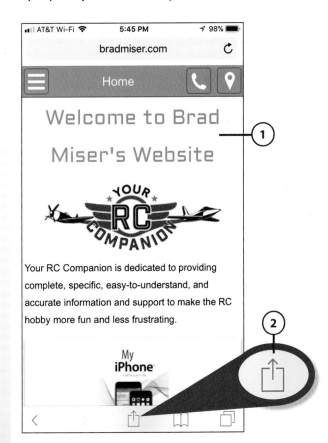

(**3**) Tap Mail. A new email message is created, and the link to the web page is inserted into the body. The subject of the message is the title of the web page.

(**4**) Complete and send the email message. (Refer to Chapter 8, "Sending, Receiving, and Managing Email," for information about the Mail app.) When the recipient receives your message, he can visit the website by tapping the link included in the email message.

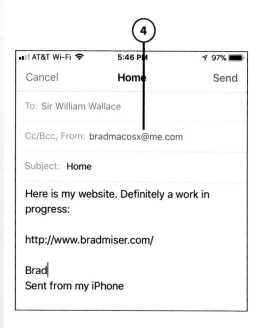

Messaging a Web Page

If you come across a page that you want to share with someone via Messages, Safari makes it easy.

1. Use Safari to navigate to a web page whose link you want to message to someone.

2. Tap the Share icon.

3. Tap Message. A new message is created, and the link to the web page is inserted.

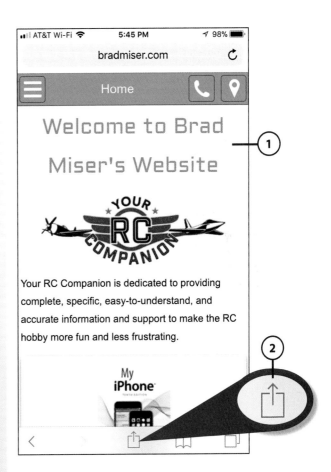

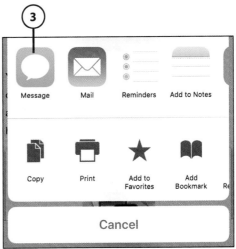

4. Address the message.

5. Enter text you want to send along with the link to the web page.

6. Tap the Send icon. Your message is sent. The recipients can visit the web page by tapping the link included in the message.

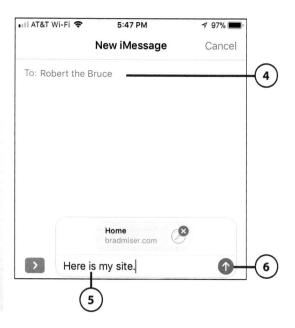

>>>Go Further
MORE WAYS TO SHARE THE WEB

If you want to share a web page in the old-fashioned way, you can print it by opening the Share menu and tapping Print (assuming you have your iPhone set up to print, as explained in Chapter 2, "Using Your iPhone's Core Features"). If you tap Copy, the web page's address is copied to the clipboard, so you can paste it into documents, emails, notes, or messages. You can also share web pages via Twitter and Facebook.

Signing In to Websites Automatically

If you enable Safari to remember usernames and passwords, it can enter this information for you automatically. When Safari encounters a site for which it recognizes and can save login information, you are prompted to allow Safari to save that information. This doesn't work with all sites; if you aren't prompted to allow Safari to save login information, you can't use this feature with the site you are visiting. When saved, this information can be entered for you automatically.

1. Move to a web page that requires you to log in to an account.

2. Enter your account's username and password.

3. Tap the icon to log in to your account, such as Continue, Sign In, Submit, Login, and such. You are prompted to save the login information.

4. Tap Save Password to save the information. The next time you move to the login page, your user-name and password are entered for you automatically. Tap Never for This Website if you don't want the information to be saved and you don't want to be prompted again. Tap Not Now (you won't always have this option) if you don't want the information saved but do want to be prompted again later to save it.

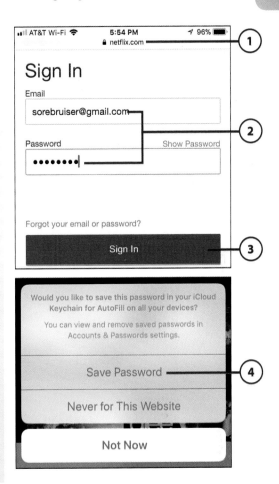

>>>*Go Further*

LETTING SAFARI CREATE PASSWORDS FOR YOU

If you have enabled the Names and Passwords setting, Safari can create passwords for you. Go to a website that requires you to create a password, such as when you register for a new account. When you tap in a field that Safari recognizes as requiring a password, tap Suggest Password. Safari presents a password for you; most of these are not easy to remember, but that doesn't matter because it is saved for you automatically so you won't have to enter it manually. If you want to use the recommended password, tap Use Suggested Password; Safari enters the password in the password and verify password fields. When syncing is enabled, the password is stored on the synced devices, too, so you are able to sign in from those devices just as easily.

Take photos and video

Configure
Camera
settings

Take photos and video and quickly
send them to others

In this chapter, you explore all the photo and video functionality that your iPhone has to offer. Topics include the following:

→ Getting started
→ Setting Camera preferences
→ Using the Camera app to take photos and video with your iPhone

Taking Photos and Video with Your iPhone

The iPhone's cameras and Camera app capture high-quality photos and video. Because you'll likely have your iPhone with you at all times, it's handy to capture photos with it whenever and wherever you are. And, you can capture video just as easily.

Whether you've taken photos and video on your iPhone or added them from another source, the Photos app enables you to edit, view, organize, and share your photos. (To learn how to use the Photos app with the great photos and video you take, see Chapter 14, "Viewing and Editing Photos and Video with the Photos App.") You'll likely find that taking and working with photos and videos are among the most useful things your iPhone can do.

Getting Started

Each generation of iPhone has had different and more sophisticated photo and video capabilities and features than the previous versions. All current versions sport high-quality cameras; in fact, there is a camera on each side of the iPhone. One takes photos of what you are looking at (the back-facing camera, located on the backside of the phone), whereas the other takes photos of what the screen is facing (the front-facing camera, which is usually for taking selfies, located on the face of the phone).

Current generations also have a flash; can zoom; take burst, panoramic, and time-lapse photos; and have other features you expect from a high-quality digital camera. The iPhone 6s and later models can also take Live Photos, which capture a small amount of video along with the photo.

The iPhone 7 and later models have image stabilization, more resolution, and other enhancements to enable them to take even higher quality photos and video with both the back-facing and front-facing cameras.

The iPhone 7 Plus, 8 Plus, and X have two back-facing cameras: one is the wide-angle camera that all models have (in different versions depending on the model), and the other camera has a telephoto lens. These two cameras give these models unique photo capabilities, including a Telephoto mode that enables you to capture much better quality photos using both optical zoom and software zoom. They also enable you to take Portrait photos in which the subject is in very sharp focus and the background in a soft blur.

The iPhone's photo and video capabilities and features are probably the largest area of differences between the various models. Because of the fairly large variation in capabilities of iPhone models that can run iOS 11, it's impossible to cover all the differences in this chapter; the iPhone 7 and 8 are used for the step-by-step tasks in this chapter. If you have a different model, some of the tasks described might not be applicable to you, or some of the details in this chapter might be different than what you see on your iPhone if it is an older model. However, all models can do most of the tasks in this chapter so even if you don't have an iPhone 7 or 8, you can still take lots of different kinds of photos and videos using the information in this chapter.

Have an iPhone 7 Plus, 8 Plus, or X?

The iPhone 7 Plus, 8 Plus, and X have some amazing photographic features and are significantly more advanced than the iPhone 7 and 8 in this area. If you have one of these models, you can get detailed step-by-step tasks to help you learn to take advantage of their unique features in the online supplement *My iPhone X*. You can download this supplement from www.informit.com/myiphoneseniors. Of course, these models can do all of the tasks described in this chapter, so its content will help you take great photos and videos just like the iPhone 7 and 8 can.

Additionally, the iPhone's photo and video capabilities have been increasingly tied into iCloud. For example, you can store your entire photo library under your iCloud account; this offers many benefits, including backing up all your photos, making it easy to access your photos from any device, and being able to quickly share your photos with others. Therefore, I've assumed you are using iCloud and have configured it to work with photos as described in Chapter 3, "Setting Up and Using an Apple ID, iCloud, and Other Online Accounts." Like differences in iPhone camera capabilities, if you don't use iCloud with your photos, some of the information in this chapter doesn't apply to you and what you see on your phone might look different than what you see in this chapter.

Setting Camera Preferences

The following table describes options in the Settings app that you can access by tapping Settings, and then tapping Camera. The default settings allow you to take photos and video without making any changes to these settings, but it's good to know where they are and what they do if you decide to change how your apps work.

Settings App Explained

To get detailed information on using the Settings app, see "Working with the Settings App" in Chapter 2, "Using Your iPhone's Core Features."

iPhone 7 Plus, 8 Plus, and X

Because of their unique capabilities, these models of iPhone have slightly different Camera settings than those shown in the table. Refer to the online supplement *My iPhone X* by going to www.informit.com/myiphoneseniors for the details of configuring the Camera settings on these models.

Camera Settings

Section	Setting	Description
Preserve Settings	Camera Mode	When this switch is on (green), the Camera app retains the mode you most recently used, such as VIDEO or PANO. When off (white), the camera is reset to the PHOTO mode each time you move into the Camera app.
Preserve Settings	Filter	When this switch is on (green), the Camera app retains the filter you most recently used, such as DRAMATIC. When off (white), the camera is reset to the ORIGINAL filter each time you move into the Camera app.
Preserve Settings	Live Photo	When this switch is on (green), the Camera app retains the Live Photo setting you used most recently, such as Off. When off (white), Live Photo is turned on automatically each time you move into the Camera app.
N/A	Grid	When this switch is on (green), you see a grid on the screen when you are taking photos with the Camera app. This grid can help you align the subject of your photos in the image you are capturing.
N/A	Scan QR Codes	When this switch is on (green), you can use the Camera app to scan QR codes that provide information about the object to which they are attached or with which they are associated. For example, many zoos and museums put QR codes on their exhibits; you can use your iPhone's camera to quickly scan these QR codes to get information about what you are looking at. When this switch is off (white), this feature is disabled.

Section	Setting	Description
N/A	Record Video	Use the options under this menu to determine how video is recorded. The options available depend on the model of iPhone you have. You can choose from among different combinations of resolution and frame rate. Higher resolution and frame rates mean better-quality video, but also larger files.
N/A	Record Slo-mo	The selections under this menu determine the resolution and frame rate for slow-motion video. Like regular video, the higher the resolution and frame rate, the better quality the resulting video is and the larger the file sizes are.
Formats	CAMERA CAPTURE	Choose High Efficiency if you want your photos to be captured in the HEIF/HEVC format so they use less storage space. Not all devices and apps can use this format, but any that are related to the iPhone (such as iPads and Macs) should be able to. This format results in smaller file sizes so you can store more photos on your iPhone. If you use photos on other types of devices or if you want to make sure your photos are compatible with as many devices and apps as possible, choose Most Compatible instead.
HDR (High Dynamic Range)	Keep Normal Photo	When this switch is on (green), the HDR (read more about this in a later sidebar) and the normal version of photos are stored. When this switch is off (white), only the HDR version of the photo is stored.

Photos Settings

You should use the Photos settings to determine what happens with your photos and videos after you capture them, such as if they are stored in your iCloud Photo Library and if photos are optimized for storage on your iPhone. See the section "Configuring Photos Settings" in Chapter 14 for a detailed explanation of these settings.

Using the Camera App to Take Photos and Video with Your iPhone

You use the Camera app to take photos and video with your iPhone. This app has a number of controls and features. Some features are easy to spot, whereas others aren't so obvious. By the end of this section, you'll know how to use these features to take great photos and video with your iPhone.

The general process for capturing photos or video follows:

1. Choose the type of photo or video you want to capture.

2. Set the options for the type of photo or video you selected.

3. Take the photos or video.

4. View and edit the photos or video you captured using the Photos app.

The information you need to accomplish steps 1 through 3 of this process is provided in tables and tasks throughout this chapter. The details for step 4 are provided in Chapter 14.

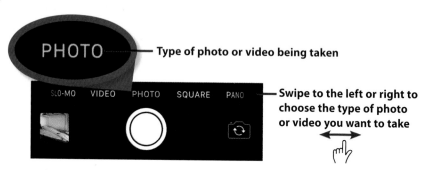

PHOTO ———— **Type of photo or video being taken**

———— **Swipe to the left or right to choose the type of photo or video you want to take**

The first step in taking photos or video is to choose the type of photo or video that you want to capture. You do this by swiping to the left or right on the selection bar just above the large Shutter icon at the bottom of the Camera app's screen, as shown in the previous figure. The option shown in yellow at the center of the screen just above the Shutter icon is the current type of photo or video you are capturing. The options available in the Camera app are explained in the following table.

Types of Photo and Video iPhones Can Capture

Type of Photo or Video	Description
TIME-LAPSE	Captures a video with compressed time so that the time displayed in the video occurs much more rapidly than "real time." This is what is often used to show a process that takes a long time, such as a plant growing, in just a few seconds.
SLO-MO	Takes slow-motion video so that you can slow down something that happens quickly.
VIDEO	Captures video at a real-time speed. The steps to take video are provided in the task "Taking Video," later in this chapter.
PHOTO	Captures still photos (or Live Photos on iPhone 6s/6s Plus or later models). Step-by-step instructions showing how to use this option are provided in the task "Taking Photos," later in this chapter.
SQUARE	Takes "square" photos in which the height and width are the same.
PANO	Takes panoramic photos that enable you to capture very wide images. An example of capturing a panoramic photo is provided in the task "Taking Panoramic Photos," later in this chapter.

Telephoto and Portrait Photos

The iPhone 7 Plus, 8 Plus, and X can also capture telephoto and portrait photos. The step-by-step instructions to take telephoto or portrait photos are provided in the online supplement *My iPhone X* that you can download by going to www.informit.com/myiphoneseniors. The icons you see on the screen when capturing these types of photos are also explained in the supplement.

When you choose the type of photo or video you want to take, there are quite a few options you can select (the options available to you depend on the specific model of iPhone you are using). When you select options, the icons you see on the screen change to reflect your selection. For example, when you choose a self-timed photo, the Self-timer icon changes to show the time delay you have selected. And, not all options are available at the same time. For example, you can't set the flash and HDR to go on at the same time because you can't take HDR images with the flash.

The following table describes the icons and tools available on the Camera app's screen. (Remember that the specific icons and tools you see depend on the type of photo or video you are capturing and the model of iPhone you are using.)

Photo and Video Options and Icons

Icon	Description
⚡	**Flash**—When you tap this icon, you see a menu with the flash options, which are Auto (the app uses the flash when required), On (flash is always used), or Off (flash is never used). Tap the option you want to use and the menu closes. When the flash is set to on, the icon is yellow.
⚡	**Flash Being Used**—When this icon appears on the screen, it indicates the flash will be used when taking a photo or video.
HDR	**High Dynamic Range (HDR)**—Tap this to set the HDR options. (You learn more about HDR in the "More on Taking Photos and Video" Go Further sidebar later in this chapter.) The options are Auto, On, or Off. When the flash is set to on, this is disabled and you see a line through the HDR icon because you can't use the flash with HDR images.
◉	**Live Photo on**—When this feature is enabled, you take Live Photos (see the "Live Photos" note following this table) and the Live Photos icon is yellow. To turn Live Photos off, tap this icon.
◉	**Live Photo off**—When disabled, you take static photos and the Live Photos icon is white. To turn Live Photos on, tap this icon.
⏱ ⏱	**Self-timer**—When you tap this icon, a menu appears on which you can choose (3s or 10s) a 3- or 10-second delay for photos. When you choose a delay, the icon is replaced with one showing the delay you set. When you tap the Shutter icon, the timer starts and counts down the interval you selected before capturing the image.

Icon	Description
	Filter—When you tap this icon, a filter selection bar appears above the Shutter icon. You can swipe on this bar to see the filters available, with the name of the filter in the center box appearing above it. You can choose from such filters as DRAMATIC WARM and VIVID COOL. Then tap a filter to apply it to the photo or video you are capturing. For example, you can apply the NOIR filter to give the photo a cool Noir-movie look. When you apply a filter, you see the image with the filter applied and you see the name of the filter above its preview on the Filter selection bar. Generally, it's better to apply filters after you take a photo so that you have an original, unfiltered version of the photo (this is covered in the task "Applying Filters to Photos" in Chapter 14).
 	Filter applied—When the Filter icon is in color, you know a filter is currently applied. You also see the filter highlighted on the selection bar. When you capture a photo using the filter, the filter preview is marked with a white dot. Tap the Filter icon to close the filter selection bar. To remove a filter, tap the Filter icon, select the ORIGINAL filter, and tap the Filter icon.
	Change Camera—When you tap this icon, you toggle between the back-facing and front-facing camera (the front-facing camera is typically used for selfies).
◯	**Shutter**—This icon changes based on the type of photo or video you are taking. For example, when you are taking a photo, this icon is white as shown. When you take a video, it becomes red. It looks a bit different for other types as well, such as Time-Lapse. Regardless of what the icon looks like, its function is the same. Tap it to start the process, such as to take a photo or start capturing video. If applicable, tap it again to stop the process, such as stopping video capture. To take burst photos, you touch and hold it to capture the burst.
00:00:06	**Timer**—When you capture video, the timer shows the elapsed time of the video you are capturing. The red dot on the left side of the time indicates you are currently capturing video.

Icon	Description
	Focus/exposure box—When you frame an image, the camera uses a specific part of the image to set the focus, exposure, and other attributes. The yellow box that appears on the screen indicates the focus/exposure area. You can manually set the location of this box by tapping on the part of the image that you want the app to use to set the image's attributes. The box moves to the area on which you tapped and sets the attributes of the image based on that area.
	Exposure slider—When you tap in an image you are framing, the sun icon appears next to the focus/exposure box. If you tap this icon, you see the exposure slider. Drag the sun up to increase the exposure or down to decrease it. The image changes as you move the slider so you can see its effect immediately.
AE/AF LOCK	**AE/AF Lock**—When you tap an image to set the location of the focus/exposure box and keep your finger on the screen after a second or so, the focus and exposure become locked based on the area you selected. This icon indicates that the exposure and focus are locked so you can move the camera without changing the focus or exposure that is used when you capture the image. Tap the screen to release the lock and refocus on another area.
	Faces found—When your iPhone detects faces, it puts this box around them and identifies the area as a face. You can use faces to organize photos by applying names to the faces in your photos.
	**Zoom slider**—You can unpinch on an image to zoom in or pinch on an image to zoom out. When you do, the Zoom slider appears on the screen. This indicates the relative level of zoom you are applying. You can also drag the slider toward the – to zoom out or drag it toward the + to zoom in.

And Now a Few Words on Live Photos

The iPhone 6s/6s Plus and later models can capture Live Photos. A Live Photo is a static image, but it also has a few of what Apple calls "moments" of video around the static image that you take. To capture a Live Photo, you set the Live function to on (it is on by default and its icon is yellow) and take the photo as you normally would. When you are viewing a Live Photo you have taken (these photos have the LIVE icon on them), touch and hold on the photo to see the motion associated with that photo. When you aren't touching and holding on a Live Photo, it looks like any other photo you've taken (except that it is marked with the LIVE icon).

Taking Photos

You can use the Camera app to capture photos, like so:

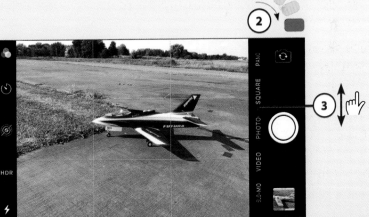

(1) On the Home screen, tap Camera.

(2) To capture a horizontal photo, rotate your iPhone so that it's horizontal; of course, you can use either orientation to take photos just as you can with any other camera.

(3) Swipe up or down (right or left if the phone is vertical) on the selection bar until PHOTO is in the center and in yellow.

(4) If you want to change the camera you are using, tap the Change Camera icon. When you change the camera, the image briefly freezes, and then the view changes to the other camera. The front-facing camera (the one facing you when you look at the screen) has fewer features than the back-facing camera has. These steps show taking a photo with the back-facing camera.

(5) Set the Flash, HDR, Live, and Self-timer options you want to use for the photo; see the previous table for an explanation of these options.

Part of the image being used to set brightness, focus, and exposure

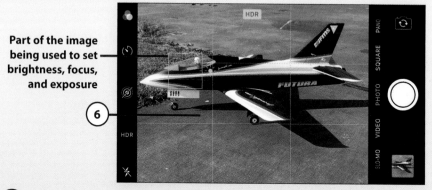

(6) Frame the image by moving and adjusting the iPhone's distance and angle to the object you are photographing; if you have the Grid turned on, you can use its lines to help you frame the image the way you want it. When you stop moving the phone, the Camera app indicates the part of the image that is used to set focus, brightness, and exposure with the yellow box. If this is the most important part of the image, you are good to go. If not, you can set this point manually by tapping where you want the focus to be (see step 9).

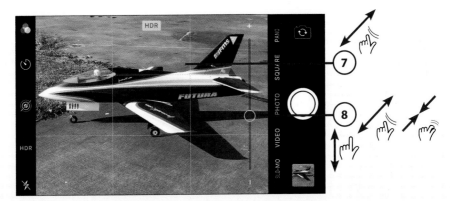

7 Zoom in by unpinching on the image. The camera zooms in on the subject and the Zoom slider appears.

8 Unpinch on the image or drag the slider toward the + to zoom in or pinch on the image or drag the slider toward the – to zoom out to change the level of zoom until it's what you want to use.

9 Tap the screen to manually set the area of the image to be used for setting the focus and exposure. The yellow focus box appears where you tapped.

10 To change the exposure, swipe up on the sun icon to increase the brightness or down to decrease it.

11 Continue making adjustments in the framing of the image, the zoom, focus point, and brightness until it is the image you want to take.

12 Tap the Shutter icon on the screen, either Volume button on the side of the iPhone, or press the center button on the EarPods. The Camera app captures the photo, and the shutter closes briefly while the photo is recorded. When the shutter opens again, you're ready to take the next photo.

13 Tap the thumbnail to see the photo you most recently captured.

(14) Use the photo-viewing tools to view the photo (see Chapter 14 for the details).

(15) If you don't want to keep the photo, tap the Trash icon to delete a photo, and then tap Delete Photo.

(16) Edit the photo by tapping Edit and using the resulting editing tools to make changes to the picture (again, see Chapter 14 for the details).

(17) Tap the Back icon. You move back into the Camera app and can take more photos.

Taking Panoramic Photos

The Camera app can take panoramic photos by capturing a series of images as you pan the camera across a scene, and then "stitching" those images together into one panoramic image. To take a panoramic photo, perform the following steps:

(1) Open the Camera app.

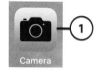

2 Swipe on the selection bar until PANO is selected. On the screen, you see a bar representing the entire image that contains a smaller box representing the current part of the image that will be captured.

3 Tap the Shutter icon. The app begins capturing the image.

4 Slowly sweep the iPhone to the right while keeping the white arrow centered on the yellow line on the screen (if you move the phone too fast, you see a message on the screen telling you to slow down). The better you keep the tip of the arrow aligned with the yellow line, the more consistent the centerline of the resulting image will be.

5 When you've moved to the "end" of the image you are capturing or the limit of what you can capture in the photo, tap the Shutter icon. You move back to the starting point and the panoramic photo is created. You can tap the panoramic image's thumbnail to view, delete, or edit it just as you can with other types of photos.

Current position in the image

The shaded bar indicates the total possible area that can be included in the image

As you move the iPhone from the start of the image to the end, keep the arrow centered on the yellow line

This box shows the image you've captured so far

Taking Video

You can capture video as easily as you can still images. Here's how.

① Open the Camera app.

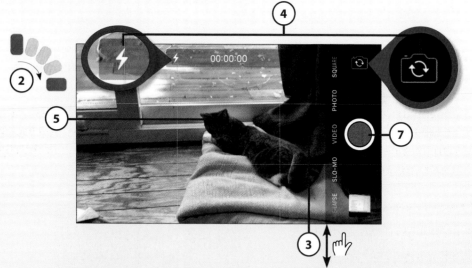

② To capture horizontal video, rotate the iPhone so that it's horizontal; of course, you can use either orientation to take video just as you can with any other video camera.

③ Swipe on the selection bar until VIDEO is selected.

④ Choose the back-facing or front-facing camera, configure the flash, or zoom in, just like setting up a still image. (The Self-timer, Grid, and HDR mode are not available when taking video.)

⑤ Tap on the screen where you want to focus.

⑥ If needed, adjust the exposure by sliding the "sun" icon up or down just like a still photo (not shown on the figure).

⑦ Tap the Shutter icon to start recording. You hear the start/stop recording tone and the app starts capturing video; you see the timer on the screen showing how long you've been recording.

Length of video

8 Take still images while you take video by tapping the white Shutter icon. (If the Live Photos preference is enabled, the photos you take are Live Photos. If not, you take static images.)

9 Stop recording by tapping the red Shutter icon again. Also, like still images, you can then tap the video's thumbnail to preview it as well as any still images you took while taking the video. You can use the Photos app's video tools to view or edit the clip. (These tasks are also explained in Chapter 14.)

Taking Photos and Video from the Lock Screen

Because it is likely to be with you constantly, your iPhone is a great camera of opportunity. You can use its Quick Access feature to quickly take photos when your iPhone is asleep/locked. Here's how:

1 When the iPhone is locked, press the Side button, touch the Touch ID/Home button, or lift your phone up (if you have a model that supports the Raise to Wake feature and it is enabled). The Lock screen appears.

2 Swipe to the left. The Camera app opens.

(**3**) Use the Camera app to take the photo or video as described in the previous tasks. You can only view the most recent photos or videos you captured from within the Camera app when your iPhone is locked; you have to unlock the phone to work with the rest of your photos.

Taking Photos and Video from the Control Center

You can get to the camera quickly using the Control Center, too.

(**1**) Swipe up from the bottom of the Home screen (all models except the iPhone X) or swipe down from the upper-right corner of the screen (iPhone X, not shown in the figure) to open the Control Center.

(**2**) Tap the Camera icon. The Camera app opens.

(**3**) Use the Camera app to take photos or video as you've learned in the previous tasks (not shown in the figures).

Taking Photos with Quick Actions (Models with 3D Touch)

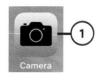

On iPhone 6s/6s Plus and later models, the Quick Access menu offers a selection of photos and video commands that you can choose right from a Home screen.

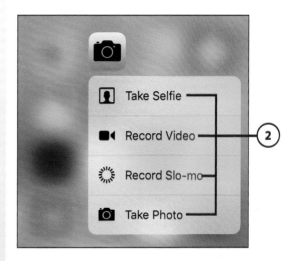

(1) Touch and hold on the Camera icon until the Quick Actions menu opens.

(2) Tap the type of photo or video you want to take. The Camera app opens and is set up for the type you selected.

(3) Use the Camera app to capture the photo or video (not shown in the figures).

Scanning QR Codes

QR (Quick Response) codes provide information about or enable you to take action on objects to which they are attached or associated. A QR scanner reads these codes and presents the information they contain. For example, rental cars usually have a QR code sticker on a window; when you scan this code, you get information about the car you are renting.

QR codes also enable you to take action, such as scanning the QR code for a Wi-Fi network and then joining it, scanning the code for an email address and then creating an email, and so on.

The Camera app can scan QR codes. After the code is scanned, you are prompted to take action on it.

The following steps show scanning a QR code for a rental car; scanning other types of QR codes is similar:

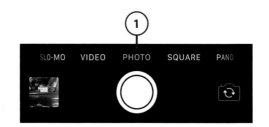

1. Open the Camera app and put it in either Photo or Square mode.

2. Frame the QR code in the camera.

3. Tap on the code to focus on it. You see a prompt about the code you scanned.

4. Tap the prompt to take action on it.

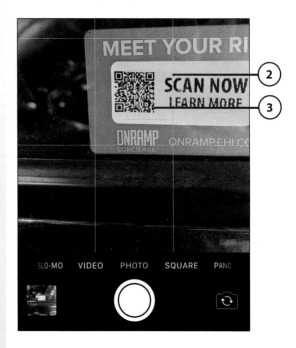

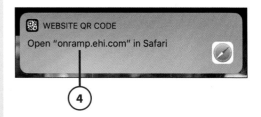

5 Complete the task you started in step 4 based on the type of code you scanned. For example, when you scan the QR code on a rental car, you might move to a website with information about the vehicle you rented. If the code is for a Wi-Fi network, you join that network. If the code contains an email address, you move into Mail and can complete the email to that address.

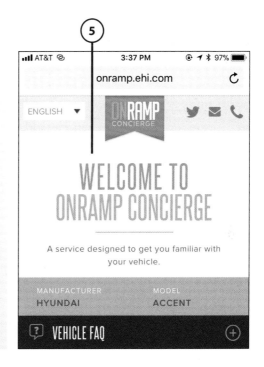

>>>Go Further
MORE ON TAKING PHOTOS AND VIDEO

The iPhone enables you to do all sorts of interesting and fun things with photos and video. Following are some additional pointers that help you make the most of this great app:

- **Set and forget**—You need to set the Flash, HDR, and most other options only when you want to change the current settings because these settings are retained even after you move out of the Camera app and back into it. The Camera Mode, Filter, and Live Photo behaviors are controlled by the Preserve Settings described earlier in this chapter.

- **HDR**—The High Dynamic Range (HDR) feature causes the iPhone to take three shots of each image with each shot having a different exposure level. It then combines the three images into one higher-quality image. HDR works best for photos that don't have motion and where there is good lighting. (You can't use the iPhone's flash with HDR images.) Also, HDR photos take longer to capture.

When the Keep Normal Photo switch in the Camera Settings is on (green), you see two versions of each HDR photo in the Photos app: One is the HDR version, and the other is the normal version. If you prefer the HDR versions, set the Keep Normal Photo switch to off (white) so that your photos don't use as much space on your iPhone, and you don't have twice as many photos to deal with.

HDR photos display the HDR icon in the upper-left corner when you view them.

- **Location**—The first time you use the Camera app, you are prompted to decide whether you allow it to use Location Services. If you allow the Camera app to use Location Services, the app uses the iPhone's GPS to tag the location where photos and video were captured. Some apps can use this information, such as the Photos app on your iPhone, to locate your photos on maps, find photos by their locations, and so on.

- **Sensitivity**—The iPhone's camera is sensitive to movement, so if your hand moves while you are taking a photo, it's likely to be blurry; iPhone 6 Plus and later models have image stabilization that mitigates this to some degree. Sometimes, part of the image will be in focus and part of it isn't, so be sure to check the view before you capture a photo. This is especially true when you zoom in. If you are getting blurry photos, the problem is probably your hand moving while you are taking them. Of course, because it's digital, you can take as many photos as you need to get it right; delete the rejects as you take them and use the Photos app to periodically review and delete photos you don't want to keep (see Chapter 14), so you don't have to waste storage room or clutter up your photo library with photos you don't want to keep.

- **Burst photos**—When you touch and hold on the Shutter icon while taking photos, a series of images is captured rapidly and you see a counter showing the number being taken. When you release the Shutter icon, a burst photo is created; the burst photo contains all of the images you captured but appears as a single image in the Photos app. You can review the images in the burst and choose to keep only the images you want to save (this task is also covered in Chapter 14).

- **Self-timer**—When you set the Self-timer option, you choose either a 3- or 10-second delay between when you tap the Shutter icon and when the image is captured. Like the other settings, the Self-timer is persistent, so you need to turn it off again when you want to stop using it.

- **Self-timer and burst**—If you set the timer, and then touch and hold on the Shutter icon for a second or so, a burst of ten photos is captured when the timer expires.

- **Slow-motion video**—You can also take slow-motion video. Choose SLO-MO on the selection bar. Set up the shot and take the video as you do with normal speed video. When you play it back, the video plays in slow motion except for the very beginning and ending. (The speed of the video is determined by the Record Slo-mo setting, described earlier.)

- **Time-lapse video**—When you choose the TIME-LAPSE option, you can set the focus and exposure level and choose the camera you want to use. You record the video just like "real time" video. When you play it back, the video plays back rapidly so you seemingly compress time.

- **Screenshots**. You can take screenshots of your iPhone's screen by pressing and holding the Touch ID/Home and Side buttons at the same time (all models except the iPhone X) or pressing and holding the Side button and upper Volume button (iPhone X). The screen flashes white and the shutter sound plays to indicate the screen has been captured. You see a thumbnail of the screen capture. You can tap this to open the screen capture to edit it; when you're finished editing it, tap Done to close the preview (tap Save to Photos to save it or Delete Screenshot if you don't want to save it). If you don't tap the thumbnail, after a couple of seconds, it disappears (you can swipe it off the screen to get rid of it immediately).

If you didn't preview the screenshot, it automatically is saved. If that happened or you chose to save the preview in the editor, the resulting image is stored in the Screenshots album. You can view the screen captures you take, email them, send them via Messages, or other tasks as you can with photos you take with the iPhone's camera.

View, edit, and share photos,
slideshows, and video

Use Messages, Mail,
and other apps to
share your photos
and video

In this chapter, you explore all the photo- and video-viewing and editing functionality that your iPhone has to offer. Topics include the following:

→ Getting started
→ Configuring Photos settings
→ Viewing, editing, and working with photos on your iPhone
→ Viewing, editing, and working with video on your iPhone
→ Using iCloud with your photos

Viewing and Editing Photos and Video with the Photos App

Chapter 13, "Taking Photos and Video with Your iPhone," explains how to take photos and video using the iPhone's Camera app. The photos and video you take with your iPhone's cameras are stored in your photo library, which you can access using the Photos app. In this chapter, you learn how to use the Photos app to view, organize, edit, and share those photos and videos.

Getting Started

The Photos app provides many useful tools that you can use to view and edit photos and video stored on your iPhone, whether you used the iPhone's camera to capture them or you downloaded them from another source, such as images attached to email messages.

As you take photos, capture video, and download photos or video onto your iPhone, you can quickly build up a large photo library. Fortunately, the Photos app automatically organizes your photos and video so that you can find specific photos or video you want to view, edit, or share quite easily. You can also manually organize photos in albums with just a few steps.

After you locate photos and video in which you are interested, you can view them in the app manually or you can use the amazing Memories feature to see collections of photos and video based on location, dates, people, and other factors.

You can edit photos and videos to fix mistakes or to just make improvements in them. You can even use additional photo editors, such as the Markup tool that enables you to draw on or add text to your photos.

You'll probably want to share photos and videos with others, and the Photos app makes that a snap, too. You can do that through other apps on your iPhone, such as Messages, or directly using iCloud's Photo Sharing tools.

Even though the Photos app provides lots of features you can use with your photos and video, it isn't hard to use, as you'll see throughout the rest of this chapter.

Configuring Photos Settings

The following table describes options in the Settings app that you can access by tapping Settings, and then tapping Photos. You can likely work with the Photos app without changing any of these, but it's good to know what and where these settings are in case you want to make changes.

Settings App Explained

To get detailed information on using the Settings app, see "Working with the Settings App" in Chapter 2, "Using Your iPhone's Core Features."

Photos Settings

Section	Setting	Description
Siri & Search	Siri & Search Suggestions	When this switch is enabled (green), information in the Photos app can be searched, used when you perform Look Ups on terms, and by Siri. If you set this switch to off (white), Photos information is not used for search or Siri Suggestions.
N/A	iCloud Photo Library	When enabled, your photos and videos are stored in your iCloud account on the cloud so that they are backed up and you can access them from multiple devices. See Chapter 3, "Setting Up and Using an Apple ID, iCloud, and Other Online Accounts," for information about configuring iCloud for your photos and video.
N/A	Optimize iPhone Storage	If you select this option, only versions of your photos that are optimized for the iPhone are stored on your phone; this saves space so that you can keep more photos and videos on your iPhone. Full resolution photos are uploaded to the cloud.
N/A	Download and Keep Originals	This option downloads and stores full resolution versions of your photos and videos on your iPhone. They consume a lot more space than optimized versions.
N/A	Upload to My Photo Stream	When enabled, all your photos are automatically uploaded to your iCloud Photo Stream when you are connected to the Internet with Wi-Fi. New photos are also downloaded from the cloud to your iPhone and other devices with this setting enabled.
N/A	Upload Burst Photos	This setting determines if all of the photos in a burst are uploaded to the cloud or only photos you tag as favorites are uploaded. Because burst photos can take up a lot of space, it's usually better to leave this disabled. If you leave this disabled, when you select favorite photos in a burst series, only those photos are uploaded.
N/A	iCloud Photo Sharing	When enabled, you can share your photos with others and subscribe to other people's Photo Streams to share their photos.

Section	Setting	Description
Cellular Data	Cellular Data	When enabled (green), photos are copied to and from your iCloud Photo Library when you are using a cellular Internet connection. If you have a limited data plan, you might want to set this to off (white) so photos are copied only when you are using a Wi-Fi network.
Cellular Data	Unlimited Updates	When enabled, updates to your photos are made constantly, which uses much more data. With this disabled, updates are made periodically, which lowers the data use.
PHOTOS TAB	Summarize Photos	When this switch is on (green), you see thumbnails for only some of the photos in a collection and the timeframe of each group is larger. If you set this to off (white), you see a thumbnail of every photo in your collections, which takes up much more screen space and you have to scroll more to move among your collections. This setting affects how you see Collections view and Years view only.
MEMORIES	Show Holiday Events	With this switch enabled (green), the Photos app attempts to collect photos taken on the holidays in your country into memories. When disabled (white), the Photos app ignores holidays when it creates memories for you.
TRANSFER TO MAC OR PC	N/A	If you select Automatic, when you sync photos to a Mac or Windows PC, the compatibility of the format is changed to improve compatibility with the computer you are transferring files to.
TRANSFER TO MAC OR PC	N/A	If you choose Keep Originals, the files are transferred without checking compatibility.

iCloud Settings

The iCloud-related settings on the Photos settings screen are the same as the Photos settings under the iCloud settings area (see Chapter 3 for details).

Viewing, Editing, and Working with Photos on Your iPhone

When you work with your photos in the Photos app, you first find and view the photos that you are interested in. You can then view those photos in a number of ways including individually or in memories. Should you want to make changes to photos, a couple of taps get you into the app's amazing editing tools so you can make bad photos better, good photos great, and, well, you get the idea.

Finding Photos to Work With by Browsing

The first step in viewing, editing, or doing other tasks with photos is finding the photos you want to work with. When you open the Photos app, you see four ways to access your photos: Photos, Memories, Shared, and Albums. You can browse these sources to find photos in which you are interested.

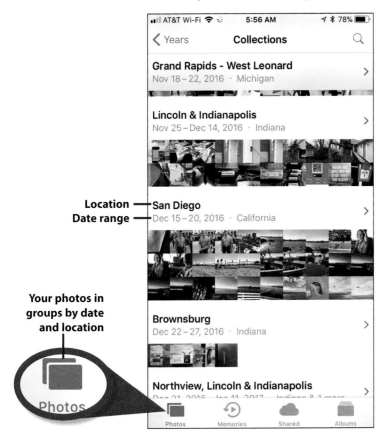

The Photos source automatically organizes photos based on the time and location associated with them (this information is embedded in the photos you take with the iPhone's camera, assuming you haven't disabled Location Services for it). The top level is Years, which shows your photos grouped by the year in which they were taken. You can then "drill down" into a year where you find collections, under which photos are organized by location and date ranges. When you tap one of these collections, you drill down and see moments, which show you the detail of a collection. At the moment level, you see and can work with the individual photos in the collection.

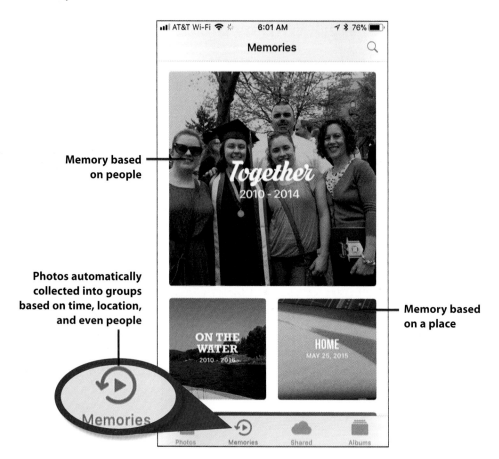

Memory based on people

Photos automatically collected into groups based on time, location, and even people

Memory based on a place

The Memories source builds collections of photos for you automatically. These collections can be based on a number of factors, such as time, location, holiday, and even people. You can view the photos in a memory individually, and the app builds slideshows automatically to make viewing your photos more interesting.

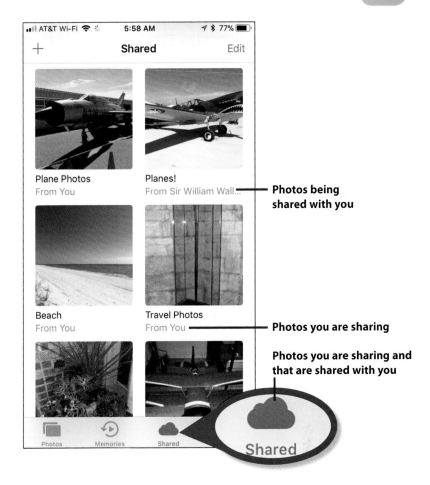

Shared shows photos you are sharing with other people and photos other people are sharing with you. For each group of photos being shared, you see the name of the group and who is sharing it (you, for photos you are sharing, or the name of the person sharing with you). When you tap a shared group, you see the photos it contains and can work with them. (Working with photo sharing is covered in detail in "Using iCloud with Your Photos" later in this chapter.)

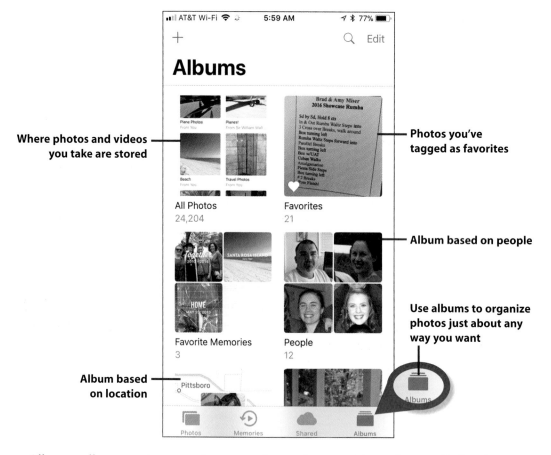

Where photos and videos you take are stored

Photos you've tagged as favorites

Album based on people

Use albums to organize photos just about any way you want

Album based on location

Albums allow you to organize your photos in a number of ways. Following are some of the albums or types of albums you might see:

- **All Photos or Camera Roll**—When you see the All Photos album, you have the iCloud Photo Library enabled so that you can use this album to see all the photos in your library. When this is not enabled, you see Camera Roll instead. When you use the iCloud Photo Library, all the photos that you've stored on the iPhone or other devices that are using the same iCloud account are stored here. If you don't use the iCloud Photo Library, the Camera Roll album contains photos and videos you've taken with the iPhone's camera or saved from other apps, such as attachments to email in Mail.

- **Favorites**—This folder contains images you have tagged as favorites by tapping their Heart icons.

- **Favorite Memories**—This folder contains memories you've tagged as favorites. This album makes it easy to get back to memories you want to view or use.

- **People**—This folder contains images based on the people in them (people are identified by the iPhone's facial recognition software).

- **Places**—This groups photos by the location at which they were captured.

- **Videos**—Videos you record are collected in this folder.

- **Live Photos**—This folder contains your Live Photos (which capture snippets of video along with the still photo).

- **Selfies**—Photos you take with the front-facing camera are stored here.

- **Panoramas**, **Slo-mo, Time-lapse, Bursts, and Screenshots**—These folders contain photos and videos of the types for which they are named.

- **Recently Deleted**—This folder is a temporary location for photos you have deleted recently. When you delete a photo, it is moved into this folder, where it remains for a period of time (how long depends on how many photos you have deleted and when you deleted them). You can recover photos from this folder if you change your mind. After the holding time passes, photos are permanently deleted and can't be recovered.

- **My Albums**—In this section, you see albums you create to manually organize photos. You can create albums for any reason and store photos within them.

Your Albums May Vary

Some apps, such as Instagram, might add their own albums to the Albums tab.

Although each of these sources looks a bit different, the steps to browse them to find the photos you want to work with are similar for most of these sources. (The Memories source is a bit different and is covered separately.) This example shows using the Photos source to browse for photos:

(1) On the Home screen, tap Photos.

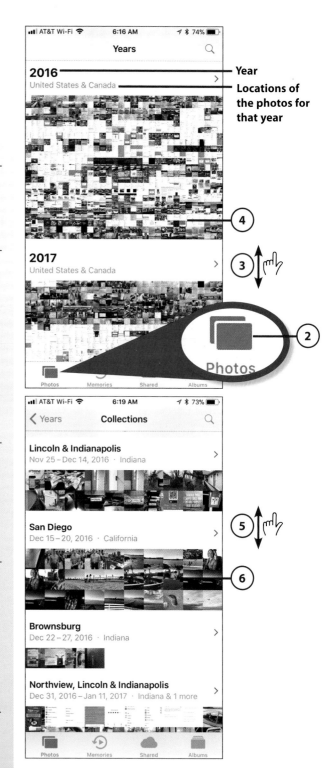

2 Tap Photos. On the Years screen, you see photos collected by the year in which they were taken. Under the year, you see a summary of the various locations where the photos were taken.

Start at the Beginning

If the title at the top of the screen isn't "Years," tap the Back icon located in the upper-left corner of the screen until it is.

3 Swipe up and down the screen to browse all the years.

4 Tap the thumbnails in the year that contains photos you want to work with. You move to the Collections screen that groups the selected year's photos based on locations and time periods.

Memories

If you want to jump directly to memories for the photos, tap a group's heading, such as the locations for a group of photos. You move into the memory view of those photos (covered later in this chapter).

5 Swipe up and down the screen to browse all the collections in the year you selected.

6 Tap the collection that contains photos you want to see. Doing so opens the Moments screen, which further breaks out the photos in the collection by location and date.

(7) Swipe up and down the screen to browse all the moments in the collection you selected.

(8) Tap a photo to view it.

(9) You're ready to view the photos in detail as described in the task "Viewing Photos Individually" later in this chapter.

Go Back

You can move back to the screens from where you came by tapping the Back icon, which is always located in the upper-left corner of the screen; this icon is named with the screen it takes you back to, it says Back, or it's just a left-facing arrow. To choose a different source, you might have to tap the Back icon a time or two as the Photos, Memories, Shared, and Albums icons at the bottom of the screen are only visible on some screens.

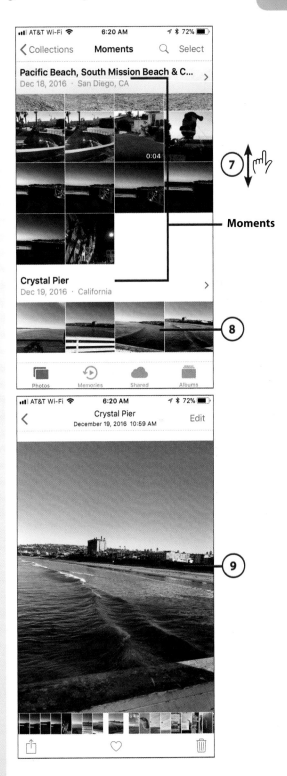

Finding Photos to Work With by Searching

Browsing photos can be a fun way to find photos, but at times you might want to get to specific photos more efficiently. The Search tool enables you to quickly find photos based on their time, date, location, and even content.

1. Continuing in the Photos app, tap the magnifying glass, which is available at the top of many of the app's screens. The Search bar opens.

2. Swipe up and down the current searches on the screen; these are created for you automatically based on your recent activity. For example, Nearby finds photos that were taken near your current location.

3. To use a current search, tap it and skip to step 5; if you don't want to use a current search, move to step 4.

4. Type your search term. This can be any information associated with your photos. As you type, collections of photos, such as location or date that match your search criteria, are listed under the Search bar. The more specific you make your search term, the smaller the set of photos that will be found.

5. Swipe up and down the screen to browse all the results.

6. Tap the results you want to explore.

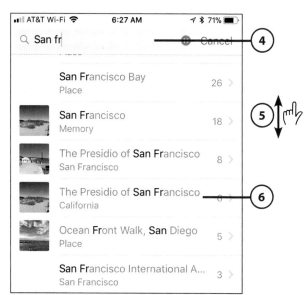

7. Tap a photo to view it.

8. View the rest of the photos in the group (covered in the next section).

9. Tap the Back icon to return to the group of photos you were viewing.

10. Tap Back to move back to the Search screen.

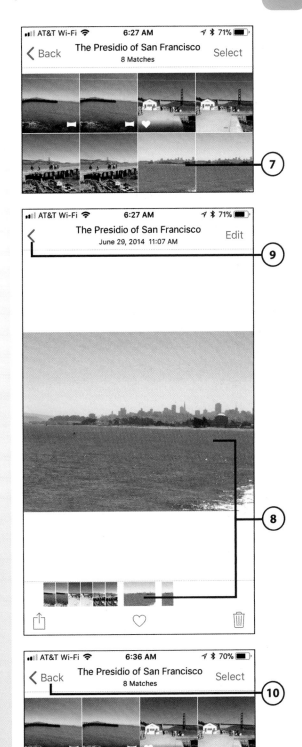

(11) Tap a different result to explore its photos.

(12) To change the search, tap in the Search bar and change the current search term (you can delete the current term by tapping the Clear [x] icon).

(13) Tap Cancel to exit the search.

Viewing Photos Individually

The Photos app enables you to view your photos individually. Here's how:

(1) Using the skills you learned in the previous tasks, open the group of photos that you want to view.

Orientation Doesn't Matter

Zooming, unzooming, and browsing photos works in the same way whether you hold your iPhone horizontally or vertically.

(2) Swipe up and down to browse all the photos in the group.

(3) Tap the photo you want to view. The photo display screen appears.

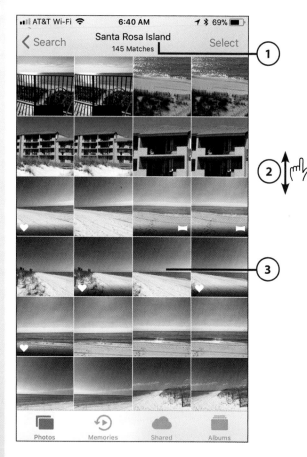

④ If it is a Live Photo, tap and hold on the screen to see the photo's motion.

⑤ To see the photo without the app's toolbars, tap the screen. The toolbars are hidden.

My, Isn't That Special?

If there is something unique about a photo, you see an icon indicating what it is on the photo when you view it. In this figure, you see the LIVE icon indicating it is a Live Photo. You might also see Burst for Burst photos, HDR for a photo captured with HDR, and so on. Keep an eye out for these icons as you explore your photos.

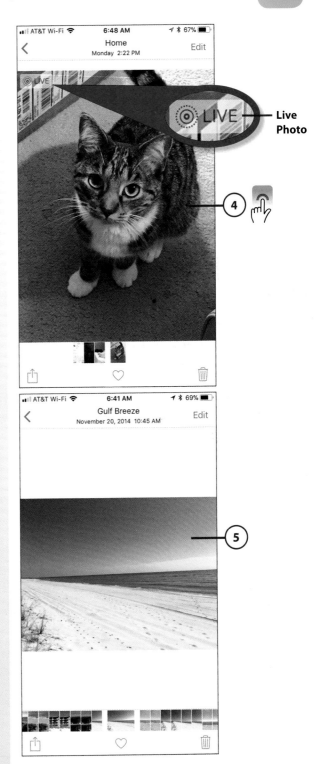

Live Photo

6 Rotate the phone horizontally if you are viewing a horizontal photo.

7 Unpinch or double-tap on the photo to zoom in.

8 When you are zoomed in, drag around the image to view different parts of the zoomed image.

9 Pinch or double-tap on the photo to zoom out.

No Zooming Please

You can't have any zoom when you swipe to move to the next or previous photo so make sure you are zoomed out all the way before performing step 10. If not, you move the photo around instead.

10 Swipe to the left to view the next photo in the group.

11 Swipe to the right to view the previous photo in the group.

12 When you're done viewing photos in the group, tap the screen to show the toolbars again.

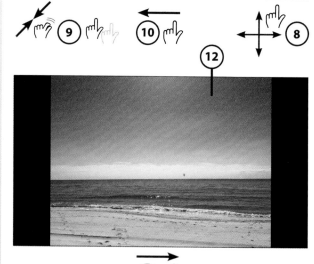

13 Swipe to the left or right on the thumbnails at the bottom of the screen to view all the photos in the current group. As you swipe, the photo you are viewing changes to be the one in the larger thumbnail at the center of the screen.

14 Tap a photo to view it.

15 Swipe up on the photo to get detailed information about it.

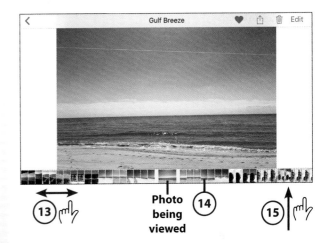

16 Tap Show Nearby Photos to see photos that were captured near the location associated with the photos you are viewing.

17 Tap the photo on the map to move to the map view (using the map view is covered in the "Working with Memories" section later in this chapter).

18 Swipe up the screen to see more details.

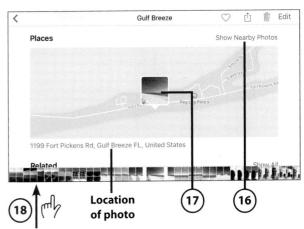

19 Tap a related memory to view it (details are provided later in this chapter).

20 Tap Show Photos from this Day to display the photos taken on the same day.

21 When you are done viewing the details, tap the Back icon.

Using 3D Touch with Photos

You can use 3D Touch (iPhone 6s and later models) to preview and open photos as follows:

1. Browse a collection of photos in the Photos app.

2. Tap and hold on a photo in which you are interested. A Peek of that photo appears.

3. To open the photo, press down slightly harder until it pops open and use the steps in the previous task to view it. (If you pop the photo open, skip the rest of these steps.)

4. To see actions you can perform on the photo preview, swipe up the image.

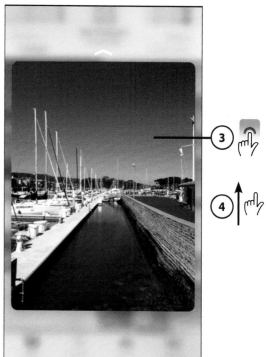

⑤ Tap the action you want to perform, such as Favorite to tag the photo as a favorite.

Working with Memories

The Memories feature automatically creates collections of photos for you to view in a number of ways. You can view them in a slideshow, individually, by selecting places, by selecting people, and so on. This feature provides lots of options and at times can be a very interesting way to view photos, because you might be surprised by some of the photos included in a particular memory.

There are a number of ways to access memories, including: tapping the Memories icon on the Dock at the bottom of the screen; tapping a heading for a group of photos when viewing years, collections, or moments; or tapping a Related item on a photo's Details page.

When you access a memory (no matter how you arrived), you see different options depending on the content of that memory. These can include:

- **Slideshow**—The photos collected in a memory play in a slideshow that plays using a theme, which has effects and a soundtrack. You can change the theme and length of the slideshow, and you can also edit it.

- **Photos**—All memories enable you to view the photos they contain just like photos collected in other kinds of groups.

- **People**—If the photos in a memory include people, the app identifies those people by facial recognition and enables you to view other photos containing those people or groups of people.

- **Groups & People**—If the photos in a memory include people that are in consistent groupings, you can use these groups to view photos containing those groupings.

- **Places**—You can use the Places tool to view the photos in a memory on a map. You can tap locations on the map where photos were taken to view those photos.

- **Related**—This section of a memory presents other memories that are somehow related to the one you are viewing. This relationship can be based on location, people, and so on.

The Photos app creates memories for you dynamically, meaning they change over time as the photos in your library change. You can save memories that you want to keep as they are. Otherwise, the memories you see change as you take more photos or edit photos you have. This keeps memories a fresh and interesting way to view your photos.

Following are examples of different ways to access memories:

- **Memories icon**—When you tap the Memories icon on the Dock, you see the Memories screen that contains the current memories the app has created and those you have saved. Tap a memory to open it.

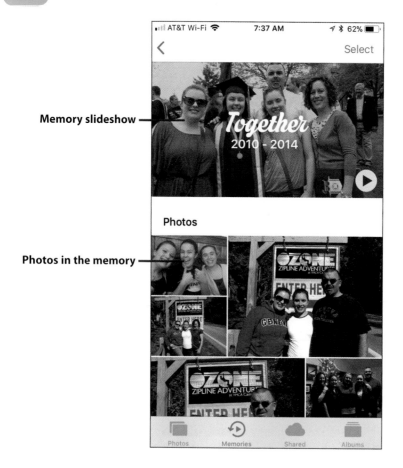

Memory slideshow

Photos in the memory

On the memory's screen, you see different tools for viewing its photos, as described in the previous list, depending on the content of the memory. For example, if there aren't any people in the photos that the app recognizes via face recognition, there won't be a People section.

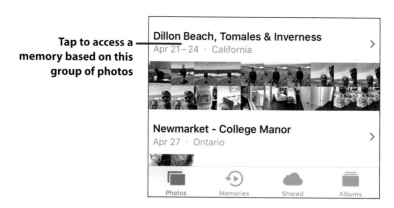

Tap to access a memory based on this group of photos

Memory containing
photos in the
selected group

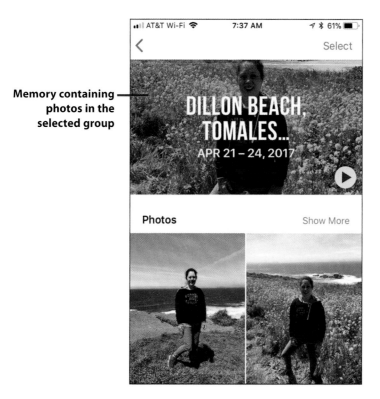

- **The heading of a group of photos**—As you learned earlier, the Photos app collects photos based on the time and location at which they were taken. As you browse these groups, you can tap on a group's heading to view the photos it contains in a memory.

You can work with memories in a similar way no matter how you open them or what kind of photos they contain. Following are examples showing how to use several of the sections you see in memories.

Watching and Changing a Memory's Slideshow

All memories have slideshows that you can watch using the following steps:

(1) Open a memory using an option described previously. Slideshows appear at the top of a memory's screen.

(2) Tap the Play icon. The slideshow begins to play. If some of the photos in the slideshow aren't currently stored on your iPhone, there might be a pause while they are downloaded (you see the Downloading status on the opening screen while this is done).

(3) To view the slideshow in landscape orientation, rotate the iPhone. As the slideshow plays, you see effects applied to the photos; videos included in the memory also play.

(4) Tap the screen to reveal the slideshow controls.

(5) To pause the slideshow, tap the Pause icon. (When paused, this becomes the Play icon that you can tap to resume the slideshow.)

(6) Swipe to the right or left on the theme bar located at the bottom of the image to change the slideshow's theme. As you change the theme you might see changes on the screen, such as a different font for the title, and hear different music while the slideshow plays.

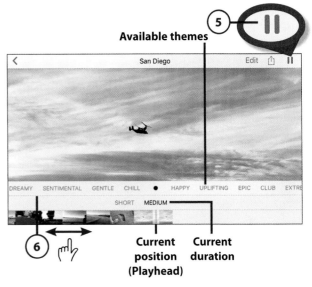

Available themes

DREAMY   SENTIMENTAL   GENTLE   CHILL   ●   HAPPY   UPLIFTING   EPIC   CLUB   EXTR

SHORT   **MEDIUM**

Current position (Playhead)   **Current duration**

7 Swipe to the right or left on the duration bar, which is located above the thumbnail images at the bottom of the screen, to change the slideshow's length. As you make changes, you see the slideshow's current length just above the theme bar.

8 Swipe to the left or right on the thumbnails at the bottom of the screen to move back or forward, respectively.

9 To restart the slideshow with the new settings, tap the Play icon.

10 Tap Edit to make manual changes to the slideshow and save the memory (see the Go Further sidebar "Make Your Own Memories" for more information).

11 Tap the Share icon and use the resulting menu to share the slideshow via AirDrop or an app; you can also save it to your iCloud Drive or Dropbox.

12 Tap the Back icon to return to the memory.

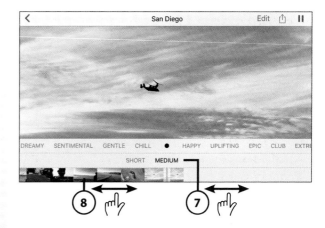

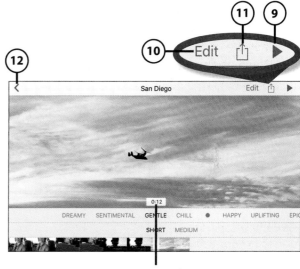

Current runtime

>>>Go Further
MAKE YOUR OWN MEMORIES

You can edit a memory's slideshow to change how it plays. Tap Edit; you might see a prompt indicating that the memory is saved to your memories; tap OK if you see this. Tap Title to change the slideshow's name and title style. Tap Title Image to change the image shown in the video's opening thumbnail. Tap Music to change its soundtrack; you can choose None to remove the soundtrack, Soundtracks to use one of the default soundtracks, or My Music to use music in your iTunes Music Library. Tap Duration to set the slideshow's playing time. Tap Photos & Videos to manually select the photos that are included; tap the Trash Can to remove a photo from the slideshow (this doesn't delete the photo from your library, only from the slideshow) or tap Add (+) to include more of the memory's photos in the slideshow (tap the Back icon when you are finished selecting photos). Tap Done to save your slideshow. When you play the slideshow, the options you selected are used. Choose Custom on the Theme bar to view the video you created.

Viewing a Memory's Photos

You can view the photos contained in a memory using the following steps:

① Open a memory using an option described previously.

② Swipe up the screen until you see the Photos section. Here you see the photos in the memory.

Show All, Tell All

If the memory has lots of photos, you might see only a summary view of them on the Photos section. Tap Show More to see all the photos. Tap Summary to return to the summary view.

3 Swipe up and down the photos section to see all the photos the memory contains.

4 Tap a photo to view it.

5 Use the techniques you learned in "Viewing Photos Individually" earlier in the chapter to work with the photos in the memory.

6 Tap the Back icon to return to the memory.

Viewing a Memory's Photos by Place

You can choose the photos in a memory to view based on the location using the Places section.

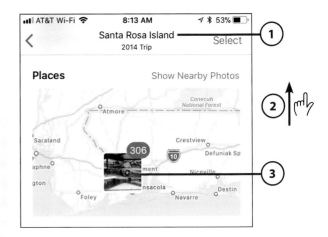

1. Open a memory using an option described previously.

2. Swipe up the screen until you see the Places section.

3. Tap a place. The map expands to fill the screen and you see more locations associated with photos in the memory.

Nearby Photos

Tap Show Nearby Photos to show other photos that were taken near the locations that you are viewing on the map, but that are not currently included in the memory. Tap Hide Nearby Photos to hide those photos again.

4. Unpinch your fingers on the screen to zoom in to reveal more detailed locations.

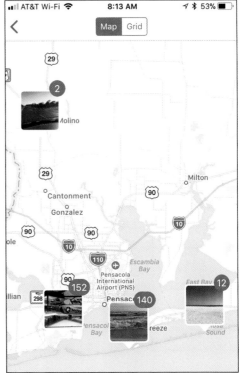

5 Swipe around the screen to move around the map.

6 Tap a location with photos to see the photos associated with it.

7 Swipe up and down the screen to browse the photos taken at the location.

8 Tap a photo to view it.

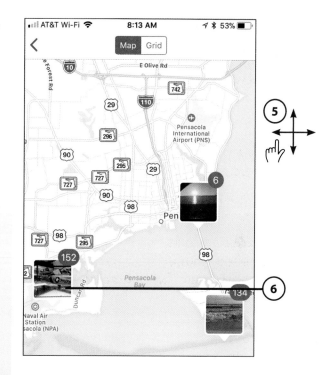

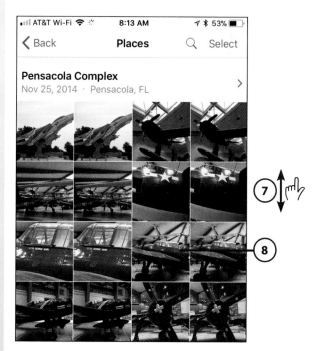

9 Use the techniques covered in "Viewing Photos Individually" earlier in the chapter to work with the photos you view.

10 Tap the Back icon to return to the place.

11 Tap Back to return to the map.

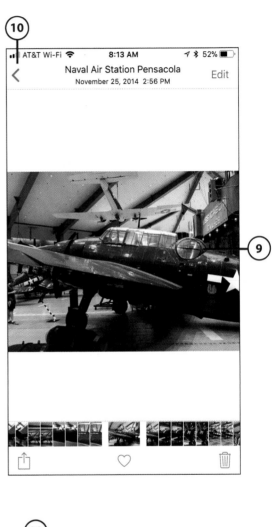

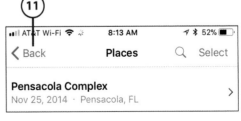

12 Tap other locations to view their photos.

13 Tap the Back icon to return to the memory.

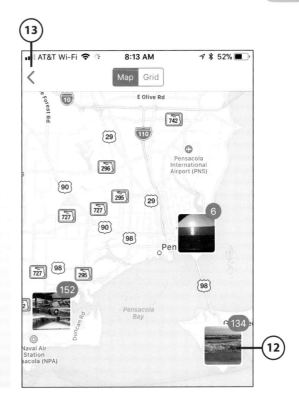

>>>Go Further

MAKING THE MOST OF YOUR MEMORIES

Here are a few more ways to make the most of your memories:

- To view memories based on people or groups of people, tap the person or group in the Groups & People or People section; you see a memory focused on the person or group you selected. Tap Add Name, enter and then tap the name of the person (if she is a contact), and tap Done. The person will be identified by name. When viewing photos containing a person, you can add more photos of a person by tapping REVIEW. You see more photos that might contain that person. Select the photos containing the person and tap Done. Any photos you confirm are added to that person's memory. (By the way, the Photos app can often identify pets in your photos and create memories focused on them.)

- Tap a memory in the Related section to see a memory that is related to the current one, such as one with photos containing the same people or in the same locations.

- Tap Add to Favorite Memories to add a memory you are viewing to the Favorite Memories album. Tap Remove from Favorite Memories to remove the memory from the Favorite Memories album.

- Tap Add to Memories to add a memory to the Memory screen. For example, when you are viewing a related memory and want to be able to get back to it quickly, tap Add to Memories. That memory appears on the Memories screen.

- Tap Delete Memory and then confirm you want to delete a memory by tapping Delete Memory again; the memory is deleted. When you delete a memory, only the memory is deleted; the photos that were in that memory remain in your photo library. (However, if you delete a photo from within a memory, that photo is deleted from your photo library, too.)

>>>*Go Further*

ROLL YOUR OWN SLIDESHOWS

The Memories feature creates slideshows that include effects and soundtracks for you automatically. However, you can create your own slideshows manually. View photos in a collection that you want to view as a slideshow; tap Select and then tap the photos you want to view in a slideshow. Tap the Share icon. Tap Slideshow. The slideshow plays. Tap the screen to show the slideshow controls. Tap Options to configure the slideshow, such as to choose music for it. When you're done configuring the slideshow, tap Done. Tap Done again when you are finished watching a slideshow.

Working with Burst Mode Photos

When you use the Burst mode to take photos, the Camera app rapidly takes a series of photos. (Typically, you use Burst mode to capture motion, where the action is happening too quickly to be able to frame and take individual photos.) You can review the photos taken in Burst mode and save any you want to keep as favorites; your favorites become separate photos just like those you take one at a time.

Here's how to identify which photos in a burst you want to keep:

1. View a Burst mode photo. Burst mode photos are indicated by the word Burst and the number of photos in the burst. (You can see all of the burst photos on your phone by opening the Bursts album.)

2. Tap Select. The burst is expanded. At the bottom of the screen, you see small thumbnails for the photos in the burst. At the top part of the screen, you see larger thumbnails of the photos; the photo in the center of the previews is marked with a downward-facing arrow. Photos marked with a dot are "suggested photos," meaning the best ones in the series according to the Photos app.

3. Swipe all the way to the right to move to the first photo in the series; swiping on the thumbnails at the bottom of the screen flips through them faster.

4. Tap a photo that you want to save. It is marked with a check mark.

5. Swipe to the left to move through the series.

6. Tap each photo you want to save; to deselect a photo so that it isn't saved, tap it so that the check mark disappears.

7. Continue reviewing and selecting photos until you've gone through the entire series.

8. Tap Done.

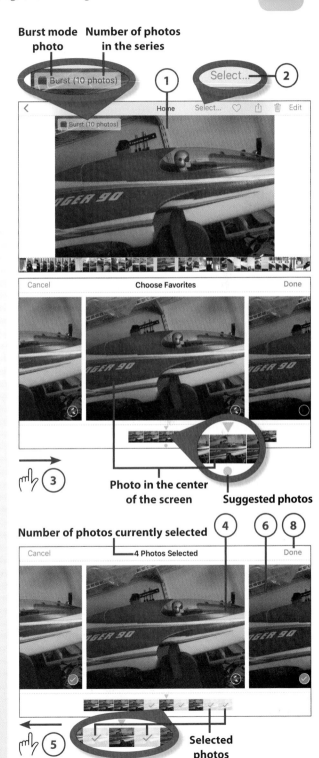

Burst mode photo
Number of photos in the series
Photo in the center of the screen
Suggested photos
Number of photos currently selected
Selected photos

9) Tap Keep Only *X* Favorites, where *X* is the number of photos you selected, or tap Keep Everything to keep all the photos in the burst. Each photo you keep becomes a separate, individual photo; you can work with these just like photos you take individually.

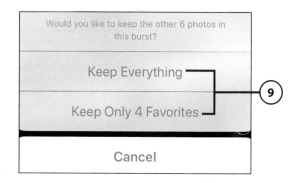

Would you like to keep the other 6 photos in this burst?

Keep Everything

Keep Only 4 Favorites

Cancel

Burst Mode Photos and Uploads to the Cloud

If the Upload Burst Photos switch on the Photos Settings screen is set to off, burst photos are not uploaded to the cloud until you go through the steps to select and save photos from a burst. The photos you selected to keep are then uploaded to the cloud just like individual photos you take.

Editing Photos

Even though the iPhone has great photo-taking capabilities, not all the photos you take are perfect from the start. Fortunately, you can use the Photos app to improve your photos. The following tools are available to you:

- **Enhance**—This tool attempts to automatically adjust the colors and other properties of photos to make them better.

- **Straighten, Rotate, and Crop**—You can rotate your photos to change their orientation and crop out the parts of photos you don't want to keep.

- **Filters**—You can apply different filters to your photos for artistic or other purposes.

- **Red-eye**—This one helps you remove that certain demon-possessed look from the eyes of people in your photos.

- **Smart Adjustments**—You can adjust the light, color, and even the black-and-white properties of your photos.

- **Markups**—You can add markups, such as redlines, drawings, and magnification to photos.

Enhancing Photos

To improve the quality of a photo, use the Enhance tool.

1. View the image you want to enhance.

2. Tap Edit.

3. Tap the Enhance icon. The image is enhanced and the Enhance icon turns yellow.

(4) If you don't like the enhancements, tap the Enhance
icon again to remove the
enhancements.

(5) Tap Done to save the enhanced
image.

**Photo is
enhanced**

Straightening, Rotating, and Cropping Photos

To change the alignment, position, and
part of the image shown, perform the
following steps:

(1) View the image you want to
change.

(2) Tap Edit.

3 Tap the Rotate/Crop icon.

4 To rotate the image in 90-degree increments, tap the Rotate tool. Each time you tap this icon, the image rotates 90 degrees in the counterclockwise direction.

5 Rotate the image within its frame by dragging the triangle to the left or right. This is often useful to straighten photos that aren't aligned quite right, but can be used for artistic effects too.

6 When the image is straightened, lift your finger from the screen. The dial shows how much you've rotated the image.

7 Crop the image proportionally by tapping the Constrain icon; to crop the image without staying to a specific proportion, skip to step 9.

8 Tap the proportion with which you want to crop the image. You use this to configure the image for how you intend to display it. For example, if you want to display it on a 16:9 TV, you might want to constrain the cropping to that proportion so the image matches the display device.

9 Drag the corners of the crop box until the part of the image you want to keep is shown in the box. If you performed step 8, the app keeps the crop box in the proportion you selected.

10 Drag on the image to move it around inside the crop box.

11 When the image is cropped and positioned as you want it to be, tap Done. The edited image is saved.

More on Straightening and Cropping Photos

To undo changes you've made, tap RESET and the photo returns to the state it was in before you started editing it. To exit the Edit mode without saving your changes, tap Cancel.

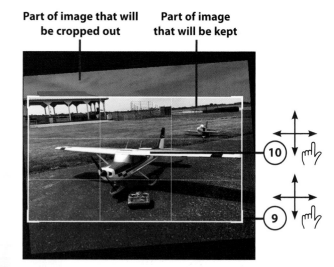

Part of image that will be cropped out **Part of image that will be kept**

Applying Filters to Photos

To apply filters to photos, do the following:

1. View the image to which you want to apply filters.

2. Tap Edit.

3. Tap the Filters icon. The palette of filters appears. If you haven't applied a filter, you see the current filter as Original.

4. Swipe to the left or right on the palette to browse all of the filters.

Filter currently applied

(5) Tap the filter you want to apply. The filter is applied to the image and you see a preview of the image as it will be with the filter; the filter currently applied is highlighted with a blue box. Keep trying filters until the image is what you want it to be.

(6) Tap Done. The photo with the filter applied is saved.

Filter currently applied

Undoing What You've Done

To restore a photo to its unedited state, tap Revert, which appears when you edit a photo that you previously edited and saved. At the prompt, tap Revert to Original, and the photo is restored to its "like new" condition.

The original version of photos is saved in your library so you can use the Revert function to go back to the photo as it was originally taken or added to the library, even if you've edited it several times.

However, you can't have the edited version and the original version displaying in your library at the same time. If you want to be able to have both an edited and original version (or multiple edited versions of the same photo), make a copy of the original before you alter it. To do this, view the photo, tap the Share icon, and tap Duplicate. You can do this as many times as you want. Each copy behaves like a new photo. If you edit one copy, the original remains available in your library for viewing or different editing.

Removing Red-Eye from Photos

When you edit a photo with people in it, the Red-eye tool becomes available (if no faces are recognized, this tool is hidden). To remove red-eye, perform the following steps:

(1) View an image with people that have red-eye.

(2) Tap Edit.

(3) Tap the Red-eye icon.

(4) Zoom in on the eyes from which you want to remove red-eye; as you zoom in, drag the photo to keep the eyes you want to fix on the screen.

5 Tap each eye containing red-eye. The red in the eyes you tap is removed.

6 Repeat steps 4 and 5 until you've removed all the red-eye.

7 Tap Done to save your changes.

Tap each red-eye

Red-eye has been corrected

Cancel   Done — 7

5

Making Smart Adjustments to Photos

You can edit your photos using the Photos app's Smart Adjustment tools. Using these tools, you can change various characteristics related to light, color, and black-and-white aspects of your photos.

1 View the image you want to change.

2 Tap Edit.

AT&T Wi-Fi   7:20 AM   95%
Home
April 8 2:29 PM   Edit — 2

1

3 Tap the Smart Adjust icon.

4 Tap the characteristic you want to change, such as Color.

Get Straight to the Point

To jump directly to a specific aspect of the area you are adjusting, tap the downward-facing arrow along the right side of the screen. On the resulting menu, tap the characteristic you want to adjust. For example, if you open this menu for Color, you tap Saturation, Contrast, or Cast to adjust those factors.

5 Swipe to the left or right to change the level of the parameter you are adjusting. As you make changes, you see the results of the change on the image.

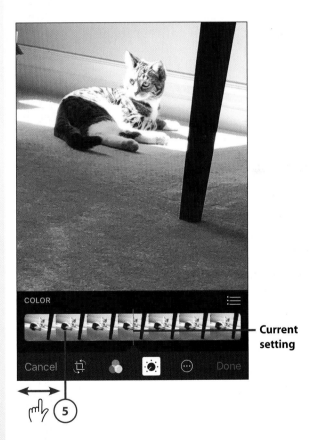

Current setting

(6) When you're done adjusting the first attribute you selected, tap the List icon.

(7) Tap one of the options under the attribute you are already working with to adjust it; or tap the downward-facing arrow under one of the other attributes, and then tap the characteristic you want to change.

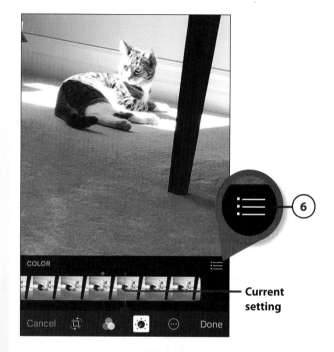

Current setting

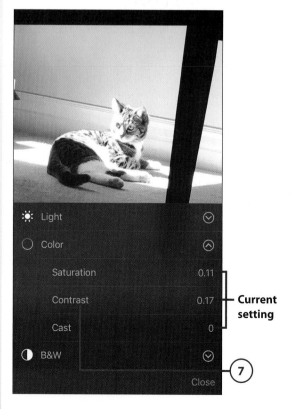

Current setting

(**8**) Swipe to the left or right to change the level of the parameter you are adjusting. As you make changes, you see the results of the change on the image.

(**9**) Repeat steps 6 through 8 until you've made all the adjustments you want to make.

(**10**) Tap Done to save the adjusted image.

Marking Up Photos

You can add markups to photos, including:

- **Draw**—You draw directly on top of photos, such as to indicate areas of interest or highlight something.

- **Magnify**—This tool magnifies a section of an image in a circle that looks kind of like an image you see through a magnifying glass.

- **Add text**—You can use the text tool to add words to an image.

With the drawing and text tools, you can choose the format of the markup, such as its color.

The following steps show the magnification and text markup tools; the drawing and other tools work similarly.

1. View the image you want to mark up.

2. Tap Edit.

3. Tap the Options (…) icon.

4. Tap Markup.

But Wait, There Might Be More

The Markup tool is the default photo editor that comes with the Photos app. Over time, other photo-editing tools will become available (check the App Store). When installed, you see them on the Photo Editing menu. Tap a tool to use it. Tap More to configure the photo-editing tools you have installed—for example, set a tool's switch to off (white) to hide it. You can also change the order in which the tools are listed on the menu.

5. Tap Add (+).

Drawing Tools

Tap the Pen or Pencil icons to draw on the photo. You can change the size and color of the lines and drag them on the screen similar to how these steps show using the text tool.

6. Tap Magnifier. The magnification circle appears.

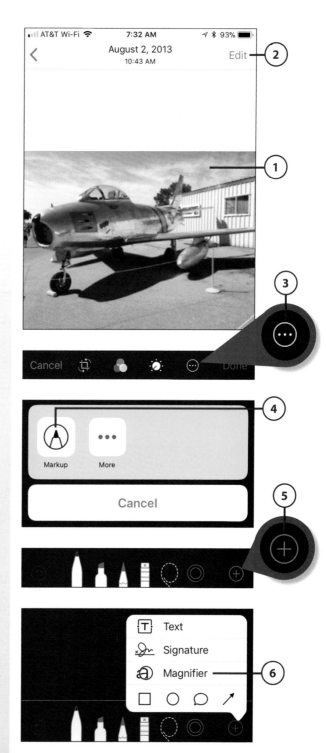

7 Drag the circle over the area of the image you want to magnify.

8 To change the size of the area being magnified, drag the blue dot away from the center of the circle to increase the area or toward the center to decrease the size of the area.

9 To change the amount of magnification being applied, drag the green dot clockwise around the circle to increase the magnification or counterclockwise to decrease it.

De-magnify

To remove a magnification markup, tap it and then tap Delete on the menu that appears.

10 Tap Add (+).

11 Tap Text. A text box appears.

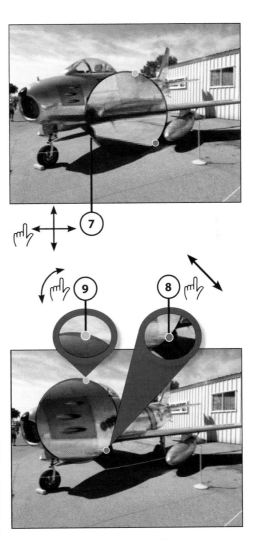

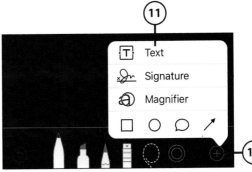

(12) Tap the text box.

(13) Tap Edit.

(14) Type the text you want to add.

(15) Tap Done.

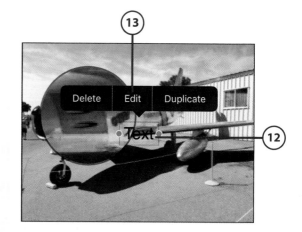

16 If it isn't selected already, tap the text.

17 Tap the Font icon.

18 Use the Font menu, Size slider, and Justification icons to format the text.

19 Tap outside the menu to close it.

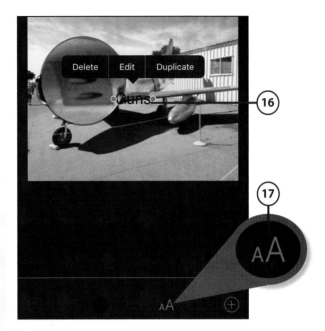

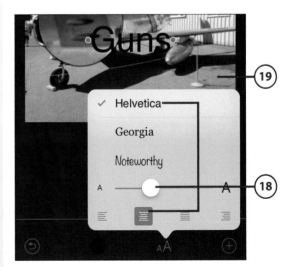

20 If it isn't selected already, tap the text.

21 Tap the Color icon (it starts as black so it is hard to see against the black background).

22 Tap the color you want to apply to the text.

23 Drag the text to where you want it to be on the photo.

24 Tap Done.

25 Tap Done to save your markups on the photo.

Editing Markups

To edit existing markups on a photo, edit the photo and open the markups tool using steps 1 through 4.

Working with Photos

Once you have photos on your iPhone, there are a lot of things you can do with them, including the following:

- Emailing one or more photos to one or more people (see the next task).

- Sending a photo via a text message (see Chapter 9, "Sending, Receiving, and Managing Texts and iMessages").

- Sharing photos via AirDrop (see the online Chapter 15, "Working with Other Useful iPhone Apps and Features").

- Sharing photos with others via iCloud (covered later in this chapter).

- Posting your photos on your Facebook wall or timeline.

- Assigning photos to contacts (see Chapter 6, "Managing Contacts").

- Using photos as wallpaper (see Chapter 5, "Customizing How Your iPhone Looks and Sounds").

- Sharing photos via tweets.
- Printing photos from your printer (see Chapter 2, "Using Your iPhone's Core Features").
- Deleting photos (covered later in this chapter).
- Organizing photos in albums (also covered later in this chapter).

Copy 'Em

If you select one or more photos and tap the Copy icon, the images you selected are copied to the iPhone's clipboard. You can then move into another app and paste them in.

You'll easily be able to accomplish any actions on your own that are not covered in detail here once you've performed a couple of those that are demonstrated in the following tasks.

Individual Versus Groups

Some actions are only available when you are working with an individual photo. For example, you might be able to send only a single photo via some apps, whereas you can email multiple photos at the same time. Any commands that aren't applicable to the photos that are selected won't appear on the screen.

Sharing Photos via Email

You can email photos via iPhone's Mail application starting from the Photos app.

1. View the source containing one or more images that you want to share.

2. Tap Select.

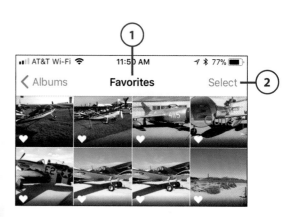

3 Select the photos you want to send by tapping them. When you tap a photo, it is marked with a check mark to show you that it is selected.

4 Tap the Share icon.

Too Many?

If the photos you have selected are too much for email, the Mail icon won't appear. You need to select fewer photos to attach to the email message.

5 Tap Mail. A new email message is created, and the photos are added as attachments.

6 Use the email tools to address the email, add a subject, type the body, and send it. (See Chapter 8, "Sending, Receiving, and Managing Email," for detailed information about using your iPhone's email tools.)

7 Tap the size of the images you want to send. Choosing a smaller size makes the files smaller and reduces the quality of the photos. You should generally try to keep the size of emails to 5MB or smaller to ensure the message makes it to the recipient. (Some email servers block larger messages.) After you send the email, you move back to the photos you were browsing.

Images from Email

As mentioned in Chapter 8, when you save images attached to email that you receive, they are stored in the All Photos or Camera Roll photo album just like photos you take with your iPhone.

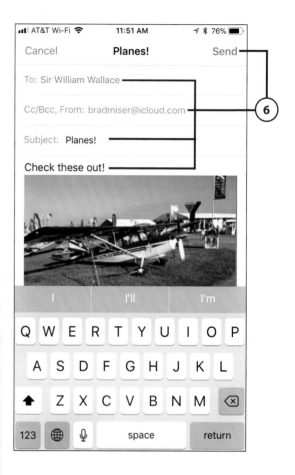

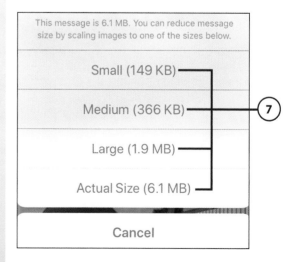

Organizing Photos in a New Album

You can create photo albums and store photos in them to keep your photos organized.

To create a new album, perform these steps:

1. Move to the Albums screen by tapping Albums on the toolbar.

2. Tap Add (+).

3. Type the name of the new album.

4. Tap Save. You're prompted to select photos to add to the new album.

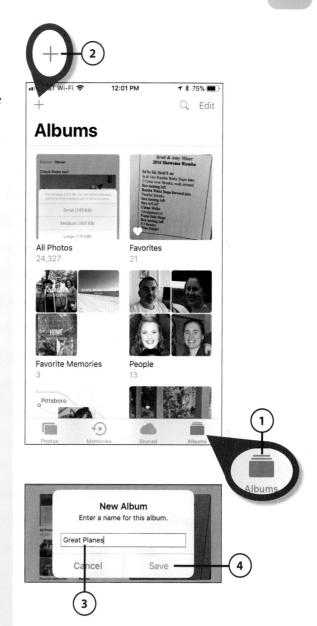

(5) Move to the source of the photos you want to add to the new album.

(6) Swipe up and down to browse the source and tap the photos you want to add to the album. They are marked with a check mark to show that they are selected. The number of photos selected is shown at the top of the screen.

(7) Tap Done. The photos are added to the new album and you move back to the Albums screen. The new album is shown on the list, and you can work with it just like the other albums you see.

Playing Favorites

To mark any photo or video as a favorite, tap its Heart icon. It fills in with blue to show you that the item you are viewing is a favorite. Favorites are automatically collected in the Favorites album, so this is an easy way to collect photos and videos you want to be able to easily find again without having to create a new album or even put them in an album. You can unmark a photo or video as a favorite by tapping its Heart icon again.

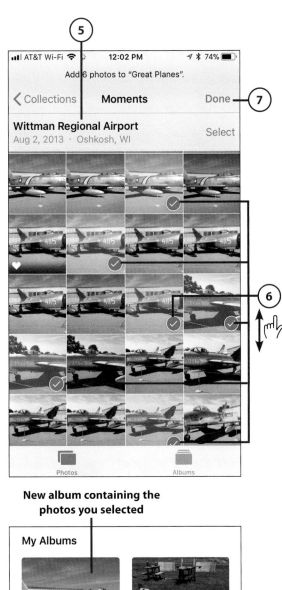

New album containing the photos you selected

Adding Photos to an Existing Album

To add photos to an existing album, follow these steps:

(1) Move to the source containing the photos you want to add to an album.

(2) Tap Select.

(3) Tap the photos you want to add to the album.

(4) Tap the Share icon.

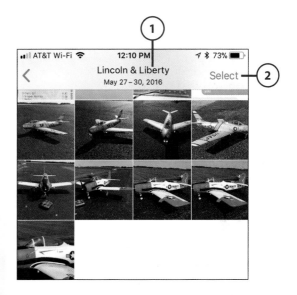

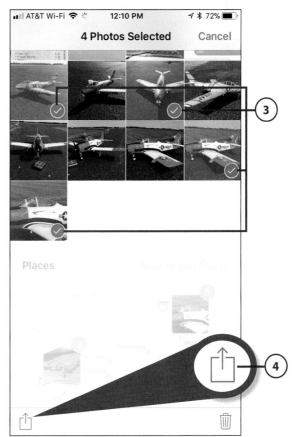

5 Swipe to the left until you see Add to Album.

6 Tap Add to Album.

7 Swipe up and down the list to find the album to which you want to add the photos.

8 Tap the album; the selected photos are added to the album. (If an album is grayed out and you can't tap it, that album was not created on the iPhone, so you can't change its contents.)

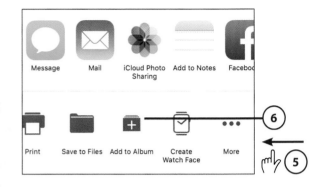

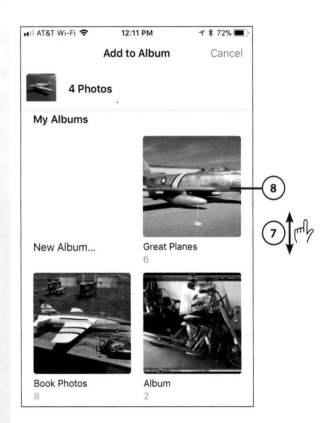

>>>Go Further

MORE ALBUM FUN

You can create a new album from photos you've already selected. Perform steps 1 through 6 and then tap New Album. Name the new album and save it. It's created with the photos you selected already in it.

You can change the order in which albums are listed on the Albums screen. Move to the Albums screen and tap Edit. Drag albums up or down the screen to reposition them. To delete an album that you created in the Photos app, tap its Unlock icon (red circle with a –) and then tap Delete Album. (This only deletes the album itself; the photos in your library remain there.) When you're done making changes to your albums, tap Done.

To remove a photo from an album, view the photo from within the album, tap the Trash Can, and then tap Remove from Album. Photos you remove from an album remain in your photo library; they are only removed from the album.

Deleting Photos

You can delete photos and videos that you don't want to keep on your iPhone. If you use the iCloud Photo Library, deleting the photos from your phone also deletes them from your photo library and from all the other devices using your library. So, make sure you really don't want photos any more before you delete them.

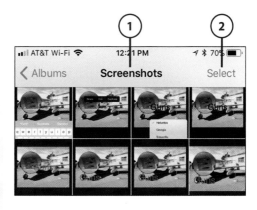

1. Open the source containing photos you want to delete.

2. Tap Select.

(3) Tap the photos you want to delete. Each item you select is marked with a check mark.

(4) Tap the Trash Can.

(5) Tap Delete *X* Photos, where *X* is the number of photos you selected. The photos you selected are deleted.

Deleting Individual Photos

You can delete individual photos that you are viewing by tapping the Trash Can, and then tapping Delete Photo.

Recovering Deleted Photos

As you learned earlier, photos you delete are moved to the Recently Deleted folder. You can recover photos you've deleted by opening this folder. You see the photos you've deleted; each is marked with the time remaining until it is permanently deleted. To restore photos in this folder, tap Select, tap the photos you want to recover, and tap Recover. Tap Recover *X* Photos, where *X* is the number of photos you selected (if you select only one, this is labeled as Recover Photo). The photos you selected are returned to the location from which you deleted them.

Deleted Means Deleted

Be aware that when you delete a photo from your iPhone, it is also deleted from your iCloud Library and all the devices sharing that library—not just from your iPhone. (After it has been deleted from the Recently Deleted folder of course.)

Viewing, Editing, and Working with Video on Your iPhone

As explained in Chapter 13, you can capture video clips with your iPhone. Once captured, you can view clips on your iPhone, edit them, and share them.

Finding and Watching Videos

Watching videos you've captured with your iPhone is simple.

1. Move to the Albums screen.

2. Tap the Videos album. Video clips display their running time at the bottom of their thumbnails. (Videos can also be stored in other albums, in collections, in memories, and so on. This Videos album collects videos no matter where else they are stored.)

3. Swipe up and down the screen to browse your videos.

4. Tap the video you want to watch.

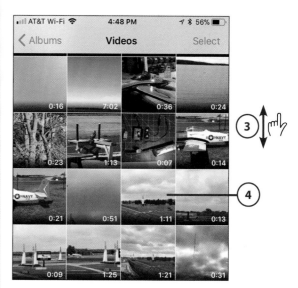

(5) Rotate the phone to change its orientation if necessary.

(6) Tap Play. The video plays. After a few moments, the toolbars disappear automatically.

(7) Tap the video. The toolbars reappear.

Deleting Video

To remove a video clip from your iPhone, select it, tap the Trash Can, and then tap Delete Video at the prompt.

(8) Pause the video by tapping Pause.

(9) Jump to a specific point in a video by swiping to the left or right on the thumbnails at the bottom of the screen. When you swipe to the left, you move ahead in the video; when you swipe to the right, you move back in the video.

Watching Slow-Motion and Time-Lapse Video

Watching slow-motion video is just like watching regular speed video except after a few frames, the video slows down until a few frames before the end at which point it speeds up again. Watching time-lapse is similar except the video plays faster instead of slower than real time.

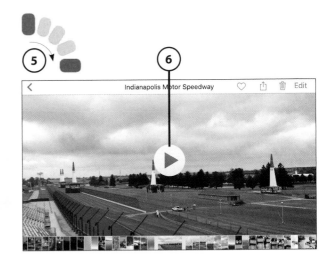

Current frame

Editing Video

You can trim a video clip to remove unwanted parts. Here's how you do it:

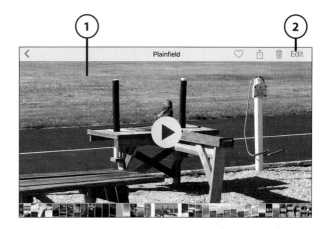

(1) View the video you want to edit.

(2) Tap Edit. If the video isn't stored on your phone, it is downloaded. When that process is complete, you can edit it.

(3) Drag the left trim marker to where you want the edited clip to start; the trim marker is the left-facing arrow at the left end of the timeline. If you hold your finger in one place for a few seconds, the thumbnails expand so your placement of the crop marker can be more precise. As soon as you move the trim marker, the part of the clip that is inside the selection is highlighted in the yellow box.

(4) Drag the right trim marker to where you want the edited clip to end.

(5) Tap Done.

(6) Tap Save as New Clip to save the trimmed clip as a new clip or Cancel to leave the clip as it was. When you save it as a new clip, the frames outside the crop markers are removed from the clip and it is added to your library as a new clip.

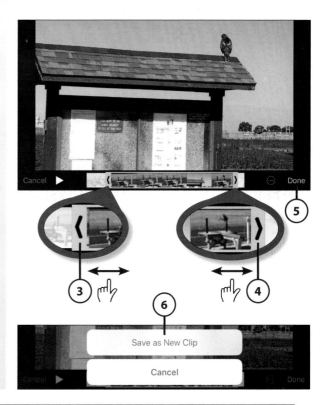

There's an App for That

For more powerful video editing on your iPhone, download the iMovie app. This app provides a much more powerful video editor. You can use themes to design a video, add music, include titles and photos, and much more.

>>>*Go Further*

SHARING VIDEO

There are lots of ways to share your videos. Select the video you want to share. Tap the Share icon. Tap how you want to share the video. There are a number of options including Messages, Mail, iCloud, iCloud Photo Sharing, YouTube, and Facebook. Follow the onscreen prompts to complete the sharing process. The options available to you might depend on the size of the video; for example, you might not be able to email a large video.

Using iCloud with Your Photos

With iCloud, your devices can automatically upload photos to your iCloud account on the Internet. Other devices can automatically download photos from iCloud, so you have your photos available on all your devices at the same time. Using iCloud with your photos has two sides: a sender and receiver. Your iPhone can be both. Photo applications (such as the Photos app on a Mac) can also access your photos and download them to your computer automatically.

In addition to backing up your photos and having all your photos available to you on all your devices, you can also share your photos and videos with others and view photos and videos being shared with you.

Sharing Your Photos

You can share your photos with others by creating a shared album. This is a great way to share photos, because others can subscribe to your shared albums to view and work with the photos you share. When you share photos, you can add them to an album that's already being shared or create a new shared album.

To create a new, empty, shared album, do the following:

1. Open the Shared source. You see the Shared screen that lists the shared albums in which you are currently participating (as either the person sharing them or subscribed to them).

2. Tap Add (+).

3. Type the title of the new album.

4. Tap Next.

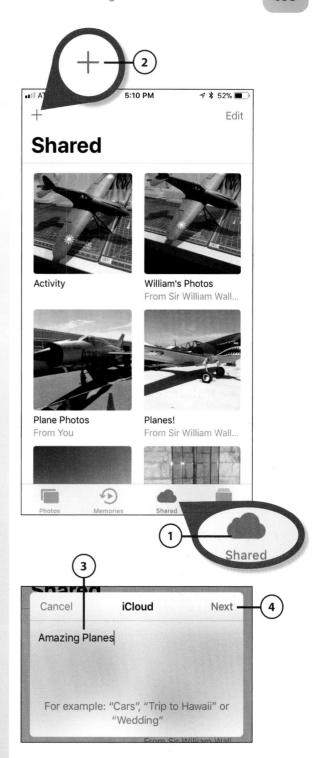

(**5**) Enter or select the email address of the first person with whom you want to share the photos.

(**6**) Add other recipients until you've added everyone you want to access the photos.

(**7**) Tap Create. The shared album is created and is ready for you to add photos. The recipients you included in the new album receive notifications that invite them to join the album.

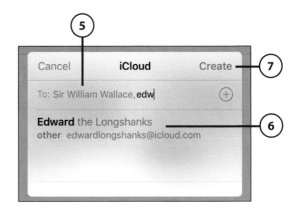

New shared album,
ready for your photos

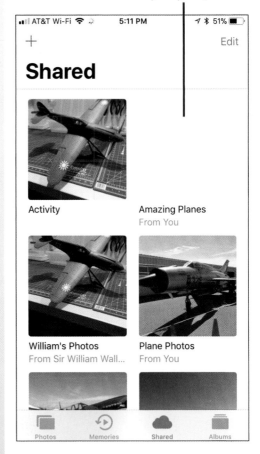

Adding Photos to a Shared Album

To add photos to an album you are sharing, perform the following steps:

1. Move to the source containing photos you want to add to a shared album.

2. Tap Select.

3. Tap the photos you want to share.

4. Tap the Share icon.

5. Tap iCloud Photo Sharing.

(6) Enter your commentary about the photos you are sharing. (Note, this commentary is associated only with the first photo.)

(7) Tap Shared Album.

(8) Swipe up and down to browse the list of shared albums available.

(9) Tap the album to which you want to add the photos.

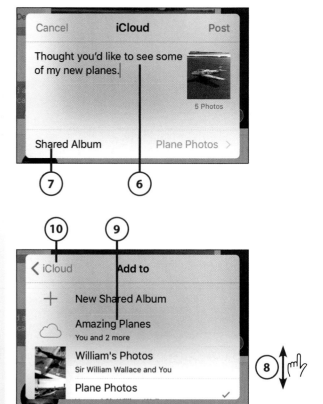

New Shared Album with Photos

You can create a new shared album with the selected photos by tapping New Shared Album.

(10) Tap iCloud.

(11) Tap Post. The photos you selected are added to the shared album. People who are subscribed to the album receive a notification that photos have been added and can view the new photos along with your commentary.

iCloud Account Required

The people with whom you share photos must have an iCloud account.

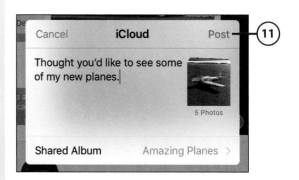

>>>Go Further

MORE ON iCLOUD PHOTO SHARING

Following are a few more pointers to help you use iCloud photo sharing:

- You can add comments to photos you are sharing. Open the shared album and tap the photo to which you want to add comments. Tap Add a comment. Type your comment and tap Send. People with whom you are sharing the photo receive a notification and can read your comments.

- To add more photos to a shared album, open the album and tap Add (+). Use the resulting screen to select the photos you want to add, include commentary, and post the photos.

- To invite people to join a shared album, open the shared album. Tap the People tab at the bottom of the screen and then tap Invite People. Enter the email addresses of the people you want to invite and tap Add.

- You can configure various aspects of a shared album by opening it and tapping the People tab at the bottom of the screen. You can see the status of people you have invited, determine if the people with whom you are sharing the album can post to it, make the album a public website, determine if notifications are sent, or delete the shared album.

Working with Photo Albums Shared with You

You can work with albums people share with you as follows:

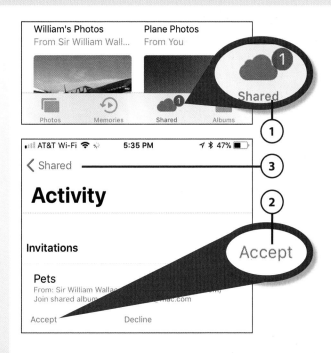

(1) Tap the notification you received, or tap the Shared source when you see a badge indicating you have activity.

(2) Tap Accept for the shared album you want to join. The shared album becomes available on your Shared tab.

(3) Tap Shared.

(4) Tap the new shared album.

(5) Tap a photo in the album.

(6) Tap Like to indicate you like the photo.

(7) Tap Add a comment. (If you previously liked the photo, you see the number of likes for it instead; tap that number to add a comment.)

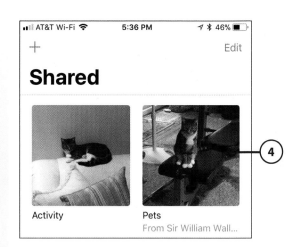

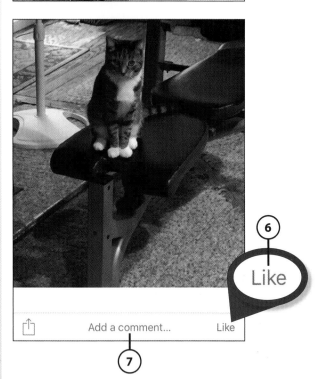

8. Type your comment.

9. Tap Send. Your comments are added to the album.

10. Tap the Back icon.

11. If the person who shared the album has allowed you to add photos to the album, tap Add (+) and post your own photos. This works just like posting to your own albums.

>>>Go Further
MORE ON PHOTOS SHARED WITH YOU

When you share other people's photos, keep the following points in mind:

- You can do most of the tasks with shared photos that you can with your own, such as emailing them, using them as wallpaper, and so on.

- To unsubscribe from an album, move to its People screen and tap Unsubscribe and confirm that is what you want to do. The shared album is removed from your iPhone.

- To see the activity associated with albums being shared with you, and those you are sharing, open the Activity Album on the iCloud Photo Sharing screen. You see new postings to the albums, when someone comments, and so on.

Glossary

3D Touch   The iPhone 6s and later models have a screen that is pressure sensitive. The 3D Touch feature enables you to press (you don't have to press hard, just apply some pressure) on the screen to perform different actions, such as opening the Quick Action menu when you press on an app's icon.

3G/4G/LTE   Names of various kinds of cellular data networks that you can use to connect your iPhone to the Internet. Your iPhone automatically uses the fastest cellular network available to it. LTE is the fastest, 4G is slightly slower, and 3G is slower than that. Because your iPhone automatically chooses a network to use, you don't need to do anything, but it is helpful to understand which network your iPhone is using.

AirDrop   Apple's technology that enables content to be easily shared among iPhones, iPads, iPod touches, and Mac computers. No complicated setup is required, you simply tap the people with whom you want to share content. For example, you can use AirDrop to quickly and easily share photos you've taken on your iPhone with other people near you. You can also use it to send content to other devices you own, such as sending a photo from your iPhone to a Mac computer.

Airplane mode   In this mode, your iPhone's cellular sending and receiving functions are disabled. You are supposed to use this mode when traveling on airplanes to ensure your iPhone doesn't interfere with the operation of the plane. You can also use it at other times, such as if you don't want to receive any phone calls.

AirPlay/Screen Mirroring   Apple's technology that enables your iPhone to broadcast to other AirPlay devices. For example, you can use AirPlay to display photos on a TV connected to an Apple TV. Or, you can show the iPhone's screen on a computer running a "reflecting" application, such as Reflector.

AirPrint   Apple's technology that enables iPhones, iPads, and iPod touches to print wirelessly without requiring any setup (such as installing printer drivers).

app   Short for application, these are programs that your iPhone runs to accomplish a wide variety of tasks. Your iPhone comes with a number of apps installed by default, such as Mail and Safari. You can download thousands of other apps from the App Store using the App Store app.

App Store   The Apple Store that enables you to find and download apps for your iPhone. The App Store app enables you to access the App Store from your iPhone.

App Switcher   The iPhone feature that enables you to quickly change apps. When you activate the App Switcher, you see the apps you are currently using or that you have recently used. You can browse the apps, and then tap one to use it. You can also use the App Switcher to force a running app to quit, such as when the app isn't performing correctly.

Apple ID   When you access iCloud, download items from the App or iTunes Stores, or access other Apple services, you need to have a user account called an Apple ID. The Apple ID consists of the email address associated with your user account and a password. You also use it to connect your iPhone to Apple services, such as iMessages.

Apple Music   Apple's subscription-based music service that enables you to use the Music app to listen to any of the music in Apple's Music Library for a monthly fee. You can listen to music by streaming it onto your iPhone. You can also download music onto your iPhone so you can listen to it without an Internet connection.

Apple Pay   This is Apple's payment service through which you can register credit and debit cards and then use those cards to make payments quickly and easily. Apple Pay is more secure than using a credit or debit card directly because your account number is not involved in Apple Pay transactions. Once configured, you can quickly pay for something by holding your phone near a register and activating the Wallet app. You can also use Apple Pay for online purchases.

badge   A red circle with a number that appears on app or folder icons that indicates the number of new "items," such as emails when it appears on the Mail app's icon or messages when it appears on the Messages app's icon.

Bluetooth   Technology that enables devices to communicate with each other wirelessly. Your iPhone uses Bluetooth to work with wireless headphones, speakers, keyboards, automobile audio systems, and much more. Using a Bluetooth device is a two-step process. First, pair the device with your phone. Second, connect to the Bluetooth device you want to use.

cellular data network   The technology that enables your iPhone to communicate data similarly to how it can place a phone call. This enables your iPhone to access the Internet from just about any location in the world. Your provider offers various types of cellular data networks that have different speeds. Your iPhone automatically manages its cellular data connection, but you can determine when the connection is used by enabling or disabling it. Cellular data is provided with your account. Many plans have a limit on the amount of data you can use per month. If you exceed this amount, you have to pay additional fees. Some accounts have unlimited data, which means you can use as much data as you want without additional charges (sometimes, surpassing a threshold results in your iPhone's connection being limited to lower speeds until the next billing cycle).

Control Center   When you swipe up from the bottom of the iPhone's screen (all models except iPhone X) or swipe down from the upper-right corner of the screen (iPhone X), the Control Center appears. You can use its controls to do things such as enabling or disabling features or modes, such as Airplane mode. You can also configure some of the icons you see on the Control Center so that you have quick access to the ones you find most useful.

Do Not Disturb mode In this mode, your iPhone doesn't ring or make other noises or sounds caused by notifications. This keeps your iPhone from bothering you at times you don't want it to, such as when you are sleeping. You can set exceptions so that important calls come in even when Do Not Disturb is turned on.

emoji Icons, such as a smiley face, that are used in emails and text messages to indicate emotion or to show an object (for example, using an icon of an airplane instead of writing the word *airplane*). The iPhone includes many emojis you can use. You can access even more by downloading and installing apps.

Face ID Introduced with the iPhone X, this is the ability for your iPhone to record "your face" on your phone so that it recognizes you. You can then perform a number of actions by "looking" at your phone. For example, you can configure Face ID so that you can unlock your iPhone by looking at its screen. (Other iPhone models support Touch ID instead.)

Facebook A social media service that people and organizations use to share information. Facebook users have a "page" on which they can present information about themselves along with photos and videos. Other people, who have been tagged as "friends," can view that information and exchange comments. Facebook is available on the iPhone through the Facebook app. It can also be used with a web browser, such as Google Chrome or Safari, on a computer.

FaceTime The app and service that enables you to easily have video conversations with others. You can use the iPhone's camera to share video content, either in "selfie" mode where your image appears on the screen or you can "show" people other images using the camera on the backside of the iPhone. The FaceTime app makes it very easy to have video conversations; you simply select the person you want talk to and see; the app handles the details for you. You can receive FaceTime requests and respond to them just like answering a phone call.

Fetch Your iPhone can receive many different kinds of information from the Internet, such as new emails, contacts, and so on. Fetch is when your iPhone retrieves information from various servers (such as email servers) at specific intervals; for example, every 15 minutes. Fetch uses less battery than Push does.

Find My iPhone The Apple service that can track the location of your iPhone and enable you to protect your iPhone by locking or erasing it. You can track your iPhone using the Find iPhone app on an iOS device, such as an iPad, or using a web browser, such as Safari or Google Chrome, on a computer.

haptic feedback   iPhone 7 and later models provide vibratory feedback for certain events. For example, when you make a selection, such as date, the phone vibrates slightly to confirm you have made a selection.

Home screens   The screens on your iPhone where app icons are stored. The Home screens are the starting point for most of the tasks you learn about in this book.

iCloud   An Apple service that provides storage space on the Internet and a host of features that enable you to share information, such as contacts and calendars, among many devices. iCloud is integrated into the iPhone; you need an account to use it (an iCloud account is free). One of the best uses for iCloud is to store photos and videos because they are backed up so you don't lose them even if something happens to your iPhone, and you can access your photos and videos from many different devices. iCloud also makes it easy to share photos and videos with other people.

iMessage   Apple's messaging service that enables you to send messages to other iMessage users. Unlike traditional text messages, iMessages are sent over the Internet, so don't have limits on the content or quantity of messages you can send. You send and receive iMessages using the Messages app. Those messages can contain text, photos, videos, graphics, and just about any other content you want to share.

Instagram   People use this social media service to share photos, video, and messages with others. You can install the Instagram app on your iPhone to make using Instagram easy and convenient.

iOS   The name of the operating system software that controls your iPhone (and iPads) and enables it to do so many wonderful things. The current version is the eleventh major release of the software, which is why it is called iOS 11.

iTunes Store   The Apple Store that provides content you can use on your iPhone, including music and movies. You can download this content using the iTunes Store app. You pay for most of the content in the iTunes Store, but you can sample most of it for free to decide if you want to purchase it. After it is downloaded, you can view or listen to the content in the associated app. For example, you can listen to music you download in the Music app.

Lightning   Apple's technology for connecting accessories, such as a charger or EarPods, to the iPhone. The iPhone has a Lightning port on the bottom side.

Lock screen   To secure the information on your iPhone, it can be locked so that a passcode is required to use most of its functionality. When you wake up a phone, you see the Lock screen that enables you to unlock the phone. You can also perform some tasks on the Lock screen, such as accessing the Widget Center.

Multi-touch interface   The technology that enables you to control and use an iPhone by touching your fingers to its screen.

Notification Center   The Notification Center displays all the notifications that have been issued recently so you can easily review them and get more detail for items in which you are most interested. You can open the Notification Center by swiping down from the top of the screen when the iPhone is unlocked or swiping up from the center of the screen when it is locked.

Notifications   There is a lot of activity happening on your iPhone. Notifications keep you informed about this activity. Notifications can be visual, audible, or vibratory. You can determine the types of notifications you receive for various events, such as when you receive new emails. You can even set up notifications for specific people, such as a sound when you receive a text from someone important.

passcode   A numeric or alphanumeric sequence that is required to unlock an iPhone to make full use of it. It is important to configure a passcode on your iPhone to secure the information stored there. You can use Touch ID or Face ID so that you don't have to enter your passcode each time you need to use it. Instead, you can touch the Touch ID/Home button (all models except iPhone X) or look at your iPhone's screen (iPhone X).

Peek   A 3D Touch movement that you use when you're looking at a preview of something, such as an email. You touch the screen with a small amount of pressure. A Peek causes a window to open that shows a preview of the object.

personal hotspot   When acting as a personal hotspot, your iPhone can share its cellular data connection with other devices so that those devices can access the Internet.

podcast   An episodic audio or video program that you can listen to or watch using the Podcasts app. You can subscribe to podcasts so that the episodes are downloaded to your phone automatically.

Pop   A 3D Touch movement similar to a Peek that happens when you apply slightly more pressure to the screen when you touch it. A Pop opens the object in its app. For example, when you are looking at a Peek of a photo and perform a Pop on it, it opens in the Photos app.

Predictive Text   The iPhone feature that attempts to predict the next text you want to type; you can tap the text on the Predictive Text bar to enter it. Predictive Text learns over time so it gets better at predicting the text you are going to write. You can use Predictive Text to type faster or to correct mistakes. Predictive Text can also recommend emojis when you type certain words, such as a plane emoji when you type the word "plane."

Push   Your iPhone can receive many different kinds of information from the Internet, such as new emails, contacts, and so on. Push is when information is moved from a server (such as an email server) directly to your iPhone as soon as the new information appears on the server. Push causes your information to be the most current, but also uses more battery than other methods.

Quick Action menu   When you press on an app's icon on an iPhone that supports 3D Touch, the Quick Action menu appears. You can choose the action you want to perform on this menu.

roaming   The provider from whom you get an account to enable your iPhone to be used for phone calls and cellular data covers a specific geographic region, such as the United States. When you take your iPhone outside of that region, a different provider provides services for you to use; this is called roaming. Roaming is important because it often involves additional charges that can be quite expensive.

selfie   A photo you take of "yourself" by using the camera on the front side of the iPhone. Selfies can include anything you want them to, but usually the person taking the photo is included in the photo, thus the name *selfie*. Selfies are very popular, especially when someone is someplace or doing something interesting or unusual. It is also common to take a selfie to capture a group of people, such as when they are sitting at a table together.

Settings app   This app enables you to configure and customize your iPhone and the apps you use.

Siri   Apple's voice recognition technology that enables you to speak to your iPhone to perform tasks and dictate text. You can perform just about any task using Siri. For example, you can place phone calls, send text messages, read text messages, get information, and so on, just by speaking to your iPhone.

Sleep   The power-saving mode the iPhone moves into after a period of inactivity or when you press the Side button while it is awake. In Sleep mode, the screen goes dark and some processes stop to conserve battery power. To use the iPhone again, you wake it. If the iPhone is both locked and asleep, you wake it and then unlock it to be able to work with it.

social media   Services and apps that enable people and organizations to share their information, photos, videos, comments, etc. Social media services can be accessed through apps on your iPhone or via web browsers, such as Google Chrome or Safari, on a computer. Popular social media services include Facebook, Twitter, and Instagram.

Touch ID   The sensor and associated software that enables you to record fingerprints and use them to enter your passcode to unlock your iPhone and passwords in various apps, such as the App Store app when you are downloading apps. All iOS 11-compatible models support Touch ID except the iPhone X, which instead uses Face ID.

Touch ID/Home button   The circular button on the bottom of the front side of the iPhone. This button serves several purposes. You press it to wake and unlock your iPhone. When you are using your iPhone, pressing it takes you to the Home screen. Pressing it twice opens the App Switcher. It can also be configured to perform other actions. On iPhone models that support Touch ID, touching a recorded fingerprint to this button enters the associated passcode or password. For example, you can unlock your iPhone simply by touching a recorded finger to the Touch ID/Home button. All models except the iPhone X have this button.

Twitter/tweet/Twitter feed   Twitter is the social media service that enables people to post and share short comments, photos, and other content (Twitter messages are called tweets) with a group of people (called followers). The followers can respond to these messages and everyone subscribed to the group sees the messages (unless they are blocked by the group's owner). These groups of messages are called a Twitter feed. You can use the Twitter app on your iPhone to follow or start a Twitter feed.

wake   To save power, your iPhone goes to sleep after a period of inactivity or when you put it to sleep. When sleeping, the iPhone's screen goes dark. To use it again, you wake it by pressing the Side button, the Touch ID/Home button, or raising the phone (if the Raise to Wake feature is enabled on your iPhone).

Wallet App   This app stores Apple Pay information along with boarding passes, store discount cards, and other information so that you can quickly use this information, such as to scan a boarding pass when boarding a plane.

wallpaper   The image you see on the Lock screen and Home screens. You can determine the images you want to see on your iPhone using the Wallpaper option in the Settings app. You can use default images that come with your iPhone or you can use any photo you take using the iPhone's cameras or that you download onto your iPhone, such as from an email.

Wi-Fi   Wi-Fi (Wireless Fidelity) technology that enables iPhones, computers, and many other devices to communicate with each other wirelessly. Your iPhone connects to Wi-Fi networks primarily in order to connect to the Internet. Wi-Fi networks are fast and make accessing the Internet easy and convenient.

Widget Center   When you swipe to the right from a Home screen or the Lock screen, the Widget Center opens. Here, you can use the widgets that are configured on your Widget Center.

widgets   Widgets are "mini" versions of the apps that are available on the Widget Center. Widgets enable you to quickly get information or accomplish a task using its app.

Index

Z

Answers to Your Technology Questions

My Windows 10 Computer for Seniors

Michael Miller

My iPad for Seniors
FIFTH EDITION

Michael Miller

My iPhone for Seniors
FOURTH EDITION

Brad Miser

My Samsung Galaxy S6 for Seniors

Michael Miller

My Samsung Galaxy S7 for Seniors

Michael Miller

My Health Technology for Seniors

Lonzell Watson

My Digital Entertainment for Seniors

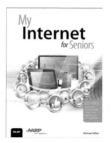

My Internet for Seniors

Michael Miller

My Smart Home for Seniors

Michael Miller

SECOND EDITION

My Social Media for Seniors

Michael Miller

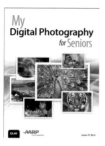

My Digital Photography for Seniors

Jason R. Rich

$24.99

WITHDRAWN
1/11/2018

... Seniors Series is a
... how-to guide books
... nd Que that respect
... without assuming
... hie. Each book in
... ntures:

... l-color photos
... tep instructions
... ps and tricks

LONGWOOD PUBLIC LIBRARY
800 Middle Country Road
Middle Island, NY 11953
(631) 924-6400
longwoodlibrary.org

LIBRARY HOURS

Monday-Friday	9:30 a.m. - 9:00 p.m.
Saturday	9:30 a.m. - 5:00 p.m.
Sunday (Sept-June)	1:00 p.m. - 5:00 p.m.

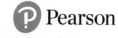

Pearson

QUe

Teach Yourself
VISUALLY™

iPhone® 8,
iPhone® 8 Plus,
and iPhone® X

by Guy Hart-Davis

Visual
®
A Wiley Brand

Teach Yourself VISUALLY™ iPhone® 8, iPhone® 8 Plus, and iPhone® X

Published by
John Wiley & Sons, Inc.
10475 Crosspoint Boulevard
Indianapolis, IN 46256

www.wiley.com

Published simultaneously in Canada

Copyright © 2018 by John Wiley & Sons, Inc., Indianapolis, Indiana

Library of Congress Control Number: 2017953998

ISBN: 978-1-119-43961-5

Manufactured in the United States of America

10 9 8 7 6 5 4 3 2 1

Trademark Acknowledgments

Contact Us

For general information on our other products and services please contact our Customer Care Department within the U.S. at 877-762-2974, outside the U.S. at 317-572-3993 or fax 317-572-4002.

For technical support please visit https://hub.wiley.com/community/support.

Sales | Contact Wiley at (877) 762-2974 or fax (317) 572-4002.

Credits

Acquisitions Editors
Riley Harding
Jody Lefevere

Project Editor
Lynn Northrup

Technical Editor
Galen Gruman

Copy Editor
Lynn Northrup

Production Editor
Athiyappan Lalith Kumar

**Manager, Content Development &
Assembly**
Mary Beth Wakefield

**Vice President, Professional
Technology Strategy**
Barry Pruett

About the Author

Guy Hart-Davis is the author of *Teach Yourself VISUALLY iPad, 4th Edition; Teach Yourself VISUALLY iPhone 7; Teach Yourself VISUALLY Android Phones and Tablets, 2nd Edition; Teach Yourself VISUALLY MacBook Pro, 2nd Edition; Teach Yourself VISUALLY MacBook Air; iMac Portable Genius, 4th Edition;* and *iWork Portable Genius, 2nd Edition*.

Author's Acknowledgments

My thanks go to the many people who turned my manuscript into the highly graphical book you are holding. In particular, I thank Riley Harding and Jody Lefevere for asking me to write the book; Lynn Northrup for keeping me on track and skillfully editing the text; Galen Gruman for reviewing the book for technical accuracy and contributing helpful suggestions; and SPi Global for laying out the book.

How to Use This Book

Who This Book Is For

This book is for the reader who has never used this particular technology or software application. It is also for readers who want to expand their knowledge.

The Conventions in This Book

1 Steps

This book uses a step-by-step format to guide you easily through each task. **Numbered steps** are actions you must do; **bulleted steps** clarify a point, step, or optional feature; and **indented steps** give you the result.

2 Notes

Notes give additional information — special conditions that may occur during an operation, a situation that you want to avoid, or a cross reference to a related area of the book.

3 Icons and Buttons

Icons and buttons show you exactly what you need to click to perform a step.

4 Tips

Tips offer additional information, including warnings and shortcuts.

5 Bold

Bold type shows command names, options, and text or numbers you must type.

6 Italics

Italic type introduces and defines a new term.

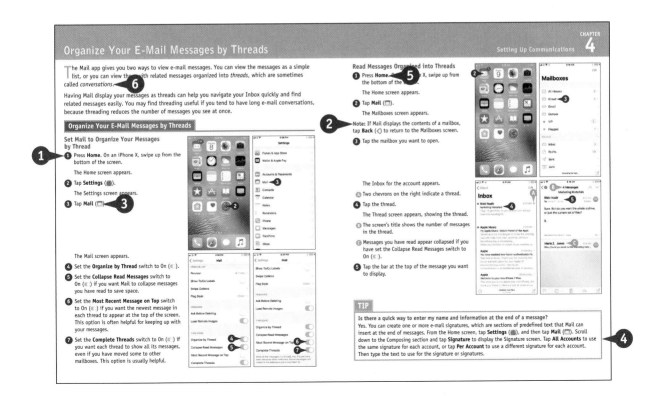

Table of Contents

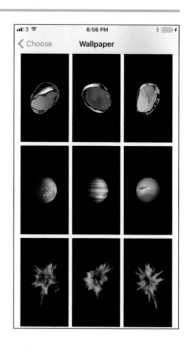

Chapter 3   Using Voice, Accessibility, and Continuity

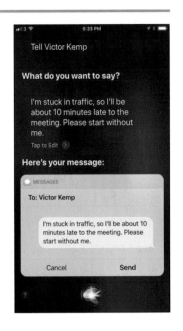

Chapter 4   Setting Up Communications

Table of Contents

Chapter 7 — Working with Apps

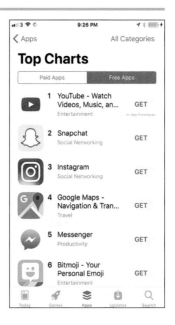

Chapter 8 — Browsing the Web and E-Mailing

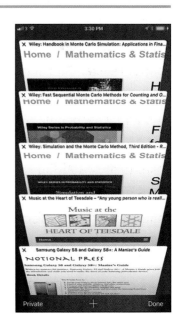

Table of Contents

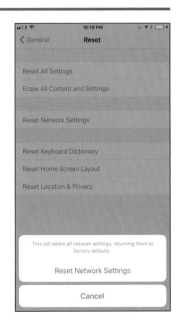

CHAPTER 1

Getting Started with Your iPhone

In this chapter, you set up your iPhone to work with your computer or iCloud. You choose items to sync and learn to use the iPhone interface.

Identify and Compare the iPhone Models

The iPhone is a series of hugely popular smartphones designed by Apple. As of this writing, Apple sells six iPhone models that differ in size, power, and price. This section explains the six models, their common features, and their differences to enable you to distinguish them and choose among them.

Understanding the Six iPhone Models

As of this writing, Apple sells six iPhone models:

- iPhone X, introduced in 2017. The iPhone X has the largest screen of the iPhone models and very thin bezels around the screen. The front camera, flash, and microphone are inset in the middle of the top edge of the screen. In the name, X is pronounced as "ten" rather than the letter.

- iPhone 8 and iPhone 8 Plus, also introduced in 2017. The iPhone 8 Plus is physically larger than the iPhone 8.

- iPhone 7 and iPhone 7 Plus, introduced in 2016. As with the iPhone 8 models, the iPhone 7 Plus is physically larger than the iPhone 7.

- iPhone SE, introduced in 2016. The iPhone SE is the most compact iPhone.

All of the iPhone models except the iPhone X have the Home button, a physical button for navigation, below the screen. The iPhone X uses gestures instead of the Home button.

iPhone X

Understanding the Common Features of the iPhone Models

Each iPhone comes with the Apple EarPods headset, which incorporates a remote control and a microphone. For all current iPhone models except the iPhone SE, the Apple EarPods headset connects via the Lightning connector, and the iPhone comes with a Lightning-to-3.5mm headphone jack adapter for connecting analog headphones via the Lightning port. For the iPhone SE and most earlier iPhone models, the headset connects via the headphone socket. Each iPhone includes a USB power adapter and a Lightning-to-USB cable. Each iPhone uses a nano-SIM card to connect to cellular networks. Each iPhone except the iPhone X has a Touch ID fingerprint reader.

Each iPhone runs iOS 11, the latest operating system from Apple, which comes with a suite of built-in apps, such as the Safari web browser and the Mail e-mail app.

The iPhone X models come in two colors: black, which is matte rather than glossy; and silver. The iPhone 8 models and iPhone 7 models come in five colors: jet black, which is glossy; black, which is matte; silver; gold; and rose gold. The iPhone SE comes in four colors: gold, silver, space gray, and rose gold.

iPhone 8 Plus

The iPhone X has dual 12-megapixel cameras on the back and a front-facing camera with extra features that enable the Face ID authentication and unlocking system.

The iPhone 8 models and the iPhone 7 models have a 12-megapixel main camera on the back and a 7-megapixel camera on the front. The iPhone 8 Plus and the iPhone 7 Plus also include a second camera unit to enable optical zoom and other features. The iPhone SE has a 12-megapixel main camera and a 1.2-megapixel front camera.

Compare the iPhone X with the iPhone 8 Models

The iPhone X has the biggest screen of any iPhone but is physically smaller than the iPhone 8 Plus. To achieve its compact size, the iPhone X has much slimmer bezels than the iPhone 8 models. On the iPhone X, the front camera module, speaker, and microphone are inset into a cutout in the top of the screen, whereas on other iPhone models they are located in the top bezel above the screen.

Unlike other iPhone models, the iPhone X has no Home button below the screen. To unlock the iPhone X, you use the Face ID authentication feature, whereas on other current iPhone models, you use the Touch ID fingerprint recognition built into the Home button. To display the Home screen on the iPhone X, you swipe up the bar from the bottom of the screen, whereas on other iPhone models, you press the Home button.

Compare the iPhone 8 Models with the iPhone 7 Models

The two iPhone 8 models, the iPhone 8 and the iPhone 8 Plus, have faster processors than the corresponding iPhone 7 models, the iPhone 7 and the iPhone 7 Plus. Although each model has a 12-megapixel main camera with the same aperture settings, the cameras on the iPhone 8 models feature improved True Tone flash with a feature called Slow Sync for more even lighting with flash.

The iPhone 8 models and iPhone 7 models have a Home button that features haptic feedback to simulate being pressed without moving. By contrast, the iPhone SE has a physical Home button that actually presses in.

The iPhone 8 is fractionally bigger and heavier than the iPhone 7; the iPhone 8 Plus is fractionally bigger and heavier than the iPhone 7 Plus. These differences are almost imperceptible but may mean that tight-fitting cases for iPhone 7 models do not fit iPhone 8 models and vice versa.

Compare the iPhone Plus Models with the Regular Models

The iPhone 8 Plus and the iPhone 7 Plus are physically larger than the iPhone 8 and the iPhone 7 and have higher-definition screens that may enable you to see greater detail in photos and other high-definition content.

As well as being larger, the iPhone Plus models are somewhat heavier than the regular models; but if you are deciding between the Plus model and the regular model, your main consideration is likely to be whether the device will fit comfortably in your hand and your pocket or purse.

The iPhone 8 Plus and iPhone 7 Plus have a dual-camera module on the back rather than a single-camera module, as the other models have. One camera has a 28mm wide-angle lens, while the other has a 56mm telephoto lens to provide optical zoom, which gives higher image quality than the digital zoom provided by enlarging pixels via software. The Plus models also have a Portrait Mode for photos that blurs out the background to emphasize the subject; the iPhone X also has Portrait Mode.

All of these models have optical image stabilization to minimize camera shake. If you shoot many photos and videos, you may find this feature useful.

continued ▶

Apart from physical size, you should consider the storage capacity of the iPhone model you are thinking of buying. Having more storage enables you to install more apps and carry more music, movies, and other files with you. Having plenty of storage is especially important for shooting videos with your iPhone.

Compare the iPhone SE with the Larger iPhone Models

The iPhone SE is physically smaller than the iPhone 8 model and the iPhone 7. Its 4-inch screen has lower resolution than the screens on the larger models. It processor, an A9 model, is relatively powerful, but less powerful than the A10 Fusion processor on the iPhone 7 and iPhone 7 Plus, which in turn is less powerful than the A11 Bionic processor on the iPhone 8 and iPhone 8 Plus.

While the rear camera on the iPhone SE has the same 12-megapixel resolution as the camera on the iPhone 8 models and iPhone 7 models, the front camera on the iPhone SE has relatively low 1.2-megapixel resolution.

All of these iPhone models have a Near Field Communication (NFC) chip that enables you to use the Apple Pay service to make payments from your iPhone.

iPhone SE

Evaluate iPhone Storage Capacity

The iPhone models are available with different amounts of storage capacity. The diagram shows sample amounts of contents.

The iPhone X, iPhone 8, and iPhone 8 Plus come in 64GB and 256GB capacities.

The iPhone 7, iPhone 7 Plus, and iPhone SE come in 32GB and 128GB capacities.

Higher capacities command substantially higher prices, so you must decide how much you are prepared to spend. Generally speaking, higher-capacity devices get more use in the long run and are worth the extra cost.

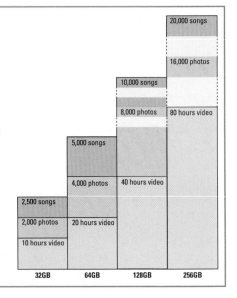

Understanding the 3D Touch Feature

The iPhone X, the iPhone 8 models, and the iPhone 7 models include a feature called 3D Touch that provides shortcuts to content and to frequently used actions for the current item and context. 3D Touch uses force sensors in the screen to detect when you press the screen firmly rather than just tapping it. For example, you can press an app icon on the Home screen to display actions for that app. For instance, press **Maps** (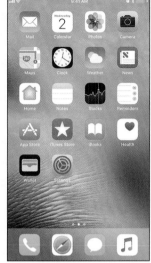) to display the pop-up menu for the Maps app. You can then tap a button in the Maps Destinations box to get directions to upcoming appointments, tap **Mark My Location** to mark your location, tap **Send My Location** to share your location with a contact, or tap **Search Nearby** to search for businesses or other places near you.

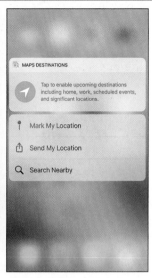

3D Touch uses two actions, Peek and Pop. Peek enables you to get a preview of content by pressing it briefly. Pop opens the content when you press harder. For example, you can press an e-mail message to display a preview of its content using Peek. If you want to open the message, you press harder until the Pop action opens the message.

Understanding the Reachability Feature

iOS includes a feature called Reachability to help you use your iPhone with one hand when necessary. With the Reachability feature enabled, double-tap **Home** — double-tap rather than double-press — to slide the screen down so that you can easily reach the top of it. After you give a command, the screen slides back up again; if you decide not to give a command, double-tap **Home** again to slide the screen back up.

To enable Reachability, first tap **Settings** (⚙), tap **General** (⚙), and then tap **Accessibility**. Toward the bottom of the Accessibility screen, tap **Reachability** to display the Reachability screen, and then set the **Reachability** switch to On (◯).

Understanding the Live Photos Feature

All of the current iPhone models include a feature called Live Photos that enables you to capture short sections of video before and after a still photo. After capturing the Live Photo, you can make the video segments play by tapping and holding the photo.

You can view your Live Photos on other Apple devices, such as your iPad or your Mac. You can also use a Live Photo as the wallpaper for your iPhone's lock screen.

After unboxing your iPhone, connect it to its charger and charge the battery fully. Then turn your iPhone on and meet its hardware controls: the Power/Sleep button, the Ringer On/Off switch, the Volume Up button, and the Volume Down button, and the Home button below the screen of all iPhone models except the iPhone X. If the store or carrier has not inserted a SIM card in the iPhone, you will need to insert a suitable card yourself (see the tip for details).

Meet Your iPhone's Hardware Controls

1 Press and hold the Power/Sleep button for a couple of seconds.

Note: The Power/Sleep button is on the right side of the iPhone X, the iPhone 8 models, and the iPhone 7 models, and on the top of the iPhone SE.

As the iPhone starts, the Apple logo appears on the screen.

Above the iPhone's screen are:

A The front-facing camera.

B The receiver speaker, which plays phone calls into your ear when you hold the iPhone up to your face.

C Below the iPhone's screen is the Home button, which you press to display the Home screen.

At the bottom of the iPhone are:

D The microphones.

E The Lightning connector.

F The speakers.

Note: On the iPhone X, the camera and receiver speaker are located in the cutout at the top of the screen.

Note: The bottom edge of the iPhone SE has a mono speaker on the right and a 3.5mm headphone socket on the left, looking from the front.

2 Turn the iPhone so that you can see its left side.

3 When you want to turn the ringer off, move the Ringer On/Off switch to the rear so that the orange background appears.

Note: Turn the ringer off when you do not want the iPhone to disturb you or the peace. Move the Ringer On/Off switch back to the front when you want to turn the ringer back on.

4 Press the Volume Up (+) button to increase the ringer volume.

Note: When the Camera app is displayed, you can press the Volume Up (+) button to take a picture with the camera.

5 Press the Volume Down (–) button to decrease the ringer volume.

6 When the lock screen appears, press **Home**. On an iPhone X, swipe up from the bottom of the screen.

The iPhone unlocks, and the Home screen appears.

TIP

How do I insert a SIM card in my iPhone?
If the store or carrier has not inserted a SIM card, insert the SIM removal tool in the SIM hole on the right side of the iPhone. If you do not have a SIM removal tool, straighten out the end of a small paperclip and use that instead. Push gently until the tray pops out, and then pull it with your fingernails. Insert the SIM in the tray, and then push the tray in fully.

Download, Install, and Set Up iTunes

To sync your iPhone with your computer, you use Apple's iTunes application. iTunes comes preinstalled on every Mac but not on PCs; to get iTunes for Windows, you download it from the Apple website and then install it on your PC.

If you do not have a computer, or you do not want to sync your iPhone with your computer, you can set up and sync your iPhone using Apple's iCloud service, as described in "Set Up Your iPhone as New Using iCloud," later in this chapter.

Download, Install, and Set Up iTunes

1 On your PC, open the web browser. This example uses the Microsoft Edge browser on Windows 10.

2 Click the Address box, type www.apple.com/itunes/download, and then press **Enter**.

The Download iTunes Now web page appears.

3 Click the check boxes (☑ changes to ☐) unless you want to receive e-mail from Apple.

4 Click **Download now**.

5 When the download finishes, click **Run** in the pop-up panel that appears.

The iTunes installation begins, and the Welcome to iTunes dialog opens.

6 Click **Next**, and then follow the steps of the installer.

Note: You must accept the license agreement to install iTunes.

The Installation Options screen appears.

7 Click **Add iTunes shortcut to my desktop** (☑ changes to ☐) unless you want this shortcut.

8 Click **Use iTunes as the default player for audio files** (☑ changes to ☐) if you do not want to use iTunes as the default audio player.

9 Click **Automatically update iTunes and other Apple software** (☑ changes to ☐) if you do not want automatic updates.

10 Click **Install**.

Note: If the User Account Control dialog opens, make sure that the Program Name is iTunes and the Verified Publisher is Apple Inc. Then click **Yes**.

The Congratulations screen appears.

11 Click **Open iTunes after the installer exits** (☑ changes to ☐) if you do not want iTunes to launch automatically when you close the installer.

12 Click **Finish**.

The installer closes.

Unless you chose not to open iTunes automatically, iTunes opens.

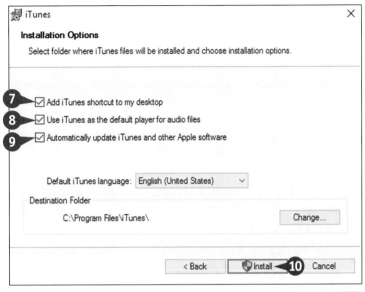

TIPS

Should I allow Apple to install updates automatically on my PC?

If this is your own PC, installing updates automatically is usually helpful. The updates may include fixes to bugs or vulnerabilities, new features, or both.

How do I set up iTunes on a Mac?

If you have not run iTunes already, click **iTunes** (♫) on the Dock. If the Dock contains no iTunes icon, click **Launchpad** (🚀) on the Dock, and then click **iTunes** (♫) on the Launchpad screen. The iTunes Setup Assistant launches. Follow the steps to set up iTunes.

Begin Setup and Activate Your iPhone

Before you can use your iPhone, you must set it up and activate it. First, you choose your language and specify your country or region. You can then either use the Quick Start feature if you have an iPhone or iPad running iOS 11 or continue setup manually. Assuming you continue manually, you connect the iPhone to the Internet through either a Wi-Fi network or the cellular network, choose whether to use Touch ID fingerprint unlocking, and choose a passcode.

Begin Setup and Activate Your iPhone

Note: If you are upgrading from an existing iPhone, see Chapter 12 for instructions on turning off Find My iPhone, backing up the iPhone fully, and resetting it.

1 Turn on the iPhone by pressing and holding the Power/Sleep button until the Apple logo appears on-screen.

2 When the initial iPhone screen appears, press **Home**. On the iPhone X, swipe up from the bottom of the screen.

The setup routine begins.

The Language screen appears.

3 Tap the language you want to use.

The Select Your Country or Region screen appears.

4 Tap your country or region.

The Quick Start screen appears.

5 If you have an iPhone or iPad running iOS 11, bring it close to the iPhone and follow the prompts. Otherwise, tap **Set Up Manually** and follow the remaining steps in this list.

The Choose a Wi-Fi Network screen appears.

6 Tap the wireless network you want to use.

Ⓐ If your Wi-Fi network does not appear because it does not broadcast its network name, tap **Choose Another Network**. You can then type the network's name.

Note: If your Wi-Fi network does not appear because it is out of range, tap **Use Cellular Connection**.

The Enter Password screen appears.

7 Type the password.

8 Tap **Join**.

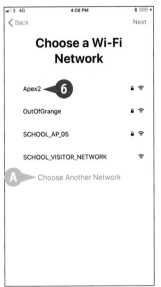

The Touch ID screen appears. On an iPhone X, the Face ID screen appears. Follow the prompts to set up Face ID, which enables you to unlock the iPhone X by holding it up to your face. Skip to step **13**.

9 Tap **Continue** if you want to use Touch ID.

Ⓑ Tap **Set Up Touch ID Later** if you do not want to set up Touch ID now.

The Place Your Finger screen appears.

10 Place your finger or thumb on the Home button, following the prompts.

The fingerprint reader scans your finger or thumb and fills in the lines as you lift and replace your finger.

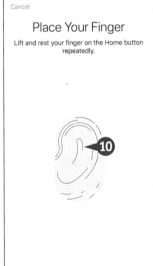

TIP

Should I use Touch ID or Face ID for unlocking my iPhone?
Using Touch ID or Face ID is usually the most convenient way of unlocking an iPhone quickly but securely. As of this writing, only the iPhone X has Face ID. All other current models of iPhone have Touch ID instead.

continued ▶

After setting up Touch ID — or Face ID on an iPhone X — and a passcode, you choose how to complete setting up the iPhone. If you have not used an iOS device before, you can set up the iPhone as a new iPhone. If you have used an iOS device, you can restore an iCloud backup or an iTunes backup of that device to the iPhone. If you have been using an Android device, you can use the Move to iOS app to move data to the iPhone.

Begin Setup and Activate Your iPhone (continued)

The Adjust Your Grip screen appears.

⑪ Tap **Continue**.

The Place Your Finger screen appears again, showing a larger fingerprint area.

⑫ Continue scanning your fingerprint, now placing the edges of your finger on the Home button.

The Complete screen appears.

⑬ Tap **Continue**.

The Create a Passcode screen appears.

⑭ To use a standard passcode, type a six-digit passcode, and then repeat it on the Re-Enter Your Passcode screen.

Ⓒ To create a different type of passcode, tap **Passcode Options**.

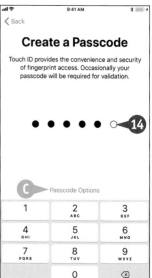

14

The Passcode Options dialog opens.

D Tap **Custom Alphanumeric Code**, **Custom Numeric Code**, or **4-Digit Numeric Code**, as appropriate, and follow the prompts to create the passcode. See the tip for advice on which type of passcode to create.

15 If the This Passcode Can Be Easily Guessed dialog opens, tap **Change Passcode** and create a stronger passcode.

After you create your passcode, the Apps & Data screen appears.

16 Tap the appropriate button:

E Tap **Restore from iCloud Backup** to set up your iPhone using a backup stored in iCloud. See the section "Set Up Your iPhone from an iCloud Backup," later in this chapter.

F Tap **Restore from iTunes Backup** to set up your iPhone using a backup stored on your computer. See the section "Set Up Your iPhone from iTunes," later in this chapter.

G Tap **Set Up as New iPhone** to set up your iPhone from scratch using iCloud. See the next section, "Set Up Your iPhone as New Using iCloud."

H Tap **Move Data from Android** to use the Move to iOS app to move data from an Android device.

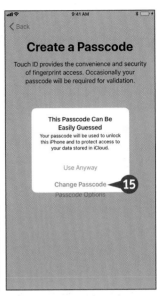

TIP

Which type of passcode should I create?

The default setting — a six-digit numeric passcode — provides adequate security for most people as long as you avoid the temptation to derive the numbers from your birthdate, which can be easily guessed. If you need stronger security, choose **Custom Numeric Code** and create a passcode of eight or more digits. For the strongest security, choose **Custom Alphanumeric Code** and create a passcode of ten or more characters. Choose **4-Digit Numeric Code** only if your iPhone contains no sensitive or valuable data at all.

I f you want to use your iPhone without syncing it to your computer, set it up using Apple's iCloud online service. With this approach, you sync your data to your account on iCloud, from which you can access it using other iOS devices, a Mac, or a web browser on any computer.

To set up a new iPhone to use iCloud, follow the instructions in the previous section to begin setup, and then continue with the instructions in this section.

Set Up Your iPhone as New Using iCloud

1 Begin setup as explained in the previous section, "Begin Setup and Activate Your iPhone."

2 On the Apps & Data screen, tap **Set Up as New iPhone**.

The Apple ID screen appears.

A You can tap **Don't have an Apple ID or forgot it?** to create a new Apple ID or get a reminder about your existing Apple ID.

B You can tap **About Apple ID and Privacy** to see information about privacy concerns.

3 Tap **Apple ID** and type your Apple ID.

C You can quickly enter widely used domains, such as .com and .edu, by tapping and holding **.** (the period key) and then sliding your finger to the appropriate domain on the pop-up panel.

4 Tap **Password** and type your password.

5 Tap **Next**.

The Apple ID Verification Code dialog opens.

6 Type the verification code sent to your other iOS device or Mac.

The Terms and Conditions screen appears.

7 Read the terms and conditions, and tap **Agree** if you want to proceed.

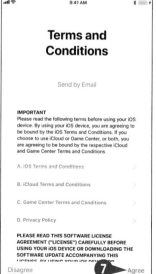

The Express Settings screen appears.

8 Tap **Continue**.

Ⓓ You can tap **Customize Settings** to choose settings that control whether apps and services may use your location data and whether your iPhone uploads anonymized usage data to help Apple improve its products.

The Apple Pay screen appears.

9 Tap **Continue**.

Ⓔ You can tap **Set Up Later in Wallet** to skip setting up Apple Pay.

The Add Card screen appears.

10 Point the rear camera lens at your credit card or debit card.

The setup routine recognizes the card details.

Ⓕ You can tap **Enter Card Details Manually** if the recognition fails or is inaccurate.

Ⓖ You can tap **Set Up Later in Wallet** to skip adding a card.

The Card Details screen appears.

11 Follow the prompts to set up Apple Pay.

The iCloud Keychain screen appears.

Ⓗ You can tap **Don't use iCloud Keychain** if you do not want to restore your passwords from iCloud to your iPhone.

12 Tap **Continue**, and then follow any prompts to set up iCloud Keychain.

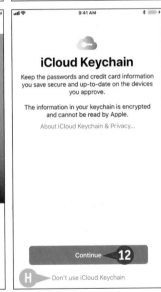

TIP

Why should I use iCloud Keychain?
iCloud Keychain gives you an easy way to store your passwords and credit card information securely on your iPhone, other iOS devices, or Mac. Instead of having to remember the password for each website, or look at a credit card when you need to enter its details, iCloud Keychain can automatically provide the details.

iCloud Keychain encrypts your data, but you must use a complex passcode to keep it secure.

continued ▶

When you set up your iPhone using iCloud, use an e-mail address that you intend to keep for the long term. This is especially important if you use the same e-mail address for the Apple ID that you use for the App Store; each app you buy is tied to that e-mail address, so if you change the address, you will need to authenticate again for each app update.

Set Up Your iPhone as New Using iCloud (continued)

The Siri screen appears.

13 Tap **Continue** and follow the prompts to set up Siri's voice recognition.

I You can tap **Set Up Later in Settings** if you do not want to turn on Siri now.

Note: You can turn Siri on or off at any point after setup.

The "Hey Siri" Is Ready screen appears.

14 Tap **Continue**.

The App Analytics screen appears.

15 Tap **Share with App Developers** if you want to share usage statistics and crash data with the developers of the apps you use. Otherwise, tap **Don't Share.**

The Meet the New Home Button screen appears.

16 Tap **Get Started**.

J You can tap **Customize Later in Settings** if you do not want to customize the Home button now.

The Choose Your Click screen appears.

17 Tap **1**, **2**, or **3**, and then press **Home** to feel the haptic feedback.

18 When you have chosen the haptic click you prefer, tap **Next**.

The first Display Zoom screen appears.

19 Tap **Choose a View**.

The second Display Zoom screen appears.

K You can tap **Standard** or **Zoomed** to switch between the views and decide which you prefer.

L You can swipe left to view other sample screens to help choose which zoom to use.

20 Tap **Next**.

The Welcome to iPhone screen appears.

21 Tap **Get Started**.

The Home screen appears, and you can begin using your iPhone.

TIP

What is Siri and should I enable it?

Siri is Apple's voice-driven assistant, which enables you to interact with your iPhone by voice. Many people find Siri useful, but if you do not, you can turn Siri off at any time. See Chapter 3 for instructions on using and customizing Siri.

Set Up Your iPhone from an iCloud Backup

If you have used an iPhone or other iOS device before, you can set up your iPhone by restoring from an iCloud backup. This backup can be from either another iPhone or iOS device or from the same iPhone.

When you restore your iPhone from an iCloud backup, you choose which backup to use — normally, the most recent one. iOS automatically restores your settings, downloads your apps from the App Store, and then installs them on the iPhone.

Set Up Your iPhone from an iCloud Backup

1 Begin setup as explained in the section "Begin Setup and Activate Your iPhone," earlier in this chapter.

2 On the Apps & Data screen, tap **Restore from iCloud Backup**.

The iCloud Sign In screen appears.

3 Type your Apple ID.

4 Type your password.

5 Tap **Next**.

The Terms and Conditions screen appears.

6 Tap **Agree**.

The Apple ID Verification Code dialog opens.

7 Type the verification code sent to your other iOS device or Mac.

The Choose Backup screen appears.

8 Tap the backup you want to use.

A You can tap **Show All Backups** to display other available backups.

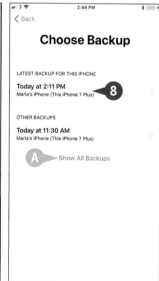

The Settings from Your Backup screen appears.

9 Tap **Continue** to proceed and restore all the settings listed.

B You can tap **Customize Settings** to choose which settings to restore to the iPhone.

The Siri screen appears.

10 Tap **Continue** and follow the prompts to set up Siri's voice recognition.

C You can tap **Set Up Later in Settings** if you do not want to turn on Siri now.

Note: You can turn Siri on or off at any point after setup.

The "Hey Siri" Is Ready screen appears.

11 Tap **Continue**.

The App Analytics screen appears.

12 Tap **Share with App Developers** if you want to share usage statistics and crash data with the developers of the apps you use. Otherwise, tap **Don't Share**.

The Restore from iCloud screen appears as iOS restores the backup to your iPhone.

Note: If iOS prompts you to enter your passcode, do so.

The iPhone restarts.

The lock screen appears. You can then unlock the iPhone and start using it.

TIP

Which iPhone backup should I use?

Normally, it is best to use the most recent backup available for this iPhone or for the iPhone whose backups you are using. But sometimes you may find a problem exists with the latest backup. In that case, try the previous backup.

Set Up Your iPhone from iTunes

Instead of setting up your iPhone using iCloud, as described in the previous two sections, you can set it up using iTunes. You can either restore an iTunes backup to the device or set up the iPhone from scratch using iTunes.

When setting up your iPhone for the first time, you can restore it from an iTunes backup of another iPhone — for example, your previous iPhone. If you have already set up this iPhone, you can restore it from its own backup.

Set Up Your iPhone from iTunes

1 Begin setup as explained in the section "Begin Setup and Activate Your iPhone," earlier in this chapter.

2 On the Apps & Data screen, tap **Restore from iTunes Backup**.

The Connect to iTunes screen appears.

3 Connect your iPhone to your computer via the USB cable.

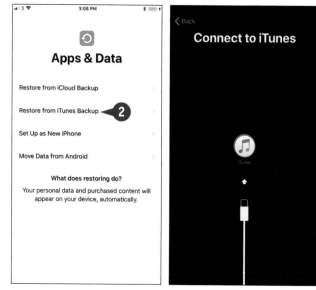

On your computer, iTunes opens or becomes active.

The Welcome to Your New iPhone screen appears.

4 Make sure the **Restore from this backup** radio button is selected (⦿).

5 Click the pop-up menu button (⬍) and select the appropriate iPhone from the menu.

6 Click **Continue**.

iTunes restores your iPhone from the backup.

When the restore is complete, your iPhone restarts.

Your iPhone's control screens appear in the iTunes window.

You can now choose sync settings for the iPhone as explained in the next section, "Choose Which Items to Sync from Your Computer."

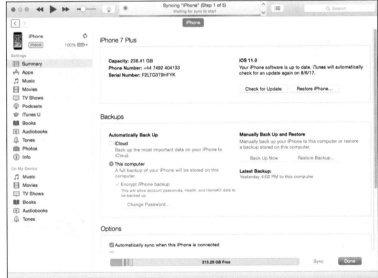

How do I set up my iPhone from scratch using iTunes?

On the Apps & Data screen, tap **Restore from iTunes Backup**, and then connect your iPhone to your computer via the USB cable. When the Welcome to Your New iPhone screen appears in iTunes on your computer, click **Set up as new iPhone** (◯ changes to ⦿). Click **Continue**. On the Sync with iTunes screen that appears, click **Get Started**. The iPhone's control screens appear, and you can set up synchronization as described in the next section, "Choose Which Items to Sync from Your Computer."

Choose Which Items to Sync from Your Computer

After specifying that you will use iTunes to sync your iPhone, as explained in the previous section, "Set Up Your iPhone from iTunes," you use the iPhone's control screens in iTunes to choose which items to sync. When setting your sync preferences, start on the Summary tab. Here, you can change your iPhone's name, choose whether to back up the iPhone to iCloud or to your computer, decide whether to encrypt the backup, and set general options for controlling syncing.

Choose Which Items to Sync from Your Computer

Connect Your iPhone and Choose Options on the Summary Tab

1 Connect your iPhone to your computer via the USB cable.

The iTunes window appears.

2 If your iPhone's control screens do not automatically appear, click **iPhone** (📱) on the navigation bar at the top of the screen.

Note: Your iPhone appears in iTunes with either a default name or the name you have given it.

The iPhone's control screens appear.

3 Click **Summary** if the Summary screen is not already displayed.

The Summary screen appears.

4 To change the iPhone's name, click the existing name, type the new name, and press **Enter** or **Return**.

5 In the Automatically Back Up area, click **iCloud** (○ changes to ◉) or **This computer** (○ changes to ◉) to specify where to back up your iPhone.

6 If you choose to back up to this computer, click **Encrypt iPhone backup** (☐ changes to ☑).

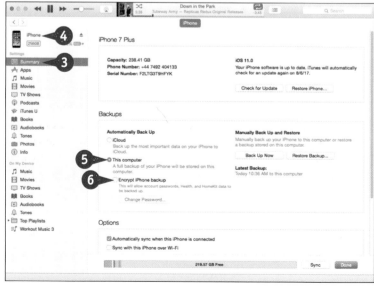

The Set Password dialog opens.

7 Type a password in the Password box and again in the Verify Password box.

8 On a Mac, click **Remember this password in my keychain** (☐ changes to ☑) if you want to save the password in your keychain.

9 Click **Set Password**.

The Set Password dialog closes.

10 Click **Automatically sync when this iPhone is connected** (☐ changes to ☑) if you want to sync your iPhone automatically when you connect it.

11 Click **Sync only checked songs and videos** (☐ changes to ☑) if you want syncing to omit any song or video whose check box you have deselected (☐).

12 Click **Convert higher bit rate songs to AAC** (☐ changes to ☑) if you want to compress larger songs to fit more on your iPhone. In the pop-up menu, choose the bit rate.

TIP

Should I back up my iPhone to my computer or to iCloud?

If you plan to use your iPhone mostly with your computer, back up the iPhone to the computer. Doing so makes iTunes store a full backup of the iPhone on the computer, so you can restore all the data to your iPhone, or to a replacement iPhone, if necessary. You can also encrypt the backup; doing so enables you to store and restore your passwords. To keep your data safe, you must back up your computer as well. For example, you can use Time Machine to back up a Mac.

Backing up your iPhone to iCloud enables you to access the backups from anywhere via the Internet, but make sure your iCloud account has enough storage to contain the backups. An iCloud backup stores less information than an iTunes backup.

continued ▶

iTunes makes it easy to choose which items to sync to your iPhone. By selecting the iPhone in the navigation bar in iTunes, and then clicking the appropriate item in the Settings area of the Source list, you can quickly choose which apps, music, movies, books, and other items to sync from your computer.

Choose Which Items to Sync from Your Computer (continued)

Choose Which Apps to Sync

1 Click **Apps**.

A You can click the pop-up menu button (⬥) and choose how to sort the apps: Click **Sort by Name**, **Sort by Kind**, **Sort by Category**, **Sort by Date Added**, or **Sort by Size**, as needed.

2 Click **Install** for each app you want to sync to the iPhone (Install changes to Will Install).

3 Scroll down the screen and click **Automatically install new apps** (☐ changes to ☑) if you want to sync new apps automatically. This is usually helpful.

Choose Which Music to Sync

1 Click **Music**.

2 Click **Sync Music** (☐ changes to ☑).

3 To load a selection of music, click **Selected playlists, artists, albums, and genres** (◯ changes to ◉) instead of **Entire music library**.

B Click **Automatically fill free space with songs** (☐ changes to ☑) only if you want to put as much music as possible on your iPhone.

4 Click the check box (☐ changes to ☑) for each playlist, artist, genre, or album to include.

Sync Books

1 Click **Books**.

The Books controls appear.

2 Click **Sync Books** (☐ changes to ☑).

3 Click **All books** (◯ changes to ◉) or **Selected books** (◯ changes to ◉).

4 If you click **Selected books**, use the controls in the Books box to choose which books to sync.

Note: You can sync photos from your computer only if you are not using the iCloud Photos feature. If you have enabled iCloud Photos, your iPhone syncs your photos through iCloud instead.

Apply Your Changes and Sync

1 Click **Apply** or **Sync**.

Note: The Apply button appears when you have made changes to the items you will sync. Click **Apply** to apply the changes and sync them.

iTunes syncs the items to your iPhone.

C The readout shows you the sync progress.

D If you need to stop the sync, click **Stop** (✖).

When the sync finishes, disconnect your iPhone.

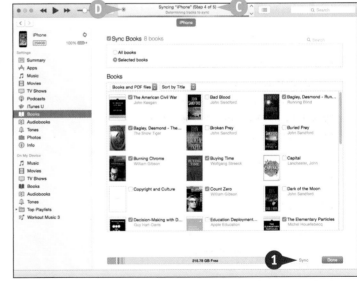

TIP

How can I fit more content on my iPhone?

You cannot install a memory card to increase your iPhone's storage capacity, but you can use the iPhone Storage feature to remove items you do not need.

Press **Home**; on an iPhone X, swipe up from the bottom of the screen. Tap **Settings** (⚙) to display the Settings screen, and then tap **General** (⚙). On the General screen, tap **iPhone Storage** to display the iPhone Storage screen. You can then follow suggestions in the Recommendations box, such as tapping **Enable** for Optimize Photos or for Offload Unused Apps, or tap buttons in the lower section to see which apps and files are consuming the most space.

Instead of syncing your iPhone with iTunes via USB, you can sync it wirelessly or "over the air." You must connect your iPhone and your computer to the same network.

To use wireless sync, you must first enable it in iTunes. You can then have the iPhone sync automatically when connected to a power source and to the same wireless network as the computer. You can also start a sync manually from the iPhone, even if it is not connected to a power source.

Sync Your iPhone with iTunes via Wi-Fi

Set Your iPhone to Sync with iTunes via Wi-Fi

1 Connect your iPhone to your computer with the USB cable.

The iTunes window appears.

2 Click **iPhone** (☐).

Note: Your iPhone appears in iTunes with the name you gave it.

The iPhone's control screens appear.

3 Click **Summary**.

The Summary screen appears.

4 Click **Sync with this iPhone over Wi-Fi** (☐ changes to ☑).

5 Click **Apply**.

iTunes applies the change.

6 Disconnect your iPhone from your computer.

Perform a Manual Sync via Wi-Fi

1 Press **Home**. On an iPhone X, swipe up from the bottom of the screen.

The Home screen appears.

2 Tap **Settings** (⚙).

The Settings screen appears.

3 Tap **General** (⚙).

The General screen appears.

4 Tap **iTunes Wi-Fi Sync**.

The iTunes Wi-Fi Sync screen appears.

5 Tap **Sync Now**.

The sync runs.

A The Sync symbol (↻) appears in the status bar.

B The readout shows which part of the sync is currently running.

6 When the sync completes, tap **General** (‹).

The General screen appears.

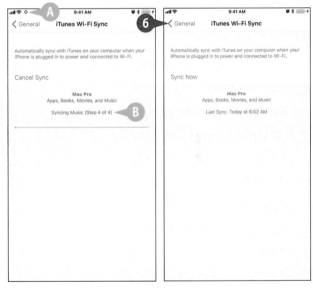

Can I sync my iPhone automatically via Wi-Fi?

Yes. To sync your iPhone automatically via Wi-Fi, connect your iPhone to a power source — for example, the iPhone power adapter. Make sure your computer is on and connected to your network, and that iTunes is running. Your iPhone automatically connects to your computer across the wireless network. iTunes syncs the latest songs, videos, and data.

To avoid interruptions, iTunes may sync your iPhone overnight. This means you need to leave your computer on for automatic syncing to occur, but it is fine for the computer to be asleep.

After you set up your iPhone with iCloud or iTunes, you are ready to start using the device. When you wake the iPhone from sleep, it displays the lock screen. You then unlock the iPhone to reach the Home screen, which contains icons for running the apps installed on the iPhone.

You can quickly launch an app by tapping its icon on the Home screen. From the app, you can return to the Home screen by pressing **Home**; on an iPhone X, you swipe up from the bottom of the screen instead. You can then launch another app as needed.

Explore the Interface and Launch Apps

1 Press **Home** with a finger or thumb you have registered for Touch ID, the fingerprint-unlocking feature. On an iPhone X, tap the screen and raise the iPhone, pointing the screen at your face.

The iPhone's screen lights up.

The lock screen appears momentarily.

The iPhone unlocks.

The Home screen appears.

Note: If you are not using Touch ID or Face ID, or you press **Home** with a nonregistered finger or thumb, the iPhone prompts you to enter your passcode. After you enter the passcode correctly, the iPhone unlocks, and the Home screen appears.

A The iPhone has two or more Home screens. The gray dots at the bottom of the Home screen show how many Home screens you have. The white dot shows the current Home screen.

2 Tap **Notes** ( ).

The Notes app opens.

Note: If you chose to sync notes with your iPhone, the synced notes appear in the Notes app. Otherwise, the list is empty until you create a note.

3 Tap **New** ( ).

A new note opens, and the on-screen keyboard appears.

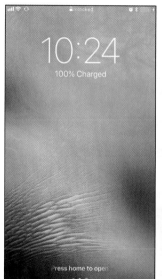

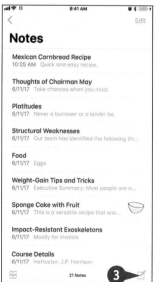

4 Type a short note by tapping the keys.

B If the middle button in the suggestion bar shows the word you want, tap `Spacebar` to accept it. If one of the other buttons shows the right word, tap that button.

5 Tap **Done**.

The on-screen keyboard closes.

6 Tap **Notes** (<).

C The Notes list appears, with your note in it.

7 Press **Home**. On an iPhone X, swipe up from the bottom of the screen.

The Home screen appears.

8 Swipe left to display the second Home screen.

Note: You can also tap at the right end of the row of dots on the Home screen to move one screen to the right. Tap at the left end to move one screen to the left.

You can now launch another app by tapping its icon.

9 Press the **Power/Sleep** button.

Your iPhone goes to sleep.

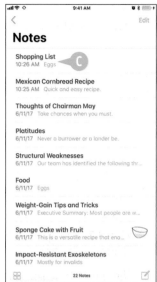

TIP

Where do I get more apps to perform other tasks?
You can find an amazingly wide selection of apps — both free and those you pay for — on Apple's App Store. See Chapter 7 for instructions on finding and downloading the apps you need.

Using Cover Sheet and Today View

Your iPhone handles many different types of alerts, such as missed phone calls, text messages, and invitations to events such as meetings. Your iPhone integrates these alerts into Cover Sheet so that you can review them easily.

The iPhone's Today View enables you to view snippets of important and helpful information, such as weather, calendar appointments, and stock updates. You can access Today View either via Cover Sheet or directly from the Home screen.

Using Cover Sheet and Today View

Open Cover Sheet and Deal with Notifications

1 Swipe down from the top of the screen.

Cover Sheet appears.

Note: See the section "Choose Which Apps Can Give Notifications" in Chapter 2 for instructions on customizing the notifications that appear on Cover Sheet.

Ⓐ You can tap **Clear** (⊗) to clear all notifications in a category such as Yesterday.

2 To remove a single notification, swipe it left.

Action buttons for the notification appear.

Ⓑ You can tap **View** to view the notification in its app.

3 Tap **Clear**.

The notification disappears from Cover Sheet.

4 Press a notification.

The Peek panel opens, together with action buttons.

5 Tap the action you want to take. For example, for an e-mail message, tap **Mark as Read** to mark the message as read.

Note: To go to the app that raised a notification, tap the notification.

6 When you finish working on Cover Sheet, press **Home**. On an iPhone X, swipe up from the bottom of the screen.

The Home screen appears.

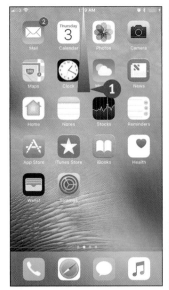

Open Today View

1 Press **Home**. On an iPhone X, swipe up from the bottom of the screen.

The Home screen appears.

Note: If the Home screen that appears is not the first Home screen, press **Home** again or swipe up again to display the first Home screen.

2 Swipe right.

C You can also tap the gray dot at the bottom of the screen.

Today View appears.

Note: You can customize the selection of widgets in Today View. See the section "Customize Today View" in Chapter 2 for details.

3 Swipe up.

Other items appear.

D You can tap a widget to go straight to the related app.

E You can tap an item such as a reminder to mark it as done.

4 Swipe left.

The Home screen appears.

TIP

What happens if I receive a notification when my iPhone is locked?
This depends on the type of notification. For most types of notifications, your iPhone displays an alert on the lock screen to alert you to the notification. Unlocking your iPhone while the alert is showing takes you directly to the notification in whatever app it belongs to — for example, to an instant message in the Messages app.

Using Control Center

ontrol Center puts your iPhone's most essential controls at your fingertips. From Control Center, you can turn Airplane Mode, Wi-Fi, Bluetooth, Do Not Disturb Mode, and Orientation Lock on or off; control music playback and volume and direct your iPhone's audio and video output to AirPlay devices; change the setting for the AirDrop sharing feature; and quickly access the Flashlight, Clock, Calculator, and Camera apps. Control Center appears as a pane that you open by swiping upward from the bottom of the screen on the Home screen or in most apps.

Using Control Center

Open Control Center

1 On an iPhone X, swipe down from the upper-right corner of the screen. On other iPhone models, swipe up from the bottom of the screen.

Control Center opens.

A You can drag the **Brightness** slider to control screen brightness. Press the **Brightness** slider to display a larger slider and the Night Shift icon (), which you can tap to turn Night Shift on or off. See the section "Configure Night Shift and Display Zoom" in Chapter 2 for information on Night Shift.

B You can drag the **Volume** slider to control audio volume.

Control Essential Settings

1 Tap **Airplane Mode** (or) to turn Airplane Mode on () or off ().

2 Tap **Wi-Fi** (or) to turn Wi-Fi on () or off ().

3 Tap **Cellular Data** (or) to turn Cellular Data on () or off ().

4 Tap **Bluetooth** (or) to turn Bluetooth on () or off ().

5 Tap **Do Not Disturb** (or) to turn Do Not Disturb Mode on () or off ().

6 Tap **Orientation Lock** (or) to turn Orientation Lock on () or off ().

7 Press the **Communications** box firmly.

The Communications panel opens.

8 Tap **AirDrop** () to change the AirDrop setting.

9 Tap **Personal Hotspot** (or) to turn Personal Hotspot on () or off ().

10 Tap outside the Communications panel.

The Communications panel closes.

Choose an AirPlay Device for Audio

ⓒ Tap the song information to go to the song in the Music app.

ⓓ Tap **Previous** (⏮) to go back to the start of the song. Tap again to play the previous song.

ⓔ Tap **Next** (⏭) to play the next song.

ⓕ Tap **Pause** (⏸) to pause playback.

❶ Press the Audio box firmly.

The Audio panel opens.

ⓖ You can drag the playhead to move through the song.

❷ Tap **AirPlay** (◎).

The list of AirPlay devices appears.

❸ Tap the audio device to use for output.

The iPhone starts playing audio on that device.

❹ Tap **Done**.

The Now Playing On panel closes.

❺ Tap the screen outside the Audio panel.

The Audio panel closes.

❻ Press **Home**. On an iPhone X, swipe up from the bottom of the screen.

Control Center closes.

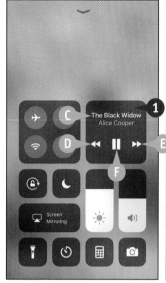
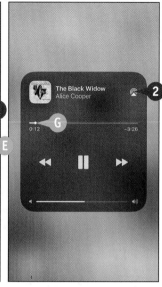

TIP

What are the buttons at the bottom of Control Center?

Tap **Flashlight** (🔦) to turn on the Flashlight. Press **Flashlight** (🔦) firmly to display the Flashlight panel, which lets you choose among four brightnesses. Tap **Timer** (⏲) to display the Timer screen in the Clock app. Press **Timer** (⏲) firmly to display the Timer panel, which enables you to set timers for preset times from 1 minute up to 2 hours. Tap **Calculator** (▦) to display the Calculator app. Tap **Camera** (📷) to display the Camera app.

Using 3D Touch

The iPhone's 3D Touch feature enables you to take actions quickly by pressing firmly with your finger on the screen instead of tapping or tapping and holding. 3D Touch gives you an alternative way to access some commands in some apps.

Only some apps offer 3D Touch actions, although Apple is encouraging developers to include 3D Touch in their apps. Similarly, only some iPhone models have 3D Touch.

Understanding Which iPhone Models Have 3D Touch

All current iPhone models except the iPhone SE have 3D Touch. iPhone models as far back as 2015's iPhone 6s and iPhone 6s Plus also have 3D Touch.

Understanding 3D Touch's Three Main Features

3D Touch has three main features:

- **Quick Actions**. These are actions you can take by pressing an app's icon on the Home screen or in another location.

- **Peek**. This feature enables you to preview the content of an item, such as an e-mail message or a photo.

- **Pop**. This feature enables you to fully open an item into which you have Peeked.

Using Quick Actions from the Home Screen

3D Touch enables you to take a variety of useful actions directly from the Home screen using the Quick Actions feature. To access Quick Actions on the Home screen, you press the appropriate app's icon firmly and then tap the Quick Action on the menu that opens.

If you firmly press an icon that does not provide any Quick Actions, the screen blinks briefly and your iPhone vibrates, as if to shake its head to say "no."

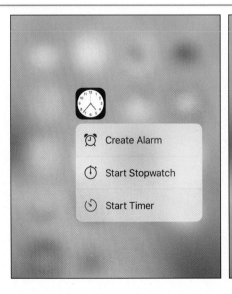

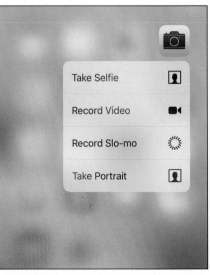

Understanding How Peek and Pop Work

When using 3D Touch, you normally begin with the Peek action, which opens the Peek panel to give you a preview of the contents of an item. The Peek panel stays open only as long as you keep pressing with the same pressure; when you lift your finger, the Peek panel closes.

Instead of lifting your finger, you can press a little harder to Pop open the item. For example, in Mail, you can 3D-Touch a message to open its Peek panel to look at its contents. You can then 3D-Touch further to Pop the message open for reading, or simply lift your finger to allow the message to close again.

Exploring 3D Touch

This book gives some examples of 3D Touch in cases where it is especially convenient. But there are many other actions you can take with 3D Touch, assuming that your iPhone model supports it.

You can explore 3D Touch further by simply pressing icons or other objects in the user interface and seeing if a Quick Actions menu opens or a Peek panel appears. When you do get the menu or the panel, evaluate whether you will be able to save time by using this feature — and if so, add it to your iPhone repertoire.

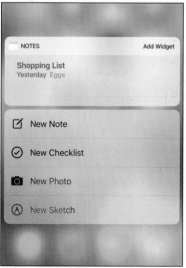

CHAPTER 2

Personalizing Your iPhone

To make your iPhone work the way you prefer, you can configure its many settings. In this chapter, you learn how to control iCloud sync, notifications, audio preferences, screen brightness, and other key aspects of the iPhone's behavior.

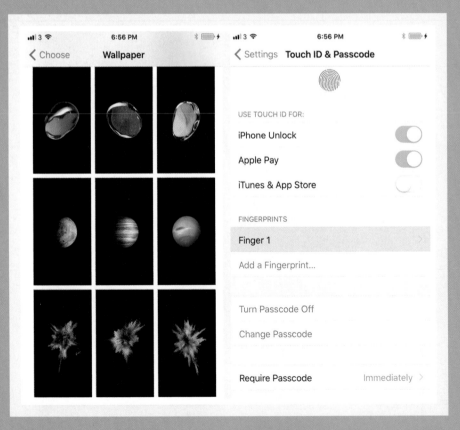

Find the Settings You Need

The iOS operating system includes many settings that enable you to configure your iPhone to work the way you prefer. The central place for manipulating settings is the Settings app, which contains settings for the iPhone's system software, the apps the iPhone includes, and third-party apps you have added. To reach the settings, you first display the Settings screen and then the category of settings you want to configure.

Find the Settings You Need

Display the Settings Screen

1 Press **Home**. On an iPhone X, swipe up from the bottom of the screen.

The Home screen appears.

2 Tap **Settings** (⚙).

The Settings screen appears.

A You can tap **Settings** (🔍) and type a setting name or keyword to locate the setting. You may need to drag down the screen to reveal the Search bar.

B The Apple ID button, which shows your Apple ID name, gives access to settings for your Apple ID and your accounts for iCloud, iTunes, and the App Store.

C The top section of the Settings screen contains settings you are likely to use frequently, such as Airplane Mode, Wi-Fi, and Bluetooth.

3 Tap and drag up to scroll down the screen.

D This section contains settings for built-in apps and features developed by Apple.

4 Tap and drag up to scroll farther down the screen. You can also swipe up to move more quickly.

E This section contains settings for apps you install. These apps can be either from Apple or from third-party developers.

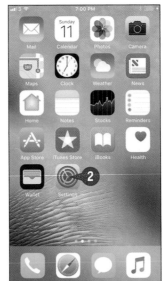

Display a Settings Screen

1 On the Settings screen, tap the button for the settings category you want to display. For example, tap **Sounds & Haptics** (🔊) to display the Sounds and Haptics screen.

2 Tap **Settings** (‹) when you are ready to return to the Settings screen.

Display the Settings for an App

1 On the Settings screen, tap the button for the app whose settings you want to display. For example, tap **Safari** (🧭) to display the Safari settings.

2 Tap **Settings** (‹) when you are ready to return to the Settings screen.

3 Press **Home**. On an iPhone X, swipe up from the bottom of the screen.

The Home screen appears again.

Note: When you next open the Settings app, it displays the screen you were last using. For convenience, it is usually best to return to the main Settings screen when you finish choosing settings.

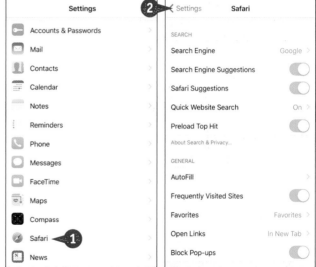

TIP

Where do I find other settings for an app?

As well as the settings that you access by tapping the button bearing the app's name on the Settings screen, some apps include settings that you configure directly within the app. For such apps, look for a Settings icon or menu item.

To configure notifications for an app, tap **Notifications** (🔔) on the Settings screen, and then tap the app's button. To configure Location Services settings for an app, tap **Privacy** (✋) on the Settings screen, tap **Location Services** (➤), and then tap the app's button.

Choose Which iCloud Items to Sync

pple's iCloud service enables you to sync many types of data — such as your e-mail account details, your contacts, and your calendars and reminders — online so you can access them from any of your devices. You can also use the Find My iPhone feature to locate your iPhone when it goes missing. To use iCloud, you set your iPhone to use your Apple ID, and then choose which features to use.

Choose Which iCloud Items to Sync

1 Press **Home**. On an iPhone X, swipe up from the bottom of the screen.

The Home screen appears.

2 Tap **Settings** (⚙).

The Settings screen appears.

3 Tap the Apple ID button. This button shows the name you have set for your Apple ID.

4 Tap **iCloud** (☁).

The iCloud screen appears.

5 In the Apps Using iCloud section, set each app's switch to On (⬤) or Off ( ), as needed.

6 Tap **Photos** (✿).

The Photos screen appears.

7 Set the **iCloud Photo Library** switch to On (⬤) to store all your photos in iCloud.

8 Tap **Optimize iPhone Storage** to store lower-resolution versions of photos on your iPhone to save space. Tap **Download and Keep Originals** if you prefer to keep original, full-quality photos on your iPhone.

9 Set the **Upload to My Photo Stream** switch to On (⬤) to upload photos to your photo stream.

10 Set the **iCloud Photo Sharing** switch to On (⬤) to use Photo Sharing.

11 Tap **iCloud** (<).

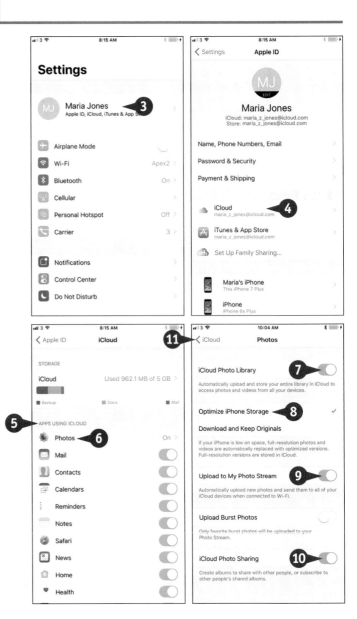

42

The iCloud screen appears again.

12 Swipe up to scroll down to the lower part of the screen.

13 Set the **iCloud Drive** switch to On (⬤) to enable iCloud Drive.

14 In the next two sections, set each app's switch to On (⬤) or Off (⬤) to control whether the app can use iCloud.

A You can tap **Look Me Up** to control which apps can look you up by your Apple ID.

B You can tap **Share My Location** to control whether iCloud shares your location.

C You can tap **Mail** to change your name in outgoing iCloud messages or choose advanced settings.

15 Swipe down to scroll up until iCloud Drive appears at the bottom of the screen.

16 Tap **Keychain** (🔑) to display the Keychain screen, set the **iCloud Keychain** switch to On (⬤), and then create a security code if prompted to do so.

17 Tap **Find My iPhone** (⬤) to display the Find My iPhone screen, set the **Find My iPhone** switch to On (⬤), and set the **Send Last Location** switch to On (⬤) or Off (⬤), as necessary.

18 Tap **iCloud Backup** (⬤).

The Backup screen appears.

19 Set the **iCloud Backup** switch to On (⬤).

20 Tap **iCloud** (‹).

The iCloud screen appears again.

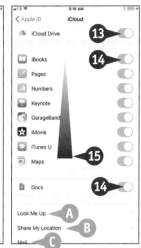

TIPS

How much space does iCloud provide?
iCloud provides 5GB of space for a free account. Content and apps you acquire from Apple do not count against this space, nor do your Photo Stream photos or songs included in iTunes Match — but iCloud Photo Sharing does count. You can buy more space by tapping **Storage**, and then tapping **Buy More Storage** on the iCloud screen that appears.

Should I turn on Find My iPhone?
Yes. Find My iPhone enables you to locate your iPhone when you misplace it or learn where it is when someone takes it. It also prevents someone else from activating your iPhone on his or her own account.

Choose Which Apps Can Give Notifications

*S*ome iPhone apps can notify you of events that occur, such as messages arriving or updates becoming available. You can choose which notifications an app gives or prevent an app from showing notifications. You can also control notification previews and choose which notifications appear on Cover Sheet, the iOS screen for current notifications, and in History, which contains older notifications.

iPhone apps use three types of notifications: badges on app icons, persistent banners, and temporary banners. See the tip for details.

Choose Which Apps Can Give Notifications

1 Press **Home**. On an iPhone X, swipe up from the bottom of the screen.

The Home screen appears.

2 Tap **Settings** (⚙).

The Settings screen appears.

3 Tap **Notifications** (🔲).

The Notifications screen appears.

Ⓐ To choose your default setting for notification previews, tap **Show Previews**, and then tap **Always**, **When Unlocked**, or **Never**, as needed.

4 Tap the app for which you want to configure notifications. This example uses **Calendar** (📅).

The screen for configuring the app's notifications appears.

5 Set the **Allow Notifications** switch to On (🔘) to enable notifications.

Note: For some apps, all the options appear on the screen for configuring the app's notifications.

6 Tap the button for the notification type you want to configure. This example uses **Upcoming Events**.

The screen for configuring that notification type appears, such as the Upcoming Events screen.

7 Tap **Sounds**.

8 Tap the sound you want to use.

B You can tap **None** for no sound.

C You can tap **Tone Store** to browse and buy tones.

D You can tap **Vibration** and choose the vibration pattern for the notification type.

9 Tap the **Back** button (<), such as **Upcoming Events** (<) in this example.

10 Set the **Badge App Icon** switch to On (◯) to show badges.

11 Set the **Show on Cover Sheet** switch to On (◯) or Off ( ), as needed.

12 Set the **Show in History** switch to On (◯) or Off ( ), as needed.

13 If you want the notifications to appear as banners, set the **Show as Banners** switch to On (◯), then tap **Temporary** or **Persistent**, as appropriate.

14 To exempt this app from your default preview setting, tap **Show Previews**.

The Show Previews screen appears.

15 Tap **Always**, **When Unlocked**, or **Never**, as needed.

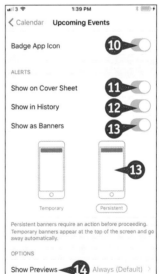

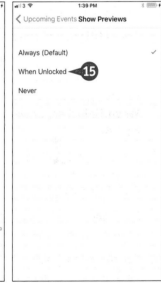

What are the three kinds of notifications?

A *badge* is a red circle or rounded rectangle that appears on the app's icon on the Home screen and shows a white number indicating how many notifications there are. A *temporary banner* is a pop-up notification that appears briefly at the top of the screen and then disappears automatically. A *persistent banner* — previously called an *alert* — is like a temporary banner, but you must dismiss it before you can take other actions on your iPhone. Whichever notification type you choose, you can set the **Sounds** switch to On (◯) to have your iPhone play a sound to get your attention.

Choose Sounds and Haptics Settings

The Sounds & Haptics screen in Settings enables you to control what audio feedback and vibration feedback your iPhone gives you. You can have the iPhone always vibrate to signal incoming calls, or vibrate only when the ringer is silent. You can set the ringer and alerts volumes, choose your default ringtone and text tone, and choose which items can give you alerts. Your iPhone can play lock sounds to confirm you have locked or unlocked your iPhone. It can also play keyboard clicks to confirm each key press.

Choose Sounds and Haptics Settings

1 Press **Home**. On an iPhone X, swipe up from the bottom of the screen.

The Home screen appears.

2 Tap **Settings** (⚙).

The Settings screen appears.

3 Tap **Sounds & Haptics** (🔊).

The Sounds & Haptics screen appears.

4 Set the **Vibrate on Ring** switch to On (🔘) or Off ( ), as needed.

5 Set the **Vibrate on Silent** switch to On (🔘) or Off ( ), as needed.

6 Tap and drag the **Ringer and Alerts** slider to set the volume.

A When the **Change with Buttons** switch is On (🔘), you can change the Ringer and Alerts volume by pressing the volume buttons on the side of the iPhone.

7 Tap **Ringtone**.

The Ringtone screen appears.

8 Tap the ringtone you want to hear.

B You can tap **Tone Store** to browse and buy ringtones.

9 Tap **Vibration**.

The Vibration screen appears.

10 Tap the vibration pattern you want.

11 If you prefer a custom vibration, tap **Create New Vibration** in the Custom area.

The New Vibration screen appears.

12 Tap a rhythm.

13 Tap **Stop**.

14 Tap **Play** to play back the vibration.

15 Tap **Save**.

The New Vibration dialog opens.

16 Type a name.

17 Tap **Save**.

The Vibration screen appears.

18 Tap **Ringtone** (﹤).

The Ringtone screen appears.

19 Tap **Sounds & Haptics** (﹤).

The Sounds & Haptics screen appears.

20 Repeat steps **7** to **19** to set other tones, such as text tones.

21 Set the **Keyboard Clicks** switch to On (◉) or Off ( ), as needed.

22 Set the **Lock Sounds** switch to On (◉) or Off ( ), as needed.

23 Set the **System Haptics** switch to On (◉) or Off ( ) to control whether your iPhone plays haptics for system controls and touches.

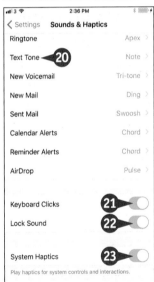

TIP

How do I use different ringtones for different callers?

The ringtone and text tone you set in the Ringtone area of the Sounds & Haptics screen are your standard tone for phone calls, FaceTime calls, and messaging calls. To set different tones for a contact, to display the Home screen tap **Phone** (📞), and then tap **Contacts**. In the Contacts list, tap the contact, tap **Edit**, and then tap **Ringtone**. On the Ringtone screen, tap the ringtone and then tap **Done**. You can also change other settings, such as the Text Tone vibration for the contact. Tap **Done** when you are finished.

Set Display Brightness and Wallpapers

To make the screen easier to see, you can change its brightness. You can also have the Auto-Brightness feature automatically set the screen's brightness to suit the ambient brightness or turn on Smart Invert Colors to counter bright lighting.

To make the screen look good, you can choose which picture to use as the wallpaper that appears in the background. You can use either a static wallpaper or a dynamic, changing wallpaper. You can set different wallpaper for the lock screen and for the Home screen.

Set Display Brightness and Wallpapers

1 Press **Home** — on an iPhone X, swipe up from the bottom of the screen — to display the Home screen.

2 Tap **Settings** (⚙) to display the Settings screen.

3 Tap **Display & Brightness** (🔠).

Note: If lighting conditions make the screen hard to see, try Smart Invert Colors. Press **Home**, tap **Settings** (⚙), and then tap **General** (⚙). Tap **Accessibility**, tap **Display Accomodations**, tap **Invert Colors**, and then set the **Smart Invert** switch to On (🔵).

4 Drag the **Brightness** slider left or right to set brightness.

5 Set the **Auto-Brightness** switch to On (🔵) or Off ( ), as needed.

6 Set the **Raise to Wake** switch to On (🔵) if you want the iPhone to wake up when you raise it.

A You can tap **Text Size** to set your preferred text size.

B You can set the **Bold Text** switch to On (🔵) to make the system text bold.

7 Tap **Settings** (‹).

The Settings screen appears again.

8 Tap **Wallpaper** (🌸).

The Wallpaper screen appears.

9 Tap **Choose a New Wallpaper**.

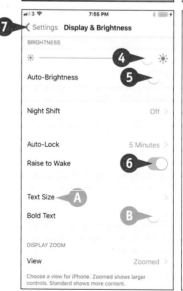

10 Tap **Dynamic**, **Stills**, or **Live** in the Apple Wallpaper area. This example uses **Stills**.

C To choose a picture from a different picture category, tap that category.

11 Tap the wallpaper you want to use.

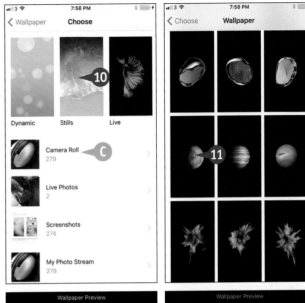

The Wallpaper Preview screen appears.

12 Tap **Still** if you want the image to have no perspective. Tap **Perspective** if you want it to have perspective, as if there is depth between the icons and the wallpaper.

13 Tap **Set**.

14 Tap **Set Lock Screen**, **Set Home Screen**, or **Set Both**. Tap **Cancel** if you do not want to proceed.

15 Press **Home**. On an iPhone X, swipe up from the bottom of the screen.

The Home screen appears.

If you changed the Home screen wallpaper, the new wallpaper appears.

Note: To see the lock screen wallpaper, press **Power/Sleep** twice.

TIP

How do I use only part of a picture as the wallpaper?

The Apple wallpapers are the right size for the screen, so you do not need to resize them. But when you use a photo for the wallpaper, you usually need to choose which part of it to display. When you choose a photo as wallpaper, the iPhone displays the Move and Scale screen. Pinch in or out to zoom the photo out or in, and tap and drag to move the picture around. When you have chosen the part you want, tap **Set**.

Configure Night Shift and Display Zoom

Blue light from the screens of devices can prevent or disrupt your body's sleep, so the iPhone includes a feature called Night Shift that reduces blue light from the screen. You can configure Night Shift to run automatically each night, manually enable it until the next day, and adjust the color temperature to look more or less warm.

On large-screen iPhones, you can choose whether to zoom the display in to a larger size or to keep it at the standard size.

Configure Night Shift and Display Zoom

1 Press **Home**. On an iPhone X, swipe up from the bottom of the screen.

The Home screen appears.

2 Tap **Settings** (⚙).

The Settings screen appears.

3 Tap **Display & Brightness** (🅰🅰).

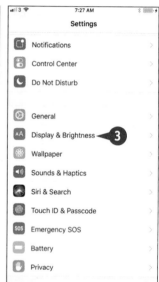

The Display & Brightness screen appears.

4 Tap **Night Shift**.

The Night Shift screen appears.

5 Drag the **Color Temperature** slider along the Less Warm–More Warm axis to set the color temperature you want for Night Shift.

A You can set the **Manually Enable Until Tomorrow** switch to On (◯) to enable Night Shift immediately.

6 Set the **Scheduled** switch to On (◯) to run Night Shift each night.

7 Tap **From, To**.

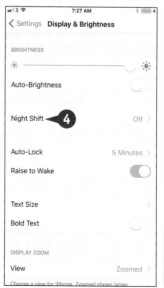

50

The Schedule screen appears.

8. Tap **Sunset to Sunrise** if you want Night Shift to follow sunset and sunrise times for your location; go to step **11**. Otherwise, tap **Custom Schedule**.

9. Tap **Turn On At** and set the time.

10. Tap **Turn Off At** and set the time.

11. Tap **Night Shift** (<).

The Night Shift screen appears.

12. Tap **Display & Brightness** (<).

The Display & Brightness screen appears.

13. Tap **View** in the Display Zoom area.

The Display Zoom screen appears.

14. Tap the unselected tab.

The preview shows the zoom effect.

B. You can swipe left or tap a dot to change the preview. The second preview shows Messages. The third preview shows Mail.

15. Tap **Set**.

The Changing Display Zoom Will Restart iPhone dialog opens.

16. Tap **Use Zoomed** or **Use Standard**, depending on which button appears.

Your iPhone restarts, but you do not need to unlock it again.

The display appears with the zoom effect you chose.

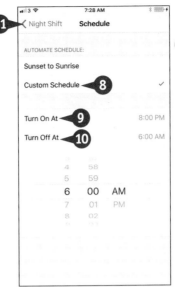

TIP

How does Night Shift know when sunset and sunrise are?
Your iPhone uses Location Services to determine your location, and then looks up the sunset time and sunrise time online. If you disable Location Services, you will need to turn on Night Shift on a custom schedule or manually.

Choose Privacy and Location Settings

Your iPhone contains a huge amount of information about you, the people you communicate with, what you do, and where you go. To keep this information safe, you need to choose suitable privacy and location settings.

Privacy settings enable you to control which apps can access your contacts, calendars, reminders, and photos. You can also choose which apps can use your iPhone's location services, and which track the iPhone's location via the Global Positioning System, or GPS.

Choose Privacy and Location Settings

1. Press **Home**. On an iPhone X, swipe up from the bottom of the screen.

   The Home screen appears.

2. Tap **Settings** (⚙).

   The Settings screen appears.

3. Tap **Privacy** (✋).

   Note: To limit how ads can track your iPhone usage, tap **Advertising** at the bottom of the Privacy screen. On the Advertising screen, set the **Limit Ad Tracking** switch to On (⬤). Tap **Reset Advertising Identifier** and then tap **Reset Identifier** in the confirmation dialog.

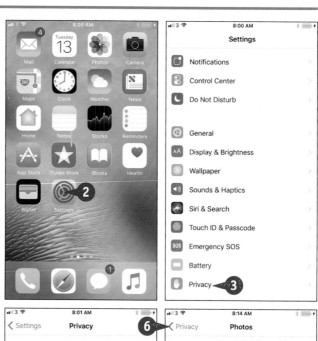

   The Privacy screen appears.

4. Tap the app or service you want to configure. This example uses **Photos** (✿).

   The screen for the app or service appears.

5. For each app, tap the switch to display the app's screen, tap **Never** to prevent access or **Read and Write** to allow access, and then tap **Back** (‹).

6. Tap **Privacy** (‹).

   The Privacy screen appears.

7. Configure other apps and services as needed.

8. Tap **Location Services**.

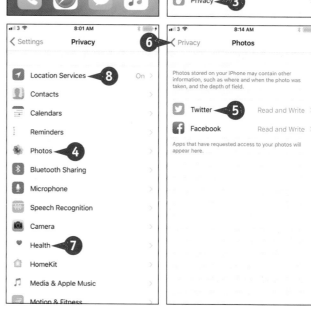

The Location Services screen appears.

9 If you need to turn location services off completely, set the **Location Services** switch to Off (　). Usually, you would leave it set to On (　).

10 Tap the app or feature you want to configure.

11 In the Allow Location Access box, tap the appropriate button, such as **While Using the App** or **Never**.

Note: The buttons in the Allow Location Access box vary depending on the app or feature.

12 Tap **Location Services** (<).

The Location Services screen appears again.

13 Set location access for other apps and features.

14 Tap **System Services**.

The System Services screen appears.

15 Set the switch for each system service to On (　) or Off (　), as needed. For example, set the set the **Location-Based Apple Ads** switch to Off (　) to turn off ads based on your location.

16 Set the **Status Bar Icon** switch to On (　) to see the Location Services icon in the status bar when an app requests your location.

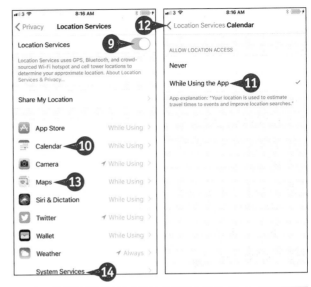

TIP

Why do some apps need to use Location Services?

Some apps and system services need to use Location Services to determine where you are. For example, the Maps app requires Location Services to display your location, and the Compass service needs your location to display accurate compass information.

If you allow the Camera app to use Location Services, it stores GPS data in your photos. You can then sort the photos by location in applications such as Photos on the Mac. Other apps use Location Services to provide context-specific information, such as information about nearby restaurants. For privacy, review the apps using Location Services and turn off any you prefer not to have this information.

Configure and Use Search

Your iPhone can put a huge amount of data in the palm of your hand, and you may often need to search to find what you need.

To make your search results more accurate and helpful, you can configure the Search feature. You can turn off searching for items you do not want to see in your search results.

Configure and Use Search

Configure Search

1 Press **Home**. On an iPhone X, swipe up from the bottom of the screen.

The Home screen appears.

2 Tap **Settings** (⚙).

The Settings screen appears.

3 Tap **Siri & Search** (✳).

The Siri & Search screen appears.

4 Swipe up to scroll down the screen.

The Siri Suggestions section appears.

5 Set the **Suggestions in Search** switch to On (🔵) if you want to see Spotlight suggestions when you search.

6 Set the **Suggestions in Look Up** switch to On (🔵) if you want to see Spotlight suggestions when you use Look Up.

7 In the list of apps, tap the app you want to configure. This example uses **Calendar** (📅).

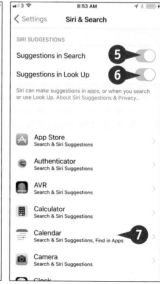

54

8 Set the **Search & Siri Suggestions** switch to On ( ) if you want Calendar content to appear in Search and Look Up and for Siri to access your Calendar data.

9 Set the **Find Events in Other Apps** switch to On ( ) if you want iOS to try to identify events.

Note: The Find in Other Apps switch appears for only some apps. Its name varies depending on the app. For example, the Find Contacts in Other Apps switch appears for the Contacts app.

10 Tap **Back** ( ).

The Siri & Search screen appears again, and you can configure other apps.

Search for Items Using Search

1 Press **Home**. On an iPhone X, swipe up from the bottom of the screen.

The Home screen appears.

2 Tap near the top of the screen and pull down.

Ⓐ The Search panel appears, with the insertion point in it.

Note: You can also start a search by swiping right from the Home screen and then tapping the Search box at the top of the screen.

The keyboard appears.

3 Type your search term.

A list of results appears.

4 Tap the result you want to view.

Which items should I search?

This depends on what you need to be able to search for. For example, if you do not need to search for music, videos, or podcasts, you can exclude the Music apps, the Videos app, and the Podcasts app from Siri & Search Suggestions.

Choose Locking and Control Center Settings

After a period of inactivity whose length you can configure, your iPhone automatically locks itself. It then turns off its screen and goes to sleep to save battery power. Setting your iPhone to lock itself quickly helps preserve battery power, but you may prefer to leave your iPhone on longer so that you can continue work, and then lock your iPhone manually. You can also choose which controls to display in Control Center and the order in which they appear.

Choose Locking and Control Center Settings

① Press **Home**. On an iPhone X, swipe up from the bottom of the screen.

The Home screen appears.

② Tap **Settings** (⚙).

The Settings screen appears.

③ Tap **Display & Brightness** (🔠).

Note: If your iPhone is managed by an administrator, you may not be able to set all the options explained here. For example, an administrator may prevent you from disabling automatic locking for security reasons.

The Display & Brightness screen appears.

④ Tap **Auto-Lock**.

The Auto-Lock screen appears.

⑤ Tap the interval — for example, **1 Minute**.

Note: Choose **Never** for Auto-Lock if you need to make sure your iPhone never goes to sleep. For example, if you are playing music with the lyrics displayed, turning off auto-locking may be helpful.

⑥ Tap **Display & Brightness** (‹).

The Display & Brightness screen appears again.

⑦ Tap **Settings** (‹).

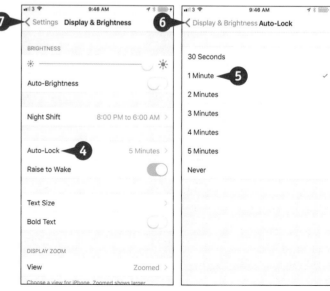

The Settings screen appears again.

8 Tap **Control Center** (icon).

The Control Center screen appears.

A The Include section shows the controls currently in Control Center that you can remove.

B The More Controls section shows controls you can add to Control Center.

9 To remove a control from Control Center, tap **Remove** (⊖), and then tap the textual **Remove** button that appears.

Note: You can also remove a control by dragging it from the Include list to the More Controls list.

10 To add a control to Control Center, tap **Add** (⊕).

C The control moves to the Include list.

11 To change the order of controls in Control Center, drag a control up or down by its handle (≡).

12 When you finish customizing Control Center, tap **Settings** (‹).

The Settings screen appears again.

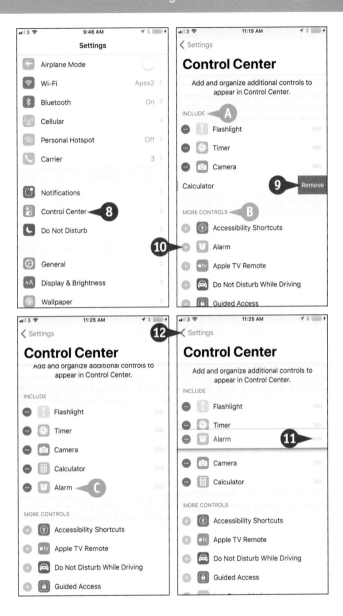

TIP

How do I put the iPhone to sleep manually?

You can put the iPhone to sleep at any point by pressing **Power/Sleep** for a moment.

Putting the iPhone to sleep as soon as you stop using it helps to prolong battery life. If you apply a passcode or other means of locking, as discussed in the section "Secure Your iPhone with Touch ID or Face ID," later in this chapter, putting the iPhone to sleep also starts protecting your data sooner.

Set Up and Use Do Not Disturb Mode

When you do not want your iPhone to disturb you, turn on its Do Not Disturb Mode. You can configure Do Not Disturb Mode to turn on and off automatically at set times each day — for example, on at 10 p.m. and off at 7 a.m. You can turn Do Not Disturb Mode on and off manually from Control Center.

You can allow particular groups of contacts to bypass Do Not Disturb Mode so they can contact you even when Do Not Disturb is on. You can also allow repeated calls to ring when Do Not Disturb is on.

Set Up and Use Do Not Disturb Mode

Configure Do Not Disturb Mode

1 Press **Home**. On an iPhone X, swipe up from the bottom of the screen.

The Home screen appears.

2 Tap **Settings** (⚙).

The Settings screen appears.

3 Tap **Do Not Disturb** (🌙).

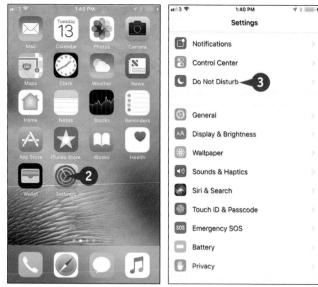

Ⓐ You can turn on Do Not Disturb by setting the **Do Not Disturb** switch to On (⬤).

Note: You can turn Do Not Disturb on and off more easily from Control Center. See the first tip.

4 Set the **Scheduled** switch to On (⬤).

5 Tap **From, To**.

6 Tap **From**.

7 Use the spin wheels to set the From time.

8 Tap **To**.

9 Set the To time.

10 Tap **Do Not Disturb** (‹).

The Do Not Disturb screen appears again.

11 In the Silence section, tap **Always** or **While iPhone is locked**, as needed.

12 Tap **Allow Calls From**.

The Allow Calls From screen appears.

13 Tap the group you will allow to call you during your quiet hours.

14 Tap **Do Not Disturb** (<).

The Do Not Disturb screen appears again.

15 Set the **Repeated Calls** switch to On (⬤) or Off ( ), as needed.

16 Tap **Settings** (<).

The Settings screen appears again.

Turn Do Not Disturb Mode On or Off Manually

1 Press **Home**.

The Home screen appears.

Note: On an iPhone X, swipe down from the upper-right corner of the screen to open Control Center.

2 Swipe up from the bottom of the screen.

Control Center opens.

3 Tap **Do Not Disturb** to turn Do Not Disturb on (⬤ changes to ⬤) or off (⬤ changes to ⬤).

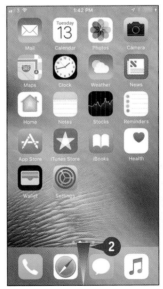

TIPS

How can I tell whether Do Not Disturb is on?

When Do Not Disturb is on, a crescent moon symbol appears in the status bar to the left of the battery readout.

How can I allow multiple groups of people to call me when Do Not Disturb is on?

The Allow Calls From screen lets you select only one group. Unless you can put all the relevant contacts into a single group, the best solution is to create a new group and add the existing groups to it. This is easiest to do in your iCloud account by working in a web browser on a computer.

Customize Today View

Today View, which you display by swiping right on the first Home screen, shows a list of widgets to provide you with quick information about the weather, the news, and your time commitments. You can configure Today View by removing widgets you do not need, adding widgets you find useful, and arranging the widgets into the order you find most helpful.

Customize Today View

1 Press **Home**. On an iPhone X, swipe up from the bottom of the screen.

The Home screen appears.

Note: If the first Home screen does not appear when you press **Home**, press **Home** again — on an iPhone X, swipe up from the bottom of the screen — to display it.

2 Swipe right.

Today View appears.

3 Swipe up to scroll down to the bottom of the screen.

More items in Today View appear.

4 Tap **Edit**.

The Add Widgets screen appears.

5 Tap **Remove** (⊖) to the left of a widget you want to remove.

The textual Remove button appears.

6 Tap **Remove**.

The widget disappears from the list.

7 Swipe up.

The More Widgets list appears.

8 Tap **Add** (⊕) to the left of a widget you want to add to Today View.

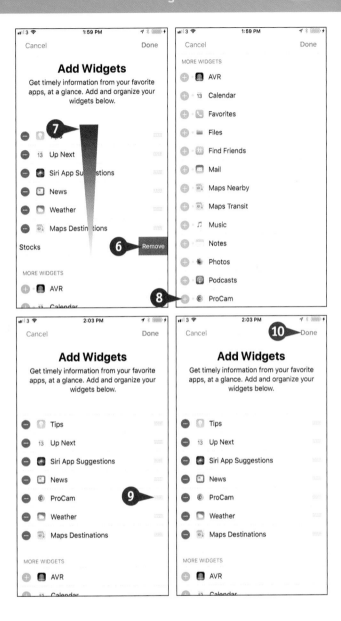

The widget appears in the upper list.

9 Tap a widget's handle (≡) and drag up or down to rearrange the widgets.

10 Tap **Done**.

Today View appears, showing the widgets in the order you specified.

TIP

How do I get more widgets to add to Today View?

The widgets in Today View come built into apps, so the only way to get more widgets is to install more apps that have widgets.

When choosing an app to add to your iPhone, consider whether the app is one for which a widget in Today View would be useful. If so, look for an app that offers a widget.

Secure Your iPhone with Touch ID or Face ID

Apple provides two methods of unlocking your iPhone quickly: Face ID on the iPhone X, and Touch ID on all other current models. Face ID uses cameras to scan your face, while Touch ID uses a scanner built into the Home button to scan your fingerprint. For either Face ID or Touch ID, you create a passcode as a backup method of unlocking your iPhone. For added security, you can set your iPhone to automatically erase its data after ten failed attempts to enter the passcode.

Secure Your iPhone with Touch ID or Face ID

1 Press **Home**. On an iPhone X, swipe up from the bottom of the screen.

The Home screen appears.

2 Tap **Settings** (⚙).

The Settings screen appears.

3 Tap **Touch ID & Passcode** (▣).

Note: This section shows an iPhone without either Touch ID or a passcode set up. Normally, you would set up either a passcode or Touch ID and a passcode during initial setup.

The Touch ID & Passcode screen appears.

Ⓐ To set up Touch ID, tap **Add a Fingerprint** and follow the prompts. You can then set the **iPhone Unlock** switch, the **Apple Pay** switch, and the **iTunes & App Store** switch to On (🔵) or Off ( ), as needed.

4 Tap **Turn Passcode On**.

Ⓑ To change the passcode type, you can tap **Passcode Options** and then tap **Custom Alphanumeric Code**, **Custom Numeric Code**, or **4-Digit Numeric Code**.

5 Type your passcode.

The iPhone displays the message *Verify Your New Passcode*.

6 Type the passcode again.

The Apple ID Password dialog opens.

7 If you want to be able to use your passcode to change your Apple ID from your iPhone, type your passcode and tap **Continue**. If not, tap **Cancel**.

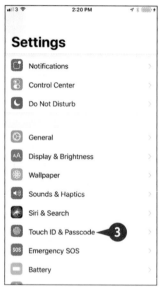

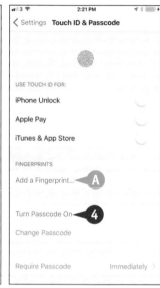

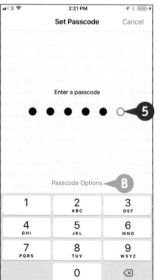

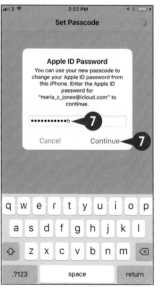

The Touch ID & Passcode screen appears.

8 If you have applied a passcode but not a fingerprint, tap **Require Passcode**.

The Require Passcode screen appears.

9 Tap the button for the length of time you want — for example, **Immediately** or **After 1 minute**.

Note: After you apply a fingerprint, the only choice on the Require Passcode screen is Immediately.

10 Tap **Touch ID & Passcode** (**<**).

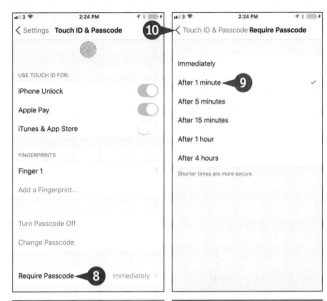

The Touch ID & Passcode screen appears.

11 Set the **Voice Dial** switch to On (⬤) or Off ( ), as needed.

12 In the Allow Access When Locked area, set the switches to On (⬤) or Off ( ), as needed.

Note: Allowing access to Wallet when your iPhone is locked enables you to make payments and reach boarding passes and similar documents more quickly when you need them.

13 If you want the iPhone to erase all its data after ten failed passcode attempts, set the **Erase Data** switch to On (⬤).

The iPhone displays a confirmation dialog.

14 Tap **Enable**.

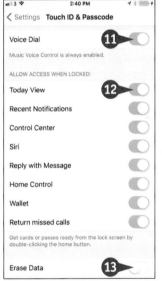

TIPS

Which type of passcode should I use?
The default, a six-digit numeric passcode, provides reasonably good security and is easy to enter. But if you need strong security, choose **Custom Numeric Code** and use 12 or more digits. For extra-strong security, choose **Custom Alphanumeric Code** and create a passcode of 12 or more characters, including upper- and lowercase letters, numbers, and symbols.

What Require Passcode setting should I choose?
Choose **Immediately** for greatest security. Choose **After 1 minute** for good security but more convenience.

Configure Restrictions and Parental Controls

Like any other computer that can access the Internet, the iPhone can reach vast amounts of content not suitable for children or business contexts. You can restrict the iPhone from accessing particular kinds of content. You can use the restrictions to implement parental controls — for example, preventing the iPhone's user from buying content in apps or watching adult-rated movies.

Configure Restrictions and Parental Controls

1 Press **Home**. On an iPhone X, swipe up from the bottom of the screen.

The Home screen appears.

2 Tap **Settings** (⚙).

The Settings screen appears.

3 Tap **General** (⚙).

The General screen appears.

4 Tap **Restrictions**.

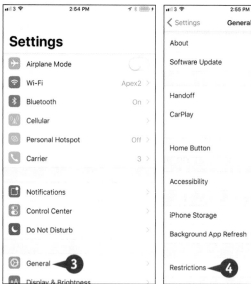

The Restrictions screen appears.

5 Tap **Enable Restrictions**.

The Set Passcode screen appears.

Note: The passcode you set to protect restrictions is different from the passcode you use to lock the iPhone. Do not use the same code.

6 Type the passcode.

Note: The iPhone shows dots instead of your passcode digits in case someone is watching.

The iPhone displays the Set Passcode screen again, this time with the message *Re-enter Your Restrictions Passcode.*

7 Type the passcode again.

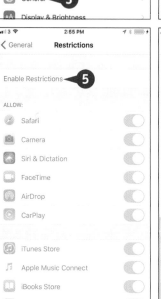

8 In the Allow area, set each switch to On (⬤) or Off ( ), as needed.

9 Scroll down to the Allowed Content area.

10 If you need to change the country used for rating content, tap **Ratings For**. On the Ratings For screen, tap the country, and then tap **Restrictions** (‹).

A You can tap **Password Settings** to choose whether to require a password for each purchase or only after a 15-minute interval, and whether to require a password for free downloads.

11 Choose settings for Music, Podcasts, News & iTunes U, Movies, TV Shows, Books, Apps, Siri, and Websites. For example, tap **Movies**.

12 Tap the highest rating you will permit.

13 Set the **Show Movies in the Cloud** switch to Off ( ) if you want to restrict the iPhone to playing movies in the TV app's library.

14 Tap **Restrictions** (‹).

15 Set the **In-App Purchases** switch to Off ( ) to prevent the user from making in-app purchases. See the first tip.

16 Choose other settings in the Privacy section.

17 Choose settings in the Allow Changes section.

18 Set the **Multiplayer Games** switch, the **Adding Friends** switch, and the **Screen Recording** switch to On (⬤) or Off ( ), as needed.

TIPS

What are in-app purchases?
In-app purchases are items you can buy directly from within apps. These are a popular and easy way for developers to sell extra features for apps, especially low-cost apps or free apps. They are also an easy way for the iPhone's user to spend money.

What do the Privacy settings in Restrictions do?
The Privacy settings in Restrictions enable you to control which apps can access the iPhone's location information, contacts, and other apps, and whether the user can change the settings.

Set Up Family Sharing and Add Members

Apple's Family Sharing feature enables you to share purchases from Apple's online services with other family members. You can also share photos and calendars, and you can use the Find My iPhone feature to find your iOS devices and Macs when they go missing.

This section assumes that you are the Family organizer, the person who gets to set up Family Sharing; invite others to participate; and pay for the content they buy on the iTunes Store, the iBooks Store, and the App Store.

Set Up Family Sharing

To set up Family Sharing, press **Home** — on an iPhone X, swipe up from the bottom of the screen — and then tap **Settings** (⚙) to open the Settings app. Tap **Apple ID** — the button bearing your Apple ID name — at the top of the Settings screen to display the Apple ID screen, and then tap **Set Up Family Sharing** (☁) to display the Family Sharing screen.

Tap **Get Started** to display the Family Setup screen. Here, you can tap **add photo** to add your photo if it is missing, or tap **Not [your name] or want to use a different ID?** to switch to a different Apple ID. When the Apple ID is correct, tap **Continue** to display the Share Purchases screen.

Sign in using the Apple ID you will use for sharing the items you buy on the iTunes Store, the iBooks Store, and the App Store. Tap **Next** to display the Terms and Conditions screen; read them and then tap **Agree** if you want to proceed. Tap **Agree** again in the Terms and Conditions dialog that opens.

On the Payment Method screen, verify that the correct payment card number appears, and then tap **Continue**. On the Share Your Location with Your Family screen, tap **Share Your Location** and follow the prompts if you want your family to be able to track you and your devices, or tap **Not Now** if you prefer privacy.

You have now enabled Family Sharing on your account. The Family Sharing screen appears, and you can add a family member to Family Sharing as explained in the next section.

Add a Family Member to Family Sharing

To add a family member, first display the Family Sharing screen in the Settings app. On an iPhone X, swipe up from the bottom of the screen; on other iPhone models, press **Home**. Tap **Settings** (⚙), tap **Apple ID** — the button bearing your Apple ID name — and then tap **Family Sharing**.

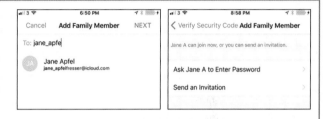

Next, tap **Family Sharing** (☁) to display the Family Sharing screen. Tap **Add Family Member** to display the Add Family Member screen. In the To box, start typing the e-mail address, and then tap the matching contact record for the family member; if there is none, finish typing the e-mail address. Tap **Next**.

If the Verify Security Code screen appears, enter your card's security code and then tap **Next**. Then, on the Add Family Member screen that appears, either tap **Ask [Name] to Enter Password** and have the family member enter her Apple ID and password on your iPhone, or tap **Send an Invitation** to send an invitation via e-mail.

Accept an Invitation to Family Sharing

When someone sends you an invitation to Family Sharing, tap **Get Started** in the e-mail message. If you are using an iOS device, the Family Sharing Invitation screen appears, and you can simply tap **Accept** to accept the invitation.

If you do not want to accept the invitation, tap **Decline** instead.

Choose Date, Time, and International Settings

To keep yourself on time and your data accurate, you need to make sure the iPhone is using the correct date and time.

To make dates, times, and other data appear in the formats you prefer, you may need to change the iPhone's International settings.

Choose Date, Time, and International Settings

Choose Date and Time Settings

1 Press **Home**. On an iPhone X, swipe up from the bottom of the screen.

The Home screen appears.

2 Tap **Settings** (⚙).

The Settings screen appears.

3 Tap **General** (⚙).

The General screen appears.

4 Tap **Date & Time**.

The Date & Time screen appears.

5 Set the **24-Hour Time** switch to On (⬤) if you want to use 24-hour times.

6 To set the date and time manually, set the **Set Automatically** switch to Off ( ).

7 Tap the bar that shows the current date and time.

Controls for setting the date and time appear.

8 Use the controls to set the date and time.

9 Tap **General** (‹).

The General screen appears.

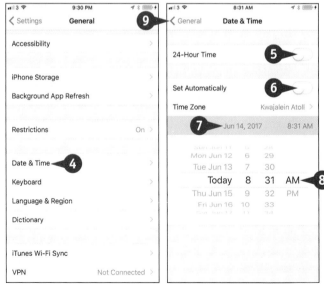

68

Choose International Settings

1 From the General screen, tap **Language & Region**.

The Language & Region screen appears.

A The Region Format Example area shows examples of the time, date, currency, and number formats for the current region.

2 Tap **iPhone Language**.

The iPhone Language screen appears.

3 Tap the language you want to use.

4 Tap **Done**.

The Language & Region screen appears.

5 Tap **Region**.

The Region screen appears.

6 Tap the region you want.

7 Tap **Done**.

The Language & Region screen appears.

TIP

How does my iPhone set the date and time automatically?

Your iPhone sets the date and time automatically by using time servers, computers on the Internet that provide date and time information to computers that request it. The iPhone automatically determines its geographical location so it can request the right time zone from the time server.

CHAPTER 3

Using Voice, Accessibility, and Continuity

Your iPhone includes the Siri personal assistant, helpful accessibility features, and integration with your Mac and Apple Watch via the Continuity feature.

Give Commands with Siri

Often, speaking is even easier than using your iPhone's touch screen — especially when you are out and about or on the move. The powerful Siri feature enables you to take essential actions by using your voice to tell your iPhone what you want. Siri requires a fast Internet connection because the speech recognition runs on servers in Apple's data center.

You can use Siri either with the iPhone's built-in microphone or with the microphone on a headset. The built-in microphone works well in a quiet environment or if you hold your iPhone close to your face, but in noisy situations you will do better with a headset microphone.

Open Siri

You can open Siri from the Home screen or any app. On the iPhone X, press and hold **Sleep/Wake** for several seconds. On other iPhone models, press and hold **Home** for several seconds. If you have connected a headset with a clicker button, you can also press and hold the headset clicker button for several seconds to invoke Siri. If you have chosen to allow Siri access when your iPhone is locked, you can also activate Siri while the lock screen is displayed.

The Siri screen appears. A tone indicates that Siri is ready to take your commands. If you enable the "Hey Siri" feature in the Settings app, you can also activate Siri by saying "Hey Siri."

Send an E-Mail Message

Say "E-mail" and the contact's name, followed by the message. Siri creates an e-mail message to the contact and enters the text. Review the message, and then tap **Send** to send it.

If you prefer, you can start the message by saying "E-mail" and the contact's name, and then pausing. Siri then prompts you for the subject and text of the message in turn.

Set an Alarm

Say "Set an alarm for 4:30 a.m." and check the alarm that Siri displays.

You can turn the alarm off by tapping its switch (changes to).

You can ask a question such as "Which alarms do I have set?" to make Siri display a list of your alarms.

Set a Reminder for Yourself

Say "Remind me" and the details of what you want Siri to remind you of. For example, say "Remind me to take my iPad to work tomorrow morning." Siri listens to what you say and creates a reminder. Check what Siri has written. If the reminder is correct, simply leave it; if not, tap **Remove** and then try again.

Send a Text Message

Say "Tell" and the contact's name. When Siri responds, say the message you want to send. For example, say "Tell Victor Kemp" and then "I'm stuck in traffic, so I'll be about 10 minutes late to the meeting. Please start without me." Siri creates a text message to the contact, enters the text, and sends the message when you say "Send" or tap **Send**.

You can also say "tell" and the contact's name followed immediately by the message. For example, "Tell Bill Sykes the package will arrive at 10 a.m."

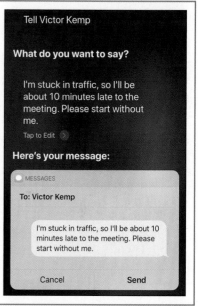

Set Up a Meeting

Say "Meet with" and the contact's name, followed by brief details of the appointment. For example, say "Meet with Don Williamson at noon on Friday for lunch." Siri listens and warns you of any scheduling conflict. Siri then sends a meeting invitation to the contact if it finds an e-mail address, and adds the meeting to your calendar after you tap **Confirm** or say "Confirm."

Dictate Text Using Siri

Ｏne of Siri's strongest features is the capability to transcribe your speech quickly and accurately into correctly spelled and punctuated text. Using your iPhone, you can dictate into any app that supports the keyboard, so you can dictate e-mail messages, notes, documents, and more. To dictate, simply tap the microphone icon (🎤), speak after Siri beeps, and then tap **Done**.

To get the most out of dictation, it is helpful to know the standard terms for dictating punctuation, capitalization, symbols, layout, and formatting.

Insert Punctuation

To insert punctuation, use standard terms: "comma," "period" (or "full stop"), "semicolon," "colon," "exclamation point" (or "exclamation mark"), "question mark," "hyphen," "dash" (for a short dash, –), or "em dash" (for a long dash, —). You can also say "asterisk" (*), "ampersand" (&), "open parenthesis" and "close parenthesis," "open bracket" and "close bracket," and "underscore" (_).

For example, say "buy eggs comma bread comma and cheese semicolon and maybe some milk period nothing else exclamation point" to enter the text shown here.

Insert Standard Symbols

To insert symbols, use these terms: "at sign" (@), "percent" (%), "greater than" (>) and "less than" (<), "forward slash" (/) and "backslash" (\), "registered sign" (®), and "copyright sign" (©).

For example, say "fifty-eight percent forward slash two greater than ninety-seven percent forward slash three" to enter the computation shown here.

Insert Currency Symbols

To insert currency symbols, say the currency name and "sign." For example, say "dollar sign" to insert $, "cent sign" to insert ¢, "euro sign" to insert €, "pound sterling sign" to insert £, and "yen sign" to insert ¥.

For example, say "convert dollar sign two hundred to UK pounds sterling" to enter the calculation shown here.

Control Layout

You can control text layout by creating new lines and new paragraphs as needed. A new paragraph enters two line breaks, creating a blank line between paragraphs. To create a new line, say "new line." To create a new paragraph, say "new paragraph."

For example, say "dear Anna comma new paragraph thank you for the parrot period new paragraph it's the most amazing gift I've ever had period" to enter the text shown here.

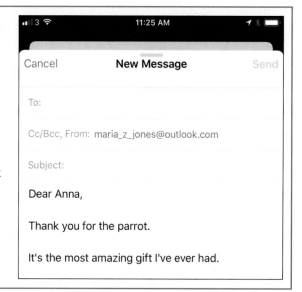

Control Capitalization

You can apply capitalization to the first letter of a word or to a whole word. You can also switch capitalization off temporarily to force lowercase:

Say "cap" to capitalize the first letter of the next word.

Say "caps on" to capitalize all the words until you say "caps off."

Say "no caps" to prevent automatic capitalization of the next word — for example, "no caps Monday" produces "monday" instead of "Monday."

Say "no caps on" to force lowercase of all words until you say "no caps off."

For example, say "give the cap head cap dining cap table a no caps french polish period" to enter the text shown here.

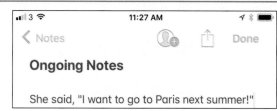

Insert Quotes and Emoticons

To insert double quotes, say "open quotes" and "close quotes." To insert single quotes, say "open single quotes" and "close single quotes." To enter standard emoticons, say "smiley face," "frown face," and "wink face."

For example, say "she said comma open quotes I want to go to Paris next summer exclamation point close quotes" to enter the text shown here.

Gather and Share Information with Siri

You can use Siri to research a wide variety of information online — everything from sports and movies to restaurants worth visiting or worth avoiding. You can also use Siri to perform hands-free calculations. When you need to share information quickly and easily, you can turn to Siri. By giving the right commands, you can quickly change your Facebook status or post on your wall. Similarly, you can send tweets on your Twitter account.

Find Information About Sports

Launch Siri and ask a question about sports. For example:

"Siri, when's the next White Sox game?"

"Did the Lakers win their last game?"

"When's the end of the NBA season?"

"Can you show me the roster for the Maple Leafs?"

Find Information About Movies

Launch Siri and ask a question about movies. For example:

"Siri, where is the movie *The Book of Henry* playing in Indianapolis?"

"What's the name of Blake Lively's latest movie?"

"Who's the star of *My Cousin Rachel*?"

"Is *Cars 3* any good?"

Find a Restaurant

Launch Siri, and then tell Siri what type of restaurant you want. For example:

"Where's the best Mexican food in Palo Alto?"

"Where can I get sushi in Albuquerque?"

"Is there a brewpub in Minneapolis?"

"Is there any dim sum within 50 miles of here?"

Address a Query to the Wolfram Alpha Computational Knowledge Engine

Launch Siri, and then say "Wolfram" and your query. For example:

"Wolfram, minus 20 centigrade in Kelvin."

"Wolfram, what is the cube of 27?"

"Wolfram, tangent of 60 degrees."

"Wolfram, give me the chemical formula for hydrogen peroxide."

Find Out What Music You Are Listening To

Launch Siri and ask a question such as "What song is this?" or "Do you know what this music is called?" Siri monitors the microphone's input, consults the Shazam music-recognition service, and returns a result if there is a match.

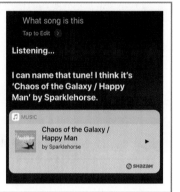

Translate to Another Language

Launch Siri, and then say "Translate to" and the name of the language, such as "Translate to Spanish." When Siri prompts you for the text, speak it. Siri announces the translated text and displays it on-screen, together with a Play button (▶) that you can tap to play the audio again.

Configure Siri to Work Your Way

To get the most out of Siri, spend a few minutes configuring Siri. You can set the language Siri uses and choose when Siri should give you voice feedback. You can also decide whether to use the Raise to Speak option, which activates Siri when you raise your iPhone to your face.

Most important, you can tell Siri which contact record contains your information, so that Siri knows your name, address, phone numbers, e-mail address, and other essential information.

Configure Siri to Work Your Way

1 Press **Home**. On an iPhone X, swipe up from the bottom of the screen.

The Home screen appears.

2 Tap **Settings** (⚙️).

The Settings screen appears.

3 Tap **Siri & Search** (🔍).

The Siri & Search screen appears.

4 Set the **Listen for "Hey Siri"** switch on On (🔘) if you want to be able to activate Siri by saying "Hey Siri!"

5 Set the **Press for Siri** switch to On (🔘) if you want to be able to summon Siri by pressing and holding the Home button.

6 Set the **Allow Siri When Locked** switch to On (🔘) if you want to use Siri from the lock screen.

7 Tap **Language**.

The Language screen appears.

8 Tap the language you want to use.

9 Tap **Siri & Search** (‹).

The Siri & Search screen appears again.

10 Tap **Siri Voice**.

The Siri Voice screen appears.

11 In the Accent box, tap the accent you want Siri to use. For example, for English (United States), you can tap **American, Australian**, or **British**.

12 In the Gender box, tap **Male** or **Female**, as needed.

13 Tap **Siri & Search** (‹).

The Siri & Search screen appears again.

14 Tap **Voice Feedback**.

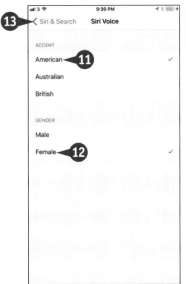

The Voice Feedback screen appears.

15 Tap **Always On**, **Control with Ring Switch**, or **Hands-Free Only**, as needed.

16 Tap **Siri & Search** (‹).

The Siri & Search screen appears again.

17 Tap **My Info**.

The Contacts screen appears, showing either the All Contacts list or the groups you have selected.

Note: If necessary, click Groups to display the Groups screen, select the groups you need, and then tap **Done**.

18 Tap the contact record that contains your information.

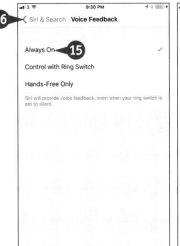

TIP

Does Apple store the details of what I ask Siri?

Yes, but not in a way that will come back to haunt you. When you use Siri, your iPhone passes your input to servers in Apple's data center in North Carolina, USA, for processing. The servers analyze your request and tell Siri how to respond to it. Apple's data center stores the details of your request and may analyze them to determine what people use Siri for and work out ways of making Siri more effective. Apple does not associate your Siri data with other data Apple holds about you — for example, the identity and credit card data you used to pay for iTunes Match.

Set Up VoiceOver to Identify Items On-Screen

If you have trouble identifying the iPhone's controls on-screen, you can use the VoiceOver feature to read them to you. VoiceOver changes your iPhone's standard finger gestures so that you tap to select the item whose name you want it to speak, double-tap to activate an item, and flick three fingers to scroll.

VoiceOver can make your iPhone easier to use. Your iPhone also includes other accessibility features, which you can learn about in the next section, "Configure Other Accessibility Features."

Set Up VoiceOver to Identify Items On-Screen

1 Press **Home**. On an iPhone X, swipe up from the bottom of the screen.

The Home screen appears.

2 Tap **Settings** (⚙).

The Settings screen appears.

3 Tap **General** (⚙).

The General screen appears.

4 Tap **Accessibility**.

The Accessibility screen appears.

5 Tap **VoiceOver**.

Note: You cannot use VoiceOver and Zoom at the same time. If Zoom is on when you try to switch VoiceOver on, your iPhone prompts you to choose which of the two to use.

The VoiceOver screen appears.

6 Set the **VoiceOver** switch to On (⃝ changes to ⬤).

7 Tap **VoiceOver Practice**.

A selection border appears around the button, and VoiceOver speaks its name.

8 Double-tap **VoiceOver Practice**.

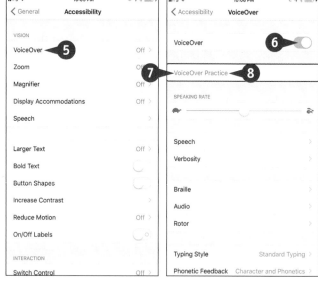

The VoiceOver Practice screen appears.

9 Practice tapping, double-tapping, triple-tapping, swiping, and flicking. VoiceOver identifies each gesture and displays an explanation.

10 Tap **Done** to select the button, and then double-tap **Done**.

The VoiceOver screen appears again.

11 Swipe up with three fingers.

The screen scrolls down.

12 Tap **Speaking Rate** to select it, and then swipe up or down to adjust the rate. Swiping up or down is the VoiceOver gesture for adjusting the slider.

13 Tap **Speech** and choose voice, pronunciations, and pitch options on the Speech screen.

14 Tap **Verbosity** and choose which items to have VoiceOver announce.

15 Set the **Always Speak Notifications** switch to On (⬤) or Off ( ), as needed.

16 Tap **Double-tap Timeout** and set the timeout for double-tapping.

17 Tap **Typing Feedback** to select it, and then double-tap.

18 In the Software Keyboards area, tap and then double-tap the feedback type you want: **Nothing**, **Characters**, **Words**, or **Characters and Words**.

19 In the Hardware Keyboards area, tap and then double-tap the feedback type you want: **Nothing**, **Characters**, **Words**, or **Characters and Words**.

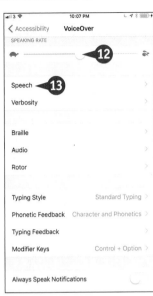

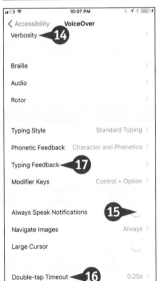

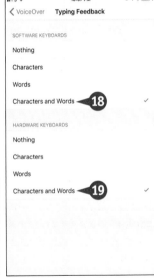

TIP

Is there an easy way to turn VoiceOver on and off?
Yes. You can set your iPhone to toggle VoiceOver on or off when you press **Home** three times in rapid sequence. At the bottom of the Accessibility screen, tap **Accessibility Shortcut** to display the Accessibility Shortcut screen. In the Triple-Click the Home Button For list, tap **VoiceOver**, placing a check mark next to it. Tap **Accessibility** (<) to return to the Accessibility screen.

Configure Other Accessibility Features

If you have trouble using your iPhone in its default configuration, explore the other accessibility features that your iPhone offers apart from VoiceOver.

To help you see the screen better, iOS provides a full-featured zoom capability. After turning on zooming, you can display the Zoom Controller to give yourself easy control of zoom, choose the zoom region, and set the maximum zoom level. You can then triple-tap the screen to zoom in and out quickly.

Configure Other Accessibility Features

Display the Accessibility Screen and Configure Zoom Settings

1 Press **Home**. On an iPhone X, swipe up from the bottom of the screen.

The Home screen appears.

2 Tap **Settings** (⚙).

The Settings screen appears.

3 Tap **General** (⚙).

The General screen appears.

Note: Apart from the accessibility features explained in this section, your iPhone supports physical accessibility features such as Switch Control and AssistiveTouch. Switch Control enables you to control your iPhone through a physical switch you connect to it. AssistiveTouch lets you use an adaptive accessory to touch the screen.

4 Tap **Accessibility**.

The Accessibility screen appears.

5 Tap **Zoom**.

The Zoom screen appears.

6 Set the **Zoom** switch to On (changes to ⚪).

A The Zoom window appears if the Zoom Region is set to Window Zoom.

7 Set the **Follow Focus** switch to On (⚪) to make the zoomed area follow the focus on-screen.

8 Set the **Smart Typing** switch to On (⚪) to make iOS switch to Window Zoom when a keyboard appears, so that text is zoomed but the keyboard is regular size.

9 Set the **Show Controller** switch to On (⚪).

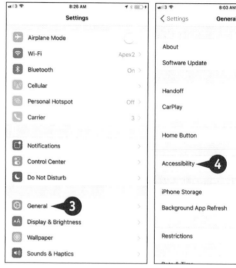

B The Zoom Controller (⊕) appears.

10 Tap **Idle Visibility**.

The Idle Visibility screen appears.

11 Drag the slider to set the visibility percentage for the Zoom Controller when it is idle.

12 Tap **Zoom** (<).

The Zoom screen appears again.

13 Tap **Zoom Region** to display the Zoom Region screen; tap **Full Screen Zoom** or **Window Zoom**, as needed; and then tap **Zoom** (<).

14 Tap **Zoom Filter**.

The Zoom Filter screen appears.

15 Tap **None**, **Inverted**, **Grayscale**, **Grayscale Inverted**, or **Low Light**, as needed.

16 Tap **Zoom** (<).

The Zoom screen appears again.

17 Drag the **Maximum Zoom Level** slider to set the maximum zoom level, such as 8×.

18 Tap **Accessibility** (<).

The Accessibility screen appears.

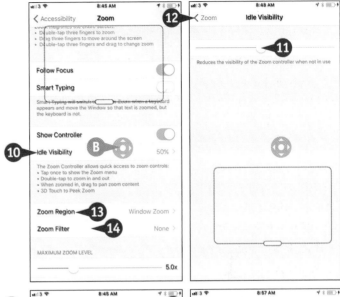

TIP

Is there an easy way to turn the Zoom feature on and off?

Yes. You can set your iPhone to toggle Zoom on or off when you press **Home** three times in rapid sequence. At the bottom of the Accessibility screen, tap **Accessibility Shortcut** to display the Accessibility Shortcut screen. In the Triple-Click the Home Button For list, tap **Zoom**, placing a check mark next to it, and then tap **Accessibility** (<). You can also use the Home triple-press to toggle the VoiceOver feature, the Invert Colors feature, the Grayscale feature, the Switch Control feature, or the AssistiveTouch feature.

continued ▶

Your iPhone includes several "display accommodations" to make the screen easier to view. These accommodations include inverting the screen colors, reducing the white point to lessen the intensity of bright colors, and applying color filters for grayscale or for the protanopia, deuteranopia, or tritanopia color blindnesses.

You can also configure visual interface accessibility settings to make items easier to see. For example, you can set a larger text size, apply shading around text-only buttons, reduce the transparency of items, and darken colors.

Configure Other Accessibility Features (continued)

Configure Display Accommodations

1 On the Accessibility screen, tap **Display Accommodations**.

The Display Accommodations screen appears.

2 Tap **Invert Colors**.

The Invert Colors screen appears.

3 Set the **Smart Invert** switch to On (⬤) if you want to invert the colors except for images, media files, and dark-themed apps.

Note: Enabling Invert Colors disables Night Shift.

4 Set the **Classic Invert** switch to On (⬤) if you want to invert all the colors, as in this example.

5 Tap **Display Accommodations** (＜).

The Display Accommodations screen appears again.

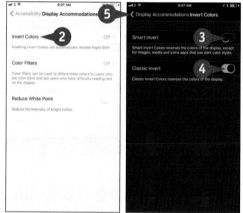

6 Set the **Reduce White Point** switch to On (⬤) if you want to reduce the intensity of bright colors.

7 Drag the slider to adjust the white point.

8 Tap **Color Filters**.

The Color Filters screen appears.

C The color chart displays colors using the filtering you apply. Swipe left for other charts.

9 Set the **Color Filters** switch to On (⬤).

The list of color filters appears.

10 Tap the filter you want to apply: **Grayscale**, **Red/Green Filter**, **Green/Red Filter**, **Blue/Yellow Filter**, or **Color Tint**.

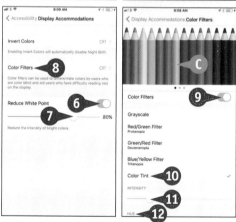

11 If the Intensity slider appears, drag it to adjust the intensity.

12 For Color Tint, drag the **Hue** slider to adjust the hue.

Configure Visual Interface Accessibility Settings

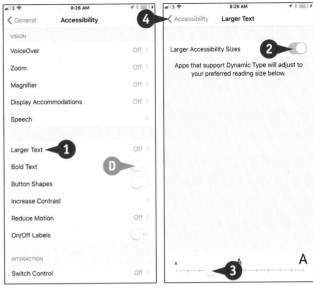

1 On the Accessibility screen, tap **Larger Text**.

The Larger Text screen appears.

2 Set the **Larger Accessibility Sizes** switch to On (changes to ○).

3 Drag the slider to set the text size.

4 Tap **Accessibility** (<).

The Accessibility screen appears.

D You can set the **Bold Text** switch to On (○) to make text appear bold. You must restart your iPhone to effect this change.

E You can set the **Button Shapes** switch to On (○) to make underlines appear under button names, as on the General button at the top of the left screen.

5 Tap **Increase Contrast**.

The Increase Contrast screen appears.

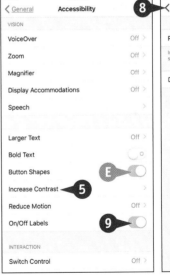

6 Set the **Reduce Transparency** switch to On (○) or Off ( ), as needed.

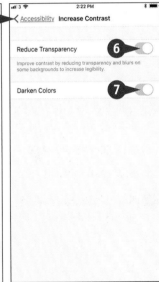

7 Set the **Darken Colors** switch to On (○) or Off ( ), as needed.

8 Tap **Accessibility** (<).

The Accessibility screen appears again.

9 Set the **On/Off Labels** switch to On (○) if you want to display I and O labels on the switches.

TIPS

How do I set up a hearing aid with my iPhone?
Tap **Hearing Devices** on the Accessibility screen to display the Hearing Devices screen. Here you can pair a hearing aid that conforms to the Made for iPhone standard; for other hearing aids, work on the Bluetooth screen, as for other Bluetooth devices.

What does the Reduce Motion feature do?
Reduce Motion reduces the amount of movement that occurs when you tilt the iPhone when displaying a screen such as the Home screen, where the icons appear to float above the background.

continued ▶

Your iPhone includes a suite of interaction features designed to make it easier for you to interact with the touch screen and other hardware components, such as the accelerometers that detect and analyze the device's movements. Changes you can make include setting the tap-and-hold duration and the repeat interval, adjusting the pressure needed for 3D Touch, and configuring the double- and triple-click speed for the Home button. You can also choose your default audio device for call audio.

Configure Other Accessibility Features (continued)

Configure Interaction Accessibility Features

1 On the Accessibility screen, tap **Touch Accommodations**.

The Touch Accommodations screen appears.

2 Set the **Touch Accommodations** switch to On (●) to enable touch accommodations.

3 Set the **Hold Duration** switch to On (●) if you need to adjust the hold duration.

Note: If the Important dialog opens, warning you that Touch Accommodations changes iPhone control gestures, tap **OK.**

4 Tap **+** or **−** to set the Hold Duration.

5 Set the **Ignore Repeat** switch to On (●) if your iPhone detects false repeat touches.

6 Tap **+** or **−** to set the Ignore Repeat interval.

7 In the Tap Assistance box, tap **Off**, **Use Initial Touch Location**, or **Use Final Touch Location**, as needed.

8 Tap **Accessibility** (<).

9 Tap **3D Touch**.

F You can set the **3D Touch** switch to Off ( ) to disable 3D Touch.

10 Drag the **3D Touch Sensitivity** slider to Light, Medium, or Firm, as needed.

G Press the image to test the 3D Touch setting.

11 Tap **Accessibility** (<) to display the Accessibility screen again.

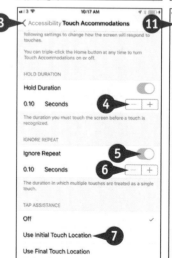
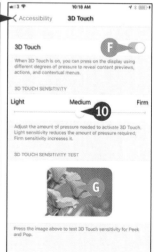

12 Tap **Shake to Undo**.

13 Set the **Shake to Undo** switch to Off ( ) if the feature undoes actions by accident.

14 Tap **Accessibility** (<).

H If you want to disable all vibration, tap **Vibration**, set the **Vibration** switch on the Vibration screen to Off ( ), and then tap **Accessibility** (<).

15 Tap **Call Audio Routing**.

The Call Audio Routing screen appears.

16 Tap the audio output device you want to use for phone calls and FaceTime audio calls — for example, tap **Bluetooth Headset**.

17 Tap **Auto-Answer Calls** and set the **Auto-Answer Calls** switch On ( ) or Off ( ), as needed.

18 Tap **Accessibility** (<).

19 Tap **Home Button**.

20 In the Click Speed section, tap **Default**, **Slow**, or **Slowest** to set the double-click speed.

21 In the Press and Hold to Speak section, tap **Siri**, **Voice Control**, or **Off**, as needed.

22 Set the **Rest Finger to Open** switch to On ( ) if you want to unlock the iPhone using Touch ID by resting your finger on the Home button rather than pressing it.

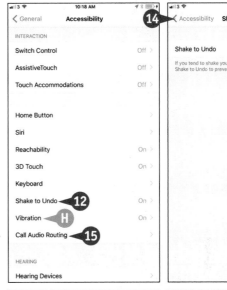

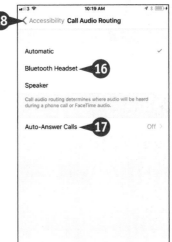

TIP

What are the Speech accessibility settings?
You can have your iPhone speak selected text or the whole screen. To enable these features, tap **Speech** on the Accessibility screen and then set the **Speak Selection** switch or the **Speak Screen** switch to On ( ). Set the **Speak Screen** switch to On ( ) to enable swiping down the screen with two fingers to make your iPhone speak all the text on-screen. Tap **Voices** to choose the speaking voice and drag the **Speaking Rate** slider to set the speaking speed. To have your iPhone speak what you type, tap **Typing Feedback** and then choose settings on the Typing Feedback screen.

87

Using Your iPhone with Your Mac

If you have a Mac, you can enjoy the impressive integration that Apple has built into iOS and the Mac's operating system, now called macOS but formerly called OS X. Apple calls this integration Continuity. Continuity involves several features, including Handoff, which enables you to pick up your work or play seamlessly on one device exactly where you have left it on another device. For example, you can start writing an e-mail message on your Mac and then complete it on your iPhone.

Understanding Which iPhone Models and Mac Models Can Use Continuity

To use Continuity, your iPhone must be running iOS 8 or a later version. Your Mac must be running Yosemite, El Capitan, Sierra, High Sierra, or a later version. Your Mac must have Bluetooth 4.0 hardware. In practice, this includes a Mac mini or MacBook Air from 2011 or later, a MacBook Pro or iMac from 2012 or later, a Mac Pro from 2013 or later, or a MacBook from 2015 or later.

Enable Handoff on Your iPhone

To enable your iPhone to communicate with your Mac, you need to enable the Handoff feature. Display the Home screen, tap **Settings** ( ) to open the Settings app, tap **General** ( ) to display the General screen, and then tap **Handoff**. On the Handoff screen, set the **Handoff** switch to On ( ).

Enable Handoff on Your Mac

You also need to enable Handoff on your Mac. To do so, click on the menu bar and then click **System Preferences** to open the System Preferences window. Click **General** to display the General pane. Click **Allow Handoff between this Mac and your iCloud devices** (changes to). You can then click **System Preferences** on the menu bar and click **Quit System Preferences** to quit System Preferences.

Make and Take Phone Calls on Your Mac

When you are using your Mac within Bluetooth range of your iPhone, Continuity enables you to make and take phone calls on your Mac instead of your iPhone. For example, when someone calls you on your iPhone, your Mac displays a call window automatically, and you can pick up the call on your Mac.

Send and Receive Text Messages from Your Mac

Your Mac can already send and receive messages via Apple's iMessage service, but when your iPhone's connection is available, your Mac can send and receive messages directly via Short Message Service (SMS) and Multimedia Messaging Service (MMS). This capability enables you to manage your messaging smoothly and tightly from your Mac.

Using Your iPhone with Your Apple Watch

Apple Watch puts timekeeping, notifications, and other essential information directly on your wrist. Apple Watch is an accessory for the iPhone — it requires an iPhone to set it up, to provide apps and data, and to give access to the cellular network and the Internet.

Apple Watch works with iPhone 5 and later models.

Pair Your Apple Watch with Your iPhone

You must pair Apple Watch with your iPhone before you can use the devices together. Press and hold the **side button** on Apple Watch until the Apple logo appears, and then wait while Apple Watch finishes starting up.

On your iPhone, display the Home screen, and then tap **Watch** (⌚) to open the Watch app. Tap **Start Pairing**, and then follow the prompts to hold Apple Watch up to your iPhone's rear camera so that the Watch app can recognize the pattern on the Apple Watch screen.

When the Your Apple Watch Is Paired screen appears, tap **Set Up Apple Watch** and complete the setup routine.

Configure Your Apple Watch Using Your iPhone

The Watch app on your iPhone enables you to configure your Apple Watch. On your iPhone, display the Home screen, tap **Watch** (⌚) to open the Watch app, and then tap **My Watch** (⌚) to display the My Watch screen.

From here, you can choose a wide range of settings. For example, you can tap **App Layout** (▦) to configure the layout of the apps on your Apple Watch's screen, or you can tap **Notifications** (▢) to choose which notifications you receive on your Apple Watch.

Install Apps on Your Apple Watch

The Watch app on your iPhone enables you to install apps on your Apple Watch — and remove them if necessary.

When you install an iPhone app that has a companion app for Apple Watch, the app's name appears on the My Watch screen. Tap the app's name to display the app's screen. You can then set the **Show App on Apple Watch** switch to On (changes to) to install the app.

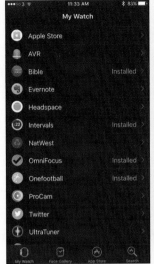

Receive Notifications on Your Apple Watch

When you receive a notification from an app you have permitted to raise notifications, your Apple Watch displays an icon showing the app and other information, such as the sender of an e-mail message. You can tap the notification to view its details.

Receive Calls on Your Apple Watch

When you receive a phone call, it rings on both your Apple Watch and your iPhone. You can tap **Accept** ( ) to pick up the call on Apple Watch or tap **Decline** ( ) to decline the call, sending it to voicemail.

CHAPTER 4

Setting Up Communications

In this chapter, you learn how to add your e-mail accounts to the Mail app and control how Mail displays your messages. This chapter also shows you how to control the way your iPhone displays your contacts; browse, search, create, and import contacts; choose options for your calendars; and set up Wallet and Apple Pay.

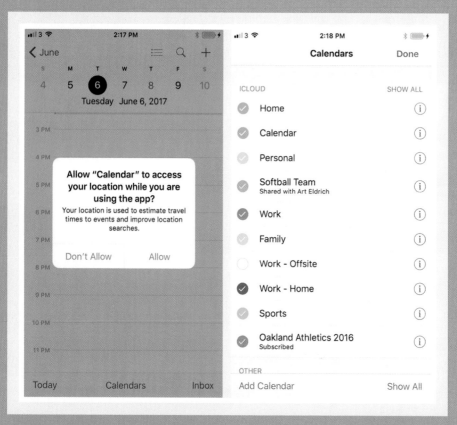

Set Up Your Mail Accounts

Usually, you set up your iCloud account while going through the initial setup routine for your iPhone. But if you have other e-mail accounts, you can set them up as explained in this section.

To set up an e-mail account, you need to know the e-mail address and password, as well as the e-mail provider. You may also need to know the addresses of the mail servers the account uses. For Microsoft Exchange, including Office 365, you must know the domain name as well.

Set Up Your Mail Accounts

1 Press **Home**. On an iPhone X, swipe up from the bottom of the screen.

The Home screen appears.

2 Tap **Settings** (⚙).

The Settings screen appears.

Note: If you have not yet set up an e-mail account on the iPhone, you can also open the Add Account screen by tapping **Mail** on the iPhone's Home screen.

3 Tap **Accounts & Passwords** (🔑).

The Accounts & Passwords screen appears.

4 Tap **Add Account**.

The Add Account screen appears.

5 Tap the kind of account you want to set up. For example, tap **Google**.

Note: Some account types have fields other than those shown here. For example, some accounts include a field for entering your name the way you want it to appear on outgoing messages. Some include a field for changing the description displayed for the account.

The screen for setting up that type of account appears.

A You can tap **More options** and then tap **Create New Account** to create a new account.

6 Tap **Enter your email** and type the e-mail address.

7 Tap **Next**.

The Password screen appears.

8 Type your password.

B You can tap **Show** () to display the password you have typed.

9 Tap **Next**.

10 If another security screen appears, such as the 2-Step Verification screen shown here, enter the required information and tap **Next**.

The configuration screen for the account appears.

11 Make sure the **Mail** switch is set to On ( ).

12 Set the **Contacts** switch, **Calendars** switch, **Notes** switch, and any other switches to On ( ) or Off ( ), as needed.

13 Tap **Save**.

The account appears on the Accounts & Passwords screen.

TIP

How do I set up a Hotmail account?
Hotmail is one of the services that Microsoft has integrated into its Outlook.com service. Tap **Outlook.com** on the Add Account screen, enter your e-mail address on the Outlook screen that appears, and tap **Next**. On the Enter Password screen, type your password and tap **Sign In**. On the Let This App Access Your Info? screen, tap **Yes**. Verify your password again if prompted. After Mail verifies the account, set the **Mail** switch, **Contacts** switch, **Calendars** switch, **Reminders** switch, and **Notes** switch to On ( ) or Off ( ), as needed, and then tap **Save**.

In the Mail app, you can choose how many lines to include in message previews, decide whether to display the To and Cc label, and control whether Mail prompts you before deleting a message. You can change the minimum font size. You can also choose whether to load remote images in messages; whether to mark e-mail addresses outside a particular domain, such as that of your company or organization; and whether to increase the indentation on messages you reply to or forward.

Control How Your E-Mail Appears

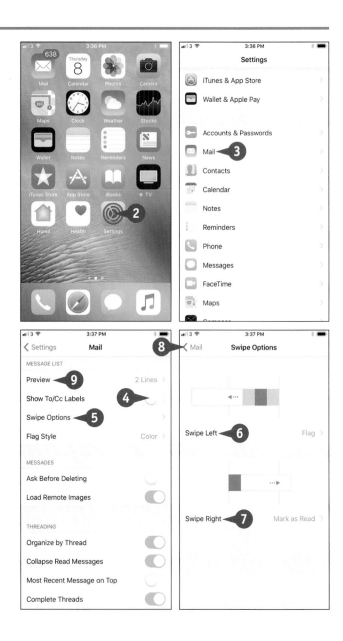

1 Press **Home**. On an iPhone X, swipe up from the bottom of the screen.

The Home screen appears.

2 Tap **Settings** (⚙).

The Settings screen appears.

3 Tap **Mail** (✉).

The Mail screen appears.

4 Set the **Show To/Cc Labels** switch to On (⬤) or Off (⬤), as needed.

5 Tap **Swipe Options**.

The Swipe Options screen appears.

6 Tap **Swipe Left**; tap **None**, **Mark as Read**, **Flag**, or **Move Message**; and then tap **Swipe Options** (〈).

7 Tap **Swipe Right**; tap **None**, **Mark as Read**, **Flag**, **Move Message**, or **Archive**; and then tap **Swipe Options** (〈).

8 Tap **Mail** (〈).

The Mail screen appears again.

9 Tap **Preview**.

The Preview screen appears.

10 Tap the number of preview lines you want.

11 Tap **Mail** ($<$).

12 Tap **Flag Style**, tap **Color** or **Shape** to control how message flags appear, and then tap **Mail** ($<$).

13 Set the **Ask Before Deleting** switch to On (⬤) or Off ( ), as needed.

14 Set the **Load Remote Images** switch to On (⬤) or Off ( ), as needed.

15 Tap **Mark Addresses**.

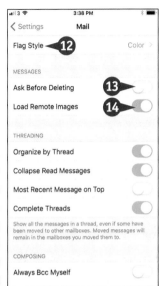

The Mark Addresses screen appears.

16 In the Mark Addresses Not Ending With box, type the domain name of your company or organization, such as surrealmacs.com.

17 Tap **Mail** ($<$).

The Mail screen appears again.

18 Tap **Increase Quote Level**.

The Increase Quote Level screen appears.

19 Set the **Increase Quote Level** switch to On (⬤) or Off ( ), as needed.

20 Tap **Mail** ($<$).

21 Tap **Settings**.

TIPS

Why might I want to turn off Load Remote Images?
Loading a remote image lets the sender know that you have opened the message. When Mail requests the remote image, the server that provides the image can log the date and time and your Internet connection's IP address, which reveals your approximate location.

What is Always Bcc Myself useful for?
Most e-mail services automatically put a copy of each message you send or forward into a folder with a name such as Sent. If your e-mail service does not use a Sent folder, set the **Always Bcc Myself** switch to On (⬤) to send a bcc copy of each message to yourself for your records.

Organize Your E-Mail Messages by Threads

The Mail app gives you two ways to view e-mail messages. You can view the messages as a simple list, or you can view them with related messages organized into *threads*, which are sometimes called *conversations*.

Having Mail display your messages as threads can help you navigate your Inbox quickly and find related messages easily. You may find threading useful if you tend to have long e-mail conversations, because threading reduces the number of messages you see at once.

Organize Your E-Mail Messages by Threads

Set Mail to Organize Your Messages by Thread

1 Press **Home**. On an iPhone X, swipe up from the bottom of the screen.

The Home screen appears.

2 Tap **Settings** (⚙).

The Settings screen appears.

3 Tap **Mail** (✉).

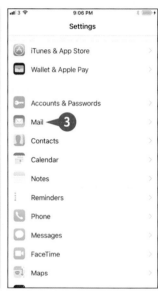

The Mail screen appears.

4 Set the **Organize by Thread** switch to On (◯).

5 Set the **Collapse Read Messages** switch to On (◯) if you want Mail to collapse messages you have read to save space.

6 Set the **Most Recent Message on Top** switch to On (◯) if you want the newest message in each thread to appear at the top of the screen. This option is often helpful for keeping up with your messages.

7 Set the **Complete Threads** switch to On (◯) if you want each thread to show all its messages, even if you have moved some to other mailboxes. This option is usually helpful.

Read Messages Organized into Threads

1 Press **Home**. On an iPhone X, swipe up from the bottom of the screen.

The Home screen appears.

2 Tap **Mail** (✉).

The Mailboxes screen appears.

Note: If Mail displays the contents of a mailbox, tap **Back** (‹) to return to the Mailboxes screen.

3 Tap the mailbox you want to open.

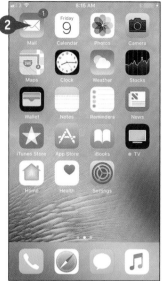
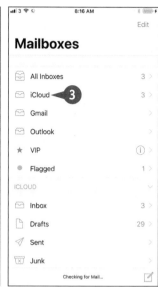

The Inbox for the account appears.

A Two chevrons on the right indicate a thread.

4 Tap the thread.

The Thread screen appears, showing the thread.

B The screen's title shows the number of messages in the thread.

C Messages you have read appear collapsed if you have set the Collapse Read Messages switch to On (⬤).

5 Tap the bar at the top of the message you want to display.

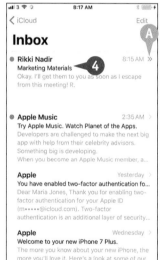

TIP

Is there a quick way to enter my name and information at the end of a message?

Yes. You can create one or more e-mail signatures, which are sections of predefined text that Mail can insert at the end of messages. From the Home screen, tap **Settings** (⚙), and then tap **Mail** (✉). Scroll down to the Composing section and tap **Signature** to display the Signature screen. Tap **All Accounts** to use the same signature for each account, or tap **Per Account** to use a different signature for each account. Then type the text to use for the signature or signatures.

Set Your Default E-Mail Account

If you set up two or more e-mail accounts on your iPhone, make sure that you set the right e-mail account to be the default account. The default account is the one from which the Mail app sends messages when you start creating a message from another app. For example, if you open the Photos app and choose to share a photo via Mail, Mail uses your default account.

You can quickly set your default e-mail account on the Mail screen in the Settings app.

Set Your Default E-Mail Account

1 Press **Home**. On an iPhone X, swipe up from the bottom of the screen.

The Home screen appears.

2 Tap **Settings** (⚙).

The Settings screen appears.

3 Tap **Mail** (✉).

The Mail screen appears.

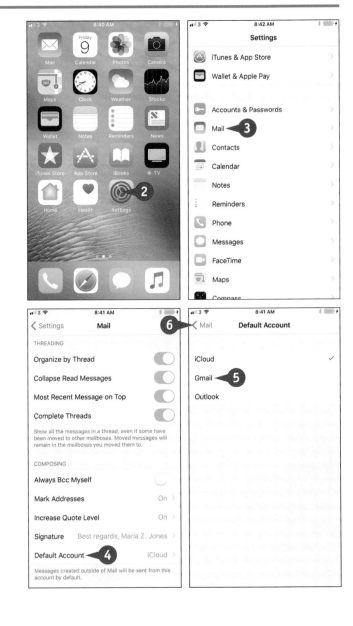

4 In the Composing section, tap **Default Account**.

The Default Account screen appears.

5 Tap the account you want to make the default.

6 Tap **Mail** (‹).

Note: To change the e-mail account for a message you are sending, tap **Cc/Bcc, From** to expand the Cc, Bcc, and From fields. Next, tap **From**, and then tap the address on the list that appears at the bottom of the screen.

Control How Your Contacts Appear

To swiftly and easily find the contacts you need, you can set your iPhone to sort and display the contacts in your preferred order. Your iPhone can sort contacts either by first name, putting Abby Brown before Bill Andrews, or by last name, putting Bill Andrews before Abby Brown. Your iPhone can display contacts either as first name followed by last name or last name followed by first name. You can also configure short names preferences for contacts.

Control How Your Contacts Appear

1 Press **Home**. On an iPhone X, swipe up from the bottom of the screen.

The Home screen appears.

2 Tap **Settings** (⚙).

The Settings screen appears.

3 Tap **Contacts** (👤).

The Contacts screen appears.

4 In the Contacts section, tap **Sort Order** or **Display Order**, depending on which order you want to set. This example uses Sort Order.

The Sort Order screen or the Display Order screen appears.

5 Tap **First, Last** or **Last, First**, as needed.

6 Tap **Contacts** (〈).

The Contacts screen appears again.

7 Tap **Short Name**.

The Short Name screen appears.

8 Set the **Short Name** switch to On (◯).

9 Tap **First Name & Last Initial**, **First Initial & Last Name**, **First Name Only**, or **Last Name Only** to specify the format for short names.

10 Set the **Prefer Nicknames** switch to On (◯) or Off ( ), as needed.

11 Tap **Contacts** (〈).

The Contacts screen appears again.

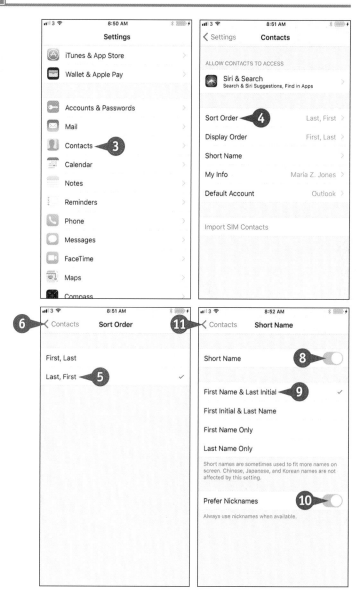

Browse or Search for Contacts

Your iPhone's Contacts app enables you to store contact data that you sync from your computer or online accounts or that you enter directly on your iPhone. You can access the contacts either via the Contacts app itself or through the Contacts tab in the Phone app.

To locate a particular contact, you can browse through the list of contacts or through selected groups, such as your friends, or use the Search feature.

Browse or Search for Contacts

Browse Your Contacts

1 Press **Home**. On an iPhone X, swipe up from the bottom of the screen.

The Home screen appears.

2 Tap **Extras** (⚙).

The Extras folder opens.

3 Tap **Contacts** (👤).

The Contacts screen appears, showing either All Contacts or your currently selected groups.

Note: You can also access your contacts by pressing **Home**, tapping **Phone** (📞), and then tapping **Contacts** (👥 changes to 👥).

A To navigate the screen of contacts quickly, tap the letter on the right that you want to jump to. To navigate more slowly, scroll up or down.

4 Tap the contact whose information you want to view.

The contact's screen appears.

Note: From the contact's screen, you can quickly phone the contact by tapping the phone number you want to use.

5 If necessary, tap and drag up to scroll down the screen to display more information.

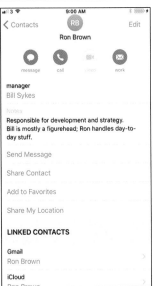

Choose Which Groups of Contacts to Display

1 From the Contacts screen, tap **Groups**.

The Groups screen appears.

2 Tap **Show All Contacts**.

Contacts displays a check mark next to each group.

Note: When you tap **Show All Contacts**, the Hide All Contacts button appears in place of the Show All Contacts button. You can tap **Hide All Contacts** to remove all the check marks.

3 Tap a group to apply a check mark to it or to remove the existing check mark.

4 Tap **Done**.

The Contacts screen appears, showing the contacts in the groups you selected.

Search for Contacts

1 From the Contacts screen, tap **Search** (🔍).

The Search screen appears.

2 Start typing the name you want to search for.

3 From the list of matches, tap the contact you want to view.

The contact's information appears.

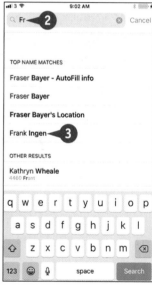

TIP

What is a linked contact?

A *linked contact* is a contact record that the Contacts app has created by combining contact records from two separate sources. For example, if your iCloud account and your Gmail account each contain a contact called Ron Brown, Contacts creates a linked contact called Ron Brown. To unlink a linked contact, tap **Edit** at the top of the screen for a contact. In the Linked Contacts area, tap **Remove** (⊖) for the appropriate contact record, and then tap **Unlink**. Alternatively, tap **Edit** and then tap **link contacts** (⊕) in the Linked Contacts area to link another contact record to the current record.

Create a New Contact

As well as syncing your existing contacts via cloud services such as iCloud or Yahoo!, your iPhone enables you to create new contact records directly on the device. For example, if you meet someone you want to remember, you can create a contact record for that person — and take a photo using the iPhone's camera. You can then sync that contact record online, adding it to your other contacts.

Create a New Contact

1 Press **Home**. On an iPhone X, swipe up from the bottom of the screen.

The Home screen appears.

2 Tap **Phone** (📞).

The Phone app opens.

3 Tap **Contacts** (👤 changes to 👥).

The Contacts screen appears.

Note: You can also access the Contacts app by tapping **Extras** (📦) on the Home screen, and then tapping **Contacts** (👤) in the Extras folder.

4 Tap **Add** (+).

The New Contact screen appears.

5 Tap **First name**.

The on-screen keyboard appears.

6 Type the first name.

7 Tap **Last name**.

8 Type the last name.

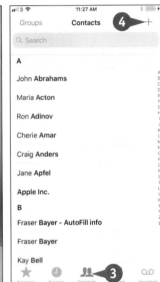

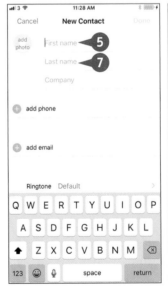

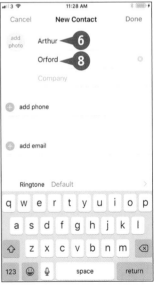

9 Add other information as needed by tapping each field and then typing the information.

10 To add a photo of the contact, tap **add photo**.

The Photo dialog opens.

11 Tap **Take Photo**.

The Take Photo screen appears.

12 Compose the photo, and then tap **Take Photo** (○).

The Move and Scale screen appears.

13 Position the part of the photo you want to use in the middle.

Note: Pinch in with two fingers to zoom the photo out. Pinch out with two fingers to zoom the photo in.

A You can tap **Retake** to take another photo.

14 Tap **Use Photo**.

The photo appears in the contact record.

15 Tap **Done**.

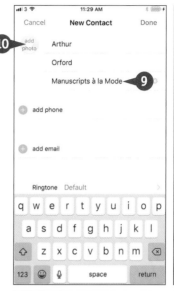

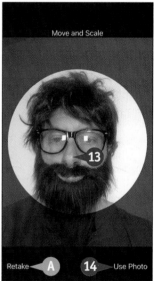

TIP

How do I assign my new contact an existing photo?

1 In the Photo dialog, tap **Choose Photo**.

2 On the Photos screen, tap the photo album.

3 Tap the photo.

4 On the Move and Scale screen, position the photo, and then tap **Choose**.

Import Contacts from a SIM Card

If you have stored contacts on a SIM card, you can import them into your iPhone. If the SIM card is a nano-SIM, the smallest common size, you can insert the SIM card in the iPhone temporarily and import the contacts. Alternatively, you can insert the iPhone's SIM card in an unlocked cell phone, copy the contacts to the SIM card, and then put the SIM card back in the iPhone. This approach enables you to use a SIM adapter to make the iPhone's nano-SIM fit in a micro-SIM or full-size SIM slot.

Import Contacts from a SIM Card

1 Press **Home**. On an iPhone X, swipe up from the bottom of the screen.

The Home screen appears.

2 Tap **Settings** (⚙).

The Settings screen appears.

3 Tap **Contacts** (👤).

The Contacts screen appears.

4 In the Contacts section, tap **Import SIM Contacts**.

5 If the Import SIM Contacts to Account dialog appears, tap the account in which you want to put the contacts.

Your iPhone imports the contacts from the SIM.

Ⓐ If you want your iPhone to suggest creating contacts from names and data found in e-mail messages, incoming calls, or contact data, tap **Siri & Search** to display the Siri & Search screen, and then set the **Find Contacts in Other Apps** switch to On (⬤).

Choose Default Alert Options for Calendar Events

Your iPhone enables you to sync your calendars via iCloud and other online services. To help keep on schedule, you can set default alert times for calendar events. You can set a different alert time for each type of event — for example, 15 minutes' notice for a regular event and a week's notice for a birthday. You can also turn on the Time to Leave feature to make the Calendar app allow travel time based on your location and current traffic.

Choose Default Alert Options for Calendar Events

1 Press **Home** — on an iPhone X, swipe up from the bottom of the screen — to display the Home screen.

2 Tap **Settings** (⚙) to display the Settings screen.

3 Tap **Calendar** (📅) to display the Calendar screen.

Ⓐ If you want your iPhone to suggest creating events from apparent event data found in apps such as Mail and Messages, tap **Siri & Search** to display the Siri & Search screen, and then set the **Find Events in Other Apps** switch to On (⬤).

Ⓑ Set the **Location Suggestions** switch to On (⬤) if you want Calendar to suggest locations for events.

4 Tap **Default Alert Times**.

The Default Alert Times screen appears.

5 Tap the event type for which you want to set the default alert time. For example, tap **Events**.

The Events screen, Birthdays screen, or All-Day Events screen appears.

6 Tap the amount of time for the alert.

7 Tap **Default Alert Times** (‹).

The Default Alert Times screen appears again.

8 Set default alert times for other event types by repeating steps **5** to **7**.

9 Set the **Time to Leave** switch to On (⬤) if you want Calendar to suggest leave times based on your location and current traffic information.

Choose Your Default Calendar and Time Zone

When you use multiple calendars on your iPhone, set your default calendar, the calendar that receives events you create outside any specific calendar. For example, if you have a Work calendar and a Home calendar, you might set the Home calendar as the default calendar.

If you travel to different time zones, use the Time Zone Override feature to specify the time zone in which to show event dates and times. Otherwise, Calendar uses the time zone for your current location.

Choose Your Default Calendar and Time Zone

1 Press **Home**. On an iPhone X, swipe up from the bottom of the screen.

The Home screen appears.

2 Tap **Settings** (⚙).

The Settings screen appears.

3 Tap **Calendar** (📅).

The Calendar screen appears.

4 Tap **Time Zone Override**.

The Time Zone Override screen appears.

5 Set the **Time Zone Override** switch to On (ⓞ).

6 Tap **Time Zone**.

The Time Zone screen appears.

7 Type the first letters of a city in the time zone.

8 Tap the search result you want.

The Time Zone Override screen appears again, now showing the city you selected.

9 Tap **Calendar** (<).

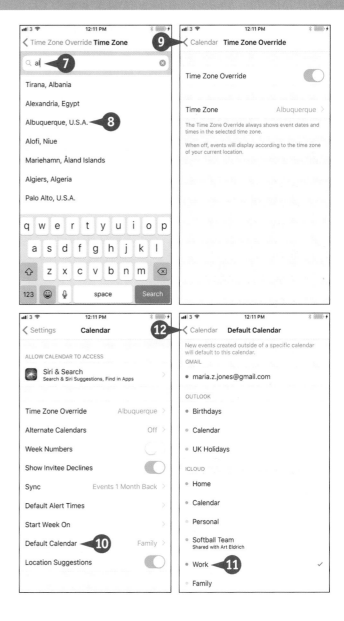

The Calendar screen appears again.

10 Tap **Default Calendar**.

The Default Calendar screen appears.

11 Tap the calendar you want to make the default.

12 Tap **Calendar** (<).

The Calendar screen appears again.

TIP

Where do I control which calendars the Calendar app displays?
You choose the calendars in the Calendar app, not in the Settings app. Press **Home** — on an iPhone X, swipe up from the bottom of the screen — to display the Home screen, tap **Calendar** (14), and then tap **Calendars**. On the Calendars screen, tap to place a check mark on each calendar you want to show. Tap to remove a check mark from a calendar you want to hide. Tap **Done** when you finish.

Set Up and Use Wallet and Apple Pay

Your iPhone enables you to make payments using the Apple Pay system and the Wallet app on your iPhone. Apple Pay can be faster and more convenient than paying with cash. It can also be more secure than paying with a credit card or debit card.

Understanding Apple Pay and Wallet

Apple Pay is Apple's electronic-payment and digital-wallet service. After setting up Apple Pay with one or more credit cards or debit cards, you can make payments using your iPhone either at contactless payment terminals or online. If you have an Apple Watch, you can use Apple Pay on that device as well.

Wallet is the app you use on your iPhone to manage Apple Pay and the digital documents you want to carry with you, such as airline tickets or store rewards cards.

Set Up Wallet

Press **Home** — on an iPhone X, swipe up from the bottom of the screen — to display the Home screen, and then tap **Wallet** (▭) to open the Wallet app.

If you have not yet set up a credit card or debit card, tap **Add Credit or Debit Card** in the Pay area of the Wallet screen. Follow the prompts to add a card to Wallet. You can add the card either by lining it up within an on-screen frame and using the camera to recognize it or by typing in the details manually. Complete the card registration by selecting the correct billing address. For some cards, you may need to contact the card provider to confirm you are setting up Apple Pay.

If you have already added a card, you can add another by tapping **Add Card** (⊕) in the upper-right corner of the screen.

After you add cards, they appear at the top of the Wallet screen.

Set Apple Pay to Use Touch ID or Face ID

After setting up Apple Pay, you can set your iPhone to use Touch ID or Face ID instead of your Apple ID password for buying items. Touch ID enables you to authenticate yourself and approve a purchase by placing one of your registered fingers on the Home button. Face ID enables you to authenticate yourself and approve a purchase by looking at your iPhone X. This is much more convenient than typing a password, especially when you are shopping in the physical world rather than online.

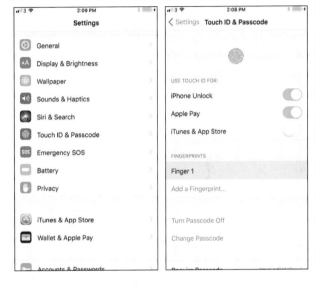

To set your iPhone to use Touch ID or Face ID for Apple Pay, press **Home** — on an iPhone X, swipe up from the bottom of the screen — to display the Home screen, and then tap **Settings** ( ) to display the Settings screen. For Touch ID, tap **Touch ID & Passcode** ( ) to display the Touch ID & Passcode screen, and then set the **Apple Pay** switch to On ( ).

Make a Payment with Apple Pay

Now that you have set up Apple Pay and configured your iPhone to use it, you can make payments by bringing your iPhone close to the contact area on a payment terminal.

When the Near Field Communication (NFC) chips on the two devices make contact, a tone sounds. Your iPhone then displays details of the transaction and prompts you to confirm it by placing your finger on the Home button so that it can verify your fingerprint or by looking at your iPhone X to use Face ID.

CHAPTER 5

Making Calls and Messaging

You can make calls by holding your iPhone to your face, by using the speakerphone, or by using a headset or your car's audio system. You can also make calls using Favorites and recent numbers, send and receive text and multimedia messages, and chat using the FaceTime feature.

With your iPhone, you can make phone calls anywhere you have a connection to the cellular network. You can dial a phone number using the iPhone's keypad, but you can place calls more easily by tapping the appropriate phone number for a contact, using the Phone app's Recents screen, using the Favorites list, or using Siri. When other people near you need to be able to hear the call, you can switch on your iPhone's speaker; otherwise, you can use the headset for privacy.

Make Phone Calls and FaceTime Audio Calls

Open the Phone App

1 Press **Home**. On an iPhone X, swipe up from the bottom of the screen.

The Home screen appears.

2 Tap **Phone** (📞).

The Phone app opens and displays the screen you used last — for example, the Contacts screen.

A Your phone number appears at the top of the Contacts list for quick reference.

Note: You can dial a call by activating Siri and speaking the contact's name or the number. See Chapter 3 for instructions on using Siri.

Dial a Call Using the Keypad

1 Tap **Keypad** (⚏ changes to ⚏).

The Keypad screen appears.

Note: On the Keypad screen, you can tap **Call** (📞) without dialing a number to display the last number dialed.

2 Tap the number keys to dial the number.

Note: You can tap **Add to Contacts** (⊕) to add this number to your Contacts list.

B If you dial a contact's number, the contact's name and phone type appear.

3 Tap **Call** (📞).

Your iPhone makes the call.

4 Tap **End** (📞) when you are ready to end the call.

Place a Call to a Contact

1 Tap **Contacts** (changes to).

The Contacts list appears.

2 Tap the contact you want to call.

The contact's info appears.

3 If FaceTime () appears, tap **FaceTime** () to place a FaceTime Audio call. Otherwise, tap **Call** ().

 You can tap a number to place a phone call to that number.

Note: You can also place a call to a phone number that the iPhone has identified — for example, by tapping an underlined phone number on a web page or in an e-mail message.

Your iPhone places the call.

 In a FaceTime Audio call, you can tap **FaceTime** () to switch to a FaceTime Video call.

4 When you are ready to end the call, tap **End** ().

Your iPhone ends the call.

The Call Ended screen appears for a moment.

The screen from which you placed the call appears — for example, the Contacts screen.

Note: To end a call for which you are using the headset, press the clicker button.

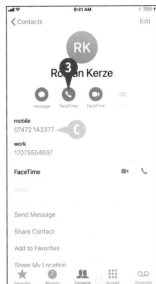

TIPS

Can I use the iPhone as a speaker phone?

Yes. Tap **speaker** (changes to) on the screen that appears while you are making a phone call. The iPhone starts playing the phone call through the speaker on the bottom instead of the small speaker at the top. Tap **speaker** (changes to) to switch off the speaker.

What is Dial Assist?

Dial Assist is a feature that automatically determines the correct local prefix or international prefix when you place a call. To turn Dial Assist on or off, press **Home**, tap **Settings** (), tap **Phone** (), and then set the **Dial Assist** switch to On () or Off ( ).

Using a Wireless Headset or Car System

Instead of using the headset that came with your iPhone, you can use a Bluetooth headset. Similarly, you can use a car system with a Bluetooth connection when using your iPhone in your vehicle. For example, many new cars have systems that include Apple's CarPlay standard, which enables the car system to act as the display and controller for a connected iPhone.

You must first pair the Bluetooth headset or car system with your iPhone, as discussed in Chapter 6.

Using a Wireless Headset or Car System

1 Turn on the wireless headset or connection and make sure it works.

2 Press **Home**. On an iPhone X, swipe up from the bottom of the screen.

The Home screen appears.

3 Tap **Phone** (📞).

The Phone app opens.

4 Dial the call. For example, tap **Contacts**, tap the contact, tap **Call** (📞), and then tap the appropriate phone number.

Note: You can also tell Siri to place the call for you.

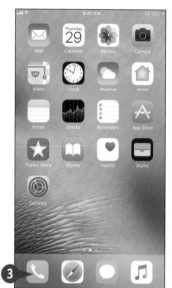

Your iPhone places the call.

The Audio dialog opens.

5 Tap the headset or other device you want to use.

The Audio dialog closes.

Ⓐ You can tap **audio** (🔊) to display the Audio dialog and switch to another audio device.

Note: If you are playing audio or video on a Bluetooth headset when you receive a call, your iPhone automatically pauses the audio or video and plays the ringtone on the headset.

Mute a Call or Put a Call on Hold

When you are on a call, you may need to mute your iPhone's microphone so that you can confer with people near you without the person at the other end of the phone call hearing.

You may also need to put a call on hold so that you can make another call or take a break from the call.

Mute a Call or Put a Call on Hold

1 Establish the phone call as usual. For example, call a contact.

2 Tap **mute** (changes to).

The iPhone mutes the call.

3 When you are ready to unmute the call, tap **mute** again (changes to).

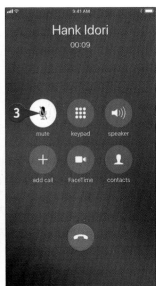

The iPhone turns off muting.

4 To put the call on hold, tap and hold **mute** (changes to) for several seconds.

The iPhone puts the call on hold.

Ⓐ The HOLD readout appears in place of the call time.

Note: After placing a call on hold, you can make another call if necessary.

5 When you are ready to take the call off hold, tap **hold** (changes to).

Make a Conference Call

As well as making phone calls to one other phone at a time, your iPhone can make calls to multiple phones at once, making either standard cellular calls or FaceTime audio calls, but not mixing the two. To make a conference call, you call the first participant, and then add each other participant in turn. During a conference call, you can talk in private to individual participants. You can also drop a participant from the call.

Make a Conference Call

1 Press **Home**. On an iPhone X, swipe up from the bottom of the screen.

The Home screen appears.

2 Tap **Phone** (📞).

The Phone app opens.

3 Tap **Contacts** (👥 changes to 👥).

The Contacts screen appears.

4 Tap the contact you want to call first.

The contact's record appears.

5 Tap **Call** (📞) on the phone number to use.

Note: You can also add a contact to the call by using Favorites, Recents, or Keypad.

Your iPhone establishes the call.

6 Tap **add call** (➕).

The Contacts screen appears.

7 Tap the contact you want to add.

The contact's record appears.

8 Tap **Call** (📞).

A The iPhone places the first call on hold and makes the new call.

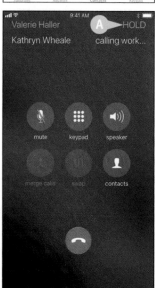

118

9 Tap **merge calls** ().

The iPhone merges the calls and displays the participants' names at the top of the screen. You can now speak to both participants.

Ⓑ You can add more participants by tapping **add call** (⊞), specifying the contact or number, and then merging the calls.

10 To speak privately to a participant, tap **Information** (ⓘ).

The Conference screen appears, showing a list of the participants.

11 Tap **Private** next to the participant.

The iPhone places the other caller or callers on hold.

Ⓒ You can tap **swap** (🔄) to swap the caller on hold and the active caller.

12 When you are ready to resume the conference call, tap **merge calls** (🔄).

The iPhone merges the calls, and all participants can hear each other again.

13 When you finish the call, tap **End** (🔴).

The iPhone ends the call.

TIPS

How do I drop a participant from a conference call?
Tap **Information** (ⓘ) to display the Conference screen, and then tap **End** next to the participant you want to drop.

How many people can I add to a conference call?
This depends on your carrier, not on your iPhone. Ask your carrier what the maximum number of participants can be.

Make Video Calls Using FaceTime

By using your iPhone's FaceTime feature, you can enjoy video chats with any of your contacts who have an iPhone 4 or later, an iPad 2 or later, an iPad mini, a fourth-generation or later iPod touch, or the FaceTime for Mac app.

To make a FaceTime call, you and your contact must both have Apple IDs. Your iPhone must be connected to either a wireless network or the cellular network. Using a wireless network is preferable because you typically get better performance and do not use up your cellular data allowance.

Make Video Calls Using FaceTime

Receive a FaceTime Call

1. When your iPhone receives a FaceTime request, and the screen shows who is calling, aim the camera at your face, and then tap **Accept** ( ).

   The Connecting screen appears.

   When the connection is established, your iPhone displays the caller full-screen, with your video inset.

2. Start your conversation.
3. Tap the screen.

   The controls appear.

4. If you need to mute your microphone, tap **Mute** (changes to).
5. Tap **Mute** again (changes to) when you want to turn muting off.
6. Tap **End** ( ) when you are ready to end the FaceTime call.

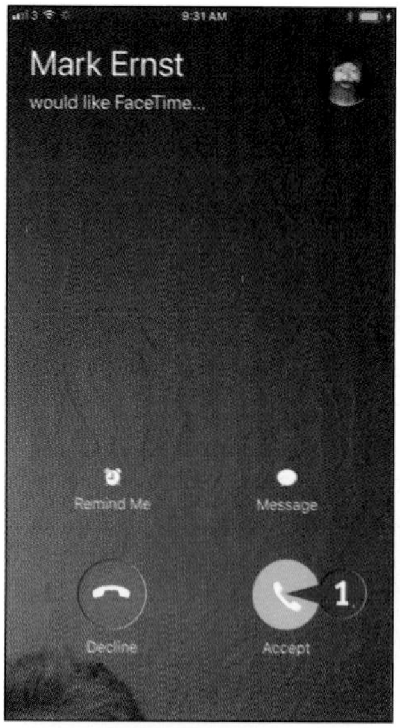

Make a FaceTime Call

1 Press **Home**. On an iPhone X, swipe up from the bottom of the screen.

The Home screen appears.

2 Tap **FaceTime** ().

The FaceTime app opens.

3 Tap **Video**.

The Video tab appears.

4 Tap the contact you want to call.

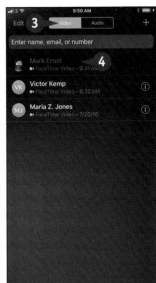

The FaceTime app starts a video call.

5 When your contact answers, smile and speak.

Ⓐ If you need to show your contact something using the rear-facing camera, tap **Switch Cameras** (📷).

6 When you are ready to end the call, tap **End** (⬛).

TIP

Are there other ways of starting a FaceTime call?

Yes. Here are two easy ways to start a FaceTime call:

- Ask Siri to call a contact via FaceTime. For example, press and hold **Home** to summon Siri, and then say "FaceTime John Smith."
- During a phone call, tap **Video** (📹).

Save Time with Call Favorites and Recents

You can dial phone numbers easily from your Contacts list, but you can save time and effort by using the Favorites and Recents features built into the Phone app.

Favorites are phone numbers that you mark as being especially important to you. Recents are phone numbers you have called and received calls from recently.

Save Time with Call Favorites and Recents

Add a Contact to Your Favorites List

1 Press **Home**. On an iPhone X, swipe up from the bottom of the screen.

The Home screen appears.

2 Tap **Phone** (📞).

The Phone app opens.

3 Tap **Contacts** (👤 changes to 👥).

The Contacts list appears.

4 Tap the contact you want to add.

The contact's record appears.

5 Tap **Add to Favorites**.

The Add to Favorites dialog opens.

6 Tap the heading for the type of favorite you want to add. This example uses **Call**.

The list of phone numbers for the contact appears.

7 Tap the phone number you want to add to your Favorites list.

The Add to Favorites dialog closes, and the iPhone creates a favorite for the contact.

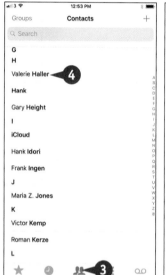

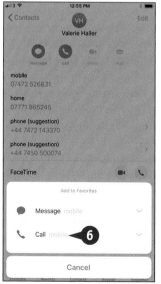

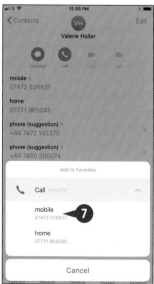

Call a Favorite

1 In the Phone app, tap **Favorites** (⭐ changes to ⭐).

The Favorites list appears.

2 Tap the Favorite you want to call.

Your iPhone places the call.

A To display the contact's record, tap **Information** (ⓘ) instead of tapping the contact's button. You can then tap a different phone number for the contact if necessary.

Call a Recent

1 In the Phone app, tap **Recents** (🕐 changes to 🕐).

The Recents screen appears. Red entries indicate calls you missed.

B Tap **Missed** if you want to see only recent calls you missed.

2 Tap the recent you want to call.

Your iPhone places the call.

C You can delete a recent by swiping its button left and then tapping the textual **Delete** button.

D If you want to clear the Recents list, tap **Edit** and then tap **Clear**. In the dialog that opens, tap **Clear All Recents**.

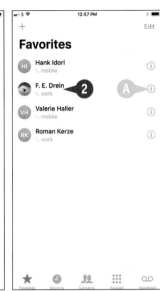
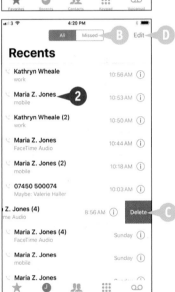
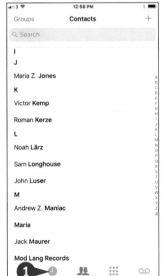

TIP

How do I remove a contact from my Favorites?

Tap **Favorites** (⭐ changes to ⭐) to display the Favorites list, and then tap **Edit**. Tap **Delete** (➖) next to the contact, and then tap the textual **Delete** button. You can also rearrange your favorites by tapping the handle (☰) and dragging up or down. Tap **Done** when you have finished changing your favorites.

Send Text and Multimedia Messages

Your iPhone can send instant messages using the Short Message Service, abbreviated SMS; the Multimedia Messaging Service, MMS; or Apple's iMessage service. An SMS message consists of only text, whereas an MMS message can contain text, videos, photos, sounds, or other data. An iMessage can contain text, multimedia content, emoji, animations, handwriting, and other features. The Messages app automatically chooses the appropriate type — SMS, MMS, or iMessage — for the messages you create and the ways you send them.

Send Text and Multimedia Messages

1 Press **Home**. On an iPhone X, swipe up from the bottom of the screen.

The Home screen appears.

2 Tap **Messages** (◯).

The Messages screen appears.

3 Tap **New Message** (◻️).

Note: Before sending an SMS or MMS message, make sure the recipient's phone number can receive such messages. Typically, you do not receive an alert if the message cannot be delivered.

The New Message screen appears.

4 Tap **Add Contact** (⊕).

The Contacts list appears.

5 Tap the contact to whose phone you want to send the message.

Note: If the contact's record contains multiple phone numbers, Messages displays the contact record. Tap the phone number to use.

Note: iMessage is available only for communicating with other users of Apple devices using their Apple IDs. SMS and MMS work with any device, but may use up your messaging allowance from your carrier.

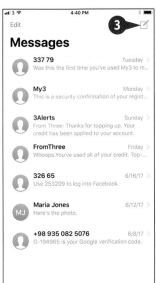

124

The contact's name appears in the To field of the New Message screen.

⑥ Tap the text field.

The text field expands, and the More button appears.

⑦ Tap in the text field, and then type your message.

⑧ Tap **More** (▶).

The other buttons reappear.

⑨ To add a photo, tap **Photo** (📷).

Note: Messages from contacts sent via iMessage appear in blue balloons. Messages from contacts sent via SMS or MMS appear in green balloons.

The Photo dialog opens.

Ⓐ You can tap **Take Photo** (○) to take a photo.

Ⓑ You can tap **Switch Cameras** (📷) to switch between the front and rear cameras.

⑩ Tap a recent photo to add it. Scroll left to view other recent photos.

Ⓒ You can tap **Photo Library** to select a photo from your photo library.

Ⓓ The photo appears in the message.

⑪ Tap **Send** (⬆).

Messages sends the message and the photo.

How can I respond quickly to an instant message?

When Messages displays a notification for an instant message, tap the notification to display the Text Message box. You can then type a reply and tap **Send** to send it.

Is there another way to send a photo or video?

Yes. You can start from the Camera app or the Photos app. Select the photo or video you want to share, and then tap **Share** (📤). On the Share sheet, tap **Message**. Your iPhone starts an MMS message containing the photo or video. You can then address and send the message.

Using Emoji and iMessage Features

The Messages app makes it easy to include *emoji* — graphical characters — in your messages. You can send emoji to users of most instant-messaging services, not just to iMessage users.

When you are sending a message to another user of the iMessage service, you can also use a wide range of features that are not available for SMS messages and text messages. These features include stickers, handwriting and sketches, animations, and Digital Touch, which enables you to send a pattern of taps or your heartbeat. You can also respond quickly to a message by using the Tapback feature.

Add Emoji to Messages

The Messages app makes it easy to add emoji to your messages. After typing text, tap **Emoji** (😀) on the keyboard. Messages highlights with color any words in the message that you can replace with emoji; tap a word to insert the corresponding emoji icon, such as 👍 for "great!"

You can also insert other emoji manually by tapping them on the emoji keyboard. Tap the buttons at the bottom of the screen, or simply scroll the emoji panel left or right, to browse the available emoji.

Send a Handwritten Message or Sketch

To send a handwritten message or sketch, tap **New** (📝) to begin a new message. Address the message to an iMessage user, tap **Apps** (Ⓐ), and then tap **Digital Touch** (⬤) to display the Digital Touch controls.

Tap **Expand** (⌒) to expand the panel to full screen, tap the color you want, and then write or draw what you want to send. Tap **Send** (⬆) to send the message.

Send a Message with Effect

To send a message with effect, write the text for the message, and then tap and hold **Send** (⬆). The Send with Effect screen appears. At the top of the screen, tap **Bubble** if you want to send a bubble with an effect such as Slam or Invisible Ink, and then tap the button for the effect; a preview then plays. To send text with a full-screen effect, tap **Screen** at the top of the screen, and then swipe left or right to reach the effect you want; again, a preview plays. When you are ready to send the message, tap **Send** (⬆).

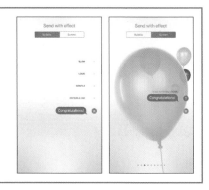

126

Send Heartbeats or Taps

To send heartbeats or taps, tap **New** (✏️) to begin a new message. Address the message to an iMessage user, tap **Apps** (Ⓐ), and then tap **Digital Touch** (●) to display the Digital Touch controls.

To send a heartbeat, tap and hold with two fingers on the screen. Messages displays a heartbeat graphic and sends a heartbeat; you do not need to tap Send (⬆️).

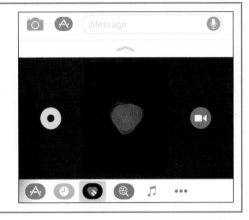

Responding Quickly Using the Tapback Feature

iMessage enables you to respond quickly to an incoming message by tapping and holding it. The Tapback panel opens, and you can tap the icon you want to send as an instant response.

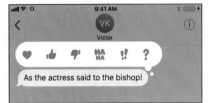

Share the Music You Are Listening To

With iMessage, you can quickly share links to the music you are enjoying on Apple Music. Tap **New** (✏️) to begin a new message, and then address the message to an iMessage user. Tap **Apps** (Ⓐ) to display the Apps panel. Swipe left or right if necessary to display the Music panel, and then tap the item you want to share. A button for the item appears in the message box. Type any explanatory or exhortatory text needed, and then tap **Send** (⬆️).

Send a Payment

With iMessage, you can send a payment to a contact. Tap **New** (✏️) to begin a new message, and then address the message to an iMessage user. Tap **Apps** (Ⓐ) to display the Apps panel. Swipe left or right if necessary to display the Apple Pay button, and then tap **Apple Pay** (Ⓟ). Use the controls to specify the amount, and then tap **Pay**. The payment ticket appears in the message box. Tap **Send** (⬆️) to send it.

Manage Your Instant Messages

essages is great for communicating quickly and frequently with your nearest and dearest and with your colleagues, so it may not take long before the interface is so full of messages that it becomes hard to navigate.

To keep your messages under control, you can forward messages to others and delete messages you do not need to keep. You can either delete messages from a conversation, leaving the conversation's other messages, or delete the entire conversation.

Manage Your Instant Messages

Delete an Entire Conversation

1 Press **Home**. On an iPhone X, swipe up from the bottom of the screen.

The Home screen appears.

2 Tap **Messages** (⬤).

The Messages screen appears.

3 Tap **Edit**.

The Messages screen switches to Edit Mode.

4 Tap the **selection button** (⬤ changes to ✓) for each conversation you want to delete.

The Delete button appears.

5 Tap **Delete**.

Messages deletes the conversation.

Ⓐ You can also delete a conversation by swiping it to the left and then tapping **Delete**.

Ⓑ You can suppress alerts for a contact by swiping a message left and then tapping **Hide Alerts**.

6 When you finish deleting conversations, tap **Done**.

Messages turns off Edit Mode.

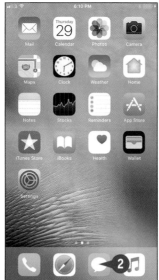

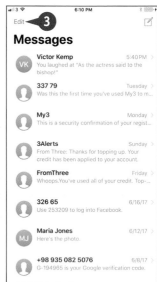

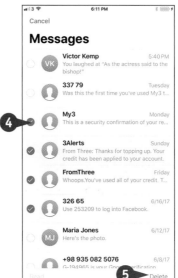

Forward or Delete One or More Messages from a Conversation

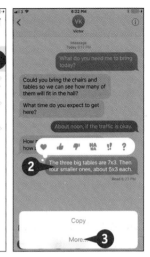

1 On the Messages screen, tap the convers⟨...⟩ contains the message or messages you w⟨...⟩

The conversation appears.

Note: You can tap in a conversation and sli⟨...⟩ finger left to display the time of each messa⟨...⟩

2 Tap and hold a message.

A dialog opens.

3 Tap **More**.

A selection button ( ) appears to the l⟨...⟩ each message.

4 Tap the **selection button** (changes t⟨...⟩ for each message you want to affect.

5 Tap **Forward** (⤳).

Messages starts a new message containi⟨...⟩ message or messages you selected.

C Instead of forwarding the selected messa⟨...⟩ you can tap **Delete** (🗑) to delete them f⟨...⟩ the conversation.

D You can also tap **Delete All** to delete all⟨...⟩ messages.

6 Address the message.

7 Type any extra text needed.

8 Tap **Send** (⬆) to send the message.

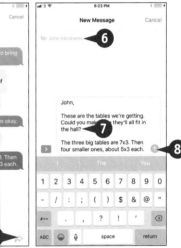

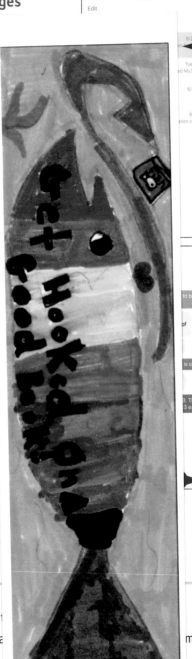

TIP

Can I resend a message?

Yes, you can resend a message in either of ⟨...⟩

- If a red icon with an exclamation point a⟨...⟩ message has not been sent. Tap the icon to try sending the message ⟨...⟩

- If the message has been sent, you can fo⟨...⟩ion. Alternatively, tap and hold the message text, and then tap **Copy** to ⟨...⟩age text field, and then tap **Paste** to paste the text. Tap **Send** to sen⟨...⟩

Choose Settings for Messages

essages includes many settings that you can configure to control the way the app looks and behaves. These settings include whether to send messages as SMS if the iMessage service is unavailable, whether to use MMS messaging, and how long to keep messages.

A key setting is whether to send read receipts for the messages you receive. You can turn read receipts on or off for Messages as a whole, but you can also make exceptions for individual contacts.

Choose Settings for Messages

1 Press **Home**. On an iPhone X, swipe up from the bottom of the screen.

The Home screen appears.

2 Tap **Settings** (⚙).

The Settings screen appears.

3 Tap **Messages** (🔵).

The Messages screen appears.

4 Set the **iMessage** switch to On (🔵) to use the iMessage service.

5 Set the **Show Contact Photos** switch to On (🔵) to display contact photos.

6 Set the **Send Read Receipts** switch to On (🔵) or Off ( ) to control whether Messages sends read receipts for all messages.

7 Tap **Text Message Forwarding**.

The Text Message Forwarding screen appears.

8 Set the switch to On (🔵) for each Mac or device you want to allow to send text messages via the iPhone.

9 Tap **Back** (‹).

The Messages screen appears again.

10 Set the **Send as SMS** switch to On (🔵) to send iMessage messages as SMS or MMS messages when iMessage is unavailable.

11 Tap **Send & Receive**.

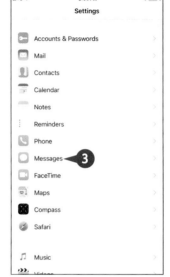

The iMessage screen appears.

12 Verify that this list shows the correct phone number and address.

13 Tap the phone number or e-mail address from which to start new conversations.

14 Tap **Messages** (<).

The Messages screen appears again.

15 Set the **MMS Messaging** switch to On (◯) to enable MMS messaging.

16 Set the **Show Subject Field** switch to On (◯) or Off (◡), as needed.

17 Set the **Character Count** switch to On (◯) or Off (◡), as needed.

18 Tap **Keep Messages**.

The Keep Messages screen appears.

19 Tap **30 Days**, **1 Year**, or **Forever**, as needed.

20 Tap **Messages** (<).

The Messages screen appears again.

21 Set the **Filter Unknown Senders** switch to On (◯) if you want to keep messages from unknown senders separate.

22 Tap **Expire** and choose **After 2 Minutes** or **Never** for audio messages.

23 Set the **Raise to Listen** switch to On (◯) or Off (◡).

24 Set the **Low Quality Image Mode** switch to On (◯) or Off (◡), as needed.

TIP

How do I control read receipts for individual contacts?

First, on the Messages screen in the Settings app, set the **Send Read Receipts** switch to On (◯) or Off (◡) to control whether Messages sends read receipts by default.

Next, in the Messages app, open a message to or from the appropriate contact. Tap **Info** (ⓘ) to display the Details screen. Set the **Send Read Receipts** switch to On (◯) or Off (◡), as needed, and then tap **Done**.

Block and Unblock Senders

Messages enables you to block any sender from whom you do not want to receive communications. You can implement blocking from the Messages app or from the Phone app. Whichever app you start from, blocking the contact prevents you from receiving notifications when the contact phones or messages you.

You can review your list of blocked senders and unblock any sender from whom you want to receive messages again.

Block and Unblock Senders

Block a Sender from the Messages App

1 Press **Home**. On an iPhone X, swipe up from the bottom of the screen.

The Home screen appears.

2 Tap **Messages** (◯).

The Messages screen appears.

Note: If the screen for a contact appears, tap **Back** (<) to display the Messages screen.

3 Tap a conversation with the contact you want to block.

The conversation opens.

4 Tap **Info** (ⓘ).

The Details screen appears.

5 Tap the contact's name.

The contact record opens.

6 Tap **Block this Caller**.

A confirmation dialog opens.

7 Tap **Block Contact**.

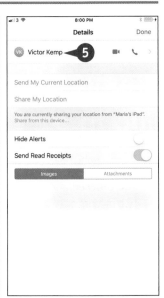

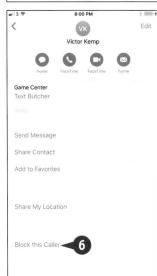

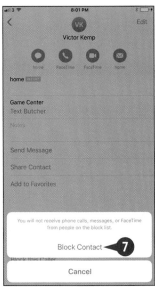

View Your Blocked List and Unblock Senders

1 Press **Home**. On an iPhone X, swipe up from the bottom of the screen.

The Home screen appears.

2 Tap **Settings** (⚙).

The Settings screen appears.

3 Tap **Messages** (💬).

The Messages screen appears.

4 In the SMS/MMS section, tap **Blocked**.

The Blocked screen appears, showing the list of contacts you have blocked.

Ⓐ You can tap **Add New** to display the contacts screen, and then tap the contact you want to block. Blocking the contact blocks all the means of contact, but you can then unblock any means of contact you wish to allow.

5 To unblock a means of contact, swipe its button to the left.

The Unblock button appears.

6 Tap **Unblock**.

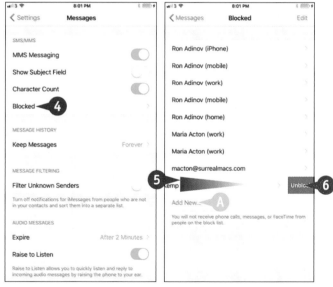

How do I block a contact in the Phone app?

In the Phone app, tap **Contacts** (👥 changes to 👥), tap the contact to display the contact record, and then tap **Block this Caller**. In the confirmation dialog that opens, tap **Block Contact**.

Set Up and Use the Emergency SOS Feature

The iPhone's Emergency SOS feature can either display the Emergency SOS screen or dial emergency services automatically when you give the Emergency SOS shortcut, five quick presses on the Power/Sleep button. Emergency SOS can also automatically text a group of emergency contacts to tell them you have dialed emergency services.

To be ready for an emergency, enable the Emergency SOS feature, configure its settings, and then set up your emergency contacts in the Health app.

Set Up and Use the Emergency SOS Feature

Set Up the Emergency SOS Feature

1 Press **Home**. On an iPhone X, swipe up from the bottom of the screen.

The Home screen appears.

2 Tap **Settings** (⚙).

The Settings screen appears.

3 Tap **Emergency SOS** (🆘).

The Emergency SOS screen appears.

4 Set the **Auto Call** switch to On (⬤) if you want to invoke the Emergency SOS shortcut to place the emergency call. Set the **Auto Call** switch to Off ( ) to display the Emergency SOS screen instead.

5 If you set the **Auto Call** switch to On (⬤), set the **Countdown Sound** switch to On (⬤) to receive a 3-second countdown before your iPhone dials emergency services.

6 Tap **Set Up Emergency Contacts in Health**.

The Medical ID screen in the Health app appears.

7 Tap **Edit**.

The Medical ID screen opens for editing.

8 Tap **add emergency contact** (➕).

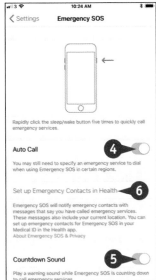

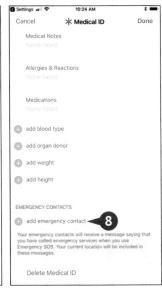

The Contacts screen appears.

9 Tap the contact you want to designate an emergency contact.

The Relationship screen appears.

10 Tap the button for the term that describes the contact's relationship to you, such as **mother**, **sister**, or **partner**.

The Medical ID screen appears again.

You can add other contacts by repeating steps **8** to **10**.

11 Tap **Done**.

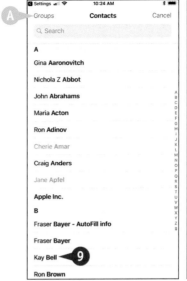

Use the Emergency SOS Feature

1 When you need to place an emergency call, press the **Power/Sleep** button five times in quick succession.

Ⓐ If you set the **Auto Call** switch to On (⬤), your iPhone starts placing an emergency call.

Ⓑ If you set the **Countdown Sound** switch to On (⬤), a 3-second countdown starts.

Ⓒ You can tap **Stop** (✕) to stop the call.

Ⓓ If you set the **Auto Call** switch to Off ( ), the Emergency SOS screen appears.

Ⓔ You can swipe **Emergency SOS** (🆘) right to place the emergency call.

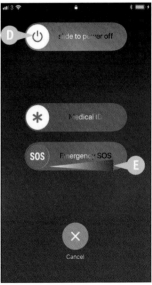

TIP

How can I quickly disable Touch ID or Face ID to prevent someone from forcing me to unlock my iPhone?

You can disable Touch ID or Face ID temporarily by pressing the **Power/Sleep** button five times to invoke the Emergency SOS feature. You must then enter your passcode to unlock the iPhone.

On the iPhone X, you can also temporarily disable Face ID by pressing the **Power/Sleep** button and the **Volume Up** button or the **Volume Down** button — or both the **Volume Up** button and the **Volume Down** button — simultaneously.

CHAPTER 6

Networking and Social Networking

You can control which cellular and wireless networks your iPhone uses and enjoy social networking wherever you go.

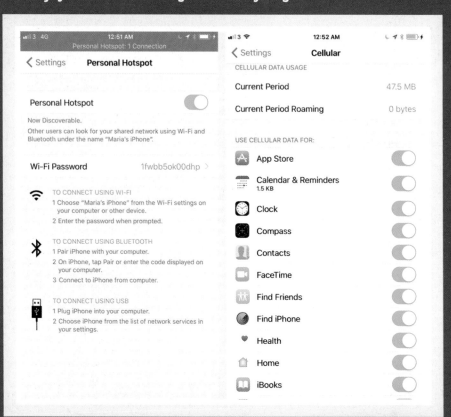

Using Airplane Mode

Normally, you will want to keep your iPhone connected to the cellular network so that you can make or receive phone calls and access the Internet. But when you do not need or may not use the cellular network, you can turn on the iPhone's Airplane Mode feature to cut off all connections.

Turning on Airplane Mode turns off Wi-Fi and Bluetooth connections as well, but you can also turn Wi-Fi and Bluetooth on and off separately when you need to.

Using Airplane Mode

1. Swipe up from the bottom of the screen. On an iPhone X, swipe down from the upper-right corner of the screen.

   Control Center opens.

   Note: You can open Control Center from within most apps. If you are using an app that blocks Control Center, display the Home screen, and then swipe up to open Control Center.

   Ⓐ You can tap **Airplane Mode** (changes to) to turn Airplane Mode on quickly.

2. Press the upper-left box.

   The Peek panel opens.

3. Tap **Airplane Mode** (changes to).

   Your iPhone turns off all cellular and wireless connections.

4. To turn on Wi-Fi, tap **Wi-Fi** (changes to).

5. To turn on Bluetooth, tap **Bluetooth** (changes to).

6. Tap the screen above the Peek panel.

   The Peek panel closes.

7. Tap the screen at the top of Control Center.

   Control Center closes.

Note: When your iPhone has a wireless network connection, it uses that connection instead of the cellular connection. This helps keep down your cellular network usage and often gives a faster connection.

Monitor Your Cellular Network Usage

If you use your iPhone extensively, you may need to monitor your usage of the cellular network to avoid incurring extra charges beyond your data allowance. You can check your current data usage and roaming data usage in the Cellular Data Usage area of the Cellular screen in the Settings app. However, you should also see if your carrier provides an app for monitoring data usage, because such apps frequently offer extra features, such as warning you when your phone is using data quickly.

Monitor Your Cellular Network Usage

1 Press **Home**. On an iPhone X, swipe up from the bottom of the screen.

The Home screen appears.

2 Press **Settings** (⚙).

The Peek panel opens.

3 Tap **Cellular Data** ((ᵂ)).

Note: You can also display the Cellular screen by pressing **Home**, tapping **Settings** (⚙), and then tapping **Cellular** (📶) on the Settings screen.

The Cellular screen appears.

4 Set the **Cellular Data** switch to On (⚪) to enable cellular data.

A The readouts in the Call Time area show the amount of time you have spent making calls since last resetting the statistics and during your phone's lifetime.

B The readouts in the Cellular Data Usage area show your cellular data usage since last resetting the statistics and how much roaming data you have used.

C You can reset your usage statistics by tapping **Reset Statistics** at the bottom of the Cellular screen.

D You can set the **Wi-Fi Assist** switch to On (⚪) to make your iPhone automatically use cellular data when the phone's Wi-Fi connection is poor.

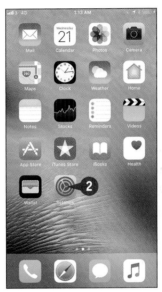

Control Cellular Data and Background Refresh

To control your iPhone's use of cellular data, you can turn cellular data on and off, and you can decide which apps can use cellular data. You can determine which apps and services use the most data, and then turn off greedy apps.

You can also use the Background App Refresh feature to control which apps refresh their content via Wi-Fi or cellular connections when running in the background rather than the foreground.

Control Cellular Data and Background Refresh

1 Press **Home**. On an iPhone X, swipe up from the bottom of the screen.

The Home screen appears.

2 Tap **Settings** (⚙).

The Settings screen appears.

3 Tap **Cellular** (📶).

Note: Turning off cellular data does not affect cellular voice services: You can still make phone calls, and GPS tracking still works.

The Cellular screen appears.

4 If you need to turn cellular data off altogether, set the **Cellular Data** switch to Off (⬤ changes to ◯).

5 Tap **Cellular Data Options**.

The Cellular Data Options screen appears.

6 Tap **Enable 4G**, **Enable LTE**, or a similar button that appears for your iPhone.

The corresponding screen appears, such as the Enable 4G screen.

7 Tap **Off**, **Voice & Data**, or **Data Only** to specify how to use the high-speed service.

8 Tap **Back** (‹).

The Cellular Data Options screen appears again.

9 Tap **Cellular** (‹).

The Cellular screen appears again.

10 If cellular data is enabled, set each app's switch to On (●) or Off ( ), as needed.

11 To see which system services have been using cellular data, tap **System Services**.

The System Services screen appears.

12 Browse the list to identify any services that hog cellular data.

13 Tap **Cellular** (<).

The Cellular screen appears.

14 Tap **Settings** (<).

The Settings screen appears.

15 Tap **General** (⚙).

The General screen appears.

16 Tap **Background App Refresh**.

The Background App Refresh screen appears.

17 Tap **Background App Refresh**; tap **Off**, **Wi-Fi**, or **Wi-Fi & Cellular Data**, as needed; and then tap **Background App Refresh** (<).

18 Assuming you chose Wi-Fi or Wi-Fi and Cellular Data, set each individual app switch to On (●) or Off ( ), as needed.

19 Tap **General** (<).

The General screen appears.

20 Tap **Settings** (<).

The Settings screen appears.

TIP

Which apps should I allow to use Background App Refresh?
Normally, you should restrict Background App Refresh to those apps for which it is important to have updated information immediately available each time you access the app. For example, if you use your iPhone for navigation, getting updated map and GPS information in the background is a good idea, whereas updating magazine subscriptions is usually a waste of cellular data.

Connect Your iPhone to a Different Carrier

Your iPhone's SIM card makes it connect automatically to a particular carrier's network, such as the AT&T network or the Verizon network. If your iPhone is not locked to a particular carrier's network, you can connect the iPhone to a different carrier's network when you go outside the area your carrier covers. For example, if you travel to the United Kingdom, you can connect your iPhone to carriers such as O2, Vodafone, Three, or EE. You may need to change the iPhone's SIM card to connect to another network.

Connect Your iPhone to a Different Carrier

1 Press **Home**. On an iPhone X, swipe up from the bottom of the screen.

The Home screen appears.

2 Tap **Settings** (⚙).

The Settings screen appears.

3 Tap **Carrier** (📞).

Note: To connect to a different carrier's network, you may need to set up an account with that carrier or pay extra charges to your standard carrier. You may also need to insert a different SIM card in your iPhone.

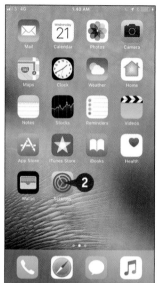

The Network Selection screen appears.

4 Set the **Automatic** switch to Off (◯ changes to ◯).

The list of available carriers appears.

5 Tap the carrier you want to use.

Note: When you want to switch back to your regular carrier, set the **Automatic** switch on the Network Selection screen to On (◯ changes to ◯).

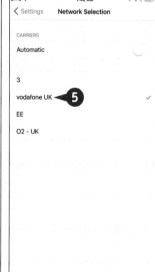

Turn Data Roaming On or Off

When you need to use your iPhone somewhere your carrier does not provide Internet service, you can turn on data roaming, which enables you to access the Internet using other carriers' networks. Data roaming may incur extra charges, especially when you use it in another country, so keep data roaming turned off and turn it on only when you need it. Normally, you will want to use data roaming only when no wireless network connection is available.

Turn Data Roaming On or Off

1 Press **Home**. On an iPhone X, swipe up from the bottom of the screen.

The Home screen appears.

2 Press **Settings** (⚙).

The Peek panel opens.

3 Tap **Cellular Data** (📶).

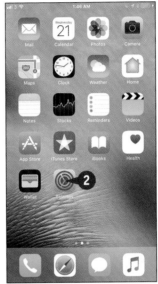

The Cellular screen appears.

A You can also turn off cellular data altogether by setting the **Cellular Data** switch to Off (⚪). Do this when you need to ensure that all apps use Wi-Fi rather than cellular connections.

4 Tap **Cellular Data Options**.

The Cellular Data Options screen appears.

5 Set the **Data Roaming** switch to On (⚪ changes to 🔵).

Note: When you need to turn data roaming off again, set the **Data Roaming** switch on the Cellular Data Options screen to Off (🔵 changes to ⚪).

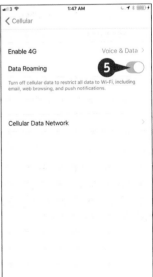

Connect Bluetooth Devices to Your iPhone

To extend your iPhone's functionality, you can connect devices to it that communicate using the wireless Bluetooth technology.

For example, you can connect a Bluetooth headset and microphone so that you can listen to music and make and take phone calls. Or you can connect a Bluetooth keyboard so that you can quickly type e-mail messages, notes, or documents. You can also connect your iPhone to another phone, to a tablet, to many cars' infotainment unit, or to a computer via Bluetooth.

Connect Bluetooth Devices to Your iPhone

Set Up a Bluetooth Device

1 Press **Home**. On an iPhone X, swipe up from the bottom of the screen.

The Home screen appears.

2 Press **Settings** (⚙).

The Peek panel opens.

3 Tap **Bluetooth** (✳).

The Bluetooth screen appears.

4 Set the **Bluetooth** switch to On (⬤ changes to ⬤).

5 Turn on the Bluetooth device and make it discoverable.

Note: Read the Bluetooth device's instructions to find out how to make the device discoverable via Bluetooth.

A Devices in the My Devices list are already paired with your iPhone. You can tap a device to connect it.

6 Tap the device's button.

B For a device such as a keyboard or a computer, the Bluetooth Pairing Request dialog opens.

7 Type the code on the device.

The iPhone pairs with the device and then connects to it.

C The My Devices list shows the device as Connected. You can start using the device.

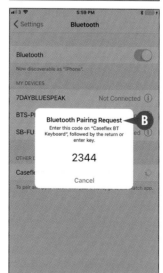

Choose the Device for Playing Audio or Taking a Call

1 Swipe up from the bottom of the screen. On an iPhone X, swipe down from the upper-right corner of the screen.

Note: This example uses the Music app.

Control Center opens.

2 Press the audio controls box.

The Peek panel opens.

3 Tap **AirPlay** ().

The list of devices appears.

4 Tap the device you want to use.

5 Tap **Done**.

The Peek panel closes.

6 Tap the screen at the top of Control Center.

Control Center closes.

TIP

How do I stop using a Bluetooth device?

When you no longer need to use a particular Bluetooth device, tell your iPhone to forget it. Press **Home**, and then tap **Settings** (⚙). Tap **Bluetooth** (ᛒ), and then tap **Info** (ⓘ) for the device. On the device's screen, tap **Forget This Device**, and then tap **Forget Device** in the confirmation dialog.

Share Items via AirDrop

irDrop enables you to share files quickly and easily with iOS devices and Macs near your iPhone. For example, you can use AirDrop to share a photo, a contact record, or an item from Wallet. You can use AirDrop in any app that displays a Share button (⬆).

You can turn AirDrop on when you need it and off when you do not. When AirDrop is on, you can choose between accepting items only from your contacts or from everyone.

Share Items via AirDrop

Turn AirDrop On or Off

1 Swipe up from the bottom of the screen. On an iPhone X, swipe down from the upper-right corner of the screen.

Control Center opens.

2 Press the upper-left box.

The Peek panel opens.

A The readout shows AirDrop's status: *AirDrop: Receiving Off*; *AirDrop: Contacts Only*; or *AirDrop: Everyone*.

3 Tap **AirDrop**.

Note: AirDrop uses Wi-Fi or Bluetooth to transfer files wirelessly without the devices having to be on the same wireless network.

The AirDrop dialog opens.

4 Tap **Receiving Off**, **Contacts Only**, or **Everyone**, as needed.

The AirDrop dialog closes.

B The AirDrop readout shows the AirDrop setting you chose.

5 Tap the screen above the Peek panel.

The Peek panel closes.

6 Tap the screen at the top of Control Center.

Control Center closes.

Share an Item via AirDrop

1 Open the app that contains the item. For example, tap **Photos** (🌸) on the Home screen.

2 Navigate to the item you want to share. For example, tap a photo to open it.

3 Tap **Share** (⬆️).

The Share sheet appears.

C In some apps, you can select other items to share at the same time. For example, in Photos, you can select other photos.

4 In the AirDrop area, tap the contact or device you want to send the item to.

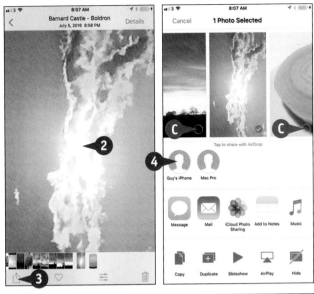

Receive an Item via AirDrop

D When someone tries to send you an item via AirDrop, the AirDrop dialog opens.

1 Tap **Accept** if you want to receive the item. If not, tap **Decline**.

E Your iPhone stores the item in the appropriate app and displays it if possible. For example, when you receive a photo, the Photos app opens and displays the photo so that you can enjoy it, edit it, delete it, or all three.

TIPS

Which devices can use AirDrop?
AirDrop works on all iPhone, iPad, and iPod touch models that have the Lightning port rather than the older, larger Dock Connector port.

Does AirDrop pose a security threat to my iPhone and data?
AirDrop encrypts files so it can transfer them securely. When using AirDrop, you choose which files — if any — you want to share from your iPhone and accept on it; other iOS devices and Macs cannot use AirDrop to grab files from your iPhone.

Share Internet Access via Personal Hotspot

Your iPhone can not only access the Internet itself from anywhere it has a suitable connection to the cellular network, but it can also share that Internet access with your computer and other devices. This feature is called *Personal Hotspot*.

For you to use Personal Hotspot, your iPhone's carrier must permit you to use it. Some carriers charge an extra fee per month on top of the standard data plan charge.

Share Internet Access via Personal Hotspot

Set Up Personal Hotspot

1 Press **Home**. On an iPhone X, swipe up from the bottom of the screen.

The Home screen appears.

2 Tap **Settings** (⚙).

The Settings screen appears.

3 Tap **Personal Hotspot** (⊚).

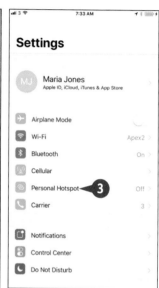

The Personal Hotspot screen appears.

4 Tap **Wi-Fi Password**.

The Wi-Fi Password screen appears.

5 Tap **Delete** (⊗) to delete the default password.

6 Type the password you want to use.

7 Tap **Done**.

The Personal Hotspot screen appears again.

8 Set the **Personal Hotspot** switch to
On (changes to ⬤).

The Personal Hotspot screen shows the
message *Now Discoverable* and displays
information for connecting computers and
devices to the hotspot.

You can now connect your computer or
other devices.

A The blue bar at the top of the screen shows
how many computers or devices are
connected to Personal Hotspot.

Stop Using Personal Hotspot

1 Press **Home**. On an iPhone X, swipe up from
the bottom of the screen.

The Home screen appears.

2 Tap the Personal Hotspot bar.

The Personal Hotspot screen appears.

3 Set the **Personal Hotspot** switch to
Off (⬤ changes to).

TIP

How else can I connect a PC or Mac to Personal Hotspot?

Usually, you can connect a PC to Personal Hotspot by simply connecting your iPhone to the PC via USB.
Windows automatically detects the iPhone's Internet connection as a new network connection and installs
any software needed.

Similarly, you can connect a Mac via USB, but you may need to configure the network connection. Control + click
or right-click **System Preferences** (⚙) on the Dock and click **Network** on the contextual menu to open the
Network preferences pane. In the left pane, click **iPhone USB**. If the Apply button is dark, click **Apply**.

If you cannot get USB to work, connect the computer via Wi-Fi or Bluetooth, if your computer has either of
those features.

Connect to Wi-Fi Networks and Hotspots

To conserve your data allowance, use a Wi-Fi network instead of the cell phone network whenever you can. Your iPhone can connect to both private Wi-Fi networks and to public Wi-Fi hotspots.

The first time you connect to a Wi-Fi network, you must provide the network's password. After that, the iPhone stores the password, so you can connect to the network without entering the password again.

Connect to Wi-Fi Networks and Hotspots

Connect to a Network Listed on the Wi-Fi Screen

1 Press **Home**. On an iPhone X, swipe up from the bottom of the screen.

The Home screen appears.

2 Press **Settings** (⚙).

The Peek panel opens.

3 Tap **Wi-Fi** (📶).

The Wi-Fi screen appears.

4 If Wi-Fi is off, set the **Wi-Fi** switch to On (changes to 🔵).

The Choose a Network list appears.

A A lock icon (🔒) indicates the network has security such as a password.

5 Tap the network you want to connect to.

Note: If the network does not have a password, your iPhone connects to it without prompting you for a password.

Note: When connecting to a Wi-Fi hotspot, you may need to enter login information in Safari. In this case, Safari usually opens automatically and prompts you to log in.

The Enter Password screen appears.

6 Type the password.

7 Tap **Join**.

Your iPhone connects to the wireless network.

B The Wi-Fi screen appears again, showing a check mark (✓) next to the network the iPhone has connected to.

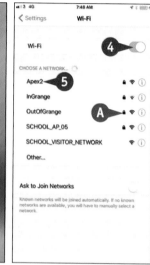

Connect to a Network Not Listed on the Wi-Fi Screen

1 On the Wi-Fi screen, tap **Other**.

The Other Network screen appears.

2 Type the network name.

Note: If the network does not use security, tap **Join**.

C The Wi-Fi signal icons (📶) on the Wi-Fi screen and in the status bar show the strength of the Wi-Fi signals. The more bars that appear in black rather than gray, the stronger a signal is.

3 Tap **Security**.

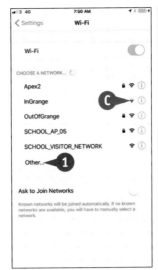

The Security screen appears.

4 Tap the security type — for example, **WPA2**.

5 Tap **Other Network** (<).

The Other Network screen appears.

6 Type the password.

7 Tap **Join**.

Your iPhone joins the network.

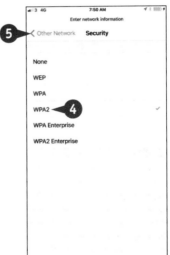

TIPS

What does the Ask to Join Networks switch control?

Your iPhone automatically connects to networks it "knows" — those it has connected to before. Set the **Ask to Join Networks** switch to On (◯) if you want your iPhone to prompt you to join unknown networks when they are available.

How do I stop using a particular wireless network?

Tap **Info** (ⓘ) to the right of the network's name on the Wi-Fi screen. On the network's screen, tap **Forget This Network**. In the dialog that opens, tap **Forget**.

Always forget a Wi-Fi hotspot you will not use again. Forgetting the hotspot helps prevent your iPhone from connecting to a malevolent hotspot that mimics the genuine hotspot.

Set Up and Enjoy Social Networking

Always in your pocket or purse if not in your hand, your iPhone is the perfect device for keeping in touch with family, friends, and acquaintances via social networking. You can install apps such as Facebook, Twitter, or WhatsApp; post updates or browse what others have posted; and share content easily from many apps, such as Photos.

Install the Social Networking Apps You Need

To start with, install the social networking apps you want to use. Press **Home** to display the Home screen, and then tap **App Store** ( ) to launch the App Store app. To find a specific app, tap **Search** (changes to), type the app's name, and then tap the appropriate search result. On the screen showing the app, tap **Get** and follow the procedure for installing the app.

Configure Settings for a Social Networking App

Many social networking apps have settings that you can configure in the Settings app. To do so, press **Home**, tap **Settings** ( ), and then tap the app's button — for example, tap **Facebook** ( ) to display the settings screen for the app. You can then configure the controls. Many apps have standard settings such as the Siri & Search switch, the Background App Refresh switch, and the Cellular Data switch. Some have other settings, such as the Upload HD switch in the Facebook app, which controls whether the app uploads high-definition video.

Some apps also have settings that you can configure within the app itself. For example, in Facebook, tap **Menu** ( ) to open the menu, and then tap **Settings** ( ).

Launch and Sign In to a Social Networking App

When you are ready to start using a social networking app, launch it by tapping its icon on the Home screen. For example, tap **Twitter** (). Follow the prompts to sign in or log in. For example, in Twitter, enter your username or Twitter handle, enter your password, and then tap **Log in**.

The app then opens, and you can start using it as normal. For example, in Twitter, tap **Tweet** ( ) to start writing a new tweet.

Share Content with a Social Networking App

You can easily share content from other apps with your social networking apps. To do so, first open the appropriate app and select the item you want to share. For example, tap **Photos** ( ) and select a photo to share. Next, tap **Share** ( ) to open the Share sheet, tap the social networking app on the Activities bar, and then follow the prompts to post the photo.

If the app does not appear on the Activities bar, tap **More** (...) at the right end of the Activities bar to display the Activities dialog. Set the app's switch to On ( ) and drag it by its handle ( ) up or down the list, as needed. Then tap **Done**.

CHAPTER 7

Working with Apps

iOS enables you to customize the Home screen, putting the icons you need most right at hand and organizing them into folders. You can switch instantly among the apps you are running, find the apps you need on Apple's App Store, and update and remove apps. You can also work easily with text and take notes.

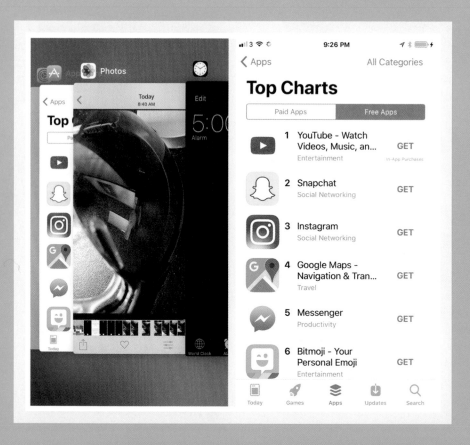

Customize the Home Screen

From the Home screen, you run the apps on your iPhone. You can customize the Home screen to put the apps you use most frequently within easy reach. You can create additional Home screens as needed and move the app icons among them. You can customize the Home screen by working on the iPhone, as described here. If you synchronize your iPhone with a computer, you can use iTunes instead. This is an easier way to make extensive changes, such as changing the order of the Home screens.

Customize the Home Screen

Unlock the Icons for Customization

1. Press **Home**. On an iPhone X, swipe up from the bottom of the screen.

   The Home screen appears.

2. Swipe left or right to display the Home screen you want to customize.

   A. You can also tap the dots to move from one Home screen to another.

3. Tap and hold the icon you want to move, without pressing the icon.

Note: You can tap and hold any icon until the apps start jiggling. Usually, it is easiest to tap and hold the icon you want to move, and then drag that icon.

   The icons start to jiggle, indicating that you can move them.

Move an Icon Within a Home Screen

1. After unlocking the icons, drag the icon to where you want it.

   The other icons move out of the way.

2. When the icon is in the right place, drop it.

   B. The icon stays in its new position.

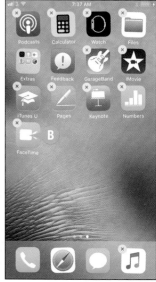

156

Move an Icon to a Different Home Screen

1 After unlocking the icons, drag the icon to the left edge of the screen to display the previous Home screen or to the right edge to display the next Home screen.

The previous Home screen or next Home screen appears.

2 Drag the icon to where you want it.

If the Home screen contains other icons, they move out of the way as needed.

3 Drop the icon.

C The icon stays in its new position.

Stop Customizing the Home Screen

1 Press **Home**. On an iPhone X, swipe up from the bottom of the screen.

The icons stop jiggling.

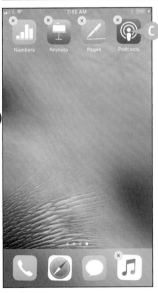

TIP

How can I put the default apps back into their original Home screen locations?
Press **Home** — on an iPhone X, swipe up from the bottom of the screen — to display the Home screen, tap **Settings** (⚙), and then tap **General** (⚙). Tap and drag up to scroll down the screen, and then tap **Reset**. On the Reset screen, tap **Reset Home Screen Layout**, and then tap **Reset Home Screen** in the dialog that opens. Press **Home** or swipe up to return to the Home screen.

Organize Apps with Folders

To organize the Home screen, you can arrange the items into folders. The iPhone's default Home screen layout includes a folder named Extras, which contains items such as the Contacts app and the Compass app, but you can create as many other folders as you need. Like the Home screen, each folder can have multiple pages, with up to nine apps on each page, so you can put many apps in a folder.

Organize Apps with Folders

Create a Folder

1 Display the Home screen that contains the item you want to put into a folder.

2 Tap and hold the item until the icons start to jiggle.

Note: When creating a folder, you may find it easiest to first put both items you will add to the folder on the same screen.

3 Drag the item to the other icon you want to place in the folder you create.

The iPhone creates a folder, puts both icons in it, and assigns a default name based on the genre, if it can identify a genre.

4 Tap **Delete** (🗙) to delete the folder name.

The keyboard appears.

5 Type the new name for the folder.

6 Tap outside the folder.

The iPhone applies the name to the folder.

7 Press **Home**. On an iPhone X, swipe up from the bottom of the screen.

The icons stop jiggling.

Note: You can quickly rename a folder by pressing it, tapping **Rename**, typing the new name, and then tapping outside the folder.

Open an Item in a Folder

1 Display the Home screen that contains the folder.

2 Tap the folder's icon.

The folder's contents appear, and the items outside the folder fade and blur.

3 If necessary, swipe left or right or tap a dot to navigate to another page in the folder.

4 Tap the item you want to open.

The item opens.

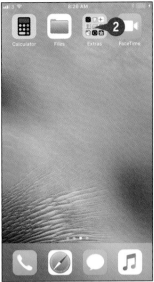

Add an Item to a Folder

1 Display the Home screen that contains the item.

2 Tap and hold the item until the icons start to jiggle.

3 Drag the icon on top of the folder and drop it there.

Note: If the folder is on a different Home screen from the icon, drag the icon to the left edge to display the previous Home screen or to the right edge to display the next Home screen.

The item goes into the folder.

4 Press **Home** to stop the icons jiggling.

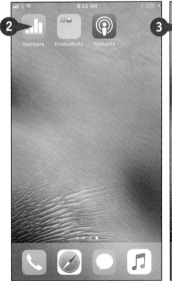

TIPS

How do I take an item out of a folder?
Tap the folder to display its contents, and then tap and hold the item until the icons start to jiggle. Drag the item out of the folder, drag it to where you want it on the Home screen, and then drop it. When you remove the last item, iOS deletes the folder automatically.

How do I create another page in a folder?
Open the folder, and then tap and hold an item until the icons start jiggling. Drag the item to the right side of the current page. A new page appears automatically.

Switch Quickly from One App to Another

You can run many apps on your iPhone at the same time, switching from one app to another as needed.

You can switch apps by pressing **Home** — or on an iPhone X, swiping up from the bottom of the screen — to display the Home screen and then tapping the icon for the next app. But the iPhone also has an app-switching screen that enables you to switch quickly from one running app to another running app. From the app-switching screen, you can also easily close one or more running apps.

Switch Quickly from One App to Another

1 Press **Home**. On an iPhone X, swipe up from the bottom of the screen.

The Home screen appears.

2 Tap the app you want to launch. This example uses **Maps** ( ).

The app's screen appears.

3 Start using the app as usual.

Note: On an iPhone X, you can switch quickly from one app to another by swiping left or right on the invisible bar at the bottom of the screen.

4 On an iPhone X, swipe up from the bottom of the screen to the middle, and then pause momentarily. On iPhone models with a Home button, press **Home** twice in quick succession.

Ⓐ The app-switching screen appears, showing a carousel of thumbnails of the open apps.

Ⓑ The icons identify the app thumbnails.

5 Swipe left or right to scroll until you see the app you want.

Note: The last app you used appears on the right side of the app-switching screen. To its right is the Home screen. To its left are the apps you have used most recently.

6 Tap the app.

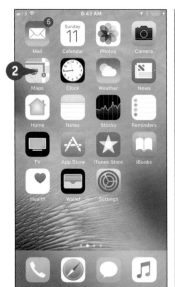

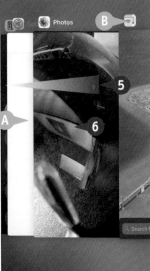

The app appears.

7 When you are ready to switch back, display the app-switching screen again. On an iPhone X, swipe up from the bottom of the screen to the middle, and then pause momentarily. On iPhone models with a Home button, press **Home** twice in quick succession.

8 Scroll left or right as needed, and then tap the app to which you want to return.

The app appears, ready to resume from where you stopped using it.

TIP

How do I stop an app that is not responding?

If an app stops responding, you can quickly close it from the app-switching screen. Press **Home** twice to open the app-switching screen. Scroll to the problem app and then drag it upward so it disappears off the screen. Tap the app you want to use or press **Home** — on an iPhone X, swipe up from the bottom of the screen — to return to the Home screen.

You can use this move to close any app that you no longer want to use, whether or not it has stopped responding. For example, if an app seems to be devouring battery power, you can use this technique to close it.

Find Apps on the App Store

The iPhone comes with essential apps, such as Safari for surfing the web, Mail for e-mail, and Calendar for keeping track of your schedule. But to get the most out of your iPhone, you will likely need to add other apps.

To get apps, you use the App Store, which provides apps that Apple has approved as correctly programmed, suitable for purpose, and free of malevolent code. Before you can download any apps, including free apps, you must create an App Store account.

Find Apps on the App Store

1 Press **Home**. On an iPhone X, swipe up from the bottom of the screen.

The Home screen appears.

2 Tap **App Store** (🅰).

The App Store screen appears.

Usually, the Today screen appears at first.

3 Tap **Apps** (≋ changes to ≋).

Ⓐ You can tap **Games** (🚀 changes to 🚀) if you want to browse games instead of apps.

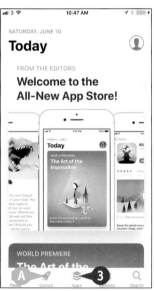

The Apps screen appears.

Ⓑ You can tap **See All** for a list to see the whole list.

4 Swipe up to scroll down until the Top Categories section appears.

Note: The Top Free list shows the free apps that App Store users are downloading. The Top Paid list shows the apps that App Store users are buying.

5 Tap **See All** in the Top Categories section.

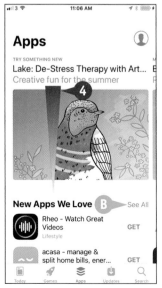

The Categories screen appears.

6 Tap the category you want to see. This example uses the **Utilities** category.

The category's screen appears.

C You can tap **See All** to view the full list.

7 Tap the app you want to view.

Note: To understand what an app does and how well it does it, look at the app's rating, read the description, and read the user reviews. Swipe the images to see screen captures from the app.

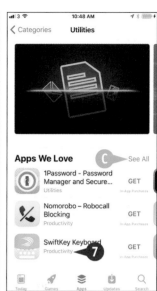

The app's screen appears.

8 Tap the price button or the **Get** button.

Note: If the iPhone prompts you to sign in, type your password and then tap **OK**.

Note: If you have not created an App Store account already, the iPhone prompts you to create one now.

The iPhone downloads and installs the app.

9 Tap **Open**.

Note: If you switch to another app while the new app downloads and installs, launch the new app from the Home screen instead.

The app opens, and you can start using it.

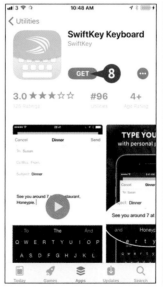

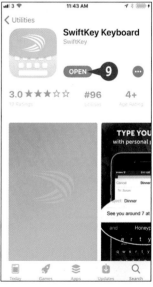

TIP

Why does App Store not appear on the Home screen or when I search for it?

If App Store (🅐) does not appear on the Home screen, and if searching for it does not show a result, the iPhone has restrictions applied that prevent you from installing apps. You can remove these restrictions if you know the restrictions passcode. Press **Home**, tap **Settings** (⚙), and then tap **General** (⚙). Scroll down, and then tap **Restrictions**. Type the passcode on the Enter Passcode screen, and then set the **Installing Apps** switch to On (changes to ⬤).

Update and Remove Apps

To keep your iPhone's apps running smoothly, you should install app updates when they become available. Most minor updates for paid apps are free, but you must often pay to upgrade to a new version of the app.

When you no longer need an app you have installed on your iPhone, you can remove it, thus recovering the space it occupied. You can remove some but not all of the built-in apps.

Update and Remove Apps

Update One or More Apps

1 Press **Home**. On an iPhone X, swipe up from the bottom of the screen.

The Home screen appears.

A The badge on the App Store icon shows the number of available updates.

2 Tap **App Store** (⊞).

The App Store screen appears.

3 Tap **Updates** (⊡ changes to ⬇).

Note: You can press **App Store** (⊞) on the Home screen and then tap **Update All** on the Peek panel to update all apps easily.

Note: You can also update apps using your computer. Connect your iPhone to the computer. In iTunes, click iPhone (▯), and then click **Apps** (⟁). Click the **Updates** tab, click **Update All Apps**, and then click **Sync**.

The Updates screen appears.

4 Tap **Update All** to apply all the available updates now.

B You can tap **Update** to update a single app.

C You can tap **Account** (⬤ or your iCloud account icon) to display the Account screen. From here, you can tap **Purchased** to display the Purchased screen, from which you can install apps you have bought previously but not yet installed on this iPhone.

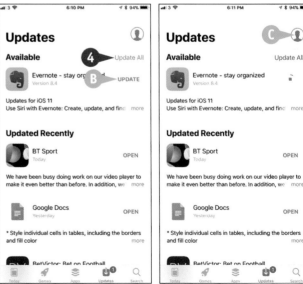

164

Remove an App from the iPhone

1 Press **Home**. On an iPhone X, swipe up from the bottom of the screen.

The Home screen appears.

2 Display the Home screen that contains the app you want to delete.

3 Tap and hold the item until the icons start to jiggle.

4 Tap **Delete** (×) on the icon.

The Delete dialog appears.

5 Tap **Delete**.

The iPhone deletes the app, and the app's icon disappears.

6 Press **Home**. On an iPhone X, swipe up from the bottom of the screen.

The icons stop jiggling.

TIP

How do I remove an app using my computer?
Connect your iPhone to your computer. Then, in iTunes on the computer, click **iPhone** (□), click **Apps** (A) in the Source list on the left, and then click **Remove** to the right of the app. Click **Sync** to effect the change.

Cut, Copy, and Paste Text

You can easily type text on your iPhone's keyboard or dictate it using Siri, but if the text already exists, you can copy and paste the text instead. This section demonstrates copying text from an e-mail message and pasting it into a Pages document.

If the text is in a document you can edit, you can either copy the text or cut it. If the text is in a document you cannot edit, you can only copy the text.

Cut, Copy, and Paste Text

Open an App and Copy Text

1 Press **Home**. On an iPhone X, swipe up from the bottom of the screen.

The Home screen appears.

Note: This example uses the Mail app, but you can cut, copy, and paste text in many other apps as well.

2 Tap **Mail** (⬛).

The Mail app opens.

3 Tap the message you want to open.

Note: Some apps also have a Copy icon and a Paste icon on the top row of the on-screen keyboard.

The message's contents appear.

4 Tap and hold a word in the section of text you want to copy or cut.

The word becomes highlighted.

Selection handles appear around the selection.

Ⓐ The formatting bar appears.

5 Drag the start handle (⏐) to the beginning of the text you want.

6 Drag the end handle (⏐) to the end of the text you want.

7 Tap **Copy**.

Your iPhone places the text on the Clipboard, a hidden storage area.

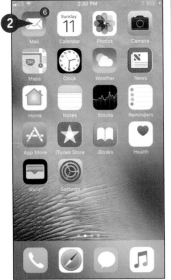

Paste the Content You Have Copied or Cut

① Press **Home**. On an iPhone X, swipe up from the bottom of the screen.

The Home screen appears.

② Tap the app into which you want to paste the text. This example uses Notes, but you can use many other apps.

The app opens.

③ Create a new document or open an existing document, as needed. For example, in Notes, tap **New** () to create a new note.

The document opens.

④ Tap where you want to paste the text.

The formatting bar opens.

⑤ Tap **Paste**.

Ⓑ The copied text appears in the document.

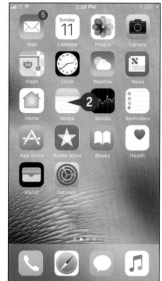

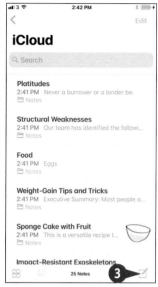

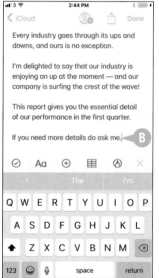

TIPS

How many items can I store on the Clipboard?

You can store only one item on the Clipboard at a time. Each item you cut or copy replaces the existing item on the Clipboard. But until you replace the existing item on the Clipboard, you can paste it as many times as needed.

Can I transfer the contents of the Clipboard to my computer?

You cannot transfer the Clipboard's contents directly to your computer, but you can easily transfer it indirectly. For example, paste it into an e-mail message and send it to yourself, or paste it into a note in the Notes app and allow the account, such as iCloud, to sync the note.

Format and Replace Text

Some apps enable you to add text formatting such as boldface, underline, italics, and strikethrough to text to make parts of it stand out. For example, you can apply formatting in e-mail messages you create using the Mail app on some e-mail services and in various apps for creating word-processing documents.

To apply formatting, you first select the text, and then choose options from the pop-up formatting bar. Some apps also offer other text commands, such as replacing a word or phrase from a menu of suggestions.

Format and Replace Text

Apply Bold, Italics, Underline, and Strikethrough

1 Tap and hold the text to which you want to apply bold, italics, underline, or strikethrough.

The formatting bar appears.

2 Tap **Select**.

Part of the text becomes highlighted, and the selection handles appear.

3 Drag the start handle (❘) to the beginning of the text you want.

4 Drag the end handle (❘) to the end of the text you want.

5 Tap **B***I*U on the formatting bar.

The formatting bar displays formatting options.

6 Tap **Bold**, *Italic*, **Underline**, or **Strikethrough**, as needed.

The text takes on the formatting you chose.

7 Tap outside the selected text to deselect it.

Note: Some apps have their own formatting tools, many of which are more extensive than the standard formatting tools shown here.

Note: Some e-mail services and notes services do not support formatting.

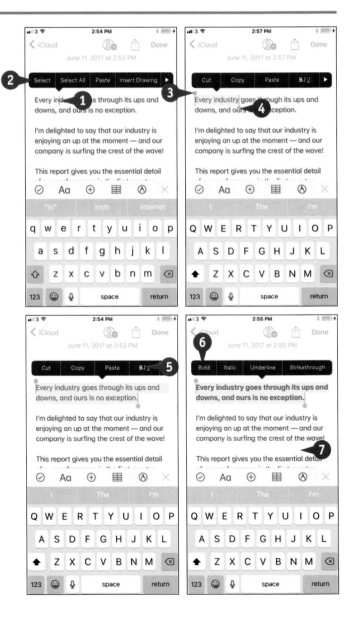

Replace Text with Suggested Words

1 Double-tap the word you want to replace.

Note: You can tap and hold anywhere in the word, and then tap **Select** on the formatting bar to select the word.

The word becomes highlighted and selection handles appear around it.

The formatting bar appears.

2 Tap **Replace**.

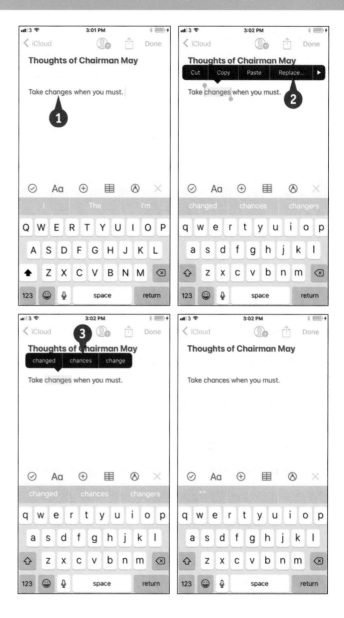

The formatting bar displays suggested replacement words.

3 Tap the word with which you want to replace the selected word.

The word you tapped appears in the text.

Note: Tap **More** (▶) to display more commands on the formatting bar. For example, in some apps, you can insert photos and videos.

TIP

What does the Quote Level button on the pop-up formatting bar in Mail do?
Tap **Quote Level** when you need to increase or decrease the quote level of your selected text. You may need to tap **More** (▶) to display the Quote Level button. When you tap Quote Level, the formatting bar displays an Increase button and a Decrease button. Tap **Increase** to increase the quote level, indenting the text more and adding a colored bar to its left, or **Decrease** to decrease the quote level, reducing the existing indent and removing a colored bar.

CHAPTER 8

Browsing the Web and E-Mailing

Your iPhone is fully equipped to browse the web and send e-mail via a Wi-Fi connection or via the cellular network.

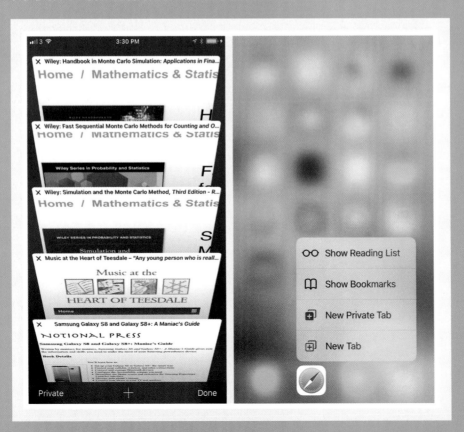

Browse the Web with Safari

Your iPhone comes equipped with the Safari app, which enables you to browse the web. You can quickly go to a web page by entering its address in the Address box or by following a link.

Although you can browse quickly by opening a single web page at a time, you may prefer to open multiple pages and switch back and forth among them. Safari makes this easy to do.

Browse the Web with Safari

Open Safari and Navigate to Web Pages

1 Press **Home**. On an iPhone X, swipe up from the bottom of the screen.

The Home screen appears.

2 Tap **Safari** (⊘).

Safari opens and loads the last web page that was shown.

3 Tap the Address box.

Note: You can enter widely used domain extensions, such as .com and .net, by tapping and holding . (the period key) and tapping the extensions on the pop-up panel that appears.

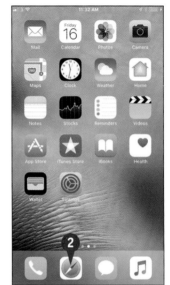

Safari selects the current contents of the Address box, and the keyboard appears.

4 Tap **Delete** (⊗) if you need to delete the contents of the Address box.

5 Type the address of the page you want to open.

Ⓐ You can also tap a search result that Safari displays below the Address box.

6 Tap **Go**.

Safari displays the page.

7 Tap a link on the page.

Safari displays that page.

Ⓑ After going to a new page, tap **Back** (‹) to display the previous page. You can then tap **Forward** (›) to go forward again.

Open Multiple Pages and Navigate Among Them

1 Tap **Pages** (▢).

Safari displays the list of open pages, each bearing a Close button (✕).

C Below the list of open pages, you can find a list of recent pages you opened on other devices that use the same iCloud account.

2 Tap **New Page** (▦).

Note: In landscape orientation, a large-screen iPhone displays a tab bar at the top of the screen. Tap the tab for the page you want to view.

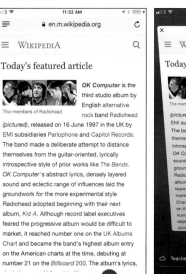

Safari opens a new page and displays your bookmarks.

3 Tap the Address box, and then go to the page you want.

Note: You can also go to a page by using a bookmark, as described in the next section, "Access Websites Quickly with Bookmarks."

The page appears.

4 To switch to another page, tap **Pages** (▢).

Safari displays the list of pages.

5 Tap the page you want to see.

D You can tap **Close** (✕) to close a page.

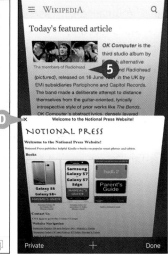

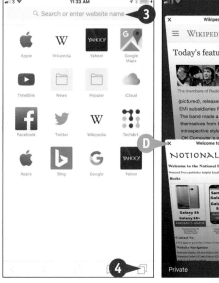

TIPS

How do I search for information?
Tap the Address box to select its current contents, and then type your search terms. Safari searches as you type; you can type further to narrow down the results, and stop as soon as you see suitable results. Tap the result you want to see, and then tap a link on the results page that Safari opens.

How can I return to a tab I closed by mistake?
Tap **Pages** (▢) to display the list of open pages, and then tap and hold **New Page** (▦). On the Recently Closed Tabs screen that appears, tap the tab you want to reopen.

Access Websites Quickly with Bookmarks

Typing web addresses can be laborious, even with the help that the iPhone's keyboard adds, so you will probably want to use bookmarks to access websites you visit often.

By syncing your existing bookmarks from your computer or online account, as described in Chapter 1, you can instantly provide your iPhone with quick access to the web pages you want to visit most frequently. You can also create bookmarks on your iPhone, as discussed in the next section, "Create Bookmarks."

Access Websites Quickly with Bookmarks

Open the Bookmarks Screen

1 Press **Home**. On an iPhone X, swipe up from the bottom of the screen.

The Home screen appears.

2 Tap **Safari** ( ).

Safari opens.

3 Tap **Bookmarks** ( ).

The Bookmarks screen appears.

Note: You can display the Bookmarks screen quickly from the Home screen by pressing **Safari** ( ) and then tapping **Show Bookmarks** on the Peek panel.

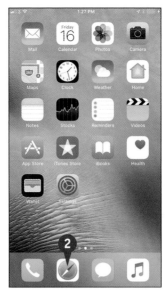

Explore Your History

1 On the Bookmarks screen, tap **History** ( ).

The History screen appears, showing a list of the web pages you have recently visited.

A You can tap a time or a day to display the list of web pages you visited then.

B You can tap **Search History** ( ) and type search terms to search for particular pages.

C You can tap a page's button to display that page.

2 Tap **Bookmarks** ( ) when you want to return to the Bookmarks screen.

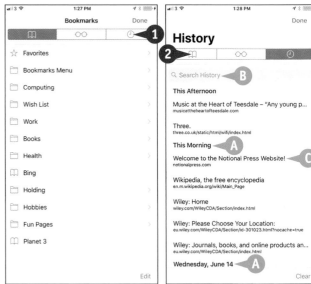

Explore a Bookmarks Category

① On the Bookmarks screen, tap the bookmarks folder or category you want to see. This example uses the **Books** folder.

The contents of the folder or category appear. For example, the contents of the Books folder appear.

② Tap the **Back** button (〈) one or more times to go back. The button's name depends on the previous folder — in this case, you would tap **All** (〈) to go back to the Bookmarks screen.

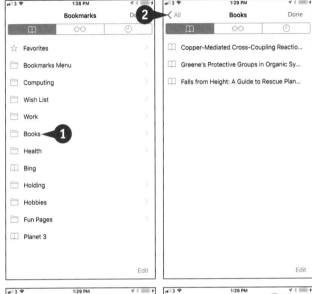

Open a Bookmarked Page

Ⓓ You can delete a bookmark by swiping it to the left and then tapping **Delete**.

① When you find the bookmark for the web page you want to open, tap the bookmark.

Ⓔ The web page opens.

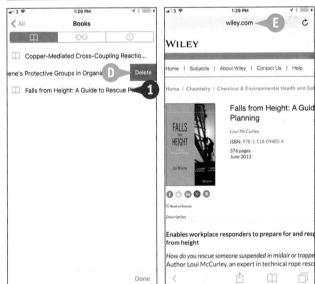

TIP

How can I quickly access a website?
Creating a bookmark within Safari — as discussed in the next section, "Create Bookmarks" — is good for sites you access now and then. But if you access a site frequently, create an icon for it on your Home screen. Open the site in Safari. Tap **Share** (⬆), tap **Add to Home Screen** (➕), type the name on the Add to Home screen, and then tap **Add**. You can then go straight to the page by tapping its icon on the Home screen.

Create Bookmarks

When you want to access a web page again easily, create a bookmark for it. If you have set your iPhone to sync bookmarks with your iCloud account, the bookmark becomes available on your computer or online account as well when you sync.

If you create many bookmarks, it is usually helpful to create multiple folders in which you can organize the bookmarks. You can create folders easily on the iPhone and choose the folder in which to store each bookmark.

Create Bookmarks

Create a Bookmark

1 Press **Home**. On an iPhone X, swipe up from the bottom of the screen.

The Home screen appears.

2 Tap **Safari** (🧭).

Safari opens and displays the last web page you were viewing.

3 Navigate to the web page you want to bookmark.

4 Tap **Share** (📤).

The Share sheet appears.

5 Tap **Add Bookmark** (📖).

The Add Bookmark screen appears.

6 Edit the suggested name, or type a new name, as needed.

7 Tap the current folder under the Location heading.

The Choose a Folder screen appears.

8 Tap the folder in which to store the bookmark.

The Add Bookmark screen appears.

9 Tap **Save**.

Create a New Folder for Bookmarks

1 In Safari, tap **Bookmarks** (▢).

The Bookmarks screen appears.

2 Tap **Edit**.

The editing controls appear.

Ⓐ You can drag a handle (═) to change the order of the bookmark folders.

Ⓑ You can tap **Delete** (⊖) and then tap the textual **Delete** button to delete a bookmark folder and its contents.

3 Tap **New Folder**.

The Edit Folder screen appears.

4 Type the name for the folder.

5 Tap the folder under the Location heading.

A screen showing the list of folders appears.

6 Tap the folder in which to store the bookmark.

The Edit Folder screen appears again.

7 Tap **All** (〈).

The Bookmarks screen appears, still with editing controls displayed.

8 Tap **Done**.

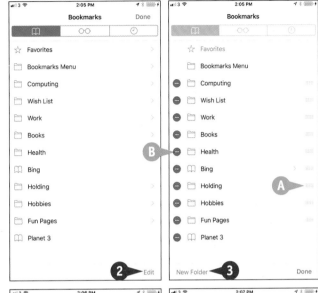

TIP

Can I change a bookmark I have created?

Yes. Tap **Bookmarks** (▢) to display the Bookmarks screen, and then navigate to the bookmark you want to change. Tap **Edit** to switch to Editing Mode. You can then tap a bookmark to open it on the Edit Bookmark screen, where you can change its name, address, or location. In Editing Mode, you can also delete a bookmark by tapping **Delete** (⊖) and then tapping **Delete**, or rearrange your bookmarks by dragging the handle (═) up or down the list. Tap **Done** when you finish editing bookmarks.

Keep a Reading List of Web Pages

afari's Reading List feature enables you to save a web page for later without creating a bookmark. You can quickly add the current web page to Reading List by using the Share sheet. Once you have added pages, you access Reading List through the Bookmarks feature. When viewing Reading List, you can display either all the pages it contains or only those you have not read.

Keep a Reading List of Web Pages

Add a Web Page to Reading List

1 Press **Home**. On an iPhone X, swipe up from the bottom of the screen.

The Home screen appears.

2 Tap **Safari** (⊘).

Safari opens and displays the last web page you were viewing.

3 Navigate to the web page you want to add to Reading List.

4 Tap **Share** (⬆).

The Share sheet appears.

5 Tap **Add to Reading List** (∞).

The first time you give the Add to Reading List command, the Automatically Save Reading List Articles for Offline Reading? dialog opens.

6 Tap **Save Automatically** if you want to save the articles so you can read them when you do not have an Internet connection, which is usually helpful. If not, tap **Don't Save Automatically**.

Safari adds the web page to Reading List.

Note: To change the Automatically Save Offline setting later, press **Home** to display the Home screen, tap **Settings** (⚙), and then tap **Safari** (⊘). Scroll down to the Reading List section and set the **Automatically Save Offline** switch to On (⬤) or Off ( ), as needed.

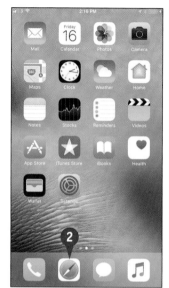

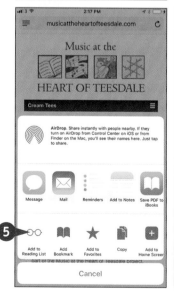

178

Open Reading List and Display a Page

1 In Safari, tap **Bookmarks** (📖).

The Bookmarks screen appears.

2 Tap **Reading List** (∞).

Note: You can quickly display the Reading List screen from the Home screen by pressing **Safari** (🧭) and then tapping **Show Reading List** on the Peek panel.

The Reading List screen appears.

3 Tap **Show All**.

Reading List displays all the pages it contains, including those you have read.

Ⓐ Pages you have read appear with gray shading.

Ⓑ You can tap **Show Unread** to display only unread pages.

4 Tap the page you want to open.

Ⓒ If you decide not to open a page from Reading List, tap **Done** to hide the Reading List screen.

TIP

How do I remove an item from Reading List?

To remove an item from Reading List, swipe it left and then tap the textual **Delete** button that appears.

You can also swipe an item right. When you do so, the Mark Read button also appears if you have not read the item; the Mark Unread button appears if you have read it. You can tap **Mark Read** or **Mark Unread** to switch the item's read status.

Navigate Among Open Web Pages Using Tabs

If you browse the web a lot, you will probably need to open many web pages in Safari at the same time. Safari presents your open pages as a list of scrollable tabs, making it easy to navigate from one page to another.

You can change the order of the tabs to suit your needs, and you can quickly close a tab by either tapping its **Close** button or simply swiping it off the list.

Navigate Among Open Web Pages Using Tabs

Open Safari and Display the List of Tabs

1 Press **Home**. On an iPhone X, swipe up from the bottom of the screen.

The Home screen appears.

2 Tap **Safari** (⊘).

Safari opens or becomes active.

Note: If Safari has hidden the on-screen controls, tap the screen and pull down a short way to display them.

3 Tap **Pages** (◻).

The list of pages appears.

Close Pages You Do Not Need to Keep Open

1 Tap **Close** (✕) on the tab for a page you want to close.

The page closes, and the tab disappears from the list.

2 Alternatively, you can tap a tab and swipe it left off the screen.

The page closes, and the tab disappears from the list.

Note: You can turn a large-screen iPhone to landscape orientation and then tap **Close** (✕) to close the current tab.

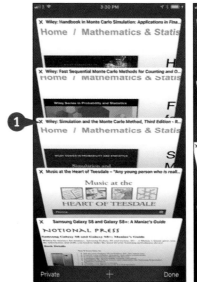

Change the Order of the Pages

1 Tap and hold the tab for a page you want to move.

The tab moves to the foreground.

2 Drag the tab to where you want it to appear in the list, and then release it.

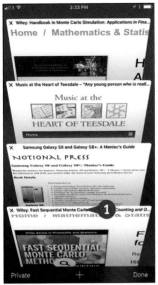

Find a Page and Display It

1 Press the tab for the page you want to display.

The Peek panel for the page opens.

2 Press harder.

The page opens.

Note: You can also turn a large-screen iPhone to landscape orientation to display the tab bar at the top of the screen. You can then tap the tab you want to view.

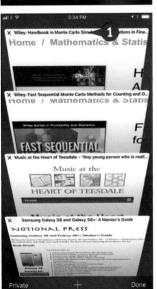

TIP

How do I return from the list of tabs to the page I was viewing before?
To return to the page you were viewing before, either tap the page's tab in the list of tabs, or tap **Done** in the lower-right corner of the screen.

Tighten Up Safari's Security

To protect yourself against websites that infect computers with malware or try to gain your sensitive personal or financial information, turn on Safari's Fraudulent Website Warning feature. You can also turn off the JavaScript programming language, which can be used to attack your iPhone. Additionally, you can block pop-up windows, which some websites use to display unwanted information; block new cookies and data; and request that sites not track your visits.

Tighten Up Safari's Security

1 Press **Home**. On an iPhone X, swipe up from the bottom of the screen.

The Home screen appears.

2 Tap **Settings** (⚙).

The Settings screen appears.

3 Tap **Safari** (🧭).

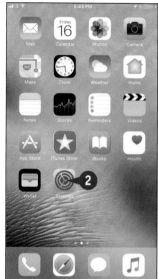

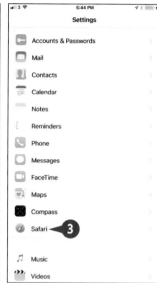

The Safari screen appears.

A The AutoFill feature enables you to save information — such as your name, address, and credit card details — for filling out web forms quickly.

4 Set the **Block Pop-ups** switch to On (🔘) to block unwanted pop-up windows.

5 Set the **Try to Prevent Cross-Site Tracking** switch to On (🔘) or Off (⚬), as needed.

6 Set the **Block New Cookies and Data** switch to On (🔘) or Off (⚬), as needed.

7 Set the **Ask Websites Not to Track Me** switch to On (🔘).

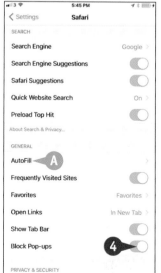

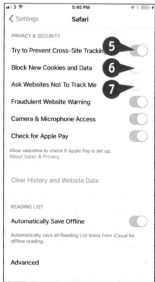

The Safari screen appears again.

8 Set the **Fraudulent Website Warning** switch to On ( ).

9 Tap **Clear History and Website Data**.

A dialog opens.

10 Tap **Clear History and Data**.

The dialog closes.

Safari clears your browsing history and data.

11 Tap **Advanced**.

The Advanced screen appears.

12 Set the **JavaScript** switch to On ( ) or Off ( ), as needed.

Note: Turning off JavaScript may remove some or most functionality of harmless sites.

13 Tap **Website Data**.

The Website Data screen appears.

B You can tap **Remove All Website Data** to remove all website data.

14 Tap **Edit**.

A Delete icon ( ) appears to the left of each website.

15 To delete a website's data, tap **Delete** ( ), and then tap the textual **Delete** button that appears.

16 Tap **Done**.

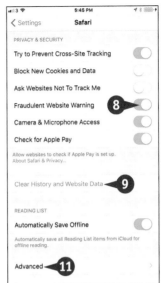

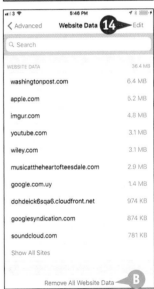

TIP

What are cookies, and what threat do they pose?
A *cookie* is a small text file that a website places on a computer to identify that computer in the future. This is helpful for many sites, such as shopping sites in which you add items to a shopping cart, but when used by intrusive or malevolent sites, cookies can pose a threat to your privacy. You may want to set the **Block New Cookies and Data** switch to Off ( ) to reduce the number of cookies Safari accepts, but be warned that doing so may prevent some legitimate sites from working properly.

Manage Your App and Website Passwords

Your iPhone can store your app and website passwords so that Safari and other apps can enter them automatically when needed, reducing the need for you to type passwords manually.

The App & Website Passwords screen in the Settings app enables you to view the list of password entries your iPhone has stored. You can view and edit a password entry, which lets you copy the password, update it, or change the sites for which it is used; delete a password; or add a new password entry.

Manage Your App and Website Passwords

1 Press **Home**. On an iPhone X, swipe up from the bottom of the screen.

The Home screen appears.

2 Tap **Settings** (⚙).

The Settings screen appears.

3 Tap **Accounts & Passwords** (🔑).

The Accounts & Passwords screen appears.

4 Tap **App & Website Passwords**.

The Touch ID for "Settings" dialog opens.

Note: If you are not using Touch ID for authentication, your iPhone prompts you to provide your passcode.

5 Apply your registered finger to the Home button.

The Passwords screen appears.

Ⓐ You can tap **Search** (🔍) and type a search term to search for a particular password.

6 Tap the password entry you want to view.

The screen for the password entry appears.

Ⓑ You can copy the username or password by tapping and holding it and then tapping **Copy** on the pop-up toolbar.

⑦ If you need to edit the username, password, or list of websites, tap **Edit**.

The fields open for editing.

⑧ Edit the username or password as needed.

⑨ To remove a website, tap **Delete** (➖) and then tap the textual **Delete** button.

⑩ Tap **Done**.

Editing Mode closes.

⑪ Tap **Passwords** (‹).

The Passwords screen appears again.

Ⓒ You can delete a password entry by swiping it left and then tapping **Delete**.

⑫ To add a new password, tap **Add Password**.

The Add Password screen appears.

⑬ Type or paste the website address.

⑭ Type or paste the username.

⑮ Type or paste the password.

⑯ Tap **Done**.

The Passwords screen appears again.

TIP

What does the Edit button on the Passwords screen enable me to do?
The Edit button on the Passwords screen enables you to delete multiple password entries at once instead of one at a time. Tap **Edit** to switch the Passwords screen to Editing Mode. You can then tap the selection circle (⃝ changes to ✓) for each password you want to delete, and then tap **Delete**.

Read E-Mail

After you have set up Mail during the initial setup routine, as described in Chapter 1, or by adding other accounts, as explained in Chapter 4, you are ready to send and receive e-mail messages using your iPhone. This section shows you how to read your incoming e-mail messages. You learn to reply to messages and write messages from scratch later in this chapter.

Read E-Mail

Read a Message and View an Attached File

1 Press **Home**. On an iPhone X, swipe up from the bottom of the screen.

The Home screen appears.

A The badge shows the number of unread messages.

2 Tap **Mail** (✉).

The Mailboxes screen appears.

Note: If Mail does not show the Mailboxes screen, tap **Back** (<) until the Mailboxes screen appears.

3 Tap the inbox you want to open.

B To see all your incoming messages together, tap **All Inboxes**.

C A blue dot indicates an unread message.

D A paperclip icon (⬯) indicates one or more attachments.

E A gray star indicates the message's sender is one of your VIPs. See the second tip for information about VIPs.

F You can tap **Filter** (⊜) to filter the messages by Unread status, displaying only unread messages. You can then tap **Unread** to apply a different filter.

4 Tap a message.

The message opens.

G You can tap **Previous** (︿) or **Next** (﹀) to display another message.

5 If the message has an attachment, tap it.

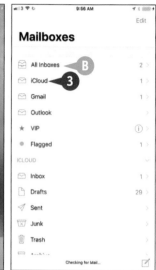

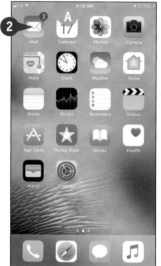

The attachment opens in the viewer.

Note: Mail's viewer can display many types of attached files, but not all files.

Note: If Mail has hidden the controls at the top of the screen, tap the screen to display the controls.

6 If you want to send the file to an app or share it with others, tap **Share** (⬆).

The Share sheet opens.

7 Tap the means of sharing, such as **Copy to Pages** (▨) for a Word document.

8 Tap **Done**.

The message appears again.

Access New Messages Quickly from the Home Screen

1 Press **Home**. On an iPhone X, swipe up from the bottom of the screen.

The Home screen appears.

2 Press **Mail** (✉).

The Peek panel opens.

Ⓗ You can also tap another button, such as **VIP**.

Ⓘ You can tap a contact whose icon bears a badge to display a new message from that contact.

3 Tap **All Inboxes**.

The All Inboxes screen appears.

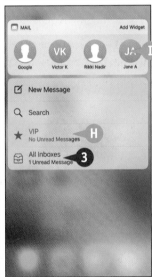

TIPS

How do I view the contents of another mailbox?
From an open message, tap **Inbox** (❮) or **All Inboxes** (❮) to return to the inbox or the screen for all the inboxes. Tap **Back** (❮) to go back to the Mailboxes screen. You can then tap the mailbox you want to view.

What is the VIP inbox on the Mailboxes screen?
The VIP inbox is a tool for identifying important messages, no matter which e-mail account they come to. You mark particular contacts as being very important people to you, and Mail then adds messages from these VIPs to the VIP inbox. To add a VIP, tap the sender's name in an open message, and then tap **Add to VIP** on the Sender screen.

Reply To or Forward an E-Mail Message

Mail makes it easy to reply to an e-mail message or forward it to others. If the message had multiple recipients, you can choose between replying only to the sender of the message and replying to the sender and all the other recipients in the To field and the Cc field, if there are any. Recipients in the message's Bcc field, whose names you cannot see, do not receive your reply.

Reply To or Forward an E-Mail Message

Open the Message You Will Reply To or Forward

1 Press **Home**. On an iPhone X, swipe up from the bottom of the screen.

The Home screen appears.

2 Tap **Mail** (✉).

The Mailboxes screen appears.

Note: When you launch Mail, the app checks for new messages. This is why the number of new messages you see on the Mailboxes screen sometimes differs from the number on the Mail badge on the Home screen.

3 Tap the inbox you want to see.

The inbox opens.

4 Tap the message you want to open.

The message opens.

5 Tap **Action** (↰).

The Action dialog opens.

Note: You can also reply to or forward a message by using Siri. For example, say "Reply to this message" or "Forward this message to Alice Smith," and then tell Siri what you want the message to say.

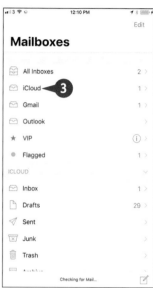

Reply To the Message

1 In the Action dialog, tap **Reply**.

A To reply to all recipients, tap **Reply All**. Reply to all recipients only when you are sure that they need to receive your reply. Often, it is better to reply only to the sender.

A screen containing the reply appears.

B Mail automatically adds your signature, if you have one.

2 Type your reply to the message.

3 Tap **Send**.

Mail sends the message.

Forward the Message

1 In the Action dialog, tap **Forward**.

A screen containing the forwarded message appears.

2 Type the recipient's address.

C Alternatively, you can tap **Add Contact** (⊕) and choose the recipient in your Contacts list.

3 Type a message if needed.

4 Tap **Send**.

Mail sends the message.

TIPS

Can I reply to or forward only part of a message?
Yes. The quick way to do this is to select the part of the message you want to include before tapping **Action** (↩). Mail then includes only your selection. Alternatively, you can start the reply or forwarded message, and then delete the parts you do not want to include.

How do I check for new messages?
In a mailbox, tap and drag your finger down the screen, pulling down the messages. When a progress circle appears at the top, lift your finger. Mail checks for new messages.

Organize Your Messages in Mailbox Folders

To keep your inbox or inboxes under control, you should organize your messages into mailbox folders.

You can quickly move a single message to a folder after reading it or after previewing it in the message list. Alternatively, you can select multiple messages in your inbox and move them all to a folder in a single action. You can also delete any message you no longer need.

Organize Your Messages in Mailbox Folders

Open Mail and Move a Single Message to a Folder

1 Press **Home**. On an iPhone X, swipe up from the bottom of the screen.

The Home screen appears.

2 Tap **Mail** (🖂).

The Mailboxes screen appears.

3 Tap the mailbox you want to open.

The mailbox opens.

A The Replied arrow (↩) indicates you have replied to the message.

B The Forwarded arrow (➡) indicates you have forwarded the message.

4 Tap the message you want to open.

The message opens.

C You can delete the message by tapping **Delete** (🗑).

5 Tap **Move** (🗀).

The Move This Message to a New Mailbox screen appears.

6 Tap the mailbox to which you want to move the message.

Mail moves the message.

The next message in the mailbox appears, so that you can read it and file it if necessary.

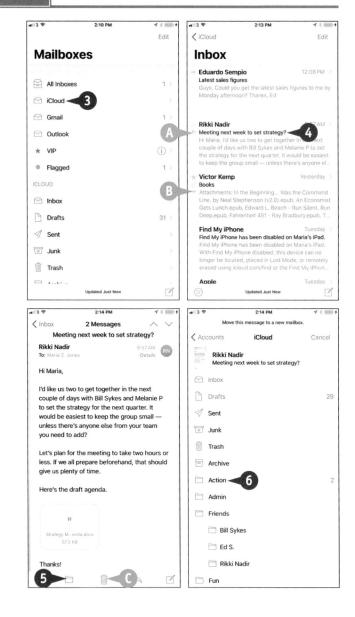

Move Multiple Messages to a Folder

1 In the mailbox, tap **Edit**.

2 Tap the selection button (⃝ changes to ✓) next to each message you want to move.

3 Tap **Move**.

4 Tap the destination mailbox.

Note: To move the messages to a mailbox in another account, tap **Accounts** on the Move This Message to a New Mailbox screen, tap the account, and then tap the mailbox.

Note: Mail studies your history of moving messages so it can suggest the folder you may want for a particular message, saving you scrolling through all your folders.

Move a Message from a Mailbox

1 In the mailbox list, tap the message and swipe to the left.

Ⓓ Tap **Trash** (🗑) to delete the message.

2 Tap **More**.

The More dialog opens.

3 Tap **Move Message**.

The Mailboxes screen appears.

4 Tap the mailbox to which you want to move the message.

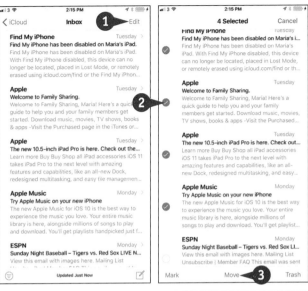

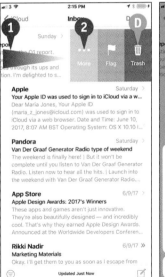

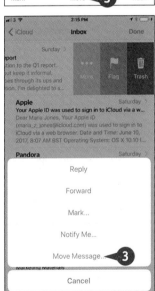

TIP

What does the Mark command in the Action dialog do?

Tap **Mark** to display the Mark dialog. You can then tap **Flag** to set a flag on the message — for example, to indicate that you need to pay extra attention to it. The flag appears as an orange dot (🟠). In the Mark dialog, you can also tap **Mark as Unread** to mark the message as not having been read, even though you have opened it; if the message is marked as unread, you can tap **Mark as Read** instead. You can also mark a message as unread or by tapping it in the message list, swiping right, and then tapping **Unread** (✉) or **Read** (📨), as appropriate.

Write and Send E-Mail Messages

Your iPhone is great for reading and replying to e-mail messages you receive, but you will likely also need to write new messages. When you do, you can use the data in the Contacts app to address your outgoing messages quickly and accurately. If the recipient's address is not one of your contacts, you can type the address manually.

You can attach one or more files to an e-mail message to send those files to the recipient. This works well for small files, but many mail servers reject files larger than several megabytes in size.

Write and Send E-Mail Messages

1 Press **Home**. On an iPhone X, swipe up from the bottom of the screen.

The Home screen appears.

2 Press **Mail** (✉).

The Peek panel appears.

3 Tap **New Message** (✎).

Note: You can also tap **Mail** (✉) and then tap **New Message** (✎) to start a new message.

The New Message screen appears.

4 Tap **Add Contact** (⊕).

The Contacts list appears.

Note: If necessary, change the Contacts list displayed by tapping **Groups**, making your choice on the Groups screen, and then tapping **Done**.

Ⓐ If the person you are e-mailing is not a contact, type the address in the To area. You can also start typing here and then select a matching contact from the list that the Mail app displays.

Note: Contacts that appear in gray have no e-mail address.

5 Tap the contact you want to send the message to.

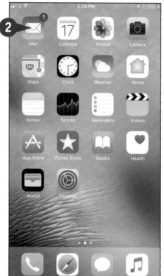

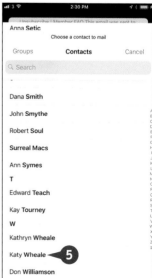

B The contact's name appears in the To area.

Note: You can add other contacts to the To area by repeating steps **4** and **5**.

6 If you need to add a Cc or Bcc recipient, tap **Cc/Bcc, From**.

The Cc, Bcc, and From fields expand.

7 Tap the Cc area or Bcc area, and then follow steps **4** and **5** to add a recipient.

C To change the e-mail account you are sending the message from, tap **From**, and then tap the account to use.

8 Tap **Subject**, and then type the message's subject.

D You can tap **Notifications** (🔔 changes to 🔔) to receive notifications when someone responds to the e-mail conversation.

9 Tap below the Subject line, and then type the body of the message.

Note: If you need to stop working on a message temporarily, tap its title bar and drag it down to the bottom of the screen. You can then work with other messages. To resume work on the parked message, tap its title bar.

10 Tap **Send**.

Mail sends the message.

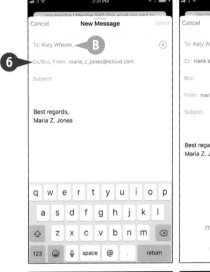

How do I attach a file to a message?

To attach a photo or video, tap and hold the message body area to display the contextual menu, and then tap **Insert Photo or Video**. On some iPhone models, you may need to tap **More** (▶) before tapping **Insert Photo or Video**.

To attach a file from iCloud Drive, tap and hold the message body area to display the contextual menu, and then tap **Add Attachment**. On some iPhone models, you may need to tap **More** (▶) before tapping **Add Attachment**.

To attach other types of files, start the message from the app that contains the file. Select the file, tap **Share** (⬆), and then tap **Mail** (✉). Mail starts a message with the file attached. You then address the message and send it.

Keeping Your Life Organized

Your iPhone includes many apps for staying organized, such as the Calendars app, the Reminders app, and the Wallet app. Other apps help you find your way, stay on time, and track stock prices, weather forecasts, and your own health.

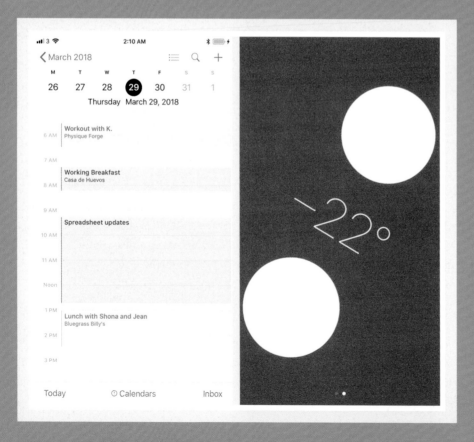

Browse Existing Events in Your Calendars

Your iPhone's Calendar app gives you a great way of managing your schedule and making sure you never miss an appointment.

After setting up your calendars to sync using iCloud or other calendar services, as described in Chapter 1, you can take your calendars with you everywhere and consult them whenever you need to. You can view either all your calendars or only those you choose.

Browse Existing Events in Your Calendars

Browse Existing Events in Your Calendars

1 Press **Home**. On an iPhone X, swipe up from the bottom of the screen.

2 Tap **Calendar** (14).

A The black circle indicates the day shown. When the current date is selected, the circle is red.

B Your events appear on a scrollable timeline.

C An event's background color indicates the calendar it belongs to.

D You can tap **Today** to display the current day.

3 Tap the day you want to see.

The events for the day appear.

4 Tap the month.

The calendar for the month appears.

E You can tap the year to display the calendar for the full year, in which you can navigate quickly to other months.

5 Scroll up or down as needed, and then tap the date you want.

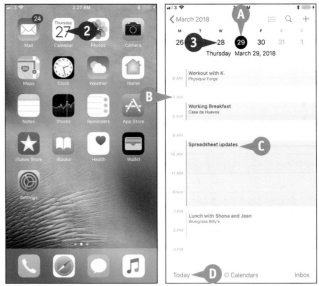

The date's appointments appear.

6 Tap **List** (≡ changes to ▥).

The appointments appear as a list, enabling you to see more.

7 Tap an event to see its details.

The Event Details screen appears.

8 To edit the event, tap **Edit**.

The Edit screen appears, and you can make changes to the event. When you finish, tap **Done**.

Choose Which Calendars to Display

1 Tap **Calendars**.

2 Tap to place or remove a check mark next to a calendar you want to display or hide.

F Tap **Show All** to place a check mark next to each calendar for all accounts. Tap **Hide All** to remove all check marks.

G Similarly, tap **Show All** or **Hide All** for an account to display or hide the account's calendars.

H The Birthdays calendar automatically displays birthdays of contacts whose contact data includes the birthday.

I You can set the **Show Declined Events** switch to On (◯) to include invitations you have declined.

3 Tap **Done**.

The calendars you chose appear.

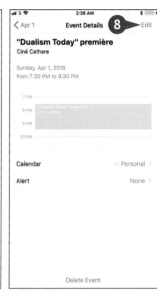

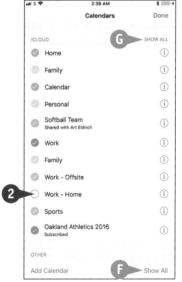

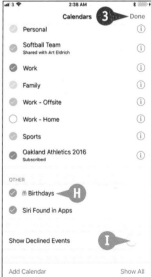

TIP

How can I quickly find an event?

In the Calendar app, tap **Search** (🔍). Calendar displays a list of your events. Type your search term. When Calendar displays a list of matches, tap the event you want to view.

Create New Events in Your Calendars

Y ou can create calendar events on your computer, or online using a web interface such as that of iCloud, and then sync the events to your iPhone. But you can also create new events directly on your iPhone.

You can create either a straightforward, one-shot appointment or an appointment that repeats on a schedule. You can also choose the calendar in which to store the appointment.

Create New Events in Your Calendars

1 Press **Home**. On an iPhone X, swipe up from the bottom of the screen.

The Home screen appears.

2 Tap **Calendar** (📅).

The Calendar screen appears.

3 Tap the day on which you want to create the new event.

Note: From the Home screen, press **Calendar** (📅) to display the Peek panel and then tap **Add Event** to start creating a new event. You will need to select the date.

Note: You can also leave the current date selected, and then change the date when creating the event.

4 Tap **New** (➕).

The New Event screen appears.

5 Tap **Title** and type the title of the event.

6 Tap **Location**.

Note: If the Allow "Calendar" to Access Your Location While You Use the App? dialog opens when you tap **Location**, tap **Allow** to use locations.

The Location screen appears.

A You can tap **Current Location** to use the current location.

7 Start typing the location.

8 Tap the appropriate match.

9 Tap **Starts**.

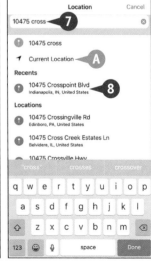

198

The time and date controls appear.

10 Tap the date and time controls to set the start time.

11 Tap **Ends**.

12 Tap the date and time controls to set the end time.

B If this is an all-day appointment, set the **All-day** switch to On (⬤).

C If you need to change the time zone, tap **Time Zone**, type the city name, and then tap the time zone.

13 Tap **Alert**.

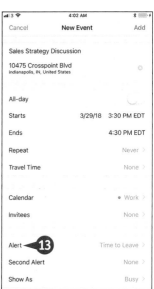

The Alert screen appears.

14 Tap **Time to Leave** if you want Calendar to calculate when you should leave, based on your location, the event's location, and the traffic conditions. Otherwise, tap the timing for the alert, such as **30 minutes before**.

The New Event screen appears.

15 Tap **Calendar**.

The Calendar screen appears.

16 Tap the calendar for the event.

The New Event screen appears again.

17 Tap **Add**.

The event appears on your calendar.

TIPS

How do I set up an event that repeats every week?

On the New Event screen, tap **Repeat**. On the Repeat screen, tap **Every Week**, placing a check mark next to it, and then tap **Done**.

How do I set a time to the exact minute instead of to the nearest 5 minutes?

On the New Event screen, tap **Starts** to display the time and date controls. Double-tap the time readout — either the hours or the minutes — to switch the minutes between 5-minute intervals and single minutes.

Work with Calendar Invitations

As well as events you create yourself, you may receive invitations to events that others create. When you receive an event invitation attached to an e-mail message, you can choose whether to accept the invitation or decline it. If you accept the invitation, you can add the event automatically to your calendar.

Work with Calendar Invitations

Respond to an Invitation from an Alert

1 When an invitation alert appears, press it.

The Peek panel displays the event's details, together with buttons for responding to the event.

2 Tap **Accept**, **Maybe**, or **Decline**, as needed.

A You can tap **Close** (✕) to close the Peek panel without tapping one of the response buttons.

Respond to an Invitation from the Inbox Screen

1 Press **Home**. On an iPhone X, swipe up from the bottom of the screen.

The Home screen appears.

2 Tap **Calendar** (14).

The Calendar screen appears.

B The Inbox button shows the number of invitations.

3 Tap **Inbox**.

The Inbox screen appears.

C You can tap **Accept**, **Maybe**, or **Decline** to deal with the invitation without viewing the details.

4 Tap the invitation whose details you want to see.

The Event Details screen appears.

5 Tap **Calendar** if you decide to accept the invitation.

The Calendar screen appears.

6 Tap the calendar to which you want to assign the event.

The Event Details screen appears again.

7 Tap **Alert**.

The Alert screen appears.

8 Tap the button for the alert interval. For example, tap **1 hour before**.

The Event Details screen appears again.

Note: To control how the event's time appears in your calendar, tap **Show As**, and then tap **Busy** or **Free**, as appropriate, on the Show As screen.

9 Tap **Accept**.

Your calendar appears, showing the event you just accepted.

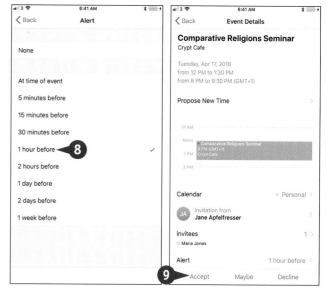

TIP

In what other ways can I respond to an invitation?

You can also respond to an invitation by pressing its alert on the lock screen and then tapping **Accept**, **Maybe**, or **Decline** in the Peek panel.

If you have an Apple Watch, it will display your calendar alerts when your iPhone is locked. You can respond to invitations on the Apple Watch as well.

Track Your Commitments with Reminders

Your iPhone's Reminders app gives you an easy way to note your commitments and keep track of them. The Reminders app comes with a built-in list called Reminders, but you can create as many other lists as you need, giving each a distinctive color.

You can create a reminder with no due time or location or tie a reminder to a due time, arriving at or leaving a location, or both. Your iPhone can remind you of time- or location-based commitments at the appropriate time or place.

Track Your Commitments with Reminders

Open the Reminders App and Create Your Reminder Lists

1 Press **Home**. On an iPhone X, swipe up from the bottom of the screen.

The Home screen appears.

2 Tap **Reminders** (⸬).

The Reminders app opens, displaying the Lists screen.

3 Tap **New** (⊞).

The Create New dialog opens.

4 Tap **List**.

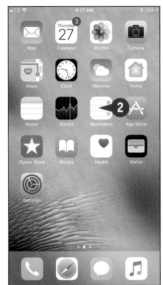

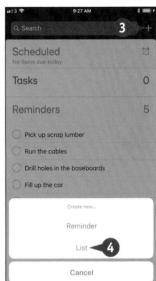

The Select Account dialog opens.

Note: If you have only one Reminders account, the Select Account dialog does not appear.

5 Tap the account in which you want to store the list.

The screen for creating the list appears.

6 Type the name for the list.

7 Tap the color to use for the list.

8 Tap **Done**.

The list appears.

Create a New Reminder

1 To create a new reminder in this list, tap the first line.

Ⓐ To return to the Lists screen so you can switch to another list, tap the tabbed pages at the bottom of the screen.

The keyboard appears.

2 Type the text for the reminder.

3 Tap **Information** (ⓘ).

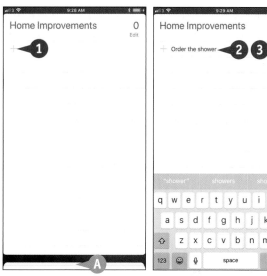

The Details screen appears.

4 To create a time-based reminder, set the **Remind me on a day** switch to On (⬜ changes to ⬤).

The Alarm and Repeat controls appear.

5 Tap **Alarm**.

The date and time controls appear.

6 Set the date and time for the reminder.

7 If you need to repeat the reminder, tap **Repeat**, choose the repeat interval on the Repeat screen, and then tap **Details** to return to the Details screen.

TIP

How do I sync my iPhone's reminders with my Mac's reminders?

You can sync your iPhone's reminders with your Mac's reminders via your iCloud account, via one or more Exchange accounts, or via both types of accounts.

On your iPhone, press **Home** — on an iPhone X, swipe up from the bottom of the screen — to display the Home screen, and then tap **Settings** (⚙) to display the Settings screen. Tap **iCloud** (☁) to display the iCloud screen, and then set the **Reminders** switch to On (⬤). On your Mac, click **Apple** () and **System Preferences** to open System Preferences. Click **iCloud** (☁) to display the iCloud pane, and then click **Reminders** (⬜ changes to ☑).

continued ▶

You can assign different priorities to your reminders to give yourself a quick visual reference of their urgency. You can also add notes to a reminder to keep relevant information at hand. When you have completed a reminder, you can mark it as completed. You can view your list of scheduled reminders for quick reference, and you can choose whether to include your completed reminders in the list. If you no longer need a reminder, you can delete it from the list.

Track Your Commitments with Reminders (continued)

8 To create a location-based reminder, set the **Remind me at a location** switch to On ( ).

Note: If Reminders prompts you to allow it to use your current location, tap **Allow**.

9 Tap **Location**.

The Location screen appears.

10 Start typing the location in the search box.

B You can tap **Current Location** to use your current location.

11 Tap the location in the list of results.

The Location screen displays a map of the location.

12 Tap **When I Arrive** or **When I Leave**, as needed.

13 Tap **Details** (‹).

The Details screen appears again.

14 To assign a priority to the reminder, tap **None, !, !!,** or **!!!**.

C To assign the reminder to a different list than the current list, tap **List**. On the Change List screen, tap the list you want to use.

15 To add a note to the reminder, tap **Notes** and then type the text.

16 Tap **Done**.

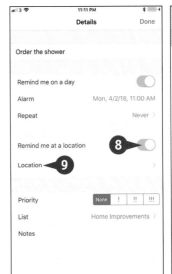

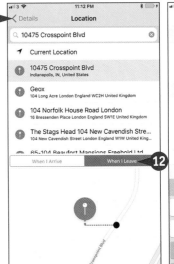

The new reminder appears on your list of reminders.

⑰ Tap **New** (▦) or anywhere on the next line to start creating a new reminder.

Ⓓ When you finish a task, tap its button (○ changes to ◉) to mark the reminder as complete.

Note: To delete a reminder, tap **Edit** on the screen that contains it. Tap **Delete** (⊖) to the left of the reminder, and then tap **Delete**.

⑱ Tap the tabbed pages at the bottom of the screen to switch to another reminder list.

View a List of Your Scheduled Reminders

① Tap **Scheduled** (⏰).

The Scheduled list appears.

② Tap the reminder you want to see.

Note: You can turn a large-screen iPhone to landscape orientation to view both your reminder lists and the current list's reminders at the same time.

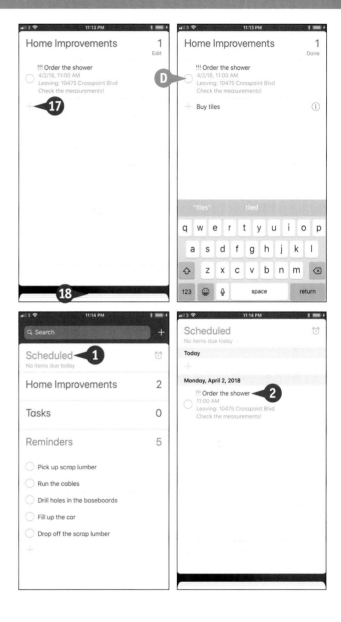

How do I change the default list that Reminders puts my reminders in?

Press **Home** — on an iPhone X, swipe up from the bottom of the screen — to display the Home screen, and then tap **Settings** (⚙) to display the Settings screen. Tap **Reminders** (⋮) to display the Reminders screen, tap **Default List** to display the Default List screen, and then tap the list you want to make the default. On the Reminders screen, you can also tap **Sync** and choose how many reminders to sync — **Reminders 2 Weeks Back, Reminders 1 Month Back, Reminders 3 Months Back, Reminders 6 Months Back,** or **All Reminders**.

Keep Essential Documents at Hand with Wallet

Wallet is an app for storing payment cards and electronic versions of essential documents such as insurance cards, boarding passes, movie tickets, and hotel reservations. As explained in Chapter 1, the iPhone's setup routine walks you through adding a payment card for Apple Pay to Wallet; you can add other cards later, as needed.

You can add documents to Wallet from built-in apps such as Mail and Safari, as shown in this section, or by using custom apps for shopping, booking hotels, and booking flights.

Keep Essential Documents at Hand with Wallet

Add a Document to Wallet

1. In Mail, tap the message with the document attached.

   The message opens.

2. Tap the document's button.

   The document appears.

3. Tap **Add**.

   Mail adds the document to Wallet.

   The message appears again.

Note: In Safari, open the web page containing the document, and then tap **Add** to add the document to Wallet.

Open Wallet and Find the Documents You Need

1. Press **Home**. On an iPhone X, swipe up from the bottom of the screen.

   The Home screen appears.

2. Tap **Wallet** (□).

   The Wallet app opens.

   The documents you have added appear.

Note: Until you add one or more documents to Wallet, the app displays an information screen highlighting its uses.

3. Tap the document you want to view.

206

A The document appears above the other documents. You can then hold its barcode in front of a scanner to use the document.

4 To see another document, tap the current top document and swipe down.

Wallet reshuffles the documents so you can see them all.

Choose Settings for a Document or Delete It

1 Tap **Information** (ⓘ).

The document rotates so you can see its back.

2 Set the **Automatic Updates** switch to On (⬤) if you want to receive updates to this document.

3 Set the **Suggest on Lock Screen** switch to On (⬤) if you want notifications about the document to appear on the lock screen.

B If you have no further need for the document, tap **Remove Pass** to remove it.

4 When you finish reviewing the document, tap **Done**.

The document rotates to display its front.

TIP

What other actions can I take with documents in Wallet?
You can share a document with other people via e-mail, instant messaging, or AirDrop. To access these features, tap **Share** (⬆), and then tap **AirDrop**, **Mail**, or **Message** on the Share sheet that appears.

Get Your Bearings with Compass

When you need to get your bearings, use the Compass app that comes installed on your iPhone. With Compass, you can establish your relationship to the points of the compass, learn your precise GPS location, and measure an angle between two points.

Compass includes the Level feature that you can use to level an object or surface precisely or to measure its current slant.

Get Your Bearings with Compass

Open Compass and Get Your Bearings

1 Press **Home**. On an iPhone X, swipe up from the bottom of the screen.

The Home screen appears.

2 Tap **Extras** (⊞).

The Extras folder opens.

3 Tap **Compass** (▦).

Note: If Compass displays a message prompting you to complete the circle to calibrate it, turn your iPhone this way and that until the circle is filled in. The compass then appears.

4 Point your iPhone in the direction whose bearing you want to take.

A The readout shows the bearing.

B You can tap the GPS location to switch to the Maps app and display the map for that location.

C The readout shows the approximate elevation above sea level.

Measure an Angle

1 On the Compass screen, tap anywhere on the compass to fix the current bearing.

D The bearing appears at the top of the compass.

2 Turn the iPhone toward the target point.

E The red arc measures the difference between the two bearings.

3 Tap anywhere to release the compass.

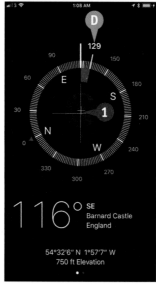

Use the Level Feature

1 From the Compass screen, tap and drag left or swipe left.

F You can also tap the gray dot to switch to the Level screen.

The Level screen appears.

G The figure shows the angle of the object or surface.

2 Tilt your iPhone toward a level position to move the circles on top of each other.

3 If the black-and-white color scheme is hard to see, tap anywhere on the screen.

The background color changes to red.

Note: You can tap again to switch the background color from red back to black.

H When you align the circles, the screen goes green.

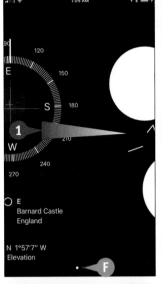

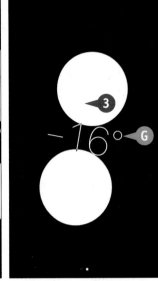

TIP

Does the Compass app use True North or Magnetic North?
The Compass app can show either True North or Magnetic North. To switch, press **Home** — on an iPhone X, swipe up from the bottom of the screen — to display the Home screen, and then tap **Settings** (⚙). In the Settings app, tap **Compass** (▦), and then set the **Use True North** switch to On (🔘) or Off ( ), as needed.

Find Your Location with Maps

Your iPhone's Maps app can pinpoint your location by using the Global Positioning System, known as GPS, or wireless networks. You can view your location on a road map, display a satellite picture with or without place labels, or view transit information. You can easily switch among map types to find the most useful one. To help you get your bearings, the Tracking feature in the Maps app can show you which direction you are facing.

Find Your Location with Maps

1 Press **Home**. On an iPhone X, swipe up from the bottom of the screen.

The Home screen appears.

2 Tap **Maps** (📍).

The Maps screen appears.

A A blue dot shows your current location. The expanding circle around the blue dot shows that Maps is determining your location.

Note: It may take a minute for Maps to work out your location accurately. While Maps determines the location, the blue dot moves, even though the iPhone remains stationary.

3 Drag the gray handle down to collapse the Search pane.

4 Place your thumb and finger apart on the screen and pinch inward.

Note: To zoom in, place your thumb and finger on the screen and pinch apart.

The map zooms out, showing a larger area.

5 Tap **Location** (⌁ changes to ➤), turning on the Location service.

6 Tap **Location** (➤ changes to ⋏).

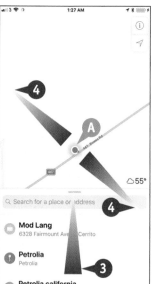

210

B The Compass icon appears (●). The red arrow indicates north.

C The map turns to show the direction the iPhone is facing, so that you can orient yourself.

7 When you need to restore the map orientation, tap **Compass** (●).

The map turns so that north is upward.

The Compass icon disappears.

8 Tap **Information** (ⓘ).

The Maps Settings dialog opens.

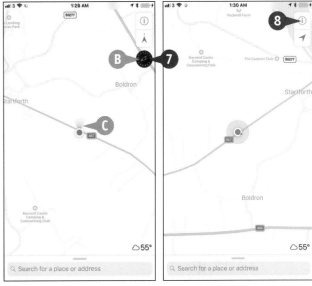

D You can tap **Transit** to display transit information for the area.

9 Tap **Satellite**.

The satellite map appears, showing photos with street and place names overlaid on them.

10 Set the **Traffic** switch to On (●) or Off ( ), as needed.

11 Set the **Labels** switch to On (●) to display labels.

12 Tap **Close** (✕).

The Maps Settings dialog closes.

Note: The satellite photos may be several years old and no longer accurate.

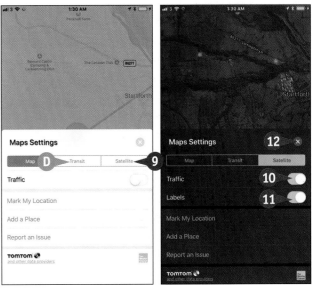

TIPS

How can I tell the scale of the map?

Place two fingers on the screen as if about to pinch outward or inward. Maps displays a scale in the upper-left corner of the screen.

How can I share my location?

Press the location you want to share. A Marked Location pin appears, and the Marked Location panel opens. Swipe up to open the Marked Location panel fully, and then tap **Share** (📤) to display the Share sheet. You can then tap the means of sharing — such as AirDrop, Message, Mail, or Twitter — and follow the prompts to send or post your location.

Find Directions with Maps

Your iPhone's Maps app can give you directions to where you want to go. Maps can also show you current traffic congestion in some locales to help you identify the most viable route for a journey.

Maps displays driving directions by default, but you can make it display public transit directions and walking directions.

Find Directions with Maps

1 Press **Home**. On an iPhone X, swipe up from the bottom of the screen.

The Home screen appears.

2 Tap **Maps** (🗺).

The Maps screen appears.

3 Tap **Search for a place or address**.

The Directions screen appears.

4 Start typing your destination.

A list of suggested matches appears.

5 Tap the correct match.

A map of the destination appears.

6 Tap **Directions**.

Note: If you want the directions to start from your current location, leave My Location in the From field. Go to step **10**.

7 Tap **My Location**.

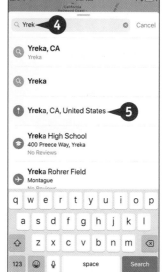

The Change Route dialog opens.

8 Tap **From** and start typing the start location for the directions.

9 Tap the correct match.

A You can tap **Switch Places** (⇅) to switch the start location and end location.

10 Tap **Route**.

A screen showing the driving directions appears.

B If multiple routes are available, tap a time button to view a different route. The time button changes to blue to indicate it is active.

C You can tap **Walk** (🚶) to see walking directions.

D You can tap **Transit** (🚆) to see transit directions.

E You can tap **Ride** (🧍) to see ride-sharing apps that are available.

11 Tap **Go**.

The first screen of directions appears.

12 Swipe left to display the next direction.

Note: When you start navigating the route, the directions change automatically to reflect your progress.

13 To finish using the directions, tap **End**.

The map appears again.

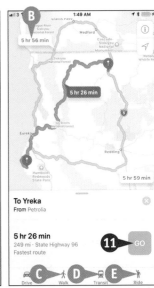

TIP

What else should I know about the directions for walking or public transit?

You should be aware that walking directions may be incomplete or inaccurate. Before walking the route, check that it does not send you across pedestrian-free bridges or through rail tunnels.

The Maps app provides transit information for only some routes. Even for these, it is advisable to double-check the information via online schedules, such as on the website or app of the transit company involved.

Explore with 3D Flyover

Maps is not only great for finding out where you are and for getting directions to places, but it can also show you 3D flyovers of the places on the map. Flyovers can be a useful way to explore a place virtually so that you can find your way around later in real life.

After switching on the 3D feature, you can zoom in and out, pan around, and move backward and forward.

Explore with 3D Flyover

1 Press **Home**. On an iPhone X, swipe up from the bottom of the screen.

The Home screen appears.

2 Tap **Maps** (icon).

The Maps screen appears.

3 Display the area of interest in the middle of the screen. For example, tap and drag the map, or search for the location you want.

4 Tap **Information** (icon).

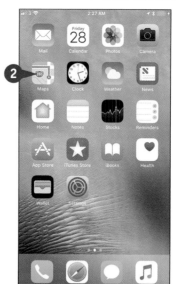

The Maps Settings dialog opens.

5 Tap **Satellite**.

The map switches to Satellite view.

6 Tap **Close** (icon).

The Maps Settings dialog closes.

7 Tap **3D**.

Note: You can also swipe up the screen with two fingers to switch to 3D view.

The map switches to 3D view.

8 Place your thumb and finger on the screen and pinch outward.

The map zooms in.

Note: You can place your thumb and finger on the screen and pinch inward to zoom out.

Note: Tap and drag to scroll the map as needed.

9 Place two fingers on the screen and twist clockwise or counterclockwise to rotate the view.

The rotated view appears.

A The Compass arrow (**⊙**) appears. You can tap it to restore the direction to north.

Note: Pan and zoom as needed to explore the area.

10 Tap and drag up with two fingers.

The viewing angle becomes shallower.

11 Tap **2D**.

The two-dimensional map reappears.

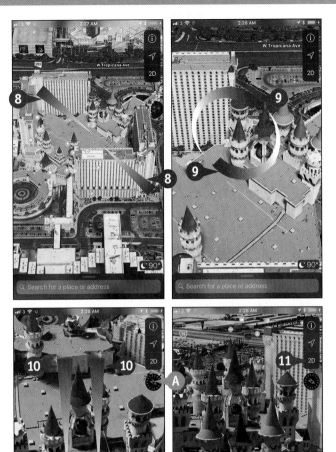

TIP

What does 3D do with the standard map?
When you swipe up the screen with two fingers to switch on Flyover with the standard map displayed, Maps tilts the map at an angle, as you might do with a paper map. In cities, building shapes appear when you zoom in on the map, enabling you to see the layout without using the full detail of the satellite photos.

Using Maps' Favorites and Contacts

When you want to return to a location easily in the Maps app, you can create a favorite for the location.

Similarly, you can add a location to your contacts, so that you can access it either from the Contacts app or from the Maps app. You can either create a new contact or add the location to an existing contact. You can also return quickly to locations you have visited recently but for which you have not created a favorite or contact.

Using Maps' Favorites and Contacts

Create a Favorite in Maps

1 Press **Home**. On an iPhone X, swipe up from the bottom of the screen.

The Home screen appears.

2 Tap **Maps** (📍).

The Maps screen appears.

3 Find the place for which you want to create a favorite. For example, tap and drag the map, or search for the location you want.

4 Press the place for which you want to create a favorite.

A The Maps app drops a pin on the place.

The Marked Location panel opens.

5 Swipe up.

The Marked Location panel opens further.

6 Tap **Favorite** (♥).

The Add to Favorites dialog opens.

7 Edit the suggested name, or type a new name.

8 Tap **Save**.

The Add to Favorites dialog closes, and the new name appears at the top of the panel.

9 Tap **Close** (✕).

The panel closes.

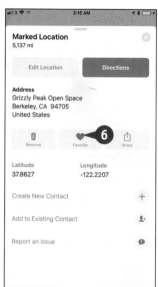

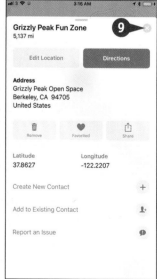

Create a Contact in Maps

1 Find the place for which you want to create a contact. For example, tap and drag the map, or search for the location you want.

2 Tap and hold the appropriate place.

The Maps app drops a pin on the place.

The Marked Location panel opens.

3 Swipe up.

The Marked Location panel opens further.

4 Tap **Create New Contact**.

B You can tap **Add to Existing Contact** and then tap the contact to which you want to add the location instead.

The New Contact screen appears.

5 Type the first name for the contact record, as needed.

6 Type the last name for the contact record, as needed.

7 Add any other information the contact record requires.

8 Tap **Done**.

The Maps app creates the contact record for the location.

The Marked Location panel appears again.

9 Tap **Close** (⊗).

The Marked Location panel closes.

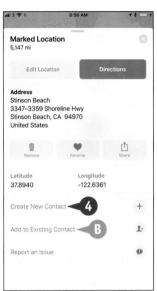

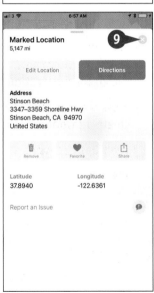

TIP

How do I go to a location for which I have created a favorite or a contact?

In the Maps app, tap **Where do you want to go?** to display the Search screen. Start typing the name of the favorite or contact, and then tap the appropriate search result.

Take Notes

Your iPhone is a great device for taking notes no matter where you happen to be. The Notes app enables you to create notes stored in an e-mail account — such as your iCloud account — or on your iPhone.

You can create straightforward notes in plain text for any account you add to Notes. For notes stored on Exchange, IMAP, or Google accounts, you can also add formatting. For notes stored in iCloud, you can add check boxes, photos, web links, and sketches.

Take Notes

1 Press **Home**. On an iPhone X, swipe up from the bottom of the screen.

The Home screen appears.

2 Tap **Notes** (⬭).

The Notes app opens.

Note: To change the account or folder in which you are working, tap **Back** (〈), and then tap the account or folder you want to use.

3 Tap **New** (✐).

A new note opens.

4 Type the title or first paragraph of the note.

5 Tap **More** (⊕).

The More bar appears.

6 Tap **Formatting** (Aa).

A You can tap **Table** (▦) to add a table.

B You can tap **Add** (⊕) to add a photo, scanned document, or sketch to the note. This adds the photo, document, or sketch as a separate item attached to the note.

C You can tap **Sketch** (Ⓐ) to draw a sketch in the note.

D You can tap **Close** (✕) when you no longer need the More bar displayed.

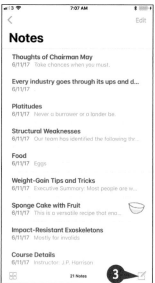

The Formatting pane appears.

7 Tap the style you want to apply to the paragraph.

The paragraph takes on the style.

8 Tap **Close** (✕).

The Formatting pane closes.

9 Tap **return**.

The insertion point moves to a new paragraph.

10 Tap **Check box** (⊘).

ⓔ The Notes app inserts a check box on the current line.

11 Type the text to accompany the check box.

12 Tap **return** twice.

The Notes app creates a new paragraph and discontinues the check boxes.

13 When you finish working on the note, tap **Done**.

The Notes app hides the keyboard.

14 Tap **Notes** (‹).

The Notes screen appears again, and you can work with other notes.

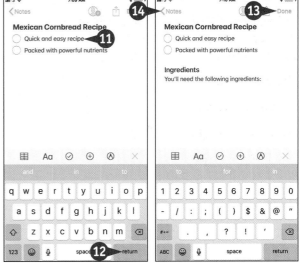

TIPS

How do I tell Siri the account for new notes?

Press **Home** — on an iPhone X, swipe up from the bottom of the screen — to display the Home screen, tap **Settings** (⚙) to display the Settings screen, and then tap **Notes** (　). On the Notes screen, tap **Default Account** to display the Default Account screen, and then tap the appropriate account; or tap **On My iPhone** to store the notes only on your iPhone. The Notes widget in Today View also uses this default account.

What other settings can I configure for Notes?

You can choose the default style for the first line in each new note. Open the Notes screen in the Settings app as explained in the previous tip, tap **New Notes Start With**, and then tap the appropriate style — **Title**, **Heading**, or **Body** — on the New Notes Start With screen.

Using Stocks, Weather, and Clock

The iPhone includes several built-in apps that enable you to keep track of important information throughout the day. You can use the Stocks app to track stock prices so that you can take immediate action when it becomes necessary. You can use the Weather app to learn the current weather conditions and forecast for your current location and for as many cities as you need. And you can use the Clock app's World Clock, Alarm, Bedtime, Stopwatch, and Timer features to track and measure time.

Using the Stocks App

The Stocks app enables you to track a customized selection of stock prices.

Tap **Stocks** (◼) on the Home screen to launch the Stocks app. The Stocks screen appears, showing the default selection of stocks.

To change the stocks displayed, tap **Info** (▤). On the Stocks configuration screen that appears, tap **Add** (+) to display the Search screen. Type the name or stock symbol of the stock you want to add, and then tap the matching entry in the list. You can tap stock handles (▤) and drag the stocks into your preferred order. Tap **percentage**, **price**, or **market cap** to control which statistic the Stocks app displays first, and then tap **Done** to return to the Stocks screen.

Using the Weather App

The Weather app lets you stay in touch with current weather conditions and forecasts for multiple locations.

Tap **Weather** (◯) on the Home screen to launch the Weather app. You can then swipe left or right at the top of the screen, or tap the dots at the bottom of the screen, to display the city you want to see. Swipe the timeline left to see later hours. Swipe up to display further details, such as sunrise and sunset times, humidity, and wind.

To customize the locations, tap **Cities** (▤). You can then tap **Add** (⊕) to add a location, swipe a location left and tap **Delete** to delete it, or tap and hold and then drag to move a city up or down the list. When you finish customizing the list, tap the city whose weather you want to display.

Using the Clock App

The Clock app, which you can launch by tapping **Clock** (○) on the Home screen, has five main features: World Clock, Alarm, Bedtime, Stopwatch, and Timer. You tap the buttons at the bottom of the screen to select the feature you want to use.

The World Clock feature enables you to easily keep track of the time in different cities. From the list, you can remove a city by swiping its button left and then tapping **Delete**. To add cities, tap **Add** (⊞) and select the city on the Choose a City screen. To change the order of the list, tap **Edit** and drag cities up or down by their handles (☰); tap **Done** when you finish.

The Alarm feature lets you set as many alarms as you need, each with a different schedule and your choice of sound. Tap **Add** (⊞) to display the Add Alarm screen, set the details for a new alarm, and then tap **Save**. On the Alarm screen, you can set each alarm's switch to On (◯) or Off (◖), as needed.

The Bedtime feature encourages you to follow consistent times for going to bed and waking. It also provides sleep analysis.

The Stopwatch feature allows you to time events to the hundredth of a second. You can switch between the analog-look stopwatch and the digital-look stopwatch by swiping left or right. Tap **Start** to start the stopwatch, tap **Lap** to mark a lap time, and tap **Stop** to stop the stopwatch.

The Timer feature enables you to count down a set amount of time and play a sound when the timer ends. You can also use the Timer to play music or other media for a set amount of time. To do this, tap **When Timer Ends**, tap **Stop Playing** on the When Timer Ends screen, and then tap **Set**.

Using the Health App

The Health app integrates with third-party hardware and software to enable you to keep tabs on many different aspects of your health, ranging from your weight and blood pressure to your nutrition, activity levels, and body mass index. Press **Home** — on an iPhone X, swipe up from the bottom of the screen — to display the Home screen, and then tap **Health** (♥) to launch the Health app.

Track Your Health with Health Data

The Health Data screen provides quick access to the health information you want to track closely.

Tap **Health Data** (⊞ changes to ⊞) to display the Health Data screen. You can then tap one of the main four areas — Activity, Mindfulness, Nutrition, or Sleep — at the top of the screen to explore the data available. Further down the screen, you can tap **Body Measurements**, **Health Records**, **Reproductive Health**, **Results**, or **Vitals** to access those categories. For example, Body Measurements enables you to track your height, weight, body mass index, body fat percentage, and lean body mass.

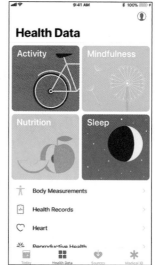

Examine Today's Statistics

The Today screen provides an easy way to look at a day's activity and vital statistics.

Tap **Today** (▦ changes to ▦) to display the Today screen, which displays the Favorites list, showing items you have designated as favorites; the Activity list, which shows items such as Resting Energy, Active Energy, and Steps; and the Vitals list, which shows any vital signs measured by your iPhone, Apple Watch, or other hardware sources you have connected to Health.

Tap a button on the Today screen to display more detail. For example, tap **Walking + Running Distance** to display the Walking + Running Distance screen, where you can view graphs for day, week, month, and year; set the **Add to Favorites** switch to On (◯) to make the item a favorite; or tap **Data Sources & Access** to examine or change the data sources used.

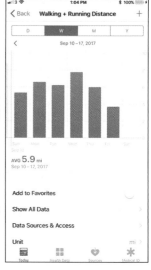

Add Data Points

The Health app can automatically accept data points from sources you approve, as explained next, but you can also add data points manually. For example, if you weigh yourself on a manual scale or have your blood pressure taken, you can add your latest readings to the Health app so that you can track your weight and blood pressure over time.

Tap **Vitals** on the Health Data screen to display the Vitals screen. You can then tap the appropriate button to reach its screen. For example, tap **Blood Pressure** to display the Blood Pressure screen. You can then tap **Add** (+) to display the Add Data screen. Enter the date, time, and systolic and diastolic pressures, and then tap the **Add** button.

Add Sources

Tap **Sources** (♡ changes to ♥) to display the Sources screen. Here you can review the list of apps that have requested permission to update the data in the Health app; you can remove any apps that you no longer want to permit to update the data. You can also review the list of hardware devices that have gotten permission to update the data — for example, your Apple Watch — and revoke permissions as needed.

Add Your Medical ID

Tap **Medical ID** (✳ changes to ✳) to display the Medical ID screen. You can then tap **Edit** to open the data for editing so that you can enter details of your medical conditions, medications, emergency contact, and blood type. Set the **Show When Locked** switch to On (◯) if you want to display your medical ID on the lock screen, enabling others to access your essential information to help if you become unwell.

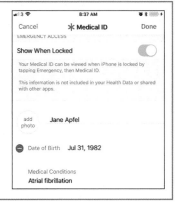

Manage Files with the Files App

The Files app enables you to work with files stored on your iPhone; files stored on network servers, such as macOS Server; and files stored on online storage services, such as iCloud Drive. You can quickly locate files by using the Recents screen, by using the Browse screen, or by searching by keyword. You can also recover recently deleted files by using the Recently Deleted Location. You navigate the Files app using similar techniques to those for navigating file-opening and file-saving features within apps.

Manage Files with the Files App

Open the Files App

1 Press **Home**. On an iPhone X, swipe up from the bottom of the screen.

The Home screen appears.

2 Tap **Files** (📁).

The Files app opens.

3 Tap **Browse** (📁 changes to 📁).

The Browse screen appears.

Note: The Recently Deleted location contains files that you have deleted recently, somewhat like the Trash on macOS or the Recycle Bin on Windows. To retrieve a deleted file, tap **Recently Deleted**, tap and hold the file, and then tap **Recover** on the command bar that appears.

Browse Files and Open Files

1 Tap **Recents** (🕐 changes to 🕐).

The Recents screen appears.

Ⓐ You can search your recent files by tapping **Search** (🔍) and then typing a search term.

Ⓑ Some of your most recent files appear at the top.

Ⓒ Older files appear listed by their tags.

2 Tap **Browse** (📁 changes to 📁).

The Browse screen appears.

Ⓓ You can search all your files by tapping **Search** (🔍) and then typing a search term.

3 Tap the location you want to browse. This example uses iCloud Drive.

224

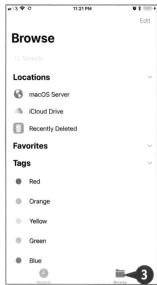

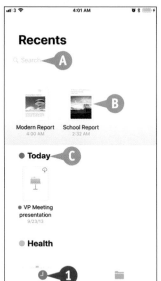

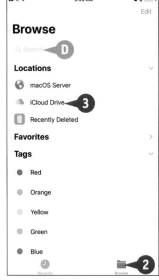

The screen for the location appears.

E You can tap **New Folder** (📁) to create a new folder in the current folder.

F You can change the sort order by tapping **Sorted by** and then tapping **Name**, **Date**, **Size**, or **Tags** in the Sort By dialog.

G You can tap **List** (☰) to display the files and folders as a list rather than as a grid.

4 Tap the folder you want to open.

The folder opens.

5 Press a file you want to preview.

Note: If you are sure which file you want to open, simply tap the file without pressing it.

The Peek panel opens, showing a preview.

6 Press further on the Peek panel.

The file opens in the default app for the file type, assuming your iPhone has such an app.

The app appears, and you can work on the file.

Note: You can open only files for which your iPhone contains a suitable app. If there is no suitable app, Files displays the file for viewing if it has a suitable viewer, but you cannot change the file.

H You can tap **Files** (◀) to return to the Files app.

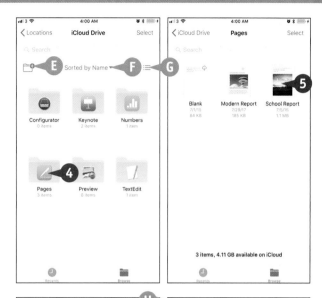

TIP

How do I add locations to the Locations list?

You add locations — such as OneDrive, Google Drive, or Dropbox — by adding accounts for those locations in the Settings app. Press **Home** — on an iPhone X, swipe up from the bottom of the screen — to display the Home screen, and then tap **Settings** (⚙) to display the Settings screen. Tap **Accounts & Passwords** to display the Accounts & Passwords screen, and then tap **Add Account.** On the Add Account screen, tap the account type. To add an account type that does not appear on the Add Account screen, tap **Other** to display the Other screen, and then tap the button for the account type, such as **Add macOS Server Account.**

continued ▶

A s well as opening a file, the Files app enables you to take other actions with a file, such as renaming it, copying it and pasting a copy, duplicating it in the same location, or moving it to another location.

The Files app also enables you to use tags to group and sort your files. The Files app comes with default tags with color names, such as Red and Orange, but you can customize the names and create new tags as needed.

Manage Files with the Files App (continued)

Take Other Actions with a File

1 Tap and hold the file you want to affect.

The control bar appears.

I Tap **Copy** to copy the file. After copying the file, navigate to the location in which you want to paste the copy, tap and hold open space, and then tap **Paste** on the control bar.

J Tap **Duplicate** to create a duplicate file in the same folder.

K Tap **Rename** to display the Rename Document screen. Type the new name, and then tap **Done**.

L Tap **Move** to display a screen for moving the file. Tap the location, and then tap **Move**.

2 For other commands, tap **More** (▶).

The remaining commands appear.

M Tap **Delete** to delete the file.

N Tap **Share** to open the Share sheet for sharing the file.

O Tap **Info** to display information about the file.

3 Tap **Tags**.

The Tags screen appears.

4 Tap each tag you want to apply to the file. Also tap any applied tag that you want to remove.

5 Tap **Done**.

The Files app displays the folder from which you started.

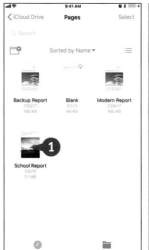

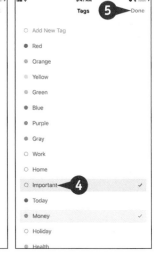

Organize Your Locations and Tags

1 Tap **Browse** (📁 changes to 📂).

The Browse screen appears.

2 Tap **Edit**.

The Browse screen switches to Edit Mode.

3 In the Locations list, set a switch to Off (🔵 changes to ⚪) if you want to hide the location.

4 Tap a handle and drag a location up or down, as needed.

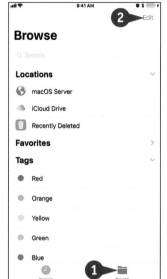

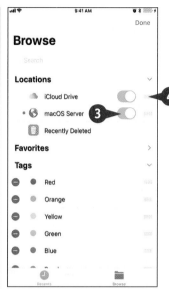

5 In the Tags list, tap **Delete** (➖) and then tap **Delete** to delete a tag.

6 To change the tag order, tap the handle (☰) and drag the tag up or down the list.

7 To rename a tag, tap it, and then type the new name.

8 When you finish editing the Browse screen, tap **Done**.

The Browse screen switches off Edit Mode.

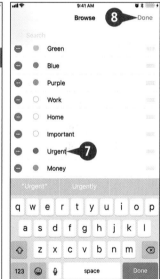

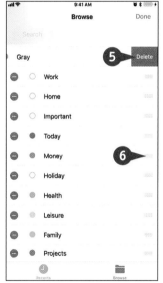

TIP

Can I move or delete multiple files at once?

Yes, you can take several actions with multiple files in the same folder. First, navigate to that folder, and then tap **Select** to switch to Selection Mode. Tap each item to select it (⚪ changes to ✅). After selecting the items, tap the appropriate button at the bottom of the screen — **Duplicate**, **Move**, **Share**, or **Delete** — and then follow the prompts to complete the action.

CHAPTER 10

Enjoying Music, Videos, and Books

As well as being a phone and a powerful handheld computer, your iPhone is also a full-scale music and video player. To play music and listen to radio, you use the Music app; to play videos, you use the TV app. You can read digital books and PDF files using the iBooks app.

Navigate the Music App and Set Preferences

The Music app enables you to enjoy music you have loaded on your iPhone, music you have stored on Apple's iTunes Match service, and music on the Apple Music Radio service.

The Music app packs a wide range of functionality into its interface. The For You feature enables you to set — and reset — your musical preferences. The Radio feature allows you to listen to Apple Music Radio. And the Connect feature lets you connect to artists online.

Navigate the Music App and Set Preferences

① Press **Home**. On an iPhone X, swipe up from the bottom of the screen.

The Home screen appears.

② Tap **Music** (🎵).

The Music app opens.

③ If Library is not selected, tap **Library** (🎵 changes to 🎵).

The Library screen appears, showing your music library.

Ⓐ You can tap an item, such as Playlists or Artists, to browse the library.

Ⓑ The Recently Added section shows items added recently.

④ Tap **Edit**.

The Library screen opens for editing.

⑤ Tap an empty selection circle to select it (◯ changes to ✅), adding that item to the Library list.

⑥ Tap a selected selection circle to deselect it (✅ changes to ◯), removing that item from the Library list.

⑦ Drag a selection handle up or down to move an item in the list.

⑧ Tap **Done**.

The Library screen displays the customized list.

⑨ Tap **For You** (🤍 changes to ❤️).

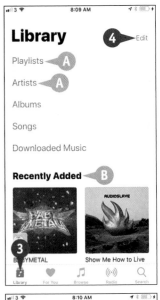

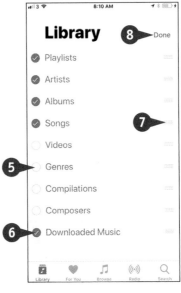

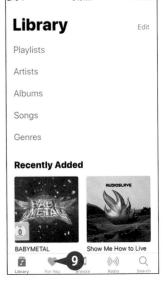

The For You screen appears, showing music suggestions for you.

Note: On the For You screen, you can scroll down to see different categories of items, such as Artist Playlists and New Releases for you. Scroll a category left to see more items in it.

C You can tap **Account** (⚇) to display the Account screen, on which you can edit your nickname for the account and set a photo to use.

10 Tap **Browse** (♫ changes to ♫).

The Browse screen appears, providing ways to browse music.

11 Tap **Radio** ((•)) changes to (•)).

The Radio screen appears.

D You can tap a station to start it playing.

Note: See the section "Listen to Apple Music Radio," later in this chapter, for more information on the Radio feature.

12 Tap **Search** (🔍 changes to 🔍).

The Search screen appears.

E You can tap the Search box and type a search term.

F You can tap a recent search to repeat it.

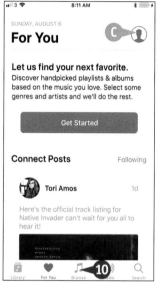

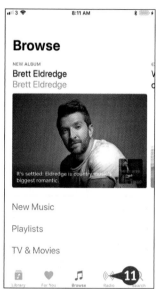

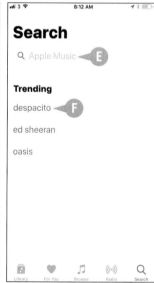

TIP

How does the Search function work?

The Search function enables you to search both your own music and the Apple Music service. Tap **Search** (🔍 changes to 🔍) to display the Search screen, and then type your search terms in the box at the top of the screen. Tap the **Apple Music** tab button to see matching searches you can perform on Apple Music; you can then tap a search to perform it. Tap the **In Library** tab button to see matching items in your music, broken down into categories such as Artists, Albums, or Songs. When you locate the item you want, tap the item to go to it.

Play Music Using the Music App

After loading music on your iPhone, as described in the section "Choose Which Items to Sync from Your Computer" in Chapter 1, you can play it back using the Music app. You can play music by song or by album, as described in this section. You can play songs in exactly the order you want by creating a custom playlist, as described in the later section, "Create a Music Playlist." You can also play by artist, genre, or composer.

Play Music Using the Music App

1 Press **Home**. On an iPhone X, swipe up from the bottom of the screen.

The Home screen appears.

2 Tap **Music** (♫).

The Music app opens.

3 Tap **Library** (📚 changes to 📚).

The Library screen appears.

4 Tap the button for the means by which you want to browse your library. This example uses **Songs**, so the Songs screen appears.

5 Tap the letter that starts the name of the item you want to play.

That section of the list appears.

A If tapping the letter displays the songs sorted by artist, tap **Sort** and then tap **Title** in the dialog that opens.

Note: You can also swipe or drag your finger up the screen to scroll down.

Note: Tap above the letter A in the navigation letters to go back to the top of the screen.

6 Tap the song you want to play.

The song starts playing.

B The song appears on the Now Playing button.

C You can tap **Pause** (❚❚) to pause the song.

D You can tap **Next** (▶▶) to skip to the next song.

7 Tap **Now Playing** — either the song name or the album art.

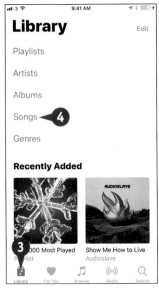

232

The Now Playing screen appears.

8 Tap and drag the playhead to move through the song.

9 Tap and drag the volume control to change the volume.

10 Tap **More** (•••).

The More pop-up panel appears.

E You can tap **Delete from Library** (🗑) to delete the song from your iPhone's library.

F You can tap **Add to a Playlist** (⊕≡) to add the song to a new or existing playlist.

G You can tap **Love** (♥) or **Dislike** (🖤) to indicate your feeling toward the song.

11 Swipe up the screen.

Other controls appear.

H You can tap **Shuffle** (⤬) to play songs in random order.

I You can tap **Repeat** (⟲) to repeat the current song or current list.

J The Up Next section shows upcoming songs. You can tap a song to play it, or drag a handle (≡) to rearrange the list.

12 Tap **Back** (⌄).

The list of songs appears again.

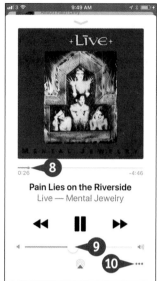

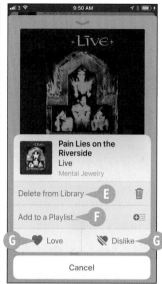

TIP

How else can I control playback?
Swipe up from the bottom of the screen to display Control Center. You can control playback using the playback buttons, and tap and drag the volume slider to adjust the volume.

Play Videos Using the TV App

To play videos — such as movies, TV shows, or music videos — you use the iPhone's TV app, which you can set up to use your existing TV provider. You can play a video on the iPhone's screen, which is handy when you are traveling; on a TV to which you connect the iPhone; or on a TV connected to an Apple TV box. Using a TV is great when you need to share a movie or other video with family, friends, or colleagues.

Play Videos Using the TV App

Set Up the TV App

1 Press **Home**. On an iPhone X, swipe up from the bottom of the screen.

The Home screen appears.

Note: If your iPhone does not have the TV app, use the Videos app ( ) instead.

Note: You can also play videos included on web pages. To do so, press **Home**, tap **Safari**, navigate to the page, and then tap the video.

2 Tap **TV** ( ).

The Welcome to the TV App screen appears.

3 Tap **Continue**.

The Sign In to Your TV Provider screen appears.

4 Tap **Sign In**.

A If you do not have a TV provider, or you do not want to sign in now, tap **Not Now**.

The Choose a TV Provider screen appears.

5 Tap your TV provider, and then follow the prompts to sign in.

The Watch Now screen appears.

6 Tap **Get Started**, and then follow the prompts to connect any TV-related apps to the TV app.

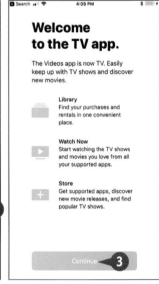

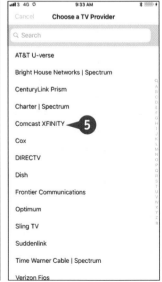

Watch a Video

1 In the TV app, tap the video source. In this example, tap **Library** (▦ changes to ▦).

The Library screen appears.

2 Tap the video category, such as **Home Videos**.

The category screen appears.

3 Tap the video you want to view.

The details screen for the video appears.

4 Tap **Play** (▶).

The video starts playing.

Note: If the video is in landscape format, turn your iPhone sideways to view the video in landscape orientation.

5 When you need to control playback, tap the screen.

The playback controls appear.

B You can drag the playhead to move through the video.

C You can drag the volume control to change the volume.

D You can tap **Pause** (❚❚) to pause playback. Tap **Play** (▶) to resume playback.

E Tap and hold **Rewind** (◀◀) to rewind the video a few seconds at a time.

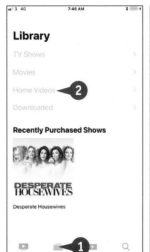

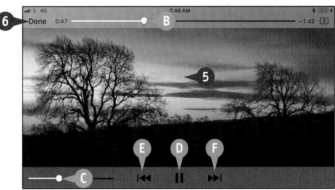

F Tap and hold **Fast-Forward** (▶▶) to fast-forward the video a few seconds at a time.

6 Tap **Done** when you want to stop playing the video.

The details screen for the video appears again.

TIPS

How do I play videos on my television from my iPhone?

If you have an Apple TV or AirPlay-compatible device, use AirPlay, as explained in the next section, "Play Music and Videos Using AirPlay." Otherwise, use the Apple Lightning Digital AV Adapter and an HDMI cable to connect your iPhone to a TV.

What other video content can I watch on my iPhone?

You can also use your iPhone to watch or listen to *podcasts*, which are video or audio programs released via the Internet. The Podcasts app enables you to access podcasts covering many different topics, and the iTunes U app is your gateway to podcasts containing educational content, some free and some paid.

Play Music and Videos Using AirPlay

U sing the AirPlay feature, you can play music from your iPhone on remote speakers connected to an AirPlay-compatible device such as an AirPort Express or Apple TV. Similarly, you can play video from your iPhone on a TV or monitor connected to an Apple TV. Even better, you can use the iOS feature called *Screen Mirroring* to display an iPhone app on a TV or monitor. For example, you can display a web page in Safari on your TV screen.

Play Music and Videos Using AirPlay

Play Music on External Speakers or an Apple TV

1 Press **Home**. On an iPhone X, swipe up from the bottom of the screen.

The Home screen appears.

2 Tap **Music** (♫).

The Music app opens.

3 Navigate to the song you want to play. For example, tap **Library** (🎵 changes to 🎵), tap **Songs**, and then tap the song.

The song appears on the Now Playing button.

4 Tap **Now Playing**.

The Now Playing screen appears.

5 Tap **AirPlay** (🔊).

The AirPlay dialog opens.

6 Tap the AirPlay device on which you want the music to play.

Your iPhone starts playing music on the device via AirPlay.

Play Video or an App on an Apple TV

1. Open the app you want to use. This example uses **Notes** ( ).

2. On an iPhone X, swipe down from the upper-right corner of the screen. On other iPhone models, swipe up from the bottom of the screen.

Note: In landscape view, swipe up once to display an arrow button in the center of the bottom of the screen. Tap this button or swipe up again to open Control Center.

Control Center opens.

3. Press **Screen Mirroring** ( ).

The Peek panel for Screen Mirroring opens.

4. Tap the Apple TV you want to use.

The Peek panel closes.

The iPhone's screen appears on the screen connected to the Apple TV.

5. Tap in the app above Control Center.

Control Center closes, and the app appears full-screen.

Note: When you are ready to stop screen mirroring, open Control Center, press **Screen Mirroring** ( ), and then tap **Stop Mirroring**.

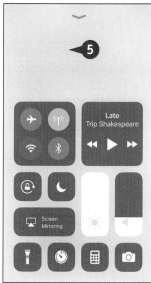

TIP

Can AirPlay play music through multiple sets of speakers at the same time?
AirPlay on the Mac or PC can play music through two or more sets of speakers at the same time, enabling you to play music throughout your home. However, as of this writing, AirPlay on the iPhone can play only to a single device at a time.

Create a Music Playlist

Instead of playing individual songs or playing a CD's songs from start to finish, you can create a playlist that contains only the songs you want in your preferred order. Playlists are a great way to enjoy music on your iPhone.

To help identify a playlist, you can add a new photo or an existing photo. Alternatively, you can let the Music app create a thumbnail from the covers of the songs you add to the playlist.

Create a Music Playlist

1. Press **Home**. On an iPhone X, swipe up from the bottom of the screen.

   The Home screen appears.

2. Tap **Music** (♪).

   The Music screen appears.

3. Tap **Library** (🎵 changes to 🎵).

   The Library screen appears.

4. Tap **Playlists**.

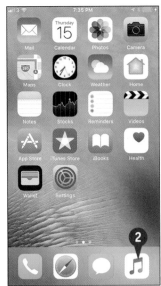

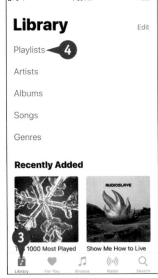

5. The Playlists screen appears.

5. Tap **New Playlist**.

   The New Playlist screen opens.

6. Tap **Playlist Name** and type the name for the playlist.

7. Optionally, tap **Description** and type a description for the playlist.

8. Optionally, tap **Photo** (📷), tap **Take Photo** or **Choose Photo**, and follow the prompts to add a photo.

9. Tap **Add Music** (⊕).

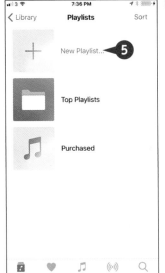

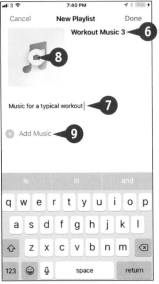

The Add Songs screen appears.

Ⓐ You can search for music by tapping **Search** (🔍) and typing your search term.

⑩ Tap the button for the means by which you want to browse your library. This example uses **Songs**.

The appropriate screen appears, such as the Songs screen.

⑪ Tap each song you want to add (➕ changes to ✓).

⑫ Tap **Done**.

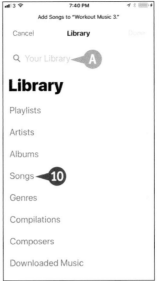

The New Playlist screen appears.

⑬ Rearrange the songs as needed by dragging each song up or down by its handle (☰).

Ⓑ You can remove a song by tapping **Remove** (➖) and then tapping the textual Remove button that appears.

⑭ Tap **Done**.

The Playlists screen appears.

⑮ If you want to listen to the new playlist, tap its button.

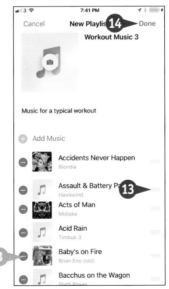

TIP

How can I add songs to an existing playlist?
Navigate to the song you want to add, and then press it. In the Peek panel, tap **Add to a Playlist** (⊕☰). The Add to a Playlist screen appears, showing your playlists. Tap the playlist to which you want to add the song. You can use the same technique to add a whole album to a playlist.

Listen to Apple Music Radio

The Radio feature in the Music app enables you to listen to the Apple Music Radio service. Apple Music Radio has two main parts, one free and one paid. The free part comprises the Beats 1 global radio station and other live radio stations. The paid part is curated, on-demand radio stations and custom radio stations, which require a subscription to the Apple Music service. An individual subscription costs $9.99 per month; a family subscription, which covers up to six people, costs $14.99 per month.

Listen to Apple Music Radio

1 Press **Home**. On an iPhone X, swipe up from the bottom of the screen.

The Home screen appears.

2 Tap **Music** (♫).

The Music app opens.

3 Tap **Radio** ((( )) changes to (( ))).

The Radio screen appears.

Ⓐ You can swipe left on the thumbnail bar to display other major stations.

Ⓑ The Featured Stations list shows stations that Apple Music Radio is currently featuring.

4 Tap **Radio Stations**.

The Radio Stations screen appears.

Ⓒ The top of the Radio Stations screen shows some featured stations such as Charting Now. Swipe left on the thumbnail bar to browse the stations.

Ⓓ The Featured Stations list shows currently featured stations.

5 Swipe up to scroll down.

The All Genres list appears.

6 Tap the genre you want to browse.

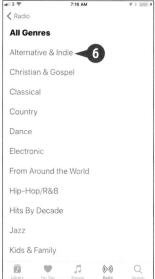

The list of stations in that genre appears.

Note: To share a station, press the station and then tap **Share Station** (⬆).

7 Tap the station you want to play.

E The current song on that station starts playing. The song appears on the Now Playing button.

F You can tap **Pause** (⏸) to pause playback.

G You can tap **Skip** (⏭) to skip to the next song.

8 Tap **Now Playing**.

The Now Playing screen appears.

H You can tap **Back** (⌄) to return to the Radio screen.

I You can drag the playhead to move through the song.

J You can drag the volume control to change the volume.

K You can tap **Add** (➕) to add the song to your library.

9 Tap **More** (•••).

The More panel appears.

L You can tap **Love** (♥) or **Dislike** (🖤) to express your feelings about the song.

M You can tap **Add to a Playlist** (⊕≡) to add the song to a playlist.

N You can tap **Create Station** ((•)) to create a station based on the song.

O You can tap **Share Song** (⬆) to share the song with others.

TIP

What do the Share Station and Share Song commands do?

The Share Station command enables you to share a link to a station on Apple Music Radio. Similarly, the Share Song command lets you share a link to a song on the iTunes Store. You can use various means of sharing, such as sending the link via Mail or Messages, posting it to Facebook or Twitter, or simply setting yourself a reminder to listen to — or avoid — the music.

Read Digital Books with iBooks

The iBooks app enables you to read e-books or PDF files that you load on the iPhone from your computer or sync via iCloud by enabling iBooks on your Mac and your iPhone to use iCloud. You can also read e-books and PDFs you download from online stores, download from web pages, or save from e-mail messages.

If you have already loaded some e-books, you can read them as described in this section. If iBooks contains no books, tap **Store** and browse the iBooks Store or sync books from your computer using iTunes.

Read Digital Books with iBooks

1 Press **Home**. On an iPhone X, swipe up from the bottom of the screen.

The Home screen appears.

2 Tap **iBooks** (📖).

iBooks opens, and a screen such as the All Books screen or the Books screen appears.

A If the Audiobooks screen or the PDFs screen appears, tap **Audiobooks** or **PDFs**. On the Collections screen that appears, tap **All Books** or **Books** to display the All Books screen or the Books screen.

3 To view the books as a list, tap **List** (☰ changes to ▦) at the top of the screen.

B You can tap **Search** (🔍) and search to locate the book you want.

The list of books appears.

C You can tap **Recent**, **Titles**, **Authors**, or **Categories** to sort the books differently.

4 Tap the book you want to open.

The book opens.

Note: When you open a book, iBooks displays your current page. When you open a book for the first time, iBooks displays the book's cover, first page, or default page.

D To change the font, tap **Font Settings** (ₐA) and work in the Font Settings dialog.

5 Tap anywhere on the screen to hide the reading controls.

The reading controls disappear.

Note: To display the reading controls again, tap anywhere on the screen.

6 Tap the right side of the page to display the next page.

Note: To display the previous page, tap the left side of the page. Alternatively, tap the left side of the page and drag to the right.

7 To look at the next page without fully revealing it, tap the right side and drag to the left. You can then either drag further to turn the page or release the page and let it fall closed.

8 To jump to another part of the book, tap **Table of Contents** (☰).

Note: Alternatively, you can drag the slider at the bottom of the screen.

The table of contents appears.

9 Tap the part of the book you want to display.

10 To search in the book, tap **Search** (🔍).

The Search screen appears.

11 Type the search term.

The list of search results appears.

12 Tap the result you want to display.

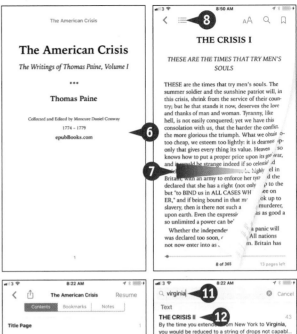

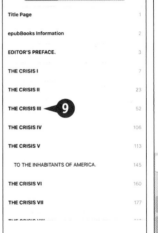

TIPS

How do I put my Mac's iBooks library on my iPhone manually?

Use iTunes to sync your books. Connect your iPhone to your Mac, and then click **iPhone** (📱) on the navigation bar. Click **Books** in the Settings list in the sidebar, and then click **Sync Books** (☐ changes ✅). To sync all your books, click **All books** (◯ changes to ◉); to sync books you choose, click **Selected books** (◯ changes to ◉) and then click each book (☐ changes to ✅).

Where can I find free e-books to read in iBooks?

On the iBooks Store, tap **Featured** and then tap **Free Books** in the Browse area. Other sources of free e-books include ManyBooks.net (www.manybooks.net), Project Gutenberg (www.gutenberg.org), and the Baen Free Library (www.baen.com/library).

CHAPTER 11

Working with Photos and Video

Your iPhone's Camera app enables you to take high-quality still photos and videos. You can edit photos or apply filters to them, trim video clips down to length, and easily share both photos and videos.

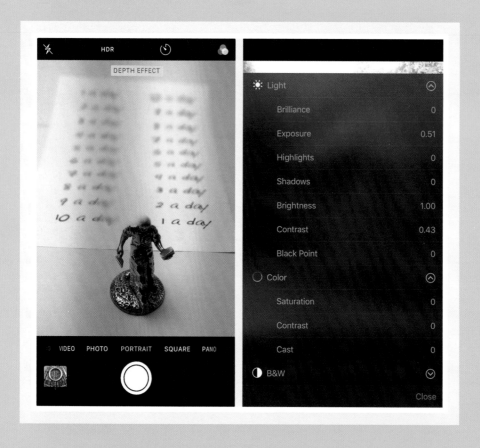

Take Photos with the Camera App

Your iPhone includes a high-resolution rear camera and a lower-resolution screen-side camera. Both cameras can take photos and videos, and the screen-side camera works for video calls, too. To take photos using the camera, you use the Camera app. This app includes a digital zoom feature for zooming in and out; a flash that you can set to On, Off, or Auto; and a High Dynamic Range (HDR) feature that combines several photos into a single photo with adjusted color balance and intensity.

Take Photos with the Camera App

Open the Camera App

1 Press **Home**. On an iPhone X, swipe up from the bottom of the screen.

The Home screen appears.

Note: From the lock screen, you can open the Camera app by swiping left.

2 Tap **Camera** (📷).

The Camera app opens and displays whatever is in front of the lens.

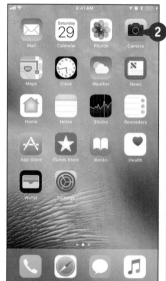

Compose the Photo and Zoom if Necessary

1 Aim the iPhone so that your subject appears in the middle of the photo area. To focus on an item not in the center of the frame, tap that item to move the focus rectangle to it.

Note: If you need to take tightly composed photos, get a tripod mount for the iPhone. You can find various models on eBay and photography sites.

2 If you need to zoom in, tap and hold the Zoom readout.

The zoom track appears.

3 Drag along the zoom track to zoom.

Note: You can also zoom in by placing two fingers together on the screen and pinching outward. To zoom out, pinch inward.

Note: On a dual-lens iPhone, tap the zoom number to zoom in quickly to 2X using optical zoom. Tap **2X** to return to 1X zoom.

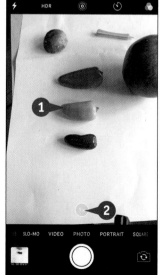

Choose Flash and HDR Settings

1 Tap **Flash** (⚡, ⚡, or ⚡).

The Flash settings appear.

2 Tap **On** to use the flash, **Auto** to use the flash if there is not enough light without it, or **Off** to turn the flash off.

3 Tap **HDR**.

The HDR settings appear.

4 Tap **Auto**, **On**, or **Off**, as needed.

Note: You cannot use the flash with HDR. Turning HDR on turns the flash off, and vice versa.

Take the Photo and View It

A HDR appears if HDR is on.

1 Tap **Take Photo** (◯).

Note: You can tap and hold **Take Photo** (◯) to take a burst of photos.

The Camera app takes the photo and displays a thumbnail.

2 Tap the thumbnail.

The photo appears.

B From the photo screen, swipe or tap a thumbnail to display another photo. Tap **Delete** (🗑) to delete the current photo.

3 Tap **Back** (❮) when you want to go back to the Camera app.

TIP

How do I switch to the front-facing camera?

Tap **Switch Cameras** (📷) to switch from the rear-facing camera to the front-facing camera. The image that the front-facing camera is seeing appears on-screen, and you can take pictures as described in this section. HDR is available for the front-facing camera; flash is available only on the some iPhone models. Tap **Switch Cameras** (📷) again when you want to switch back to the rear-facing camera.

Take Live, Timed, Portrait, and Panorama Photos

The Camera app's Live Photo feature enables you to capture several seconds of video around a still photo. Live Photo is great for photographing moving subjects or setting the scene.

The self-timer feature lets you set the app to take a burst of 11 photos after a delay of 3 seconds or 10 seconds, which is good for group shots and for avoiding camera shake. You can also capture panoramas, time-lapse movies, and — on some iPhone models only — portrait photos with blurred backgrounds.

Take Live, Timed, Portrait, and Panorama Photos

Open the Camera App, Take a Live Photo, and View It

1 Press **Home**. On an iPhone X, swipe up from the bottom of the screen.

The Home screen appears.

2 Tap **Camera** ( ).

The Camera app opens.

3 Tap **Live** (changes to).

Note: Live Photo starts recording video as soon as you enable the feature. Live Photo discards the video except for the segments before and after photos you shoot.

Ⓐ The Live badge appears briefly.

4 Take **Take Photo** ( ).

The Camera app captures the Live Photo.

5 Tap the photo's thumbnail.

The photo opens.

The Live Photo segment plays.

6 Tap and hold the photo to play the Live Photo segment again.

7 Tap **Back** ( ).

The Camera app appears again.

Take a Timed Photo

1 Tap **Timer** ().

The Timer settings appear.

2 Tap **3s** or **10s** to set the delay.

The delay appears next to the Timer icon.

3 Tap **Take Photo** (◯).

Note: The Camera app displays an on-screen countdown, and the rear flash flashes to indicate the countdown to the subject.

When the countdown ends, the Camera app takes a burst of 11 photos.

Note: The timer remains set until you change it.

Take a Portrait Photo

1 Tap **Portrait**.

Note: If Portrait does not appear, your iPhone does not support this feature.

Camera adjusts the focus to blur the background.

Note: If the subject is too close to the iPhone, Camera displays the prompt *Move farther away*. Do so.

B The Depth Effect readout appears.

2 Tap **Take Photo** (◯).

Camera takes a photo.

Note: To take a square photo, such as a photo for a contact record, tap **Square**.

TIPS

How do I take panorama photos?
Tap **Pano**. Holding the iPhone in portrait orientation, aim at the left end of the panorama. Tap **Take Photo** (◯); gradually move the iPhone to the right, keeping the white arrow on the horizontal line; and then tap **Stop** (◯).

How do I take time-lapse movies?
Tap **Time-Lapse**; if you cannot see Time-Lapse, drag the current setting to the right first. Set the iPhone up on a tripod or other steady holder, aim it at the subject, and then tap **Start** (■). When you have captured enough, tap **Stop** (■) to stop shooting.

You can use the Filter feature in the Camera app to change the look of a photo by applying a filter such as Vivid, Dramatic Warm, Mono, Silvertone, or Noir.

You can apply a filter either before taking the photo or after taking it. If you apply the filter before taking the photo, you can remove the filter afterward; the filter is an effect applied to the photo, not an integral part of the photo.

Apply Filters to Your Photos

1 Press **Home**. On an iPhone X, swipe up from the bottom of the screen.

The Home screen appears.

2 Tap **Camera** (📷).

The Camera app opens.

3 Tap **Filters** (◉).

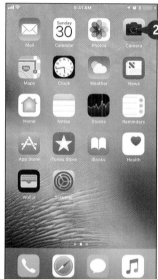

The Filters screen appears.

4 Tap the filter you want to preview.

Camera applies the filter to the screen.

5 Tap the filter you want to apply.

6 Tap **Take Photo** (◯).

7 Tap the photo's thumbnail.

The photo appears.

8 Tap **Edit**.

The Edit Photo screen appears, showing the editing tools.

9 Tap **Filters** ().

The Choose Filter screen appears.

10 Tap the filter you want to apply.

Note: Tap **Original** if you want to remove filtering.

11 Tap **Done**.

iOS saves the change to the photo.

12 Tap **Back** (<) to return to the Camera app.

TIP

Is it better to apply a filter before taking a photo or after taking it?
This is up to you. Sometimes it is helpful to have the filter effect in place when composing a photo so that you can arrange the composition and lighting to complement the filtering. Other times, especially when you do not have time to experiment with filters, it is more practical to take the photos and then try applying filters afterward.

Edit Your Photos

To improve your photos, you can use the powerful but easy-to-use editing tools your iPhone includes. These tools include rotating a photo to a different orientation, straightening it by rotating it a little, and cropping off the parts you do not need.

You can access the editing tools either through the Recently Added album in the Photos app or through the Photos app. To start editing a photo, you open the photo by tapping it, and then tap **Edit**.

Edit Your Photos

Open a Photo for Editing

1 Press **Home**. On an iPhone X, swipe up from the bottom of the screen.

The Home screen appears.

2 Tap **Photos** (🌼).

The Photos app opens.

3 Navigate to the photo you want to edit.

Ⓐ If the photo is part of a burst, the Burst readout appears. You can tap **Select** to select another photo from the burst instead of the default photo.

4 Tap **Edit**.

The Editing controls appear.

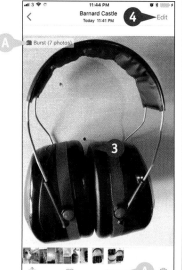

Crop, Rotate, and Straighten a Photo

1 Tap **Crop** (🔲).

The tools for cropping, straightening, and rotating appear.

Ⓑ You can tap **Rotate** (◰) to rotate the photo 90 degrees counterclockwise.

2 Tap and hold the degree dial.

Ⓒ The grid appears.

3 Drag the degree dial left or right to straighten the photo.

Ⓓ You can tap **Reset** to reset the photo.

4 Tap and hold an edge or corner of the crop box.

E The nine-square grid appears. This is to help you compose the cropped photo.

5 Drag the edge or corner of the crop box to select only the area you want to keep.

Enhance the Colors in a Photo

1 Tap **Auto-Enhance** (changes to).

iOS enhances the colors.

Note: Tap **Auto-Enhance** again (changes to) if you want to remove the color change.

Note: You can tap and hold the photo to display the original photo for as long as you hold. Displaying the original helps you see the effects of your changes.

TIP

What does the three-squares button on the cropping screen do?
The button with three squares (▭) is the Aspect button. Tap **Aspect** (▭) when you need to crop to a specific aspect ratio, such as a square or the 16:9 widescreen aspect ratio. In the Aspect dialog that opens, tap the constraint you want to use. iOS adjusts the current cropping to match the aspect ratio. You may then need to move the portion of the photo shown to get the composition you want. If you adjust the cropping, tap **Aspect** (▭) again and reapply the aspect ratio.

continued ▶

The Red-Eye Reduction feature enables you to restore feral eyes to normality. The Enhance feature enables you to adjust a photo's color balance and lighting quickly using default algorithms that analyze the photo and try to improve it. The Enhance feature often works well, but for greater control, you can use the Light settings and the Color settings to tweak the exposure, highlights, shadows, brightness, black point, contrast, vibrancy, and other settings manually.

Edit Your Photos (continued)

Remove Red Eye from a Photo

Note: You may need to zoom in on the photo in order to touch the red-eye patches accurately.

1 Tap **Red-Eye Reduction** (🚫).

iOS prompts you to tap each eye.

2 Tap each red eye.

iOS removes the red eye.

3 Tap **Red-Eye Reduction** (👁).

iOS turns off the Red-Eye Reduction tool.

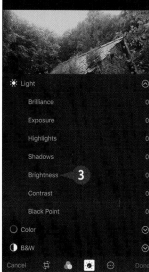

Adjust the Colors in a Photo

1 Tap **Adjust** (⚙).

The Adjust controls appear.

2 Tap **Expand** (⊙) on the Light bar.

Note: To adjust all the light settings at once, using Photos' automated adjustments, tap **Light**.

The Light settings appear.

3 Tap the setting you want to adjust. This example uses **Brightness**.

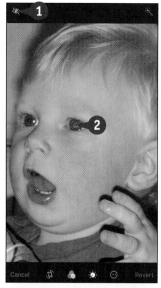

254

4 Drag the scale to adjust the setting.

Following this example, the photo becomes brighter.

5 Tap **List** (▤).

The list of Light settings appears.

6 Tap **Expand** (⊙) on the Color line.

Note: To adjust all the color settings at once, using Photos' automated adjustments, tap **Color**. Similarly, you can tap **B&W** to adjust all the black-and-white settings at once.

The list of Color settings appears.

7 Tap the setting you want to adjust. This example uses **Saturation**.

8 Drag the scale to adjust the setting.

9 Tap **List** (▤).

The list of settings appears, and you can adjust further settings as needed.

TIPS

How do I save the changes I have made to a photo?
When you finish making changes to a photo, tap **Done** to save the changes.

How do I get rid of changes I have made to a photo?
Tap **Cancel**, and then tap **Discard Changes** in the confirmation dialog that opens.

Capture Video

As well as capturing still photos, the Camera app can capture high-quality, full-motion video in either portrait orientation or landscape orientation. You launch the Camera app as usual, and then switch it to Video Mode for regular-speed shooting or to Slo-Mo Mode to shoot slow-motion footage. You can use flash, but it is effective only at close range for video. After taking the video, you can edit the clip by trimming off any unwanted frames at the beginning and end.

Capture Video

1 Press **Home**. On an iPhone X, swipe up from the bottom of the screen.

The Home screen appears.

2 Tap **Camera** (📷).

The Camera screen appears, showing the image the lens is seeing.

Ⓐ Tap **Slo-Mo** if you want to shoot slow-motion footage.

3 Tap **Video**.

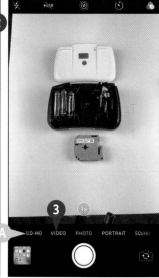

The video image and video controls appear.

4 Aim the camera at your subject.

Ⓑ If you need to use the flash for the video, tap **Flash** (⚡, ⚡, or ✕), and then tap **Auto** or **On**.

Note: To focus on a particular area of the screen, tap that area.

5 Tap **Record** (⏺).

Ⓒ The camera starts recording, and the time readout shows the time that has elapsed.

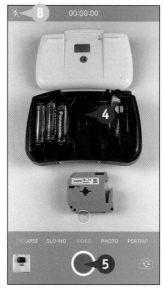

6 To zoom in, tap and hold the Zoom readout, and then drag along the zoom track.

Note: You can also zoom by placing your thumb and forefinger on the screen and pinching apart or pinching together.

D To take a still photo while shooting video, tap **Take Photo** (○).

7 To finish recording, tap **Stop** (◉).

The Camera app stops recording and displays a thumbnail of the video's first frame.

8 Tap the thumbnail.

The video appears.

9 Tap **Play** (▶).

The video starts playing.

10 Tap anywhere on the screen to display the video controls. These disappear automatically after a few seconds of not being used.

Note: To trim the clip down to only the section you need, tap **Edit**. Tap and hold the left trim handle (‹) so that its background turns yellow, and then drag it to the starting frame. Drag the right trim handle (›) to the ending frame. Tap **Done**, and then tap **Save as New Clip**.

11 When you finish viewing the video, tap **Back** (‹).

The Camera app appears again.

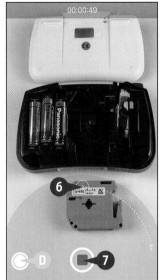

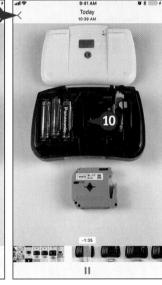

TIPS

How can I pause shooting a video?

As of this writing, you cannot pause while shooting. Either shoot separate video clips or trim out unwanted footage afterward.

What does the bar of miniature pictures at the bottom of the video playback screen do?

The navigation bar gives you a quick way of moving forward and backward through the video. Tap the thumbnails and drag them left or right until the part of the video you want to view is at the vertical blue playhead bar. You can use the navigation bar either when the video is playing or when it is paused.

Y ou can use the Photos app to browse the photos you have taken with your iPhone's camera, photos you have synced using iTunes or via iCloud's Shared Streams feature, and images you save from e-mail messages, instant messages, or web pages.

You can browse your photos by dates and locations using the smart groupings that Photos creates. Each Year grouping contains Collections, which contain Moments, which contain your photos. Alternatively, you can browse by albums, as explained in the section "Browse Photos Using Albums," later in this chapter.

Browse Photos Using Years, Collections, and Moments

1 Press **Home**. On an iPhone X, swipe up from the bottom of the screen.

The Home screen appears.

2 Tap **Photos** (❀).

The Photos app opens.

3 Tap **Photos** (▭ changes to ▰).

The Photos screen appears, showing the Years list.

4 Tap the year you want to open.

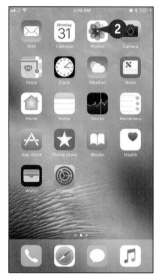

The Collections screen for the year appears.

5 Tap the collection you want to open.

Note: Scroll up or down as needed to see other collections.

The Moments screen for the collection appears.

6 Tap the photo you want to view.

The photo opens.

Ⓐ You can tap **Edit** to edit the photo, as explained earlier in this chapter.

Ⓑ You can tap **Share** (⬆) to share the photo, as explained later in this chapter.

Ⓒ You can tap **Favorite** (♡ changes to ♥) to make the photo a favorite.

Ⓓ You can tap **Trash** (🗑) to delete the photo.

Note: The Trash icon does not appear for photos you cannot delete, such as photos in a shared photo stream.

7 In the thumbnail bar, tap the photo you want to view.

Note: You can also swipe left or right to display other photos.

The photo appears.

8 Tap **Back** (‹).

The Moments screen appears.

Note: You can scroll up or down to display other moments.

9 Tap **Collections** (‹).

The Collections screen appears.

Note: You can scroll up or down to display other collections.

10 Tap **Years** (‹).

The Years screen appears, and you can navigate to another year.

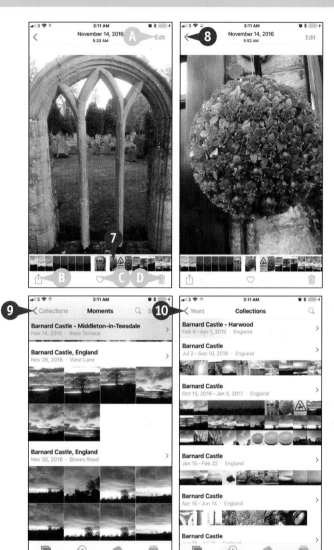

TIP

How can I move a photo to a different year?

To move a photo to a different year, you need to change the date set in the photo's metadata. You cannot do this with the Photos app, but you can change the date with a third-party app such as Pixelgarde, which is free from the App Store at this writing. Alternatively, if you sync the photos from your computer, you can change the date in the photo on your computer. For example, in Photos on the Mac, select the photo, click **Image** on the menu bar, and then click **Adjust Date and Time**.

Browse Photos Using Memories

The Memories feature in the Photos app presents a movie of photos from a particular period of time, such as a given year or a trip to a certain geographical location.

You can customize the settings for a memory. You can either customize them quickly by choosing roughly how long a memory should be and what atmosphere it should have, or you can take complete control and specify exactly which items to include and which music to play.

Browse Photos Using Memories

1 Press **Home**. On an iPhone X, swipe up from the bottom of the screen.

The Home screen appears.

2 Tap **Photos** (✿).

The Photos app opens.

3 Tap **Memories** (⊙ changes to ⊙).

The Memories screen appears.

4 Tap the memory you want to view.

The screen for the memory opens.

Ⓐ You can tap **Show All** to show all the photos.

Ⓑ You can tap **Select** to select the photos you want to include.

5 Tap **Play** (▶).

The memory starts playing.

6 Tap the screen.

The customization controls appear.

7 Tap the desired mood, such as **Happy** or **Gentle**.

8 Tap **Short**, **Medium**, or **Long**, as needed.

9 For greater control, tap **Edit**.

The Edit screen appears.

10 Choose settings for Title, Title Image, Music, Duration, and Photos & Videos.

11 Tap **Done**.

Browse Photos Using the Map

The Camera app automatically stores the GPS location in each photo and video you take, enabling the Photos app to sort your photos and videos by their locations. Starting from any photo, you can display other nearby photos, identifying them by their locations on the map. You can then browse the photos taken in a particular location.

Browse Photos Using the Map

1 In the Photos app, navigate to the photo from which you want to start browsing.

2 Swipe up.

The Places section and the Related section for the photo appear.

A The map in the Places section shows the area in which the photo was taken.

B The Related section shows photos related to the photo from which you started.

3 Tap **Show Nearby Photos**.

The Map screen appears.

C You can tap **Grid** to display the places as a list.

4 Tap **Show Nearby Photos**.

The Photos app displays nearby photos on the map.

5 Tap the place you want to view.

The photos in the place appear.

Note: You can tap **Show All** to display all the photos in a group.

6 Tap the photo you want to view.

The photo opens.

Browse Photos Using iCloud Photo Sharing

Your iPhone's Photos app includes a feature called iCloud Photo Sharing that enables you to share photos easily with others via iCloud and enjoy the photos they are sharing. You can add other people's shared albums to the Photos app on your iPhone by accepting invitations. You can then browse the photos those people are sharing.

The section "Share Photo Streams with Other People," later in this chapter, shows you how to share your own photos via iCloud Photo Sharing.

Browse Photos Using iCloud Photo Sharing

Accept an Invitation to a Shared Album

1 When you receive an invitation to subscribe to shared photos, open the e-mail message in Mail.

2 Tap **Subscribe**.

The Photos app becomes active.

The Shared screen appears.

3 Tap the shared album.

The album opens.

Ⓐ You can tap **People** to view the list of people with whom the album is shared.

4 Tap the thumbnail for the photo you want to view.

The photo opens.

Ⓑ You can tap **Share** (📤) to share the photo with others.

Ⓒ You can tap **Add a comment** if you want to add a comment on the photo.

Ⓓ You can tap **Like** to like the photo.

Note: Swipe left or right to display other photos.

5 Tap **Back** (‹).

The album's screen appears again.

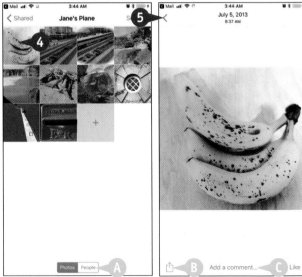

262

Browse the Latest Activity on iCloud Photo Sharing

1 In the Photos app, tap **Shared** (☁ changes to ☁).

The Shared screen appears.

2 Tap **Activity**.

Note: The Activity item shows new activity on your shared albums. When you add a shared album, the Activity thumbnail shows the new album's thumbnail.

The Activity screen appears.

3 Swipe up to scroll down.

Other items appear.

4 Tap a photo.

The photo opens.

5 Tap **Activity** (〈).

The Activity screen appears.

6 When you finish browsing the latest activity, tap **Shared** (〈).

The Shared screen appears.

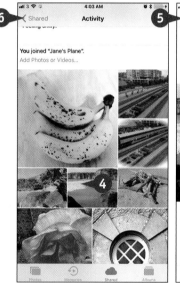

How do I remove a shared album?

In the Photos app, tap **Shared** (☁ changes to ☁) to display the Shared screen. Tap **Edit** to turn on Editing Mode, and then tap **Delete** (⊖) to the left of the stream you want to remove. In the Unsubscribe From dialog that opens, tap **Unsubscribe**. Tap **Done** to turn off Editing Mode.

Along with browsing by collections and browsing shared albums, you can browse your photos by albums. The Camera app automatically stores each conventional photo you take in the All Photos album, each burst photo in an album called Bursts, and each video in an album called Videos. You can also create other albums manually from your photos or sync existing albums from your computer.

Browse Photos Using Albums

Open the Photos App and Browse an Album

1 Press **Home**. On an iPhone X, swipe up from the bottom of the screen.

The Home screen appears.

2 Tap **Photos** (🏵).

The Photos app opens.

3 Tap **Albums** (🔲 changes to ⬛).

The Albums screen appears.

4 Tap the album you want to browse. This example uses the Favorites album.

Note: The All Photos album contains all the photos you take; photos you save from web pages, e-mail messages, instant messages, and social media apps; and photos you edit from other people's streams.

The album appears.

Note: The People album contains faces identified in photos. You can browse the photos in which a particular person appears.

5 Tap the photo you want to view.

The photo opens.

Note: Swipe left to display the next photo or right to display the previous photo.

6 Tap **Back** (‹).

The album appears.

7 Tap **Albums** (‹).

The Albums screen appears.

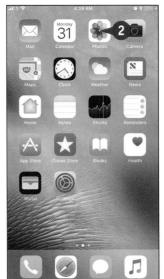

Create an Album

1 In the Photos app, tap **Albums** (▥ changes to ▤).

The Albums screen appears.

2 Tap **New** (+).

The New Album dialog opens.

3 Type the name to give the album.

4 Tap **Save**.

The screen for adding photos appears.

5 Tap the source of the photos. For example, tap **Albums**, and then tap the album.

6 Tap each photo to add to the collection, placing ✓ on each.

7 Tap **Done**.

ⓐ The album appears on the Albums screen.

How can I move through a long list of photos more quickly?

You can move through the photos more quickly by using momentum scrolling. Tap and flick up with your finger to set the photos scrolling. As the momentum drops, you can tap and flick up again to scroll further. Tap and drag your finger in the opposite direction to stop the scrolling.

How can I recover photos I deleted by mistake?

Tap **Albums**, and then tap **Recently Deleted**. In the Recently Deleted album, tap **Select**, tap the photos, and then tap **Recover**. Alternatively, tap **Recover All** to recover all the photos without selecting any.

I f you have an iCloud account, you can use the My Photo Stream feature to upload your photos to iCloud, making them available to all your iOS devices and your computer.

After you turn on My Photo Stream on your iPhone, other iOS devices, and your Macs or PCs, Photo Stream automatically syncs your 1,000 most recent photos among your devices and your computers.

Share Photos Using My Photo Stream

Turn On My Photo Stream on Your iPhone

1 Press **Home**. On an iPhone X, swipe up from the bottom of the screen.

The Home screen appears.

2 Tap **Settings** (⚙).

The Settings screen appears.

3 Tap **Apple ID**, the button bearing your Apple ID name.

The Apple ID screen appears.

4 Tap **iCloud** (☁).

The iCloud screen appears.

5 Tap **Photos** (❀).

The Photos screen appears.

Ⓐ You can set the **iCloud Photo Library** switch to On (⬤) to store your photo library in iCloud. You do not need to do this to use My Photo Stream.

6 Set the **Upload to My Photo Stream** switch to On (⬤).

Ⓑ You can set the **Upload Burst Photos** switch to On (⬤) to upload all bursts of photos instead of only favorite bursts.

7 If you also want to share your iCloud photo streams with others, set the **iCloud Photo Sharing** switch to On (⬤). See the next section, "Share Photo Streams with Other People," for more information.

8 Tap **iCloud** (‹).

The iCloud screen appears.

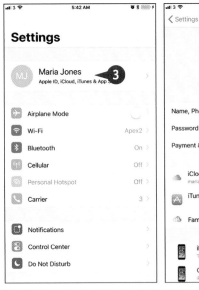

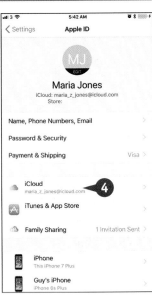

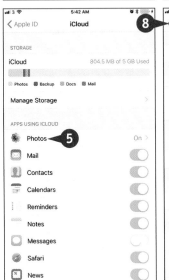

Set Your Mac to Upload Photos to Your Photo Stream

1 Click **Apple** (🍎) and then click **System Preferences** (⚙).

The System Preferences window opens.

2 Click **iCloud** (☁).

The iCloud pane appears.

3 Click **Photos** (☐ changes to ☑).

4 Click **Options**.

The Options dialog opens.

5 Click **iCloud Photo Library** (☐ changes to ☑) to use iCloud Photo Library.

6 Click **My Photo Stream** (☐ changes to ☑).

7 If you want to share photo streams with others, click **iCloud Photo Sharing** (☐ changes to ☑).

8 Click **Done**.

9 Click **System Preferences** and **Quit System Preferences**.

10 Click **Photos** (❋) on the Dock.

11 In Photos, click **Shared**.

The Shared screen appears, showing your streams and your family and friends' streams.

TIP

How do I use Photo Stream in Windows?

On Windows, you must install Apple's iCloud for Windows software, which you can download from www.apple.com/icloud/setup/pc.html. Then click **Start**, click **All Apps**, and then click **iCloud Photos**.

In the iCloud Photos window, click **Open iCloud**. Type your Apple ID and password and then click **Sign in**. Click **Photos** (☐ changes to ☑). Click **Options** to display the Photos Options dialog. Click **My Photo Stream** (☐ changes to ☑) and **iCloud Photo Sharing** (☐ changes to ☑). Click **Change** and select the folder for photos, if necessary. Click **OK** and then click **Apply**.

Share Photo Streams with Other People

After turning on iCloud Photo Sharing as described in the previous section, you can create shared photo albums, invite people to subscribe to them, and add photos.

You can also control whether subscribers can post photos and videos to your shared photo album, decide whether to make the album publicly available, and choose whether to receive notifications when subscribers comment on your photos or post their own.

Share Photo Streams with Other People

1 Press **Home**. On an iPhone X, swipe up from the bottom of the screen.

The Home screen appears.

2 Tap **Photos** (❀).

The Photos app opens.

3 Tap **Shared** (☁ changes to ☁).

The Shared screen appears.

4 Tap **New** (+).

The iCloud dialog opens.

5 Type the name for the album.

6 Tap **Next**.

Another iCloud dialog opens.

7 Tap **Add Contact** (⊕) to display the Contacts screen, and then tap the contact to add.

8 Repeat step **7** to add other contacts as needed. You can also type contact names or tap names that the list automatically suggests.

9 Tap **Create**.

The Shared screen appears.

10 Tap the new album.

The album's screen appears.

11 Tap **Add** (+).

The Moments screen appears, with the selection controls displayed.

Note: You can navigate to other collections or albums as needed.

12 Tap each photo you want to add.

13 Tap **Done**.

Another iCloud dialog opens.

14 Type the text you want to post with the photos.

15 Tap **Post**.

The album's screen appears.

16 Tap **People**.

The People screen appears.

Ⓐ To invite others to the album, tap **Invite People**.

17 Set the **Subscribers Can Post** switch to On (⬤) or Off ( ), as needed.

18 Set the **Public Website** switch to On (⬤) or Off ( ) to control whether to make the album publicly accessible on the iCloud.com website.

19 Set the **Notifications** switch to On (⬤) or Off ( ), as needed.

20 Tap **Shared** (⟨).

The Shared screen appears.

TIP

If I make a photo album public, how do people find the website?

When you set the **Public Website** switch on the People screen for a photo album to On (⬤), a Share Link button appears. Tap **Share Link** to display the Share sheet, and then tap the means of sharing you want to use — for example, Messages, Mail, Twitter, or Facebook.

fter taking photos and videos with your iPhone's camera, or after loading photos and videos on the iPhone using iTunes, you can share them with other people.

This section explains how to tweet photos to your Twitter account, assign photos to contacts, use photos as wallpaper, and print photos. Chapter 6 explains how to share items via the AirDrop feature.

Share and Use Your Photos and Videos

Select the Photo or Video to Share

1. Press **Home**. On an iPhone X, swipe up from the bottom of the screen.

   The Home screen appears.

2. Tap **Photos** (✹).

3. On the Photos screen, tap the item that contains the photo or video you want to share. For example, tap an album such as **Favorites**.

4. Tap the photo or video you want to share.

5. Tap **Share** (⬆) to display the Share sheet.

Share a Photo on Twitter

Ⓐ You can tap the selection button (○ changes to ✓) to include another item in the sharing.

1. On the Share sheet, tap **Twitter** (🐦).

   The Twitter dialog opens.

2. Type the text of the tweet.

3. Tap **Post**.

   Your iPhone posts the tweet to Twitter.

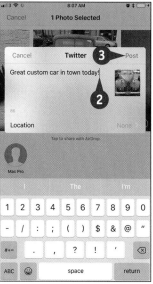

Assign a Photo to a Contact

1 On the Share sheet, tap **Assign to Contact** (⬤).

The list of contacts appears.

2 Tap the contact to which you want to assign the photo.

The Move and Scale screen appears.

3 If necessary, move the photo so that the relevant part appears centrally.

4 If necessary, pinch in to shrink the photo or pinch out to enlarge it.

5 Tap **Choose**.

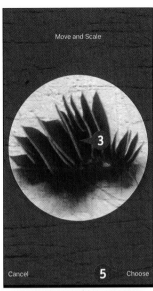

Set a Photo as Wallpaper

1 On the Share sheet, tap **Use as Wallpaper** (▢).

The Move and Scale screen appears.

2 Move the photo to display the part you want.

3 If necessary, pinch in to shrink the photo or pinch out to enlarge it.

4 Tap **Still** if you want the photo to be still, or tap **Perspective** to use perspective movement.

5 Tap **Set**.

The Set Wallpaper dialog appears.

6 Tap **Set Lock Screen**, **Set Home Screen**, or **Set Both**, as needed.

TIP

How do I print a photo?

Display the photo you want to print, and then tap **Share** (⬆) to display the Share sheet. Tap **Print** (🖨) to display the Printer Options screen. If the Printer readout does not show the correct printer, tap **Select Printer** and then tap the printer. Back on the Printer Options screen, tap **Print** to print the photo.

Play Slide Shows of Photos

Your iPhone can not only display your photos, but also play a sequence of photos as a slide show. You can choose which theme to use, which music to play, and whether to repeat the slide show when it reaches the end. You can adjust the running speed of the slide show as a whole, but you cannot adjust individual slides.

Play Slide Shows of Photos

① Press **Home**. On an iPhone X, swipe up from the bottom of the screen.

The Home screen appears.

Note: To play your photos on a bigger screen, either use AirPlay to play a TV connected to an Apple TV or use the Apple Lightning Digital AV Adapter and an HDMI cable to connect your iPhone to a TV or monitor with an HDMI input.

② Tap **Photos** (✿).

The Photos app opens.

③ Navigate to the photo with which you want to start the slide show. For example, tap **Photos** (▦ changes to ▦), tap the appropriate year, tap the appropriate collection, and then tap the moment that contains the photo.

The moment or other photo collection opens.

④ Tap the photo you want to use at the beginning of the slide show.

The photo opens.

⑤ Tap **Share** (⬆).

The Share sheet appears.

⑥ Tap **Slideshow** (▶).

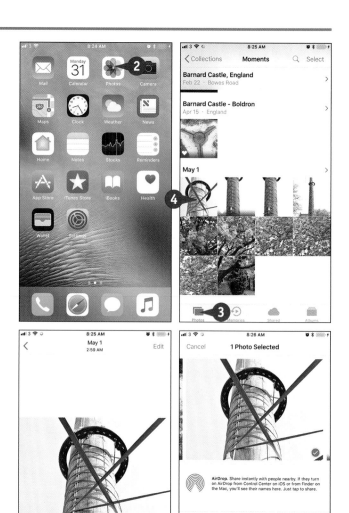

The slide show starts playing, using the default theme and music.

⑦ Tap the screen.

The controls appear.

Ⓐ You can tap **AirPlay** (⊡) to play the slide show to an Apple TV.

⑧ Tap **Options**.

The Slideshow Options screen appears.

⑨ Tap **Theme**.

The Themes screen appears.

⑩ Tap the theme you want.

The Slideshow Options screen appears.

⑪ Tap **Music** and choose the music to play.

⑫ Set the **Repeat** switch to On (◯) if you want the slide show to repeat.

⑬ Drag the **Speed** slider as needed to change the speed.

⑭ Tap **Done**.

The slide show resumes, using the settings you chose.

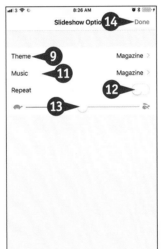

TIP

How do I choose music for a slide show?

First, choose the theme for the slide show, as explained in the main text. When you choose the theme, Photos automatically selects the theme's default music as the music for the slide show.

Next, tap **Music** on the Slideshow Options screen to display the Music screen. Here, you can either tap a different theme's music in the Theme Music list or tap **iTunes Music** to select music from your iTunes Music library.

CHAPTER 12

Advanced Features and Troubleshooting

You can connect your iPhone to VPNs and Exchange Server, troubleshoot problems, and locate it when it goes missing. You can also manage your Apple ID.

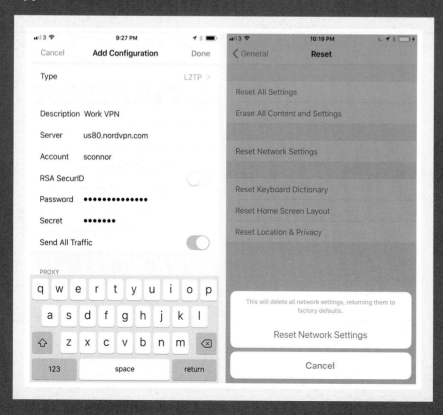

Connect to a Network via VPN

Virtual private networking, or VPN, enables you to connect your iPhone securely to a network across the Internet. For example, you can connect to a network at your workplace — or to your home network, if you set up a VPN server on it.

To set up a VPN connection, you enter the settings, username, and password in the Settings app. You normally get this information from the network's administrator.

Connect to a Network via VPN

Set Up the VPN Connection on the iPhone

1. Press **Home**. On an iPhone X, swipe up from the bottom of the screen.

   The Home screen appears.

2. Tap **Settings** (⚙).

   The Settings screen appears.

Note: After you have set up a VPN configuration, the VPN switch appears in the top section of the Settings screen. You can connect to the currently selected virtual private network by setting the switch to On (⚪ changes to ⚫).

3. Tap **General** (⚙).

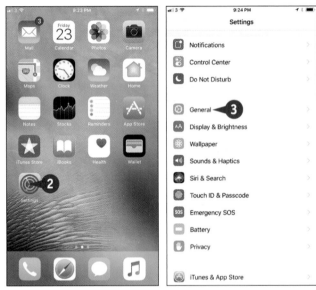

   The General screen appears.

4. Toward the bottom of the screen, tap **VPN**.

   The VPN screen appears.

5. Tap **Add VPN Configuration**.

Note: If your iPhone already has a VPN configuration you want to use, tap it, and then go to step **1** of the next set of steps, "Connect to the Virtual Private Network."

The Add Configuration screen appears.

6 Tap **Type**.

The Type screen appears.

7 Tap the VPN type: **IKEv2**, **IPSec**, or **L2TP**.

8 Tap **Add Configuration** (〈).

The Add Configuration screen appears again.

9 Fill in the details of the virtual private network.

Note: Set the **Send All Traffic** switch to On (◉) if you want your iPhone to send all Internet traffic across the virtual private network after you connect.

10 Tap **Done**.

The VPN configuration appears on the VPN screen.

Connect to the Virtual Private Network

1 On the VPN screen, set the **Status** switch to On (⚪ changes to ◉).

The iPhone connects to the virtual private network.

Ⓐ The VPN indicator appears in the status bar.

2 Work across the network connection as if you were connected directly to the network.

3 To see how long your iPhone has been connected, or to learn its IP address, tap **Information** (ⓘ).

4 Tap **VPN** (〈) to return to the VPN screen.

5 When you are ready to disconnect from the virtual private network, set the **Status** switch to Off (◉ changes to ⚪).

TIPS

Is there an easier way to set up a VPN connection?
Yes. An administrator can provide the VPN details in a configuration profile. This is a settings file that the administrator either installs directly on your iPhone or shares via e-mail or a website so that you can install it. Installing the profile adds its settings, such as the VPN details or the settings needed to connect to an Exchange Server system, to your iPhone. You can then connect to the virtual private network.

What can I do if my iPhone cannot connect to my company's VPN type?
Look in the App Store for an app for that VPN type.

Connect Your iPhone to Exchange Server

You can set up your iPhone to connect to Exchange Server or Office 365 for e-mail, contacts, calendaring, reminders, and notes.

Before setting up your Exchange account, ask an administrator for the connection details you need: your e-mail address, your password, the server name if required, and the domain name if required. You may be able to set up the account using only the e-mail address and password, but often you need the server name and domain as well.

Connect Your iPhone to Exchange Server

1 Press **Home**. On an iPhone X, swipe up from the bottom of the screen.

The Home screen appears.

2 Tap **Settings** (⚙).

The Settings screen appears.

Note: If you have not yet set up an e-mail account on the iPhone, you can also open the Add Account screen by tapping **Mail** (✉) on the iPhone's Home screen.

3 Tap **Accounts & Passwords** (🔑).

The Accounts & Passwords screen appears.

4 Tap **Add Account**.

The Add Account screen appears.

5 Tap **Exchange**.

Note: You can also set up an Exchange account using a configuration profile file that an administrator provides.

The Exchange screen appears.

6 Type your e-mail address.

7 Type a descriptive name for the account field.

8 Tap **Next**.

Another screen appears.

9 Type your password.

10 Tap **Next**.

Note: If Mail needs more information, another screen appears. Type the server's address; type the domain, if it is needed; and type your username. Then tap **Next**.

The Exchange screen appears.

11 Set the **Mail** switch to On (⬤) or Off ( ).

12 Set the **Contacts** switch to On (⬤) or Off ( ).

13 Set the **Calendars** switch to On (⬤) or Off ( ).

14 Set the **Reminders** switch to On (⬤) or Off ( ).

Note: If the Notes switch appears, set it to On (⬤) or Off ( ), as needed.

15 Tap **Save**.

Ⓐ The new account appears on the Mail screen.

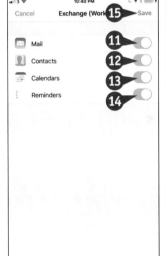

TIPS

How do I know whether to enter a domain name when setting up my Exchange account?
You need to ask an administrator, because some Exchange implementations require you to enter a domain, whereas others do not.

How do I set up an Office 365 e-mail account?
Use the method explained in this section, but use outlook.office365.com as the server's address. Your username is typically your full e-mail address; if in doubt, ask an administrator.

Update Your iPhone's Software

Apple periodically releases new versions of the iPhone's software to fix problems, improve performance, and add new features. To keep your iPhone running quickly and smoothly, and to add any new features, update its software when a new version becomes available.

You can update your iPhone's software either directly on the iPhone or by using iTunes on your computer. Both the iPhone and iTunes notify you automatically when an update is available. You can also check for updates manually.

Update Your iPhone's Software

Update Your iPhone's Software on the iPhone

1 Press **Home**. On an iPhone X, swipe up from the bottom of the screen.

The Home screen appears.

A The badge on the Settings icon indicates that an update is available.

2 Tap **Settings** (⚙).

The Settings screen appears.

3 Tap **General** (⚙).

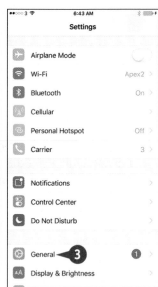

The General screen appears.

4 Tap **Software Update**.

The Software Update screen appears.

5 Tap **Install Now**.

The installation procedure begins.

6 Follow the prompts to complete the installation.

Update Your iPhone's Software Using iTunes on Your Computer

1 Connect your iPhone to your computer via the USB cable.

The iPhone appears on the navigation bar in iTunes.

A dialog appears, telling you that a new software version is available.

2 Click **Update**.

iTunes downloads the new software, extracts it, and begins to install it.

When the installation is complete, iTunes displays a dialog telling you that the iPhone will restart in 15 seconds.

3 Click **OK**, or wait for the countdown to complete.

The iPhone restarts, and its button then appears on the navigation bar in iTunes.

4 Disconnect your iPhone from the USB cable. You can now start using the iPhone as usual.

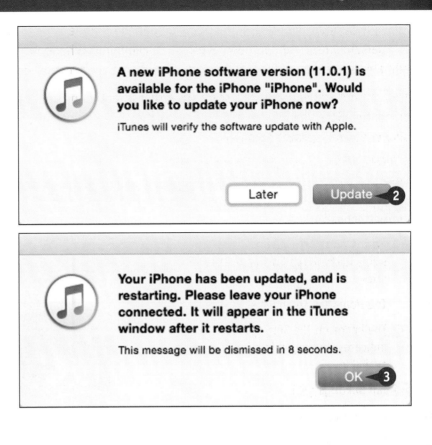

A new iPhone software version (11.0.1) is available for the iPhone "iPhone". Would you like to update your iPhone now?

iTunes will verify the software update with Apple.

Later | Update **2**

Your iPhone has been updated, and is restarting. Please leave your iPhone connected. It will appear in the iTunes window after it restarts.

This message will be dismissed in 8 seconds.

OK **3**

TIP

How do I make iTunes check for a new version of my iPhone's software?
Connect your iPhone to your computer via the USB cable so that the iPhone appears on the navigation bar in iTunes. Click **iPhone** to display the Summary screen, and then click **Check for Update** in the upper area.

Extend Your iPhone's Runtime on the Battery

To extend your iPhone's runtime on the battery, you can reduce the power usage by dimming the screen; turning off Wi-Fi, Bluetooth, and cellular data when you do not need them; and setting your iPhone to go to sleep quickly. When the battery reaches 20 percent power, your iPhone prompts you to turn on Low Power Mode, which disables background app refreshing, slows down the processor, and turns off some demanding graphical features. You can also enable Low Power Mode manually anytime you want.

Extend Your iPhone's Runtime on the Battery

Dim the Screen

1 Press **Home**. On an iPhone X, swipe up from the bottom of the screen.

The Home screen appears.

2 On an iPhone X, swipe down from the upper-right corner of the screen. On other iPhone models, swipe up from the bottom of the screen.

Control Center opens.

3 Swipe down the **Brightness** control.

The screen brightness decreases.

4 Tap **Close** (⌄) or anywhere at the top of the screen.

Control Center closes.

Turn Off Wi-Fi, Bluetooth, and Cellular Data

1 Press **Home**. On an iPhone X, swipe up from the bottom of the screen.

The Home screen appears.

2 On an iPhone X, swipe down from the upper-right corner of the screen. On other iPhone models, swipe up from the bottom of the screen.

Control Center opens.

A You can turn off all communications by tapping **Airplane Mode** (✈ changes to ✈).

3 To turn off Wi-Fi, tap **Wi-Fi** (📶 changes to 📶).

4 To turn off Bluetooth, tap **Bluetooth** (✳ changes to ✳).

5 To turn off cellular data, tap **Cellular Data** (◉ changes to ◉).

6 Tap **Close** (⌄) or anywhere at the top of the screen.

Control Center closes.

Turn On Low Power Mode Manually

1 Press **Home**. On an iPhone X, swipe up from the bottom of the screen.

The Home screen appears.

2 Press **Settings** (⚙).

The Peek panel opens.

3 Tap **Battery** (🔋).

The Battery screen appears.

Ⓑ You can set the **Battery Percentage** switch to On (⚪) to display the battery percentage in the status bar.

4 Set the **Low Power Mode** switch to On (⚪ changes to ⚪).

The first time you set the Low Power Mode switch to On, the Low Power Mode dialog opens.

5 Tap **Continue**.

Your iPhone enables Low Power Mode.

Ⓒ The battery icon appears yellow to indicate that the iPhone is using Low Power Mode.

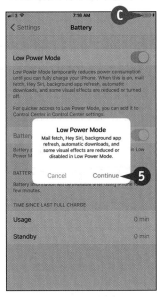

TIP

What else can I do to save power?

If you do not need your iPhone to track your location, you can turn off the GPS feature. Press **Home**, tap **Settings** (⚙), and then tap **Privacy** (✋) to display the Privacy screen. Tap **Location Services** (➤) to display the Location Services screen, and then set the **Location Services** switch to Off (⚪).

You can also set a short time for Auto-Lock. Press **Home**, tap **Settings** (⚙), tap **Display & Brightness** (🔠), and then tap **Auto-Lock**. Tap a short interval — for example, **1 Minute**.

Back Up and Restore Using Your Computer

When you sync your iPhone with your computer, iTunes automatically backs up the iPhone's data and settings, unless you have chosen to back up your iPhone to iCloud instead.

If your iPhone suffers a software or hardware failure, you can use iTunes to restore the data and settings to your iPhone or to a new iPhone, an iPad, or an iPod touch. You must turn off the Find My iPhone feature before restoring your iPhone.

Back Up and Restore Using Your Computer

Back Up Your iPhone

1 Connect your iPhone to your computer via the USB cable or via Wi-Fi.

The iPhone appears on the navigation bar in iTunes.

2 Click **iPhone** (☐) on the navigation bar.

The iPhone's management screens appear.

3 Click **Summary** if the Summary screen is not yet shown.

4 Click **Back Up Now**.

iTunes backs up your iPhone.

Turn Off the Find My iPhone Feature on Your iPhone

1 Press **Home**. On an iPhone X, swipe up from the bottom of the screen.

The Home screen appears.

2 Tap **Settings** (⚙).

The Settings screen appears.

3 Tap **Apple ID**, the button bearing your Apple ID name.

The Apple ID screen appears.

4 Tap **iCloud** (☁).

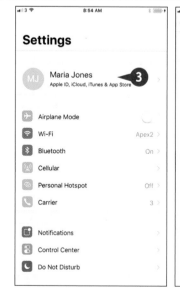

The iCloud screen appears.

5 Tap **Find My iPhone** (⊘).

The Find My iPhone screen appears.

6 Set the **Find My iPhone** switch to Off
(⬤ changes to ◯).

The Apple ID Password dialog opens.

7 Type the password for your Apple ID.

8 Tap **Turn Off**.

The iPhone turns off the Find My iPhone feature.

Restore Your iPhone

1 On the Summary screen in the iPhone's
management screens, click **Restore iPhone**.

iTunes asks you to confirm that you want to
restore the iPhone to its factory settings.

2 Click **Restore**.

iTunes backs up the iPhone's data, restores
the software on the iPhone, and returns the
iPhone to its factory settings.

Note: Do not disconnect the iPhone during the
restore process. Doing so can leave the iPhone
in an unusable state.

3 On the Welcome to Your New Phone screen, click
Restore from this backup (◯ changes to ⬤).

4 Click ⬍ and choose your iPhone by name.

5 Click **Continue**.

iTunes restores the data and settings to your iPhone.

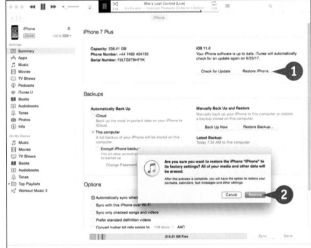

Your iPhone restarts, appears on the navigation
bar in iTunes, and then syncs.

6 Disconnect the iPhone.

TIP

How can I protect confidential information in my iPhone's backups?

On the Summary screen in iTunes, click **Encrypt iPhone backup** (☐ changes to ☑). In the Set Password dialog,
type the password, and then click **Set Password**. iTunes then encrypts your backups using strong encryption.

Apart from protecting your confidential information, encrypting your iPhone also saves your passwords
during backup and restores them to the iPhone when you restore the device.

Back Up and Restore Using iCloud

Instead of backing up your iPhone to your computer, you can back it up to iCloud, preferably via Wi-Fi, but optionally — if you have a generous data plan — via the cellular network. If your iPhone suffers a software or hardware failure, you can restore its data and settings from backup.

You can choose which items to back up to iCloud. You do not need to back up apps, media files, or games you have bought from the iTunes Store, because you can download them again.

Back Up and Restore Using iCloud

1 Press **Home**. On an iPhone X, swipe up from the bottom of the screen.

The Home screen appears.

2 Tap **Settings** (⚙️).

The Settings screen appears.

3 Tap **Apple ID**, the button bearing your Apple ID name.

The Apple ID screen appears.

4 Tap **iCloud** (☁️).

Note: The 5GB of storage in a standard free iCloud account is enough space to store your iPhone's settings and your most important data and files.

The iCloud screen appears.

5 Tap **Photos**.

The Photos screen appears.

6 Set the **iCloud Photo Library** switch to On (◯) if you want to store all your photos in iCloud.

7 If you enable iCloud Photo Library, tap **Optimize iPhone Storage** or **Download and Keep Originals**, as needed.

8 Set the **Upload to My Photo Stream** switch to On (◯) if you want to upload all your new photos.

9 Set the **iCloud Photo Sharing** switch to On (◯) if you want to share albums with others via iCloud.

10 Tap **iCloud** (<).

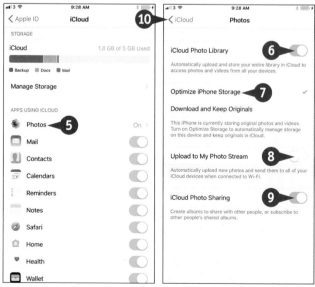

286

The iCloud screen appears again.

A If you need more storage space, tap **Manage Storage** to display the Manage Storage screen, and then tap **Buy More Storage**.

11 In the Apps Using iCloud section, set each app's switch to On (⬤) or Off ( ), as needed.

12 In the nameless lower sections, set each app's switch to On (⬤) or Off ( ), as needed.

13 Set the **iCloud Drive** switch to On (⬤).

14 At the bottom of the Apps Using iCloud section, tap **iCloud Backup** (⟳).

The Backup screen appears.

15 Set the **iCloud Backup** switch to On (⬤).

16 If you want to back up your iPhone now, tap **Back Up Now**.

Your iPhone begins backing up its contents to iCloud.

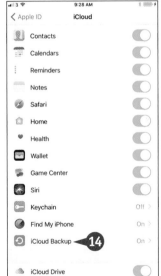

TIP

How do I restore my iPhone from its iCloud backup?

First, reset the iPhone to factory settings. Press **Home**, tap **Settings** (⚙), tap **General** (⚙), tap **Reset**, and then tap **Erase All Content and Settings**. Tap **Erase iPhone** in both the first and the second confirmation dialogs. When the iPhone restarts and displays its setup screens, choose your language and country. On the Set Up iPhone screen, tap **Restore from iCloud Backup**, and then tap **Next**. On the Apple ID screen, enter your Apple ID, and then tap **Next**. On the Choose Backup screen, tap the backup you want to use — normally, the most recent backup — and then tap **Restore**.

Reset Your iPhone's Settings

If your iPhone malfunctions, you can reset its network settings, reset the Home screen's icons, reset your keyboard dictionary, reset your location and privacy settings, or reset all settings to eliminate tricky configuration issues. If your iPhone has intractable problems, you can back it up, erase all content and settings, and then set it up from scratch. You can also erase your iPhone before selling or giving it to someone else; you must turn off Find My iPhone first.

Reset Your iPhone's Settings

Display the Reset Screen

1 Press **Home**. On an iPhone X, swipe up from the bottom of the screen.

The Home screen appears.

2 Tap **Settings** (⚙).

The Settings screen appears.

Note: If your iPhone is not responding to the Home button or your taps, press and hold the **Sleep/Wake** button and **Home** for about 15 seconds to reset the iPhone.

3 Tap **General** (⚙).

The General screen appears.

4 Tap **Reset**.

The Reset screen appears.

You can then tap the appropriate button: **Reset All Settings**, **Erase All Content and Settings**, **Reset Network Settings**, **Reset Keyboard Dictionary**, **Reset Home Screen Layout**, or **Reset Location & Privacy**.

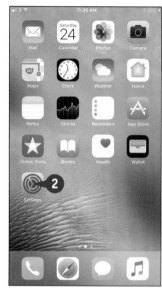

Reset Your Network Settings

1 On the Reset screen, tap **Reset Network Settings**.

Note: If your iPhone prompts you to enter your passcode at this point, do so.

A dialog opens, warning you that this action will delete all network settings and return them to their factory defaults.

2 Tap **Reset Network Settings**.

iOS resets your iPhone's network settings.

Restore Your iPhone to Factory Settings

Note: If you intend to sell or give away your iPhone, turn off Find My iPhone before restoring your iPhone to factory settings. See the second tip.

1 On the Reset screen, tap **Erase All Content and Settings**.

Note: Enter your passcode if prompted to do so.

A dialog opens to confirm that you want to delete all your media and data and reset all settings.

2 Tap **Erase iPhone**.

A second dialog opens.

3 Tap **Erase iPhone**.

iOS wipes your media and data and restores your iPhone to factory settings.

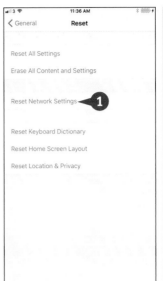

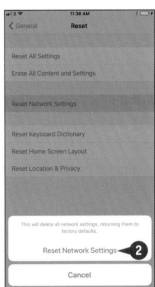

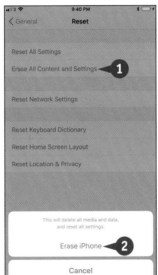

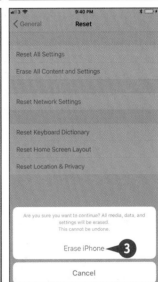

TIPS

Does the Reset All Settings command delete my data and my music files?

No. When you reset all the iPhone's settings, the settings go back to their defaults, but your data remains in place. But you need to set the iPhone's settings again, either by restoring them using iTunes or by setting them manually, in order to get your iPhone working the way you prefer.

How do I turn off the Find My iPhone feature?

Press **Home**, tap **Apple ID** — the button bearing your Apple ID name — and then tap **iCloud** ( ). Tap **Find My iPhone** ( ), and then set the **Find My iPhone** switch to Off (changes to).

Troubleshoot Wi-Fi Connections

To avoid exceeding your data plan, use Wi-Fi networks whenever they are available instead of using your cellular connection.

Normally, the iPhone automatically reconnects to Wi-Fi networks to which you have previously connected it and maintains those connections without problems. But you may sometimes need to request your iPhone's network address again, a process called *renewing the lease* on the IP address. You may also need to tell your iPhone to forget a network, and then rejoin the network manually, providing the password again.

Troubleshoot Wi-Fi Connections

Renew the Lease on Your iPhone's IP Address

1 Press **Home**. On an iPhone X, swipe up from the bottom of the screen.

The Home screen appears.

Note: You can sometimes resolve a Wi-Fi problem by turning Wi-Fi off and back on. Swipe up from the bottom of the screen to open Control Center, tap **Wi-Fi** (🛜 changes to 🛜), and then tap **Wi-Fi** again (🛜 changes to 🛜).

2 Press **Settings** (⚙️).

The Peek panel opens.

3 Tap **Wi-Fi** (🛜).

The Wi-Fi screen appears.

4 Tap **Information** (ⓘ) to the right of the network for which you want to renew the lease.

The network's screen appears.

5 Tap **Renew Lease**.

The Renew Lease dialog opens.

6 Tap **Renew Lease**.

7 Tap **Wi-Fi** (‹).

The Wi-Fi screen appears.

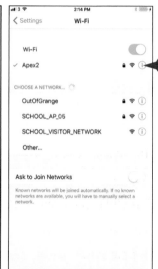

Forget a Network and Then Rejoin It

1 On the Wi-Fi screen, tap **Information** (ⓘ) to the right of the network.

The network's screen appears.

2 Tap **Forget This Network**.

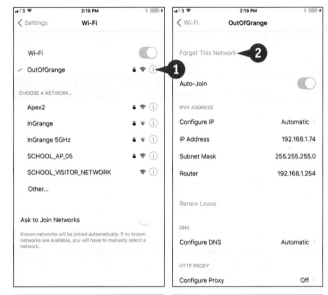

The Forget Wi-Fi Network dialog opens.

3 Tap **Forget**.

The iPhone removes the network's details.

4 Tap **Wi-Fi** (‹).

The Wi-Fi screen appears.

5 Tap the network's name.

The Enter Password screen appears.

6 Type the password for the network.

7 Tap **Join**.

The iPhone joins the network.

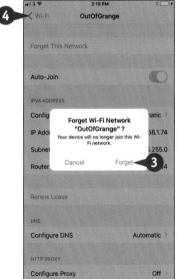

TIP

What else can I do to reestablish my Wi-Fi network connections?

If you are unable to fix your Wi-Fi network connections by renewing the IP address lease or by forgetting and rejoining the network, as described in this section, try restarting your iPhone. If that does not work, reset your network settings, as described earlier in this chapter, and then set up each connection again manually.

Locate Your iPhone with Find My iPhone

If you have an iCloud account, you can use the Find My iPhone feature to locate your iPhone if it has been lost or stolen. You can also display a message on the iPhone — for example, to tell the finder how to contact you — or remotely wipe the data on the iPhone.

To use Find My iPhone, you must first set up your iCloud account on your iPhone, and then enable the Find My iPhone feature.

Locate Your iPhone with Find My iPhone

Turn On the Find My iPhone Feature

1 Set up your iCloud account on your iPhone as discussed in "Set Up Your iPhone as New Using iCloud" in Chapter 1.

Note: You may have turned on the Find My iPhone feature when setting up your iCloud account.

2 Press **Home**. On an iPhone X, swipe up from the bottom of the screen.

The Home screen appears.

3 Tap **Settings** (⚙).

The Settings screen appears.

4 Tap **Apple ID**, the button that bears your Apple ID name.

The Apple ID screen appears.

5 Tap **iCloud** (☁).

The iCloud screen appears.

6 Tap **Find My iPhone** (◉).

The Find My iPhone screen appears.

7 Set the **Find My iPhone** switch to On (◯ changes to ◯).

8 Set the **Send Last Location** switch to On (◯ changes to ◯) if you want your iPhone to send Apple its location when the battery runs critically low.

9 Tap **iCloud** (〈).

The iCloud screen appears.

10 Tap **Apple ID** (〈).

The Apple ID screen appears.

Locate Your iPhone Using Find My iPhone

1 On a computer, open a web browser, such as Microsoft Edge, Internet Explorer, Chrome, or Safari.

Note: On an iOS device, use the Find My iPhone app to locate a missing iPhone. You cannot use an Android device.

2 Click the Address box.

3 Type www.icloud.com and press Enter in Windows or Return on a Mac.

The Sign in to iCloud web page appears.

4 Type your username.

5 Type your password.

6 Click **Sign In** (→).

The iCloud site appears, displaying either the Home page or the page you last used.

Note: If you have set up two-step verification on your Apple ID, the Verify Your Identity screen may appear. Click the device to use for verification, and then enter the code sent to the device on the Enter Verification Code screen. In the Trust This Browser? dialog that opens, click **Trust** or **Don't Trust**, as appropriate.

Note: If iCloud displays a page other than the Home page, click **iCloud** and then click **Find iPhone** (◉) on the pop-up panel. Go to step **8**.

7 Click **Find iPhone** (◉).

 TIP

Is it worth displaying a message on my iPhone, or should I simply wipe it?
Almost always, it is definitely worth displaying a message on your iPhone. If you have lost your iPhone and someone has found it, that person may be trying to return it to you. The chances are good that the finder is honest, even if he has not discovered that you have locked the iPhone with a passcode. That said, if you are certain someone has stolen your iPhone, you may prefer simply to wipe it, using the technique explained next.

continued ▶

Find My iPhone is a powerful feature you can use when your iPhone goes missing.

If Find My iPhone reveals someone has taken your iPhone, you can wipe its contents to prevent anyone from hacking into your data. However, know that wiping your iPhone prevents you from locating the iPhone again — ever — except by chance. Wipe your iPhone only when you have lost it, you have no hope of recovering it, and you must destroy the data on it.

Locate Your iPhone with Find My iPhone (continued)

The iCloud Find My iPhone screen appears.

8 Click the pop-up menu at the top. Normally, this shows All Devices at first.

The My Devices pop-up panel appears.

9 Click your iPhone.

Ⓐ Your iPhone's location appears.

The Info dialog appears, showing when the iPhone was last located.

10 If you want to play a sound on the iPhone, click **Play Sound** (🔊). This feature is primarily helpful for locating your iPhone if you have mislaid it somewhere nearby.

Ⓑ A message indicates that the iPhone has played the sound.

Lock the iPhone with a Passcode

1 Click **Lost Mode** (🔒) in the Info dialog.

The Lost Mode dialog appears, prompting you to enter a phone number where you can be reached.

2 Optionally, click **Number** and type the number.

3 Click **Next**.

The Lost Mode dialog prompts you to enter a message.

4 Type a message to whoever finds your iPhone.

5 Click **Done**.

iCloud sends the lock request to the iPhone, which locks itself.

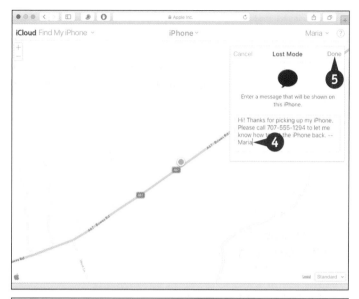

Remotely Erase Your iPhone

1 Click **Erase iPhone** (🗑) in the Info dialog.

The Erase This iPhone? dialog opens.

Note: If this iPhone is the last trusted device for your Apple ID, the Erase Last Trusted Device? dialog opens instead of the Erase This iPhone? dialog. Read the warning about having to use your Recovery Key to access your Apple ID. If you are sure you want to erase the iPhone, click **Erase**.

2 Click **Erase**.

iCloud sends the erase request to the iPhone, which erases its data.

TIP

Can I remotely wipe the data on my iPhone if I do not have an iCloud account?

No, not remotely, but you can make the iPhone wipe itself. Set a passcode for the iPhone, as discussed in the section "Secure Your iPhone with Touch ID or Face ID" in Chapter 2, and then set the **Erase Data** switch on the Touch ID & Passcode screen to On (⬤). This setting makes the iPhone automatically erase its data after ten successive failed attempts to enter the passcode. After five failed attempts, the iPhone enforces a delay before the next attempt; further failures increase the delay.

Manage Your Apple ID

Your iPhone uses your Apple ID for authentication and authorization. Using the Apple ID screen in the Settings app, you can review your Apple ID information and change it if necessary. For example, you may need to change your display name, add a payment method or shipping address, or verify that two-factor authentication is enabled for security. You can also edit the phone numbers and e-mail addresses at which you are reachable via iMessage, FaceTime, and Game Center.

Manage Your Apple ID

1 Press **Home**. On an iPhone X, swipe up from the bottom of the screen.

The Home screen appears.

2 Tap **Settings** (⚙).

The Settings app opens.

3 Tap **Apple ID**, the button that shows your Apple ID name.

The Apple ID screen appears.

Ⓐ To add a photo or update an existing photo, tap the account icon. In the Photo dialog that opens, tap **Take Photo** or **Choose Photo**, as appropriate, and then follow the prompts.

Note: At the bottom of the Apple ID screen is a Sign Out button that you can tap to sign out of your account.

4 Tap **Name, Phone Numbers, Email**.

Note: If the Sign In to iCloud dialog opens, type your password and then tap **OK**.

The Name, Phone Numbers, Email screen appears.

Ⓑ You can tap **Name** and edit your name.

Ⓒ You can add phone numbers and e-mail addresses to the Reachable At list by tapping **Edit** and then tapping **Add Email or Phone Number**.

5 In the News & Announcements section, set the switches to On (◉) or Off ( ) to control which messages you receive.

6 Tap **Apple ID** (❮).

The Apple ID screen appears again.

7 Tap **Password & Security**.

The Password & Security screen appears.

D You can tap **Change Password** and follow the prompts to change your Apple ID password.

8 Verify that the Two-Factor Authentication button shows On. If not, follow the prompts to enable two-factor authentication.

E You can tap **Edit** and then change your trusted phone numbers.

F You can tap **Get Verification Code** to get a code for signing in on another device or at iCloud.com.

9 Tap **Apple ID** (<).

The Apple ID screen appears.

10 Tap **Payment & Shipping**.

The Payment & Shipping screen appears.

G You can tap **Add Card** to add a payment method.

H You can tap **Add a Shipping Address** to add a shipping address.

11 Tap **Apple ID** (<).

The Apple ID screen appears.

12 Tap the button for your phone.

The Device Info screen appears.

13 Verify that the Find My iPhone button shows On. If not, tap **Find My iPhone** and set the **Find My iPhone** switch to On (⬤).

I You can view your phone's details.

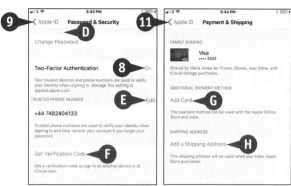

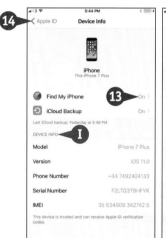

14 Tap **Apple ID** (<).

The Apple ID screen appears.

15 Tap **iTunes & App Stores**.

The iTunes & App Stores screen appears.

16 In the Automatic Downloads area, set each switch to On (⬤) or Off ( ) , as needed.

TIPS

How do I use a different Apple ID for the iTunes and App Store?

On the iTunes & App Stores screen, tap **Apple ID**. In the Apple ID dialog that opens, tap **Sign Out**. Tap **Apple ID** again to open the Apple ID Sign-in Requested dialog. Type the Apple ID and password you want to use, and then tap **Sign In**.

What does the Offload Unused Apps switch control?

Set the **Offload Unused Apps** switch to On (⬤) if you want iOS to delete apps you have not used for a while. iOS keeps any documents you created in the app.

Index

Index